FISCAL FEDERALISM IN CANADA

Analysis, Evaluation, and Prescription

Edited by André Lecours, Daniel Béland, Trevor Tombe, and Eric Champagne

Featuring insights from some of the top specialists in the country, *Fiscal Federalism in Canada* unpacks numerous complexities of fiscal federalism in Canada. The book features key regional and provincial perspectives, while taking into account Indigenous realities, the three territories, and municipal affairs. The contributing authors go beyond the major federal transfers to examine the financing of education, cities, infrastructure, and housing.

This volume shows that fiscal federalism is much more than simply an aggregate of individual programs and transfers. It highlights the role of actors other than the federal and provincial governments and recalls the importance of territoriality. The book pays close attention to the political dimension of fiscal federalism in Canada, which is at the heart of how the federation functions and is essential to its governance. Fiscal federalism is central to the funding of critical programs through intergovernmental transfers, but it is also the focus of political debates on territorial redistribution. In tackling essential questions, *Fiscal Federalism in Canada* contributes to the so-called second-generation fiscal federalism literature, taking stock of the critical sociological and political issues at its core.

ANDRÉ LECOURS is a professor of political studies at the University of Ottawa.

DANIEL BÉLAND is the director of the McGill Institute for the Study of Canada and James McGill Professor in the Department of Political Science at McGill University.

TREVOR TOMBE is a professor of economics and a research fellow at the School of Public Policy at the University of Calgary.

ERIC CHAMPAGNE is an associate professor of public administration at the School of Political Studies and the director of the Centre on Governance at the University of Ottawa.

Fiscal Federalism in Canada

Analysis, Evaluation, and Prescription

EDITED BY ANDRÉ LECOURS, DANIEL BÉLAND,
TREVOR TOMBE, AND ERIC CHAMPAGNE

UNIVERSITY OF TORONTO PRESS
Toronto Buffalo London

© University of Toronto Press 2023
Toronto Buffalo London
utorontopress.com

ISBN 978-1-4875-5124-7 (cloth)   ISBN 978-1-4875-5126-1 (EPUB)
ISBN 978-1-4875-5125-4 (paper)   ISBN 978-1-4875-5128-5 (PDF)

Library and Archives Canada Cataloguing in Publication

Title: Fiscal federalism in Canada : analysis, evaluation, and prescription / edited by André Lecours, Daniel Béland, Trevor Tombe, and Eric Champagne.
Names: Lecours, André, 1972– editor. | Béland, Daniel, editor. | Tombe, Trevor, editor. | Champagne, Eric (Professor of public administration), editor.
Description: Includes bibliographical references and index.
Identifiers: Canadiana (print) 20230496903 | Canadiana (ebook) 20230496997 | ISBN 9781487551254 (paper) | ISBN 9781487551247 (cloth) | ISBN 9781487551261 (EPUB) | ISBN 9781487551285 (PDF)
Subjects: LCSH: Intergovernmental fiscal relations – Canada.
Classification: LCC HJ795.A1 F57 2023 | DDC 336.1/850971 – dc23

Cover design: Will Brown
Cover image: Raymond Hui/Unsplash

We wish to acknowledge the land on which the University of Toronto Press operates. This land is the traditional territory of the Wendat, the Anishnaabeg, the Haudenosaunee, the Métis, and the Mississaugas of the Credit First Nation.

University of Toronto Press acknowledges the financial support of the Government of Canada, the Canada Council for the Arts, and the Ontario Arts Council, an agency of the Government of Ontario, for its publishing activities.

Canada Council for the Arts
Conseil des Arts du Canada

ONTARIO ARTS COUNCIL
CONSEIL DES ARTS DE L'ONTARIO
an Ontario government agency
un organisme du gouvernement de l'Ontario

Funded by the Government of Canada
Financé par le gouvernement du Canada

In memory of Richard Bird

Contents

List of Figures and Tables xi

Acknowledgments xv

1 Introduction: Fiscal Federalism under the Microscope 3
   ANDRÉ LECOURS, DANIEL BÉLAND, TREVOR TOMBE,
   AND ERIC CHAMPAGNE

2 The Struggle for Equity That Saved the Federation 29
   MARY JANIGAN

3 Fiscal Federalism and the Federal Spending Power: A Legal and
   Constitutional Analysis 50
   PETER C. OLIVER

4 The Challenges and Opportunities Facing Canada's Fiscal Arrangements
   after COVID-19 77
   TREVOR TOMBE

5 The Canada Health Transfer: Past, Present, and Future 93
   ROBIN BOADWAY

6 Ceremonial Fiscal Federalism: Social Assistance and the Canada Social
   Transfer 112
   MICHAEL J. PRINCE

7 Living on Equalization Payments: How Hard Is It for Receiving Provinces
   to Anticipate Future Equalization Revenues? 132
   MARCELIN JOANIS

viii   Contents

8   Canadian Fiscal Federalism and the Provinces' Natural Resource
    Revenues   155
    JAMES FEEHAN

9   Fiscal Federalism, Governance, and Provincial Debt   176
    KYLE HANNIMAN

10 Fiscal Federalism in Canada's North: Understanding Territorial Formula
    Financing   192
    CHRISTOPHER YURRIS, DANIEL BÉLAND, AND TREVOR TOMBE

11 Leading the Way: First Nations in Canadian Fiscal Federalism   215
    DONN. L. FEIR AND DAVID SCOONES

12 Long-Term Care Reform in Canada in the Wake of COVID-19: The
    Poverty of the National Standards Solution   237
    ANTHONY BRETON AND PATRIK MARIER

13 Cities in Canadian Fiscal Federalism: The Forgotten Partner   263
    ENID SLACK

14 Coming Full Circle: Federalism and Responsibility for Housing   284
    STEVE POMEROY

15 Public Infrastructure Financing and Multilevel Governance in
    Canada   306
    ERIC CHAMPAGNE AND ARACELLY DENISE GRANJA

16 Financing Education in Canada   326
    JENNIFER WALLNER

17 Childcare in a Decentralized Federation: Who Pays?   342
    JENNIFER ROBSON

18 Diversity in Adversity: Fiscal Federalism, the Four Atlantic Provinces, and
    Canada's Great Demographic Imbalance   375
    RICHARD SAILLANT

19 Quebec's Fiscal Federalism Trilemma   395
    ALAIN NOËL

20 Fiscal Fortunes: An Ontario Perspective on Federal-Provincial
    Transfers   413
    TRACY SNODDON

21 Canadian Fiscal Federalism and Alberta's Latest Attempt to Get a Fair(er) Deal   438
   KEN BOESSENKOOL

22 Canadian Fiscal Federalism in Comparative Perspective   451
   ALAN FENNA

23 Pressures, Challenges, and Policy Recommendations: Improving Fiscal Federalism in Canada   476
   ANDRÉ LECOURS, DANIEL BÉLAND, TREVOR TOMBE, AND ERIC CHAMPAGNE

Contributors   483

Index   489

Figures and Tables

Figures

4.1 Federal Transfers to Provincial Governments   81
4.2 Economic Convergence across Provinces in 2020   82
7.1 Year-Over-Year Change in Equalization Payments to the Five Core Beneficiaries, 2001–21   142
7.2 Forecasting Error: Overestimation or Underestimation for Fiscal Years in Provincial Budgets   143
7.3 Revisions to the Quebec Budget t-1 Estimate for Fiscal Year t – Overestimation or Underestimation   146
8.1 Residential Electricity Rates, 2020   166
9.1 Net Provincial Debt to GDP and Interest Payments to Revenues   178
10.1 Per Capita Government Health Expenditures, 2019   203
11.1 Increases in Fiscal Capacity – The Cumulative Number of First Nations Passing a Tax Law   223
11.2 Estimated Percentage Point Change in the Likelihood of Passing a COVID-19 Response Law in 2020–1   226
13.1 Distribution of Municipal Revenues, Canada, 2009–20   268
15.1 Basic Infrastructure Investments, 2009–20   314
15.2 Infrastructure Investments, Comparison between Major Sectors, 2009–20   315
15.3 Net Stock of Basic Infrastructure by Level of Government, 2020   316
17.1 Maximum CCED Value ($2021) for a Young Child (under Age 7) and Labour Force Participation of Women 25 to 44 Years of Age, 1966–2020   349
17.2 Relative Shares of Real Total Spending on ELCC, Quebec, 2012–18   359

17.3 Relative Shares of Real Total Spending on ELCC, Ontario, 2012–18   360
17.4 All Public Spending and Public Plus Household Spending per Licensed Space, Quebec, 2010–11 to 2019–20   361
17.5 All Public Spending and Public Plus Household Spending per Licensed Space, Ontario, 2010–11 to 2019–20   362
18.1 Provincial Health-Care Spending Per Capita by Age Groups, Canada, 2018   386
19.1 Quebec's Fiscal Federalism Trilemma   399
19.2 Quebec Per Capita Equalization Entitlements, 1957–8 to 2021–2   401
19.3 Major Social Transfers to Quebec (Cash Component) in Real Per Capita Dollars, 1981–2021   404
19.4 Share of Federal Transfers in Quebec's Consolidated Revenues, 2000–1 to 2021–2   409
20.1 Federal Net Debt and Major Cash Transfers to Provinces, 1981–2022   415
20.2 Federal Cash Transfers to Provinces and Ontario   416
20.3 Alberta's Non-Renewable Resource Revenues   419
20.4 Share of Federal Transfers, by Type, 2020–1   422

Tables

4.1 Fiscal Responses to COVID-19   79
4.2 Safe Restart Agreement Funding Categories   80
8.1 Major Federal Transfers to Provincial Governments, 2021–2   160
8.2 Impacts of the Fiscal Capacity Cap on Newfoundland and Labrador and Saskatchewan Equalization Entitlements, 2021–2   165
8.3 Estimated Impact on 2021–2 Equalization Payments Due to Inclusion of Forgone Water Power Rentals   167
10.1 Summary of TFF Grant Calculation for 2022–3   200
12.1 Characteristics of the Provincial Quality of Care Standards Analysed   242
12.2 Summary of Standards Identified in the Four Provinces   245
12.3 Structure-Related Standards Categories   246
12.4 Process-Related Standards Categories   249
12.5 Outcome-Related Standards Categories   251
13.1 Distribution of Municipal Expenditures, Canada, 2020   267
13.2 Selected Additional Municipal Revenues by Province   269
15.1 Types of Policy Instruments for Federal Investment in Municipal Infrastructure   318

17.1	Mean Variance between Provincial ELCC Spending Allocations and Actual Expenditures Reported in Public Accounts	351
17.2	Summary of Total Public Real Spending on ELCC, Selected Jurisdictions	353
17.3	Summary of Licensed ELCC Spaces, Selected Jurisdictions	353
17.4	Details of Federal Real Spending on ELCC	354
17.5	Details of Provincial Real Spending on ELCC in Quebec	355
17.6	Details of Provincial Real Spending on ELCC in Ontario	356
18.1	Selected Population Age Structure Characteristics, Canada and Provinces, 1946–2040	377
18.2	Growth in Real GDP, Real GDP Per Capita, and Labour Force, 1981–2010 and 2010–19	379
18.3	Net Debt in the Four Atlantic Provinces, Fiscal Years 2009–10 and 2019–20	381
20.A1	Changes to Federal Transfers: Health, Post-Secondary Education, and Welfare, 1980 to Present	432
20.A2	Changes to Federal Transfers: Equalization, 1980 to Present	433
20.A3	Changes to Federal Transfers: FSP, DFAA, and Temporary COVID-19 Measures, 1980 to Present	433

Acknowledgments

This book has its origins in a conference titled "Fiscal Federalism in Canada," which was held virtually between 21 and 23 October 2021 under the auspices of the University of Ottawa's Centre on Governance and its federalism and multilevel governance research axis. The authors wish to express their most sincere gratitude to Anna Bogic and Mahyar Sherafat Naseri from the Centre on Governance and to the University's IT team for the logistical management of the event. The conference was financially supported by the Secrétariat du Québec aux relations canadiennes and the University of Ottawa's Alex Trebek Forum for Dialogue. The Faculty of Social Sciences and the Office of the Vice-President, Research and Innovation at the University of Ottawa, the Forum of Federations, the McGill Institute for the Study of Canada, and the University of Calgary's School of Public Policy also contributed to the success of the event, which brought together some of Canada's leading scholars and experts on a wide range of fiscal federalism topics. We want to thank all these backers and partners for their support, as well as the nine graduate students who facilitated the virtual workings of the conference. We thank Ally Hays-Albertstat and Christopher Yurris for their research assistance. We also thank Daniel Quinlan at the University of Toronto Press for supporting this ambitious project and two anonymous referees who commented on the manuscript and helped us improve its general structure and quality. Finally, we gratefully acknowledge financial support for this project from the Social Science and Humanities Research Council Insight Grant 435-2019-0100.

We dedicate this book to the late Richard Bird, a luminary of fiscal federalism studies, who participated at the opening roundtable of the 2021 University of Ottawa conference. In his memory, we hope that this book will become a central and enduring reference on fiscal federalism in Canada and serve to stimulate both public and expert debate in our country.

André Lecours, Daniel Béland, Trevor Tombe, and Eric Champagne

FISCAL FEDERALISM IN CANADA

Analysis, Evaluation, and Prescription

1 Introduction: Fiscal Federalism under the Microscope

ANDRÉ LECOURS, DANIEL BÉLAND, TREVOR TOMBE, AND ERIC CHAMPAGNE

Canada is a country of multiple territorial cleavages. The French-English cleavage and nationalism in Quebec have long structured Canadian political life (Cardinal 2008; McRoberts 2001). Settler colonialism has created a deeply imbalanced relationship between Indigenous and non-Indigenous Canadians (Coulthard 2014; Harris 2020). Federalism has generated political communities in the form of provinces as well as territories (Cairns 1977; Henderson 2008). The diversity of political economies and cultural traditions has contributed to the emergence of regionalism, particularly in the West (Brodie 1990; Gibbins and Berdhal 2003). Against this complex backdrop of political cleavages and communities, it is unsurprising that fiscal federalism has generated conflict in Canada. In fact, quarrels around the territorial distribution and redistribution of financial resources are, as Mary Janigan discusses in chapter 2, as old as Canada itself (see also Janigan 2012). There is, therefore, a timeless quality to debates around fiscal federalism in Canada.

Simultaneously, part of the multifaceted impact of the COVID-19 crisis is that it has created new fiscal challenges and calls for fiscal federalism reform (Béland et al. 2020). The pandemic has exacerbated long-standing tensions within Canadian fiscal federalism and "revealed even greater cracks in the system. We are seeing considerable fiscal pressures on governments with critical responsibilities but without the necessary resources they need to combat this pandemic. This misalignment of revenues and expenditure responsibilities is most severe for municipalities" (Béland, Dahlby, and Orsini 2020). To the problem of municipal finance, we can add federal funding for health care as one of many sources of political tension within fiscal federalism that was amplified by the COVID-19 crisis. While provinces have long requested a faster and greater increase in federal health transfers, the pandemic has made this issue even more urgent, in part because of the situation prevailing in the relatively neglected long-term care sector. In this context, in late 2020 and early 2021, the ten provinces stepped up their campaign to pressure Ottawa to do more on health care funding through the bold proposal of immediately increasing the health-care federal transfers by $28 billion per year. The starting point of the premiers was clear: "Once upon a time, the federal government contributed 50 per cent of the cost of medicare; now it contributes only 22 per cent. The provinces, it seems, are being generous by requesting that the feds need only raise their share to 35 per cent" (McIntosh 2021). Yet, although it is clear that health-care costs are increasingly rapidly, McIntosh (2021) points out that the premiers' argument "misrepresents the actual history of how federal transfers for health care evolved" through obfuscation of past transfers of tax points for health-care financing from Ottawa to the provinces. The debate about the exact role of the federal government in health care is therefore ongoing.

Thus, in the context of the post–COVID-19 pandemic, fiscal federalism is in a peculiar place. The pandemic has upended budgets (federal, provincial, and municipal), creating serious deficit and debt challenges. It has amplified provincial pressure for increasing federal transfers, primarily the Canada Health Transfer (CHT), as well as escalated criticism of equalization from Alberta and Saskatchewan, since the drop in the price of oil during the first waves of the pandemic contributed to reducing territorial disparities while the overall equalization pool kept increasing. The pandemic has also raised serious questions about the structuring and financing of long-term care (Béland and Marier 2020). Crises are often critical junctures for political and economic development, and the pandemic may just represent one such fork in the road in the evolution of fiscal federalism in Canada (Béland et al. 2020).

Canadian fiscal federalism sits largely outside the formal constitutional framework (Oliver, Macklem, and Des Rosiers 2017), but it is central to a decentralized federation with significant territorial diversity like Canada, where intergovernmental transfers play such a crucial role in ensuring the delivery of quality public services.

Canada is exceptional in the world of federations for its degree of decentralization (Dardanelli et al. 2019). This decentralization is visible not only in legislation and administration but also in the fiscal sphere (Perry 1997; Watts 2008; Béland et al. 2017). A high percentage of provincial revenues are ownsource, and the major transfers are largely unconditional (Lecours 2019). At the broadest level, fiscal federalism in Canada has been shaped by provincial governments, which represent genuine political communities that tend to value autonomy. If strong provinces fed by the significant regional diversity of the country have shaped fiscal federalism in the country, multinationalism (Gagnon and Iacovino 2007), specifically the presence of Quebec (Boucher and Noël 2021), has represented the major bulwark against the type of fiscal centralization experienced by mononational federations such as Australia and the United States (Fenna 2019; Kincaid 2019). It is unsurprising, then, that fiscal federalism is strongly and consistently challenged in Canada, with (as this volume demonstrates) various provinces having different perspectives on the nature, structure, and legal foundations of fiscal arrangements and transfers.

Certainly, transfers from the federal to the provincial governments are necessary. Federations are typically characterized by a "vertical fiscal gap" insofar as the spending of constituent unit governments in their constitutionally specified areas tends to exceed their own-source revenues, whereas the revenues generated by federal governments often exceed the cost of their constitutionally mandated responsibilities. As a consequence, all federations operate transfers between the federal and constituent unit governments. These transfers have historically taken different forms (Perry 1997; Stevenson 2006), but, since 2004, they have largely been block grants of a mostly unconditional nature meant to support health care (the CHT) as well as higher education, child services, and social assistance (the Canada Social Transfer, CST). As mentioned earlier, the CHT is a particularly politically charged transfer considering both the long-term weight of health care for provincial governments and the particular demands placed on health-care systems by the COVID-19 pandemic.

Like most other advanced industrialized federations (the United States being the notable exception: Théret 1999; Béland and Lecours 2014c), Canada has an equalization program designed to reduce the consequences of territorial economic disparities, which can be considerable in a country where natural resources (especially oil and gas) are unevenly located across provinces.[1] Equalization, together with the CHT and the CST, form a *system* of transfers (Béland et al. 2017). Equalization is often referred to as "the glue that holds our federation together" (Expert Panel 2006, 1), but it has nonetheless sometimes found itself in the crosshairs of some provincial governments, particularly Alberta's, as the 2021 referendum clearly shows. Discussions around equalization raise important programmatic questions tackled in this volume, such as the treatment of natural resources in the calculation of provincial fiscal capacity as well as the (un)predictability of payments from year to year and its impact on provincial budgets. In a broader perspective, these discussions also involve the question of the appropriate level of territorial redistribution in the Canadian federation. Equalization in Canada has to find a balance between provincial autonomy, a fundamental principle of the federation (Béland and Lecours 2011), and territorial solidarity. This perilous exercise is a microcosm of federalism's constant attempt to balance self-rule and shared rule (Elazar 1987).

As discussed, in this collection, in addition to the CHT, CST, and equalization, fiscal federalism in Canada involves the partial and sometimes occasional financing by the federal government of specific policy sectors such as housing, infrastructure, municipalities, and early learning and childcare (Pomeroy 2001, 2017; Bojorques, Champagne, and Vaillancourt 2009; Champagne 2013; Champagne and Choinière 2016; Champagne and Tellier 2017; Bird and Slack 2017; Boessenkool and Robson 2021). This financing is well received by some provinces for bringing extra and welcome resources, but it is much less well received by others, since it may distort their policy priorities or simply come with conditions deemed unacceptable. Quebec governments consistently and as a matter of principle oppose, and struggle against, conditionality, even contesting the notion of federal spending power that allows financing in constitutionally assigned provincial jurisdictions (Noël 2008). Clearly, there are significant fiscal federalism issues beyond the major transfers.

One such issue is the challenges faced by municipalities. The political position of municipalities has always been ambiguous in Canada (Champagne 2012), something that also applies in relation to their place within the fiscal federalism framework. Their financial situation is precarious. Canada's major cities, especially, have seen their responsibilities increase considerably over the past decades. In addition to their traditional service delivery duties (basic infrastructure, parks and recreation, public safety, garbage collection and recycling), they have seen a multitude of social, economic, and environmental responsibilities fall into their lap in the face of new urban issues. These issues include affordable housing and homelessness; air quality, energy consumption, and climate change; immigration and societal integration; urban Aboriginal communities; and transit. They typically require a multilevel response (Horak and Young 2012), even though the formal constitutional status of Canadian municipalities has remained unchanged (they are still "creatures of the provinces") and they are quite fiscally dependent upon the federal and provincial governments (Slack 2017).

Any examination of fiscal federalism in Canada should also consider the plight of First Nations.[2] First Nations issues have, for good reasons, become an important focus of Canadian politics in recent years. Colonial and assimilationist policies (Macdonald 2014; Feir 2016) have generated political marginalization, social and cultural dislocations, and economic frailty for First Nations. The struggle of First Nations against colonialism (Alfred and Corntassel 2005; Coulthard 2014) has put pressure on the Canadian state. Their position in the Canadian federal system – as rights holders in virtue of treaties or historical presence on the lands without representing, in constitutional terms, constituent units of the federation – is inherently ambiguous (Otis and Papillon 2013). Hence, the financing of First Nations is a unique and crucial endeavour that adds complexity to fiscal federalism in Canada. This complexity is also the case for the country's three territories, which have their own Territorial Formula Financing (TFF) and are home to a diversity of Indigenous peoples.

The main goal of this volume is to encourage and contribute to scholarly research, policy debate, and public understanding on fiscal federalism in Canada. For this purpose, we have gathered a varied and multidisciplinary group of specialists to explore political and economic issues linked to the design, process, actors, and components of fiscal federalism in Canada, as well as to the policy content and political dynamics associated with it. The book provides analysis, evaluation, and some prescriptions. From an analytical perspective, the authors shed light on how fiscal federalism works and why it works the way it does. From an evaluation angle, they weigh in on the strengths and weaknesses of fiscal arrangements, transfers, and processes. Finally, the book also points to ways in which fiscal federalism in Canada could be improved.

Fiscal Federalism: Multidimensionality and Multidisciplinarity

This volume builds upon and contributes to a rich literature on fiscal federalism (Bird 1986; Bird and Vaillancourt 1998; Ahmad and Brosio 2006, 2015; Shah 2007; Boadway and Shah 2007, 2009; Bird and Vaillancourt 2006; Anderson 2010; Sorens 2011; Jametti and Joanis 2016; Watts 2018; Yilmaz and Zahir 2020). This literature has evolved from being economics-dominated to multidisciplinary (Valdesalici 2019, 95), with political scientists, historians, and legal scholars all making important contributions (Rodden 2006; Weingast 2009, 2014; Sorens 2016; Béland et al. 2017; Valdesalici and Palermo 2018; Janigan 2020).[3] The present volume very much contributes to the disciplinary diversification of the field.

The "first-generation" fiscal federalism literature, dominated by economists, was very much focused on the optimal allocation of revenue and expenditure responsibilities across different orders of government (Musgrave 1959; Oates 1972; McLure 1983). It emphasized how central governments tend to have advantages over constituent unit governments in conducting macroeconomic policy on account of their authority over monetary policy, exchange rates, and international trade. In addition, this literature argued that the case for decentralization was strongest when the provision of public goods or services has only local effects. In this context, constituent unit governments can tailor programs to reflect the preferences of their residents, and they may potentially be more accountable to them (Tiebout 1961). This literature also suggested a limited role for subnational governments in redistributive taxation. These are, of course, broad theoretical principles. In practice, research has shown that the way and the extent to which these principles are put into practice varies across time and space (Shah and Boadway 2006). An exploration of some of the specific issues explored by this literature and the subsequent research it sparked is valuable.

The earlier economics-dominated literature on fiscal federalism looked extensively at whether and when decentralized approaches to raising government revenues are appropriate (appropriateness was typically defined in terms of efficiency). In doing so, it explored the "tax assignment problem" (McLure 1983), generally finding the mobility of workers and capital across constituent units to be a particularly important variable. A key argument is that there might be a shift in where individuals choose to live if constituent unit taxes are not directly related to benefits received, something that may detract from a country's overall productivity (Tiebout 1956; Boadway and Flatters 1982; Albouy 2012; Tombe and Winter 2021). Constituent unit governments should therefore rely on taxation of mobile individuals and businesses that are closely connected to the benefits of living in the jurisdiction, and redistributive taxes, such as highly progressive income taxation, should be undertaken by higher levels of government (Chernick 1992; Oates 1996). More recent work argues for an important, though circumscribed, role for redistributive subnational taxation (Milligan and Smart 2019).

There is also an extensive literature (not strictly limited to, but incorporating important elements of, fiscal questions) on the program expenditure side (Tiebout 1956; Musgrave 1969; Oates 1972; Epple and Nechyba 2004; Boadway and Tremblay 2011). This literature has found strong reasons for decentralizing many public policy sectors (Hubbard and Paquet 2010). For one thing, having a diversity of designs or even menus of public policies allows for experimentation, discovery, and learning (Hueglin and Fenna 2015, 43). Constituent units as public policy "laboratories" is an old idea (Bryce 1901) but one that remains an active source of research today (Boyd and Olive 2021). The literature has also identified downsides in the decentralization of policy. Competition and externalities between constituent unit governments, for example, may mean an underprovision of certain important public goods, such as environmental protection (Banzhaf and Chupp 2012). As federal governments tend to want to expand their presence in many areas of constituent unit jurisdiction – including in Canada, most recently with childcare – the age-old federalism question of what order of government should perform which policy task remains tremendously important. The pandemic may represent a critical juncture in the evolution of the division of roles and responsibilities in federal systems (Chattopadhyay et al. 2022; Steytler 2022), which could have important implications for fiscal federalism.

The literature on fiscal federalism, and on federalism more broadly, has consistently remarked that federal governments tend to levy significantly higher levels of revenue than their own program expenditure responsibilities require (Watts 2008; Fenna 2012; Hueglin and Fenna 2015, 170–1; Yilmaz and Zahir 2020). This vertical fiscal gap, or imbalance, has drawn the attention of both economists and political scientists seeking to theorize its origins and ascertain its effects (Boadway and Tremblay 2006; Noël 2009; Fenna and Hollander 2013). To address this gap, federations conduct financial transfers from federal to constituent unit governments. In the last two decades or so, research on these transfers and on broader questions of fiscal architecture has coincided with the "second-generation" fiscal federalism (Weingast 2009, 2014; Eccleston and Krever 2017; Valdesalici 2019, 95), which views fiscal arrangements as the products of politics and state-building rather than as neutral objects abstracted from their social, cultural, and political contexts (Watts 2000, 2008; Joanis 2018). Such research has addressed, among other things, the question of the impact of fiscal arrangements on the autonomy of constituent units (McKinnon 1997), on their fiscal performance (Rodden 2002), on their prosperity (Weingast 2009), and on the quality of their democracy (Weingast 2009). It has been strongly influenced by the "market-preserving" federalism model (Weingast 1995; Qian and Weingast 1997), which is normatively geared towards enhancing market mechanisms and establishes an "optimal" fiscal architecture design featuring strongly autonomous constituent units firmly integrated into the national market and facing hard budget constraints (Weingast 2009, 281). Despite the popularity of this model, Wallner and Boychuk (2014) found that, contrary to the expectations set by the market-preserving federalism model, three economically successful federations (Canada, the United States, and Australia) showed considerable divergence.

Fiscal and economic territorial disparities between constituent units, and the equalization schemes designed to mitigate their consequences, have drawn the attention of a diversity of scholars who have tackled questions about the origins, design, governance, and efficiency of horizontal fiscal redistribution mechanisms (Boadway and Flatters 1982; Shah 2007; Dafflon 2008, 2012; Hepp and von Hagen 2012; Béland and Lecours 2011, 2013, 2014c; Yilmaz and Zahir 2020). Some authors have also tackled the often politically tricky question of the treatment of natural resources in various equalization systems (Fenna 2011; Anderson 2012; Eccleston and Woolley 2014; Trojbicz 2021).

There exists a multidisciplinary scholarship, which includes contributions from political philosophers, political scientists, and economists, that explores the relationship between, on the one hand, fiscal federalism and, on the other hand, self-determination and secessionism or, to take it from the other angle, national unity (Castells 2001; Stauffer 2001; Bird and Ebel 2006; Sorens 2016; Lecours and Béland 2019). This scholarship has explored issues of territorial redistribution in multinational contexts (Boucher and Noël 2021), that is, in countries where a significant proportion of citizens identify with a nation other than the one projected by the state. In these contexts, normative concerns about fairness and justice have been considered particularly salient (Grégoire and Jewkes 2015).

Canada and Fiscal Federalism

As one of the oldest, most stable, and most prosperous federations in the world, Canada is a central case in the study of fiscal federalism (Ahmad and Brosio 2006; Shah 2007; Anderson 2012; Ruiz Almendral and Vaillancourt 2013; Eccleston and Krever 2017; Yilmaz and Zahir 2020; Trojbicz 2021). Scholars have used the Canadian case to make contributions to comparative fiscal federalism on taxation (Vaillancourt and Guimond 2013); austerity (Brown 2017); and fiscal transfers (Boadway 2007), including equalization (Béland and Lecours 2011, 2013) and, perhaps most particularly, the question of the treatment of natural resources in these fiscal transfers (Plourde 2012; Joanis and Vaillancourt 2020; Béland, Lecours, and Brassard-Dion 2021). The study of Canadian fiscal federalism has also been a fundamental component of the broader literature on Canadian federalism, as scholars of Canadian federalism have acknowledged the crucial importance of the fiscal component (Stevenson 2009; Hueglin 2021). Not only are fiscal arrangements and transfers central for understanding Canadian federalism, but, in Canada, fiscal federalism is part and parcel of generating knowledge about the country (see, for example, Théret 1999).

In this spirit, researchers have examined Canadian fiscal federalism from a variety of angles, including taxation (Hale 2001; Tellier 2016); budgets, borrowing, and public finances (Doern, Maslove, and Prince 2013; Hanniman 2018; Tellier 2020); fiscal arrangements (Bird and Vaillancourt 2001; Vaillancourt and Rault 2003; Lazar 2005; Bird and Vaillancourt 2006; Snoddon and Hobson 2010); and the historical and contemporary evolution of fiscal federalism more broadly (Perry 1997; Stevenson 2006; Janigan 2020), including the numerous reforms to its various components over the years (Maxwell 1937; Moore, Perry, and Beach 1966; Banting, Brown, and Courchene 1994; Perry 1997; Tombe 2018; Brown 2020).

The scholarship on fiscal federalism in Canada has a few distinctive features. The first is a focus, by legal scholars and political scientists, on the federal spending power. Here, scholars have looked at, and in some cases questioned, the legal and constitutional existence of this power (Petter 1989; Noël 2008; Courchene 2008) as well as the effect of its use on national unity (Telford 2003). The second distinctive feature of the study of fiscal federalism in Canada is the emphasis, particularly on the part of Quebec scholars, on the vertical fiscal gap as an imbalance that needs to be addressed. The charge led by the Quebec government in the early 2000s to "fix" the fiscal imbalance, culminating in the Séguin Commission (Commission sur le déséquilibre fiscal 2002), triggered a lot of scholarly interest for that question (for example, St-Hilaire 2005; Noël 2009). The third is equalization. Equalization in Canada has recently been termed "a controversial and contested policy success" (Béland, Lecours, and Tombe 2022, 225). There has always been much to examine about equalization, including the design and the evolution of the program (Courchene 1983, 1984, 2007; Béland and Lecours 2010; Béland et al. 2017), potential reforms (Feehan 2020), its governance (Béland and Lecours 2011), the intergovernmental relations around it (Lecours and Béland 2010), and the difficult question of natural resources (Boadway, Flatters, and Leblanc 1983; Locke and Hobson 2004; Courchene 2004, 2005, 2006; Boessenkool 2002; Béland and Lecours 2014b; Eisen, Emes, and Whalen 2020). The fourth distinctive feature of the study of fiscal federalism in Canada is how it features in national unity issues. In this context, scholars have questioned how nationalism in Quebec has been accommodated through equalization (Béland and Lecours 2014a; Béland et al. 2017; Bird 2018), how equalization has affected national cohesion more broadly (Bird and Vaillancourt 2001), and how it has factored into Western alienation (Gibbins and Berdhal 2003; Janigan 2012, 2020; Béland and Lecours 2021).

This volume seeks to add to all these angles for analysing fiscal federalism in Canada. In addition, some of the authors look at more specific issues and targeted transfers. For example, population aging (Saillant 2016; Marier 2021) and health funding (Tombe 2020; Mou 2021) present long-run challenges for many provincial governments, and the exact role of the federal government is the object of much debate. Financial arrangements with First Nations are an important part of their aspirations for self-government and the broader reconciliation promises, and federal policy is undergoing significant renewal (Indigenous Services Canada, 2021). Finally, the pandemic may represent a critical juncture for Canada's fiscal arrangements (Béland et al. 2020), and scholars have, in this context, been mulling over reforms in federal-provincial transfers (Goldberg and Speer 2020) and in long-term care (Busby 2021). As we consider the future of Canadian federalism (Goodyear-Grant and Hanniman 2019; Gagnon and Poirier 2020), the fiscal element is of crucial importance.

This multidisciplinary volume is strongly rooted in the idea that fiscal federalism is not only, and not mostly, a technical enterprise but rather that, both in its process and product, it is strongly shaped by, while being constitutive of, Canadian politics. The volume pays attention to a variety of actors (individual politicians, political parties, provinces, First Nations, experts, and civil society leaders) considered significant in the production, reproduction, and, sometimes, the transformation of fiscal federalism in Canada. It situates these actors in their political and institutional environment in order to fully understand their preferences, objectives, and strategies. The volume also pays attention to how ideas about the Canadian federation and political community, as well as identities (territorial and otherwise), shape politics around fiscal federalism.

Outline of the Book

The volume begins by situating Canadian fiscal federalism in its historical, constitutional, and contemporary COVID-19 perspectives.

In chapter 2, Mary Janigan looks at the origins of equalization. Janigan understands the federal equalization program as a creative resolution to the acrimonious debates over revenue-sharing between poorer and richer provinces. Before 1957, the federal government's approach of ad hoc grants and loans could not effectively mitigate the consequences of territorial economic disparities, something outlined by the Royal Commission on Dominion-Provincial Relations in its 1940 report for constitutional change. Instead, Ottawa forged deals with individual provinces so they would "rent" taxes to the federal government in return for block grants. After Quebec was the only province to not renew the tax rental agreements in 1952, the creation of an equalization program providing unconditional transfers to poorer provinces became the permanent, albeit partial, solution to the long-standing problem of territorial inequality. In chapter 3, Peter Oliver examines the constitutional basis for the federal transfers that make up fiscal federalism. Some transfers, such as equalizations payments, are underpinned by a constitutional provision, whereas the legal basis for others is linked to the federal spending power. The chapter explains that the federal spending power comes in different forms and that the sources of the power are not clear. The chapter also points out that the Supreme Court of Canada is reluctant to view spending as a justiciable matter, even as it occasionally refers to the spending power. In chapter 4, Trevor Tombe surveys the state of federal-provincial finances using the latest available data and evaluates how current fiscal arrangements responded to the pandemic. The chapter argues that, despite the massive fiscal and economic shock of the pandemic, Canada's fiscal arrangements remained relatively robust and withstood recent challenges fairly well. Targeted, though ad hoc, increases in federal transfers to provincial, territorial, and municipal governments absorbed a significant portion of subnational fiscal costs from the pandemic. At the same time, the pandemic revealed where change may be most needed, and the chapter evaluates several possible reforms to improve the design and delivery of major federal transfers.

Next, the volume examines the major federal-provincial transfers. Perhaps no single such transfer is as important as the Canada Health Transfer (CHT), which Robin Boadway examines in chapter 5. Despite its name, the notional attribution of the CHT to provincial health-care expenditures means little in practice. The conditions of the Canada Health Act are limited, and the primary role of the CHT, Boadway notes, is to address the vertical fiscal gap. The CHT helps bridge this gap but in a way that has gradually declined over time. The chapter concludes by exploring some potential reforms, ranging from increasing the size of the CHT, to incorporating measures of expenditure needs, to changing the conditions that the federal government attaches to CHT funding. As Canada recovers from the COVID-19 pandemic, and as populations age rapidly across the country, the CHT should occupy much of our attention. Complementing the CHT is the other pillar of major vertical federal transfers: the Canada Social Transfer (CST), or – as Michael Prince describes it in chapter 6 – the "poor cousin" of the larger programs. Following a rich history, described in detail in the chapter, the CST has evolved to serve a largely ceremonial function. It nominally supports provincial social assistance programs, but, like the CHT, the program comes with few strings attached. Moreover, as Prince argues, it lacks vision, a clear policy objective, and effective governance arrangements between federal and provincial governments. With a renewal on the horizon for 2024, Prince discusses several reform options that may be considered. These range from maintaining the status quo, to adding measures of fiscal need to the allocation of CST, to the more dramatic option of shifting all social assistance expenditures to the federal government. In addition to the vertical fiscal gap, there are differences between provincial governments' ability to raise revenues. Canada's equalization system helps bridge these horizontal gaps. This program is the subject of recurring, and often intense, debates, but what is rarely considered is the challenge it may pose for provincial budget forecasts. In chapter 7, Marcelin Joanis provides new and systematic estimates of the difficulty in forecasting provincial equalization payments. These "equalization errors" can be significant, and they vary across provinces. Reforms to improve the stability and predictability of the program – ranging from prefunding the program, to creating an independent body for managing arrangements, to reforming the entire formula to reflect macroeconomic variables rather than a representative tax system – are, Joanis argues, worth considering.

The next two chapters unpack two recurrent dilemmas facing fiscal federalism in Canada. First, in chapter 8, James Feehan describes the complications posed by natural resource revenues. These large but unevenly distributed revenue sources exacerbate already significant fiscal capacities across provinces. Incorporating such revenues into equalization is fundamentally more difficult than other revenue sources. Various design choices have attempted to grapple with this issue, and the chapter reviews this history and the strengths and weaknesses of the current systems. The central challenge that remains is one of incentives for provincial governments: raising more natural resource revenues results in smaller equalization payments. This consequence may lead to choices that artificially lower such revenues, which Feehan argues may be the case with respect to hydroelectricity. There is no simple solution to these issues, but Feehan concludes by noting that an independent arm's-length agency may be a productive way forward. The creation of an arm's-length agency is also a potential solution to a second challenge for fiscal federalism in Canada presented in chapter 9 by Kyle Hanniman. With the pandemic, there is renewed attention paid to the long-term sustainability of provincial finances. Hanniman argues that, while increasing federal transfers may appear to be a solution to provincial fiscal challenges, such support may undermine fiscal discipline even further. This dilemma raises problems of governance that are particularly acute in Canada, given its limited capacity to constrain borrowing. An arm's-length agency responsible for monitoring the transfer system and advising the federal government on its reform could help reconcile federal support and provincial discipline by strengthening the federation's problem-solving capacity and helping harden provincial budget constraints. The feasibility and potential effectiveness of this approach is critically examined in the chapter.

One significant feature of this book is the consideration of emerging issues and new actors in the analysis of fiscal federalism in Canada. New issues resulting from changes in the economy, demography, environment, and politics of Canada have resulted in the federal government funding national programs, sometimes within provincial jurisdictions. Newer actors in Canadian fiscal federalism include First Nations and municipalities. The next few chapters look at these emerging issues and newer actors. In some instances, the federal government holds and uses significant leverage on emerging issues, while in other instances it is content to stay on the sidelines.

In chapter 10 on the territories, Christopher Yurris, Daniel Béland, and Trevor Tombe turn to Territorial Formula Financing (TFF), which provides annual transfers to the three territories. Compared to other core elements of fiscal federalism in Canada such as equalization, TFF has a low public profile and is not a source of overt territorial conflict. Yet, as suggested in the chapter, TFF should be studied, as it intersects with key issues such as devolution, demographic change, reconciliation, and the development of natural resources. The chapter maps these complex issues in order to offer a broad overview of TFF and fiscal federalism in Canada's North. It shows that TFF is a fascinating component of fiscal federalism in Canada that deserves more scholarly and policy attention moving forward. Chapter 11 focuses on a prominent topic: the place of First Nations in Canadian fiscal federalism. In this chapter, Donn. L. Feir and David Scoones analyse, from a historical perspective, the most recent advances in the relationship between the federal government and First Nations, proposing new funding models to support First Nations' self-government. This question requires a better understanding and recognition of the current capacity of First Nations in Canada to generate and manage own-source revenues. Chapter 12 focuses on the federal government's most recent long-term care initiatives in the wake of COVID-19. Anthony Breton and Patrik Marier analyse the management of long-term care services, which was a massive challenge for many provinces during the pandemic. Breton and Marier observe that such services are not formally a federal responsibility, although, during the pandemic, the military was called upon to help out some provinces. The pandemic has led the federal government to contemplate intervening more significantly in long-term care by formulating new conditions for provinces accessing federal funds. Breton and Marier put into perspective the historical role of the provinces in this sector by proposing alternative solutions to improving the quality of long-term care in Canada.

The next three chapters focus on dimensions of particular relevance to the municipal sector. Enid Slack in chapter 13 explores the fiscal gap between cities and federal and provincial governments. She shows that cities have increasing responsibilities, which require resources that largely exceed their fiscal capacity. Slack's main argument is that, given their increasing responsibilities, cities rely too much on property taxes and intergovernmental transfers. She suggests it is time to review the roles and responsibilities of all levels of government to ensure that cities have the fiscal instruments they need to match their expenditure responsibilities. In chapter 14, Steve Pomeroy examines another critical issue for cities: housing. He takes a historical perspective to describe the role of the federal and provincial governments in housing policies and programs, particularly on social housing. His analysis highlights the varying positions of the federal government in this area over the years, with an emphasis on the most recent federal refocus. This refocus tends to reaffirm the role of the federal government, particularly in programs to assist the homeless and households in need. In chapter 15, Eric Champagne and Aracelly Denise Granja examine public infrastructure financing in Canada from a multilevel governance perspective. They describe how basic infrastructure financing requires shared contributions from all three levels of government, which makes financing packages and project implementation much more complicated. They propose a typology of the most prominent financing instruments and note the pressure on Canadian municipalities to maintain infrastructure over the medium and long term.

Chapter 16 by Jennifer Wallner looks at the funding of elementary and secondary education in Canada. While the federal government has traditionally supported some initiatives in higher education, the author notes that elementary and secondary education is almost exclusively a provincial responsibility, an arrangement peculiar to Canada since central governments usually play a more significant role in education within most federations. Wallner is interested in interprovincial variations in education financing but, at the same time, notes that a focus on the principle of universality has helped produce strong and consistent results across time and space. In the cases of education for First Nations and for official minority language communities, she suggests that the federal government should rethink its arrangements and practices. Jennifer Robson's chapter 17 focuses on early learning and childcare (ELCC). Though an area of provincial jurisdiction, federal and private expenditures are heavily involved in this policy sector. This mix of financing arrangements makes ELCC policies as complex to analyse as they are varied across provinces. In the chapter, Robson effectively combines several data sources of information on ELCC systems and financing arrangements to paint one of the clearest pictures available of these systems in Canada. The analysis suggests the recent federal goal of becoming an equal partner with provinces on ELCC expenditures may be challenging, especially in provinces that already have high levels of public ELCC expenditures like Quebec. Regardless, increased federal expenditures in this area, Robson argues, appear to make the ELCC systems more resilient.

Next, the volume explores key provincial and regional perspectives on fiscal federalism in Canada. Canada is a highly decentralized federation featuring significant provincial and regional economic, demographic, social, and political diversity. Although we could not offer a view from all provinces on fiscal federalism, the four chapters illustrate the sheer diversity of provincial and regional perspectives.

In chapter 18 on the Atlantic provinces, Richard Saillant explains how demographic aging and the economic and budgetary challenges stemming from it are a major source of concern in this poorer region of the country, which has historically benefited from federal equalization payments. Moreover, as Saillant suggests, each of the four Atlantic provinces has adopted a distinct fiscal trajectory to address relatively similar demographic, economic, and fiscal challenges. His analysis stresses the importance of political agency in addressing major demographic and economic challenges within the broader institutional context of fiscal federalism. Turning to Quebec, Alain Noël in chapter 19 emphasizes the importance of provincial autonomy as a political imperative that shapes the province's preferences on fiscal federalism. This discussion leads Noël to introduce what he calls Quebec's fiscal federalism trilemma, which features a tension between autonomy, vertical equity, and horizontal equity. As Noël shows, while this trilemma remains largely implicit in political discourse, it does underlie Quebec's relatively coherent policy orientations on fiscal federalism. Yet, as he suggests, the three objectives are difficult to reconcile, and the overall policy orientations are dynamic in nature because successive Quebec governments can emphasize different components of the trilemma to reflect their own priorities.

Next, dealing with Ontario, Tracy Snoddon's chapter 20 emphasizes the concerns about fiscal federalism that have become dominant for successive provincial governments since the early 1980s. These concerns relate to the seemingly unfair fiscal treatment of the province relating to its net fiscal contribution to Canada, in part through the federal Equalization Program, and they involve the quest over time for adequate, stable, and sustainable federal transfers to Ontario. In her analysis, Snoddon evaluates these concerns before discussing how the COVID-19 situation might exacerbate political tensions over fiscal federalism in relation to Ontario and beyond.

From Alberta come even more acute concerns about fiscal federalism from the perspective of a traditionally wealthier province. As Ken Boessenkool shows in chapter 21, Alberta's understanding of fiscal federalism is closely tied to natural resources. Another specific aspect of Alberta's perspective on fiscal federalism is the existence of sentiments of regional political alienation and the sense that, while both Alberta and Quebec strongly advocate for strong provincial autonomy, the latter has much more clout in Ottawa than the former in shaping fiscal federalism. As Boessenkool shows, since the beginning of the Justin Trudeau era, political resentment in Alberta towards the federal Liberal government and its environmental policies has exacerbated both traditional criticisms of equalization and the belief that the province is not treated fairly within the federation. This situation leads Boessenkool to discuss what a "fair deal" for Alberta could look like.

Finally, Alan Fenna in chapter 22 offers reflections on Canadian fiscal federalism by placing it in a comparative perspective. Fenna examines the extent to which Canadian fiscal federalism corresponds to a set of "best practices." On the vertical side, Fenna judges that Canada is very close to such best practices with a small vertical fiscal gap and low conditionality on transfers. There is, however, a weakness in that these transfers are not always the subject of any binding intergovernmental agreement. On the horizontal side, Fenna concludes that it is really impossible to say what constitutes best practices and, therefore, whether Canada conforms to them. He judges that equalization in the country is good if one considers what is politically feasible. In chapter 23, a conclusion highlights the main contributions of the volume and puts forward some recommendations for fiscal federalism in Canada.

NOTES

1 Equalization does not aim to reduce economic inequalities between provinces (there are other policies designed to do that, namely industrial and regional economic development policies) but simply to mitigate their consequences. By ensuring that citizens can receive public services of comparable quality at comparable levels of taxation, independent of their province of residence, equalization helps poorer provinces retain their population.
2 The Inuit and the Métis are also Indigenous peoples, but they have a different relationship history with the Canadian state.
3 A major multidisciplinary research project on fiscal federalism, featuring a comparison of several federations as well as the European Union and led by Stefan Griller from the Faculty of Law at the University of Salzburg, was unfolding at the time of writing. For information, see https://fiscalfederalism.eu/.

REFERENCES

Ahmad, Ehtisham, and Giorgio Brosio, eds. 2006. *Handbook of Fiscal Federalism*. Cheltenham, UK: Edward Elgar.
– eds. 2015. *Handbook of Multilevel Finance*. Cheltenham, UK: Edward Elgar.
Albouy, David. 2012. "Evaluating the Efficiency and Equity of Federal Fiscal Equalization." *Journal of Public Economics* 96, nos. 9–10: 824–39. https://doi.org/10.1016/j.jpubeco.2012.05.015.
Alfred, Taiaiake, and Jeff Corntassel. 2005. "Being Indigenous: Resurgence against Colonialism." *Government and Opposition* 40, no. 4: 597–614. https://doi.org/10.1111/j.1477-7053.2005.00166.x.

Anderson, George. 2010. *Fiscal Federalism: A Comparative Introduction*. Oxford: Oxford University Press.
– ed. 2012. *Oil and Gas in Federal Systems*. Don Mills, ON: Oxford University Press.
Banting, Keith, Douglas M. Brown, and Thomas Courchene, eds. 1994. *The Future of Fiscal Federalism*. Kingston, ON: School of Policy Studies.
Banzhaf, H. Spencer, and B. Andrew Chupp. 2012. "Fiscal Federalism and Interjurisdictional Externalities: New Results and an Application to US Air Pollution." *Journal of Public Economics* 96, nos. 5–6: 449–64. https://doi.org/10.1016/j.jpubeco.2012.01.001.
Béland, Daniel, Bev Dahlby, Steve Orsini. 2020. "COVID-19 Will Force a Change to Canada's Fiscal Arrangements." *Policy Options*, 7 May 2020. https://policyoptions.irpp.org/magazines/may-2020/covid-19-will-force-a-change-to-canadas-fiscal-arrangements/.
Béland, Daniel, and André Lecours. 2010. "Logiques institutionnelles et politiques publiques: Le programme de péréquation d'hier à aujourd'hui." *Politiques et Sociétés* 29, no. 3: 3–20. https://doi.org/10.7202/1003554ar.
– 2011. "The Ideational Dimension of Federalism: The 'Australian Model' and the Politics of Equalization in Canada." *Australian Journal of Political Science* 46, no. 2: 199–212. https://doi.org/10.1080/10361146.2011.567974.
– 2013. "The Institutional Politics of Territorial Redistribution: Federalism and Equalization Policy in Australia and Canada." *Canadian Journal of Political Science* 46, no. 1: 93–113. https://doi.org/10.1017/S000842391300019X.
– 2014a. "Accommodation and the Politics of Fiscal Equalization in Multinational States: The Case of Canada." *Nations and Nationalism* 20, no. 2: 337–54. https://doi.org/10.1111/nana.12049.
– 2014b. "Equalization and the Politics of Natural Resources: Balancing Provincial Autonomy and Territorial Solidarity." In *Canada: The State of the Federation 2012*, edited by Loleen Berdhal, André Juneau, and Carolyn Hughes Tuohy, 99–115. Montreal and Kingston: McGill-Queen's University Press.
– 2014c. "Fiscal Federalism and American Exceptionalism: Why Is There No Federal Equalization Program in the United States?" *Journal of Public Policy* 34, no. 2: 303–29. https://doi.org/10.1017/S0143814X14000038.
– 2021. "L'Alberta, l'aliénation de l'Ouest et le programme fédéral de péréquation: Identités territoriales, cadrage idéologique et inscription à l'agenda politique." *Politique et Sociétés* 40, no. 3: 177–96. https://doi.org/10.7202/1083028ar.
Béland, Daniel, André Lecours, and Nikola Brassard-Dion. 2021. "Canada." In *Oil Wealth and Federal Conflict in American Petrofederations*, edited by Beni Trojbicz, 101–21. Amsterdam: Elsevier.
Béland, Daniel, André Lecours, Gregory P. Marchildon, Haizhen Mou, and M. Rose Olfert. 2017. *Fiscal Federalism and Equalization Policy in Canada: Political and Economic Dimensions*. Toronto: University of Toronto Press.

Béland, Daniel, André Lecours, Mireille Paquet, and Trevor Tombe. 2020. "A Critical Juncture in Fiscal Federalism? Canada's Response to COVID-19." *Canadian Journal of Political Science* 53, no. 2: 239–43. https://doi.org/10.1017/S0008423920000323.
Béland, Daniel, André Lecours, and Trevor Tombe. 2022. "The Federal Equalization Program as a Controversial and Contested Policy Success." In *Policy Success in Canada: Cases, Lessons, Challenges*, edited by Evert Lindquist, Michael Howlett, Grace Skogstad, Geneviève Tellier, and Paul 't Hart, 225–44. Oxford: Oxford University Press.
Béland, Daniel, and Patrik Marier. 2020. "COVID-19 and Long-Term Care Policy for Older People in Canada." *Journal of Aging & Social Policy* 32, nos. 4–5: 358–64. https://doi.org/10.1080/08959420.2020.1764319.
Bird, Richard M. 1986. "On Measuring Fiscal Centralization and Fiscal Balance in Federal States." *Environment and Planning C: Politics and Space* 4, no. 4: 389–404. https://doi.org/10.1068/c040389.
– 2018. "Equalization and Canada's Constitution: The Tie That Binds?" *Canadian Tax Journal* 66, no. 4: 847–69. https://doi.org/10.2139/ssrn.3262830.
Bird, Richard M., and Robert D. Ebel. 2006. "Fiscal Federalism and National Unity." In *Handbook of Fiscal Federalism*, edited by Ehtisham Ahmad and Giorgio Brosio, 499–520. Cheltenham, UK: Edward Elgar.
Bird, Richard M., and Enid Slack. 2017. *Financing Infrastructure: Who Should Pay?* Montreal and Kingston: McGill-Queen's University Press.
Bird, Richard M., and François Vaillancourt, eds. 1998. *Fiscal Decentralization in Developing Countries*. Cambridge: Cambridge University Press.
– 2001. "Fiscal Arrangements for Maintaining an Effective State in Canada." *Environment and Planning C: Politics and Space* 19, no. 2: 163–97. https://doi.org/10.1068/c0052.
– 2006. "Changing with the Times: Success, Failure, and Inertia in Canadian Federal Arrangements, 1945–2002." In *Federalism and Economic Reform: International Perspectives*, edited by Jessica S. Wallach and T.N. Srinivasan, 189–248. New York: Cambridge University Press.
Boadway, Robin. 2007. "Canada." In *The Practice of Fiscal Federalism: Comparative Perspectives*, edited by Anwar Shah, 98–124. Montreal and Kingston: McGill-Queen's University Press.
Boadway, Robin, and Frank Flatters. 1982. "Efficiency and Equalization Payments in a Federal System of Government: A Synthesis and Extension of Recent Results." *Canadian Journal of Economics* 15, no 4: 613–33. https://doi.org/10.2307/134918.
Boadway, Robin, Frank Flatters, and Alfred Leblanc. 1983. "Revenue Sharing and the Equalization of Natural Resource Revenues." *Canadian Public Policy* 9, no. 2: 174–80. https://doi.org/10.2307/3550994.
Boadway, Robin, and Anwar Shah, eds. 2007. *Intergovernmental Fiscal Transfers: Principles and Practice*. Washington, DC: World Bank.

– 2009. *Fiscal Federalism: Principles and Practice of Multiorder Government*. Cambridge: Cambridge University Press.

Boadway, Robin, and Jean-François Tremblay. 2006. "A Theory of Fiscal Imbalance." *FinanzArchiv/Public Finance Analysis* 62, no. 1: 1–27. https://doi.org/10.1628/001522106776667004.

– 2011. "Reassessment of the Tiebout Model." *Journal of Public Economics* 96, nos. 11–12: 1063–78. https://doi.org/10.1016/j.jpubeco.2011.01.002.

Boessenkool, Kenneth J. 2002. "Ten Reasons to Remove Nonrenewable Resources from Equalization." Speaking Notes for Remarks at the Montreal Conference on Regional Equalization, Montreal, 24 October 2001. Sponsored by the Atlantic Institute for Market Studies, the Frontier Centre for Public Policy, and the Montreal Economic Institute. https://www.iedm.org/files/011025boessenkoolpaper.pdf.

Boessenkool, Kenneth J., and Jennifer Robson. 2021. "Aggressive Incrementalism: Strengthening the Foundations of Canada's Approach to Childcare." C.D. Howe Institute Commentary 595. https://doi.org/10.2139/ssrn.4094422.

Bojorques, Fabio, Eric Champagne, and François Vaillancourt. 2009. "Federal Grants to Municipalities in Canada: Nature, Importance and Impact on Municipal Investments from 1990 to 2005." *Canadian Public Administration* 53, no. 3: 439–55. https://doi.org/10.1111/j.1754-7121.2009.00091.x.

Boucher, François, and Alain Noël, eds. 2021. *Fiscal Federalism in Multinational States: Autonomy, Equality, and Diversity*. Montreal and Kingston: McGill-Queen's University Press.

Boyd, Brendan, and Andrea Olive. 2021. *Provincial Policy Laboratories: Policy Diffusion and Transfer in Canada's Federal System*. Toronto: University of Toronto Press.

Brodie, Janine. 1990. *The Political Economy of Canadian Regionalism*. Toronto: Harcourt Brace Jovanovich.

Brown, Douglas M. 2017. "The Financial Crisis and the Future of Federalism in Canada." In *The Future of Federalism: Intergovernmental Fiscal Relations in an Age of Austerity*, edited by Richard Eccleston and Richard Krever, 73–94. Cheltenham, UK: Edward Elgar.

– 2020. "Fiscal Federalism: The Importance of Balance." In *Canadian Federalism: Performance, Effectiveness, and Legitimacy*, edited by Herman Bakvis and Grace Skogstad, 251–81. Toronto: University of Toronto Press.

Bryce, James. 1901. *The American Commonwealth*. London: Macmillan.

Busby, Colin. 2021. "Could Down-Payment Federalism Help Kickstart Reform in Long-Term Care?" *Policy Options*, 28 May 2021. https://policyoptions.irpp.org/magazines/may-2021/could-down-payment-federalism-help-kickstart-reform-in-long-term-care/.

Cairns, Alan C. 1977. "The Government and Societies of Canadian Federalism." *Canadian Journal of Political Science* 10, no. 4: 695–726. https://doi.org/10.1017/S0008423900050861.

Cardinal, Linda. 2008. "Bilinguisme et territorialité: L'aménagement linguistique au Québec et au Canada." *Hermès* 51, no. 2: 135–40. https://doi.org/10.4267/2042/24187.

Castells, Antoni. 2001. "The Role of Intergovernmental Finance in Achieving Diversity and Cohesion: The Case of Spain." *Environment and Planning C: Politics and Space* 19, no. 2: 189–206. https://doi.org/10.1068/c0053.

Champagne, Eric. 2012. "L'organisation et les structures gouvernementales dans le contexte canadien: Fédéralisme, centralisation et décentralisation." In *L'administration contemporaine de l'État: Une perspective canadienne et québécoise*, edited by Pierre Tremblay, 17–39. Montreal: Presses de l'Université du Québec.

– 2013. "Les programmes d'infrastructures municipales du gouvernement fédéral: Une analyse de la gouvernance multiniveau au Canada." *Télescope* 19, no. 1: 43–61. https://doi.org/10.7202/1017151ar.

Champagne, Eric, and Olivier Choinière. 2016. "Le financement des infrastructures municipales et les défis du fédéralisme fiscal canadien." *Revue Gestion et Management Public* 4, no. 3: 25–36. https://doi.org/10.3917/gmp.043.0025.

Champagne, Eric, and Geneviève Tellier. 2017. "La longue marche vers l'autonomie financière des municipalités canadiennes: L'exemple des transferts fédéraux en infrastructures municipales." In *L'autonomie financière des collectivités territoriales*, edited by Marc Leroy, 360–83. Paris: Economica.

Chattopadhyay, Rupak, Felix Knüpling, Diana Chebenova, Liam Whittington, and Phillip Gonzalez, eds. 2022. *Federalism and the Response to COVID-19: A Comparative Analysis*. New Delhi: Routledge India.

Chernick, Howard. 1992. "A Model of the Distributional Incidence of State and Local Taxes." *Public Finance Quarterly* 20, no. 4: 572–85. https://doi.org/10.1177/109114219202000412.

Commission sur le déséquilibre fiscal. 2002. *Pour un nouveau partage des moyens financiers au Canada*. Québec: Commission sur le déséquilibre fiscal.

Coulthard, Glen. 2014. *Red Skin, White Masks: Rejecting the Colonial Politics of Recognition*. Minneapolis: University of Minnesota Press.

Courchene, Thomas. 1983. "Canada's New Equalization Program: Description and Evaluation." *Canadian Public Policy* 9, no. 4: 458–75. https://doi.org/10.2307/3551131.

– 1984. *Equalization Payments: Past, Present, and Future*. Toronto: Ontario Economic Council.

– 2004. "Confiscatory Equalization: The Intriguing Case of Saskatchewan's Vanishing Energy Revenues." *Choices* 10, no. 2. Montreal: Institute for Research on Public Policy. https://irpp.org/research-studies/confiscatory-equalization/.

– 2005. *Resource Revenues and Equalization: Five-Province vs. National-Average Standards, Alternatives to the Representative Tax System, and Revenue-Sharing Pools*. IRPP Working Paper Series, no. 2005-04. Montreal: Institute for Research on Public Policy. https://irpp.org/research-studies/resource-revenues-and-equalization/.

– 2006. "Energy Prices, Canadian Federalism and Equalization: Comparing Canada's Energy Price Shocks." *Queen's Law Journal* 31, no. 2: 644–95. https://irpp.org/wp-content/uploads/2014/09/courchene_QLJ.pdf.

- 2007. "A Short History of Equalization." *Policy Options* (March): 22–9. http://irpp.org/wp-content/uploads/sites/2/assets/po/equalization-and-the-federal-spending-power/courchene.pdf.
- 2008. "Reflections on the Federal Spending Power: Practices, Principles, Perspectives." *Queen's Law Journal* 34, no. 1: 75–124.

Dafflon, Bernard. 2008. "Fiscal Capacity Equalization in Horizontal Fiscal Equalization Programs." In *Intergovernmental Fiscal Transfers: Principles and Practice*, edited by Robin Boadway and Anwar Shah, 361–96. Washington, DC: The World Bank.

- 2012. "Solidarity and the Design of Equalization: Setting out the Issues." eJournal of Tax Issues 10, no. 1: 138–64. https://www.business.unsw.edu.au/research-site/publications-site/ejournaloftaxresearch-site/Documents/paper8_v10n1_Dafflon.pdf.

Dardanelli, Paolo, John Kincaid, Alan Fenna, André Kaiser, André Lecours, Ajay Kumar Singh, Sean Mueller, and Stephan Vogel. 2019. "Dynamic De/Centralization in Federations: Comparative Conclusions." *Publius: The Journal of Federalism* 49, no. 1: 194–219. https://doi.org/10.1093/publius/pjy037.

Doern, G. Bruce, Allan M. Maslove, and Michael J. Prince. 2013. *Public Budgeting in the Age of Crises: Canada's Shifting Budgetary Domains and Temporal Budgeting*. Montreal and Kingston: McGill-Queen's University Press.

Eccleston, Richard, and Richard Krever, eds. 2017. *The Future of Federalism: Intergovernmental Fiscal Relations in an Age of Austerity*. Cheltenham, UK: Edward Elgar.

Eccleston, Richard, and Timothy Woolley. 2014. "From Calgary to Canberra: Resource Taxation and Fiscal Federalism in Canada and Australia." *Publius: The Journal of Federalism* 45, no. 2: 216–43. https://doi.org/10.1093/publius/pju039.

Eisen, Ben, Joel Emes, and Alex Whalen. 2020. *Measuring the Equalization Clawback on Natural Resource Revenue in Have-Not Provinces*. Vancouver, BC: The Fraser Institute.

Elazar, Daniel. 1987. *Exploring Federalism*. Tuscaloosa: University of Alabama Press.

Epple, Dennis, and Thomas Nechyba. 2004. "Fiscal Decentralization." In *Handbook of Regional and Urban Economics*, vol. 4, edited by J.V. Henderson and Jacques-François Thisse, 2423–80. London: Elsevier

Expert Panel on Equalization and Territorial Formula Financing. 2006. "Executive Summary." In *Achieving a National Purpose: Putting Equalization Back on Track*, 1–11. Ottawa: Department of Finance Canada. https://publications.gc.ca/collections/Collection/F2-176-2006E.pdf.

Feehan, James. 2020. *Canada's Equalization Program: Political Debates and Opportunities for Reform*. IRPP Insight, no. 30. Montreal: Institute for Research on Public Policy. https://irpp.org/wp-content/uploads/2020/01/Canada%E2%80%99s-Equalization-Program-Political-Debates-and-Opportunities-for-Reform.pdf.

Feir, Donna L. 2016. "The Long-Term Effect of Forcible Assimilation Policy: The Case of Indian Boarding Schools." *The Canadian Journal of Economics* 49, no. 3: 433–80. https://doi.org/10.1111/caje.12203.

Fenna, Alan. 2011. "Fiscal Equalisation and Natural Resources in Federal Systems." *Public Policy* 6, nos. 1–2: 71–80. https://espace.curtin.edu.au/bitstream/handle/20.500.11937/16936/172962_50163_Fenna-Resources_HFE2011.pdf.
– 2012. "The Character of Australian Federalism." eJournal of Tax Issues 10, no. 1: 12–20. http://www.austlii.edu.au/au/journals/eJlTaxR/2012/2.pdf.
– 2019. "The Centralization of Australian Federalism 1901–2010: Measurement and Interpretation." *Publius: The Journal of Federalism* 49, no. 1: 30–56. https://doi.org/10.1093/publius/pjy042.
Fenna, Alan, and Robyn Hollander. 2013. "Dilemmas of Federalism and Dynamics of the Australian Case." *Australian Journal of Public Administration* 72, no. 3: 220–7. https://doi.org/10.1111/1467-8500.12024.
Gagnon, Alain-G., and Raffaele Iacovino. 2007. *De la nation à la multination: Les rapports Québec-Canada*. Montreal: Éditions du Boréal.
Gagnon, Alain-G., and Johanne Poirier, eds. 2020. *Canadian Federalism and Its Future: Actors and Institutions*. Montreal and Kingston: McGill-Queen's University Press.
Gibbins, Roger, and Loleen Berdhal. 2003. *Western Visions, Western Futures: Perspectives on the West in Canada*. 2nd ed. Toronto: Toronto University Press.
Goldberg, Jonah, and Sean Speer. 2020. "Reforming Canadian Fiscal Federalism: The Case for Intergovernmental Disentanglement." *Ontario 360 Policy Papers*, 12 November 2020. https://on360.ca/policy-papers/fiscal-federalism/.
Goodyear-Grant, Elizabeth, and Kyle Hanniman, eds. 2019. *Canada at 150: Federalism and Democratic Renewal*. Montreal and Kingston: McGill-Queen's University Press.
Grégoire, Jean-François, and Michael Jewkes, eds. 2015. *Recognition and Redistribution in Multinational Federations*. Leuven, BE: Leuven University Press.
Hale, Geoffrey. 2001. *The Politics of Taxation in Canada*. Toronto: University of Toronto Press.
Hanniman, Kyle. 2018. "Is Canadian Federalism Market-Preserving? The View from the Bond Market." In *Federalism and the Welfare State in a Multicultural World*, edited by Elizabeth Goodyear-Grant, Richard Johnston, Will Kymlicka, and John Myles, 49–72. Montreal and Kingston: McGill-Queen's University Press.
Harris, Cole. 2020. *A Bounded Land: Reflections on Settler Colonialism in Canada*. Vancouver: UBC Press.
Henderson, Ailsa. 2008. *Nunavut: Rethinking Political Culture*. Vancouver: UBC Press.
Hepp, Ralf, and Jürgen von Hagen. 2012. "Fiscal Federalism in Germany: Stabilization and Redistribution Before and After Unification." *Publius: The Journal of Federalism* 41, no. 2: 234–59. https://doi.org/10.1093/publius/pjr004.
Horak, Martin, and Robert Young, eds. 2012. *Sites of Governance: Multilevel Governance and Policy Making in Canada's Big Cities*. Montreal and Kingston: McGill-Queen's University Press.
Hubbard, Ruth, and Gilles Paquet, eds. 2010. *The Case for Decentralized Federalism*. Ottawa: University of Ottawa Press.

Hueglin, Thomas O. 2021. *Federalism in Canada: Contested Concepts and Uneasy Balances*. Toronto: University of Toronto Press.

Hueglin, Thomas O., and Alan Fenna. 2015. *Comparative Federalism: A Systematic Inquiry*. 2nd ed. Toronto: University of Toronto Press.

Indigenous Services Canada. 2021. "Establishing a New Fiscal Relationship." Indigenous Services Canada, Government of Canada. https://www.sac-isc.gc.ca/eng/1499805218096/1521125536314.

Jametti, Mario, and Marcelin Joanis. 2016. "Electoral Competition as a Determinant of Fiscal Decentralisation." *Fiscal Studies* 37, no. 2: 285–300. https://doi.org/10.1111/j.1475-5890.2015.12061.

Janigan, Mary. 2012. *Let the Eastern Bastards Freeze in the Dark: The West versus the Rest since Confederation*. Toronto: Knopf Canada.

– 2020. *The Art of Sharing: The Richer versus the Poorer Provinces since Confederation*. Montreal and Kingston: McGill-Queen's University Press.

Joanis, Marcelin. 2018. "The Politics of Checkbook Federalism: Can Electoral Considerations Affect Federal-Provincial Relations?" *Public Finance Review* 46, no. 4: 665–91. https://doi.org/10.1177/1091142116679728.

Joanis, Marcelin, and François Vaillancourt. 2020. "Federal Finance Arrangements in Canada: The Challenges of Fiscal Imbalance and Natural Resource Rents." In *Intergovernmental Transfers in Federations*, edited by Serdar Yilmaz and Farah Zahir, 109–33. Cheltenham, UK: Edward Elgar.

Kincaid, John. 2019. "Dynamic De/Centralization in the United States, 1790–2010." *Publius: The Journal of Federalism* 49, no. 1: 166–93. https://doi.org/10.1093/publius/pjy032.

Lazar, Harvey, ed. 2005. *Canadian Fiscal Arrangements: What Works, What Might Work Better*. Montreal and Kingston: McGill-Queen's University Press.

Lecours, André. 2019. "Dynamic De/Centralization in Canada, 1867–2010." *Publius: The Journal of Federalism* 49, no. 1: 57–83. https://doi.org/10.1093/publius/pjx046.

Lecours, André, and Daniel Béland. 2010. "Federalism and Fiscal Policy: The Politics of Equalization in Canada." *Publius: The Journal of Federalism* 40, no. 4: 569–96. https://doi.org/10.1093/publius/pjp030.

– 2019. "From Secessionism to Regionalism: The Changing Nature of Territorial Politics in Western Australia." *Regional and Federal Studies* 29, no. 1: 25–44. https://doi.org/10.1080/13597566.2018.1443918.

Locke, Wade, and Paul Hobson. 2004. *An Examination of the Interactions between Natural Resource Revenues and Equalization Payments: Lessons for Atlantic Canada*. IRPP Working Papers Series, no. 2004-10. Montreal: Institute for Research on Public Policy. https://irpp.org/wp-content/uploads/assets/research/canadian-federalism/new-research-article/wp2004-10.pdf.

MacDonald, David B. 2014. "Genocide in the Indian Residential Schools: Canadian History through the Lens of the UN Genocide Convention." In *Colonial Genocide in Indigenous America*, edited by Andrew Woolford, Jeff Benvenuto, and Alexander Laban Hinton, 306–24. Durham, NC: Duke University Press.

Marier, Patrik. 2021. *The Four Lenses of Population Aging*. Toronto: University of Toronto Press.

Maxwell, James. 1937. *Federal Subsidies to the Provincial Governments in Canada*. Cambridge, MA: Harvard University Press.

McIntosh, Tom. 2021. "The Disingenuous Demands of Canada's Premiers for $28 Billion in Health-Care Funding." *The Conversation*, 28 March 2021. https://theconversation.com/the-disingenuous-demands-of-canadas-premiers-for-28-billion-in-health-care-funding-157024.

McKinnon, Ronald L. 1997. "Market-Preserving Federalism in the American Monetary Union." In *Macroeconomic Dimensions of Public Finance*, edited by Mario Blejer and Teresa Ter-Minassian, 73–93. London: Routledge.

McLure, Charles. 1983. *Tax Assignment in Federal Countries*. Canberra: Australian National University.

McRoberts, Kenneth. 2001. "Canada and the Multinational State." *Canadian Journal of Political Science* 33, no. 4: 683–713. https://doi.org/10.1017/S0008423901778055.

Milligan, Kevin, and Michael Smart. 2019. "An Estimable Model of Income Redistribution in a Federation: Musgrave Meets Oates." *American Economic Journal: Economic Policy* 11, no. 1: 406–34. https://doi.org/10.1257/pol.20160600.

Moore, A. Milton, J. Harvey Perry, and Donald Beach. 1966. *The Financing of the Canadian Federation: The First Hundred Years*. Toronto: Canadian Tax Foundation.

Mou, Haizhen. 2021. "Canada Health Transfer: Background and Future." *What Now?*, 13 May 2021. Calgary: Canada West Foundation. https://cwf.ca/research/publications/what-now-canada-health-transfer-background-and-future/.

Musgrave, Richard. 1959. *The Theory of Public Finance*. New York: McGraw-Hill.

– 1969. "Theories of Fiscal Federalism." *Public Finance* 24, no. 4: 521–32.

Noël, Alain. 2008. "How Do You Limit a Power That Does Not Exist." *Queen's Law Journal* 34, no. 1, 391–412.

– 2009. "Balance and Imbalance in the Division of Financial Resources." In *Contemporary Canadian Federalism: Foundations, Traditions, Institutions*, edited by Alain-G. Gagnon, 273–302. Toronto: University of Toronto Press.

Oates, Wallace. 1972. *Fiscal Federalism*. New York: Harcourt Brace Jovanovich.

– 1996. "Taxation in a Federal State: The Tax-Assignment Problem." *Public Economics Journal* 1: 55–60.

Oliver, Peter, Patrick Macklem, and Nathalie Des Rosiers, eds. 2017. *The Oxford Handbook of the Canadian Constitution*. New York: Oxford University Press.

Otis, Ghislain, and Martin Papillon. 2013. *Fédéralisme et gouvernance autochtone*. Quebec City: Presses de l'Université Laval.

Perry, David. 1997. *Financing the Canadian Federation, 1867 to 1995: Setting the Stage for Change*. Toronto: Canadian Tax Foundation.

Petter, Andrew. 1989. "Federalism and the Myth of the Spending Power." *Canadian Bar Review* 68: 448–79. https://cbr.cba.org/index.php/cbr/article/download/3450/3443/3450.

Plourde, André. 2012. "Canada." In *Oil and Gas in Federal Systems*, edited by George Anderson, 88–120. Don Mills, ON: Oxford University Press.

Pomeroy, Steve. 2001. *Toward a Comprehensive Affordable Housing Strategy for Canada*. Ottawa: Caledon Institute of Social Policy.

– 2017. *Envisioning a Modernized Social and Affordable Housing Sector in Canada*. Discussion Paper. Ottawa: Carleton University Centre for Urban Research and Education (CURE). https://carleton.ca/cure/wp-content/uploads/Envisioning-a-strengthened-social-housing-sector-FINAL-Oct-2018.pdf.

Qian, Yingyi, and Barry R. Weingast. 1997. "Federalism as a Commitment to Preserving Market Incentives." *Journal of Economic Perspectives* 11, no. 4: 83–92. https://doi.org/10.1257/jep.11.4.83.

Rodden, Jonathan. 2002. "The Dilemma of Fiscal Federalism: Grants and Fiscal Performance around the World." *American Journal of Political Science* 46, no. 3: 670–87. https://doi.org/10.2307/3088407.

– 2006. *Hamilton's Paradox: The Promise and Peril of Fiscal Federalism*. Cambridge: Cambridge University Press.

Ruiz Almendral, Violeta, and François Vaillancourt. 2013. *Autonomy in Subnational Income Taxes: Evolving Powers, Existing Practices in Seven Countries*. Montreal and Kingston: McGill-Queen's University Press.

Saillant, Richard. 2016. *A Tale of Two Countries: How the Great Demographic Imbalance Is Pulling Canada Apart*. Halifax: Nimbus.

Shah, Anwar, ed. 2007. *The Practice of Fiscal Federalism: Comparative Perspectives*. Montreal and Kingston: McGill-Queen's University Press.

Shah, Anwar, and Robin Boadway. 2006. *Intergovernmental Fiscal Transfers: Principles and Practice*. Washington, DC: The World Bank.

Slack, Enid. 2017. *How Much Local Fiscal Autonomy Do Cities Have? A Comparison of Eight Cities around the World*. IMFG Perspectives, no. 19. Toronto: Institute on Municipal Finance and Governance, Munk School of Global Affairs, University of Toronto. https://imfg.munkschool.utoronto.ca/research/doc/?doc_id=432.

Snoddon, Tracy, and Paul Hobson. 2010. "Cost-Sharing and Federal-Provincial Fiscal Relations." In *The 2009 Federal Budget: Challenge, Response and Retrospect*, edited by Charles M. Beach, Bev Dahlby, and Paul A.R. Hobson. Kingston, ON: John Deutsch Institute, Queen's University.

Sorens, Jason. 2011. "The Institutions of Fiscal Federalism." *Publius: The Journal of Federalism* 41, no. 2: 207–31. https://doi.org/10.1093/publius/pjq016.

– 2016. "Secession Risk and Fiscal Federalism." *Publius: The Journal of Federalism* 46, no. 1: 25–50. https://doi.org/10.1093/publius/pjv037.

Stauffer, Thomas. 2001. "Intergovernmental Fiscal Relations in Fragmented Societies: The Case of Switzerland." *Environment and Planning C: Politics and Space* 19, no. 2: 207–22. https://doi.org/10.1068/c0054.

Stevenson, Garth. 2006. "Fiscal Federalism and the Burden of History." Selected Proceedings from the Conference "Fiscal Federalism and the Future of Canada,"

28–29 September 2006, Institute of Intergovernmental Relations, Queen's University, Kingston, ON. https://www.queensu.ca/iigr/sites/iirwww/files/uploaded_files/Stevenson.pdf.

– 2009. *Unfulfilled Union: Canadian Federalism and National Unity*. Montreal and Kingston: McGill-Queen's University Press.

Steytler, Nico, ed. 2022. *Comparative Federalism and Covid-19: Combating the Pandemic*. London: Routledge.

St-Hilaire, France. 2005. "Écarts et déséquilibres fiscaux: La nouvelle donne du fédéralisme canadien." *Options politiques*, 1 October 2005.

Telford, Hamish. 2003. "The Federal Spending Power in Canada: Nation-Building or Nation-Destroying?" *Publius: The Journal of Federalism* 33, no. 1: 33–44. https://doi.org/10.1093/oxfordjournals.pubjof.a004976.

Tellier, Geneviève. 2016. "Légitimité et contestations fiscales: Succès et échec des réformes de la taxe de vente dans les provinces canadiennes de l'Ontario et de la Colombie-Britannique." *Revue Gestion & Management Public* 4, no. 3: 75–89. https://doi.org/10.3917/gmp.043.0075.

– 2020. "La transparence budgétaire sous l'ère Trudeau." *Études canadiennes/Canadian Studies* 89: 65–86. https://doi.org/10.4000/eccs.3928.

Théret, Bruno. 1999. "Regionalism and Federalism: A Comparative Analysis of the Regulation of Economic Tensions between Regions by Canadian and American Federal Intergovernmental Transfer Programmes." *International Journal of Urban and Regional Research* 23, no. 3: 479–512. https://doi.org/10.1111/1468-2427.00209.

Tiebout, Charles. 1956. "A Pure Theory of Local Expenditures." *The Journal of Political Economy* 64, no. 5: 416–24. https://doi.org/10.1086/257839.

– 1961. "An Economic Theory of Fiscal Decentralization." In *Public Finances: Needs, Sources, and Utilization. A Conference of the Universities-National Bureau Committee for Economic Research*, 79–96. Princeton, NJ: Princeton University Press.

Tombe, Trevor. 2018. "'Final and Unalterable' – But Up for Negotiation: Federal-Provincial Transfers in Canada." *Canadian Tax Journal* 66, no. 4: 871–917. https://financesofthenation.ca/wp-content/uploads/2020/06/871_18CTJ4_FON.pdf.

– 2020. "Provincial Debt Sustainability in Canada: Demographics, Federal Transfers, and COVID-19." *Canadian Tax Journal* 68, no. 4: 1083–1122. https://doi.org/10.32721/ctj.2020.68.4.fon.

Tombe, Trevor, and Jennifer Winter. 2021. "Fiscal Integration with Internal Trade: Quantifying the Effects of Federal Transfers in Canada." *Canadian Journal of Economics* 54, no. 2: 522–56. https://doi.org/10.1111/caje.12491.

Trojbicz, Beni, ed. 2021. *Oil Wealth and Federal Conflict in American Petrofederations*. London: Elsevier.

Vaillancourt, François, and David Guimond. 2013. "Setting Personal Income Tax Rates: Evidence from Canada and Comparison with the United States of America." In *Autonomy in Subnational Income Taxes: Evolving Powers, Existing Practices in Seven*

Countries, edited by Violeta Ruiz Almendral and François Vaillancourt, 100–20. Montreal and Kingston: McGill-Queen's University Press.

Vaillancourt, François, and Stéphanie Rault. 2003. "The Regional Dimensions of Federal Intergovernmental and Interpersonal Transfers in Canada, 1981–2001." *Regional and Federal Studies* 13, no. 43: 131–52. https://doi.org/10.1080/13597560308559449.

Valdesalici, Alice. 2019. "The Peregrinations of Fiscal Federalism: Past, Present and Future of a Research Agenda." In *A Research Agenda for Federalism Studies*, edited by John Kincaid, 93–105. Cheltenham, UK: Edward Elgar.

Valdesalici, Alice, and Francesco Palermo, eds. 2018. *Comparing Fiscal Federalism*. Leiden, BE: Brill.

Wallner, Jennifer, and Gerard W. Boychuk. 2014. "Comparing Federations: Testing the Model of Market-Preserving Federalism on Canada, Australia, and the United States." In *Comparing Canada: Methods and Perspectives on Canadian Politics*, edited by Luc Turgeon, Martin Papillon, Jennifer Wallner, and Stephen White, 198–221. Vancouver: UBC Press.

Watts, Ronald. 2000. "Federal Financial Relations: A Comparative Perspective." In *Canada: The State of the Federation 1999/2000*, edited by Harvey Lazar, 371–80. Montreal and Kingston: McGill-Queen's University Press.

– 2008. *Comparing Federal Systems*. 3rd ed. Montreal and Kingston: McGill-Queen's University Press.

– 2018. "Comparative Research and Fiscal Federalism." In *Comparing Fiscal Federalism*, edited by Alice Valdesalici and Francesco Palermo, 376–81. Leiden, BE: Brill.

Weingast, Barry R. 1995. "The Economic Role of Political Institutions: Market-Preserving Federalism and Economic Development." *Journal of Law, Economics, and Organization* 11, no. 1: 1–31. https://web.stanford.edu/~jrodden/oslo/weingast_mpf.pdf.

– 2009. "Second Generation Fiscal Federalism: The Implications of Fiscal Incentives." *Journal of Urban Economics* 65, no. 3: 279–93. https://doi.org/10.1016/j.jue.2008.12.005.

– 2014. "Second Generation on Fiscal Federalism: Political Aspects of Development and Economic Development." *World Development* 53: 14–25. https://doi.org/10.1016/j.worlddev.2013.01.003.

Yilmaz, Serdar, and Farah Zahir, eds. 2020. *Intergovernmental Transfers in Federations*. Cheltenham, UK: Edward Elgar.

2 The Struggle for Equity That Saved the Federation

MARY JANIGAN

In the early 1950s, an uneasy federal official cobbled together a nightmare summary for his bosses on what was dangerously wrong with Canada. The senior official – who was almost certainly the renowned John James Deutsch – could see that the economy was booming as consumers flocked to purchase the latest luxury goods. But the enduring inequalities between the richer and the poorer provincial governments were now increasingly evident. Overall, the provincial governments were spending roughly two-thirds more than they did in 1940. Yet the poorer ones could not keep up. They might impose "arbitrary and discriminatory taxation," which could disrupt interprovincial trade (John James Deutsch Fonds 1955, 22).[1] Some might even find their solvency and autonomy at risk, which could threaten the federation's very existence (22).

Ottawa had to deal with a rapidly changing federation. It could no longer address inequalities between the provinces in the same arbitrary way that it had deployed since Confederation. It needed to renew its tax-rental deals with the provinces, collecting key provincial taxes in return for a portion of the revenues and compensatory grants. Otherwise, the inequalities among the provinces would become "intolerable" (John James Deutsch Fonds 1955, 22). But Ottawa also needed to acknowledge, as an earlier royal commission had urged, that there should be a "franker recognition of regional differences of wealth and income and a more vigorous effort on the part of the Dominion to reduce these disparities" (12).

The answer to those prescient warnings came in 1956 when Ottawa explicitly abandoned the notion that it should treat all provinces equally. It had discreetly ignored that revered political principle previously when times were difficult. But now its non-conditional equalization grants openly addressed the revenue-raising differences among the provinces. In the name of equity, those grants enabled the poorer provinces to provide roughly similar levels of services as the richer provinces for roughly similar levels of taxation.

That innovative approach preserved national unity, quelling festering resentments, especially within Quebec, which had not allowed Ottawa to collect its taxes through the tax-rental deals in peacetime. The extra funds (barely) allowed the poorer provinces to participate in national shared-cost programs such as Hospital Care and Unemployment Assistance, which later became the Canada Assistance Plan. Federal cabinet minister J.W. Pickersgill (1975, 307) asserts that Prime Minister Louis St-Laurent regarded the program "as his crowning achievement in federal-provincial relations, to which he had devoted so much of his time and energy since 1945." Equalization became the foundation stone of the modern federation – and its very existence ensured that the role of government in society was strengthened.

This chapter will trace the turbulent history of the disputes between the richer and the poorer provinces. The first section will examine the quarrels that erupted before Confederation and almost disrupted it. The second section will follow the ensuing arguments across the decades into the early 1920s as economic and social conditions evolved rapidly. The third section will concentrate upon the plight of the Maritimes, which vividly illustrated the need for reform. The fourth section will span much of the Great Depression, when it became apparent that the poorer provinces could not cope with the social and economic toll. The fifth section will examine the Royal Commission on Dominion-Provincial Relations, which called for National Adjustment Grants to address fiscal needs in the poorer provinces. It will also look briefly at models for those proposed grants, especially the Australian approach to fiscal inequality.

The sixth section will trace the history of the wartime tax-rental deals into peacetime, when John Deutsch was part of the team that devised equalization despite widespread Finance Ministry opposition. Finally, it will itemize the social programs that developed once the poorer provinces had more funds – and the principle of equalization could be applied to federal assistance. In effect, equalization was the almost perfect combination of equity and efficiency: no one had to move to another province in search of better health care or a better education. The program has endured through the disruptions of the COVID-19 pandemic and Alberta's non-binding referendum in 2021, which called in vain for the removal of the principle of equalization from the Canadian Constitution[2] (see chapters 4 and 21 by Trevor Tombe and Ken Boessenkool, respectively, in this volume). The grants remain one of the crucial, if unrecognized, links that bind together the nation.

Confederation

From the beginning, the wealthier Maritime provinces balked at the prospect of tying their fate to that of the fractious United Canada, which was composed of anglophone Ontario and francophone Quebec (Upper and Lower Canada). As Nova Scotia journalist and politician Joseph Howe complained in 1866, that province was deeply divided by "the antagonism of races arbitrarily bound together, shaken by incompatibility of temper" (1866, 6). He predicted that Maritimers would find themselves stranded in a nation where they were outnumbered, and their political clout would be insignificant. Ontario and Quebec could always put aside their differences so that "the Centre of power and influence will always be in [the Province of] Canada" (35).

Federation would mean the ruin of the sea-trading Maritime economy: Maritimers applied only light duties to British manufactured products, while Canada imposed high duties. With federation, Ottawa would take over the collection of customs duties and tariffs, and it would surely raise them. Maritimers would be forced to buy Canadian manufactured goods at steep prices – and Canada's higher fees could affect their lucrative export markets for fish and timber. Howe was in despair: it would require "the wisdom of Solomon and the energy and strategy of Frederick the Great" to preserve the new nation (1866, 10).

Many politicians in Atlantic Canada shared that foreboding. How could they find sufficient funds to fulfil their responsibilities within a federation that would take over the collection of duties and tariffs? How would they cope if Ontario and Quebec saddled them with taxation to pay Canada's large debts for railroads? From the start, fiscal inequality among the provinces was a strong motif of the federation. As historian Christopher Moore notes, the Confederation bargain gave "blunt evidence" of federal primacy: "Although the Maritime provinces had substantial net assets and the Canadas substantial liabilities, [Confederation] transferred to the federal government most of the assets and liabilities of the old provinces ... [T]he sea-trading Maritimes needed low tariffs much more than the revenue-hungry Canadas did" (Moore 1997, 128).

Provincial politicians in the Maritimes were desperate for the assurance that they would be able to fulfil such duties as hospital construction. Some, like Howe, anxiously tried to derail Confederation. But the British government paid little attention. It could no longer defend Canada against possible American incursions, if only because the expense and the distance were prohibitive. It was dismantling its protectionist tariffs, easing away from its mercantilist ties with Canada. As well, in an industrializing era that required massive investments in infrastructure, the deadlock between Upper and Lower Canada "demonstrated the inadequacy of existing institutions and structures of government" (Norrie, Owram, and Emery 2008, 143). In unity, the colonies might find strength – and vaguely common cause. For the United Kingdom, Confederation was a done deal.

But Nova Scotia and New Brunswick had one advantage: Canadian politicians were well aware of the potency of the anti-Confederation appeal. To defuse that threat, they resorted to an arbitrary and chaotic system of subsidies, which would continue for decades. Negotiators dangled extra compensation for the recalcitrant Maritimes as an inducement to bring the country into being: Nova Scotia Premier Charles Tupper and New Brunswick Premier Leonard Tilley were promised unusually large grants to meet government expenses, which were calculated "on no determinable basis, and favored the Maritime provinces very considerably" (John James Deutsch Fonds 1955, 2).

The special treatment continued. When the Dominion of Canada came into existence on 1 July 1867, New Brunswick received a "special grant" of $63,000 for ten years, for which there was "no determinable basis ... except as the price to bring it into union" (John James Deutsch Fonds 1955, 3). There was no special grant for Nova Scotia. But in January 1869, Joseph Howe and his fellow Nova Scotia Member of Parliament Archibald W. McLelan secured a financial agreement with Finance Minister John Rose that promised "better terms." Nova Scotia received a "special grant" of $83,000 per year for ten years, and Ottawa increased the per capita basis for the province's "debt allowance," which was a subsidy that initially rewarded the more frugal provinces for lower debts when Ottawa took over those debts. That increase brought Nova Scotia into line with New Brunswick: "One of the anomalies of the original arrangements" (4).

The third major statutory subsidy at Confederation was a simple per capita payment based upon the census population of 1861. In 1864, during rounds of hard bargaining over the federation's proposed revenues and responsibilities, Canadian politicians had urged Maritime finance ministers to reduce their bottom-line revenue needs to a bare minimum (Heaman 2017, 44). Those estimates were already low, taking little account of the provinces' social responsibilities, especially for their poorer citizens. The negotiators bickered until they decided upon eighty cents per person for each province. Payments to each of the Maritime provinces would increase until their census populations reached 400,000.[3] These specific numbers were embedded in the Constitution, even though inflation and population growth would eventually erode that value.

Those three subsidies were the principal ones at Confederation: the per capita grants, the subsidies to cover the cost of governance, and the debt allowances. In Nova Scotia and New Brunswick, subsidies amounted to 80 to 90 per cent of total revenues at the outset. In Ontario and Quebec, which had significant revenues from natural resources, they comprised from one-half to two-thirds of provincial funds (John James Deutsch Fonds 1955, 3).

Ottawa had already discovered how to tinker discreetly with the cherished principle of equality among the provinces. In its subsidy calculations, it had increased the assumed population of a province so that it could increase its per capita grants, and it had offered special grants to its two Maritime members. But no government even dared to demand a specific program that would formally address fiscal inequalities. That was unthinkable.

From Confederation into the Mid-1920s

It was inevitable that federal subsidy provisions would vary, often dramatically, as new provinces joined the federation. When Manitoba entered in 1870, it received subsidies totalling $67,200 per year, but there was a provision to increase the basic eighty-cent subsidy to match the 1881 census, and thereafter until the population reached 400,000 (John James Deutsch Fonds 1955, 4).[4] A year later, British Columbia joined Confederation with $116,000 per year in subsidies plus an extra $100,000 per year, ostensibly for the right of way for the eventual railroad. In 1873, debt-laden Prince Edward Island joined with an unusually generous debt allowance. It also received a "special grant" of $45,000 to compensate for the absence of Crown lands (4).

These subsidies were never enough, given population growth and inflation. Perhaps more troubling, depression conditions descended upon Canada in 1873 and lasted for almost twenty-five years. Every federation government wanted more money. By 1874, statutory subsidies represented 92 per cent of New Brunswick revenues, 81 per cent of Nova Scotia's, 75 per cent of Prince Edward Island's, 62 per cent of British Columbia's, and 40 to 50 per cent of Quebec's and Ontario's revenues (John James Deutsch Fonds 1955, 5). Ottawa scrambled to placate. In 1884, it increased the debt allowances for Ontario and Quebec, and it raised Manitoba's subsidy in lieu of resource control in 1885.

But the provinces continued to plead. In October 1887, Quebec Premier Honoré Mercier invited the first ministers to a conference on provincial rights in Quebec City. Prime Minister Sir John A. Macdonald sagely declined to attend. The premiers unanimously adopted twenty-two meticulous resolutions, including demands for higher subsidies. They forwarded their demands to Ottawa. Macdonald ignored them.

Meanwhile, the value of the federal subsidies continued to dwindle. In 1902, undeterred, the provincial premiers gathered for the first time since their meeting in Quebec City. The major topic was subsidies – and the premiers resolved to push Prime Minister Sir Wilfrid Laurier for more funds. Laurier formally acknowledged their demands, but he did nothing to remedy their frustration and growing anger. In 1905, Ottawa carved the provinces of Saskatchewan and Alberta out of the North-West Territories while retaining control of their natural resources. By 1906, as an *average* proportion of provincial revenues, the value of the subsidies had slipped from about one-half in 1867 to one-quarter (John James Deutsch Fonds 1955, 6).

But Laurier could not hold out against the continuing pressure. Premiers across the nation were fending off demands for paved roads, hospitals where patients did not get sicker, and better schools. They wanted to raid Ottawa's piggy bank. In 1906, two premiers who were among Laurier's Liberal allies told him to stop dawdling if he wanted to keep his friends. The provinces were fed up. At Laurier's invitation, the premiers convened on Monday, 8 October 1906 in Ottawa. Laurier greeted them, offered to discuss their eventual resolutions, and left them to their talks.

The nine premiers were blunt. As Ontario Premier James Whitney observed, Laurier had brushed them off in 1902, but "under our system it can never be too late to apply a remedy, where one is called for" (Whitney 1907, 6–7). So far, so good. The premiers essentially endorsed the resolutions from their 1902 conference, asking for higher per capita payments for everyone. In a special plea, the three Prairie provinces also begged for higher subsidies for their governments because their populations were growing and their infrastructure needs were escalating.

They were drowned out. British Columbia Premier Richard McBride interrupted the proceedings, demanding extra funds by arguing that the per capita cost of running *his* government was five times higher than the average costs of other provinces. Laurier accepted British Columbia's demand for special treatment "owing to the vastness of her territory, to its mountainous character, and the sparseness of her population" (Laurier 1907, 12). Eight of the nine premiers then agreed to ask Ottawa for an extra $100,000 per year for ten years for British Columbia. McBride brushed off his peers' request as inadequate. His fellow premiers seethed. McBride appeared petulant and greedy. Worse, any changes to the basic subsidy required a constitutional amendment, which Britain had to approve. Laurier's Constitution Act of 1907 spelled out a new formula: the subsidy would increase as provincial populations grew; the maximum amount would take effect when the population in any province exceeded 1.5 million.

Laurier also granted that extra $100,000 per year for ten years to British Columbia. He got little thanks. McBride actually lobbied against this change in London. At his behest, Britain removed a declaration in the legislation that the subsidy levels were "a final and unalterable settlement" – but the phrase remained in the schedule attached to the bill.[5] It was a very small victory: those new subsidy levels could never have survived anyway in an inflationary world with a growing population. The higher subsidies would purportedly allow all premiers to tackle the wrenching problems of their industrializing age.

But there was a trickier problem in the Constitution Act of 1907 that no one envisaged. What would happen if the population of any region remained stagnant, but the cost of providing improved services escalated? The Maritimes would soon complain about that exact difficulty. But the time for big changes before the First World War had passed. The history of fiscal federalism and the poorer and richer provinces is littered with ironies.

Ottawa and the provinces skittered through the war and the early turbulent years of the peace. But the federation partners were not happy. They emerged from a Dominion-Provincial Conference in November 1918 with virtually no resolution to their fiscal woes. They struggled through a post-war recession when it was already becoming clear that the traditional supports of church and family could barely meet the needs of unemployed and unemployable people in industrialized and manufacturing communities.

Society was changing faster than the capacity of any government to address those needs, and that was when the flaws in Canada's fiscal federalism became glaringly apparent.

The Maritimes and Their Woes

The three Maritime provinces were in disastrous shape during the 1920s. Nearly 150,000 people left the region in search of better lives. (As the economy worsened in the 1930s, many of them returned home in defeat; Conrad and Finkel 2008, 200, 211.) The Maritimes could not afford programs, such as the Old Age Pension, that the richer provinces and Ottawa adopted. And they were resentful. In 1923, in Halifax, Liberal-Conservative Member of the Legislative Assembly H.W. Corning demanded a referendum on Nova Scotia's secession from Canada: The province was not receiving fair treatment in "freight rates, railway shipping and other activities upon which the prosperity of the Province depended." Worse, Nova Scotia "was forced to support the policy of protective duties that were mainly beneficial to upper Provinces, while increasing the cost of living at home with no balancing benefits" (*Globe* 1923, 1).

For decades, those provinces had complained about low subsidies, their waning political clout, and Ottawa's nonchalant neglect. But the situation was far different in the 1920s: Regional manufacturers had survived Ottawa's high tariff walls because the Moncton-based Intercolonial Railway had provided low-cost transportation since the mid-1870s. Maritime manufacturers could compete in Western and Central Canada because their basic freight rates were 20 to 50 per cent lower than those in Ontario (Forbes 1989a, 102). Capital investment in Maritime manufacturing had actually *quadrupled* between 1900 and 1920 (102).

But after the war, Ottawa had united the nation's struggling railways into one entity, tucking the Maritime railway under the de facto jurisdiction of its Board of Railway Commissioners. When Central Canadian manufacturers and Prairie farmers demanded lower freight rates similar to those on the Intercolonial, Ottawa simply hiked Maritime rates. Worse, in 1920, the railway commissioners boosted national freight rates by 40 per cent. Between 1916 and September 1920, Maritime basic freight rates rose between 140 and 216 per cent (Forbes 1989b, 103).

Atlantic Canada seethed. The protest against freight rates pulled together labour and business groups, along with farmers and fishers, *against* the rest of the country (Forbes 1989b, 113). In the 1921 federal election, the federal Liberals exploited this anger, winning twenty-five of the region's thirty-one ridings in a protest against Conservative rail-rate hikes. But typically, Prime Minister Mackenzie King dawdled. By August 1925, the price of inaction was apparent. Three provincial Liberal governments had fallen within three years. In the federal election of 29 October 1925, the Liberals slipped from twenty-three Maritime seats to six. Voters in the three Maritime provinces had sent a strong message.

Rattled and chastened, King appointed a Royal Commission on Maritime Claims in April 1926. Chaired by British industrialist Sir Andrew Duncan, the commission reported that the Maritime provinces were partly responsible for their own woes. Duncan refused to blame Confederation for the relatively unequal prosperity and development among the provinces. It was a significant finding for future Dominion-Provincial quarrels over fiscal inequality.

Still, the commission called for an *interim* lump sum increase in the federal subsidy, pending in-depth examination; immediate freight rate reductions of 20 per cent; and renewed transportation subsidies for Maritime coal (Duncan 1926, 19, 22, 25). In the spring of 1927, however, King's cabinet objected to the cost of Duncan's plan. In effect, cabinet "changed Duncan's program for Maritime rehabilitation into a plan for Maritime pacification" (Forbes 1980, 176). Still, King raised the region's annual subsidies by $1.6 million, on an interim basis, and cut most freight rates by 20 per cent. And he shrewdly declared that he was adopting Duncan's measures "virtually in their entirety" (177). At the time, few Maritimers noticed the difference between what he said and what he actually did.

By November 1927, at a Dominion-Provincial Conference, King could afford to placate the provinces. First, the nine provincial premiers endorsed the Duncan report, ensuring that those temporary grants to the Maritimes became permanent (Dominion-Provincial Conferences 1951, 23–6). That special increase in subsidies to handle fiscal inequalities set a precedent for the first tentative version of equalization in the tax-rental agreements of the 1940s.

King also secured provincial agreement to transfer control over natural resources from Ottawa to the three Prairie provinces. That put them in a position of constitutional equality with the other six provinces after six decades of fierce disputes. The nine premiers also agreed with Ottawa's plan to return the railway lands to British Columbia, which had surrendered them to Ottawa in the nineteenth century.

The Depression and Provincial Inequality

And then along came the Depression. King was largely oblivious to the escalating unemployment rate, along with the miseries of the families on relief, and he lost the 1930 election to Conservative leader R.B. Bennett. King deserved to lose. But Bennett was also unfortunate to win at a time when Ottawa's responsibility for social ills was hotly disputed and constitutionally unclear. During his first years in office, Bennett was dangerously cautious about taking action.

The prime minister did meet frequently with the provincial premiers during his tenure – although little was seemingly accomplished. Their first gathering in April 1931 was devoted to constitutional discussions. That seems incongruous. But the Bennett government had already appropriated $20 million for relief and infrastructure projects in 1930–1 and then extended those provisions into 1931–2 with $42.7 million for relief (*Labour Gazette* 1935, 24).

In April 1932, as the Depression deepened, Bennett spelled out the federal financial position at a Dominion-Provincial Conference on relief. Ottawa had already added $119 million to the 1931–2 federal debt – and the Dominion was "not disposed to assume responsibility for the unemployment problem" (Marchington 1932, 1–2). That assertion surely startled many Canadians who remembered Bennett's election vow to combat unemployment "or perish in the attempt" (Boyko 2010, 198). Subsequent conferences went nowhere. In January 1933, the delegates recommended that federal assistance for direct relief should continue because of the "unprecedented economic conditions" (Dominion-Provincial Conference 1933, 1). But, while some provinces wanted more federal help, other provinces "[did] not feel that an increase should be asked for" (1). The premiers from the richer and the poorer provinces were effectively deadlocked.

The dissension simmered. The fiscal inequalities among the provinces were so brutally apparent and crippling that joint action with Ottawa to remedy any social need – with the crucial exception of relief – was literally unthinkable (Dominion-Provincial Conference 1933, 1–2). But no province dared to ask for a specific federal program to ease fiscal inequality. Instead, they pleaded for additional grants for unemployment relief or increased subsidies because of fiscal need. Sometimes, they argued – to no avail – that the political clout of the other federation partners had relegated them to the role of underdogs. They did *not* address fiscal inequality as a permanent condition within the federation.

At the next Dominion-Provincial Conference in mid-January 1934, the three Maritime premiers asked Bennett for a royal commission to consider "a revision of the financial arrangements between the Dominion Government and the Maritime Provinces."[6] There existed the "dire necessity of all the provinces finding new sources of revenue" (*Ottawa Journal* 1934, 4). They were almost drowned out because the three Prairie provinces and British Columbia were edging closer to defaulting on their bond interest.

All premiers finally recognized that the fiscal inequalities among the provinces were wrenching. Ottawa agreed to continue its aid to the Western provinces with the formal blessing of *all* participants, including wealthier Quebec and Ontario. Special ad hoc subsidies to alleviate desperate inequalities were becoming the norm. But there was no general principle, no formula, and no impartial adjudicator to determine the amount. Bennett also agreed to set up a subcommittee on Maritime rights. He dawdled. Finally, on 14 September 1934, the prime minister set up a three-person royal commission, under the chairmanship of former finance minister Sir Thomas White, to deal "as speedily as possible" with the call for revised financial arrangements (White 1935, vi).

Nova Scotia Premier Angus Macdonald could not wait: in July, he appointed his own three-person royal commission, under the chairmanship of Leeds University economist John Harry Jones, to scrutinize "the adequacy of present financial arrangements" between Ottawa and the province (Province of Nova Scotia 1934, 4). Four months later, in early December, the Jones Commission reported that three main factors had contributed to the province's "relative economic decline: tariff policies, transportation costs, and centralized, protected industries" (Henderson 2007, 63). But there were no real solutions to catch the dispirited public's fancy.

Two months later, the White Commission reported, less than five months after it had started its hectic examination of the Maritime provinces. Nova Scotia Premier Macdonald had told the commission that, since Confederation, "financial necessity" was the basis of "most if not all" federal revisions of the subsidy to meet the provinces' fiscal needs (White 1935, 5). The commission firmly rejected that assertion, arguing that, if true, provinces could spend as much as they wanted and then demand money to meet their deficits: "Power to spend must entail responsibility for expenditures" (6).

Still, the report admitted that the three provincial governments had been "frugal" – and that they were handicapped by their "isolated economic position with respect to the rest of Canada, a stationary or declining population and less per capita wealth and taxable capacity than most if not all of the other provinces" (White 1935, 12). Extra federal funds might promote education and public welfare services, along with economic efficiency, and lead to reduced taxation (20).

In effect, some form of equalization would benefit all Canadians. The White Commission recommended an increase in the subsidies for all three Maritime provinces, based upon "considerations of fairness and equity" and "the economic disadvantages to which the Maritime Provinces are particularly subject" (White 1935, 20). The Bennett government heeded that call, increasing Prince Edward Island's annual payments in the wake of the Duncan Commission hikes from $125,000 to $275,000; New Brunswick's went from $600,000 to $900,000; and Nova Scotia's from $875,000 to $1.3 million (4, 21).[7]

But Bennett's largesse and his astonishing late-term denunciations of capitalism could not save him in the 1935 election. Back in power, Prime Minister Mackenzie King summoned the premiers to Ottawa, promised virtually nothing except an increase in federal grants for relief, dismissed the gathering – and, soon after, reversed a portion of that increase. He would not meet the premiers again until January 1941.

But King could not rid himself of the problem of fiscal inequality so easily. Finance Ministry and Bank of Canada officials were uneasily aware that the three Prairie provinces were teetering on the brink of default. They considered such solutions as the Australian Loan Council model: in 1929, the Australian Commonwealth government had taken over all state debts and then put responsibility for all future federal or state borrowings under the council. It soon became clear, however, that compulsory federal oversight was not a welcome prospect for the provinces.

When Alberta vehemently resisted the proposed Loan Council terms in return for a federal loan of $2.85 million, Finance Minister Charles Dunning denied the request. On 1 April 1936, the Alberta government defaulted on its bonds (Library and Archives Canada 1937, 6). That default would mark a generation of Depression-era Alberta politicians *and* their successors. A government of Prairie farmers that had taken pride in paying its debts was now effectively insolvent.

By the end of December 1936, it was clear that both Manitoba and Saskatchewan might share the same fate if they did not receive immediate federal help. King resisted mightily – he even demanded Bank of Canada reports on their fiscal situation. But, in the end, on 16 February 1937, King announced temporary financial aid for the two provinces and the creation of the Royal Commission on Dominion-Provincial Relations or, as it is often called after its two chairmen, the Rowell-Sirois Commission. As King later stipulated, the commission was to undertake "a re-examination of the economic and financial basis of Confederation and of the distribution of legislative powers in the light of the economic and social developments of the last seventy years" (Royal Commission on Dominion-Provincial Relations [1940] 1954, 1:9).

The five commissioners were indomitable. From 29 November 1937 to 1 December 1938, they crisscrossed the nation, listening to witnesses in every provincial capital, while recording 10,702 pages of evidence from eighty-five days of hearings. They read 427 briefs and ordered studies from thirty-six experts as well as in-depth looks at how other federations, especially Australia, handled fiscal inequalities. Canberra had created the renowned Commonwealth Grants Commission in 1933 to distribute federal funds to the poorer states (Fransen 1984, v). Canada still pays close attention to Australia, even though it makes roughly equal use of tax sharing and fiscal transfers to raise the fiscal capacity of states while Canada mainly deploys transfers from the federal budget (Anderson 2009, 88).

The Commission Report and Wartime

For the commissioners, it was an arduous and often stressful odyssey. But by the time their report debuted in May 1940, Canada was at war – and King did not want to contemplate their radical blueprint for the ideal federation: Ottawa should centralize revenues from income taxes and succession duties, and assume responsibility for unemployed employables and old age pensions. Ottawa should take over current provincial debts.

Most important, provinces should receive "lump sum, annual, unconditional National Adjustment Grants (NAGs) for the support of education and welfare at an average national standard" (Lepawsky 1940, 77). Ottawa would assess each province's spending to determine its per capita fiscal needs in comparison to the national average. Each province should be "put in a financial position to provide, if it chose, a level of provincial services at average national standards without subjecting its citizens to provincial taxation above the national average" (Smiley 1962, 56).

The royal commission had finally jettisoned the dangerous fiction that all provinces were theoretically equal: the poorer provinces would require more financial assistance, especially as social programs expanded in response to the muted but already growing demands from advocacy groups. "This call for a redistribution of the nation's wealth and the establishment of national standards in social services ... earned Rowell-Sirois its reputation as a blueprint for the Canadian welfare state" (Struthers 1983, 205). The NAGs would also become one model for equalization, albeit with a different formula for establishing entitlements. The report was nudging Canada towards a crucial first step in expanding social security.

The report defended the proposals against the claim that such possible change, constitutional or otherwise, would penalize the provinces: "The only true independence is financial security."[8] It also bridged a dangerous gulf. "Although the commission was careful to dismiss the notion that the Dominion was directly responsible as such to a province for the adverse effects of federal policy on it," observed political scientist David Milne (1998, 186), "it nonetheless argued that Ottawa should support a province in fiscal need, particularly where part of the cause can be shown to flow from federal policy."

In another valuable contribution, the report documented how much Canadian society had changed since the subsidy debates at Confederation. From 1874 to 1937, total per capita government expenditures had "increased by eleven times" (Royal Commission on Dominion-Provincial Relations [1940] 1954, 1:245). The cost of education and public welfare had gone from "the almost negligible figure of $4-million to $360-million" (1:245). But Ottawa's share of the total cost of government had fallen from two-thirds to less than one-half – and that included federal contributions to the provinces for relief and old age pensions (1:245). The provinces' limited tax base had left them in an impossible position: they could not afford what they now had to deliver.

It was all too much for King. He reluctantly called a Dominion-Provincial Conference for January 1941 to discuss the report's recommendations. When three premiers objected vehemently to the proposed changes – to King's secret satisfaction – they were set aside. Instead, Finance Minister James Ilsley announced that he would invoke the War Measures Act to take over the collection of key provincial taxes. Ottawa made five-year tax-rental deals with individual provinces, based on one of two options.

Under the first option, grants were based on the revenues from key taxes collected in 1941 within a province's boundaries, which was "the antithesis of equalization" because it was based on each province's own tax collection (Courchene 1984, 27). Under the second, grants were based on the net cost of servicing the province's debt in 1940–1, minus the succession duties that it collected in that year. "It is possible to argue that the availability of a choice of options embodied some consideration of fiscal need," explains political economist Thomas Courchene (1984, 27).

Former senior finance official R.M. Burns (1980, 29) noted that Ottawa "had always been reluctant to acknowledge fiscal need per se as a basis for grants to the provinces, preferring adjustments to statutory subsidies or special grants to acknowledge any fundamental disabilities within the federation." But the grants that Ottawa had bestowed on the Maritimes in the late 1920s and the mid-1930s – in response to the Duncan and White reports – had already recognized special needs, at least indirectly.

Now, officially, Ottawa crossed this rhetorical bridge: the rental agreements effectively replaced the special grants to the West and the awards to the Maritimes with subsidies based on *existing* fiscal need. The tax-rental deals ensured that poorer provinces would now get *extra* revenues in return for cooperating with Ottawa. But, as the senior federal official who was probably Deutsch noted, National Adjustment Grants would have relieved "the social and economic disparities between regions of Canada" because "the largest payments would go to the least wealthy provinces" (John James Deutsch Fonds 1955, 17). Instead, with the tax-rental deals, "the largest payments would be received by the provinces where the tax fields had most value" (18).

Peacetime Woes

The federation remained largely stalled in peacetime. Ottawa had introduced unemployment insurance and family allowances in wartime – but those were payments that it could make directly to individuals. The Dominion-Provincial Conference of 1945–6, despite months of arduous and increasingly ill-tempered negotiations, made virtually no progress in remedying the state of fiscal federalism. Mackenzie King had tabled an extensive list of social proposals in return for permanent tax concessions from the provinces. But when many objected fiercely, he was secretly pleased and put aside those proposals.

Instead, Ottawa offered to renew the tax-rental deals with individual provinces; all except Ontario and Quebec signed the next five-year deals. King largely ignored the increasingly vociferous demands from numerous groups such as women's organizations and trade unions for expanded social security. In May 1948, however, he unveiled federal health-care grants totalling $30 million per year to all provincial governments. Ottawa earmarked the money for surveys of the health status and needs of Canadians, hospital construction, and the free diagnosis and treatment of selected disorders such as tuberculosis (Naylor 1986, 153). For the retiring King, it was the first step in a long road ahead for his successor, Louis St-Laurent.

In the early 1950s, however, the new prime minister found himself in an increasingly difficult standoff with Quebec Premier Maurice Duplessis. In June 1951, in the wake of the report from the Royal Commission on National Development in the Arts, Letters and Sciences, the prime minister offered $7 million in per capita federal grants to Canadian universities, which would provide roughly fifty cents per student (*Globe and Mail* 1951). The Quebec government reluctantly agreed to administer the funds with Ottawa for the 1951–2 year at the urging of Quebec's francophone universities. Thereafter, Duplessis refused to renew the arrangement.[9]

Quebec was leading the post-war provincial resistance to Ottawa's use of its spending power. The assertion of provincial rights against a predatory federal government predated Confederation. But this powerful Quebec nationalist movement was evolving throughout the 1950s because of the clash of two postwar forces. Ottawa's decision "to forge ahead with Keynesian-inspired fiscal and monetary policies and the creation of a highly centralized social welfare state" were changing federal-provincial relations. Neo-nationalists viewed this new federalism as "a serious threat to provincial autonomy and therefore to the French-Canadian nation" (Behiels 1985, 185–6). Ottawa was encroaching on Quebec's right to protect its language and culture (Simeon and Robinson 1990, 125, 129, 140–5).

Quebec was the only province that did not sign the third tax-rental agreements, which ran from 1952 to 1957. Ottawa did offer an abatement of 7 per cent on corporate taxes and 5 per cent on personal income taxes to Quebec taxpayers (Bélanger 2001; Ottawa had offered an abatement of 5 percentage points to Ontario and Quebec for the 1947–52 tax-rental deals). But Duplessis refused to create a provincially administered personal income tax – "no matter how small" (Behiels 1985, 196). The province lost more than $76 million in revenue from compensatory grants between 1947 and 1952 because of Duplessis's stand on the tax-rental deals (199).

The premier resisted. He established the pivotal provincial Royal Commission of Inquiry on Constitutional Problems, which Judge Thomas Tremblay chaired. In late 1953, before their final report, the commissioners urged Duplessis to resist Ottawa's fiscal domination. In 1954, Duplessis brought in a provincial income tax equal to 15 per cent of the federal rate. It was a direct challenge: Quebec taxpayers would be hit with "double taxation" unless Duplessis could accomplish "the difficult task" of convincing the St-Laurent government to allow them to deduct their provincial tax from their federal tax (Behiels 1985, 199). Duplessis also contended that Quebec had priority in the field of direct taxation.

Initially, St-Laurent reacted disdainfully. In September 1954, he challenged Duplessis in a speech to the Quebec Reform Club. He was open to settling the dispute – but he refused to recognize Quebec's claim to priority over direct taxes. He also asserted: "Quebec is a province like the others" (Black 1998, 436).[10] After an outraged reaction in Quebec, St-Laurent knew that he had to settle the impasse gracefully. Ottawa offered to reduce its income tax by 10 per cent for all provinces where a provincial income tax was levied – and to apply that move retroactively to Quebec for 1954.

The peace offering worked. On 19 January 1955, Duplessis accepted this truce and subsequently agreed to delete the assertion of provincial priority in direct taxation from the provincial income tax act (Privy Council Office 1955, 4). That scuffle "had wider significance. For the first time since the war, Ottawa had to draw back and temper its new national policy [of tax-rental accords and compensatory grants] to take the demands of a province into account" (Linteau et al. 1991, 282).

But St-Laurent knew he had to make a lasting peace with Quebec and, by extension, with all provinces that did not want to sign future tax-rental deals. In a pivotal letter to the other premiers on 14 January 1955, after his pact with Duplessis, St-Laurent declared that Ottawa would not cling to the principle of those deals "to the exclusion of any better alternative arrangement if one could be found" (Burns 1980, 111–12).[11] But Ottawa "had no intention of abandoning the *objective* of the tax rental agreements which is to make it financially possible for all provinces, whatever their tax base, to perform their constitutional functions themselves and *to provide a reasonable Canadian level of provincial services without an abnormal burden of taxation*. That is the foundation of the policy of the federal government" (111–12; emphasis added).

R.M. Burns (1980, 112), who was then director of the federal-provincial relations division in the Department of Finance, stressed: "This was the first official acknowledgement by the federal government of its adoption of equalization as a basic and explicit principle ... since its acceptance of the Rowell-Sirois recommendations in 1941." That is true. There had been adjustments to the Maritime provinces' subsidies in the 1920s and 1930s in the name of generosity. But St-Laurent's letter recognized the concept of fiscal inequality among the provinces and defined how to measure it in terms of tax revenues. He wanted to remove the compensatory grant from the tax-rental deals – and to make it available to all poorer provinces. Officials toyed with formulas and examined ways to equalize revenues in a federal state, including the models of the Australian Commonwealth Grants Commission and the proposed National Adjustment Grants of the Rowell-Sirois Commission.

St-Laurent also met twice with the premiers in October 1955 and March 1956. At the first gathering, he summarized the federation's dilemma with dignity and eloquence. "Second only to national security are the demands of social security, *which the public expects of both Canada and the provinces in great measure*," he declared (St-Laurent 1955, 8; emphasis added). Fiscal arrangements were "the heart of our problem ... The public now expects both levels of government to do things which require high taxes" (13). Canadians wanted "the good life" that the federal Liberals had promised at the end of the Second World War and, with the exception of expanded old age pensions in the early 1950s, had largely failed to deliver.

In the end, equalization payments to the poorer provinces were first based upon the average per capita revenues from three key taxes in the two wealthiest provinces of Ontario and British Columbia. The first cheques went out on 1 April 1957. Wealthy Ontario and the poorer Maritime provinces objected, but Ottawa did not need provincial permission to send out non-conditional payments with no application forms (see chapter 3 by Peter Oliver in this volume).

The equalizing star of fiscal federalism was born. And the results were immediately apparent. In 1956, Ottawa introduced the Unemployment Assistance Act. Initially, the federal government paid 50 per cent of the costs of provincial relief whenever the number of people on relief exceeded 0.45 per cent of a province's population. (The extra group was deemed to represent the unemployed employables; Progressive Conservative Party 1962.) All provinces had signed agreements by 1959 after Ottawa removed the exemption of 0.45 per cent (see chapter 6 by Michael Prince in this volume).

In 1957, St-Laurent introduced the Hospital Insurance and Diagnostic Services Act, which offered to share half the costs of a specific set of hospital and diagnostic services on the condition of universal coverage. By 1 January 1961, all provinces had joined. Quebec was the last (Canadian Museum of History 2010).

In October 1966, Ottawa abolished direct grants to universities and instead agreed to make annual grants to provinces equal to 50 per cent of those universities' operating costs with an escalating minimum of $14 per capita of the provincial population. As former federal policy advisor Tom Kent noted ruefully, those amounts escalated rapidly by an average of more than 20 per cent annually during the first five years (Kent 1988, 390; see also chapter 16 by Jennifer Wallner in this volume).

In 1965, the Established Programs (Interim Arrangements) Act allowed provinces to opt out of shared-cost programs with compensation. Only Quebec opted to levy its own taxes for key programs, with federal taxes adjusted in turn, and equalization payments were altered to ensure that the province was not penalized for the lesser amounts that its taxes raised (Kent 1988, 296).

In 1966, the Medical Care Act set four conditions for federal support for provincial programs: public administration, portability between provinces, comprehensiveness, and universal coverage "on uniform terms and conditions" (Naylor 1986, 234). When the act took effect in 1968, Ottawa provided one-half of the average per capita costs for services provided by doctors outside hospitals. Within six years, all provinces were participating. The Canada Health Act of 1984 consolidated hospital and medical insurance, and penalized provinces that allowed extra billing and user fees (see chapter 5 by Robin Boadway in this volume).

Conclusion

The history of fiscal federalism is really the chronicle of how the federation members finally agreed on sharing among the poorer and richer governments. Those rancorous debates, which included the occasional threat of secession, extended from the bitter pre-Confederation discussions on subsidies through the First World War, the Depression, the Second World War, and into Ottawa's efforts to continue its wartime tax-rental deals in peacetime. When Quebec refused to participate in those deals, it lost substantial amounts of compensatory grants – and became increasingly bitter. Meanwhile, Ottawa was facing intense pressure from national advocacy groups to modernize the federation to meet the social and economic demands of the times.

Over the objections of many senior Finance Ministry officials, but with the support of John James Deutsch, Prime Minister Louis St-Laurent solved that dilemma by separating the grants from the tax collection agreements, extending them to all poorer provinces as equalization and ensuring that they were non-conditional with a relatively transparent formula (Pickersgill 1975, 309).[12] He defused multiple stresses upon the federation. Poorer provinces now had almost enough funding to participate in national shared-cost programs for health care, post-secondary education, and social assistance. Social security expanded across the nation.

Fiscal inequality among the provinces has not disappeared; nor has the bitter squabbling about sharing. But once Ottawa openly addressed those inequalities with equalization, once it resolved to bring a measure of equity to the poorer members of the federation, it preserved national unity. And it allowed all Canadians to share in the benefits of expanded social care. It was a long, arduous, and rewarding road, the gift from the generation that survived the Second World War to make a better world.

NOTES

1 The author devotes much space to the Royal Commission on Dominion-Provincial Relations, which is another indication that Deutsch was the author, because he was research director of that royal commission.
2 The referendum did not demand changes to the equalization formula, which was the key issue for many Albertans.
3 British North America Act, 1867, clause 118.
4 The Manitoba Act 1870, clause 25.
5 British North America Act, 1907, Schedule.
6 "Letter of the Three Maritime Premiers to the Prime Minister of Canada, January 16, 1934," as quoted in *Report of the Royal Commission on Financial Arrangements*

between the Dominion and the Maritime Provinces (White 1935, vi). See also "Maritime Subsidy Held Inadequate" in *The Globe*, 16 January 1934, 3.
7 See also *Review of Dominion Provincial Financial Arrangements* (John James Deutsch Fonds 1955, 8).
8 Robert Wardhaugh and Barry Ferguson (2021) maintain that the commission wanted to avoid formal constitutional change wherever possible. Instead, governments should engage in voluntary agreements, delegating or jointly administering functions.
9 Ottawa continued to offer the money from 1953 to 1959, and Duplessis continued to refuse. When the premier died, the funds, which had been set aside, were transferred to the province (Black 1998, 338–9).
10 J.W. Pickersgill (1975, 256) quotes a slightly different version of the remarks: St-Laurent believed "that the province of Quebec can be a province like any other."
11 "Letter from Louis St-Laurent to All Provincial Premiers with the Exception of Quebec Premier Maurice Duplessis, 14 January 1955," as quoted in Burns (1980, 111–12).
12 Pickersgill says that Deutsch was with the Finance Ministry, but he was actually with the Treasury Board.

REFERENCES

Anderson, George. 2009. *Fiscal Federalism: A Comparative Introduction*. Oxford: Oxford University Press.
Behiels, Michael D. 1985. *Prelude to Quebec's Quiet Revolution: Liberalism Versus Neo-Nationalism, 1945–1960*. Montreal and Kingston: McGill-Queen's University Press.
Bélanger, Claude. 2001. "Canadian Federalism: The Tax Rental Agreements of the Period of 1941–1962 and Fiscal Federalism from 1962 to 1977." *Quebec History*. Marianopolis College. http://faculty.marianopolis.edu/c.belanger/quebechistory/federal/taxrent.htm.
Black, Conrad. 1998. *Render Unto Caesar: The Life and Legacy of Maurice Duplessis*. Toronto: Key Porter Books.
Boyko, John. 2010. *Bennett: The Rebel Who Challenged and Changed a Nation*. Toronto: Key Porter Books.
Burns, R.M. 1980. *The Acceptable Mean: The Tax Rental Agreements, 1941–1962*. Toronto: The Canadian Tax Foundation.
Canadian Museum of History. 2010. "Politics and History." In *Making Medicare: The History of Health Care in Canada, 1914–2007*. Canadian Museum of History. https://www.historymuseum.ca/cmc/exhibitions/hist/medicare/medic-4h22e.html.
Conrad, Margaret, and Alvin Finkel. 2008. *History of the Canadian Peoples*. Vol. 2, *1867 to the Present*. 5th ed. Newmarket, ON: Pearson Education Canada.
Courchene, Thomas J. 1984. *Equalization Payments: Past, Present and Future*. Toronto: Ontario Economic Council.

Dominion-Provincial Conference. 1933. "Resolutions of the Dominion-Provincial Conference, Ottawa, January 17–19, 1933." Library and Archives Canada, RG47, Vol. 67.
– 1951. *Dominion-Provincial Conferences: November 3–10, 1927; December 9–13, 1935; January 14–15, 1941.* Ottawa: Edmond Cloutier.
Duncan, Andrew. 1926. *Report of the Royal Commission on Maritime Claims.* Ottawa: F. A. Acland.
Forbes, Ernest. 1979. *Maritime Rights: The Maritime Rights Movement, 1919–1927: A Study in Canadian Regionalism.* Montreal and Kingston: McGill-Queen's University Press.
– 1989a. "Misguided Symmetry: The Destruction of Regional Transportation Policy for the Maritimes." In *Challenging the Regional Stereotype: Essays on the 20th Century Maritimes*, 114–35. Fredericton, NB: Acadiensis Press.
– 1989b. "The Origins of the Maritime Rights Movement." In *Challenging the Regional Stereotype: Essays on the 20th Century Maritimes*, 100–13. Fredericton, NB: Acadiensis Press.
Fransen, David. 1984. "'Unscrewing the Unscrutable': The Rowell-Sirois Commission, the Ottawa Bureaucracy, and Public Finance Reform, 1935–1941." PhD diss., Department of History, University of Toronto.
Globe. 1923. "Wants Nova Scotia Separate Dominion: Conservative Member of N.S. Assembly Moves That Province Secede." *The Globe*, 20 April 1923, 1.
Globe and Mail. 1951. "Universities to Receive $7,000,000 Ottawa Aid; CBC Also to Get Help." *Globe and Mail*, 20 June 1951, 3.
Heaman, Elsbeth. 2017. *Tax, Order, and Good Government: A New Political History of Canada, 1867–1917.* Montreal and Kingston: McGill-Queen's University Press.
Henderson, Stephen T. 2007. *Angus L. Macdonald: A Provincial Liberal.* Toronto: University of Toronto Press.
Howe, Joseph. 1866. *Confederation in Relation to the Interests of the Empire.* London: Edward Stanford.
John James Deutsch Fonds. 1955. *Review of Dominion Provincial Financial Arrangements.* Queen's University Archives, Box 81, File 770.
Kent, Tom. 1988. *A Public Purpose: An Experience of Liberal Opposition and Canadian Government.* Montreal and Kingston: McGill-Queen's University Press.
Labour Gazette. 1935. "Survey of Federal Relief Activities since 1930." Library and Archives Canada, RG47, Vol. 60, File Conferences.
Laurier, Wilfrid. 1907. "Address to Joint Conference, Friday, October 12, 1906." Sessional Paper 29a, Interprovincial Conference Minutes, 1906, 11–12. In *Sessional Papers, Volume 12, Third Session of the Tenth Parliament of the Dominion of Canada, 1906–7.* Ottawa: House of Commons. https://publications.gc.ca/collections/collection_2018/parl/x12-3/X12-3-12-1907-eng.pdf.
Lepawsky, Albert. 1940. "Review of *Canadian Federalism in Transition: Report of the Royal Commission on Dominion-Provincial Relations.*" *Public Administration Review* 1, no. 1: 76–81. https://doi.org/10.2307/972581.

Library and Archives Canada. 1937. "Summary of Assistance Requested of and Given by the Dominion to Province of Alberta since September 3, 1935." Memo dated 26 February 1937. Library and Archives Canada. P-1-1-10. Provincial Matters – Alberta – Miscellaneous – P – 1-1-10. RG 19. Vol. 3985. N. N., 6.

Linteau, Paul-André, René Durocher, Jean-Claude Robert, and François Ricard. 1991. *Quebec since 1930*. Toronto: James Lorimer.

Marchington, William. 1932. "Joint Public Works as Relief Measure to Be Discontinued? Dominion Will Confine Operations to Direct Assistance to Unemployed, Ottawa Learns – Provincial Delegates Confer with Federal Government; No Work, No Help, Is to Be Slogan." *The Globe*, 11 April 1932, 1–2.

Milne, David. 1998. "Equalization and the Politics of Restraint." In *Equalization: Its Contribution to Canada's Economic and Fiscal Progress*, edited by Robin W. Boadway and Paul A.R. Hobson, 175–203. Kingston, ON: John Deutsch Institute for the Study of Economic Policy, Queen's University.

Moore, Christopher. 1997. *1867: How the Fathers Made a Deal*. Toronto: McClelland & Stewart.

Naylor, David C. 1986. *Private Practice, Public Payment: Canadian Medicine and the Politics of Health Insurance, 1911–1966*. Montreal and Kingston: McGill-Queen's University Press.

Norrie, Kenneth, Douglas Owram, and J.C. Herbert Emery. 2008. *The History of the Canadian Economy*. 4th ed. Toronto: Nelson, Thomson.

Ottawa Journal. 1934. "Ask Provinces to Look After Own Financing: Desire of Federal Government Is to Shift Responsibility Back Gradually." *Ottawa Journal*, 18 January 1934, 1.

Pickersgill, Jack. 1975. *My Years with Louis St. Laurent: A Political Memoir*. Toronto: University of Toronto Press.

Privy Council Office. 1955. "Cabinet Conclusions, January 20, 1955, Top Secret, RG2." Ottawa: Privy Council Office, Series A-5-a, Vol. 2657, Access Code: 12.

Progressive Conservative Party of Canada. 1962. *Getting Things Done for Canada and Canadians: An Outline of Progressive Conservative Government Action, 1957–1962 – The Greatest Era of Expansion in Canada's History*. https://www.poltext.org/sites/poltext.org/files/plateformesV2/Canada/CAN_PL_1962_PC.pdf.

Province of Nova Scotia. 1934. *Report of the Royal Commission: Provincial Economic Inquiry*. Halifax: Provincial Secretary, King's Printer.

Royal Commission on Dominion-Provincial Relations. (1940) 1954. *Report of the Royal Commission on Dominion-Provincial Relations*. 3 vols. Ottawa: King's Printer.

Simeon, Richard, and Ian Robinson. 1990. *State, Society, and the Development of Canadian Federalism*. Toronto: University of Toronto Press.

Smiley, Donald. 1962. "The Rowell-Sirois Report, Provincial Autonomy, and Post-War Canadian Federalism." *The Canadian Journal of Economics and Political Science* 28, no. 1: 54–69. https://doi.org/10.2307/139263.

St-Laurent, Louis. 1955. "Proceedings of the Federal-Provincial Conference 1955, Ottawa, October 3, 1955, Plenary Conferences Conference of October 3, 1955, Summary Record of Proceedings." Library and Archives Canada, RG19, Vol. 3880, File: 5515-04 (55/2)-3.

Struthers, James. 1983. *No Fault of Their Own: Unemployment and the Canadian Welfare State 1914–1941*. Toronto: University of Toronto Press.

Wardhaugh, Robert, and Barry Ferguson. 2021. *The Rowell-Sirois Commission and the Remaking of Canadian Federalism*. Vancouver: UBC Press.

White, Thomas. 1935. *Report of the Royal Commission on Financial Arrangements between the Dominion and the Maritime Provinces*. Ottawa: J. O. Patenaude. https://publications.gc.ca/collections/collection_2014/bcp-pco/CP32-142-1935-eng.pdf

Whitney, James. 1907. "Memorandum on Behalf of the Province of Ontario." In *Sessional Paper 29a: Interprovincial Conference Minutes, 1906*, 4–7. Ottawa: House of Commons.

3 Fiscal Federalism and the Federal Spending Power: A Legal and Constitutional Analysis

PETER C. OLIVER

Introduction

What is the legal and constitutional basis for the range of federal transfers that together constitute fiscal federalism? Some transfers, such as equalization payments, are provided for (or at least contemplated) in the constitutional text (section 36 of the Constitution Act, 1982). The basis for other transfers is less clear, or in some eyes non-existent. If such a basis exists, it lies in the much discussed but little understood "federal spending power."

Other chapters in this volume discuss the reasons why the federal spending power is politically controversial (see, for example, chapters in this volume by Janigan, Boadway, Slack, Pomeroy, Wallner, and Robson). This chapter takes that political controversy as read and attempts instead to focus more narrowly on the legal and constitutional aspect, though politics and law are never far apart in practice. Those who doubt the existence of a federal spending power may have ulterior motives for doing so, but they have every right to question and probe its legal and constitutional basis. For example, partisans of small government (for example, Kellock and Leroy 2006) point out that, if a federal spending power existed, it would be spelled out clearly in the Constitution. Furthermore, they suggest that, if there are only exceptional specific references to federal transfers to provinces, that must be the full extent of it, there being no *general* spending power in their view. Staunch defenders of provincial jurisdiction (for example, Lajoie 1988; Québec 2002) stress that Ottawa cannot do indirectly that which it is constitutionally prohibited from doing directly (Turcotte 2015) – that is, interfere with matters under provincial jurisdiction – so if Ottawa cannot legislate in relation to what happens in higher education, for example, then it should not be able to achieve the same results by means of federal spending.

These seem to be powerful objections. And yet, the federal spending power is still a key component of Canadian federalism, especially fiscal federalism, and the courts clearly approve of its existence. How do we make sense of this?

The main answer is that, tempting as it may be, we have to try not to rush to conclusions, favourable or unfavourable, in the legal and constitutional sphere. Accordingly, this chapter attempts to break down the issue of the legal and constitutional basis of the federal spending power by asking a series of more detailed questions and exploring a range of new issues that flow from that analysis.

Section 1 addresses the key preliminary question regarding what we mean when we speak of the federal spending power. Section 2 then asks where we should look if we wish to assess the legal and constitutional basis, if any, for the federal spending power. Section 3 explores the relevant rules of Canadian legal federalism and considers the point at which federal spending becomes controversial constitutionally speaking (with regard to the conditionality of spending, for example). Section 4 looks at what our highest courts have said thus far regarding the substantive validity and justiciability (that is, whether the matter is apt for judicial consideration) of the federal spending power. Section 5 then addresses the question of what legal and constitutional issues are likely to come to the fore if the federal spending power is directly and definitively considered by the Supreme Court of Canada at some moment in the future.

1. The Meaning of the "Federal Spending Power"

The most frequently cited definition of the federal spending power originally appeared in 1969: "the power of Parliament to make payments to people or institutions or governments for purposes on which it does not necessarily have the power to legislate" (Trudeau 1969, 4). There are a number of problems with this definition.

First, it does not separate ordinary federal legislation based in section 91 of the Constitution Act, 1867, on the one hand, and executive spending on the basis of a prior appropriation, on the other. It refers only to *Parliament* and its spending power. The failure to make this distinction may be significant if the power to spend is distinct from the power to authorize the amounts of the various expenditures, as will be discussed in Section 2.

Second, the 1969 definition deliberately, though somewhat cryptically, prevaricates on whether indeed Parliament has a plenary power to legislate under the label "federal spending power": "make payments ... for purposes on which it does not *necessarily* have the power to legislate." This last phrase could be interpreted to mean that the term "federal spending power" is appropriately used whenever there is a *dispute* as to whether Parliament has a putative power to make payments, but with the assumption that a court could eventually confirm a definitive positive or negative answer. Or, more likely, the qualifier "necessarily" simply suggests that such answers are not as easily arrived at in an era where flexible and cooperative federalism, rather than a federalism of watertight compartments, is the norm (Wright 2018; Boudreault 2020; Section 3 below).

Finally, a possible nuance in this definition, and one that needs to be further explored, is that the label attached to a *spending item* (whether executive or legislative) does not always lead to the same conclusion as if that label were in relation to a *legislative or regulatory item*. We already see this nuance in relation to the taxation side of the equation: Parliament may *tax* capital gains on items such as *sales* of securities, even though Parliament could not otherwise *legislate* so as to regulate those sales. Is the same true regarding spending? We will see that the answer appears to be "yes."

This chapter begins with the widest possible definition, narrowing only insofar as the legal and constitutional analysis permits. Therefore, for present purposes, I would include in that definition both spending by the executive based on a prior appropriation and parliamentary legislation regarding spending. And, in order to avoid confusion, I would opt to substitute the neutral term "items" for "purposes," given the significance of the latter term in the characterization of legislation for division of powers purposes, as we shall see in Section 3. Accordingly, I would adapt the 1969 definition of the federal spending power so as to refer to "the power of *the federal government and* Parliament to make payments to people or institutions or governments *with respect to items* over which Parliament does not necessarily have the power to legislate." I have not removed the ambiguous word "necessarily." I will instead attempt to resolve that ambiguity over the course of the chapter.

With that definition in mind, we can now consider the most likely contenders for the legal and constitutional basis for the federal spending power in Section 2. I will then situate those answers in the modern era of Canadian federalism in Section 3, before going on to look at the courts' perspective – past, present, and future – in Sections 4 and 5. We will see in these last three sections that one of the issues that proves to be especially controversial (and not judicially clarified to the extent that we might want) is the presence of varying degrees of conditionality in federal spending.

2. The Legal and Constitutional Basis for the Federal Spending Power

Specific Constitutional Provisions

Are there any specific sections of the Constitution that provide a legal basis for the federal spending power? Part VII of the Constitution Act, 1867 referred to federal spending in a number of places. For example, section 118 stated that certain "sums shall be paid yearly by Canada to the several Provinces for the Support of their Government and Legislatures," and section 119 provided for grants to New Brunswick alone. The Constitution Act, 1907 both confirmed and widened the former power (so as to add new provinces, a new formula, and a reference to "local purposes").

Were transfers to the provinces limited to the amounts set out initially in sections 118 and 119 and subsequently in the Constitution Act, 1907? Some have argued that the answer was and still is "yes" (Kellock and Leroy 2006). As early as 1869, Ontario politician, Edward Blake, MP, arguing on behalf of the Opposition Liberals, contended that the Conservative government's payments to keep Nova Scotia in Confederation were unconstitutional for the simple reason that they were not specifically provided for in the Constitution Act, 1867. Blake's arguments failed politically due to, first, a widespread desire not to see Nova Scotia secede and, second, the alignment of votes in the House of Commons favouring the government led by Sir John A. Macdonald. But they were also rejected when put to the Colonial Office in legal form (Parliament of Canada 1869, 726; United Kingdom 1869, 9014). The latter's legal opinion was issued by the attorney general, Sir Robert Collier, a future member of the Judicial Committee of the Privy Council (JCPC) and subsequently the author of the first JCPC decision regarding Canada. Blake, Macdonald, and their colleagues subsequently treated the Colonial Office opinion as authoritative (Parliament of Canada 1870, 760).

It is hard to imagine, given the complex and changing needs of a young federation, that federal transfers to the provinces would be limited to the narrow terms contemplated by sections 118 and 119. The federal government had since 1867 frequently made payments to provinces, based on appropriations by Parliament, above and beyond the specific terms of the Constitution (see chapter 2 by Janigan in this volume). The need to end the sometimes-unprincipled nature of those payments prompted the 1907 constitutional amendment, but even in 1907 there was no expectation, even in the mind of the instigator of that amendment, Prime Minister Wilfrid Laurier, that future federal transfers would be limited to the new arrangements (House of Commons 1906–7, 5308).

We can point to one further express constitutional basis for federal spending in relation to fiscal federalism. Section 36 of the Constitution Act, 1982 put the by-then decades-old system of equalization on a more solid constitutional footing. While section 36 did not itself grant Parliament a power to transfer funds to the provinces, in that it left the division of powers as it was before 1982, it clearly presumed the existence of such a power; otherwise, it would have been setting out a constitutional commitment to an unconstitutional practice. Some commentators have taken the view that section 36 (or at the very least the power that section 36 implies) confirms the existence of a wider federal spending power (Boadway 1998, 38; Courchene 2008, 103; Kong 2008, 372–3; Nader 1996), although at least one commentator has indicated that the wider power is also constrained by section 36 (Kong 2017). While the existence of section 36 weighs heavily against those who try to question the legality of equalization (Kellock and Lemay 2006), it is perhaps prudent to assume that it provides no more than confirmation of an independent constitutional footing for equalization and to refrain for the moment from making further assumptions regarding what it might say in relation to a wider federal spending power (Banting 2008, 158n1; Bérard 2016).

With respect to that wider federal spending power, and consistent with the alterations to the definition of the spending power discussed in Section 1 of this chapter, I will consider the executive's spending powers before moving on to discuss Parliament's powers in that regard.

The Executive's Spending Power

Although much of the focus of our legal and constitutional analysis will be with regard to section 91 of the Constitution Act, 1867 and the power of Parliament to legislate regarding its own property, the federal spending story is by no means exclusively a legislative matter. In fact, although, according to our British-rooted constitutional traditions, all funds distributed by the government have to be approved or "appropriated" by Parliament, once this approval has occurred, spending is largely in the domain of the executive. What was and is the source of the executive's powers in relation to spending?

There are three possible bases for executive power in relation to spending, and these are essentially the same sources that we would look to when speaking of the executive's powers more generally. They are, respectively: the Crown prerogative, common law (or third-source) powers, and powers delegated under primary legislation.

The first of these sources, the Crown prerogative, is also the first in time historically. It reminds us once again that, although Parliament has come to perform a critical overseeing role, spending was and is to a great extent an executive function. The Crown prerogative can be defined, for present purposes, as the residue of powers formerly held by the sovereign that have not been superseded by parliamentary enactment (Dicey 2013, 188). We need hardly cite chapter and verse to confirm that spending was a central power of British (and other) monarchs (but for more, see Chitty 1820; Daintith and Page 1999).

As we have noted, Parliament came to insist on approving (appropriating) the amounts where executive spending was concerned, but the prerogative power to carry out that spending remained in executive hands. Spending (beyond appropriation) takes in a wide array of modalities, terms, and conditions: from who cuts the cheques, in what amounts and under what circumstances, to distribution and accounting. It involves spending that is local, national, *and* international. All of this would have at one time been covered by the Crown prerogative, and some of those powers remain exclusively in executive hands, to the extent that Parliament has not pre-empted them (Forcese 2017, 154–5). It is worth pausing to consider the wide array of spending powers and duties that historically resided in the executive, because (by virtue of the principle of parliamentary sovereignty) this same subject matter forms part of the legislative jurisdiction residing in Parliament (and the legislatures) that will be discussed below. As we note there, and as will become clearer in Sections 3, 4, and 5, as long as the Canadian Parliament is legislating with respect to the modalities, terms, and conditions of spending in relation to its own funds, as opposed to in relation to the substance of a provincial matter, Parliament appears to have jurisdiction.

I have so far been speaking of the Crown prerogative in a broad-brush way. However, some British and Commonwealth constitutional scholars make a further important distinction. They say that, strictly speaking, the term "Crown prerogative" should only be used to describe powers that were unique to the sovereign, such as the power to declare war or issue passports. Powers to contract, purchase, spend, and make gifts are, so it is said, powers that all persons, including moral persons, have and that the Crown therefore holds as well (*Halsbury's Laws* 2018, 348; *Verreault & Fils* 1977, 47). These last powers are referred to as common law (or third-source; Harris 2007) powers.

In one view, the existence of prerogative and/or common law powers means that, above and beyond Parliament's appropriations, the federal government (executive) does not need to identify any further legal and constitutional basis for its spending. It can make gifts and unilaterally add conditions to those gifts, or it can sign agreements with provinces on what might be the terms of such payments. This view was first associated with Frank (F.R.) Scott, who stated that such gifts or contracts "derive from doctrines of the Royal Prerogative and the common law" (Scott 1955, 6). Scott's view is usually referred to as an argument based solely in the prerogative (without qualifying that term; Kong 2008, 310; Lajoie and Molinari 1978, 596; Ryan and Slutsky 1964–6, 303; Smiley and Burns 1969, 471; Smiley 1962, 61; Telford 2003, 29; Turcotte 2015, 114), perhaps because it is well known that, ever since the seventeenth century, it is the courts (and therefore the common law) that determine the existence and extent of the prerogative (*Case of Proclamations* 1610). However, it is best to read Scott as including what some now refer to as common law (or third-source) powers in his usage of the expression "Crown prerogative and common law." Leading Canadian textbook writers François Chevrette and Peter Hogg have lent their support to the common law (or third-source) rather than the generic Crown prerogative view (Chevrette 1988, 156; Hogg 2007, 6.8).

Does it matter whether an argument such as Scott's is based in the Crown prerogative, broadly understood, or in the Crown's common law (or third-source) powers? After all, either one would appear to provide an answer to the traditional lawyers' question: "where did you (in this case the executive) get the power you are claiming?" The significance of such distinctions lies in whether one or the other classification removes the need to justify the relevant spending power in division of power terms.

Regarding the Crown prerogative in the generic sense used above, an argument can be made, and has been made (Québec 2002, 4), citing Privy Council case law

(*Maritime Bank* 1892), to the effect that the Crown prerogative in a federal system divides along jurisdictional lines. According to this argument, even a federal spending power based in the Crown prerogative would have to respect the division of powers. But far from being fatal to the spending that is at issue, it would simply revive the question (discussed in greater detail below) regarding whether the executive is acting in relation to the modalities, terms, and conditions of spending its own funds or whether its primary focus is in relation to a provincial head of power. Furthermore, given what we know of the history of executive spending powers, that history supports plenary spending jurisdiction provided the power exercised is indeed in relation to the spending of federal funds (Scott 1990).

Moving on to consider the discrete category of common law (or third-source) powers, it is easier to argue that these are not controlled by the division of powers. Common law powers are ones that individuals and moral persons have, and that the Crown is said to possess as well, without any need to have recourse to the prerogative. Are common law powers the sort of Holy Grail that some pro-federal advocates have been looking for in order to ground the federal spending power (*Verreault & Fils* 1977)?

It would seem that there are at least a few good reasons to continue the search. First, the common law (or third-source) theory is not without its critics. Some argue that there are only two sources of executive power: prerogative and delegated (which I will discuss briefly below). In this view, the spending-related powers said to be third source should be regarded as "ancillary" to known prerogative powers (Sedley 2015, ch. 6) and consequently, in Canada, controlled by the division of powers. Second, and more significantly perhaps, the sceptical view regarding third-source powers has recently found favour in a country that shares our British constitutional tradition. In the case known as *Chaplains*, the Australian High Court rejected the view that the central government could spend as it wished on the basis of a third-source power (*Williams* 2012). Third, there is an argument that, in this day and age, even common law third-source powers in the hands of government deserve constitutional treatment that is distinct from that which applies to private actors (Sedley 2015, ch. 6). Finally, such distinct constitutional treatment would have to respect the federal principle that was so memorably highlighted in the *Secession Reference* of 1998. The upshot of all this is that, while common law (or third-source) powers may provide a legal justification for wide-ranging spending powers retained by the executive, it is less clear that such sourcing releases them from federalism concerns. However, as noted earlier, it is perfectly consistent with those federalism concerns that the executive (or Parliament supplanting it) deal with the many modalities, terms, and conditions regarding spending its funds as long as in doing so it does not in pith and substance regulate a provincial matter. The answer to our main question would appear to lie in the federalism analysis that will be discussed in Section 3, but this tour through executive powers is a useful reminder as to how much subject matter there is that properly falls under the heading "spending."

The third and final legal and constitutional basis for executive powers is the easiest to understand. It is where the executive, a minister of the Crown, for example, is clearly the object of delegated (in this case spending-related) powers in legislation. To the extent that the other two bases for executive spending powers – prerogative and third source – are considered wanting or obscure for reasons discussed above, there will be a temptation to place executive spending powers on a stronger and clearer statutory basis. This is in fact what has occurred in many cases (see, for example, Canada Strategic Infrastructure Fund Act, s. 4; Canada Student Financial Assistance Act, ss. 5, 14; Federal-Provincial Fiscal Arrangements Act, s. 24.8). Are payments made under these provisions constitutionally invalid because they are payments in relation to items such as local infrastructure, education, and health services that fall to be regulated under section 92 of the Constitution Act, 1867? Or are they valid because they are primarily in relation to how Parliament spends its money, with merely incidental effects on matters within provincial jurisdiction? We will see that there is strong judicial support for the latter perspective. In determining the validity of federal provisions, it is vital to keep in mind that, in addition to the outward-facing end-of-line aspect of spending (the provinces, organizations, individuals, and the *items* to which the infrastructure spending, for example, is directed), there is also an important range of inward-facing (that is, directed at federal officials) aspects relating to all the modalities, terms, and conditions of the spending process regarding those items. Whether legislation is in pith and substance aimed at the former or the latter would appear to be an important part of the constitutional analysis.

In asking these questions, we have returned to terrain that is more familiar to constitutional lawyers and political scientists, that is, the constitutional division of powers. However, we can already see that there may be unique challenges in determining the pith and substance of a spending provision as compared to, say, provisions creating criminal offences or regulating international trade. In order to equip ourselves to answer these questions, we will discuss in Section 3 the constitutional rules and principles in relation to contemporary Canadian federalism. But first, having already considered the historical source of spending in the constitutional powers of the executive, it will now be important to discuss briefly the supervening constitutional powers of Parliament.

Parliament's Spending Power

The following are sections of the Constitution Act, 1867 that have been put forward as providing support for a federal spending power (Driedger 1981, 124–7; Hogg 2007, 6.8; Jackman 2000, 95–7; Kent 2008, 16; Magnet 1978, 478; Smiley and Burns 1969, 472; Schwartz 1987, 64; Trudeau 1969, 12): sections 91(1A) "the public debt and property"; 91(3) "the raising of money by any mode or system of taxation"; 94 "legislation for uniformity of laws" in all provinces except Quebec; 102 "Consolidated Revenue Fund to be appropriated for the public service of Canada in the manner and subject to the charges in this Act provided"; and 106 "subject to the several payments by this Act charged on the Consolidated Revenue Fund of Canada the same shall be appropriated by the Parliament for the public service." Other authors deny that there is any constitutional basis for such a spending power (Kellock and Leroy 2006; Lajoie 1988, 170; Noël 2008a, 2008b; Petter 1989, 461; Québec 2002, 9; Québec 2004, 3; Bérard 2016). A further small group of authors (notably Adam 2008) carve out a hybrid position based on section 94 of the Constitution Act, 1867, according to which federal authorities may have a spending power in areas of provincial jurisdiction with regard to common law provinces but not (following the logic of section 94) with regard to Quebec civil law.

As we will see in Section 4, the Supreme Court of Canada has shown a marked preference for anchoring the federal spending power under sections 91(1A) "the public debt and property" and 91(3) "the raising of money by any mode or system of taxation," and it is easy to see why. Section 91(1A) effectively sets out Parliament's legislative jurisdiction regarding federal assets and liabilities, and this without the sorts of limitations that one sees in sections 92(2) and 92(9) (Macdonald 2008, 263–4; Kong 2017, 436). Federal assets clearly include not just real property but also federal funds (as maintained in the Consolidated Revenue Fund referred to in sections 102 and 106).

If sections 91(1A), 91(3), 94, 102, and 106 do not together underpin federal jurisdiction with regard to spending, then the federal residual (or peace, order, and good government [POGG]) power (Choudhry 2008, 377; Hogg 2007, 6.8) is available (though basing jurisdiction in the national concern branch of POGG is admittedly more difficult in the wake of the *GGPPA References* 2021). Without going into detail regarding this power, it perhaps suffices for the moment to say that it is hard to imagine any Constitution that does not provide legislatures, federal and provincial, with jurisdiction to make laws regarding the modalities, terms, and conditions of their own spending.

Though it might appear that I have too quickly confirmed the legal and constitutional basis for the federal spending power, I have not yet done so. Thus far, I have merely confirmed a fairly clear federal power underpinning legislation in relation to federal property (including the modalities, terms, and conditions of spending the funds that, in part, constitute that property). Still to be answered is the question regarding the point at which federal legislation in relation to such spending becomes in constitutional terms legislation in relation to matters over which Parliament does *not* have power to legislate. As noted earlier by way of analogy, federal taxation in relation to the sale of securities is valid, whereas federal legislation regulating contracts of sale of securities is not. More will be said in relation to the equivalent spending-related analysis in Section 3.

This brief survey of potential legal and constitutional bases for the federal spending power included a description of the historically significant power of the executive to spend once Parliament has appropriated the relevant funds. We have seen that understanding executive powers in relation to spending helps us to understand the likely (broad) contours of the legislative powers discussed in the latter part of this Section.

3. The Federal Spending Power and Canadian Federalism

The division of powers is governed by at least two ideas that require nuance and explanation, as alluded to earlier when the definition of the federal spending power was discussed. The first nuance is that, although legislation *involves or affects* matters within provincial jurisdiction, it does not necessarily mean that the legislation is *in relation to* such matters. This distinction is a question of the characterization (and classification) of legislation, of primary objects and effects, and secondary or ancillary objects and effects. The second nuance is that, even though a *province* can legislate in relation to a matter (for example, spending on health), it does not necessarily mean that *Parliament* cannot legislate in relation to the same or similar matter. As we shall see, this second point is a question of flexible or cooperative federalism and doctrines such as double aspect.

The Characterization (and Classification) of Legislation

Characterization (and classification) of legislation is perhaps the most fundamental technique in Canadian legal federalism. It determines whether any given legal measure is *valid* or not. The validity of such measures is determined according to a familiar two-step process. Although almost every legal federalism case could be cited as authority for this two-step process, I have taken most of what follows from one of the most recent cases decided by the Supreme Court of Canada (*Reference re Genetic Non-Discrimination Act* [*GND*] 2020).

First, we must characterize the measure. Characterization involves identifying its "pith and substance," its "true subject matter." To do this, we have to look at both the *purpose* ("leading feature or true character"; *GND* 2020, [28–9]) and the *effects* (both the legal and the practical effects) of the measure in question (*GND* 2020, [30]). As the word "leading" indicates, this process recognizes that usually "the challenged law has multiple features" (*GND* 2020, [31]). The court must determine "which of these features is most important" (*GND* 2020, [31]). Second, having determined the leading feature of the measure, we must classify it under the appropriate head of power.

It has already been noted, by way of analogy, that federal measures in relation to tax may have an essential tax purpose (raising revenue by taxing capital gains), even as they affect provincial matters (regulating contracts of sale of shares). There may, of course, be circumstances in which the tax aspect and the contractual aspect are both strong, making it hard to determine a single pith and substance (*Reference re Exported Natural Gas Tax* 1982, 1073–4), or where the tax aspect is instead a smokescreen for an attempt to regulate property and civil rights (*Unemployment Insurance Reference* 1937). The former scenario raises the issue of the double aspect doctrine and is consistent with validity, while the latter leads to invalidity. Assuming that there is a federal power to enact measures with respect to public property (including how funds are spent), we have to consider the same sorts of questions as were just canvassed regarding taxation. What is the pith and substance of the legislation? Is it in relation to the wide range of modalities, terms, and conditions in relation to spending and therefore assigned to section 91(1A), for example, or is it in relation to a provincial head of power? And we must sometimes consider whether it is appropriate to speak of a double aspect.

Flexible or Cooperative Federalism and Its Doctrines

We have already reminded ourselves of the key concepts regarding the constitutional validity of federal measures and emphasized that the mere presence of a provincial recipient of federal spending or even the presence of a competing provincial purpose within a federal law is by no means fatal to its validity. But it is also important to remember that the analysis we call characterization (and classification) takes place within the context of flexible or cooperative federalism rather than the rigid, zero-sum demarcation of jurisdictional borders that attracted the familiar label "watertight compartments," a label that reflects an approach that has "long since been overtaken" (*GND* 2020, [22]). As the Supreme Court of Canada stated recently, the more flexible principle of cooperative federalism and the doctrines associated with it "have been developed in part to account for the increasing complexity of modern society" and reflect "the political and cultural realities of Canadian society" (*GND* 2020, [22]). The main characteristic of the current view is that it "accommodates overlapping jurisdiction and encourages intergovernmental cooperation" (*Reference re Securities Act* 2011, [57]).

What are the doctrines associated with flexible and cooperative federalism? We could include the ancillary powers doctrine, the weakening of the test for conflict as affects the paramountcy doctrine, and the recent downgrading of the interjurisdictional immunity doctrine, but these are less relevant to the federal spending power. More pertinently, we have already seen that, though the pith and substance doctrine distinguishes between the primary and secondary purposes and effects of a measure, the federal and provincial aspects in a federal law may sometimes be equally important, such that we can say, citing the double aspect doctrine, that Parliament and the provinces could put in place a similar or even an identical measure (*Multiple Access* 1982). What these doctrines imply, more concretely, is that it is not unusual, constitutionally speaking, for a federal measure to have effects on subject matters, facts, activities, or items that are also potentially the subject of provincial measures (*Desgagnés* 2019, [84–7]; *Pan-Canadian Securities Reference* 2018, [114]; *GGPPA Reference* 2021, [125]). The cumulative result of these doctrines is that federal and provincial lawmakers have more jurisdictional space within which to manoeuvre, overlapping federal and provincial laws are normal and expected, and conflicts resulting in federal paramountcy are rare.

In the next section, I will attempt to summarize how the JCPC, Supreme Court of Canada, and the Courts of Appeal of Alberta and Quebec have dealt with the legal and constitutional basis for the federal spending power thus far.

4. The Courts and the Federal Spending Power: The Past

I begin, as so many discussions of the federal spending power do, with the *Unemployment Insurance Reference* from the 1930s. The subject matter of the reference, the Employment and Social Insurance Act, 1935, was mostly to do with matters such as the creation of a commission, the organization by the commission of employment offices, the detailed elaboration of a new unemployment insurance scheme, measures of collaboration regarding medical care, and further regulations and reports. Only the Schedules to the Act focused on matters that could more easily be linked to the modalities, terms, and conditions of spending: defining unemployment, setting out weekly rates of contributions and rules as to payment and recovery of contributions paid by employers, and enacting rates of unemployment benefit.

It is not surprising, then, that the pith and substance of this particular legislation was eventually characterized as the insurance and regulation of the day-to-day affairs of particular businesses, a matter of clear provincial jurisdiction under section 92(13). However, the *Unemployment Insurance Reference* left open the question as to when federal legislation would be deemed to be in relation to federal spending rather than (as here) in relation to provincial matters. Kerwin J. stated by way of *obiter dicta*, speaking for a majority of the Supreme Court of Canada declaring the legislation invalid:

> It is quite true that Parliament, by properly framed legislation may raise money by taxation and *dispose of its public property in any manner it sees fit*. As to the latter point, it is evident that the Dominion may grant sums of money to individuals or organizations and that the first may be accomplished *by such restrictions and conditions as Parliament may see fit to enact*. It would then be open to the proposed recipient to decline the gift or to accept it subject to such conditions. As to the first

point, it is also undoubted, I conceive, that Parliament, by properly framed legislation, may raise money by taxation, and this may be done either generally or for the specific purpose of providing funds wherewith to make grants either before or after the conferring of the benefit. But in my view, after a careful consideration of ... the Act, in substance Parliament does not purport to do either of those things ... [T]he very pith and substance ... deals with unemployment insurance. (*Unemployment Insurance Reference* SCC 1936, 457–8; emphasis added)

Speaking for the JCPC, Lord Atkin agreed in general terms with the propositions just stated regarding federal powers to tax and spend: "That the Dominion may impose taxation for the purpose of creating a fund for special purposes, and may apply that fund for making contributions in the public interest to individuals, corporations or public authorities, could not as general proposition be denied" (*Unemployment Insurance Reference* JCPC 1937, [5]). However, like the majority in the Supreme Court of Canada, the JCPC was of the view that this particular legislation, though incidentally dealing with federal spending, was *primarily* aimed at affecting the civil rights of employers and employees by way of an insurance scheme, and therefore properly within provincial jurisdiction.

If we move ahead half a century, we can find cases that illustrate the other side of the balance. For example, in *Winterhaven Stables v. A.G. Canada* 1989, the plaintiff, appellant, and taxpayer, Winterhaven Stables, challenged a range of federal "spending statutes," including the Canada Assistance Plan, the Canada Health Act, and the Federal-Provincial Fiscal Arrangements and Federal Post-Secondary Education and Health Contributions Act, claiming that they were invalid as being beyond the power of the Parliament of Canada. The appellant argued that, by means of such spending and the conditionality associated with it, Parliament was indirectly legislating in respect of matters within provincial jurisdiction. The Attorney General of Canada replied by arguing that, while the statutes in question might have *effects* on matters within exclusive provincial jurisdiction, they were not legislation *in relation to* them (that is, in terms of their pith and substance).

Irving J.A., for a unanimous Alberta Court of Appeal, began by citing Professor Elmer Driedger to the effect that "Canadian governments (of all levels) have never restricted spending to matters within their legislative competence" and "certainly not in areas in which there may be a double aspect" (*Winterhaven* 1989, 543, referring to Driedger 1981). Irving J.A. stated that the question was effectively one regarding the pith and substance of the legislation and whether the presence of conditions in relation to federal funding meant that the legislation was in fact a colourable attempt to encroach on provincial jurisdiction rather than a legitimate attempt to set national standards regarding federal spending. He cited both section 36 of the Constitution Act, 1982 and section 106A of the then-viable Meech Lake Accord as more recent recognition of the long-standing practice by Canada and the provinces of developing shared-cost programs within provincial jurisdiction, and he then asked the historically and politically informed question behind the constitutional issue: "With the background of a long-standing convention whereby Canada and the provinces have negotiated for the establishment of national shared-cost projects, can it be suggested that the 'spending statutes' here in issue are *ultra vires*?" (*Winterhaven* 1989, 543). In his view the answer was "no." He agreed with the finding of the trial judge regarding the pith and substance of the impugned legislation, quoting the latter directly: "In my view the legislation under review is not legislation in relation to provincial matters of health, post-secondary education and welfare but is legislation [to] provide financial assistance to provinces to enable them to carry out their responsibilities" (543). From this characterization, the classification flowed and with it confirmation of the validity of the federal laws, again quoting the trial judge: "Parliament has the authority to legislate in relation to its own debt and its own debt and property. It is entitled to spend the money that it raises through proper exercise of its taxing power in the manner that it chooses to authorize" (543). Regarding the conditionality of the financial assistance, Irving J.A. once again agreed with the trial judge, quoting him directly:

> [Parliament] can impose conditions on such disposition so long as the conditions do not amount in fact to a regulation or control of a matter outside federal authority. The federal contributions are now made in such a way that they do not control or regulate provincial use of them. As well there are opting out arrangements that are available to those provinces who choose not to participate in certain shared-cost programs. (*Winterhaven* 1989, 543)

Accordingly, the appeal failed, and leave to appeal to the Supreme Court of Canada was subsequently denied.

Over the next twenty to twenty-five years, the Supreme Court of Canada had more frequent occasion to consider the federal spending power. While many of the Court's references were by way of *obiter dicta*, the accumulated acknowledgment of the federal spending power is hard to ignore. It is not possible in this relatively short chapter to go through each of these cases. If we were to summarize the various judicial pronouncements, the following propositions would seem justified:

- There is a federal spending power (*YMHA* 1989, 46; *CAP* 1991, [85]; *Finlay* 1993, 78; *Eldridge* 1997, [25]; *Chaoulli* 2005, [16]).
- It can be anchored in sections 91(1A), 91(3), and 106 of the Constitution Act, 1867 (*YMHA* 1989, 46) or can be said to be "inherent" (*Eldridge* 1997, [25]).
- Parliament can impose conditions on spending provided that those conditions do not in fact amount to what is, in pith and substance, regulation or

control of a matter outside federal authority (*YMHA* 1989, 47; *Finlay* 1993, 29; *Eldridge* 1997, [25]).
- The decision to grant (or not grant) money should not be construed as an intention to regulate (*CAP* 1991, [84]).
- There is a distinction between (valid) federal conditions designed to promote provincial legislation that achieves substantial compliance with federal objectives and (invalid) federal conditions designed to dictate the precise terms of provincial legislation (*Finlay* 1993, 78).
- The mere fact that federal legislation impacts on interests beyond the jurisdiction of Parliament is insufficient on its own to justify a finding of invalidity (*CAP* 1991, [84]).
- Supervision of the spending power is not a separate head of constitutional review above and beyond division of powers and Charter review (*CAP* 1991, [85]).

In 2006, the Quebec Court of Appeal applied many of these propositions in an important decision concerning the federal spending power. In *Confédération des syndicats nationaux v. Canada (Procureur général)*, hereafter referred to as *CSN*, the appellant unions sought to have certain provisions of the federal Employment Insurance Act declared invalid. Specifically, they challenged the "active measures" in the legislation, that is, those designed to fight unemployment and not simply to compensate unemployed persons. Robert C.J.Q., with whom Gendreau and Brossard JJ.A. agreed, rejected the unions' contentions. He first determined that provisions dealing with employment service, work-sharing programs, and training measures were designed to reduce the risk of unemployment and were therefore clearly anchored under the federal unemployment insurance power. The provisions with respect to employment benefits were more problematic. Of these, income replacement benefits could still fall under the federal power; however, initiative promotion programs (such as self-employment assistance and skills loans or grants) were probably *prima facie* invalid as being beyond the unemployment insurance power. At this point, the Chief Justice noted that they could nonetheless be justified in virtue of the federal spending power (*CSN* 2006, 125). He cited the Supreme Court of Canada decision in *YMHA* (1989) by way of support for this conclusion, noting at the same time the limits on the spending power set out in that case. He drew from *YMHA* the conclusion that Parliament can intervene with regard to provincial jurisdiction by means of its spending power provided that its intervention does not amount to an attempt to regulate the domain, citing Brun and Tremblay (2001) by way of further support (*CSN* 2006, 131–3). The Chief Justice helpfully noted that, according to some commentators, there is a spectrum between simple expenditure and constraining regulation (*CSN* 2006, 135) while, less helpfully, refraining from detailing that spectrum. With regard to the federal principle emphasized in the *Secession Reference* (1998), he noted, first, that Ottawa and the provinces (not including Quebec) had negotiated a framework for the spending power as recently as 1999, the Social Union Framework Agreement (SUFA), though such agreements were not enforceable by courts, and, second, Sopinka J.'s statement in the *CAP Reference* to the effect that it was not the courts' role to review the spending power if a law does not otherwise violate the Charter or division of powers. On appeal before the Supreme Court of Canada, LeBel J., speaking for a unanimous court, was of the view that the full range of challenged provisions and payments were justifiable under the federal unemployment insurance power. Accordingly, there was no need to consider the federal spending power and its application to those provisions and payments (*CSN* SCC 2008, 39, 49).

In 2010, when the Supreme Court of Canada came to consider whether the federal government had paid its appropriate share of costs under the by-then defunct Canada Assistance Plan, neither the appellant, Attorney General of Quebec, nor LeBel J. in rendering the court's judgment, questioned either the validity of the *CAP* or the constitutionality of the cost-sharing measures set out in it (*Attorney General of Quebec* 2011).

That is not to say that the spending power has become a constitutional non-issue. We can anticipate that spending power issues will emerge in future litigation. Accordingly, it may be helpful to bring together some of the points already made by assessing what legal and constitutional issues are likely to come to the fore if the federal spending power comes to be considered by the Supreme Court of Canada at some moment in the future.

5. The Courts and the Federal Spending Power: The Future

Given the importance of spending in the politics and economics of Canadian federalism, it is surprising, on the one hand, how few times the constitutionality of the spending power has come before the courts and, on the other hand, how dismissive some accounts are regarding such appeal-level jurisprudence as already exists. To say that the Supreme Court of Canada has often discussed the spending power, but only by way of *obiter dicta*, underestimates and understates the extent to which Canadian courts have provided support and justification for the federal spending power, as discussed in the previous section.

Let us imagine that the constitutionality of the Canada Health Act came to be considered by the Supreme Court of Canada at some moment in the future. The constitutionality of the Canada Health Act is in many ways a useful case study. Health is one of the main public services alluded to in section 36 of the Constitution Act, 1982 and a key element of fiscal federalism. Parliament and the provincial legislatures share responsibility for health, but the provision of health services via hospitals (other than marine hospitals), doctors, nurses, orderlies, and so forth is a matter of provincial responsibility. And the federal act certainly has effects at the level of the organization of the health-care system and the delivery of health services.

For some observers, this last observation is enough for them to conclude that the act, and similar legislation, is unconstitutional. However, as we saw in Section 3, effects do not determine the pith and substance of legislation unless the weight of those effects causes us to question the purported purpose of the act. Nor is it the case that *any* federal legislation involving federal spending is valid. Legislation that is in pith and substance an attempt to regulate health services in the province would be unconstitutional, as seen, for example in *Reference re Assisted Human Reproduction Act* (2010).

Characterization

The pith and substance, or "true subject matter," is identified by looking to both the purpose (*GND* 2020, [28]) and the effects (*GND* 2020, [30–1]) of the legislation in question. It is often the case that a "challenged law has multiple features" (*GND* 2020, [31]), and in such circumstances the court must determine "which of these features is most important" (*GND* 2020, [31]). To determine a law's purpose, the court can examine both intrinsic (for example, the text of the law, the title, preamble, and structure; *GND* 2020, [34]) and extrinsic evidence (for example, parliamentary proceedings and government publications; *GND* 2020, [34]). Both legal (flowing from the provisions) and practical (resulting from the application of the provisions) effects are relevant (*GND* 2020, [51]).

So, by way of illustration, and beginning with the intrinsic evidence, the long title of the Canada Health Act emphasizes spending – modalities, terms, and conditions: "An Act relating to cash contributions by Canada and relating to criteria and conditions in respect of insured health services and extended health care services." The preamble emphasizes that it is not Parliament's intention to impair provincial powers in its attempt to ensure "future improvements in health ... with cooperative partnership of governments, health professionals, voluntary organizations and individuals," to promote "continued access to quality health care without financial or other barriers," and to encourage all this by "assisting the provinces in meeting the costs thereof." Section 3 of the act speaks of the facilitation of access to health services by removing "financial or other barriers." Section 4 sets out the "purpose of this Act": "to establish criteria in respect of health services and extended health care services provided under provincial law that must be met before a full cash contribution may be made." Section 5 indicates that "subject to this Act ... a full cash contribution is payable by Canada to each province for each fiscal year." A "cash contribution" is defined in section 2 of the act and means "the cash contribution in respect of the Canada Health Transfer that may be provided to a province under ... the *Federal-Provincial Fiscal Arrangements Act*)." The latter act (in section 24) sets out the methodology for calculating the entire Canada Health Transfer (see chapter 5 by Boadway in this volume) and provides that amounts payable under that part of the act "may be paid by the Minister out of the Consolidated Revenue Fund at times and in the manner that may be prescribed." Section 25 in turn sets out the circumstances in which cash contributions may be reduced or withheld and refers back to section 15 of the Canada Health Act. Section 15 provides that cash contributions may be reduced or withheld if the Governor in Council is of the view that a provincial health-care insurance plan does not satisfy the criteria set out elsewhere in the act (public administration, comprehensiveness, universality, portability, and accessibility). Finally, in order to qualify for a full cash contribution, section 18 indicates that "no payments may be permitted by the province ... in respect of insured health services that have been subject to extra-billing," while section 19 also specifies that "user charges must not be permitted." And where a province fails to comply with the conditions regarding extra-billing and user charges, section 20 provides that "there shall be deducted from the cash contribution to the provinces for a fiscal year an amount that the Minister ... determines to have been charged through extra billing ... [or] in respect of user charges." Any such deductions are then to be accounted for separately in respect of each province in the Public Accounts.

We see in these provisions both the well-known outward-facing aspects of the act that influence provincial behaviour but also the overwhelming number of references to inward-facing aspects, that is, the modalities, terms, and conditions that federal officials must heed before distributing, reducing, or withholding cash contributions to the provinces.

In terms of extrinsic evidence, we might look in particular to statements in the House of Commons by the federal minister of Health and National Welfare. For example, in response to pressure by the NDP to expand the soon-to-be introduced legislation so as to include preventive and alternative health care, Minister Bégin replied that it could not be done through the Canada Health Act "because of the division of powers." "[T]he Constitution only permits us the basic conditions attached to the spending power" (Parliament of Canada 1983, 27940).

Accordingly, it may fairly be said that the primary purpose of the Canada Health Act is to set out in a clear manner the modalities, terms, and conditions according to which federal funds aimed at ensuring equal access by all Canadians across the country to quality health services should be distributed or, in certain circumstances, withheld. This information is a guide to both the federal officials who distribute those funds and to the provinces who expect to continue to receive them. There is clearly a hope that, by setting out these terms, the principles and aims of the act will be heeded at the provincial level, but the act does not set out to *enact* those principles and aims by means of provisions intended to be enforceable in the provinces (*Finlay* 1993, 78). Furthermore, as the Supreme Court noted in the *CAP* case, courts are not called upon under our Constitution to interpret the effects of political pressures. It is easy to see why. For example, a shared-cost infrastructure program may be an unwelcome recalibration of provincial budget priorities for some provincial governments at one moment or a welcome federal contribution to existing provincial infrastructure programs at another moment under other political leadership (Receiver General for Canada 2012, section 1.4).

Classification

I began this section by noting that the provision of health-care services is primarily a provincial matter (without forgetting that the federal authorities have responsibility to provide health-care services to the military, to prisoners, and to Indigenous peoples). We have just seen that, while the Canada Health Act evinces a clear concern for the availability and affordability of health services for all Canadians across the country, it is not designed to dictate the precise terms of provincial legislation (*Finlay* 1993, 78). A contrary conclusion would require the court to speculate as to the effect of spending decisions, something that it has expressed a reluctance to do (*CAP* 1991, [84–5]). Furthermore, the bulk of the act appears to be about the modalities, terms, and conditions of federal spending. As we saw earlier regarding the federal taxation power, it may be the case, as here, that there is a non-negligible federal desire to see a particular result regarding health services; however, provided that the federal act is not *primarily* about the regulation of health services, the legislation is valid. The mere fact that federal legislation impacts on interests beyond the jurisdiction of Parliament is insufficient on its own to justify a finding of invalidity (*CAP* 1991, [84]). And the decision to grant (or not grant) money should not be construed as an intention to regulate (*CAP* 1991, [84]). Accordingly, the act can be classified under sections 91(1A), 91(3), and 106 of the Constitution Act, 1867 (*YMHA* 1989, 46) or, if need be, as an inherent power under POGG (*Eldridge* 1997, [25]; Hogg 2007, 6.8).

It is important to make a distinction between legislating regarding health services and legislating regarding *spending* in relation to health services, just as one has to make a distinction between legislating regarding sales contracts and *taxing* capital gains under section 91(3). One needs to ask whether the Canada Health Act is more like the Employment and Social Service Act in the *Unemployment Insurance Reference* or whether it is more like the spending statutes that have repeatedly been the subject of approving references in the Courts of Appeal and Supreme Court of Canada. It has already been noted that the 1930s statute was primarily designed to set up a new insurance structure, leaving spending matters to a Schedule. As we have seen in considering characterization, the Canada Health Act focuses primarily on the modalities, terms, and conditions that would assist federal public servants in knowing how, when, where, and in what amounts to make important transfers to the provinces.

Cooperative Federalism and the Double Aspect Doctrine

The Canada Health Act does not regulate a matter within provincial jurisdiction. Nor does it attempt to create a new health-care system in each of the provinces. In the terms of the *Finlay* decision, noted in the previous Section, the act sets out (valid) federal conditions designed to promote provincial legislation that achieves substantial compliance with federal objectives rather than (invalid) federal conditions designed to dictate the precise terms of provincial legislation (*Finlay* 1993, 78). As Minister Bégin said in the early 1980s, the act does not attempt to implement direct changes because Parliament does not have power to do so (Parliament of Canada 1983). It takes the provincial health-care systems as they are and sets out the terms and conditions on which the federal government is willing to continue allocating substantial funds to the provinces to ensure that good quality health care is available to all Canadians wherever they live. In doing so, it supports the aims set out in section 36 of the Constitution Act, 1982. Robert C.J.Q.'s image of a spending-related spectrum between simple expenditure and constraining regulation acknowledges that federal legislation can go too far, but Canadian courts have confirmed on multiple occasions that the Canada Health Act is within bounds.

It is sufficient to validate the Canada Health Act as legislation in respect of federal property (Flood, Lahey, and Thomas 2017, 452–7). But it should not be forgotten that Parliament has other important powers that allow it to legislate by way of direct regulation in the health sphere (sections 91[7], [11], [24], [27] and POGG). As noted previously, the Supreme Court of Canada has on multiple occasions reminded us that cooperative and flexible federalism often leads to overlapping jurisdiction, even as it reminds us that the double aspect doctrine is relevant where health is concerned. Federal legislation must be validly anchored, but we should expect to see it coexist in the health sector alongside provincial law.

A further word should be said about the federal principle, one of the unwritten constitutional principles highlighted in cases such as the *Secession Reference* (1998). The Supreme Court of Canada has recently ruled out using such unwritten principles to strike down legislation (*City of Toronto* 2021). More importantly, the analysis set out above applies to the federal spending power the same doctrines of legal federalism that apply in other contexts, which is to say that the federal principle is respected.

Conclusion

This chapter set out to examine the legal and constitutional basis for the federal spending power. The answer turned out to involve an understanding of both the primarily British historical origins of spending in our parliamentary system and the contemporary context of Canadian constitutional law. From the historical context we learned that spending, like taxation, is a complicated subject matter in its own right, whose origins lie initially in legally vast powers that at one time resided in the Crown. Over time, Parliament acquired an essential role regarding spending in the requirement that all spending is the subject of a parliamentary appropriation, but Parliament did not otherwise impose legislative substitutes for all the various aspects of spending. Those have emerged more gradually, both in the United Kingdom and in Canada. In Canada, Parliament's power to legislate regarding spending is grounded in the division of powers. We have seen that sections 91(1A), 91(3), and 106 of the Constitution Act, 1867, supplemented if need be by the POGG power, provide that grounding.

Having identified relevant heads of power, it is still important to keep in mind that the federal spending power is a general power to legislate regarding the spending of federal property (here, moneys held in the Consolidated Fund) rather than a power to legislate only regarding spending on items over which Parliament has the power to legislate. I have tried to illustrate what is wrong with the latter formulation by using the analogy of taxation. The federal taxing power is not the power to legislate regarding taxation only if that taxation is in relation to people and things over which Parliament has the power to legislate. If that were the case, Parliament could not tax the capital gains of contracts of sale or tax property held by individuals or corporations.

Parliament's present ability to legislate regarding spending is related to the Crown's former and present ability to spend. In the United Kingdom, the Crown could effectively spend with regard to matters (including foreign objects) over which it could not effectively legislate. In Canada, as illustrated by the debates in 1869 regarding Nova Scotia, both the federal and provincial Crowns could spend with regard to matters over which they could not legislate. (Canada could, for example, send funds to assist victims of the Crimean War, and Quebec could send funds to assist victims of flooding in the Red River settlement; Parliament of Canada 1869, 737.) Parliament can then legislate to replace those former executive powers with statutory rules, and when it does so, it can replace the full length and breadth of those Crown powers. Accordingly, as we have just seen, Parliament can legislate regarding spending on health services, even if it cannot legislate, in order to directly regulate health services in the provinces.

A further point in relation to the legal and constitutional basis for the spending power is that, for at least the past half-century, Canadian constitutional law has moved clearly beyond the era of watertight compartments. The current era of flexible and cooperative federalism is characterized by overlapping federal and provincial jurisdiction and more frequent invocation of the double aspect doctrine. What this means more concretely is that, even if one insists, contrary to Supreme Court case law, that federal legislation regarding spending on certain items should be analysed in just the same way as legislation otherwise regulating those items, one has to take into account contemporary constitutional realities, including the fact that the existence of provincial jurisdiction regarding health does not preclude Parliament from legislating regarding health using its own powers.

I have not spoken in this chapter about the many political attempts over the years to structure the federal spending power. Nor have I discussed the full range of literature contesting and supporting the federal spending power. This omission is due to both the legal and constitutional emphasis of this chapter and what I deem to be the clear signals that have emerged from our highest courts.

If one were to plot the legal and political acceptability of the federal spending power on separate axes, one would see, on the one hand, that one has to travel to the far end of the legal axis before one encounters, for example, a level of conditionality that would vitiate federal spending legislation regarding items within provincial jurisdiction. On the other hand, on the related political axis, federal spending power runs into powerful political objections from some provinces when even low levels of conditionality are introduced. What this point means is that, even if the federal spending power is legally and constitutionally secure, we should probably expect discussions regarding how best to structure this important power to carry on for some time at the political level, perhaps eventually even resulting in legal or constitutional reform.

Acknowledgments

Thanks are due to former University of Ottawa students Jordan Birenbaum, Marie-France Chartier, Don Ferguson, Gabrielle White, and Jonathan Pinkus for excellent research assistance and to professors Colleen Flood, Hoi Kong, André Lecours, and Vanessa MacDonnell for helpful comments on an earlier draft. I alone am responsible for any remaining errors or omissions, of course. Part of this research was supported by a grant from the Social Science and Humanities Research Council.

REFERENCES

Articles, Books, Chapters in Books, Government Publications, and Debates

Adam, Marc-Antoine. 2008. "The Spending Power, Co-operative Federalism and Section 94." *Queen's Law Journal* 34, no. 1: 175–224.
Banting, Keith. 2008. "The Three Federalisms and Intergovernmental Decision-Making." In *Canadian Federalism: Performance, Effectiveness, and Legitimacy*, edited by Herman Bakvis and Grace Skogstad, 137–60. Don Mills, ON: Oxford University Press.
Bérard, Frédéric. 2016. "Addressing the Elephant in the Room: Spending Power in Canada." *National Journal of Constitutional Law* 36, no. 2: 287–330.

Boadway, Robin. 1998. "Delivering the Social Union: Some Thoughts on the Federal Role." *Policy Options* 19: 37–9.

Boudreault, Julien. 2020. "Flexible and Cooperative Federalism: Distinguishing the Two Approaches in the Interpretation and Application of the Division of Powers." *National Journal of Constitutional Law* 40, no. 1: 1–35.

Brun, Henri, and Guy Tremblay. 2001. *Droit constitutionnel*. 4th ed. Cowansville, QC: Yvon Blais.

Chevrette, François. 1988. "Contrôler le pouvoir fédéral de dépenser: Un gain ou un piège?" In *L'adhésion du Québec à l'accord du lac Meech: Points de vue juridiques et politiques*, edited by Réal A. Forest and Jean Bazin, 153–61. Montreal: Éditions Thémis.

Chitty, Joseph. 1820. *A Treatise on the Law of the Prerogatives of the Crown; and the Relative Duties and Rights of the Subject*. London: J. Butterworth.

Choudhry, Sujit. 2008. "Constitutional Change in the 21st Century: A New Debate over the Spending Power." *Queen's Law Journal* 34: 375–90.

Courchene, Thomas J. 2008. "Reflections on the Federal Spending Power: Practices, Principles, Perspectives." *Queen's Law Journal* 34, no. 1: 75–123.

Daintith, Terrence, and Alan Page. 1999. *The Executive in the Constitution: Structure, Autonomy, and Internal Control*. Oxford: Oxford University Press.

Dicey, Albert V. 2013. *The Law of the Constitution*. Edited by J.W.F. Allison. Oxford: Oxford University Press.

Driedger, Elmer A. 1981. "The Spending Power." *Queen's Law Journal* 7: 124–34.

Flood, Colleen, William Lahey, and Bryan Thomas. 2017. "Federalism and Health Care in Canada: A Troubled Romance?" In *The Oxford Handbook of the Canadian Constitution*, edited by Peter C. Oliver, Patrick Macklem, and Nathalie Des Rosiers, 449–74. Oxford: Oxford University Press.

Forcese, Craig. 2017. "The Executive, the Royal Prerogative and the Constitution." In *The Oxford Handbook of the Canadian Constitution*, edited by Peter C. Oliver, Patrick Macklem, and Nathalie Des Rosiers, 151–70. Oxford: Oxford University Press.

Halsbury's Laws of England. 2018. "Statutes and Legislative Process," 2. Acts of the United Kingdom Parliament, (6) Operation of Acts, (ii) Functions of the Executive, C. Statutory Powers, 348. Ram doctrine.

Harris, Bruce V. 2007. "The 'Third Source' of Authority for Government Action Revisited." *Law Quarterly Review* 123: 225–50.

Hogg, Peter W. 2007. *Constitutional Law of Canada*. Scarborough, ON: Thomson Carswell.

House of Commons. 1906–7. *Official Report of the Debates of the House of Commons of the Dominion of Canada, Third Session, Tenth Parliament, 1906–7*. Vol. LXXX. Ottawa: S.E. Dawson, King's Printer. https://parl.canadiana.ca/view/oop.debates_HOC1003_03.

Jackman, Martha. 2000. "Constitutional Jurisdiction over Health in Canada." *Health Law Journal* 8: 95–117.

Kellock, Burton H., and Sylvia LeRoy. 2006. *Questioning the Legality of Equalization.* Vancouver, BC: Fraser Institute. https://www.fraserinstitute.org/sites/default/files/QuestioningLegalityEqualization.pdf.

Kent, Tom. 2008. "The Harper Peril for Canadian Federalism." *Policy Options* 29, no. 2: 11–16.

Kong, Hoi L. 2008. "The Spending Power, Constitutional Interpretation and Legal Pragmatism." *Queen's Law Journal* 34, no. 1: 305–74.

– 2017. "The Spending Power in Canada." In *The Oxford Handbook of the Canadian Constitution*, edited by Peter C. Oliver, Patrick Macklem, and Nathalie Des Rosiers, 433–46. Oxford: Oxford University Press.

Lajoie, Andrée. 1988. "L'impact des Accords du Lac Meech sur le pouvoir de dépenser." In *L'adhésion du Québec à l'Accord du Lac Meech*, edited by Réal A. Forest and Jean Bazin. Montreal: Éditions Thémis.

Lajoie, Andrée, and Patrick A. Molinari. 1978. "Partage constitutionnel des compétences en matière de santé au Canada." *Canadian Bar Review* 56: 579–602. https://www.canlii.org/fr/doctrine/doc/1978CanLIIDocs31.

Macdonald, Roderick A. 2008. "The Political Economy of the Federal Spending Power." *Queen's Law Journal* 34: 249–303.

Magnet, Joseph Eliot. 1978. "The Constitutional Distribution of Taxation Powers in Canada." *Ottawa Law Review* 10: 473–534. https://rdo-olr.org/wp-content/uploads/2018/01/olr_10.1_magnet.pdf.

Nader, Aymen. 1996. "Providing Essential Services: Canada's Constitutional Commitment under Section 36." *Dalhousie Law Journal* 19, no. 2: 306–72. https://core.ac.uk/download/pdf/288305084.pdf.

Noël, Alain. 2008a. "Éliminer le pouvoir de dépenser." *Options Politiques*, 1 March 2008. https://policyoptions.irpp.org/magazines/obama-and-clinton/eliminer-le-pouvoir-de-depenser/.

– 2008b. "How Do You Limit a Power That Does Not Exist." *Queen's Law Journal* 34, no. 1: 391–412.

Parliament of Canada. 1869. *House of Commons Debates, Second Session, First Parliament.* Vol. 2, 15 April–22 June 1869. Ottawa: Parliament of Canada. https://parl.canadiana.ca/browse/eng/c/debates/01-2

– 1870. *House of Commons Debates, Third Session, First Parliament.* Vol. 1, 15 February–12 May 1870. Ottawa: Parliament of Canada. https://parl.canadiana.ca/browse/eng/c/debates/01-3.

– 1983. *House of Commons Debates, First Session, Thirty-Second Parliament.* Vol. 24, 12 September–19 October 1983. Ottawa: Parliament of Canada. https://parl.canadiana.ca/view/oop.debates_HOC3201_24/974.

Petter, Andrew. 1989. "Federalism and the Myth of the Spending Power." *Canadian Bar Review* 68, no. 3: 448–79. https://cbr.cba.org/index.php/cbr/article/view/3450.

Québec, Commission sur le déséquilibre fiscal. 2002. "Le 'pouvoir fédéral de dépenser' et ses implications." In *Pour un nouveau partage des moyens financiers au Canada*

(*Rapport final*), 121–31. Quebec: Commission sur le déséquilibre fiscal. https://www.groupes.finances.gouv.qc.ca/desequilibrefiscal/fr/document/rapport_final.htm.

Québec, Secrétariat aux affaires intergouvernementales canadiennes. 2004. "Remise en question des fondements du pouvoir fédéral de dépenser." Allocution prononcée par le ministre délégué aux Affaires intergouvernementales canadiennes et aux Affaires autochtones du Québec dans le cadre du colloque *Redistribution au sein de la fédération canadienne*, Toronto, 6 February 2004. https://www.sqrc.gouv.qc.ca/secretariat/salle-de-nouvelles/discours/details.asp?id=21.

Receiver General for Canada. 2012. *Public Accounts of Canada*. Vol 1, *Summary Report and Consolidated Financial Statements*. Ottawa: Government of Canada. https://epe.lac-bac.gc.ca/100/201/301/public_accounts_can/pdf/2012/49-eng.pdf

Ryan, Edward F., and Barry V. Slutsky. 1964–6. "Canada Student Loan Act – Ultra Vires?," *University of British Columbia Law Review* 2, no. 2: 299–306.

Schwartz, Bryan. 1987. "Fathoming Meech Lake." *Manitoba Law Journal* 17, no. 1 (Special Issue): 1–106. https://themanitobalawjournal.com/wp-content/uploads/articles/MLJ_17.1%20(Special%20Issue)/Fathoming%20Meech%20Lake.pdf.

Scott, Frank R. 1955. "The Constitutional Background of Taxation Agreements." *McGill Law Journal* 2: 1–10. https://lawjournal.mcgill.ca/article/the-constitutional-background-of-taxation-agreements/.

Scott, Stephen A. 1990. "Queens as Nursing-Mothers: Public Expenditure under the Canadian Constitution." Paper presented at the conference on "The Power of the Purse: Financial Incentives as Regulatory Instruments," Calgary, AB, 12–13 October 1990.

Sedley, Stephen. 2015. "*Lions under the Throne: Essays on the History of English Public Law*." Cambridge: Cambridge University Press.

Smiley, Donald V. 1962. "The Rowell-Sirois Report, Provincial Autonomy, and Post-War Canadian Federalism." *Canadian Journal of Economics and Political Science* 28, no. 1: 54–69. https://doi.org/10.2307/139263.

Smiley, Donald V, and Ronald M Burns. 1969. "Canadian Federalism and the Spending Power: Is Constitutional Restriction Necessary?" *Canadian Tax Journal* 17: 468–82.

Telford, Hamish. 2003. "The Federal Spending Power in Canada: Nation-Building or Nation-Destroying." *Publius: The Journal of Federalism* 33, no. 1: 23–44. https://doi.org/10.1093/oxfordjournals.pubjof.a004976.

Trudeau, Pierre Elliott. 1969. *Federal-Provincial Grants and the Spending Power of Parliament*. Ottawa: Queen's Printer.

Turcotte, Marc-André. 2015. *Le pouvoir fédéral de dépenser: Ou comment faire indirectement ce qu'on ne peut faire directement*. Montreal: Yvon Blais.

United Kingdom Colonial Office. 1886. *Opinions: 1866 to 1873*. No. 590, 10 August 1869. London: Colonial Office.

Wright, Wade K. 2018. "Federalism(s) in the Supreme Court of Canada in the McLachlin Era." *Supreme Court Law Review* 96: 213–48.

Cases

AUSTRALIA
Williams v. Commonwealth of Australia [2012] HCA 23.

CANADA
Attorney General of Quebec v. Canada, 2011 SCC 11.
(*CAP Reference*) *Reference re Canada Assistance Plan (B.C.)*, [1991] 2 SCR 525.
Chaoulli v. Quebec (Attorney General), [2005] 1 SCR 791.
City of Toronto v. Ontario (Attorney General), 2021 SCC 34.
Confédération des syndicats nationaux c. Canada (Procureur général), 2006 QCCA 1454; 2008 SCC 68.
Desgagnés Transport Inc. v. Wartsila Canada Inc., 2019 SCC 58.
Eldridge v. British Columbia, [1997] 3 SCR 624.
Finlay v. Canada (Minister of Finance), [1993] 1 SCR 1080.
(*Genetic Non-Discrimination Reference*) *Reference re Genetic Non-Discrimination Act*, 2020 SCC 17.
(*GGPPA Reference*) *Reference re Greenhouse Gas Pollution Pricing Act*, 2021 SCC 11.
(*Maritime Bank*) *Liquidators of Maritime Bank v. Receiver General of New Brunswick*, [1892] AC 437 (JCPC).
Multiple Access v. McCutcheon, [1982] 2 SCR 161.
Pan-Canadian Securities Regulation Reference, 2018 SCC 48.
Reference re Assisted Human Reproduction Act, [2010] 3 SCR 457.
Reference re Exported Natural Gas Tax, [1982] 1 SCR 1004.
Reference re Securities Act, 2011 SCC 66.
(*Secession Reference*) *Reference re Secession of Quebec*, [1998] 2 SCR 217.
(*Unemployment Insurance Reference* JCPC) *Reference re Employment and Social Insurance Act* (sub nom, *A.G. Canada v. A.G. Ontario*) [1937] AC 326 (JCPC).
(*Unemployment Insurance Reference* SCC) *Reference re Employment and Social Insurance Act* (sub nom, *A.G. Canada v. A.G. Ontario*) [1936] SCR 427.
Verreault & Fils v. Attorney General of the Province of Quebec [1977] 1 RCS 41.
Winterhaven Stables v. A.G. Canada, [1989] 1 WWR 193.
YMHA Jewish Community Centre of Winnipeg Inc. v. Brown, [1989] 1 SCR 1532.

UNITED KINGDOM
Case of Proclamations, (1610) EWHC KB J22.

Statutes

CANADA
Canada Assistance Plan, RSC 1985, c. C-1 (formerly RSC 1970, c. C-1).
Canada Health Act, SC 1984, c. 6.

Canada Strategic Infrastructure Fund Act, SC 2002, c. 9, s. 47.
Canada Student Financial Assistance Act, SC 1994, c. 28.
Federal-Provincial Fiscal Arrangements Act, RSC, 1985, c. F-8.
Federal-Provincial Fiscal Arrangements and Federal Post-Secondary Education and Health Contributions Act, 1977, RSC 1976–77, c. 10.

Constitutional Texts (including Amendments)

Constitution Act, 1867, 30 & 31 Vict., c. 3. (UK).
Constitution Act, 1907, Edw. VII, c. 11 (UK).
Constitution Act, 1982, Schedule B to the Canada Act 1982 (UK), 1982, c. 11.

4 The Challenges and Opportunities Facing Canada's Fiscal Arrangements after COVID-19

TREVOR TOMBE

Introduction

Periods of intense economic and fiscal disruption repeatedly create both challenges and opportunities for fiscal arrangements in Canada. Designing arrangements that effectively weather unexpected developments is an ongoing challenge for any federation, especially one as diverse as Canada (see chapter 2 by Mary Janigan in this volume). But through regular reforms spanning generations, Canada's fiscal arrangements have evolved to a relatively robust state and have withstood the shock from COVID-19 relatively well. This chapter will survey the state of federal-provincial finances following COVID-19 and evaluate how current fiscal arrangements responded. Using the latest available fiscal information and forecasts, I explore where existing programs succeeded and where the pandemic revealed or exacerbated existing gaps. I find that, overall, federal transfer arrangements were unable to respond to the fiscal pressures or COVID-19 in the short term. The federal government instead opted for ad hoc transfer arrangements that pushed 2020 transfers to over $111 billion and over 5 per cent of Canada's economy – larger than at any other point in Canadian history. In addition to these ad hoc arrangements driven by the expediency of the moment, the federal government responded to revenue pressures of provincial governments by materially expanding support through its pre-existing (though previous insubstantial) Fiscal Stabilization Program.

Much of the increase in federal transfers during the pandemic was temporary, but there remain many implications of COVID-19 for fiscal arrangements in Canada that have yet to be determined. This chapter will explore notable pressures in three programs: equalization, fiscal stabilization, and health transfers. Looking to the medium and long run, the pandemic may also present an opportunity to enact reforms today to address long simmering fiscal challenges facing all governments in Canada. In particular, the long-run sustainability of provincial finances has increasingly been a source of concern. By increasing the fiscal burdens on provinces, especially those with higher pre-COVID-19 debt levels and older populations, the pandemic may have increased the importance of redesigning fiscal arrangements to ensure long-run sustainability. Modest reforms to federal transfers may follow. I therefore evaluate several reforms to improve the design and delivery of major federal-provincial transfer programs. Though fiscal arrangements weathered the pandemic well, the potential reforms I explore may help ensure a more predictable and formula-driven system of arrangements that are able to respond to future shocks. The chapter will then conclude on two additional, but important, issues. First, given the rising level of public indebtedness, which is manageable for most governments but may not be for all, this chapter will also detail several important considerations for improving provincial debt management in Canada. Second, the fast-moving developments during the crisis may also highlight the importance of ongoing analysis and reporting, which may be better facilitated by an arm's-length entity than by any specific government.

I begin the analysis with a broad overview of the nature of changes to fiscal arrangements following COVID-19 before turning to specific issues related to individual transfer programs and potential reforms going forward.

Fiscal Supports by Canadian Governments

The fiscal implications of COVID-19 have been substantial in Canada and around the world. The federal deficit for 2020–1, for example, reached 14.9 per cent of the gross domestic product (GDP), which vastly exceeds any other fiscal year in Canadian history outside of those during the Second World War (Government of Canada 2022). Provincial governments have also experienced significant fiscal pressures, with aggregate deficits reaching 2.1 per cent (Government of Canada 2022). Both revenues and expenditures have led to this situation, and both sides of the budget are worth considering closely.

On the expenditure side, the direct costs of the pandemic response and associated health-care costs have been large. But direct payments and liquidity support to individuals and businesses have been even more so. The latest estimates from the federal government's *Budget 2022* and the *Economic and Fiscal Update 2021* summarize the main components of each order of government's fiscal response (Government of Canada 2022, 2021). I report a summary of those values in Table 4.1. Overall, the federal government's responses account for nearly 82 per cent of total direct expenditures, nearly three-quarters of the value of tax deferrals, and nearly all liquidity support programs. The bulk of expenditure pressures from the pandemic have therefore been nationalized.

On the revenue side, the fiscal implications of the pandemic have also been disproportionately borne by the federal government. In fiscal year 2020–1, for

Table 4.1. Fiscal Responses to COVID-19 ($ billion)

Fiscal Response	Federal	Provincial and Territorial	Total
Direct Measures	346.0	86.0	432.0
Tax Deferrals	85.1	31.5	116.6
Credit Support	80.6	2.6	83.2
Total	511.7	120.1	631.8

Source: Government of Canada (2021), Table 3.2.

example, federal revenues fell modestly compared to 2019–20, but provincial revenues actually increased (Finances of the Nation 2022b). This increase is not because the tax bases of provincial governments were more insulated from COVID-19 than those of the federal government. Provincial governments did, for example, experience a decline of over 9 per cent (nearly $10 billion) in revenues from taxes on goods and services (Tombe 2021). But offsetting much of this decline has been a significant increase in federal grants to provincial and territorial governments. These grants have not been explicitly aimed to compensate for revenue declines – more on the scope for a program designed for this purpose later – but instead have been largely shared-cost arrangements to help provinces with sharply rising expenditure pressures. In addition to direct grants to provincial governments, the federal government's support of individuals and businesses helped provincial budgets indirectly. Those transfers were taxable by provincial personal and corporate income tax systems, which explains the 3 per cent and 8.1 per cent increase in both revenue categories that year, respectively (Tombe 2021).

Increased federal transfers have involved several distinct programs and have added to significant sums. To date, the federal government has transferred over $28 billion to provinces in direct support of their COVID-19 responses through major transfers (Government of Canada 2021, chart 3.5). This amount is significant as it exceeds every other major federal transfer program except the Canada Health Transfer (CHT). Equalization, by comparison, is $20.5 billion for this same fiscal year. These federal support payments to other governments have been composed of several separate programs, each aiming at providing support in different ways. Early in the pandemic, a $500 million payment in support of critical health-care delivery needs was the first of many such programs. Later payments included $19.9 billion for the Safe Restart Agreement, $2 billion for the Safe Return to Class Fund, $3 billion for the Essential Workers Support Fund, $1.7 billion in targeted support for the oil and gas industry, and more. The Safe Restart Agreement itself is composed of a variety of individual components, as shown in Table 4.2.

Table 4.2. Safe Restart Agreement Funding Categories

Broad Category	Description	Amount ($ million)
Personal Protective Equipment (PPE) Costs	Funding to purchase PPE for essential workers, including in health and non-health sectors	7,500
Testing and Contact Tracing	Funding to increase testing and contact tracing capacity through hiring additional staff and purchasing supplies and equipment	4,300
Public Transit	Cost-sharing arrangement to support local public transit operations	2,400
Municipalities	Support to municipal governments	2,000
Health-Care Capacity	Offset higher health-care costs due to COVID-19	1,200
Sick Leave	Support individuals who cannot work through the Canada Recovery Sickness Benefit	1,100
Vulnerable Populations	Increase funding supports to home care, long-term care, social supports, and other programs	740
Childcare	Supporting childcare services offset additional salary and equipment costs	625
Total		19,865

Source: Government of Canada (2020, 6).

These federal supports for provincial, territorial, and municipal governments have pushed federal transfers to their highest levels in Canadian history. While the full fiscal implications of the pandemic are not yet fully known – especially considering the continuing disruptions from new variants appearing through 2022 – combining information released by governments through various public announcements, quarterly data from Statistics Canada, and my own projections can provide a reasonable estimate of the effect of COVID-19 on federal transfers. As a share of overall GDP, federal transfers reached 5.1 per cent of GDP – materially higher than any prior year and a larger increase within a single year than any since the 1941 Wartime Tax Rental Agreements. I display the full series in Figure 4.1, which updates estimates from Tombe (2018) and made available through Finances of the Nation (n.d.).

The ad hoc nature of these transfers, however, makes the sharp increase during COVID-19 distinct from many earlier arrangements. Full federal discretion over amounts and criteria were established in real time, and no government could count on specific amounts of support prior to specific federal decisions being taken. Future changes that expand or formalize emergency federal financial support would mitigate uncertainty facing provincial governments and

Figure 4.1. Federal Transfers to Provincial Governments (Percentage of GDP)

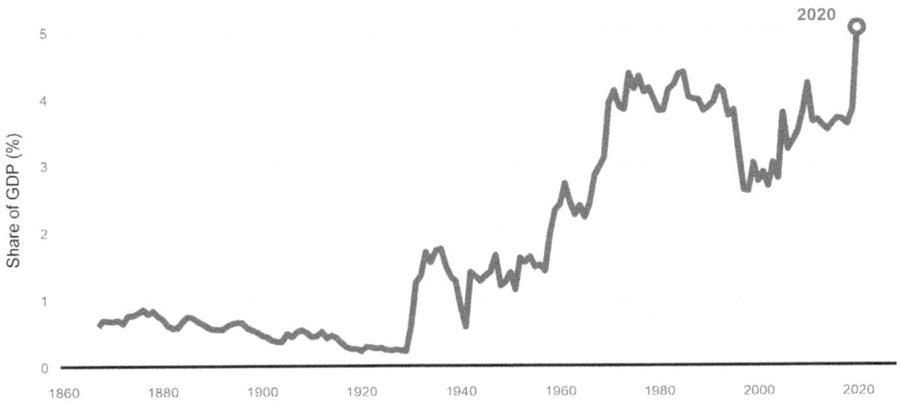

Source: Own calculations from Finances of the Nation (n.d.).

potentially alleviate pressure on the federal government during periods of crisis where its attention may be better allocated elsewhere. Before turning to specific program reforms that may help achieve this support, it is important to appreciate that COVID-19 and the economic and fiscal disruptions were not uniform across provinces. This disparity will have important implications for existing formula-driven fiscal arrangements that may also motivate future reforms.

Convergence in Fiscal Capacity

Fiscal capacity convergence during the pandemic was significant, and Canada may have reached the lowest level of horizontal inequality across provinces since at least the 1960s. Indeed, using data from Finances of the Nation (2022a), I find inequality in per capita GDP across provinces (as measured by a Schutz Index) is smaller than at any point since 1926. The reason is simple: higher income regions experienced a substantially larger economic shock from COVID-19 than lower income regions. Figure 4.2 clearly illustrates how provincial economic contractions were disproportionately larger in provinces with higher initial levels of economic activity.

This convergence will have direct implications for fiscal arrangements in general and for equalization payments. To see this change, a useful measure of inequality relevant for fiscal arrangements in Canada is the Schutz Index. It measures the share of something that must be reallocated to achieve perfect equality. In terms of provincial fiscal capacity inequality, it captures the share of overall provincial and local revenues that must be shifted across

Figure 4.2. Economic Convergence across Provinces in 2020

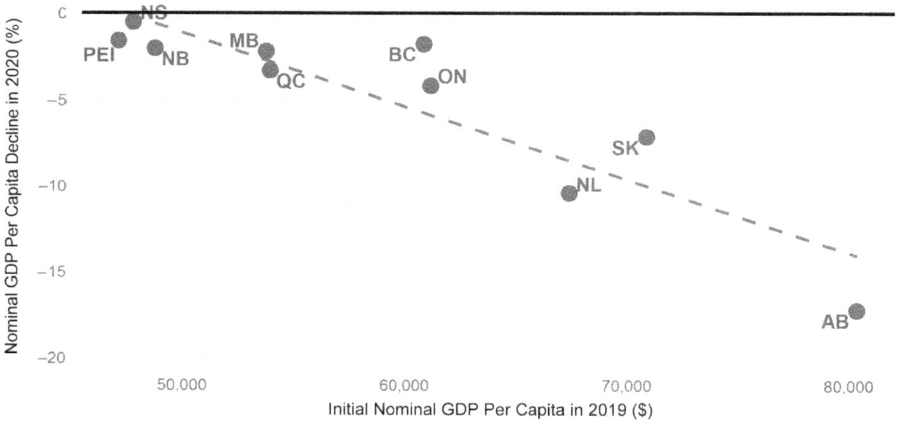

[Scatter plot with x-axis "Initial Nominal GDP Per Capita in 2019 ($)" ranging from 50,000 to 80,000, and y-axis "Nominal GDP Per Capita Decline in 2020 (%)" ranging from -20 to 0. Data points: NS near 0; PEI, NB, MB, QC around -3 to -4; BC, ON around -3 to -4; SK around -8; NL around -11; AB around -16. Dashed trend line slopes downward from upper-left to lower-right.]

Sources: Own calculations from Statistics Canada data tables 36-10-0221-01 and 17-10-0005-01.
Note: AB = Alberta; BC = British Columbia; MB = Manitoba; NB = New Brunswick; NS = Nova Scotia; ON = Ontario; PEI = Prince Edward Island; QC = Quebec; SK = Saskatchewan.

provinces to achieve identical per capita levels of revenue-raising capacity. I constructed this estimate since suitable data began in 1967, along with an estimate for 2020 based on the latest projections for nominal GDP growth for that year. Prior to COVID-19, the Schutz Index of inequality ranged from a low of just under 0.06 following the oil price declines that began in 2014 to a high of 0.15 in 1980. In 2018–19, for example, a Schutz Index value of 0.058 means that 5.8 per cent of the total provincial revenues of over $370 billion would need to be reallocated to equalize per capita fiscal capacity. At $21.5 billion, this amount illustrates well the rough magnitude of the equalization program that prevailed in recent years, which is a point I will return to shortly. But in 2020, I find a Schutz Index value of less than 0.052, which is nearly 8 per cent lower than the lowest degree of inequality measured since 1967.

To appreciate the implications of this dramatic convergence, one must look to the core of the equalization formula. This program seeks to support provinces with below average revenue-raising capacities as measured by their per capita revenue yields at national average tax rates. Based on this calculation, the federal government distributes payments based on a province's per capita fiscal capacity relative to the national average. While the mathematical details do not concern us here, it turns out that, under such an arrangement, the total dollars paid will equal the product of total fiscal capacity across all ten provinces and the Schutz Index of fiscal capacity inequality. Decreasing levels of inequality will therefore be reflected in fewer equalization payments. Specifically, changes in total payments are given by the following:

$$\%\Delta(\text{Total equalization payments})$$
$$\approx \%\Delta(\text{Schutz Index of Inequality})$$
$$+ \%\Delta(\text{Total provincial and local revenue to be equalized})$$

All else being equal, a substantial decrease in horizontal fiscal capacity inequality will correspond to a substantial decrease in the magnitude of total equalization payments in Canada. Another, though equivalent, way to see this figure is through the effect of COVID-19 on the national average per capita fiscal capacity. In 2019–20, it was just over $10,000 per person. But for 2020–1, I estimate it was $9,700. Since lower income provinces experienced a smaller economic shock from the pandemic relative to higher income regions, the difference between their measured fiscal capacity and the average will correspondingly shrink. Prince Edward Island, for example, was roughly $3,400 per person below the national average in 2019–20 but only $3,000 per person below average in 2020–1. But all else is not equal. The equalization program contains several provisions that weaken the connection between payments and horizontal inequality across provinces.

Since the financial crisis, when Ontario became an equalization-receiving province, the program has featured a fixed pool of dollars available to be paid. This pool is not static, to be clear, but is indexed to a three-year moving average of nominal GDP growth in Canada. The pool means that, instead of total payments being determined by the product of total provincial and local revenues and the Schutz Index of fiscal capacity inequality, the total is determined merely by a predetermined initial value and subsequent national economic growth. This provision has been a source of concern for many provinces, as it historically meant payments were smaller than they otherwise would have been. Between 2009–10 and 2017–18, for example, the fixed pool resulted in a cumulative $16.7 billion fewer equalization payments to recipient provinces. But following the oil price declines through COVID-19, the inequality across provinces has decreased below the predetermined fixed pool amounts. In 2018–19, the first year where this decline occurred, payments under the formula were $17.2 billion, but there was $19 billion available. The $1.8 billion difference was distributed in the form of what are called "adjustment payments." COVID-19 enlarged these payments further. For 2022–3, for example, they will approach $2.1 billion.

Recent developments following the worst of COVID-19, however, may change this picture. Through 2021 as vaccination rates increased rapidly throughout much of the world, the pace of economic recovery was strong. This recovery, combined with Russia's invasion of Ukraine early in 2022, led global oil prices to rapidly increase. Indeed, I find the year-over-year change in the Bank of Canada's commodity price index in 2021 and (through to June) 2022 to be higher than any previous annual increase in Canadian history (Macdonald 2017; Bank of Canada 2022b). This increase will lead to unprecedented levels of natural resource revenues for commodity-producing provinces and potentially more than reverse the decline in inequality across provinces.

Regardless of this recent development, though, the rapid contraction in fiscal capacities revealed a problematic feature of the current formula. To appreciate this problem, consider the experience of Newfoundland and Labrador and Saskatchewan. While these provinces did not qualify for payments in 2022–3, they only barely avoided it. I estimate that, if Saskatchewan's non-resource revenue fiscal capacity were a mere 0.1 per cent smaller in 2020–1, it would have qualified. Once this qualification happens, an interesting quirk in the formula might kick in, resulting in adjustment payments for Ontario.

To appreciate this quirk, consider a discontinuity contained within the formula. For the purposes of the 2022–3 equalization payments, which incorporate data for the three fiscal years ending in 2020–1, Saskatchewan's three-year weighted average non-resource fiscal capacity was $10.373 billion. If it were instead $10.369 billion, and all other values remained unchanged, then very little would happen to equalization payments to any province. But if their resource revenues dropped to $10.368 billion, then, in addition to Saskatchewan qualifying for payments ($89 million), I estimate Ontario would receive $1.09 billion in equalization despite no change in its underlying fiscal situation. It turns out that the critical threshold in this fiscal year is $10.368722 billion in Saskatchewan's non-resource fiscal capacity. Fall just a fraction below that amount and Ontario would receive $1.09 billion in equalization. More problematically, these payments to Ontario come at the expense of lower payments than would otherwise be the case to other recipient provinces, especially for Quebec, whose payments decrease significantly – again, despite no change in its underlying fiscal situation. This sharp, and arguably problematic, discontinuity that was only narrowly avoided during COVID-19 may motivate federal reforms before the scheduled March 2024 renewal of federal-provincial fiscal arrangements in Canada.

There are several potential reforms to consider. One possibility would involve simply removing adjustment payments from the program and returning to the 2007 formula, which largely mirrored recommendations from an expert panel. In the short term, this solution may exacerbate fiscal challenges faced by some of Canada's smaller and lower income regions. Later in this chapter, I will highlight some uniquely challenging circumstances facing Newfoundland and Labrador. Removing adjustment payments may end up shrinking the amount received by some provinces at a time when they might most need such support.

Another option may be to incorporate something akin to the personal income override that applied to fiscal years in the late 1970s and early 1980s before the introduction of the 1982 formula. This provision restricted provinces whose average incomes were above the national average from receiving equalization payments, which at the time affected only Ontario. Incorporating such a provision into the allocation of adjustment payments would, in effect, remove Ontario's ability to qualify,[1] which would potentially affect Saskatchewan. Although Saskatchewan's 2020 average income is slightly below average, recent increases in commodity prices may change that level. But high commodity prices would also lead the province to not qualify anyway, so implementing a personal income override in the allocation of adjustment payments *for those provinces who do not otherwise qualify for payments* would then, in practice, likely remove payments only to Ontario.

In any case, the pandemic and the subsequent economic and fiscal developments may have raised important questions regarding the smooth functioning of Canada's Equalization Program. This development is not new, of course. The specific design of equalization has always struggled to confront the unique properties of natural resource revenues (see chapter 8 by James Feehan in this volume).

Fiscal Stabilization and COVID-19

As new ad hoc federal transfers have mitigated the effect of rising COVID-19–related expenditures on provincial budgets, the primary way in which the pandemic has adversely affected provincial finances has been through decreased revenues. The sharp slowdown in economic activity resulting from public health measures and from changes in consumer behaviour have meant lower employment, fewer hours worked, less consumer spending, and vanishing corporate profits. Revenues from taxes on income and consumption declined markedly in the early months of the pandemic. In addition, disruptions to certain kinds of revenue-generating activities for provincial governments, such as casinos or government business enterprises, have added to the revenue declines. Though later data revisions changed the picture, as I'll discuss shortly, by early 2021 it appeared that, over the nine final months of 2020 (that is, from the second quarter to the fourth quarter), data from Statistics Canada's (2023) government finance statistics showed provincial own-source revenues fell by over $23 billion compared to the same nine-month period in 2019. This decrease represented a decline of nearly 7.5 per cent, with particularly sharp revenue declines recorded in the second quarter, leading to large increases in provincial borrowing and increasing interest in federal support for provincial revenue declines through a previously rarely used program called the Fiscal Stabilization Program.

Since 1967, the Fiscal Stabilization Program has provided a kind of revenue insurance to provincial governments. Initially, if revenues declined by more than 5 per cent, then the federal government would cover any excesses. Adjustments would be made for any policy changes made by provincial governments, such as tax rate reductions, to ensure the federal government was only exposed to relatively exogenous shocks that lowered provincial revenues. The underlying rationale for such a program is twofold: risk pooling and lower debt costs. As with any type of insurance arrangement, to the extent that financial risks across provinces are uncorrelated, there are gains to pool risks together. Paying in good times to ensure one is cushioned in the bad can increase the welfare of all. Providing such insurance is the role the federal government is implicitly playing through the original stabilization program. In addition to risk pooling, the stabilization program serves to shift the burden of public debt accumulation to the federal government. When revenues decline, there is typically an unavoidable increase in government borrowing due to the resulting budget deficits. As provincial debt yields are normally higher than federal yields, it is less costly to use federal borrowing to cover such shortfalls. For perspective, each $1 billion shifted from provincial borrowing to federal borrowing lowers the aggregate fiscal cost of servicing this debt by roughly $10 million per year.

To be sure, as with any insurance-type arrangement, moral hazard concerns weigh heavily. By insulating provincial governments from the full consequences of revenue volatility, the federal government may incentivize provinces to make choices that increase that volatility. An over-reliance on natural resource revenues by certain governments is a notable example of this hazard. Potentially motivated by this concern, the federal government enacted numerous changes to the original structure of the stabilization program to limit its exposure. Through the 1970s, it decreased the coverage of natural resource revenue declines, for example, by increasing the threshold reduction from 5 per cent for overall revenues to 50 per cent for resource revenues. By the 1980s, following British Columbia's stabilization payment in 1982–3 of roughly $60 per capita, the federal government limited all subsequent payments under the program to not exceed this limit. Such stop-loss limits, as they would be called in a standard insurance arrangement, are not uncommon, but the federal government's $60 per capita limit, which was not adjusted for inflation, gradually eroded the real value of the program. By the oil price declines and revenue drops in Alberta and Newfoundland and Labrador in 2015–16 and 2016–17, the effective insurance through the stabilization program was highly limited.

Pressure to ease limits on stabilization payments grew louder in oil-producing provinces, and COVID-19 accelerated and broadened provincial demands for an expanded program since many provinces appeared on track to become recipients. While it is not fully clear who may qualify, it appeared likely that the four large provinces of Ontario, Quebec, British Columba, and Alberta each would, along with potentially Newfoundland and Labrador and Saskatchewan. Given the $60 per capita limit, payouts and support to these governments would cover only a small fraction of the expected losses due to COVID-19. With this pandemic as a truly exogenous event, the case to expand the scope of coverage was strong. In response, the federal government lifted the cap to $166 per person in 2018, indexed subsequently to national nominal GDP growth. For the 2022–3 fiscal year, for example, I estimate this cap will be just over $200 per capita – based on the *Budget 2022* projection for nominal GDP that year. This indexation approach will help ensure the stabilization program does not atrophy again.

These changes to the stabilization program are meaningful, though it now appears most provinces will not require the support. The disruptions from COVID-19 were large, but as discussed earlier, the taxation revenues of provincial governments fared well (indeed, increasing) on account of benefits to individuals and businesses being taxable. In future years, the probability of experiencing a revenue decline sufficiently large to exceed the new higher limit is low. Using changes in economic activity as a proxy for changes in provincial non-resource revenues, I find that, based on the historical experiences of provincial governments, only Alberta has a reasonable prospect of revenue declines on that scale, largely because of fiscal choices it voluntarily makes that exacerbate budget volatility in the province.

There are several trade-offs to consider when expanding a program like stabilization. On the one hand, the federal government is sensibly averse to exposing itself to fiscal costs resulting from provincial budget decisions. Merely covering revenue shortfalls risks encouraging provincial governments to make choices that increase volatility. But, on the other hand, this issue is not an insurmountable challenge, as one could design stabilization in a way that responds to fiscal capacity – such as in equalization – rather than actual revenue. Alternatively, one could use a macro-based formula for stabilization that makes payments based on measures of provincial GDP decline rather than changes in revenue.

The pandemic may have highlighted a particularly valuable role played by a program like stabilization, but even it will not be used on the scale some expected (such as Tombe 2020a). There was also monetary support. Large-scale interventions by the Bank of Canada in provincial debt markets allowed provincial credit markets to continue to function during the early phase of the crisis. Through its Provincial Bond Purchase Program and the Provincial Money Market Purchase Program, Canada's central bank provided support to provincial governments far beyond what has been done in previous years by purchasing nearly $19 billion in provincial government bonds by May 2021 (Bank of Canada 2022a). By May 2022, the Bank of Canada's total holdings of provincial bonds declined to $14 billion. The Fiscal Stabilization Program, were it to be sufficiently large and formula driven, provides an alternative support for provincial credit markets. If investors have confidence that provincial governments would be insulated by the federal government from the worse fiscal consequences of severe economic contractions, then their willingness to purchase provincial bonds would increase.[2] It is not clear whether a reformed stabilization program would have been sufficient to forestall the credit market challenges that provincial governments faced early in the pandemic, but it is a possibility to consider carefully when examining future reforms to this or related programs.

Debt Sustainability and Fiscal Federalism

The magnitude of fiscal responses by all levels of governments raised concerns around the long-run sustainability of government debt in Canada. From April to December 2020, general government outstanding debt in Canada increased by nearly $420 billion. This increase amounted to nearly 25 per cent over the span of only nine months. The federal government accounted for much of this increase, rising nearly $340 billion over that period, while provincial governments saw a collective increase of just over $80 billion. By the first quarter of 2022, total government debt increased by nearly $600 billion compared to two years earlier.[3] While provincial debt increases were not as large as the federal increases, they may represent a more difficult fiscal challenge to overcome. Indeed, early in the pandemic, some provinces – notably Newfoundland and Labrador – faced unusually challenging credit market conditions, and borrowing rates rose while market liquidity declined (Cochrane and Antle 2020).

In future years, the sustainability of provincial debts will depend on whether the cost of carrying and servicing this debt grows more quickly than a provincial government's ability to pay, typically reflected in a rising debt to GDP ratio. Prior to COVID-19, provincial governments were facing significant fiscal pressures due to an aging population and rising health-care costs. Expenditures on health, after all, typically account for roughly two-fifths of provincial government operations. As an increasingly large share of the population enters higher aged categories – where average per person health expenditure is substantially higher – rising health costs is difficult to avoid. Current projections suggest that health cost increases could be in the order of roughly three percentage points of GDP over the next three decades from population aging alone (Tombe 2020b). In addition to rising health-care costs, an aging population will also mean a smaller share of the population will be employed. From Statistics Canada's (2022) projection, the working-age share of Canada's population may decline from its current level of 66 per cent to less than 61 per cent by 2050. This decline is a material drag on economic growth – lowering the pace of growth by roughly 0.3 per cent each year, resulting in an economy that is over 7 per cent smaller by 2050 than it would have been without this reduction in labour force participation. To be sure, policies to encourage labour market activity among older aged individuals can mitigate this decline, but the dual challenge of rising health costs and slowing rates of economic growth create a long-lasting structural gap between provincial revenues and program expenditures.

Such long-run primary deficits will require that provinces adjust their finances to remain sustainable. Tax rate increases or slowing the pace of expenditure growth will be required to ensure the pace of future debt increases does not substantially exceed growth in provincial economies. Many provinces will be able to address these fiscal challenges, but the pressure on some may require federal assistance.[4] Newfoundland and Labrador faces a uniquely challenging fiscal environment due to its low population growth (and potential for population declines) combined with a more rapidly aging population than any other province. Out migration is part of the challenge. According to the medium (M1) scenario by Statistics Canada's (2022) latest projection, which I select for illustrative purposes, Newfoundland and Labrador's population may shrink over 12 per cent by 2043, and nearly 43 per cent of the decline is accounted for by fewer individuals aged twenty to thirty-nine years. Such changes in the province's population increase the difficulty of funding public services, as taxes paid by these individuals who leave to live elsewhere are paid to the provincial government where they reside. The burden of Newfoundland and Labrador's already elevated debt will also consequently increase for those who remain.

Perhaps surprisingly, the pandemic has not fundamentally changed the long-term fiscal trajectory of provincial governments. The increase in debt this year is not trivial, to be sure, but it is offset by faster growth in current fiscal transfers. The CHT is indexed to a three-year moving average of national nominal GDP but is subject to a 3 per cent growth floor.[5] The pandemic caused a large economic contraction in 2020, and the floor was binding for some time. But from 2022–3 onwards, a faster rate of growth will occur due to the higher-than-normal recovery growth rates in 2021 and later. So, while the CHT will be lower than previously projected for the next few years, it will grow larger in time. By 2026–7, for example, the federal government projects it may reach $56 billion in total – which totals approximately $12 billion more between 2021 and 2026 than pre-pandemic projections (Government of Canada 2022, 234). Over a longer horizon, I estimate this amount will grow to eventually increase the CHT by the equivalent of 0.1 per cent of GDP per year in perpetuity. This increase is substantial. Its present value over the next fifty years, for example, is equivalent to roughly 4 per cent of GDP today[6] – larger than the COVID-19-related increase in provincial debt in 2020.

While COVID-19 may not have adversely affected the long-run provincial debt outlook, there remains an opportunity to reform current transfer arrangements to address pre-existing fiscal challenges provincial governments faced. Examining new fiscal arrangements to ensure provincial sustainability in the face of a rapidly aging population will be a priority for governments in the coming years. Adjusting health transfers to be responsive to not only demographics but also interprovincial population flows may be a part of the solution.

Conclusion

Exploring all the ways in which COVID-19 has disrupted Canada and the world will occupy researchers and analysts for decades. The financial and fiscal implications alone will take time to fully appreciate, and this chapter has been but a narrow look at a small selection of issues. Despite this uncertainty, federal transfers and broader fiscal arrangements will almost surely be reformed further as policy makers increasingly move on from the immediate pressures of the crisis. Whatever the specifics of such reforms are, the fast-moving developments during the crisis may have also highlighted the importance of real-time objective analysis and reporting. Governments may therefore wish to consider improving data collection, consolidation, reporting, and analysis. One option is for an arm's-length entity (not unlike the Commonwealth Grants Commission in Australia) that can accomplish this important work, as suggested by Béland and Lecours (2016) and others. The Canadian Institute for Health Information (CIHI), for example, performs this valuable service for health care (CIHI 2021). Regardless, federal transfers to other governments in Canada, as a share of our economy, were larger in 2020 than at any point in Canadian history. Ensuring we remain committed to continually improving these arrangements will be critical for Canada's future prosperity.

NOTES

1 The 2021 Census of Population, reported in Statistics Canada data table 98-10-0068-01 ("Income Statistics for Detailed Income Sources and Taxes by Age and Gender: Canada, Provinces and Territories, Census Metropolitan Areas and Census Agglomerations with Parts," https://doi.org/10.25318/9810006801-eng), found that average individual total income in Ontario in 2020 was $56,350 – above the national average of $54,450. Alberta also had above-average total incomes.
2 For another look at how uncertainty in federal-provincial fiscal relations affects provincial budgeting, see chapter 7 by Marcelin Joanis in this volume. For provincial debt and governance issues, see chapter 9 by Kyle Hanniman.
3 I base my calculations on Statistics Canada data table 36-10-0605-01 ("Debt Securities Issues by Sector, Currency, Maturity, Type of Interest Rate and Market of Issuance, Quarterly," https://doi.org/10.25318/3610060501-eng).

4 For a closer look at demographics and fiscal federalism issues facing Canada's Atlantic provinces, see chapter 18 by Richard Saillant in this volume.
5 For a much more detailed analysis of the Canada Health Transfer, see chapter 5 by Robin Broadway in this volume.
6 This estimate comes with much uncertainty. I report it here to illustrate that the present value of the increase in the CHT the pandemic's economic disruptions created can plausibly exceed the additional debt accumulated by provincial governments.

REFERENCES

Bank of Canada. 2022a. "Bank of Canada Assets and Liabilities: Month-End (formerly B1)." Accessed 14 July 2022. https://www.bankofcanada.ca/rates/banking-and-financial-statistics/bank-of-canada-assets-and-liabilities-month-end-formerly-b1/.
– 2022b. "Commodity Price Index." Accessed 13 July 2022. https://www.bankofcanada.ca/rates/price-indexes/bcpi/.
Béland, Daniel, and André Lecours. 2016. "Canada's Equalization Policy in Comparative Perspective." *IRPP Insight* no. 9, 15 September 2016. https://irpp.org/research-studies/insight-no9/.
CIHI (Canadian Institute for Health Information). 2021. *National Health Expenditure Trends, 2020*. Ottawa: CIHI.
Cochrane, David, and Rob Antle. 2020. "'Out of Time': How a Pandemic and an Oil Crash Almost Sank Newfoundland and Labrador." *CBC News*, 1 April 2020. https://www.cbc.ca/news/politics/newfoundland-labrador-oil-pandemic-covid-coronavirus-dwight-ball-1.5516620.
Finances of the Nation. n.d. "Aggregate Federal Transfers." Finances of the Nation. https://financesofthenation.ca/historical-federal-transfers/
– 2022a. *FON Macroeconomic Database*. Accessed 7 July 2022. https://financesofthenation.ca/macrodata/.
– 2022b. *Government Revenue and Expenditure Database*. Accessed 7 July 2022. https://financesofthenation.ca/real-fedprov/.
Government of Canada. 2020. *Fall Economic Statement 2020*. Ottawa: Department of Finance Canada.
– 2021. *Economic and Fiscal Update 2021*. Ottawa: Department of Finance Canada.
– 2022. *Budget 2022: A Plan to Grow Our Economy and Make Life More Affordable*. Ottawa: Department of Finance.
Macdonald, Ryan. 2017. "A Long-Run Version of the Bank of Canada Commodity Price Index, 1870 to 2015." Analytical Studies Branch Research Paper Series. Ottawa: Statistics Canada. https://www150.statcan.gc.ca/n1/pub/11f0019m/11f0019m2017399-eng.htm.

Statistics Canada. 2022. "Table 17-10-0057-01: Projected Population, by Projection Scenario, Age and Sex, as of July 1 (x 1,000)." https://doi.org/10.25318/1710005701-eng.
- 2023. "Table 10-10-0015-01: Statement of Government Operations and Balance Sheet, Government Finance Statistics (x 1,000,000)." https://doi.org/10.25318/1010001501-eng.

Tombe, Trevor. 2018. "Final and Unalterable – But Up for Negotiation: Federal-Provincial Transfers in Canada." *Canadian Tax Journal* 66, no. 4: 871–917. https://papers.ssrn.com/sol3/papers.cfm?abstract_id=3309712.
- 2020a. "The Need to Review Canada's Fiscal Stabilization Program for Provinces after COVID-19" *What Now? Policy Briefs*, 5 August 2020. Canada West Foundation. https://cwf.ca/research/publications/what-now-the-need-to-review-canadas-fiscal-stabilization-program-for-provinces-after-covid-19/.
- 2020b. "Provincial Debt Sustainability in Canada: Demographics, Federal Transfers, and COVID-19." *Canadian Tax Journal* 68, no. 4: 1083–122. https://doi.org/10.32721/ctj.2020.68.4.fon.
- 2021. "The Effect of COVID on Provincial Finances." Finances of the Nation, 26 November 2021. https://financesofthenation.ca/2021/11/26/covid-prov-fiscal/.

5 The Canada Health Transfer: Past, Present, and Future

ROBIN BOADWAY

1. Introduction and Context

The Canada Health Transfer (CHT) is part of a broader system of federal-provincial fiscal arrangements and contributes to various aspects of them. The CHT serves three main objectives. It provides conditional financial support for provincial health program spending; it contributes to vertical fiscal balance; and it contributes to horizontal fiscal balance. In doing so, it complements other elements of the fiscal arrangements. Our discussion of the role of the CHT in the Canadian federation will emphasize these three objectives and examine how the CHT addresses them alongside other elements of the federal-provincial transfer system.[1] To understand how the CHT interacts with and complements other major fiscal transfers, we summarize key features of these transfers.

We begin in this section with a summary of the evolution of the CHT. We then briefly outline the key features of the CHT and other main transfers. Finally, we present some stylized facts about the role of the CHT in the financing of provincial government budgets. Section 2 outlines in more detail the place of the CHT in the federal-provincial fiscal arrangements. In section 3, we explore the three main roles of the CHT mentioned above, and section 4 presents three policy options designed to enhance the ability of the CHT to contribute to vertical and horizontal balance and to the financing of provincial health programs.

Evolution of the CHT

Federal-provincial transfers in support of health and social programs began in the 1950s. Under the Hospital Insurance and Diagnostic Services Act of 1957, the federal government shared half the cost of designated provincial hospital services. The Medicare Act of 1966 did the same for doctors' services provided outside of hospitals. All provinces shortly thereafter instituted publicly funded hospital and doctors' services programs. Part of the federal contribution was based on a province's own health expenditures, and part was based on the average of all provinces' expenditures. These shared-cost transfers induced all provinces to adopt public hospital and medical care programs. The Canada Assistance Plan (CAP) of 1966 shared half the costs of provincial social assistance programs provided they were based on need and precluded any residency requirement. Similarly, the federal government shared half the cost of current expenditures on post-secondary education with the provinces, albeit with a cap on the rate of growth implemented in 1972.[2]

In 1977, health and post-secondary education shared-cost programs were replaced with Established Programs Financing (EPF). Federal funding took the form of equal amounts of cash and equalized tax transfers and, at least for equalization-receiving provinces, was equivalent to equal per capita transfers. When the Canada Health Act (CHA) was enacted in 1984, full eligibility for EPF transfers required that provincial public health insurance programs be publicly administered, universal, accessible, and comprehensive, and that coverage be maintained for persons who move between provinces. The provinces are also precluded from allowing user fees and double billing. EPF and CAP were combined to form the Canada Health and Social Transfer (CHST) in 1995 as part of the federal austerity plan to deal with the budget deficit. Shared-cost CAP funding was eliminated, and the CHST was financed by a combination of cash transfers and equalized tax points, such that provinces received equal per capita support. The CHA conditions continued to apply to the notional share of the CHST intended to support provincial health expenditures, and mobility conditions applied to transfers for provincial social assistance and social services.

In 2004, the CHST was divided into the CHT and the Canada Social Transfer (CST), with 62 per cent allocated to the CHT and the remainder to the CST. The CST included support for social assistance and services as well as post-secondary education.[3] This disaggregation was meant to improve transparency and accountability, although of course the funds were fungible. The form of federal funding as well as the conditions on the use of the funds were unchanged. In the same year, the federal government introduced a five-year Health Reform Transfer to support primary health, home care, and catastrophic drug coverage. This transfer was incorporated into the CHT in 2005, and the amount of the CHT was increased and subject to a 6 per cent annual escalator. The CHT moved to an equal per capita cash transfer by 2014. In 2017, the rate of growth of the CHT was changed to a three-year moving average of nominal gross domestic product (GDP), with a minimum guarantee increase of 3 per cent per year. In 2007, the CST was increased in size, and the escalator was set at 3 per cent per year, where it currently stands. Both the CHT and the CST will be reviewed in 2024.

Summary of the CHT, Equalization, and the CST

As discussed further below, the CHT along with Equalization and the CST together contribute to vertical and horizontal balance, so it is worth briefly characterizing these programs. The design of the CHT is remarkably simple. It is an equal per capita transfer notionally allocated to support provincial health expenditures, mainly hospital and medical programs. The allocation is notional since the funds are fungible. The CHT is not intended to cover other provincial health expenditures such as pharmaceuticals, dental care, or long-term care. It grows annually at a rate equal to a three-year moving average of GDP, with a guaranteed minimum increase of 3 per cent. The transfer is, in principle, a conditional block transfer, but the conditions are both very general and mainly indicative. Full receipt of the CHT requires that provinces adhere to the terms of the CHA mentioned above.

Health care is an exclusive legislative responsibility of the provinces, and the conditions imposed by the CHA are considered by the federal government not to violate provincial legislative authority. The provinces, after all, can refuse to take the funds. The CHT is authorized by federal statute, and the federal government settles disputes. Settlement involves the occasional withholding of some CHT transfers from provinces whose health-care systems are deemed to violate the CHA, usually because of user fees for some health services. Provinces retain considerable discretion in the design of their health-care systems and exercise it independently of both the federal government and of each other. The choice of health services to insure varies from province to province, as does their means of delivery. Despite that, residents of one province are guaranteed coverage when visiting other provinces, although the mobility of health service providers is less than perfect. The integrity of the CHA has stood up reasonably well as the share of federal financing of provincial health care has dwindled. Whether the federal government will continue to have the moral and political authority to exercise its spending power into the future, or to expand it, is an open question.

Like the CHT, the CST is an equal per capita transfer. It is intended to provide federal financial support for provincial social assistance and services, post-secondary education, early childhood development, and childcare. CST funds are notionally allocated to those categories, although in practice they are fungible. The transfer provides largely indicative support to provincial social programs. The only condition is a general one requiring that provincial social assistance programs satisfy a mobility requirement. There are no conditions attached to provincial post-secondary education funding. Provinces can and sometimes do give preferential treatment to in-province post-secondary education students. The CST grows at 3 per cent annually, unlike the CHT, which as mentioned grows at GDP growth rate. The fact that both the CHT and the

CST are equal per capita transfers is relevant when we discuss the role of the CHT below. The Canada Community-Building Fund (CCBF; formerly the Gas Tax Fund) is another equal per capita transfer, currently set at $2.2 billion. As discussed further below, it is intended to support municipal infrastructure projects and is channelled through the provinces.

Equalization is also a per capita transfer, but the per capita amounts available to each province differ by provincial tax capacity. The latter refers to the per capita amount that would be raised by applying national average provincial tax rates to the main provincial tax bases. A province's per capita equalization entitlement is the difference between its tax capacity and the national average. Only provinces whose per capita tax capacities fall below the national average are eligible for equalization transfers. However, aggregate equalization payments are also constrained to grow at the rate of GDP growth, and all provincial entitlements are adjusted in equal per capita amounts to ensure that the growth rate is met. Historically, that has meant that equalization payments are less than entitlements, though in the recent past the opposite has been the case. Overall, aggregate federal transfers grow at between 3 per cent and the rate of growth of nominal GDP, since the three main components do.

Some Stylized Facts

The CHT is the largest federal-provincial fiscal transfer, amounting to roughly $42 billion in 2020–1. It is over twice as large as Equalization (about $20 billion) and three times as large as the CST (about $15 billion). Taken together, the CHT, CST, and Equalization are worth about $2,100 for each Canadian. Looked at differently, CHT transfers constitute 12 per cent of total federal expenditures, while the CHT, CST, and Equalization together amount to about 23 per cent. Transfers from the federal government made up about 21 per cent of total provincial revenues in 2020–1, down from about 26 per cent in the early 1970s. These amounts vary among provinces owing mainly to Equalization.[4]

The relative financial positions of the federal and provincial governments have evolved over the past three decades. In the mid-1990s, the federal debt to GDP ratio was almost 60 per cent and that of the provinces was close to 40 per cent. By 2018, the federal debt to GDP ratio had fallen to about 35 per cent, while that of the provinces rose to 43 per cent. These amounts will be significantly higher due to the COVID-19 pandemic, which raises the issue of whether federal and provincial finances are sustainable given current taxation and government expenditure policies. The Parliamentary Budget Officer (2020b) has recently reported on the fiscal sustainability of the federal government and the provinces, where fiscal sustainability means that the debt to GDP ratio does not increase continuously under current policies. Their estimates apply to the post-pandemic setting, assuming that pandemic response measures are withdrawn as promised and no new programs are introduced. Their calculations show that the federal government's fiscal situation is sustainable. It could permanently increase spending or reduce taxes by 0.8 per cent of GDP and stabilize the debt to GDP ratio at the pre-pandemic level of 28 per cent. On the other hand, the aggregate of subnational government budgets is not currently sustainable, largely due to rising health-care costs. Subnational governments would have to permanently reduce spending or increase taxes by 0.5 per cent of GDP to stabilize their aggregate debt to GDP level at the pre-pandemic level of 24 per cent. Alternatively, federal-provincial transfers could rise more rapidly. We return to this issue later.

The CHT constitutes about 22 per cent of provincial health expenditures, compared to 50 per cent when medicare and hospital insurance were introduced in the 1960s and financed by cost-sharing. The Council of the Federation (2021) projected that the CHT will decline to about 20 per cent of provincial health expenditures by 2030 and less than 18 per cent by 2040. This projection is based on their estimate that health-care expenditures will rise by about 5 per cent per year until 2040. This increase exceeds the rate of GDP growth, which is the rate at which the CHT grows. The council proposed that the CHT increase by $28 billion in 2020–1 so that it would rise to 35 per cent of provincial health expenditures, and thereafter grow at 5 per cent per year.

In contrast to the Council of the Federation, the Parliamentary Budget Officer (2020a) estimates that the CHT makes up about 32.3 per cent of provincial-territorial health spending in CHT-targeted areas, where the latter includes only those expenditures that are defined by the CHA as being eligible for contributions from the federal government. These include mainly hospitals, physicians, and a specific number of extended health-care services. In practice, provincial health programs are considerably broader than that, indicating that provinces do not feel constrained by the CHA definition of supported health spending.

2. The CHT and Federal-Provincial Fiscal Relations

As we have stressed, the CHT is part of a larger system of federal-provincial fiscal arrangements. Along with two other main transfers, Equalization and the CST, they represent the main instruments used to achieve horizontal and vertical balance in the federation. All three consist of transfers allocated to provinces on the basis of some measure of need and revenue capacity financed from federal general revenues. Need is captured solely by population size, since all three transfers are allocated on a per capita basis. Although revenue capacity is unique as a determinant of equalization entitlements, it also enters indirectly through the financing of all transfers. Revenue capacity implicit in federal financing is based on capacities to raise federal revenue in each province. All three programs are equalizing. Equalization transfers go to provinces whose own revenue-raising capacities are below the national average. Both the CHT and CST are equal per capita transfers funded from federal general revenues. Since higher income provinces pay more per capita in federal tax revenues, the CHT and CST implicitly equalize differences in provincial revenue-raising capacity as measured by ability to raise federal revenues in each province. The CHT/CST system differs from Equalization in two main ways: (1) it takes no account of provincial disparities in natural resource revenues;[5] and (2) it implicitly equalizes high fiscal-capacity provinces down as well as low fiscal-capacity provinces up since, in per capita terms, the former pay more in taxes than they receive in transfers, and vice versa for the latter.

Other federal-provincial transfers include fiscal stabilization, specific-purpose grants, and grants for infrastructure. The Fiscal Stabilization Program transfers limited amounts of funds to provinces whose own-source revenues have changed in a given year. Given the restrictions on the size of these transfers – the current limit of $166 per capita indexed to GDP growth and the limited stabilization of falls in natural resource revenues – they provide minimal insurance protection to provinces whose revenues fluctuate. Grants in support of infrastructure differ from the other major transfers in the sense that they are generally not ongoing but are legislated as need arises.[6] They are also unique in the sense that they target, in part, municipal infrastructure.

An ongoing source of support for municipal infrastructure is the CCBF.[7] It was initially funded by revenues obtained from the federal gasoline excise tax but now comes from general revenues. Payments are made to the provinces, who pass them onto their municipalities. They are intended to provide a steady flow of funds for municipal infrastructure spending. The total annual transfer of about $2.2 billion is allocated on an equal per capita basis (though with a minimum guaranteed level for Prince Edward Island and the territories). The funds must be used for infrastructure projects that fall within categories defined by the federal government. Their allocation within provinces is determined by a series of bilateral federal-provincial-territorial agreements. Even though the funds are targeted towards specific infrastructure projects, they free up revenues that the provinces might otherwise have provided to municipalities; in that sense, they are partially fungible. For our purposes, we can think of the CCBF as a component of the group of equal per capita transfers to the provinces along with the CHT and CST.

Various forms of federal-provincial agreements are also relevant for our evaluation of the CHT. One is the set of bilateral tax harmonization agreements between the federal government and several provinces. Under the tax collection agreements (TCAs) for the personal and corporate tax, agreeing provinces undertake to adopt the federal tax base while retaining the freedom to set their own tax rates and, to some extent, their rate structures and tax credits. Five provinces have also adopted a harmonized sales tax (HST), which also entails substantial tax base harmonization along with considerable discretion to set provincial tax rates. Harmonized personal, corporate, and sales taxes are all administered by the Canada Revenue Agency. Both the TCAs and the HST include formulas for allocating provincial tax revenues among provinces when taxpayers operate in more than one province. These tax harmonization agreements, along with harmonization of refundable tax credits delivered through the tax system, contribute greatly to the efficiency of the Canadian economic union. In that sense, they complement the Canada Free Trade Agreement of 2017, which is an intergovernmental trade agreement whose purpose is to reduce barriers to the free movement of goods, services, labour, and capital across provincial borders. As well, there are various bilateral agreement in areas like training and labour regulation.

Finally, one feature of Canada's federal-provincial fiscal arrangements that bears noting is the relative roles of the federal and provincial governments in initiating them. A common feature is that the federal government acts as a first mover, even in areas where it shares jurisdiction with the provinces. Tax harmonization agreements are a case in point. In each of the personal income tax, corporation income tax, and HST, the federal government encouraged provinces to harmonize their tax bases with that of the federal government in return for a single tax administration and the efficiencies that entails. The ability of the federal government to induce provinces to join tax harmonization arrangements is arguably related to the fact that it occupies a dominant share of the relevant tax room. As tax room has been turned over to the provinces, they have argued for – and received – more discretion in setting their tax rates. Similarly, one might argue that the ability, for better or worse, of the federal government to use its spending power to achieve some degree of harmonization of social policies is related to the extent to which federal financing contributes to provincial social program costs. Although the Equalization and Fiscal Stabilization Programs are strictly federal, even here the political consensus for these programs is affected by the size of the horizontal imbalances they address, which is in turn related to the size of the vertical balance. The first-mover advantage that the federal government exercises is also affected by the extent to which the provinces speak with a common voice. The Council of the Federation provides some institutional support for provinces developing a common approach.

3. The Roles of the CHT

On the surface, the CHT is a conditional block transfer intended to be a federal contribution to provincial health-care expenditures and to encourage provinces to abide by the principles set out in the CHA. However, that characterization both overstates the spending power role of the CHT and fails to recognize its broader role as a key component of federal-provincial fiscal arrangements. Contrary to when federal health transfers were first introduced, the amount of the CHT is no longer directly related to provincial health expenditure. The notional attribution of the CHT to provincial health expenditures is mainly indicative of intentions: provinces are free to use the funds as they see fit. Although entitlement to the CHT is conditional on provinces abiding by the conditions set out in the CHA, these conditions consist mainly of broad principles whose meaning is open to interpretation. The federal government is the arbiter and decides on penalties against non-abiding provinces, but it is questionable whether it has either the financial clout or the political license to impose detailed requirements on provincial health-care programs. It is also questionable whether, as a matter of fiscal federalism policy, the federal government should use the spending power in the health area more intensively and unilaterally, although a collaborative approach need not be ruled out.[8] The CHT probably does buy some ability to apply moral suasion and political persuasion on the provinces, backed up by the threat of financial sanctions. But the power of that moral suasion wanes as the share of federal financing of provincial health spending falls.

The more substantial contribution the CHT makes to federal-provincial fiscal arrangements is through its effect on vertical and horizontal balance. The CHT is one of the main vehicles used by the federal government – along with the CST, Equalization, and the CCBF – to achieve vertical balance. It is a complement to the division of tax room between the federal government and the provinces: the share of federal tax room is directly related to the level of federal transfers. It enables the provinces to finance their program spending with less pressure on own-source revenues. Vertical balance is a term that refers to a satisfactory size of the vertical gap, that is, the difference between provincial expenditure requirements and own-source revenues as reflected in the size of federal-provincial fiscal transfers.[9] There is no uniquely preferred size of the ideal vertical fiscal gap. Over the post-war period, the size of the gap has gradually fallen to the point where provinces on average finance about 80 per cent of their expenditures from own-source revenues, as we have noted. The size of the gap differs by province, which raises the complementary issue of horizontal balance to which we return below. As measured by the vertical fiscal gap, Canada is one of the most decentralized federations in the world, surpassed only by Switzerland. Given current design features of federal-provincial transfers, the vertical gap will gradually fall. Is that a cause for concern?

The vertical gap has consequences for the efficiency and equity of the Canadian economic union. It has implications for policy harmonization. The resilience and evolution of existing tax and transfer harmonization measures depend on the provinces being willing to abide by federal influence over a common tax base, a common set of transfer programs delivered through the tax system, and a common tax-collecting authority. The larger the share of tax room the provinces occupy, the greater will be the likelihood that they will want to impose tax measures that favour their residents over those of other provinces. Some tax competition can be a good thing in disciplining governments. But excessive tax competition can introduce inefficiencies and inequities that arise from the temptation to free-ride or engage in beggar-thy-neighbour policies. A harmonized tax-transfer system contributes to efficiency in the economic union by removing barriers from interprovincial trade and investment. It also allows for a basic amount of fairness in the redistributive features of the tax system while retaining the right for provinces to satisfy province-specific tax-transfer policies.

The existence of sizeable federal transfers also affords the federal government some moral authority to persuade provinces to abide by common national norms in the design of their social and other programs, which is the intent with respect to provincial health-care programs. The perception of a sizeable federal contribution through the CHT may influence the ability of the federal government, for example, through public pronouncements, to persuade the provinces to conform with the CHA. The federal contribution reinforces the notion that important national equity and efficiency objectives are being addressed by provincial health programs. The same might be said for provincial welfare and post-secondary education programs assisted by the CST or for municipal infrastructure spending supported by the CCBF. While no conditions are imposed on provincial post-secondary education programs, the CST perhaps supports the idea that these programs have a national dimension. With some exceptions, provinces have largely refrained from discriminating against out-of-province students in universities and colleges. The contrast with the treatment of foreign students is instructive.

It is one thing to recognize that the ability of the federal government to influence provincial program design is affected by the level of federal transfers. It is another to say that federal influence is always desired. Provinces obviously and justifiably have different preferences for the design of social programs and tax-transfer systems reflecting their heterogeneous constituencies. There are also advantages of decentralization per se, such as the benefits of experimentation, policy innovation, and yardstick competition. The choice of vertical balance needs to trade off the benefits of decentralization to achieve these objectives and to address provincial preferences against the fact that there are also national equity and efficiency objectives at stake, such as those enunciated in section 36(1) of the Constitution Act, 1982.[10] The federal government bears shared responsibility for these objectives, even though the instruments for addressing them are exclusive legislative responsibilities of the provinces. Federal-provincial gap-filling transfers contribute to those objectives. Of course, the trade-off between the benefits of decentralization and the benefits of national coordination can vary among provinces, and this divergence may be recognized by asymmetric arrangements.[11]

A vertical fiscal gap also recognizes differences in the ability to borrow by the two levels of government and the implications that has for fiscal sustainability. Those differences are also related to the constraints facing provinces in raising revenues compared with the federal government. Fiscal sustainability issues can arise because of long-term or short-term effects. Over the longer term, provincial expenditure responsibilities have tended to grow relative to federal ones. That is a consequence of the constitutional division of responsibilities that assigns to the provinces responsibility for key public services like health and education, which have grown relatively more rapidly than federal expenditure responsibilities. This disparity is expected to continue as the population ages. Given that the rate of increase in federal-provincial transfers has been less than that of provincial expenditures, provinces have been required to finance more of their own expenditures, and pressures of tax competition have constrained their ability to do so in a sustainable way. Maintaining a satisfactory vertical fiscal gap contributes to the long-run sustainability of provincial finances, and it recognizes the advantages the federal government might have in raising capital.

In the short term, economic shocks tend to apply especially to the revenue side. This trend has two implications. First, the greater are provincial own-source revenues, the larger are the effects of a revenue shock. A larger vertical gap provides a limited shield against revenue shocks by reducing provincial own-source revenue requirements. Second, the response to provincial revenue shocks can be addressed by other transfer programs. Traditionally, Equalization has been touted as a program for insuring provinces against revenue shocks. However, evidence has shown that it is inadequate and can even be destabilizing (Boadway and Hayashi 2004; Smart 2004). While equalization might offset the volatility of a given province's revenues, a province's equalization entitlement itself is volatile to the extent that it depends on changes in other provinces' revenues that affect national average revenue capacity. Revenue-stabilization is better addressed by fiscal equalization. The current program has well-known deficiencies that could and should be addressed (Dahlby 2019; Tombe 2020). The need for fiscal stabilization is related to the extent of provincial reliance on own-revenues and the vertical fiscal gap. It is also related to the volatility of purely provincial sources of revenues, especially natural resource revenues.

The benefits of maintaining an adequate fiscal gap to address the above objectives must be weighed against some possible downsides. One is the concern that the federal government will use its financial pre-eminence to intrude excessively into areas of provincial jurisdiction and interest. Provinces may oppose unilateral changes to harmonized tax bases and tax credits. They may also be subject to unannounced changes to the level of federal-provincial transfers, for example, those that essentially transfer fiscal problems from the federal government to the provinces in times of crisis. Another concern is that the reliance of provinces on federal transfers may lead them to behave as if they had a soft budget constraint. If so, they may exercise too little caution in their spending plans, anticipating that, if they find themselves in financial difficulty, the federal government will be bound to bail them out. Evidence suggests that this expectation is a well-founded belief. Hanniman (2015) argued, based on interviews with rating agencies and on observed federal-provincial interest rate differentials, that capital markets anticipate that the federal government would bail out provinces unable to meet their obligations. The possibility of a soft budget constraint can be mitigated by the federal government adhering to a formula-driven transfer system, including fiscal stabilization, and by resisting bilateral financial deals to respond to provincial budgetary problems after the fact. The point is that there are benefits and costs associated with a vertical fiscal gap, so a compromise is inevitable. We return below to mechanisms for mitigating the soft budget constraint by reducing the need for federal bailouts.

The CHT also has implications for horizontal balance. As mentioned, the CHT system is equivalent to a net system of equalization based on ability to raise federal tax revenues as the representative tax system rather than provincial revenue-raising ability. In other words, funds are obtained by the federal government based on federal revenue capacity in each province and turned over to all provinces in equal per capita amounts. This process implicitly redistributes from provinces with higher fiscal capacity to those with lower fiscal capacity, thereby equalizing low-income provinces up and high-income provinces down. Thus, as an equalization system, the CHT is based both on revenue capacity as measured by capacity to generate federal tax revenue and on need as measured by population, and it applies symmetrically to all provinces. It differs from the Equalization Program in omitting purely provincial revenue sources, like resource revenues and property taxes, and in that sense is incomplete. The CST shares the equalizing features of the CHT, so it is the combined CHT/CST that is relevant.

The complementarity of the CHT and CST to Equalization has one further dimension. Lower levels of these transfers entail a lower vertical fiscal gap, which in turn implies that provinces will be more reliant on own-source revenues. This implication will increase horizontal imbalance since different provinces have different fiscal capacities to raise own-source revenues. The consequence is that the smaller are the CHT and CST, the greater are the demands put on the equalization system. Since the federal share of the tax room will fall as the CHT and CST fall, the ability of the federal government to finance equalization will be made more difficult.

4. Policy Options for the CHT

To summarize the above discussion, the CHT serves three main functions. First, it provides federal financial support for provincial health programs subject to some general conditions set out in the CHA. Second, it is a major determinant of vertical balance in the federation, along with the CST, Equalization, the CCBF, and the division of tax room. Third, it contributes to horizontal balance in a way that complements Equalization, the CST, and the CCBF. In each of these three areas, some policy options can be identified, beginning with the latter two, which are less contentious.

Reforming the CHT to Improve Vertical Balance

The share of provincial health expenditures financed by the CHT has eroded over the years and will continue to do so under the current formula.[12] The rate of growth of health expenditures exceeds the CHT rate of growth now and for the foreseeable future. This imbalance would be true even if the coverage of provincial health systems retained their current form. The COVID-19 pandemic has persuaded many policy makers – and to some extent the public – that the current system leaves too many people vulnerable to shocks and escalating health costs. There have been calls for expanding coverage to areas like pharmacare, long-term care, home care, and dental care. Moving in that direction would put further pressure on provincial budgets.

Increasing CHT transfers could stave off the decline of the federal contribution to health care and in the process address the erosion of the vertical fiscal gap. We have argued that a vertical fiscal gap contributes to tax harmonization, federal-provincial policy coordination, a well-functioning internal economic union, and fiscal stability, and therefore to national efficiency and equity objectives. As mentioned earlier, the Parliamentary Budget Officer (2020b) has observed that, contrary to federal finances, aggregate provincial budgets are not fiscally sustainable. The provinces will have to either permanently reduce expenditures or increase revenues to correct the situation. These circumstances support a permanent increase in the vertical fiscal gap. A reallocation of funds from the federal government to the provinces could address the long-run fiscal problems faced by the provinces without jeopardizing federal fiscal sustainability. While in principle this readjustment could be achieved by turning over tax room to the provinces, that would weaken the integrity of the economic and social union by increasing horizontal imbalance and pressures for fiscal competition and tax fragmentation.

The alternative is to increase federal-provincial fiscal transfers. This solution could be achieved by an increase in both the level of the CHT and its growth rate. The Council of the Federation (2021) proposed an increase in the CHT by enough to cover about 35 per cent of provincial health expenditures. Based on 2020–1 figures, this proposal would require an increase of about $28 billion. At the same time, the council proposed that the CHT escalator be increased to 5 per cent per year. An alternative would be to set the escalator at a moving average of aggregate provincial health expenditures.

A possible downside to increasing the fiscal gap is that it could increase provincial fiscal dependency on federal transfers and lead to soft budget constraints. As mentioned, there is compelling evidence that capital markets and rating agencies expect that the federal government would bail out provinces who face a financial crisis, and provinces may realize that as well. Avoiding this situation would require that the federal government be able to commit to not bailing out provinces in distress so that provinces foresee that they will have a responsibility to deal with financial crises. A reformed Fiscal Stabilization Program, while insuring provinces against exogenous shocks, might also encourage imprudent behaviour. To address this issue, Hanniman (2020) has proposed a two-pronged policy reform to deal with provincial fiscal sustainability problems without encouraging imprudent behaviour.[13] It would combine an increase in federal transfers with the creation of a conditional bailout facility that would be available in times of financial stress to finance provincial deficits at federal interest rates. The facility would be conditional in the sense that participating provinces would have to agree to a fiscal consolidation plan. The conditional bailout plan would essentially buy time for provinces to solve their own problems. This reform is a promising approach to mitigate the soft budget constraint problem, though many details would have to be worked out, including enforcement mechanisms.

Reforming the CHT for Horizontal Balance

A main goal of horizontal balance is to satisfy the federal obligation enunciated in section 36(2) of the Constitution Act, which states: "Parliament and the government of Canada are committed to the principle of making equalization payments to ensure that provincial governments have sufficient revenues to provide reasonably comparable levels of public services at reasonably comparable levels of taxation."

The economic rationale for this obligation is based on the complementary ideas of fiscal equity and fiscal efficiency. Equalization reduces differentials in net fiscal benefits from provincial government policies, which fosters both the equal treatment of equals across the federation (fiscal equity) and the efficient interprovincial allocation of resources (fiscal efficiency). These principles should be interpreted in terms of equalizing provincial capacities to provide public services rather than equalizing actual tax and expenditure policies. Provinces retain the power to exercise their fiscal capacities as they see fit.[14] Equalization achieves this obligation to some extent, but it has two main shortcomings. First, since it is a gross system, it brings all have-not provinces to a national average revenue capacity, leaving the rest with above-average revenue capacity. Second, equalization is calculated in per capita terms, which is equivalent to assuming that the needs for and costs of public services are proportional to population.

The CHT can partially address these deficiencies. As mentioned above, the CHT implicitly equalizes all provinces to a national average revenue capacity, where revenue capacity is based on the ability to raise federal revenues within the province. This approach is obviously not fully satisfactory since it omits from the revenue standard natural resource revenues, which are a major determinant of horizontal imbalance.[15] Nonetheless, the CHT/CST system is a partial complement to Equalization.

The CHT could, however, bring needs and/or costs into consideration, and since it applies to all provinces, it can equalize both down and up on this basis. Incorporating needs and costs for health-care expenditures into the CHT is particularly appropriate since these differences are pronounced in the provision of health care. In principle, CHT per capita allocations could be based on the relative per capita costs of providing health care among provinces. To do so precisely would be complicated, since different provinces provide different levels of health services.[16] Some representative level of health services would have to be defined, and that would be contentious. Instead, a more parsimonious approach could be taken by focusing on the main sources of cost differences. One of these might be the age composition of the population. Using estimates of the relative costs of providing health care to different age groups, one could condition per capita CHT transfers on relative cost differences based on the age distribution of the population.

A second factor, emphasized by Courchene (2013), is the difference in wage costs among provinces. Since wages make up a substantial share of health-care expenditures, conditioning per capita CHT payments on relative wage rates would go some way to equalizing differences in the cost of providing health care. Using wage costs in the health sector to determine CHT entitlements would give rise to incentives for provinces to increase health wages and salaries. A proxy approach that avoids this method would be to use an index of private sector wages and salaries to condition per capita CHT transfers.

Calculating provincial per capita shares using a combination of age and wage cost adjustments would go a considerable way to satisfying the commitments of section 36(2). A similar approach could be applied to the CST. Adjusting for needs and costs would be contentious, since it involves a zero-sum reallocation. It would be important that the process of calculating the adjustments be transparent and involve provincial input. The same could be said of equalization calculations.

Getting the per capita allocation right is key to addressing horizontal balance. Together with setting the overall size of the CHT and its escalation rate, both horizontal and vertical balance are achieved. Equally important is the length of time for which the formula should apply. A formula-based federal-provincial fiscal transfer system that is subject to only periodic revision is an important commitment device to minimize both soft provincial budget constraints and the temptation for the federal government to arbitrarily cut transfers to solve its own budgetary problems. Some federations constrain the federal government further through arm's-length grants councils, like the

Australian Commonwealth Grants Commission. This model has been considered in the past by various bodies and ruled out (see, for example, Expert Panel on Equalization 2006). As a means of infusing the transfer setting process with transparency and a long-term perspective, it should not be taken off the table.

Reforming the CHT as a Conditional Block Grant

Provinces' health spending is not constrained by the categories designated by the CHA. They have taken the initiative to provide additional forms of health coverage such as pharmaceuticals, dental care, eye care, hearing care, diagnostic services, and services provided by medical professionals other than doctors. These other forms of publicly provided health care differ among provinces according to local needs and preferences, and they need not abide by the terms of the CHA. They need not be universal – some may apply only to seniors, to children, or to low-income persons – and they may have user fees. Nonetheless, they comprise part of the health services provided by the province, and they contribute to the escalating costs of provincial health care. As with CHA-designated health services, a case can be made for federal support. These additional health services are complements to hospital and doctor services, and they contribute to equity objectives, including equality of opportunity, which are of national interest (cf. section 36[1]). They also contribute to efficiency in the economic union to the extent that health services provided in one province would be accessible by out-of-province visitors or workers. Moreover, they account for much of the projected growth of provincial heath expenditures and the implications that has for fiscal sustainability of provincial finances.

In this context, the question arises as to whether the federal government should use the CHT as a device for encouraging new provincial health programs, and if so, how. The kinds of national programs advanced include those mentioned: pharmacare, long-term care for the elderly and disabled, home care, and dental care. Virtually all the new programs being proposed are already offered in partial forms by most, if not all, provinces. Requiring them to abide by the terms of the CHA would involve making them universal, fully publicly provided, and free of user fees. They would not be new public programs designed from scratch, and their institution would affect provinces differently. The use of the federal spending power via extending the scope of the CHT would be a blunt, and probably controversial, instrument.

Alternative, more flexible approaches could be considered that could combine additional federal financing with maximum provincial discretion. The model used for the CCBF or the various tax harmonization agreements is one possibility. The CCBF provides a common per capita amount to each province to be used for municipal infrastructure projects based on bilateral federal-provincial-territorial agreements. The types of projects funded differ across provinces, although all fall under a broad list of eligible project areas. Though the funding is of the block form rather than based on cost-sharing, there is nonetheless some requirement that the funds be spent as promised, which entails some provincial accountability. The CHT could conceivably be augmented to provide federal block funding in support of additional provincial health-care services that fall under an agreed list of program areas. But the provinces could strike very different agreements with the federal government to reflect both their current practices and their special needs and preferences. Whether CHA-type conditions should be used to encourage provincial compliance is a matter for debate, as would be the desirability of any accountability requirements imposed on the provinces.

As an alternative, looser restrictions could be imposed on increases in CHT funding. The federal government could simply nominally assign funding increments as being in support of specific provincial programs, such as long-term care or pharmacare, possibly even announcing that they were intended to support universal programs in the stated areas. The provinces would then have the discretion to abide by the intentions of the funding, and enforcement would be left to political or moral persuasion. This approach would be analogous to federal CST support for provincial post-secondary education programs, where no conditions are imposed, or for social assistance and social services, where only minimal conditions are imposed. Indeed, the same mobility conditions could apply to augmented CHT transfers as apply to CST transfers in support of provincial welfare programs.

5. Concluding Comments

The perspective we have adopted in this chapter is that the CHT is one component of a coherent system of federal-provincial fiscal relations that includes other transfers and intergovernmental agreements. Together they aim to foster equity and efficiency in the Canadian economic union. We have identified three main objectives to which the CHT contributes. The first is vertical balance, which balances the benefits of federal transfers and tax room against the benefits of provincial fiscal discretion. The second is horizontal balance, which aims to achieve fiscal equity and efficiency by providing provinces with the fiscal capacity to provide comparable public services at comparable levels of taxation while retaining the ability to choose province-specific policies. The third is to provide targeted support for provincial public health-care programs that satisfy broad conditions.

We have suggested that the most pressing reform is to address the vertical imbalance reflected in the unsustainable fiscal positions of the provinces relative to the federal government. A reasonable approach would be to increase the size and rate of increase in the CHT. This increase would address the vertical imbalance in a way that is most compatible with fostering horizontal balance and federal support for provincial health programs. It would also give the provinces the opportunity to expand health care to meet emerging needs like care for the elderly and pharmaceuticals. Consideration must also be given to exploring instruments capable of mitigating potential soft budget constraint problems.

NOTES

1 We speak about the provinces, but much of what we say also applies to the three territories. The First Nations represent another order of government. The fiscal federalism issues facing First Nations are different and are discussed by Donn. L. Feir and David Scoones in chapter 11. Municipal governments represent another tier of government, and issues of vertical and fiscal balance similar to what we discuss in this chapter apply to them. Enid Slack discusses the fiscal federalism issues faced by municipal governments in chapter 13.
2 Prior to the mid-1960s, the federal government had made an equal per capita transfer to universities rather than to the provinces.
3 The CST is discussed in more detail by Michael Prince in chapter 6.
4 Source: Canadian Tax Foundation (n.d.).
5 The implications of provincial natural resource revenues for fiscal federalism are discussed by James Feehan in chapter 8.
6 The financing of public infrastructure in the Canadian federation is discussed by Eric Champagne and Aracelly Denise Granja in chapter 15.
7 For a summary of the Gas Tax Fund, see Dupuis (2016). The Gas Tax Fund has been renamed the Canada Community-Building Fund as of 29 June 2021. See also "The Canada Community-Building Fund" on the Infrastructure Canada website (https://www.infrastructure.gc.ca/plan/gtf-fte-eng.html).
8 A broad analysis of the spending power is given by Peter C. Oliver in chapter 3.
9 The relationship between vertical fiscal balance and the vertical fiscal gap is explored in detail in Boadway (2005).
10 Section 36(1) states: "Without altering the legislative authority of Parliament or of the provincial legislatures, or the rights of any of them with respect to the exercise of their legislative authority, Parliament and the legislatures, together with the government of Canada and the provincial governments, are committed to (a) promoting equal opportunities for the well-being of Canadians; (b) furthering economic development to reduce disparity in opportunities; and (c) providing essential public services of reasonable quality to all Canadians."
11 See the discussion of the Quebec case by Alain Noël in chapter 19.
12 As noted earlier, if only health expenditures in CHA-designated areas are included, the erosion of federal support is much less apparent, as pointed out by the Parliamentary Budget Officer (2020a). This view seems to be an unduly narrow interpretation

of federal support, given that the areas designated by the CHA were based on those covered by the medicare programs of the 1960s, and extended care services were added later.
13 See also the discussion by Kyle Hanniman in chapter 9.
14 A detailed discussion of the principles and practice of equalization can be found in Boadway and Shah (2009).
15 The importance of provincial resource revenues for federal-provincial fiscal arrangements is discussed by James Feehan in chapter 8.
16 For an analysis of how incorporating needs and costs for health care might be done, see Gusen (2012).

REFERENCES

Boadway, Robin. 2005. "The Vertical Fiscal Gap: Conceptions and Misconceptions." In *Canadian Fiscal Arrangements: What Works, What Might Work Better*, edited by Harvey Lazar, 51–80. Montreal and Kingston: McGill-Queen's Press.
Boadway, Robin, and Masayoshi Hayashi. 2004. "An Evaluation of the Stabilization Properties of Equalization in Canada." *Canadian Public Policy* 30, no. 1: 91–109. https://doi.org/10.2307/3552582.
Boadway, Robin, and Anwar Shah. 2009. *Fiscal Federalism: Principles and Practice of Multiorder Governance*. Cambridge: Cambridge University Press.
Canadian Tax Foundation. n.d. "Government Revenue and Expenditure." *Finances of the Nation*. https://financesofthenation.ca/real-fedprov/.
Council of the Federation. 2021. *Increasing the Canada Health Transfer Will Help Make Provinces and Territories More Financially Sustainable Over the Long Term*. Report of the Provincial and Territorial Ministers of Finance to the Council of the Federation. https://www.canadaspremiers.ca/wp-content/uploads/2021/03/PT_Finance_Report.pdf.
Courchene, Thomas J. 2013. *Surplus Recycling and the Canadian Federation: Addressing Horizontal and Vertical Fiscal Imbalances*. Fiscal Transfer Series. Mowat Publication 69. Toronto: The Mowat Centre, School of Public Policy and Governance, University of Toronto. https://mowatcentre.munkschool.utoronto.ca/surplus-recycling-and-the-canadian-federation/.
Dahlby, Bev. 2019. "Reforming the Federal Fiscal Stabilization Program." *SPP Briefing Paper* 12, no. 18. Calgary: School of Public Policy, University of Calgary. https://doi.org/10.11575/sppp.v12i0.68076.
Dupuis, Jean. 2016. *The Gas Tax Fund: Chronology, Funding and Agreements*. In Brief Series. Publication No. 2016-99-E. Ottawa: Library of Parliament. https://publications.gc.ca/collections/collection_2016/bdp-lop/eb/YM32-5-2016-99-eng.pdf.
Expert Panel on Equalization and Territorial Formula Financing. 2006. *Achieving a National Purpose: Putting Equalization Back on Track*. Ottawa: Department of Finance. https://publications.gc.ca/collections/Collection/F2-176-2006E.pdf.

Gusen, Peter. 2012. *Expenditure Need: Equalization's Other Half*. Fiscal Transfer Series. Toronto: The Mowat Centre, School of Public Policy and Governance, University of Toronto. https://hdl.handle.net/1807/99138.

Hanniman, Kyle. 2015. *Calm Counsel: Fiscal Federalism and Provincial Credit Risk*. Mowat Research 104. Toronto: The Mowat Centre, School of Public Policy and Governance, University of Toronto. https://hdl.handle.net/1807/99325.

– 2020. *Strengthening Canada's Fiscal Resilience*. Essay no. 4, Inaugural Essay Series. Montreal: Institute for Research on Public Policy. https://centre.irpp.org/research-studies/strengthening-canadas-fiscal-resilience/.

Parliamentary Budget Officer. 2020a. *Federal Support through Major Transfers to Provincial and Territorial Governments*. Ottawa: Office of the Parliamentary Budget Officer. https://www.pbo-dpb.ca/en/publications/RP-2021-020-S--federal-support-through-major-transfers-to-provincial-territorial-governments--soutien-federal-principaux-transferts-aux-gouvernements-provinciaux-territoriaux.

– 2020b. *Fiscal Sustainability Report 2020: Update*. Ottawa: Office of the Parliamentary Budget Officer. https://www.pbo-dpb.ca/en/publications/RP-2021-033-S--fiscal-sustainability-report-2020-update--rapport-viabilite-financiere-2020-mise-jour.

Smart, Michael. 2004. "Equalization and Stabilization." *Canadian Public Policy* 30, no. 2: 195–208. https://doi.org/10.2307/3552392.

Tombe, Trevor. 2020. "An (Overdue) Review of Canada's Fiscal Stabilization Program." *IRPP Insight* 31. https://doi.org/10.26070/wqe9-8225.

6 Ceremonial Fiscal Federalism: Social Assistance and the Canada Social Transfer

MICHAEL J. PRINCE

In Canadian fiscal federalism, the Canada Social Transfer (CST) is politically a poor cousin overshadowed by more prominent governmental and organized interest concerns over health care, equalization, and early learning and childcare. Despite a rich history of policy innovation, the existing intergovernmental transfer for social assistance is a fiscal mechanism with certain myths surrounding it. For social assistance policy systems across the country, the CST has a ceremonial function. It may create a respectable appearance of helping some vulnerable Canadians, yet it lacks a substantive vision, actual policy objectives, and effective intergovernmental governance. Looking ahead to the 2024 renewal for the CST, a new arrangement for social assistance needs to be widely discussed and explicitly informed by values of social justice. To encourage debate, this chapter identifies a range of reform options, including moving social assistance to the federal government and transforming it to an income-tested benefit as part of a social security or basic income guarantee agenda.

Social Assistance and Fiscal Federalism

Social assistance in Canada goes by many names, both traditionally and today: the dole, cash relief, municipal aid, public welfare, emergency relief, temporary assistance, social welfare, disability assistance, and more. Funded from general tax revenues, social assistance is government-administered financial support (and community-delivered welfare services) for low-income individuals and families generally outside or on the margins of the labour force. Clientele include persons with significant disabilities, those chronically unemployed and the "unemployable," mothers with children, older persons, and Indigenous people on and off reserves. Subject to various conditions and investigations, support can involve basic income assistance for food, clothing, and utilities; shelter assistance; and emergency hardship support. Other possible components are the provision of goods and services, such as legal aid, residential welfare institutions (homes for the aged, the disabled, and licensed nursing homes), employment-related expectations and work activity programs, and earnings exemptions to encourage labour force participation (although often frustrated by steep benefit reduction rates on other sources of income and assets).

Social assistance programs are selective in their coverage of the population and means or needs tested for eligibility and provision (Laidley and Aldridge 2020). They are the last resort public programs in Canada's social security system for people whose needs are not met by earnings or by social insurance programs such as employment insurance, workers' compensation, or the Canada Pension Plan. In reality, social assistance is the program of only resort or first resort for many people in Canada struggling in dire conditions (Prince 2015). In the history of welfare states, social assistance is the bête noire of income security policy: disreputable, intrusive, complex, and stigmatizing, imposing controls, perpetuating stereotypes, and reinforcing dependencies.

The constitutional situation in Canada for social assistance is that both orders of government have applied this technique of income security in their own areas of legislative jurisdiction. The federal government is or has been directly involved in providing social assistance programs for veterans, First Nations, the unemployed, the elderly, and children. On First Nations, see chapter 11 by Donn L. Feir and David Scoones in this volume. More notably, the provinces and territories are involved in their own programs of income assistance and social welfare services. While social assistance is a co-jurisdiction in some respects, from a fiscal federalism perspective it is a shared area of jurisdiction, with a role by federal taxation and spending powers in areas of primarily provincial responsibility. Indeed, from the 1920s the federal spending power facilitated the development of categorical social assistance programs in provinces. Overall, strong elements of provincial authority and decentralization characterize the program design and delivery in the social assistance field, especially so in social services, which is an exclusive field of provincial jurisdiction. Federal fiscal support for social assistance and social services has been provided in five design forms of public finance: cost-shared specific grants in aid to provinces; cost-shared general transfers to provinces; non-matching block transfers to provinces; tax point abatements (which only Quebec opted for); and direct transfers to civil society organizations, individuals, and families within areas of federal and provincial jurisdiction.

Over the last hundred years, Canadian fiscal federalism for social assistance has undergone considerable transformation along several dimensions and across three broad periods.

- From the 1920s into the 1960s came an incremental series of specific categorical cost-shared arrangements together with the provinces and municipalities, which had various federal conditions and controls. There were both temporary forms of assistance and permanent longer term programs of income support. During this period, social assistance policy development saw the creation and modest extension of limited social rights to certain categories of citizens for very basic income support and the advancement of provincial welfare administrative capacity.

- From 1966 to 1996, there was a more ambitious approach to social assistance policy making with the Canada Assistance Plan (CAP), a comprehensive, open-ended, and cost-shared arrangement (for most of this time) that had comparatively fewer federal conditions. This reform saw the consolidation of previous categorical social assistance programs and the expansion of coverage under federal-provincial agreements to other groups in need and to a range of social welfare services. A federal cap on the CAP transfers in 1990 sparked a period of unilateral federal expenditure restraint and thus intergovernmental conflict in this and other areas of fiscal federalism.
- From the late 1990s to the present period, we have had the Canada Health and Social Transfer (CHST) and the CST, notionally a block fund transfer with no cost-matching requirements and only one federal condition, for provincial and territorial social assistance and related social services, combined with post-secondary education and early learning and childhood development. More than about expenditure retrenchment, at least in the initial years of this period, the CST represents the replacement of the previously established model of fiscal arrangements in social assistance. When CAP ended in 1996, it marked the finale to the longest running conditional grant relationship in the history of federal-provincial fiscal arrangements, a relationship begun in the 1920s. An instrument familiar in other areas of fiscal federalism was now adopted for social assistance and social services: a closed-end block fund. Whereas the CAP exemplified a social policy and practice agenda, the CST is essentially a fiscal mechanism of revenue sharing.

During the COVID-19 pandemic in 2020 and 2021, governmental actions revealed the powerful persistence of residual practices and reactive politics in social assistance policy across nearly the entire country. Most provincial governments offered little if any additional direct financial help for social assistance recipients; more significantly from a fiscal federalism perspective, almost all provinces fully or partially clawed back federal emergency relief benefits from people on social assistance. The CST's effectiveness as a transfer for social assistance and social services is unclear and raises questions as to the future role of Ottawa and intergovernmental transfers in supporting citizens living in poverty and struggling with other forms of unmet essential needs. Chapter 4 by Trevor Tombe in this volume considers more deeply the challenges facing Canadian fiscal arrangements in the post–COVID-19 era. Before we look ahead, we need to review some history to appreciate the political memories and narratives in this field as well as the present context and future policy options.

Categorical Fiscal Federalism in Social Assistance: 1920s–60s

The initial history of intergovernmental transfers for social assistance provision spans from 1920 to the mid-1960s. In addition to cost-shared programs, each order of government had a categorical program of means-tested social assistance funded solely by that government; in the case of the provinces, it was the mothers' allowance, the first modern social assistance program adopted by most provinces; for the federal government, it was the war veterans' allowance, introduced in 1930 (Guest 1997). This mixed pattern of provision indicates that social assistance is a policy technique of income maintenance deployed by both orders of government within their areas of responsibility.

This period had the following key developments in social assistance policy making through fiscal federalism:

- The federal government's entry into intergovernmental transfers for social assistance was from 1919 to 1922, with grants in aid on a cost-sharing basis, initially to municipalities and then to municipalities and provinces for direct relief for the unemployed. During the Great Depression, the federal government entered into annual ad hoc arrangements with the provinces for the emergency provision of direct relief to destitute people. Cost-sharing ratios varied by year in the 1930s and, at times, by region, and both Conservative and Liberal governments in Ottawa made unilateral changes to the financing arrangements. Ottawa's share of governmental spending on relief among the three levels went from about 14 per cent to over 41 per cent, coupled with a shift away from vouchers and in-kind support and towards cash payments (Grauer 1939, 14).
- The first enduring federal cost-sharing arrangement in social assistance was enacted in 1927, creating old age pensions for the needy elderly that amounted to a federal reimbursement of 50 per cent of the costs of a provincial program, excluding administration. The federal government set general eligibility requirements, such as age and residency requirements, and fixed maximum benefit amounts, while provinces determined the actual benefit levels and, with a means-testing approach, administered the delivery of benefits. By the end of the 1930s, the old age pension was by far the largest of the federal transfer programs to the provinces – greater in amount than the statutory subsidies (the financial arrangements of Confederation) and the conditional grants for agricultural instruction, employment service, highways, technical education, and venereal disease control combined (Eggleston and Kraft, 1939, 60, 65). The Old Age Assistance Act replaced the old age pension program in 1952 for persons aged between sixty-five and sixty-nine, while a new universal Old Age Security program began for those aged seventy and over, for which the federal government assumed full

financing and administration. Selective old age assistance continued to be provincially administered using a means test and was cost-shared with the federal government.
- Other categorical cost-shared programs introduced by the Canadian government were for blind persons (1937/1951) and disabled persons (1954). All provinces quickly passed enabling legislation and entered into agreements for these benefit programs. These arrangements included maximum limits on monthly payments, residency requirements, and means testing and delivery by the provinces (and municipalities in some jurisdictions). For the blind persons' allowances, the federal government assumed 75 per cent of costs of the benefit; for the disabled persons' allowance, it was 50 per cent excluding administration. The federal government in 1952 also began cost-sharing on a 50 per cent basis for social services related to the vocational rehabilitation of persons with disabilities (Prince 2016).
- The Unemployment Assistance Act of 1956 committed Ottawa to cost-sharing with provinces (and municipalities) on a matching basis of 50 per cent of the cost of income assistance to able-bodied "unemployed employables." Foreshadowing policy design elements in the Canada Assistance Plan a decade later, the unemployment assistance scheme moved away from means testing, adopting a needs test to determine eligibility. It also offered open-ended cost-sharing on federal contributions, along with no ceiling stipulated on monthly benefits, to encourage increases in provincial assistance rates. There were fewer conditions, although one condition specified that the length of residence in a province or municipality could not be a prerequisite for receiving assistance (Carter 1971, 38–9; Smiley 1963, 10, 31–4).
- Until the 1950s, coverage under old age pensions, allowances for blind persons, unemployment relief, and unemployment insurance excluded Indigenous people. That systemic segregation changed officially with expanded eligibility under the categorical social assistance programs introduced in the 1950s. Then in 1965, the federal cabinet authorized the Department of Indian Affairs "to enter in to cost-sharing agreements with the provinces for the extension of welfare services on reserve. Ontario was the only province to undertake such an agreement: the 1965 Canada-Ontario Memorandum of Agreement Respecting Welfare Programs for Indians." Under the agreement, "the federal government reimburses the province for 100 per cent of the cost of administering social assistance and a selected list of social services for on-reserve Indians" (Moscovitch and Webster 1995, 37).
- The Established Programs (Interim Arrangements) Act of 1965 offered provinces the option to opt out of conditional grant programs and compensation with federal abatement of personal income tax points, thereby transferring equivalent tax room to a provincial government for funding such programs. Quebec was the only province to make use of this program – indeed, the

federal measure was in direct response to Quebec demands – and the Quebec government contracted out of numerous established shared-cost programs, including the four categorical social assistance programs. Quebec received two tax points for old age assistance and the blind and disabled persons programs, and a further two points for unemployment assistance (Black 1975, 142; Simeon 1972, 108, 142–3).

These developments are politically significant for several reasons. With the introduction of categorical social assistance programs came the building up of provincial administrations and relationships between provincial governments and particular target populations, each with their own social policy history and politics across jurisdictions (Boychuk 1998; Rice and Prince 2013, 47–56). Fiscal federalism contributed to a segmentation of the "deserving poor" into seven target groups. Some groups were not cost-shared: dependent mothers with children, burnt-out war veterans, and status Indians. Others groups were the poor elderly, blind persons, the permanently disabled, and unemployed employable persons. Interprovincial networks emerged among welfare program administrators, sharing knowledge of these categorical arrangements, lessons, and concerns. With provincial program experience and capacity came policy and practice innovations in various provinces in the 1950s and early 1960s, complaints over rigidities in the existing conditional grant arrangements, and calls for reform in social assistance policy at the federal level. This quiet administrative revolution in welfare provision and intergovernmental relations was of central importance in the negotiations over and design of the Canada Assistance Plan.

Comprehensive Social Assistance and Fiscal Federalism: 1966–96

The Canada Assistance Plan (CAP) came into existence in April 1966, and all provinces signed agreements with the federal government by the summer of 1967. While federal authorities largely initiated categorical social assistance programs, CAP followed provincial ideas and resulted in considerable intergovernmental negotiations, the ultimate example of cooperative federalism during that time in Canadian politics (Dyck 1976). CAP simplified the array of categorical programs and eased perceived rigidities by consolidating the old age assistance, blind persons' allowance, disabled persons' allowance, and unemployment assistance programs as well as adding a fifth categorical program, mothers' allowance, previously financed entirely by the provinces. Over the 1970s, the CAP replaced all of these categorical social assistance programs across the provinces. Also, in 1966 "the federal government reduced the pensionable age (under the Old Age Security Act) from 70 to 65 years, coming down by one-year steps over a five-year period, thus removing a substantial burden from the provinces" for their costs of old age assistance (Carter 1971, 38).

As a more comprehensive approach, CAP immediately extended coverage of federal cost-sharing to an estimated 200,000 needy mothers with dependent children; 50,000 children in child welfare agencies; a host of rehabilitation and preventive social services; work activity programs; and new costs of administration and training of provincial and, where applicable, municipal welfare personnel (social workers and program administrators). Though the CAP was an expansive policy reform, it did not cost-share all social services; for example, addiction or substance use services, correctional services, and mental health services were not covered (Carter 1971, 39; Guest 1997, 85–91).

Categories of need for specific groups were no longer required for federal sharing of costs for provincial programs of assistance provided by or at the request of provincially approved agencies (including municipalities) and welfare services provided by provincially approved agencies. The program provided benefits to needy Canadians with no pre-existing qualifications or conditions attached to eligibility other than economic need. Provinces could set their own rates of assistance.

As for national standards, CAP "did provide, and largely on provincial terms, large sums of federal money for expanding and redesigning welfare systems attuned primarily to each province's appreciation of its particular needs, rather than to Canada-wide priorities dictated by Ottawa" (Black 1975, 81). The few federal conditions included annual reporting requirements and the prohibition of residency requirements for social assistance, although reporting processes were nothing new and several provinces had done away with residency requirements in their welfare systems. The general absence of national standards in CAP reflected agreement among federal and provincial officials "that public assistance was primarily a provincial responsibility," and so "few federal controls on the provinces were ever proposed. Moreover, most of the remainder gave way under the combined resistance of Quebec, some other provinces, and federal Finance officials" (Dyck 1976, 599). Federal controls removed included the idea of a national standard of income adequacy for social assistance benefits across the country (Bella 1979, 450). Another noteworthy fiscal feature of CAP was that it did not contain a differential cost-sharing formula to address interprovincial inequities and differences in fiscal capacity. The idea had been proposed by welfare ministers from the Atlantic provinces and their senior officials, and endorsed by federal welfare officials, but it was rejected by federal finance officials and by some of the larger provinces (Dyck 1976, 599).

Over the thirty-year history of CAP, there were efforts to reform the intergovernmental transfer arrangement. In each case, social assistance fiscal federalism was just one part of larger constitutional, intergovernmental, or governmental processes. The mid-1970s saw the last great exercise in federal-provincial diplomacy in the field of social assistance. The reform proposals for CAP were all unrealized, falling victim to jurisdictional issues of the federation or, more frequently, to federal government concerns of exercising a measure of budgetary restraint on transfers to other governments. As a result, a political narrative emerged that CAP was increasingly dated and needed to be reviewed and reformed (Government of Canada 1994a).

The Turbulent 1990s: Capping, Contesting, Cutting, Then Killing CAP

While intergovernmental relations under CAP began in the 1960s in a spirit of fiscal sharing and expansion, it emphatically ended in the 1990s in a controversial temper of fiscal offloading and unilateral expenditure restrictions.

The 1990 federal budget outlined a two-year Expenditure Control Plan that, while exempting major direct social transfers to persons (elderly, families, veterans, and unemployed), directly affected CAP. Although CAP payments to lower income provinces were exempted, as were expenditures on social assistance for First Nations and Inuit programs, payments to "the fiscally stronger provinces" of Alberta, British Columbia, and Ontario, the non-equalization receiving provinces, were constrained to a 5 per cent annual growth rate, initially for two fiscal years. The regime of a 50/50 cost-sharing of eligible provincial spending in all ten provinces would resume on 1 April 1992. However, the 1991 federal budget announced the extension of the annual growth ceiling through to 1994–5 and specified that thereafter CAP transfers in these three provinces would grow roughly in line with increases in the gross national product. The other seven provinces continued to have unrestrained access to federal funds for CAP.

The provinces directly affected, along with a few others and some Indigenous organizations, legally challenged the federal restrictions on CAP. A reference case went first to the British Columbia Court of Appeal and then before the Supreme Court of Canada in December 1990 for an authoritative judicial opinion on the constitutionality of the unilateral restrictions by federal authorities on social assistance transfers to provinces. Provinces argued there was a legitimate expectation that the federal government would not limit its obligations under the multi-decade CAP without the consent of provinces affected. However, the Supreme Court unanimously held that this principle applied to administrative bodies but not to the legislative process. As a federal statute within the jurisdiction of Parliament, the CAP had no constitutional nature the Court said in their judgement. The federal government had the authority to limit its obligations under the fiscal arrangement for reasons of austerity by virtue of the principle of parliamentary sovereignty. The Supreme Court added: "The Court should not, under the 'overriding principle of federalism,' supervise the federal government's exercise of its spending power in order to protect the autonomy of the provinces. Supervision of the spending power is not a separate head of judicial review" (Supreme Court of Canada 1991).

From the limit on CAP, the 1992 budget estimated cumulative savings to the federal treasury at $2.3 billion up to 1995–6. The 1993 federal budget tried to offer some reassurance, indicating Ottawa would not impose any additional restraint measures on major federal transfers to provinces. Nonetheless, the 1994 budget revised estimated savings from the limit on CAP to $2.8 billion and added that entitlements would be no higher in 1996–7 than in 1993–4. After four years, the limit on CAP for the three provinces resulted in $5.8 billion in lost transfers, most of the loss being in Ontario. Ottawa was now reimbursing less than 30 per cent of social assistance costs in Ontario, effectively "an amount largely unrelated to actual provincial spending on welfare" (Maslove 1996, 300).

Through the federal budgetary process, Ottawa signalled securing at least $1.5 billion in savings from CAP and Established Programs Financing (EPF) post-secondary cash transfers in 1996–7 and, in a footnote, mentioned that EPF post-secondary and CAP "may be modified or replaced pursuant to the social security review" (Government of Canada 1994b, 40). Ironically, these messages were under a heading called "Establishing a Predictable Environment for Reform." A former senior federal official recalled that "the federal Finance ministry overwhelmingly controlled the process of decision-making and the policy content associated with those measures" (Lazar 2000, 120). With the unilateral change to the social assistance transfer regime, a constitutional reference case, a severe economic recession, and a change in federal government, the early 1990s were anything but a predictable environment for reform to fiscal federalism and social policy. A far bigger budgetary shock, however, was about to come.

Ceremonial Social Assistance and Fiscal Federalism: 1996–2020s

Termination of CAP and EPF in 1995–6 and their replacement with a super block fund, the Canada Health and Social Transfer (CHST), was the most provocative and controversial product of federal-provincial relations of the decade. Once again, the announcement came through a federal budget in February 1995. CAP transfers were to be limited to their 1994–5 levels, with just one condition – the prohibition of a residency test for applicants to social assistance.

In contrast to the collaborative design and harmonious adoption of CAP in 1966, the abrupt and unilateral arrival of the CHST could be called the ultimate in coercive federalism in the 1990s, even though the abolition of CAP virtually eliminated conditionality in the field of social assistance. Federal-provincial relations leading to the CHST and following were acrimonious, with intense conflict and distrust. Intergovernmental discussions and modifications did occur in later years, especially around health-care funding and early childhood development. The CHST was born from a unilateral action by Ottawa with little consultation with provincial officials and political leaders. While the 1995 budget declared that replacing CAP was "to complete the gradual evolution away from cost-sharing to block funding in areas of provincial responsibility" (Government of Canada 1995, 52–3), the change was far from slow and steady for governments operating in the present day. The timing was rapid, with no bargaining. Central agency officials in Ottawa were the driving force rather than health, Indian affairs, or social welfare officials across both orders of government (Dyck 1976; Lazar 2000).

In contrast to the expansionary design of CAP, the CHST was a contraction in financing and a narrowing in policy objectives for social assistance and social services. It was about offloading and limiting federal payments with a closed-end block fund, not the equal sharing of costs and incentives for growing welfare services. As Boadway (1986, 42–3) notes, "block funding does remove the incentive effect of matching grants that induce provinces to spend more in those areas." For provincial governments, "the relative cost of putting money into welfare rather than other activities ... increased" (Maslove 1996, 290). With that change in transfer design also came the loss of CAP's counter-cyclical stabilization function (Hobson and St-Hilaire 2000). What the CHST shared in origins with the CAP was responding to provincial demands for flexibility, although with significantly different processes and fiscal outcomes. The CHST bundled together social assistance and social services with health care and post-secondary education. With the demise of CAP, the last major intergovernmental cost-sharing program was gone, ending a nearly seventy-year history in fiscal federalism. For countless social policy observers, welfare groups, social workers, and poverty advocates, these changes were more than retrenchment; they represented a wholesale replacement of the paradigmatic fiscal policy for social assistance in federal-provincial relations. As a symbol, the CHST aroused deeply held concerns about what was lost and anxieties about the future of social welfare in Canada.

The CHST Years: 1996–2004

Initially, CHST funds were to be allocated in the same proportions as under the combined CAP and EPF transfers in 1995–6 (with CAP transfers limited to their 1994–5 levels), and funding was to be set for the next two years. This allocation represented a 30 per cent reduction or an approximately $6 billion reduction in cash transfers to the provinces. The 1996 federal budget unveiled a new five-year arrangement for 1998–9 to 2002–3 along with an $11 billion cash floor, which the 1998 budget raised to $12.5 billion. With federal budgets in surplus and provincial government and public concerns persisting over health care, the 1999 budget announced an $11.5 billion increase in funding for the CHST over five years explicitly for health care. Another cash supplement of $2.5 billion to support health care and post-secondary education came in the 2000 budget, and further investments in 2001 followed on agreements by first ministers for health-care renewal and early childhood development. Annual CHST cash transfers were to increase by 35 per cent from $13.5 billion in 2000–1 to $21 billion in 2005–6. No additional investments in the CHST were for social assistance. Looking at cash transfers pre-CHST and for the 1996–2004 period, Hobson and St-Hilaire (2000, 175) concluded: "It might be argued that the CHST does not embody any federal commitment toward provincial welfare expenditures."

The federal government's decision in 2003 to split the CHST and create two distinct transfers, one for health, the Canada Health Transfer (CHT), and the other for social programs, the CST, came from a first ministers meeting on health care. The impetus was to create greater transparency and accountability around federal health transfers to the provinces. In this sense, the CST was the residue in the larger politics of publicly funded health care and intergovernmental relations. Cash and tax transfers provided through the CHST were apportioned between the CHT and CST based on provincial spending patterns. Accordingly, 38 per cent of the CHST was for the CST, and the one principle to prohibit residency requirements for social assistance continued.

The CST Years: 2004–24 and Beyond?

In 2007–8, the CST was placed on an equal per capital formula for the allocation of cash funds to provinces and territories, thereby eliminating any component for cost or need differences. Additional investments through the CST came for early childhood development in the 2007 budget and for post-secondary education in the 2008 budget. Yet again, no additional investments came for social assistance, even during the severe recession of 2008–9 (Rice and Prince 2013, 178–84). An annual automatic escalator of 3 per cent has applied to the CST since 2009–10, and the 2010 federal budget affirmed the CST would grow at 3 per cent per year to 2014–15, a pledge extended in the next year's budget to 2016–17. The 2014 budget confirmed the renewal of the CST (and the CHT) for another ten years, subject to review in 2024. Announcements around the escalator and renewal communicated a predictable and stable long-term funding context for both Ottawa and the provinces and territories.

On matters of social assistance and social services, federal policy makers in recent decades have concentrated *outside the CST* on four kinds of measures:

- Some initiatives focus on improving work incentives for the welfare and working poor. For example, the Working Income Tax Benefit was introduced in 2006, enhanced to lower financial hindrances to find and keep a job, and then replaced with the expanded Canada Workers Benefit (CWB) in 2018. At the time, the federal government stated it would "continue to work with interested provinces and territories to harmonize benefits and help support the transition from social assistance and into work" (Government of Canada 2018, 35). Indeed, through reconfiguration agreements, four jurisdictions so far have made changes to the design of the CWB. The CWB was further enhanced in the 2021 budget and, in 2022–3, will provide $3.6 billion in support. Likewise, one of the aims of increasing the refundable medical expense supplement was to offset the possible loss of benefits under provincial social assistance programs when recipients enter the labour force.

- To address income support and poverty reduction for families with children, the National Child Benefit, introduced in 1998 (Boychuk 2002), and its successor in 2016, the Canada Child Benefit (CCB), is the preferred federal policy instrument, rather than transfers to the provinces and territories. As a share of maximum total welfare incomes in 2019 across provinces, the CCB for a single parent with one child represents between 26 per cent in Quebec to 36 per cent in Nova Scotia; and for a couple with two children, the CCB represents 29 per cent in Quebec to 41 per cent in New Brunswick (Laidley and Aldridge 2020), making the CCB a significant element in the social safety nets of each province. According to the federal government, the CCB has lifted 435,000 children out of poverty (Government of Canada 2022, 10). In 2022–3, the CCB is projected at $25.2 billion, an amount significantly greater than the approximate $6.4 billion of the CST nominally allocated for social assistance to the provinces and territories.
- A few other measures involve federal grants and contribution funding to community organizations that deliver social services and to funding social services and income assistance for First Nations on reserve and Inuit families. In addition are funds to support Indigenous early learning and childcare.
- Some technical initiatives address interactions between federal tax measures and provincial social assistance programming. The most significant of these was Ottawa obtaining the agreement of provinces and territories to not claw back Registered Disability Savings Plan benefits by reducing social assistance payments of eligible recipients with disabilities. Other examples include the tax treatment of trusts and estates, kinship care programs, and the Canada Caregiver Credit.

During the COVID-19 pandemic in 2020–1, the issue of provincial claw-backs of a federal income support measure arose in a much less satisfactory way with the federal government's Canada Emergency Response Benefit (CERB). Gillian Petit and Lindsay Tedds (2021, 1) explain: "Persons who applied to CERB received $2,000 per four-week period, for a maximum of 28 weeks, regardless of actual lost earnings. Because some income assistance recipients were eligible for the CERB, this made it necessary for each provincial income assistance program to determine how to treat the CERB for eligibility and benefit purposes." Although the federal government formally asked that provinces and territories not impose a claw-back of CERB benefits for people on social assistance, only one province and two territories (British Columbia, the Northwest Territories, and the Yukon) fully exempted the CERB. Four provinces partially exempted the CERB (Alberta, Manitoba, Ontario, and Quebec), and the four other provinces and one territory (Newfoundland and Labrador, Prince Edward Island, Nova Scotia, New Brunswick, and Nunavut) did not exempt the federal COVID-19 cash payments from offsets to recipients of social assistance. This issue is also relevant to the subsequent Canada Recovery Benefits launched by the federal government in 2020 and extended through 2021.

For a workable fiscal federalism and social assistance policy, the pandemic offers sombre reflections. Not only did "the CERB [allow] provinces to shift some of the financial [responsibility] for income assistance onto the federal government," Petit and Tedds (2021, 2) observe, but "provincial income assistance programs that chose to partially exempt or not exempt the CERB penalized income assistance recipients who were meeting the goals of income assistance. Income assistance recipients who worked prior to the pandemic were making an effort at becoming self-sufficient, a goal recognized by income assistance programs. By making recipients receiving the CERB ineligible for income assistance or reducing their benefits, this penalized them for having worked pre-pandemic."

This mix of exemptions and claw-backs of a national emergency income benefit illustrates the workings of the "last resort" logic of social assistance and shows how it influences the federal spending power. A case of executive federalism failure, it marks the inability or unwillingness of elected leaders and senior officials across governments to harmonize policy measures. It also suggests shallow support for egalitarian sentiments and poverty alleviation among provincial government elites. Perhaps this situation is a predictable consequence of the CST promoting provincial autonomy and priorities. That said, it may be placing too much weight on the significance of the CST in intergovernmental relations in Canada. If anything, the CST has ceremonial and symbolic effects.

The CST as Ceremonial Social Policy

What makes the CST ceremonial is that it is a financial device effectively decoupled from social assistance and social services. The CST is more the stuff of elementary public finance than contemporary social assistance policy. Basically, in Canada, conditionality is rather weak, even in areas such as health care, where national norms do exist. Within the CST, social assistance is politically and fiscally marginal, overshadowed on the national policy agenda by post-secondary education and by early learning and childhood development. The National Welfare Council, a citizens' advisory body to the federal minister responsible for income security, was abolished in 2012. A strong political sense of social assistance being a jointly financed policy undertaking among governments is absent today. There are no federal or shared intergovernmental objectives on social assistance services to build resiliency and prevent dependency. There are no specific commitments on sharing costs for basic income provision, disability-related supports, health-care services for persons in need, or research and evaluation. No longer are national statistics on provincial and territorial social assistance spending published by government.

What Hobson and St-Hilaire (2000, 160) wrote of the CHST applies more so to the CST with its fewer conditions: "rather than an instrument of social policy ... [it] is little more than a mechanism for distributing federal revenues back to provincial governments." There is no guarantee between the flow of federal funds into provincial consolidated revenue funds and the disbursements for the policy choices of a province. CST funds are inherently fluid and potentially interchangeable in myriad ways. Funding share distinctions among postsecondary education, childcare, early childhood development, and social assistance and social services are far from watertight budgeting compartments. The annual 3 per cent increase to the CST could be taken to mean an equal funding lift across all these policy areas in one or more provinces or an enhanced investment in just one or two of these areas in one or more provinces, or it could be no increase in real terms in one or more provinces. Asking if the CST is good or bad social policy misses a more basic question: as an unconditional block fund (like Equalization too), how do we know it is about social policy at all?

Unlike the other major transfers (CHT and Equalization), the CST holds relatively low symbolism. Especially with social assistance, there is no political discourse that speaks of social assistance as a nation-building instrument or as a source of civic pride. The history of fiscal federalism in social assistance added greatly to province building. Where public attention and policy demands on social assistance do occur is within individual provinces (Boychuk 1998, 2015). Nor is the CST talked about as a robust instrument of social integration that generates spheres of affective bonds and positive shared experiences across the country. There never has been a pan-Canadian safety net system for all low-income households. Unlike health care with its immediate mass relevance to the general population, most Canadians are distant bystanders of social assistance. The CST indirectly and indistinctly links the federal government to individuals and families in need of adequate social support. Programmatically and culturally, the CST's predecessor grant arrangements contributed to social differentiation and welfare stigmatization (Rice and Prince 2013). The public identities that social assistance systems still produce are too often troubled identities associated with subsistence, shame, surveillance, and struggle. If the CST contributes to "defining the nature of the Canadian communities on which the federation rests" (Banting 2005, 30), for many people in the realm of social assistance it is surely a problematic function that undermines solidarity on the ground.

As with other intergovernmental transfers, certain myths surround the CST. One of the most durable is that the overall federal contribution each year includes counting the value of federal income tax points turned over to the provinces in 1977 in relation to the then EPF arrangement. Federal finance documents routinely report this myth, representing the CST as something more substantial, more generous than it really is, suggesting what the provinces are getting this year from Ottawa as compared to tax points given several decades ago. Statements that the CST supports specific areas of post-secondary education, childcare and early childhood development, and social assistance and social services is undermined by the fact that the CST is a block fund that gives provinces and territories great flexibility in budgeting and program design and delivery. In chapter 17, Jennifer Robson examines the question of who pays for childcare in our decentralized federation. Claims that the CST rests on shared national objectives are not reflected in intergovernmental agreements for most policy areas in this block fund. We may have an idea of the public purposes for early learning and childcare, but we are none the wiser as to the collective goals for social assistance. Moreover, since the start of the century, there has been a notable absence of federal-provincial diplomacy in the social assistance field.

Concluding Observations

Important normative issues hover over the future of federal transfers, intergovernmental relations, and social assistance. What is the public interest informing the CST? As a block fund, it symbolizes a specified federal contribution with indefinite provincial autonomy. The emphasis on federal affordability and local flexibility are appropriate values, to be sure, but what of equal opportunities for the well-being of Canadians? With the demise of 50/50 cost-sharing under CAP, provinces and people in need lost a risk-sharing and automatic counter-cyclical policy instrument against macroeconomic shocks, such as the sudden slowdown of the economy associated with the COVID-19 pandemic. The CST offers another kind of stability, one anchored in public accounts rather than political economy, in the form of predictable annual increases in cash transfers. The CST is projected to grow from $15.9 billion in 2022–3 to $17.9 billion in 2026–7, in line with the legislated escalator of 3 per cent per year (Government of Canada 2022, 232). Federal transfers for social assistance have never adjusted for disparities in revenue capacity among provinces, although the idea has been periodically raised as a reform over the decades. Thus, horizontal equity in social assistance – the principle that "disadvantaged citizens in different parts of the country can expect reasonably similar levels of social protection" (Boychuk 1998, 99) – has long been constrained by marked differences in provincial fiscal capacity as well as by considerations of provincial jurisdiction and concerns of financial control by federal authorities.

If social assistance was at the centre of fiscal federalism rather than on the margins, what might that mean for intergovernmental relations and the federal spending power? What is the place of the CST and any successor transfer in relation to Canada's recently adopted official poverty rate, the Market Basket Measure (MBM), and to federal and provincial poverty reduction strategies? Research confirms that numerous types of households reliant on social assistance are living in deep poverty with disposable incomes less than 75 per cent of the MBM (Laidley and Aldridge 2020, 15–16). What will a modernization of employment insurance, possibly with increased coverage and improved benefit rates, mean for social assistance caseloads and protection for low-income workers? Does having post-secondary education, childcare, early learning, social assistance, and social services combined in one block fund actually promote transparency and accountability to federal or provincial publics? Heavy reliance on annual federal budgets for developing and announcing policy decisions about the CST marginalizes intergovernmental and parliamentary forums that could allow for engagement by civil society organizations. Another fundamental issue is how to reconcile fiscal federalism and settler colonialism to Indigenous rights of self-determination.

Future options for the federal role in social assistance policy can be found in works by academics, think tanks, parliamentary committees and the Office of the Parliamentary Budget Officer, and professional associations. Ideas include the following:

- continuing the block transfer and adding new federal investments both in and outside the CST (House of Commons 2017, 2021; McIsaac, Kapoor, and Das 2021);
- adding a feature in a new CST that fiscally equalizes for differences in need across all provinces (Hobson and St-Hilaire 2000);
- revising the Indian welfare agreements and making new investments for Indigenous peoples on and off reserves (Papillon 2015; House of Commons 2021);
- enacting federal legislation and negotiating a new intergovernmental agreement with principles and targeted expenditures specifically for social care services (Moscovitch and Thomas 2018); and
- moving social assistance to the federal government and transforming its design as part of a major basic income guarantee agenda (Boadway, Cuff, and Koebel 2018; Pasma and Regehr 2019; MacEwen et al. 2020).

These options are distinct though overlapping and potentially could be combined in different policy agendas over the short term to the longer term. The scope and scale of these options contradict the present comparatively low profile of the CST. Here I can just briefly comment on a few of them; each requires more policy analysis and public debate.

A recommendation by the House of Commons Standing Committee on Finance harkens back to categorical social assistance programming. Before the 2021 federal budget, the committee proposed that the federal government "adopt a series of targeted income supports for groups in need, including Canadians living with disabilities, youth aging out of care, women fleeing from violence, those who have lost income, who cannot work because they are sick and ineligible for employment insurance (EI) sickness benefits, or are able and willing to work but are unable to secure employment." In contrast to past categorical programs, most probably these support programs would be income tested and federally financed and delivered. Committee members also recommended "increasing financial assistance and support for Indigenous peoples living in urban and off-reserve environments" along with enhancements to EI and other federal programs (House of Commons 2021).

For reforming the CST and social assistance, various economists propose uploading responsibility for the financing and delivery of social assistance to the national level. If the federal government financed it entirely, perhaps provinces would accept it. "The federal government, already primarily responsible for delivering income security programs, could take on social assistance cash support as well" (MacEwen et al. 2020, 19). Social services currently funded under the CST would presumably continue in some intergovernmental block grant arrangement with one or more of childcare, early learning, and post-secondary education. In a policy redesign, a federal income-tested benefit for working-age adults (aged eighteen to sixty-four) would replace the income support component of provincial and territorial social assistance programs (see also Boadway, Cuff, and Koebel 2018; Pasma and Regehr 2019). This new federal income benefit would be in addition to the CCB for families with children and youth, and the Old Age Security/Guaranteed Income Supplement program for seniors. This proposal certainly speaks to administrative efficiency, equity, mobility, and social citizenship. If an adequate and dignified level of income support across the country is a worthwhile social project, then direct federal provision informed by Canada's official poverty line is a tangible form of fiscal federalism, much more so than the current ceremonial quality of the CST.

REFERENCES

Banting, Keith. 2005. "Canada: Nation-Building in a Federal Welfare State." In *Federalism and the Welfare State: New World and European Experiences*, edited by Herbert Obinger, Stephan Leibfried, and Francis G. Castles, 89–137. Cambridge: Cambridge University Press.

Bella, Leslie. 1979. "The Provincial Role in the Canadian Welfare State: The Influence of Provincial Social Policy Initiatives on the Design of the Canada Assistance Plan."

Canadian Public Administration 22, no. 3: 439–52. https://doi.org/10.1111
/j.1754-7121.1979.tb01827.x.

Black, Edwin R. 1975. *Divided Loyalties: Canadian Concepts of Federalism*. Montreal and Kingston: McGill-Queen's University Press.

Boadway, Robin. 1986. "Federal-Provincial Transfers in Canada: A Critical Review of the Existing Arrangements." In *Fiscal Federalism*, edited by Mark R. Krasnick, 1–47. Toronto: University of Toronto Press.

Boadway, Robin, Katherine Cuff, and Kourtney Koebel. 2018. "Designing a Basic Income Guarantee for Canada." In *Federalism and the Welfare States in a Multicultural World*, edited by Elizabeth Goodyear-Grant, Richard Johnston, Will Kymlicka, and John Myles, 101–29. Montreal and Kingston: McGill-Queen's University Press.

Boychuk, Gerard William. 1998. *Patchworks of Purpose: The Development of Provincial Social Assistance Regimes in Canada*. Montreal and Kingston: McGill-Queen's University Press.

– 2002. "Social Union, Social Assistance: An Early Assessment." In *Building the Social Union: Perspectives, Directions and Challenges*, edited by Tom MacIntosh, 51–67. Regina, SK: University of Regina Press.

– 2015. "Federal Policies, National Trends, and Provincial Systems: A Comparative Analysis of Recent Developments in Social Assistance in Canada, 1990–2013." In *Welfare Reform in Canada: Provincial Social Assistance in Comparative Perspective*, edited by Daniel Béland and Pierre-Marc Daigneault, 35–52. Toronto: University of Toronto Press.

Carter, George E. 1971. *Canadian Conditional Grants since World War II*. Toronto: Canadian Tax Foundation.

Dyck, Rand. 1976. "The Canada Assistance Plan: The Ultimate in Cooperative Federalism." *Canadian Public Administration* 19, no. 4: 587–602. https://doi.org/10.1111/j.1754-7121.1976.tb01877.x.

Eggleston, Wilfrid, and C.T. Kraft. 1939. *Dominion-Provincial Subsidies and Grants: A Study Prepared for the Royal Commission on Dominion-Provincial Relations*. Ottawa: J.O. Patenaude. https://publications.gc.ca/site/fra/9.894913/publication.html.

Government of Canada. 1994a. *The Budget Plan*. Ottawa: Department of Finance Canada. https://www.budget.canada.ca/pdfarch/1994-plan-eng.pdf.

– 1994b. *Improving Social Security in Canada: A Discussion Paper*. Ottawa: Human Resources Development Canada.

– 1995. *Budget Plan*. Ottawa: Department of Finance Canada. https://www.budget.canada.ca/pdfarch/budget95/binb/budget1995-eng.pdf.

– 2018. *Equality and Growth: A Strong Middle Class*. Ottawa: Department of Finance Canada. https://www.budget.canada.ca/2018/docs/plan/budget-2018-en.pdf.

– 2022. *Budget 2022: A Plan to Grow Our Economy and Make Life More Affordable*. Ottawa: Department of Finance Canada. https://www.budget.canada.ca/2022/pdf/budget-2022-en.pdf.

Grauer, Albert Edward. 1939. *Public Assistance and Social Insurance: A Study Prepared for the Royal Commission on Dominion-Provincial Relations*. Ottawa: J.O. Patenaude. https://publications.gc.ca/site/eng/9.894803/publication.html.

Guest, Dennis. 1997. *The Emergence of Social Security in Canada*. 3rd ed. Vancouver: UBC Press.

Hobson, Paul A.R., and France St-Hilaire. 2000. "The Evolution of Federal-Provincial Fiscal Arrangements: Putting Humpty Together Again." In *Toward a New Mission Statement for Canadian Fiscal Federalism*, edited by Harvey Lazar, 159–88. Montreal and Kingston: McGill-Queen's University Press.

House of Commons Canada. 2017. *Breaking the Cycle: A Study on Poverty Reduction*. Seventh Report of the Standing Committee on Human Resources, Skills and Social Development and the Status of Persons with Disabilities. 42nd Parliament, 1st Session. https://publications.gc.ca/collections/collection_2017/parl/xc67-1/XC67-1-1-421-7-eng.pdf.

– 2021. *Investing in Tomorrow: Canadian Priorities for Economic Growth and Recovery*. Report of the Standing Committee on Finance. 43rd Parliament, 2nd Session. https://www.ourcommons.ca/Content/Committee/432/FINA/Reports/RP11058298/finarp01/finarp01-e.pdf.

Laidley, Jennefer, and Hannah Aldridge. 2020. *Welfare in Canada, 2019*. Toronto: Maytree Foundation.

Lazar, Harvey. 2000. "The Social Union Framework Agreement and the Future of Fiscal Federalism." In *Toward a New Mission Statement for Canadian Fiscal Federalism*, edited by Harvey Lazar, 99–128. Montreal and Kingston: McGill-Queen's University.

MacEwen, Angella, Mark Rowlinson, Andrew Jackson, and Katrina Miller. 2020. *Basic Income Guarantee: A Social Democratic Framework*. Ottawa: Broadbent Institute.

Maslove, Allan M. 1996. "The Canada Health and Social Transfer: Forcing Issues." In *How Ottawa Spends, 1996–97: Life Under the Knife*, edited by Gene Swimmer, 283–301. Ottawa: Carleton University Press.

McIsaac, Elizabeth, Garima Talwar Kapoor, and Surma Das. 2021. *Shaking Up the Systems: Fighting Poverty in Post-Pandemic Canada*. Maytree's Submission to the National Advisory Council on Poverty. Toronto: Maytree.

Moscovitch, Allan, and Ginette Thomas. 2018. *A New Social Care Act for Canada: 2.0*. Report prepared for the Canadian Association of Social Workers (CASW). Ottawa: CASW.

Moscovitch, Allan, and Andrew Webster. 1995. "Aboriginal Social Assistance Expenditures." In *How Ottawa Spends, 1995–96: Mid-Life Crisis*, edited by Susan D. Phillips, 209–36. Ottawa: Carleton University Press.

Papillon, Martin. 2015. "Playing Catch-up with Ghosts: Income Assistance for First Nations on Reserve." In *Welfare Reform in Canada: Provincial Social Assistance in Comparative Perspective*, edited by Daniel Béland and Pierre-Marc Daigneault, 323–38. Toronto: University of Toronto Press.

Pasma, Chandra, and Sheila Regehr. 2019. *Basic Income: Some Policy Options for Canada*. Ottawa: Basic Income Canada Network.

Petit, Gillian, and Lindsay Tedds. 2021. "Fiscal Policy Trends: COVID-19 & Trends in Income Assistance Caseloads." *School of Public Policy Publications* 14, no. 1. Calgary: The School of Public Policy, University of Calgary. https://doi.org/10.11575/sppp.v14i.71907.

Prince, Michael J. 2015. "Entrenched Residualism: Social Assistance and People with Disabilities." In *Welfare Reform in Canada: Provincial Social Assistance in Comparative Perspective*, edited by Daniel Béland and Pierre-Marc Daigneault, 289–303. Toronto: University of Toronto Press.

– 2016. *Struggling for Social Citizenship: Disabled Canadians, Income Security, and Prime Ministerial Eras*. Montreal and Kingston: McGill-Queen's University Press.

Rice, James J., and Michael J. Prince. 2013. *Changing Politics of Canadian Social Policy*. Toronto: University of Toronto Press.

Simeon, Richard. 1972. *Federal-Provincial Diplomacy: The Making of Recent Policy in Canada*. Toronto: University of Toronto Press.

Smiley, Donald V. 1963. *Conditional Grants and Canadian Federalism: A Study in Constitutional Adaptation*. Canadian Tax Paper 32. Toronto: Canadian Tax Foundation.

Supreme Court of Canada. 1991. *Reference Re Canada Assistance Plan (BC) [1991] 2 SCR 525*. Ottawa: Supreme Court of Canada.

7 Living on Equalization Payments: How Hard Is It for Receiving Provinces to Anticipate Future Equalization Revenues?

MARCELIN JOANIS

1. Introduction: Canada's Complex Brand of Equalization

In large, diverse federations such as Canada, a well-functioning equalization scheme is known to be a key feature to enable a high degree of decentralization in the provision of public services. Conversely, weak or limited equalization is bound to act as a centralization force. With few exceptions, federations typically feature some form of equalization scheme, although with fairly wide variations in program details.

Among the many possible brands of equalization, it is probably fair to say that Canada picked a complex one. Equalization payments are based on detailed calculations that involve modelling the tax system of a "representative" province. The Equalization Program compensates provinces whose tax bases included in the calculations yield a tax capacity that falls short of a national standard (currently the ten-province average). This process is, in essence, how the program has functioned historically – let us refer to it as the "traditional" or "formula-based" functioning of the program.

Hence, the equalization payment that a province can expect at a given point in time depends on an array of fiscal variables. Five tax bases and their associated tax rates (for four of them) currently make up the "representative tax system" (RTS): personal income, corporate income, sales, property, and natural resources. A different approach is followed for natural resources, with fiscal capacity evaluated using actual resource revenues.

At the heart of forecasting equalization payments lies the ability to forecast these fiscal variables, some of which are more prone to fluctuations than others (natural resource revenues, for instance). Each, in turn, may involve forecasting countless economic and demographic variables. Population data play a special role in these calculations since tax capacity deficiencies are computed on a per capita basis, such that equalization payments to a province depend on population estimates.

The Equalization Program's inherent complexity has pros and cons. On the bright side, it features a sophistication that allows, through the RTS, for a rather detailed account of provincial fiscal practices. But that approach also has drawbacks. First, the large number of parameters involved, and the often non-trivial interactions among them, imply that the program has had an inherent tendency to display high variability in the short run. Since 2007, payments made to provinces have followed a three-year weighted average of two-year lagged data to attenuate that problem and smooth payments over time. Second, complexity raises transparency issues, which, some have argued (Kotsogiannis and Schwager 2008; Joanis 2018), creates room for political games. The experience of the past two decades lends support to that conjecture.

While many parameters have changed over time (for example, there used to be thirty-three tax bases before that was simplified to five in 2007; the standard once was a two-province or a five-province average; and so on),[1] a key aspect of the traditional approach (alluded to previously) had been the program's aim to fully compensate tax capacity deficiencies regardless of the aggregate amount being paid to all receiving provinces. The traditional functioning thus implies that, with reference to the federal purse, the Equalization Program tends to be more costly when horizontal (across provinces) fiscal imbalance is higher and cheaper when that imbalance is lower.

However, with a brief hiatus in the mid-2000s following the tabling of the O'Brien report (EPETFF 2006), the main thread of the Equalization Program has been the federal government's ability to isolate itself from cost pressures associated with widening horizontal fiscal imbalance, accomplished by imposing a cap on the overall annual cost of the program, thus adding an additional layer of complexity to an already complex formula. With the cap in place, the program may not fully compensate receiving provinces' deficiencies in tax capacity.

Further ad hoc tweaks have been introduced over time. The main equalization formula considers only 50 per cent of natural resource revenues, but a province can elect to have its payments calculated based on 100 per cent of these revenues. There is also an "individual" cap on a province's payments that applies should that province end up with a post-equalization fiscal capacity above that of a non-receiving province. The result, it can be argued, while still founded on the traditional approach (as revamped in 2006 by the O'Brien taskforce), at times looks more like a makeshift of add-ons introduced progressively than a genuine formula-based program. All in all, forecasting equalization payments is a tour de force, let alone predicting the effect that specific economic trends will have on a province's equalization payments in the future.

This chapter approaches equalization from the perspective of long-time receiving provinces. What does it mean to rely on such a revenue source? To what extent are payments variable from year to year? And, related, how hard is it to forecast future payments from such a complex program? To provide elements of answers to these questions, the chapter focuses on the five provinces that have continuously received equalization payments over the long run: the three Maritime provinces, Manitoba, and Quebec. Data from the last twenty years are considered in addition to analysis of provincial budget documents. Section 2 briefly surveys previous analyses of the issue by researchers and the provinces, with section 3 taking an in-depth look at budget language pertaining to equalization in Prince Edward Island (PEI) budgets. Section 4 turns to the numbers, with a focus on annual variations and the annual budget cycle. Section 5 extends the analysis beyond the annual budget cycle to discuss the emerging issue of medium-run fiscal plans. Some concluding remarks are given in section 6.

2. Previous Analyses of the Issue by Researchers and the Provinces

Research

A limited literature is concerned with revenue forecasts at the subnational level, let alone the specific issues raised by federal transfers. Two notable Canadian contributions are Couture and Imbeau (2009) and Robson and Omran (2020).

Robson and Omran (2020) is the latest (at the time of writing) in a series of annual assessments of the accuracy of federal and provincial budget forecasts conducted by the C.D. Howe Institute. Interestingly, provinces that are most dependent on federal transfers are the "best" at forecasting their revenue overall. While Robson and Omran's analysis does not allow for a disaggregation by revenue source, the authors note: "Not surprisingly, provinces with economies more oriented towards natural-resource industries, which are more cyclical, volatile, and benefited from better-than-expected demand and prices during most years in this period, recorded the largest overshoots" (6).

While the role played by natural resources is not directly tested by Couture and Imbeau's (2009) analysis of the determinants of provinces' revenue forecast errors, the broader issue of economic uncertainty emerges as the dominant force in their regression results. Unsurprisingly, annual gross domestic product (GDP) growth is negatively correlated with budget forecast errors (leading to underestimation of actual revenues). That result is consistent with all international papers that the authors cite in their comprehensive literature review, which includes papers on the United States, Britain, and Sweden. Their results for the 1994–2004 period suggest a positive correlation between provincial "dependency on transfers" (transfers as a share of provincial revenue) and revenue overestimation: "Provincial governments seemed to be optimistic vis-à-vis the possibility of the federal government increasing its transfers, which was the pervasive issue in provincial-federal relations at the time. Thus, expecting an improvement in federal transfers, more dependent provinces tended to overestimate their revenues" (164).

While not dealing with equalization forecasts per se, a closely related literature is concerned by the stabilization properties of equalization. In the Canadian context, Boadway and Hayashi (2004) empirically show that the equalization formula in place at the time tended to increase the variability of provincial revenues, at least for some revenue sources. Both the forecasting and stabilization issues are discussed in an annex to the O'Brien report.[2] Finally and more generally, this chapter is related to the literature that studies the politics of Canadian fiscal federalism and federal-provincial negotiations (see, for example, Lecours and Béland 2010; Esselment 2013; Rioux Ouimet 2014; Jametti and Joanis 2020; Joanis 2018).

Provinces

The specific issue addressed in this chapter, the variability of equalization payments and the difficulty to forecast them, occupied a central place in the fiscal imbalance debate of the early 2000s. The final report of Quebec's Commission on Fiscal Imbalance (2002) is perhaps the quintessential testament of the spirit of the times. Also called the Séguin Commission after its president, Yves Séguin, the commission's report devotes a few pages to the issue (96–9, English translation). It underscores a central concern: "It is difficult for the provinces that by definition are less affluent and whose overall revenue often depends to a significant extent on payments under this program to manage such erratic changes" (97).

According to the commission's analysis, three factors explained the variability of equalization around the turn of the millennium:

1 *The formula*: "It is normal that business cycles and changes in the economic situation affect equalization entitlements and payments."
2 *Data revisions*: "The second factor in the variability of equalization, namely the mechanics of revising data, is much more difficult to accept." The report details the revision process of Quebec's equalization entitlements for 1997–8 in its Table 16: from $3,878 million in the first estimate in February 1997, entitlements had risen to $4,745 million by September 2000's final estimate, a 22 per cent increase.
3 *Policy changes*: "Completely unexpected technical changes can also add to the uncertainty." (Commission on Fiscal Imbalance 2002, 98)

The report speaks of "spectacular variations" (98) and of payments that "vary widely over time" (96). In the decade leading to the Séguin Commission, equalization payments to Quebec had displayed year-over-year variations as high as 28.8 per cent in 2000–1 and as low as 18.5 per cent the year before (97, chart 36). According to the commission, this variability was not a minor issue: "When such variability is caused not by the economic situation but by deficiencies in revision or calculation methods, it is clearly unacceptable" (99). The commission's conclusion regarding the variability of equalization read as follows: "The brutal increases and reductions announced at regular intervals by the government that administers the program and attributable to more or less obscure calculations or estimates place the recipient provinces in a difficult position. The Commission sees this as a technical problem, as well as a lack of transparency in the calculations" (99).

Quebec was not the only province to complain about the unpredictability of equalization payments at the time. Similar arguments found their way into various provincial budgets of the era and into subsequent documents produced by the Council of the Federation and others. As a rather representative example of this issue, the next section uses PEI budgets as a case study of the evolution of budget language related to equalization over time.

3. Budget Language on Equalization: PEI as a Case Study

As the province that benefits the most from equalization per capita, PEI provides an interesting case study on how the province engages with the challenges of public finances that are highly dependent on equalization. Language used in the province's budgets provides a lively account of these challenges and their evolution over time.

In the early 2000s, equalization receipts in PEI varied widely. They decreased by as much as 15.3 per cent in 2002–3, only to increase in a similar fashion in 2004–5 (15.6 per cent). On average, the annual variation in absolute value reached 7.8 per cent between 2002–3 and 2006–7. Within the one-year budget cycle, the annual variation in absolute value reached 6.4 per cent over the same period.[3]

In her budget tabled 26 March 2002, PEI's Finance Minister Patricia J. Mella (Progressive Conservative) was especially critical of equalization's jumpiness, carefully documenting its sources:

Madam Speaker, the Federal Government provides provinces with revised estimates of their equalization entitlements twice a year. These federal estimates fluctuate widely from estimate to estimate with the result that we have learned to use our own information in an *effort to more reliably predict our revenues and plan for the future*. (PEI 2002, 5; emphasis added)

Madam Speaker, Members may recall that in January of this year provinces were unexpectedly informed of the misallocation of federal income tax to some provinces that resulted from a *federal accounting error* in the administration of capital

Living on Equalization Payments 137

gains tax from Mutual Fund Trusts. We were informed that this resulted in an estimated overpayment of Equalization to us of some $6 million. Madam Speaker, we still have received no indication of how this will impact on our Equalization in the coming year. (PEI 2002, 8; emphasis added)

The population numbers from the 2001 Census have just been released, and Madam Speaker, they also have potentially large impacts on major federal transfers. On top of these challenges, all provinces continue to have serious disagreements with our federal friends over the ceiling on Equalization and the inadequacy of the CHST transfer. (PEI 2002, 8; emphasis added)

We estimate that our Equalization payments will be considerably below their 2001–2002 level and that *calculation is highly uncertain*. Still, the Federal Government insists on applying a *ceiling* to payments. In addition, other federal transfers are clouded in uncertainty. (PEI 2002, 9; emphasis added)

In her last budget, Minister Mella continued on the same theme: "Madam Speaker, I noted a year ago that many aspects of our Provincial Budget are subject to *the policies and complexities of federal programming*" (PEI 2003, 3; emphasis added). Interestingly, Minister Mella highlighted the consequences of equalization's unpredictable behaviour:

Madam Speaker, while this is good news for the provincial finances in 2002, Equalization was a serious problem. Equalization, our largest revenue, was budgeted to be $255 million in 2002–2003, down by $27 million from the previous year. *It was largely because of this expected fall in revenue that we introduced the Workforce Adjustment Program, reduced programming in some areas and implemented significant reductions in the capital budget.* These measures were undertaken to reduce current costs and contain costs for the future. (PEI 2003, 6; emphasis added)

Madam Speaker, it is evident that the Equalization program remains a serious problem for the Province. It is easily our largest revenue source, it is very volatile, and it is very difficult to predict. *Frankly, it makes Budgeting on Prince Edward Island a nightmare.* (PEI 2003, 7; emphasis added)

Some progress, however, was acknowledged:

Madam Speaker, I am pleased to say that we have achieved some success already. The ceiling that was imposed on Equalization in 1982 will be permanently removed. This was announced by the Prime Minister on February 5, 2003 at the time of the First Ministers' Health discussions. (PEI 2003, 8)

Mitch Murphy (Progressive Conservative) took over essentially the same rhetoric in 2004:

> Mr. Speaker, I am convinced that our present fiscal arrangement with the Federal Government is significantly flawed, and this is the major contributor to our fiscal challenges. The current federal/provincial dispute on fiscal imbalance was triggered by the 1995 Federal Budget, which was the centre-piece of Ottawa's strategy for restoring federal public finances. (PEI 2004a, 2)

> We have been told by the Federal Government that they will take steps to lessen the volatility and improve the stability of transfer payments. If this is the case, it will be helpful in managing the provincial budget. (PEI 2004a, 3)

As part of a reminder of provincial demands for the 2004 renewal of the fiscal arrangements, Minister Murphy noted:

> We wanted measures incorporated to reduce the volatility of entitlements and to allow for improved ability to predict payments. (PEI 2004a, 3)

> The Federal Government claims that a move to a ten province standard is not affordable. It is difficult to accept this argument. (PEI 2004a, 4)

> Provinces are concerned with the destabilizing effect on provincial finances of substantial and unpredictable fluctuations in Equalization revenues, caused by data shocks and methodological changes to tax bases that often have multi-year impacts. Provinces and territories proposed remedial measures in consultation with the Federal Government that also reflects the principles of adequacy, accuracy and responsiveness to changing fiscal circumstances.
>
> Receiving provinces have witnessed significant volatility in their Equalization revenue in recent years and Prince Edward Island has felt this volatility more acutely than others. *Equalization is the province's largest revenue source and it is also its most volatile, making budget targets difficult to reach.*
>
> The federal proposal is to base payments on a three-year moving average. This measure will be phased-in to have full effect in 2007–08. When fully implemented, payments to provinces will be delayed by two years on average compared to the current system ... Prince Edward Island supported the need to improve the predictability of entitlements. However, we feel that the federal proposal to stabilize payments by simply averaging entitlements from previous years does not address the underlying volatility of the program. (PEI 2004b, Budget Paper B, 6–7)

The following year, the 2005 budget acknowledged significant progress on the equalization front:

> The upshot of these difficult negotiations is that significant improvements in federal transfers through Equalization and Health transfers were accomplished in the past year. (PEI 2005a, 3)

> The new framework provides financial certainty to provinces for two years and prescribes the total amount of Equalization in future. Provinces could face major changes to their entitlements depending on the recommendations by the expert panel concerning allocation. Prince Edward Island is the most dependant province on Equalization revenue and has the most at risk from changes to the allocation of Equalization beyond 2005-06. (PEI 2005b, Budget Paper B, 7)

> The new framework for Equalization and the concessions that were made to provinces with natural resources have resulted in large variations in fiscal capacities among equalization receiving provinces, in favour of provinces with large natural resource revenues. (PEI 2005b, Budget Paper B, 7)

In what would be the final budget of PEI's Progressive Conservative government, Minister Murphy commented on the consequences of the election of a Conservative government in Ottawa:

> During the Federal election campaign, Prime Minister Harper committed that PEI would be no worse off than it would be with the current legislation. Our budget number of $286.2 million reflects that fact. The Province looks forward to the reports of two task forces established to review the equalization formula. (PEI 2006a, 5)

> Large swings in program payments resulting from revised estimates of fiscal capacity spanning several years can play havoc on provincial budgets. PEI supports measures that improve predictability of payments. (PEI 2006b, Budget Paper B, 2)

Despite the election of a Liberal government in PEI in 2007, there was a clear toning down of the rhetoric on equalization from the 2007 budget onwards. It is not before his third budget, in 2009, that Wesley J. Sheridan (Liberal) raised significant criticisms on the Equalization Program:

> Madame Speaker, the Government of Prince Edward Island is concerned that the Federal restraint that was imposed on equalization will unduly restrict this revenue source in future years. I will continue to press this concern with my Federal counterpart. (PEI 2009, 32)

In 2011, the topic of equalization returned again to Minister Sheridan's budget address:

> Our challenges, Madame Speaker, are being compounded by unilateral and, we believe, unfair reductions in core federal transfers, notably Equalization ... Federal measures taken in 2009, including an artificial ceiling on the Equalization program, are denying our Province any year-over-year increase in revenues, costing us over $51 million to date. (PEI 2011, 5)

Additional concerns were again raised in the 2012 budget:

> Currently, Madame Speaker, we believe that some decisions taken by the Federal Government are causing the program to fall short of its constitutional obligation. (PEI 2012, 10)

> Madame Speaker, on several occasions I have expressed my concern to the Federal Minister that Prince Edward Island is more severely affected by restraints on the Equalization program than any other province. (PEI 2012, 11)

Interestingly, complaints regarding equalization are seldom found in PEI budgets after 2012. Overall, these excerpts from PEI budgets collected above provide a revealing (though province specific) timeline of the main issues that have been raised over the past two decades by equalization-receiving provinces. The next section turns to the analysis of equalization revenue data for the five provinces targeted by this study.

4. The Numbers: Annual Variations and the Annual Budget Cycle

Data Sources and Calculations

Provincial budget documents are the primary source of both text and data for this chapter. To facilitate data collection, various editions of the (now discontinued) annual monograph *Finances of the Nation* by the Canadian Tax Foundation have been used (Treff and Perry 2002–12). These monographs featured annual summaries of provincial budgets, which now continue as a feature in the *Canadian Tax Journal* (Morgan 2014–19; Lin 2020). Finance Canada public data have also been used to confirm final figures and details (add-ons, adjustments, and so on) in some years.

Year-Over-Year Fluctuations

Over the past two decades, equalization payments received by individual provinces have displayed significant year-over-year fluctuations (Figure 7.1). In percentage terms, the highest yearly absolute-value variation in payments was to Quebec from 2006 to 2007 (+29.3 per cent).

Overall, these data reveal four phases:

1 *2001–3*: The 2000 decade opened with declining equalization payments, featuring most of the biggest yearly declines of the period, reaching 23.5 per cent for Quebec in 2003, 15.3 per cent for PEI in 2002, 14.8 per cent for Nova Scotia also in 2002, 9.4 per cent for New Brunswick in 2003, and 3.8 per cent for Manitoba in 2002. Only three provinces experienced one yearly increase over these three years (New Brunswick, Manitoba, and PEI).
2 *2004–9*: Compensating the previous period's decline, the second phase of the 2000 decade saw the highest yearly increases of the period, reaching 29.3 per cent for Quebec in 2007, 28.1 per cent for New Brunswick in 2004, 20.1 per cent for Manitoba also in 2004, 18.4 per cent for Nova Scotia again in 2004, and 15.6 per cent for PEI in 2004. Over that period, only in 2005 were there some yearly declines (for four out of the five provinces).
3 *2010–16*: The post–financial crisis period marked the return of yearly declines for the five core receiving provinces mainly because of the GDP cap and Ontario's economic woes. With the ceiling provisions in place, Ontario's payments came at the expense of other receiving provinces in a sort of zero-sum game.[4]
4 *2017–21*: With Ontario not qualifying for payments during that period, all five core receiving provinces experienced significant increases in equalization payments.

Forecasting Errors over the Annual Budget Cycle

A major issue in the 1990s and early 2000s, short-run forecasting of equalization payments became mostly trivial after 2007 following the O'Brien report, as can be seen from Figure 7.2. While "forecasting errors"[5] within the one-year budget cycle could still be as high as 20 per cent in absolute value in 2004, they were lower on average in the following three years. After 2007, where one-year forecasting errors were non-zero in Quebec (10.8 per cent underestimation) and New Brunswick (2.9 per cent underestimation), forecasting errors fell to zero in most years for most provinces. This decline is a consequence of the federal government routinely announcing transfer payments to each province in December for the upcoming fiscal year, thus allowing provinces to incorporate the numbers in their budgets usually tabled in the spring. Two noteworthy exceptions are Quebec in 2011–12 and 2013–14, and Nova Scotia over the 2011–19 period.

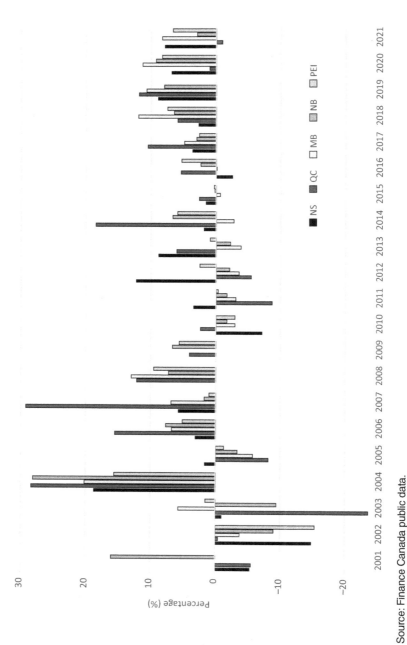

Figure 7.1. Year-Over-Year Change in Equalization Payments to the Five Core Beneficiaries, 2001–21

Source: Finance Canada public data.
Note: MB = Manitoba; NB = New Brunswick; NS = Nova Scotia; PEI = Prince Edward Island; QC = Quebec.

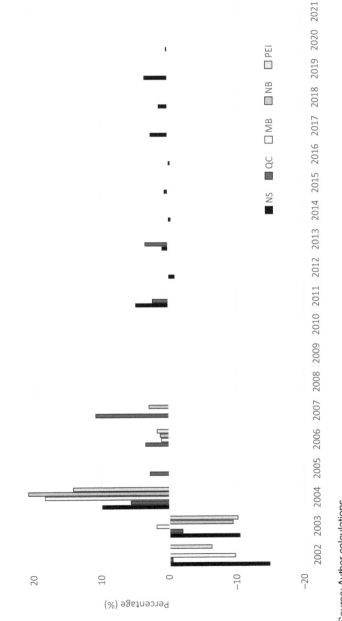

Figure 7.2. Forecasting Error: Overestimation (−) or Underestimation (+) for Fiscal Years in Provincial Budgets

Source: Author calculations.
Note: MB = Manitoba; NB = New Brunswick; NS = Nova Scotia; PEI = Prince Edward Island; QC = Quebec.

Quebec did receive Total Transfer Protection (TTP) payments in 2011–12 and in 2012–13. As described by Finance Canada, TTP ensures that "total major transfers[6] in one of these years are no lower than in the prior year." Quebec's revision of its equalization payments between its budgets of 2011 and 2012 was related to revisions by Finance Canada of the breakdown between Quebec's equalization and TTP payments for that year. Quebec's *Plan budgétaire 2012–2013* describes the adjustment that was made, which is linked to a Statistics Canada error (Quebec 2012, C.22).[7] For 2013–14, the forecasting error was due to the decision by a newly elected minority government to anticipate the tabling of the 2013–14 budget to 20 November 2012. As a consequence, a spring fiscal update had to be tabled, in which equalization payments were revised upwards by $255 million. This revision is justified in details in *Le point sur la situation économique et financière du Québec – Printemps 2013* (Quebec 2013, B.14).[8]

The case of Nova Scotia is more intricate. Within the budget cycle, forecasting errors started to creep back in with the 2011–12 fiscal year, coinciding with the year that the province started to receive Cumulative Best-of Guarantee (CBOG) payments. The 2012 budget described the situation as follows: "The 'guarantee' essentially ensures that the province will do no worse under the Equalization formula put in place in 2007–2008 than it would under the formula in place when the Offshore Accord was signed in 2005 – the 'Interim' approach. The Guarantee is in effect from 2008–2009 to the end of 2019–2020, to coincide with the term of the Offshore Accord" (Nova Scotia 2012, 1.10). The 2019 budget offered some additional background: "As part of a clarification reached with the Government of Canada on October 10, 2007, commencing with the 2008–09 fiscal year, Nova Scotia is entitled to receive an additional payment from the federal government if the cumulative value of the Equalization formula in effect at the time the Offshore Accord was signed (the Interim approach) exceeds the cumulative value of the Expert Panel approach" (Nova Scotia 2019, 30).

The CBOG mechanism created uncertainty in the short run, leading to the within-budget-cycle forecasting errors observed for Nova Scotia. For instance, the 2020 budget revisions are described as follows: "Federal Source Ordinary Revenues are forecast to be $56.4 million higher than the 2019–20 Budget Estimates, primarily resulting from a decrease in the Cumulative Best-of Guarantee payment of $66.4 million" (Nova Scotia 2020, 18) This amount fully explains the increase in equalization payments between the budget estimate and the final numbers for 2019–20. As mentioned in the previous year's 2019 budget, the "second and final estimate for the value of the 2019–20 payment will be made by the federal government in March 2020" (Nova Scotia 2019, 31). Thus, over the CBOG period, Nova Scotia's final equalization payments were not known before the beginning of the fiscal year.

In the 2021–2 budget (Nova Scotia 2021), for the first time in a decade, there was no revision to the previous budget's equalization estimate (that is, 2020–1), as the CBOG ended on 31 March 2020.

5. Beyond the Annual Budget Cycle: The Emerging Issue of Medium-Run Fiscal Plans

The data analysed in the previous section reveal that the introduction of the O'Brien formula in the mid-2000s has somewhat decreased the volatility of equalization payments from the point of view of receiving provinces, the data showing less extreme variations. The use of lagged data has also solved, with exceptions, the uncertainty that previously existed within the annual budget cycle.

Over the same period, however, many provinces have followed the advice of international organizations, such as the International Monetary Fund (IMF) and the Organisation for Economic Co-operation and Development (OECD), and introduced pluriannual fiscal planning. The core equalization-receiving provinces have experimented with medium-term fiscal plans at different points in time.

Quebec

Unlike most provinces, Quebec has for quite some time presented a detailed budget forecast a year in advance, that is, a forecast for fiscal year t in budget t-1, which means that data for three fiscal years are published in budget documents (and even five years for some aggregates; Quebec 2022).

This reporting practice allows us to analyse Quebec's forecasting performance with respect to next fiscal year's equalization revenues. The data plotted in Figure 7.3 again reveal a striking difference before and after 2009. The 2005–8 period displays underestimation of next year's equalization revenues in the 20 to 30 per cent range, peaking at 29.2 per cent in 2007–8. That era of large "positive surprises" every year was followed, between 2009 and 2013, by an era of mostly negative surprises – especially for fiscal year 2012–13 (−8.1 per cent). Positive surprises returned from 2014 to 2018, with three years above 5 per cent. The most recent period reveals three small negative surprises.

Since the 2018 election, Quebec has gone further by adopting the practice of pre-electoral reports audited by the province's auditor general. Interestingly, the 2018 report does provide a four-year forecast of equalization payments. Quebec's auditor general's opinion on that particular forecast (Vérificateur géneral du Québec 2018, 25) highlights a high degree of uncertainty due to the program's inherent complexity (*"les prévisions de la péréquation sont*

Figure 7.3. Revisions to the Quebec Budget *t*-1 Estimate for Fiscal Year *t* – Overestimation (−) or Underestimation (+)

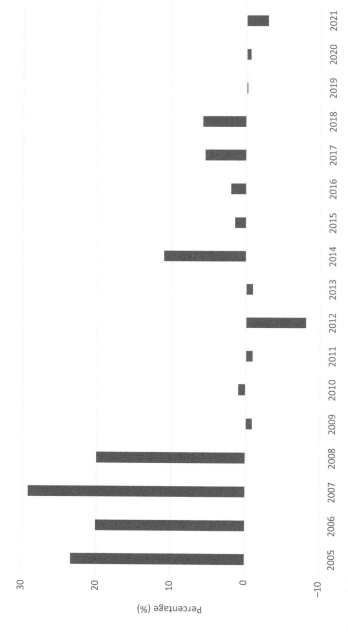

Source: Author calculations.

empreintes d'un degré d'incertitude élevé en raison de la complexité inhérente de ce programme"). She also notes the risk associated with the importance of population data in the calculations (*"vu l'importance de la variable population dans le calcul, il y a un risque que les prévisions soient modifiées"*; 27). The discretionary nature of the Total Transfer Protection is also flagged as a risk to the forecast.[9]

Nova Scotia

For a long continuous period, Nova Scotia has had a four-year fiscal plan, updated annually in the budget. While no distinct projection of federal transfers is provided, the budget texts typically provide indications related to the medium-run prospects for equalization. Here are a few examples, from the 2011 budget onwards:

- *2011*: "Equalization payments are expected to rise over the next few years, and the province is forecasting the receipt of Cumulative Best-of Guarantee payments during this period, as well. Reductions in federal trusts and declining Offshore Accord payments will partially offset increases" (Nova Scotia 2011, 1.7).
- *2012*: "Over the past three fiscal years, Equalization payments have been supported by Total Transfer Protection from the federal government to mitigate year-over-year declines in the total value of major federal transfers – Equalization, Canada Health Transfer, and Canada Social Transfer. The Equalization program is scheduled to be renewed in 2014–2015" (Nova Scotia 2012, 1.10).
- *2013*: "Growth in revenues from the equalization program is expected to be relatively strong over the next few years. This can be attributed to the growth in the size of the overall program – the 3-year average growth rate in national nominal GDP – as well as the impact of the province's reduced offshore natural resource revenues on the calculation of entitlements. In 2011–2012, the province began receiving payments under the Cumulative Best-of Guarantee. The province is forecast to continue to receive significant annual payments over the medium term. While significant, these payments are projected to gradually decline over the medium term as the Expert Panel approach formula is currently expected to grow faster than the Interim approach formula" (Nova Scotia 2013, 1.6–1.7).
- *2014 to 2016*: "Growth in federal transfer revenues will remain relatively flat for the foreseeable future, primarily as a result of the province's declining share of the national population and lower revenues for the offshore accord and cumulative best-of guarantee payments" (Nova Scotia 2014, 5; 2015, 6; 2016, 9).

Every year, the risks associated with the forecasts are also listed in the Nova Scotia budget. Risks pertaining to equalization have been described in that section of the budget over time in the following manner:

- *2002–4*: "Changes in data as it relates to 33 different tax bases; changes in population; economic activity in NS versus the standard provinces" (Nova Scotia 2002, A21; 2003, A20; 2004, A22).
- *2005–6*: "Equalization is fixed; no adjustment to the estimate" (Nova Scotia 2005, A19; 2006, B26).
- *2007*: "Fixed by the federal government" (Nova Scotia 2007, B20).
- *2008 onwards*: "One-estimate one-payment approach" (Nova Scotia 2008, 3.14; 2009, 3.15; 2010, 3.16; 2011, 3.15; 2012, 3.17; 2013, 3.13; 2014, 34; 2015, 40; 2016, 40; 2017, 42; 2018, 42; 2019, 39; 2020, 39; 2021, 41).

Other Provinces

In his 2010 budget, PEI Finance Minister Wesley J. Sheridan introduced the notion of a "four-year fiscal plan" towards a return to budget balance in connection with fixed-date elections and pre-election audited financial statements (PEI 2010, 5). In New Brunswick, a three-year forecast was provided in the 2014 pre-election report (New Brunswick 2014). In both of these cases, detailed breakdown of federal transfer projection was not provided.

What is made clear by the rise of provincial medium-term budget planning is that, while the "one-payment one-estimate" approach does solve most short-run issues (less than one year), reliable medium- and long-term projections of federal transfers will be increasingly needed. Within this context, the Equalization Program's variability remains a significant concern for receiving provinces in their ability to anticipate future trends in payments from the federal government.

6. Conclusion

Why do equalization payments vary? First and foremost, equalization payments vary because they are quite simply meant to. An equalization program must be responsive to the varying economic fortunes of provinces. Yet, payments are also affected by how the various data that feed the formula are treated and updated over time. And the program is in constant evolution, with changes being made to the formula quasi-continuously. Thus, for provinces, there exists uncertainty about the future evolution of transfers.

In recent decades, the federal government has succeeded in isolating itself to a large extent from unexpected pressures related to federal transfers. In particular, the equalization envelope doesn't fluctuate with the degree of horizontal fiscal imbalance anymore.

But from the provinces' point of view, do we now have better predictability of the program? The analysis of this chapter has shown that the predictability issue of the early 2000s has changed in nature but is still present, although in a different form. Forecasting equalization remains a challenge for any projection exercise that extends beyond the one-year horizon.

The complexity of the RTS approach and the multiple tweaks and add-ons that appear and disappear over time are the main culprits here. While the RTS is desirable in principle, history shows that it appears hard to sustain for technical and political reasons. Would a macro approach work better? In Joanis (2018), I focused on the political economy aspects of federal transfers (including Equalization). My conclusion was as follows: "Transfer programs appear to have become a more politically charged topic in recent years. Political pressures are constantly exerted on the federal government by both the electorate and the provinces, periodically leading to ad hoc changes to the fiscal arrangements. All could arguably gain from a less political and more rational approach to the fiscal arrangements" (685). The kind of policy uncertainty that is a byproduct of such political bargains is one force behind the variability documented in this chapter. Some of the policy options surveyed in the conclusion to Joanis (2018) – an independent body for managing the fiscal arrangements, pre-funding the Equalization Program, a macro approach to replace the RTS – are all worthy of further analysis in terms of variability and predictability.

NOTES

1 See Joanis (2018) for a comprehensive list of changes to the Equalization Program in the twenty-first century. In Joanis and Vaillancourt (2020), we provide more details on the specifics of Canada's federal-provincial programs, including Equalization.
2 EPETFF (2006), Annex 8: Improving Predictability and Stability.
3 See section 4 for more details on these calculations and results for other provinces.
4 Ontario received its first equalization payments in 2009–10, and its share of the program's total envelope eventually reached around 20 per cent.
5 "Forecasting errors" are everywhere presented based on the following calculation: Forecast error (per cent) = (Real − Forecast) / Forecast x 100. These numbers allow for an interpretation in terms of positive or negative fiscal "surprises" after a forecast has been formulated.
6 "Total major transfers comprise Equalization, Canada Health Transfer, Canada Social Transfer and prior year Total Transfer Protection" (Finance Canada, n.d.).

7 "Au budget du 17 mars 2011, le Québec a inscrit des montants de 7 639 M$ en péréquation et de 545 M$ désignés comme un paiement de protection pour l'année 2011-2012, tel que le gouvernement fédéral l'avait annoncé aux provinces en décembre 2010. Le 21 mars 2011, le gouvernement fédéral a informé le Québec qu'il corrigeait une erreur de Statistique Canada par rapport à l'année 2011-2012 : le paiement de péréquation au Québec a donc été augmenté de 176 M$, pour atteindre 7 815 M$, alors que le paiement de protection a été diminué du même montant, à 369 M$" (Quebec 2012, C.22).

8 "Pour 2013-2014, la révision s'explique essentiellement par une révision à la hausse de 255 millions de dollars des paiements de péréquation annoncée par le gouvernement fédéral en décembre 2012 par rapport à ce qui avait été prévu au budget de novembre 2012. Cette révision positive résulte, entre autres, d'une amélioration de la situation économique de l'Ontario, qui vient augmenter sa capacité fiscale relative, ce qui se traduit par des gains de péréquation pour les autres provinces bénéficiaires. De 2009-2010 à 2011-2012, la part de l'Ontario à l'assiette de l'impôt sur le revenu des sociétés a connu une hausse significative. Dans le cadre de la péréquation, cette amélioration relative profite aux autres provinces bénéficiaires, dont le Québec" (Quebec 2013, B.14).

9 "En vertu de la loi, lorsque la somme des versements de péréquation effectués aux provinces bénéficiaires est inférieure à l'enveloppe totale de l'année précédente, indexée selon la moyenne de croissance du PIB nominal canadien, le fédéral peut verser un montant de rajustement. Ce choix étant discrétionnaire, il y a un risque que ces montants de rajustement ne soient pas versés" (Vérificateur général du Québec 2018, 27).

REFERENCES

Boadway, Robin, and Masayoshi Hayashi. 2004. "An Evaluation of the Stabilization Properties of Equalization in Canada." *Canadian Public Policy/Analyse de Politiques* 30, no. 1: 91–109. https://doi.org/10.2307/3552582.

Commission on Fiscal Imbalance. 2002. *A New Division of Canada's Financial Resources (Final Report)*. Quebec: Government of Quebec. https://www.groupes.finances.gouv.qc.ca/desequilibrefiscal/en/pdf/rapport_final_en.pdf.

Couture, Jérôme, and Louis M. Imbeau. 2009. "Do Governments Manipulate Their Revenue Forecasts? Budget Speech and Budget Outcomes in the Canadian Provinces." In *Do They Walk Like They Talk? Speech and Action in Policy Processes*, edited by Louis M. Imbeau, 155–66. New York: Springer-Verlag.

EPETFF (Expert Panel on Equalization and Territorial Formula Financing). 2006. *Achieving National Purpose: Putting Equalization Back on Track*. Ottawa: Department of Finance Canada. https://publications.gc.ca/collections/Collection/F2-176-2006E.pdf.

Esselment, Anna Lennox. 2013. "A Little Help from My Friends: The Partisan Factor and Intergovernmental Negotiations in Canada." *Publius: The Journal of Federalism* 43, no. 4: 701–27. https://doi.org/10.1093/publius/pjs041.

Finance Canada. n.d. "Federal Transfers to Provinces and Territories." Ottawa: Finance Canada. https://www.canada.ca/en/department-finance/programs/federal-transfers.html.

Jametti, Mario, and Marcelin Joanis. 2020. "Elections and *de facto* Expenditure Decentralization in Canada." *Economics of Governance* 21 no. 3: 275–97. https://doi.org/10.1007/s10101-020-00241-8.

Joanis, Marcelin. 2018. "The Politics of Chequebook Federalism: Can Electoral Considerations Affect Federal-Provincial Transfers?" *Public Finance Review* 46, no. 4: 665–91. https://doi.org/10.1177/1091142116679728.

Joanis, Marcelin, and François Vaillancourt. 2020. "Federal Finance Arrangements in Canada: The Challenges of Fiscal Imbalance and Natural Resource Rents." In *Intergovernmental Transfers in Federations*, edited by Farah Zahir and Serdar Yilmaz. Cheltenham, UK: Edward Elgar Publishing.

Kotsogiannis, Christos, and Robert Schwager. 2008. "Accountability and Fiscal Equalization." *Journal of Public Economics* 92, no. 12: 2336–49. https://doi.org/10.1016/j.jpubeco.2007.12.013.

Lecours, André, and Daniel Béland. 2010. "Federalism and Fiscal Policy: The Politics of Equalization in Canada." *Publius: The Journal of Federalism* 40 no. 4: 569–96. https://doi.org/10.1093/publius/pjp030.

Lin, David. 2020. "Finances of the Nation: Survey of Provincial and Territorial Budgets, 2019–20." *Canadian Tax Journal* 68, no. 1: 185–250. https://doi.org/10.32721/ctj.2020.68.1.fon.

Morgan, Vivien. 2014–2019. "Finances of the Nation: Survey of Provincial and Territorial Budgets." *Canadian Tax Journal.*

New Brunswick. 2014. *Pre-Election Economic and Fiscal Outlook, 2014–15 to 2017–18.* Fredericton, NB: Department of Finance. https://www2.gnb.ca/content/dam/gnb/Departments/fin/pdf/Publications/PreElectionEconomicAndFiscalOutlook.pdf.

Nova Scotia. 2002. *Nova Scotia Budget for the Fiscal Year 2002–2003.* Halifax: Government of Nova Scotia. https://beta.novascotia.ca/sites/default/files/documents/budget-archive/Budget-2002-Budget-Address.pdf.

– 2003. *Nova Scotia Budget for the Fiscal Year 2003–2004.* Halifax: Government of Nova Scotia. https://beta.novascotia.ca/sites/default/files/documents/budget-archive/Budget-2003-Budget-Address.pdf.

– 2004. *Nova Scotia Budget for the Fiscal Year 2004–2005.* Halifax: Government of Nova Scotia. https://beta.novascotia.ca/sites/default/files/documents/budget-archive/Budget-2004-Budget-Address.pdf.

– 2005. *Nova Scotia Budget for the Fiscal Year 2005–2006.* Halifax: Government of Nova Scotia. https://beta.novascotia.ca/sites/default/files/documents/budget-archive/Budget-2005-Budget-Address.pdf.

- 2006. *Nova Scotia Budget: Assumptions and Schedules for the Fiscal Year 2006–2007.* Halifax: Government of Nova Scotia. https://beta.novascotia.ca/sites/default/files/documents/budget-archive/Budget-2006-Assumptions-Schedules.pdf.
- 2007. *Nova Scotia Budget: Assumptions and Schedules for the Fiscal Year 2007–2008.* Halifax: Government of Nova Scotia. https://beta.novascotia.ca/sites/default/files/documents/budget-archive/Budget-2007-Assumptions-Schedules.pdf.
- 2008. *Nova Scotia Budget: Assumptions and Schedules for the Fiscal Year 2008–2009.* Halifax: Government of Nova Scotia. https://beta.novascotia.ca/sites/default/files/documents/budget-archive/Budget-2008-Assumptions-Schedules.pdf.
- 2009. *Nova Scotia Budget: Assumptions and Schedules for the Fiscal Year 2009–2010.* Halifax: Government of Nova Scotia. https://beta.novascotia.ca/sites/default/files/documents/budget-archive/Budget-2009-Assumptions-Schedules.pdf.
- 2010. *Budget Assumptions and Schedules for the Fiscal Year 2010–2011.* Halifax: Government of Nova Scotia. https://beta.novascotia.ca/sites/default/files/documents/budget-archive/Budget-2010-Assumptions-And-Schedules.pdf.
- 2011. *Budget Assumptions and Schedules for the Fiscal Year 2011–2012.* Halifax: Government of Nova Scotia. https://beta.novascotia.ca/sites/default/files/documents/budget-archive/Budget-2011-Assumptions-and-Schedules.pdf.
- 2012. *Budget Assumptions and Schedules for the Fiscal Year 2012–2013.* Halifax: Government of Nova Scotia. https://beta.novascotia.ca/sites/default/files/documents/budget-archive/Budget-2012-Budget-Assumptions-And-Schedules.pdf.
- 2013. *Balanced Budget 2013–2014: Budget Assumptions and Schedules for the Fiscal Year 2013–2014.* Halifax: Government of Nova Scotia. https://beta.novascotia.ca/sites/default/files/documents/budget-archive/Budget-2013-Budget-Assumptions-and-Schedules.pdf.
- 2014. *Budget Assumptions and Schedules for the Fiscal Year 2014–2015.* Halifax: Government of Nova Scotia. https://beta.novascotia.ca/sites/default/files/documents/7-803/budget-assumptions-and-schedules.pdf.
- 2015. *Budget Assumptions and Schedules for the Fiscal Year 2015–2016.* Halifax: Government of Nova Scotia. https://beta.novascotia.ca/sites/default/files/documents/7-805/budget-assumptions-and-schedules.pdf.
- 2016. *Budget 2016–2017: Working Together for a Stronger Nova Scotia.* Halifax: Government of Nova Scotia. https://beta.novascotia.ca/sites/default/files/documents/7-810/budget-assumptions-and-schedules.pdf.
- 2017. *Budget 2017–2018: Opportunities for Growth.* Halifax: Government of Nova Scotia. https://beta.novascotia.ca/sites/default/files/documents/6-468/ftb-bfi-033-en-budget-2017-2018.pdf.
- 2018. *Budget 2018–19: Stronger Services and Supports.* Halifax: Government of Nova Scotia. https://beta.novascotia.ca/sites/default/files/documents/6-1293/ftb-bfi-035-en-budget-2018-2019.pdf.
- 2019. *Budget 2019–20.* Halifax: Government of Nova Scotia. https://beta.novascotia.ca/sites/default/files/documents/6-1692/ftb-bfi-039-en-budget-2019-2020.pdf.

Living on Equalization Payments 153

- 2020. *Budget 2020–21: Better Together*. Halifax: Government of Nova Scotia. https://beta.novascotia.ca/sites/default/files/documents/6-2046/ftb-bfi-041-en-budget-2020-2021.pdf.
- 2021. *Budget 2021–22*. Halifax: Government of Nova Scotia. https://beta.novascotia.ca/sites/default/files/documents/6-2635/ftb-bfi-043-en-budget-2021-2022.pdf.

PEI (Prince Edward Island). 2002. "The Budget Address." *Prince Edward Island 2002 Budget: A Balanced Response to Difficult Times*. Presented to the Legislative Assembly of Prince Edward Island, 26 March 2002. https://www.princeedwardisland.ca/sites/default/files/publications/2002_budget_address.pdf.
- 2003. "The Budget Address." *Prince Edward Island 2003 Budget: Fiscal Responsibility in the New Millennium*. Presented to the Legislative Assembly of Prince Edward Island, 10 April 2003. https://www.princeedwardisland.ca/sites/default/files/publications/2003_budget_address.pdf.
- 2004a. "The Budget Address 2004." In *Prince Edward Island 2004 Budget: Working Together for a Secure Tomorrow*. Presented to the Legislative Assembly of Prince Edward Island, 30 March 2004. https://www.princeedwardisland.ca/sites/default/files/publications/2004_budget_address.pdf.
- 2004b. "Budget Paper B: Federal Fiscal Issues." In *Prince Edward Island 2004 Budget: Working Together for a Secure Tomorrow*. Presented to the Legislative Assembly of Prince Edward Island, 30 March 2004. https://www.princeedwardisland.ca/sites/default/files/publications/2004_budget_address.pdf.
- 2005a. "The Budget Address." In *Prince Edward Island 2005 Budget: A Plan to Protect the Priorities of Islanders*. Presented to the Legislative Assembly of Prince Edward Island, 7 April 2005. https://www.princeedwardisland.ca/sites/default/files/publications/2005_budget_address.pdf.
- 2005b. "Budget Paper B: Federal Fiscal Issues." In *Prince Edward Island 2005 Budget: A Plan to Protect the Priorities of Islanders*. Presented to the Legislative Assembly of Prince Edward Island, 7 April 2005. https://www.princeedwardisland.ca/sites/default/files/publications/2005_budget_address.pdf.
- 2006a. "The Budget Address." In *Prince Edward Island 2006 Budget: On Course, On Target*. Presented to the Legislative Assembly of Prince Edward Island, 30 March 2006. https://www.princeedwardisland.ca/sites/default/files/publications/2006_budget_address.pdf.
- 2006b. "Budget Paper B: Federal Fiscal Issues." In *Prince Edward Island 2006 Budget: On Course, On Target*. Presented to the Legislative Assembly of Prince Edward Island, 30 March 2006. https://www.princeedwardisland.ca/sites/default/files/publications/2006_budget_address.pdf.
- 2009. *Prince Edward Island 2009 Budget: Investing in Islanders*. Presented to the Legislative Assembly of Prince Edward Island, 16 April 2009. https://www.princeedwardisland.ca/sites/default/files/publications/2009_budget_address.pdf.
- 2010. *Prince Edward Island 2010 Budget: Securing the Future*. Presented to the Legislative Assembly of Prince Edward Island, 23 April 2010. https://www.princeedwardisland.ca/sites/default/files/publications/2010_budget_address.pdf.

- 2011. *Prince Edward Island Budget Address 2011: Moving Forward Together.* Presented to the Legislative Assembly of Prince Edward Island, 6 April 2011. https://www.princeedwardisland.ca/sites/default/files/publications/2011_budget_address.pdf.
- 2012. *Prince Edward Island Budget Address 2012.* Presented to the Legislative Assembly of Prince Edward Island, 18 April 2012. https://www.princeedwardisland.ca/sites/default/files/publications/2012_budget_address.pdf.

Quebec. 2012. *Plan budgétaire 2012–2013.* Quebec: Government of Quebec. http://www.budget.finances.gouv.qc.ca/Budget/2012-2013/fr/documents/Planbudgetaire.pdf.

- 2013. *Le point sur la situation économique et financière du Québec – Printemps 2013.* Quebec: Government of Quebec. http://www.finances.gouv.qc.ca/documents/Autres/fr/AUTFR_lepoint2013.pdf.
- 2022. "Budget and Update Archive." Government of Quebec. https://www.quebec.ca/en/government/ministere/finances/publications/budget-update.

Rioux Ouimet, Hubert. 2014. "Quebec and Canadian Fiscal Federalism: From Tremblay to Séguin and Beyond." *Canadian Journal of Political Science* 47, no. 1: 47–69. https://doi.org/10.1017/S0008423914000237.

Robson, William B.P., and Farah Omran. 2020. *Busted Budgets: Canada's Senior Governments Can't Stick to Their Fiscal Plans.* Commentary 581. Toronto: C.D. Howe Institute. https://www.cdhowe.org/sites/default/files/2021-12/Commentary_581.pdf.

Treff, Karin, and David B. Perry. 2002–12. *Finances of the Nation.* Toronto: Canadian Tax Foundation.

Vérificateur général du Québec. 2018. *Rapport sur le rapport préélectoral 2018.* Quebec: Vérificateur général du Québec. https://www.vgq.qc.ca/Fichiers/Publications/rapport-preelectoral/2018/fr_Rapport2018-aout2018.pdf.

8 Canadian Fiscal Federalism and the Provinces' Natural Resource Revenues

JAMES FEEHAN

Introduction

Canadian fiscal federalism is complex and multidimensional. There can be sharp disagreement and conflict among its main actors. Provincial governments resent the federal government's discretionary authority regarding fiscal arrangements as well as federal intrusions, whether real or perceived, into areas of provincial jurisdiction. Provinces not sufficiently supporting national initiatives, as defined by Ottawa, can frustrate the federal government. Disagreements have spilled over to political campaigns and the courts. Ultimately, however, and sometimes after costly conflict, there is compromise and resolution.

This chapter deals with just one of the issues that have challenged fiscal federalism from time to time. It has to do with provincial natural resource revenues and, more broadly, jurisdiction over natural resources within provincial boundaries. Natural resources in the territories and Aboriginal interests regarding resource developments are subjects beyond the scope of this chapter.

The next section provides a historical background on natural jurisdiction and revenues. It is followed by a brief overview of fiscal federalism in Canada. Then two subsequent sections deal with specific aspects of fiscal federalism, namely, equalization and fiscal stabilization. Finally, some brief observations and conclusions end this chapter.

Background

In the mid-1860s, the governments of three North American British colonies – the Province of Canada, Nova Scotia, and New Brunswick – agreed to unite as one country. They decided on a federal form of governance, and in 1867, at their request, the British Parliament passed the British North America Act, now the Constitution Act, 1867, whereby the Dominion of Canada was created. There would be a federal government with various powers and responsibilities, while these three entities would retain their own governments as provinces. The three creators would become four as the Province of Canada was divided into Quebec and Ontario, each being geographically much smaller than its current size. Quebec was limited to the south and north shores of the St. Lawrence River, while Ontario was comprised of what is now southern Ontario plus a band of territory along the northern shores of the Great Lakes.

The responsibilities and powers of these four provinces were also defined in the act. Each province retained ownership of its Crown lands and jurisdiction over natural resources within its borders. Specifically, section 109 of the Constitution Act, 1867 states: "All Lands, Mines, Minerals, and Royalties belonging to the several Provinces of Canada, Nova Scotia, and New Brunswick at the Union, and all Sums then due or payable for such Lands, Mines, Minerals, or Royalties, shall belong to the several Provinces of Ontario, Quebec, Nova Scotia, and New Brunswick in which the same are situate or arise."

In addition, there is section 125, which states: "No Lands or Property belonging to Canada or any Province shall be liable to Taxation." This section prevents one level of government from taxing the other. Thus, the federal government cannot tax provincially owned resources.

Within the seven years following 1867, Canada became much larger. By 1870, Great Britain had transferred Rupert's Land and the North-Western Territory to it. A smaller version of present day Manitoba was created out of that area, but otherwise all those massive lands were under direct federal jurisdiction. In 1871 and 1873, respectively, the governments of the British colonies of British Columbia and Prince Edward Island joined Canada as provinces. Both kept their ownership of Crown lands and jurisdiction over natural resources as per section 109. In subsequent years, the federal government relinquished a great deal of territory. Between 1874 and 1912, it greatly enlarged Ontario and Quebec by giving them their vast northern areas. Also, in 1905, two new provinces – Saskatchewan and Alberta – were carved out of federal possessions. These created provinces, along with Manitoba, which had been greatly enlarged by federal territorial transfers, initially were not ceded natural resource jurisdiction. That constitutional asymmetry was rectified in 1930. Apparently Ottawa had retained ownership of resources to use as policy levers to encourage settlement and development in those three provinces (Hall 2015); Tough (2004, section 2) provides a historical background to the federal transfer of resources to the created provinces. Finally, the Dominion of Newfoundland joined Canada as a province in 1949, and, as with the original and other joining provinces, it retained jurisdiction over natural resources, although later there would be disagreements about ownership of and jurisdiction over offshore resources. In short, provincial jurisdiction over natural resources has always been a defining characteristic of Canadian federalism.

Having provincial jurisdiction over natural resource management and development is not difficult to justify. Geography makes resource development and exploitation local. Governments that are closer to their impacts are better placed to control the development of those resources. This logic is consistent with the original design of Canadian federalism. Historically, provinces saw their resources as spurs to economic development, as means to attract people and investment, with revenue potential playing a secondary role (see Cairns 1992, 57–60). The phenomenon of massive natural resource revenue windfalls does not seem to have been in play in the federation's first century. That did not happen until after 1970.

In 1974, the Organization of Petroleum Exporting Countries (OPEC) successfully used its market power to increase the world price of oil; it was able to further ratchet up the price in 1979. Alberta and, to a lesser extent, Saskatchewan had substantial oil and gas resources. The high oil prices attracted investment to the oil and gas sectors, and the governments of those two provinces made large revenue gains from oil and gas royalties. The federal government's response to the heightened oil price was problematic. It sought to deny the reality of the global price increase by keeping the Canadian price of crude oil below the world price. Doing so would keep consumption higher than otherwise and deter domestic production. Such price controls are far removed from microeconomic principles, which demonstrate their inherent inefficiency. In addition, the federal government created its own oil company, Petro-Canada, in 1975 and introduced the National Energy Policy (NEP) in 1980. The NEP and related policies included limiting deductibility of provincial royalty revenues from federal corporate income tax, offering incentives for oil companies to shift their exploration and development activities to territory under federal jurisdiction, and imposing oil export taxes. Alberta and Saskatchewan's oil and gas royalty revenues were greatly diminished from what they otherwise would have been, effectively being transferred to the federal government and to oil consumers throughout Canada.[1] In short, the federal government sought to exercise control over a provincial natural resource and to obtain a significant portion of provincial windfall revenues associated with that resource.

Consequently, this period was characterized by heated political clashes and debates about who should benefit from natural resource revenues.[2] There was litigation between the federal government, with the support of some oil-consuming provinces, and Alberta and Saskatchewan. Meanwhile, the federal government and the provinces of Nova Scotia (NS) and Newfoundland and Labrador (NL) were at odds over jurisdiction over the then undeveloped offshore oil and gas resources adjacent to those provinces. In 1982, the federal government sought a ruling from the Supreme Court of Canada on its jurisdiction over resources in the offshore areas of NL. To the frustration of that province, the Supreme Court ruled in favour of the federal government.[3]

Eventually, due to a combination of changes in government and policy, along with declining world oil prices from 1980 to 1985, the conflicts were largely resolved. The NEP was moderated and ended by 1985. Maintaining domestic crude oil prices below world prices ceased to be a federal policy objective, and other controversial federal interventions were phased out. Additionally, agreements were reached with NS, in 1986, and NL, in 1985, on joint management of offshore oil and gas, as well as providing for those provinces to collect offshore royalties as if they owned them.[4] These agreements were not as generous as the massive federal transfer of territory to Ontario and Quebec in the late nineteenth and early twentieth century, but they satisfied all parties at the time. Also, the new Constitution Act, 1982 contained a new provision, section 92(A), that clarified and strengthened provincial jurisdiction with respect to natural resources.[5]

The process of realizing those resolutions was difficult and costly. Historically, provincial resource revenues were not a major point of contention in federal-provincial relations. The oil price shocks were new. At that time, the magnitude of the increase in world prices, the expectation that those prices would trend higher, the size of the potential financial windfall to the oil-producing provinces, and the difficult adjustment that consuming provinces would have to make all combined to create a novel challenge. As discussed, the federal government of the day did not handle it well. The evidence of its failure is the short life of the aggressive policies that it introduced and the fact that no federal government, whatever the political party, attempted such policies when subsequent oil price shocks occurred.

Nevertheless, natural resource booms can be especially problematic in a federation. As Boadway (2007) points out, a regional resource boom can be challenging even in a unitary state but more so in a federal one, especially where provinces own the resources. One question that arises is the extent to which any windfall resource revenues ought to be shared with the rest of the country. The federal government would obtain revenues via its corporate income tax and other generally applicable taxes, but the bulk of the revenue would be in provincial government royalties, which are constitutionally beyond federal reach. Another complication relates to how a provincial government might use its windfall gains. One danger is what Boadway describes as "asymmetric tax competition." That is to say, windfall oil and gas revenues could be used to attract industries from other provinces via low tax rates, subsidies, and ample supply of supportive infrastructure. This type of competition would be economically undesirable in cases where such industry would otherwise have no natural advantage from such relocation, and it would adversely affect the regions from which such industry would be diverted. Whether and to what extent this phenomenon has occurred is an empirical question, but provincial ownership of and rights to resource windfalls make it a potential phenomenon that would not otherwise arise. On the other hand, asymmetric tax competition can arise whenever a province is rich, not necessarily natural resource revenue rich.

Huge windfalls were not in play during the 1986–2005 period. World oil prices had moved much lower in 1986 and, while not stable, had little discernible upward or downward trend up to 2005. In fact, in 1988 the federal government aided NL's offshore oil industry with financial assistance for its first offshore oil development, Hibernia, and provided further support for it through an equity buy-in in 1992. In early 2005, the federal government gave more concessions to NL and NS. It enhanced their offshore accords, which resulted in greater revenue benefits from their royalties on offshore oil and gas production.[6] Admittedly, these latter federal concessions did come after an acrimonious confrontation between NL and the federal government.[7] Still, this confrontation was unlike the 1973–81 conflicts, where disputes arose because of federal efforts to limit the revenue windfalls accruing to oil and gas–producing provinces.

Oil prices surged after 2005 and, while volatile, were generally in excess of US$100 a barrel until 2015. As a result, large increases in royalty revenues accrued to the producing provinces, particularly Alberta, but also Saskatchewan and NL. Lessons had been learned from experience, and NEP-type federal intervention did not reoccur. Nevertheless, matters of natural resource revenues, including but not limited to oil and gas, still give rise to federal-provincial conflicts and complicate fiscal federalism.[8] The remainder of this chapter focuses on current interaction between natural resource revenues and fiscal federalism.

The Current State of Fiscal Federalism

Fiscal federalism has various definitions. In broad terms, it refers to the financing arrangements that allow different levels of government to have sufficient funds to carry out their constitutionally mandated responsibilities. The main legislative mechanism for implementing fiscal federalism in Canada is the Federal-Provincial Fiscal Arrangements Act. That federal legislation's core elements are provisions for federal transfer payments to provincial and territorial governments. Transfers to the provincial governments fall into four categories:[9]

- Canada Health Transfer (CHT), which helps fund provincial governments' medical and hospital care programs;
- Canada Social Transfer (CST), which helps fund provincial governments' social welfare programs and their support for post-secondary education;
- Equalization Program, which allots unconditional payments to those provincial governments that are determined to have relatively weak "fiscal capacities";
- Fiscal Stabilization Program (FSP), which also allots unconditional payments, made to provincial governments that experience extraordinarily large declines in own-source revenues on a year-over-year basis.

Table 8.1. Major Federal Transfers to Provincial Governments, 2021–2

Transfer Payment	$ Millions	% of Federal Government Revenue
Canada Health Transfer	42,982	12.8
Canada Social Transfer	15,423	4.6
Equalization	20,911	6.2
Fiscal Stabilization	0	0.0
Total	79,316	23.6

Source: Finance Canada (2020a); excludes CHT and CST to territorial governments.

The design and magnitude of these transfer payments are determined solely by the federal government.[10] Provincial governments are consulted on program renewals but have no authority in their regard. Table 8.1 gives the projected payments for fiscal year 2020–1. The last column of the table shows that the sums involved are significant relative to total federal government revenue.

Both the CHT and CST, which come with some federally imposed but broad conditions, are essentially equal per capita transfers to the provincial governments. As such, there is no direct relation to provincial governments' financial circumstances. Provincial natural resource revenues do not come into play in determining the magnitude of these transfers. That is not to say that these transfers are satisfactory to the provinces. Provincial governments argue that the level of support from those two transfers is too small a contribution relative to the high and growing cost of the health and social programs that they deliver in accordance with their constitutional mandates. Some even see the federal conditionality as an intrusion into their areas of jurisdiction. These are matters of the vertical fiscal (im)balance, namely, the disharmony between (a) the federal government's advantage in raising revenues and its objective of having leverage to incentivize minimum national standards on provincial health and social programs, and (b) provincial governments' autonomy and need for revenue to provide the social, health, and other public services for which they are responsible.

By contrast, natural resource revenues have been controversial with respect to the equalization and fiscal stabilization payments. As shown in Table 8.1, equalization payments take a significant portion of federal revenues. While no fiscal stabilization payments were made in 2020–1, they are potentially important and became controversial during the COVID-19 pandemic as several provinces saw huge declines in their own-source revenues. Both programs incorporate provincial natural resource revenues in their design, and not without controversy. These are the respective subject matters of the following two sections.

Equalization Payments and Natural Resource Revenues

The Equalization Program began in 1957, but its modern form dates from 1967. In broad terms, payments are made to provincial governments with fiscal capacities that are weaker than others. Fiscal capacity is determined as a provincial government's estimated per capita revenue calculated under the assumption that its tax rates are the average of those across all provinces. Thus, fiscal capacity is a hypothetical number, but, importantly, it is an indicator of a province's ability to raise revenue. When a provincial government's fiscal capacity is less than a certain norm or "standard," it is entitled to a per capita equalization payment based on the difference. The standard is typically the actual average per capita revenue across a select group of provinces; this group has comprised all ten, two, or five provinces at different times according to the federal government's choice. The practice is for the federal government to revisit its formula for determining equalization payments every five years, although it makes changes in the intervening years at its discretion.

The intent of such payments is to reduce the horizontal fiscal imbalance, namely, the discrepancies in provincial governments' abilities to raise per capita revenue if they used similar tax rates. The practice of making equalization payments was formalized in the Constitution Act, 1982, section 36(2), which states: "Parliament and the government of Canada are committed to the principle of making equalization payments to ensure that provincial governments have sufficient revenues to provide reasonably comparable levels of public services at reasonably comparable levels of taxation."

Until the 1970s, natural resource revenues were not particularly problematic with respect to equalization. The federal government did take account of resource revenues starting in 1962.[11] It felt that some provincial governments that would have otherwise qualified for equalization had adequate overall revenues due to resource revenues. As Courchene (1984, 41) observes, this circumstance applied specifically to Alberta. That caused a spat between Alberta and Ottawa, but much more heated conflicts arose a decade later.

The oil price shocks of the 1970s led to various attempts by the federal government to obtain a greater share of oil and gas revenues as well as to keep oil prices below world market levels. These measures cut into producing provinces' large windfalls, especially Alberta's. However, oil revenues in those provinces still went up substantially. The effect of this increased revenue was large enough to raise the standard in the equalization formula, which in turn meant larger entitlements to equalization-qualifying provinces. To limit such increases, the federal government exercised its discretion to make cost-saving changes to the formula. Among the various changes were the following:

- In 1974, rather than use actual oil and gas revenues in the standard, the federal government used only one-third of increases in oil and gas revenues resulting from higher prices above 1973 levels.

- In 1977, the formula changed so only half of provincial non-renewable resource revenue would be used in the formula, which is approximately equivalent to valuing those revenues at half their actual price.
- In 1982, the federal government moved to a five-province standard (in place of the ten-province one in use since 1967), in which Alberta and the four Atlantic provinces were excluded, the net effect of which was to remove the bulk of oil and gas revenues from the standard, thereby lowering it.

These measures mitigated the growth in equalization payments that would otherwise have occurred (Economic Council of Canada 1982, 15). The five-province standard combined with the moderation of oil prices from 1982 to early 2000s took the pressure off the federal government's equalization payments budget.[12]

The current formula for equalization payments is largely the result of a comprehensive review by a panel of independent experts, chaired by Al O'Brien. The Expert Panel on Equalization and Territorial Formula Financing was appointed in 2005 and presented its comprehensive report the following year (EPETFF 2006). Its carefully considered recommendations, which included a return to a ten-province standard, were adopted in 2007. They remain embodied in the subsequent formulas but with various federal government modifications. The formula is normally reviewed and renewed every five years, and the federal government can use its discretion to make changes at that time or indeed during the time between renewals.

The following three-stage summary of the formula's application will help highlight the mechanisms that were put in place to deal with natural resource revenues. The summary is based on the formula for five years, 2019–20 to 2023–4. (Amounts are all in per capita terms unless otherwise stated.)

Stage 1. Initial Determination of Equalization Entitlements

For each province, the difference between the ten-province standard for each of four major categories of taxes (personal income, business income, consumption and property, and other taxes) and the province's corresponding fiscal capacity is determined.[13] Then these differences are added to obtain what may be referred to as the province's fiscal capacity gap (FCG). Natural resource revenue, the fifth category, is handled differently. Actual revenues are used, and the difference between the per capita total of all provinces' natural resource revenues and each province's per capita natural resource revenue is calculated. That difference can be called the province's natural resource revenue gap (NRRG).

Using these figures, a province's potential equalization payment is calculated as the greater of (a) its FCG plus one-half of its NRRG or (b) its FCG alone. If both numbers are negative, the province is not entitled to equalization.

Otherwise, it receives the larger of (a) and (b), subject to modifications that may occur in two subsequent stages.

Stage 2. Reductions Due to the Application of the Fiscal Capacity Cap

The fiscal capacity cap (FCC) is determined by finding from among the non-recipient provinces the one that has the lowest sum of fiscal capacity (based on the four tax groups) and per capita natural resource revenue.[14] That lowest sum is the FCC. Once determined, the FCC is compared to the sum of each recipient's (a) fiscal capacity, (b) per capita natural resource revenue, and (c) stage 1 equalization entitlement. To the extent that this sum exceeds the FCC, a province's potential equalization payment is reduced. The reduction, or "claw-back," is equal to either the gap between that three-component sum and the FCC or the total equalization payment, whichever is smaller.

Stage 3. Adjustments for the Total Equalization Funding Allotment

In this final adjustment, the total of all payments as determined to this point is compared to a pre-determined budget allocation.[15] If the total is more than the allocation, then equalization payments to recipient provinces are reduced on an equal per capita basis until the budget constraint is met. If the sum is less than the budget constraint, then the excess funds – "adjustment payments" – are allocated to all the recipients on an equal per capita basis but with the following provision. Should doing so move the recipients above the FCC, then the excess is also shared on an equal per capita basis with the province that sets the FCC; this provision ensures that no "have" province falls behind any recipient. Hence, in some years, Ontario received adjustment payments even though it otherwise did not qualify to be a recipient.

There are many ongoing debates about equalization. The remainder of the section is limited to ones related to natural resources. To that end, three issues are identified and discussed: the "better of the two" approach, the "FCC trap," and the treatment of hydroelectricity revenues.

First, within the stage 1 calculation, a province's initial entitlement is the larger of those amounts resulting from two different formulas: one where natural resource revenues are not included at all and one where 50 per cent of those revenues are included. This "better of the two" approach was not recommended by the Expert Panel. Its recommendation was to use the 50 per cent method. The option to ignore natural resource revenues entirely, when to a province's advantage, was implemented by the (Conservative) federal government when it adopted the Expert Panel framework in 2007. It was a discretionary move and stemmed from an election campaign promise. The option is unfair insofar as it treats provinces on an inconsistent basis. The metric of one province's fiscal capacity can be different from another's.

That inequity was worsened by the same government's subsequent decision to pre-set total annual equalization funding. In 2009, it deemed that the total equalization payout would grow at the same rate as the three-year average growth rate of nominal gross domestic product (GDP). That makes equalization allocation a zero-sum arrangement and, hence, created the need for the "adjustment payments." This pre-set total payout exacerbates the inequity because, with a fixed amount to allocate, to the extent the "better of" feature benefits one province, it does so at the expense of other recipients; without the fixed total, it would have been at the expense of the federal government. No federal government has addressed these matters since their adoption.

The second issue may be described as the "FCC trap." As noted above, the Expert Panel had recommended that only 50 per cent of natural resource revenues be included in the equalization formula. This recommendation was a compromise between the notion that all revenues should be included in the formula in order to accurately gauge the extent of the horizontal imbalance and the recognition that full inclusion of natural resource revenues would entail an approximate dollar-for-dollar loss in a recipient's equalization entitlement whenever its natural resource revenues increased. Considering that natural resources are provincial property and provincial governments should not face disincentives in developing their resources, the Expert Panel decided that the 50 per cent rule was a reasonable compromise (EPETFF 2006, annex 7). The 50 per cent rule also limits cost fluctuation for the federal government in the event of a resource price spike, because only 50 per cent of total resource revenues are subject to equalization. Recipient provinces would also benefit. A recipient of equalization would see a 50 per cent reduction in its equalization for every dollar increase in resource revenue and therefore obtain a net marginal revenue benefit. However, the Expert Panel also recognized that this arrangement could result in a recipient of equalization being made better off than a non-recipient. To avoid the apparent inequity, the panel devised the FCC.

The FCC limits the net revenue benefits of the preferential treatment of natural resource revenues by imposing a dollar-for-dollar loss in equalization as a recipient's resource revenues increase. As explained, this claw-back is triggered when a recipient's equalization entitlement, fiscal capacity, and natural resource revenue combined exceeds the FCC. In short, the formula, as designed by the Expert Panel, is generous to a recipient with resource revenues by allowing resource revenues to accrue beyond the standard but only up to the FCC, after which any increase in natural resource revenues is offset by an equal reduction in equalization payments.

Since its inception, the FCC has been binding for a number of resource rich provinces, causing partial reductions or complete elimination of pre-FCC equalization entitlements. In 2021–2, two provinces were affected by the FCC, namely, Saskatchewan and NL. Table 8.2 summarizes how. Rows 1 and 2 show

Table 8.2. Impacts of the Fiscal Capacity Cap on Newfoundland and Labrador and Saskatchewan Equalization Entitlements, 2021–2 (per capita)

Calculation of Equalization Entitlements from Pre- to Post-FCC	Newfoundland and Labrador ($)	Saskatchewan ($)
(1) Pre-FCC equalization; natural resource revenue excluded	1,072	563
(2) Pre-FCC equalization; 50% of resource revenue included	197	37
(3) Pre-FCC equalization entitlement – greater of rows (1) and (2)	1,072	563
(4) Sum of four tax-based fiscal capacity, natural resource revenues, and pre-FCC equalization entitlement	11,733	11,037
(5) FCC (Ontario's fiscal capacity including all its natural resource revenue)	10,122	10,122
(6) The lesser of row (3) or the excess of row (4) over row (5)	1,072	563
(7) Post-FCC equalization entitlement: row (3) minus row (6)	0	0
(8) Post-FCC fiscal position: row (4) minus row (6)	10,661	10,474

the equalization entitlements when calculated with natural resource revenue excluded and with 50 per cent included, respectively. In both cases, the exclusion of natural resource revenues is more advantageous, which results in the pre-FCC equalization entitlement shown in row 3. Moving to the second stage of the process, row 4 shows the resulting fiscal position of each province, assuming it receives the pre-FCC entitlement. However, the FCC, as in row 5, is less than the pre-FCC entitlement. Consequently, the entitlement is reduced; see row 6. Both provinces are ahead of the FCC by more than their respective pre-FCC entitlements, so their post-FCC entitlements are zero; see row 7. Nevertheless, it is worth noting that, at the end of the process, both provinces' fiscal capacities inclusive of all their resource revenues remain above the FCC; see row 8.

In the above cases, natural resource revenue in excess of the FCC is offset on a dollar-for-dollar basis through reduction in equalization entitlements. This offset can be described as a "trap" zone, in which there is no marginal revenue benefit from increased natural resource revenues until equalization is reduced to zero. It raises the question of whether provinces should be assured of always receiving some positive incremental revenue benefits whenever their natural revenues increase. This benefit does not happen when revenues push provinces into the FCC trap zone. Reducing equalization entitlements by something less

Figure 8.1. Residential Electricity Rates, 2020

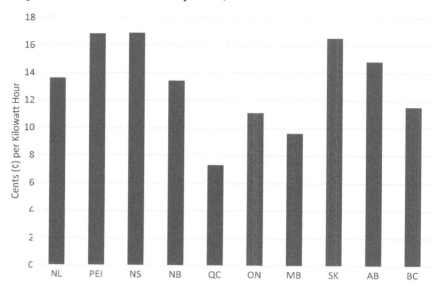

Source: Hydro-Quebec (2020, 22).
Note: AB = Alberta; BC = British Columbia; MB = Manitoba; NB = New Brunswick; NL = Newfoundland and Labrador; NS = Nova Scotia; ON = Ontario; PEI = Prince Edward Island: QC = Quebec; SK = Saskatchewan.

than on a dollar-for-dollar basis – even something as high as 90 cents per dollar – would recognize the principle of positive *marginal* revenue benefits from resource revenues. In short: the FCC is too severe.

The third natural resource issue relates to the measure of provincial hydroelectric revenues. Some provinces are well endowed with hydroelectric resources, and hydroelectricity is largely consumed in the province of generation, which is quite unlike other major sources of natural resource revenues such as minerals and oil and gas. Therefore, lower electricity rates will benefit resident household consumers and businesses. Governments in hydro-rich provinces, therefore, have an incentive to adopt low electricity rate policies. That can be accomplished by charging low water power rentals as well as by public ownership of hydroelectric companies, which are not subject to corporate income tax. This situation has led to calls for reform of equalization (see, for example, Holle 2012).

Figure 8.1 illustrates the differences in residential electricity rates across the provinces.[16] Quebec has the lowest rate, followed by Manitoba. Both provinces,

Canadian Fiscal Federalism and the Provinces' Natural Resource Revenues 167

Table 8.3. Estimated Impact on 2021–2 Equalization Payments Due to Inclusion of Forgone Water Power Rentals (millions)

Province	Actual Equalization – Column 1 ($)	Adjusted for Forgone Hydro Revenue: Total Payments Constant – Column 2 ($)	Adjusted for Forgone Hydro Revenue: Formula-Determined Total – Column 3 ($)
Newfoundland and Labrador	0	0	0
Prince Edward Island	484	528	492
Nova Scotia	2,315	2,587	2,366
New Brunswick	2,274	2,493	2,315
Quebec	13,119	9,057	7,116
Ontario	0	3,309	0
Manitoba	2,719	2,937	2,625
Saskatchewan	0	0	0
Alberta	0	0	0
British Columbia	0	0	0
Total	20,911	20,911	14,914

Source: Author's calculations based on Finance Canada's unpublished equalization tables.

especially Quebec, have large hydroelectric resources, which serve as each province's primary source of electricity generation. Both provinces tout their low electricity prices (see Hydro-Quebec 2021, 39; Manitoba Hydro 2020, 37). Quebec and Manitoba rates are approximately 3.8 cents and 1.5 cents per kilowatt hour lower than Ontario's, respectively. These differences are potential rough indicators of the underlying value of uncollected water power rentals that are passed along to consumers via low electricity prices. Based on the within-province sales of electricity, these imply forgone revenues of $6.80 billion and $0.33 billion for Quebec and Manitoba, respectively.[17]

Table 8.3 gives the estimated impacts across all provinces of these potential higher revenues if incorporated into the equalization formula. Column 1 gives the actual 2021–2 equalization payments. Column 2 shows the effect of including additional revenues of $6.8 billion and $0.33 billion to the natural resource revenues of Quebec and Manitoba, respectively, assuming that the total equalization budget remains fixed at $20.9 billion. The change in distribution is quite pronounced. Quebec's payment falls from $13.1 billion to $9.1 billion, and Ontario receives $3.3 billion (in adjustment payments only).

The last column in Table 8.3 illustrates the results if the fixed budget of $20.9 billion were not imposed. In that case, the total outlay for the program would be $14.9 billion. That is a substantial saving, and arises from not having to scale up payments to match the greater budget. Interestingly, the payments to the other recipient provinces change little relative to the actuals in column 1.

The exercise results reported in Table 8.3 are crude approximations. Depending on assumptions regarding the value of unrealized potential waterpower revenues, the estimates could vary considerably.[18] Still, this exercise is illustrative. Given the enormity of Quebec's hydro resources, even a few cents per kilowatt hour can have a substantial impact on the total equalization payout and its allocation. In-depth analysis would be necessary to estimate reasonably accurate values of those potential revenues, which could turn out to be much less or more than herein.

Two further comments on hydropower follow. First, low electricity rate policies in hydro-rich provinces have a long history in Canada. They predate the Equalization Program, so such policies were not adopted to obtain higher equalization payments. Second, even if the federal government were to adjust the equalization formula to reflect potential, rather than actual, water power rental revenue, a provincial government could still choose to maintain its low pricing policy. However, such underpricing is not best policy. If a resource is underpriced, then use of that resource will be economically inefficient. The price should reflect the resource's social marginal cost, and if that is not the case, then economic benefits are not maximized. On that basis, Boyer (2005) argued that the logic behind Quebec's low-price regime is flawed and that raising the price of electricity could generate benefits for everyone there. Perhaps losses in equalization payments as shown in Table 8.3 could deter proper pricing, although a complete explanation is likely more complex.

Fiscal Stabilization Payments

As shown in Table 8.1, fiscal stabilization payments to the provinces for 2021–2 were zero. That has not always been so. From 1982–3 to 2021–2, the average annual payment has been $66.2 million, and all provinces have received at least one payment over those years. Over that period, the highest annual payment to a province was in 1995–6: $367 million to Ontario. The most recent beneficiaries are Saskatchewan and Alberta, which received $39 million and $251 million, respectively, in 2016–17. These amounts are very small relative to those provinces' revenues and suggest that the program is not achieving its purpose; however, as will be discussed, recent reforms may result in retroactive payments to some provinces that suffered large revenue reductions during the COVID-19 pandemic.

The Fiscal Stabilization Program (FSP) dates back to 1957; see Tombe (2020) for its history. Its purpose is to provide "protection to provinces in the event of extraordinary year-over-year declines in revenues" (Finance Canada 2016).

More precisely, the revenues are own-source provincial government revenues. Natural resources revenue considerations are particularly prominent in the program for two reasons: first, in many cases the extraordinary declines in provincial revenues are due to natural resource shocks; and second, since 1977, natural resource revenues have been treated differently in the payments formula from other provincial revenues. In general terms, natural resource revenue has to fall by more than 50 per cent from the previous year before there is any chance of compensation from the FSP for the loss in excess of 50 per cent; the hurdle for other revenues is 5 per cent. Then there is a general constraint on payments, namely, a maximum per capita payout. That cap was fixed at $60 until 2019–20.[19] Additionally, the payment is for one year only. If revenues do not recover in the next year, there is no further payment – revenues would have to fall further for that to be a possibility.

In short, it has been very difficult for provinces, particularly resource rich ones, to qualify for fiscal stabilization payments, and even if qualified, the payments are meagre relative to the province's revenues. For example, in 2016–17, Saskatchewan received a $39 million payment, but its own-source revenue was $10.6 billion, and Alberta was paid $251 million against own-source revenue of $34.3 billion; at the time, those provinces were running deficits of $1.2 billion and $10.8 billion, respectively.[20] This situation led governments of those two provinces to highlight the lack of federal help with their deficits and misguidedly attack the Equalization Program (Feehan 2020).

Against the background, experts recently offered opinions on how the FSP could be improved. Dahlby (2019) suggests the following reforms:

- remove the cap on FSP payments;
- treat all own-source revenue the same, rather than the current practice with respect to natural resource revenues; and
- calculate the change in revenue relative to a moving average of the previous five years, rather than only the preceding year.

Additionally, using an insurance framework, Dahlby proposes to retain a deductible and impose a less than 100 per cent coverage rate. He suggests that these two parameters should be chosen to mitigate the moral hazard problem. That is to say, provinces might rely excessively on highly volatile revenues if they are too cushioned by the FSP when those revenues fall.

Tombe (2020) agreed that it is time for reform and that the cap on payments should be removed or at least substantially increased. This reform could be in addition, or an alternative, to decreasing the deductible. However, while recognizing that a 50 per cent decline in natural resource revenue is a "high bar," he does not recommend reducing it due to concerns about moral hazard. Boadway (2020) also takes this perspective, arguing that the resource rich provinces can self-insure against extraordinary declines in revenues by saving a sufficient amount of resource revenue in a sovereign wealth fund.

There is no doubt that the moral hazard argument is logically sound. The question is how much does it matter. Eligibility for provinces with high resource revenue is highly restrictive and, on top of that, the cap on payments can come into play. Easing up on these severe restrictions somewhat is highly unlikely to encourage an increase in any provincial fiscal irresponsibility. Additionally, it is worth emphasizing that all provinces should be capturing the economic rent arising from their natural resources. They should not be dissuaded from relying on resource revenues, even if that means volatile revenues in some cases, notably oil and gas. Saving windfalls in "rainy day" accounts that could be relied upon in downturns would deal with that volatility, but some assistance through the FSP beyond the paltry amounts provided during its existence is desirable. Moreover, provinces with high resource royalty revenues are not always "have" provinces or in a fiscal position to accumulate substantial savings – for example, Saskatchewan in 1993 or Newfoundland and Labrador in 2020.

The federal government, following appeals from various provincial governments and the Council of the Federation, implemented a number of modifications to the FSP in its 2020-1 budget. As with other federal-provincial transfers, these changes were ultimately at Ottawa's discretion. One significant change was an increase in the cap. Retroactively, it was raised from $60 per capita to $166 for 2018, and thereafter it increases annually in line with any positive growth in nominal GDP per capita. There are some other minor and technical changes as well. These modifications are improvements and timely enough to assist provinces that suffered revenue decline in 2020-1 due to the COVID-19 pandemic. Estimated payments in that year were $4.55 billion but would have been $1.64 billion without the reforms (Parliamentary Budget Officer 2021, 3).

On the other hand, the cap is still not generous, and the reforms did not address the differential treatment of natural resource revenues. As previously, payments remain dependent on three natural resource revenue scenarios, which were only slightly changed. These scenarios, which are all in terms of year-over-year changes and subject to the cap, are as follows:

1 If resource revenue *falls by less than 5 per cent* (previously: *does not fall*), then the FSP is the amount by which own-source revenue falls in excess of 5 per cent.
2 If resource revenue *falls by between 5 and 50 per cent* (previously: *falls by up to 50 per cent*), the FSP is the amount by which own-source revenue, other than resource revenue, falls in excess of 5 per cent.
3 If resource revenue falls by more than 50 per cent (unchanged), then the FSP is the change in own-source non-resource revenue plus the amount by which resource revenue falls in excess of 50 per cent.

These changes fail entirely to address the 50 per cent hurdle. This aspect of the program ought to be reconsidered, taking into account the severity of the hurdle and the importance of incentivizing provinces to fully collect resource rents, as well as the moral hazard concern.

Observations and Conclusions

On a positive note, the clash over provincial natural resource revenues, notably those from oil and gas, seems to have been permanently resolved. Federal attempts to capture and limit provincial windfall oil revenues during the 1970s brought that issue to climax. The ensuing federal-provincial conflicts were not productive, but eventually reasonable accommodations were achieved. The NEP ended and section 92(A) was included in the Constitution. That clarification of provincial jurisdiction and the lessons learned from the aggressive federal intervention in the oil and gas sector at that time make a repeat of such conflicts over natural resource revenues very unlikely.

On the other hand, new tensions are in play due to environmental initiatives. Federal policies, such as more stringent environmental assessments of major industrial and resource development projects and the recent introduction of carbon taxation, can be particularly onerous for resource rich provinces. These policies reduce or eliminate the commercial viability of some resource developments and drive up the cost of production for current operations. This situation has negative implications for resource revenues and economic growth in the resource rich provinces. While it is appropriate to ensure that the natural resource sector, like all other sectors, bear the environmental cost of their activities, the disproportionate burden on some provinces will be a challenge for federalism.

Meanwhile, swings in natural resource revenues will continue to complicate fiscal federalism. As discussed, the 50 per cent natural resource inclusion rule in equalization has been helpful, but the severity of the FCC and the issue of hydro rents have not been addressed. In short, Ottawa chooses what it does and does not want to deal with. Similarly, the recent changes to the FSP were at Ottawa's discretion, and it chose not to deal with the severe hurdle with respective to dramatic declines in natural resource revenues. This wide scope for the federal government to use its discretion in deciding which fiscal arrangements to change, and how, leads to this chapter's concluding suggestion.

Béland and Lecours (2012) proposed that an arm's-length agency be established to deal with equalization. They point to Australia's Commonwealth Grants Commission as a model. At least two chapters in this volume touch on that suggestion. Tombe (chapter 4) implies it would be of some help. Fenna (chapter 22) is sceptical. On the other hand, Feehan (2020) agreed that such an arrangement should be considered and urged that its mandate go beyond equalization to encompass the FSP as well as the CHT and CST. A national institution that is credible and independent could depoliticize the process, study ongoing and new challenges, and, especially, limit federal discretion. It could help resolve issues such as the treatment of water power revenues in equalization, the severity of the FCC, the treatment of natural resource revenues in the FSP, and more broadly advise on the adequacy of funding for all major fiscal transfers related to the horizontal and vertical balances.

NOTES

1 Nevertheless, their royalty revenues were substantial enough to produce large budget surpluses. Alberta's revenues were so substantial that it created the Alberta Heritage Savings Trust Fund.
2 Using a province-building versus centralization paradigm, Simeon (1980) gives a concise overview of the issues at play at the time.
3 NL had already started a similar case in the Newfoundland Court of Appeal, which also ruled in favour of federal jurisdiction. Fitzgerald (1991) reviews those cases and argues that both courts' rulings erred in law, but the political settlement, the Atlantic Accord 1985, constituted a partial victory for that province.
4 Those provincial governments also received additional benefits, including time-limited federal compensation for losses of equalization payments as provincial royalty revenues accrued from offshore oil and gas production.
5 Cairns et al. (1985) provides a background and an assessment of section 92A.
6 See the Nova Scotia and Newfoundland and Labrador Additional Fiscal Equalization Offset Payments Act, https://laws-lois.justice.gc.ca/eng/acts/n-27.5/page-1.html.
7 See CBC, "Maple Leaf Flags Removed in Offshore Feud," 23 December 2004, https://www.cbc.ca/news/canada/maple-leaf-flags-removed-in-offshore-feud-1.494970.
8 For a recent contribution on the same subject matter, see Joanis and Vaillancourt (2020).
9 Outside the Fiscal Arrangements Act, there is also the federal Canada Community-Building Fund (formerly the Gas Tax Fund), which provides funds for local infrastructure through bilateral agreements with the provinces
10 The three territorial governments also receive the CHT and CST. In lieu of equalization payments, each receives a Territorial Formula Financing grant. Territories are not covered by the Fiscal Stabilization Program.
11 Before 1962, equalization payments were limited to consideration of three provincial revenue sources: personal income tax, corporate income tax, and succession duties. In 1962, one half of natural resource revenues was incorporated, making it a fourth source. In 1967, equalization was extended to include a much broader range of revenue sources.

12 For more on the treatment of natural resource revenues prior to 2004, see Feehan (2005).
13 A three-year weighted average of these figures is used for the calculation, where the years are three past years, lagged two years, with the most recent year given a 50 per cent weight and the other two weighted at 25 per cent each. This process tends to smooth payments and allows time to accumulate accurate data for estimation of fiscal capacities.
14 This province is usually Ontario. When that is not the case, the FCC is set at an average across the sum of total fiscal capacities, resource revenues, and equalization payments of those provinces determined to be potential recipients in stage 1. In 2009, the federal government introduced this measure when it appeared that Ontario would qualify for equalization.
15 Starting with an initial aggregate budget, the federal government in 2009 decided to increase the equalization allocation according to the three-year moving average growth rate of nominal gross domestic product (GDP).
16 Differences in non-residential rates follow a similar pattern.
17 In-province sales were approximately 172 and 22 million megawatt hours in Quebec and Manitoba, respectively (see Hydro-Quebec 2021, 99; Manitoba Hydro 2020, 36).
18 Various scenarios can be explored using Trevor Tombe's online equalization simulator (see Tombe 2021).
19 When the cap is binding, the federal government may provide an interest-free loan for the excess.
20 Data on own-source revenue and deficits are from Finance Canada (2020b, Tables 25 and 26).

REFERENCES

Béland, Daniel, and André Lecours. 2012. *Equalization at Arm's Length*. Fiscal Transfers Series. Mowat Publication No. 48. Toronto: Mowat Centre for Policy Innovation, University of Toronto.

Boadway, Robin. 2007. "Natural Resource Shocks and the Federal System: Boon and Curse?" *Fiscal Federalism and the Future of Canada, Selected Proceedings from the Conference – September 28–29, 2006*. Kingston, ON: Institute of Intergovernmental Relations, Queen's University. https://www.queensu.ca/iigr/sites/iirwww/files/uploaded_files/boadway.pdf.

– 2020. "The Case against Enhancing Fiscal Stabilization for Resource Revenues." *C.D. Howe Institute Intelligence Memorandum*, 15 January 2020. https://www.cdhowe.org/sites/default/files/IM-Boadway-2020-1-15.pdf.

Boyer, Marcel. 2005. "Raise Electricity Prices in Quebec – and Benefit Everyone." *C.D. Howe ebrief*, 16 March 2005. https://www.cdhowe.org/sites/default/files/attachments/research_papers/mixed//ebrief_13_english.pdf.

Cairns, Robert D. 1992. "Natural Resources and Canadian Federalism: Decentralization, Recurring Conflict, and Resolution." *Publius: The Journal of Federalism* 22, no. 1: 55–70. https://www.jstor.org/stable/3330233.

Cairns, Robert D., Marsha A. Chandler, and William D. Moull. 1985. "The Resource Amendment (Section 92A) and the Political Economy of Canadian Federalism." *Osgoode Hall Law Journal* 23, no. 2: 253–74. https://digitalcommons.osgoode.yorku.ca/cgi/viewcontent.cgi?article=1901&context=ohlj.

Courchene, Thomas J. 1984. *Equalization Payments: Past, Present, and Future*. Special Research Report. Toronto: Ontario Economic Council.

Dahlby, Bev. 2019. *Reforming the Federal Fiscal Stabilization Program*. SPP Briefing Paper 12, no. 18: 1–20. Calgary: School of Public Policy, University of Calgary. https://www.policyschool.ca/wp-content/uploads/2019/06/Fiscal-Stabilization-Dahlby-final2.pdf.

Economic Council of Canada. 1982. *Financing Confederation: Today and Tomorrow*. Ottawa: Supply and Services Canada.

EPETFF (Expert Panel on Equalization and Territorial Formula Financing). 2006. *Achieving a Natural Purpose: Putting Equalization Back on Track*. Ottawa: Department of Finance. https://publications.gc.ca/collections/Collection/F2-176-2006E.pdf.

Feehan, James. 2005. "Equalization and the Provinces' Natural Resource Revenues: Partial Equalization Can Work Better." In *Canadian Fiscal Arrangements: What Works, What Might Work Better*, edited by Harvey Lazar, 185–208. Montreal-Kingston: McGill-Queen's University Press.

– 2020. "Canada's Equalization Program: Political Debates and Opportunities for Reform." *IRPP Insight* 30, 28 January 2020. https://doi.org/10.26070/zp9t-zt92.

Finance Canada. 2016. "Backgrounder: The Fiscal Stabilization Program." https://www.canada.ca/en/department-finance/news/2016/02/backgrounder-the-fiscal-stabilization-program.html.

– 2020a. "Federal Support to Provinces and Territories." https://www.canada.ca/en/department-finance/programs/federal-transfers/major-federal-transfers.html.

– 2020b. "Fiscal Reference Tables 2020." https://www.canada.ca/en/department-finance/services/publications/fiscal-reference-tables/2020.html.

Fitzgerald, E.A., 1991. "The Newfoundland Offshore Reference: Federal-Provincial Conflict over Offshore Energy Resources." *Case Western Reserve Journal of International Law* 23, no. 1: 1–64. https://scholarlycommons.law.case.edu/jil/vol23/iss1/1/.

Hall, D.J. 2015. "Natural Resources Transfer Acts." *The Canadian Encyclopedia*. https://www.thecanadianencyclopedia.ca/en/article/natural-resources-transfer-acts-1930.

Holle, Peter. 2012. "Artificially Cheap Hydro Power, Your Equalization Dollars at Work." *National Post*, 29 May 2012. https://nationalpost.com/opinion/peter-holle-artificially-cheap-hydro-power-your-equalization-dollars-at-work.

Hydro-Quebec. 2020. *Comparison of Electricity Prices in Major North American Cities: Rates in Effect April 1, 2020.* Quebec: Hydro-Quebec. https://www.hydroquebec.com/data/documents-donnees/pdf/comparison-electricity-prices.pdf.

– 2021. *Annual Report 2020.* Quebec: Hydro-Quebec. https://www.hydroquebec.com/data/documents-donnees/pdf/annual-report-2020-hydro-quebec.pdf.

Joanis, Marcelin, and François Vaillancourt. 2020. "Federal Finance Arrangements in Canada: The Challenges of Fiscal Imbalance and Natural Resource Rents." In *Intergovernmental Transfers in Federations,* edited by Serdar Yilmaz and Farah Zahir, 109–33. Cheltenham, UK: Edward Elgar Publishing.

Manitoba Hydro. 2020. *Navigating Change and Challenges with Action: Manitoba Hydro-Electric Board 69th Annual Report for the Year Ended March 31, 2020.* Winnipeg: Manitoba Hydro. https://www.annualreports.com/HostedData/AnnualReportArchive/m/manitoba-hydro_2020.pdf.

Parliamentary Budget Officer. 2021. "Legislative Costing Note." Fiscal Stabilization Program – Indexing the Maximum Per Capita Payment. Ottawa: Office of the Parliamentary Budget Officer. https://www.pbo-dpb.ca/en/publications/LEG-2021-057-S-fiscal-stabilization-program-indexing-maximum-per-capita-payment–programme-stabilisation-fiscale-indexation-paiement-maximal-habitant.

Simeon, Richard. 1980. "Natural Resource Revenues and Canadian Federalism: A Survey of the Issues." *Canadian Public Policy/Analyse de Politiques* 6: 182–91. https://doi.org/10.2307/3549918.

Tombe, Trevor. 2020. "An (Overdue) Review of Canada's Fiscal Stabilization Program." *IRPP Insight* 31, February 2020. https://centre.irpp.org/research-studies/an-overdue-review-of-canadas-fiscal-stabilization-program/.

– 2021. "A New Tool to Understand Equalization Payments in Canada." *Finances of the Nation,* 23 February 2021. https://financesofthenation.ca/2021/02/23/new-equalization-tool/.

Tough, Frank. 2004. "The Forgotten Constitution: The Natural Resources Transfer Agreements and Indian Livelihood Rights, ca. 1925–1933." *Alberta Law Review* 41, no. 4: 999–1048. https://doi.org/10.29173/alr1316.

9 Fiscal Federalism, Governance, and Provincial Debt

KYLE HANNIMAN

1. Introduction

Provincial debts in Canada are unsustainable. Most provinces will need to take significant measures to stabilize them. But what is the ideal path of fiscal adjustment? Is it a path Canada's fiscal federal and governance structures support? And if not, what, if anything, can be done?

The provinces should adopt a gradual path to fiscal consolidation. This path is the most appropriate, I will argue, given the interest rate environment and the structure of the global economy. But a gradual path still requires substantial levels of fiscal capacity and discipline. And Canada's current fiscal federal framework does not provide enough of either. The vertical fiscal imbalance robs the provinces of fiscal capacity, while the belief, widely held among provincial bondholders, that Ottawa is unlikely to let a province default weakens fiscal discipline.

In resolving this problem, federal policy makers face a provincial debt dilemma. Increasing provincial transfers is the only reliable way to enhance provincial fiscal capacity. But it will not strengthen market discipline and may soften provincial budget constraints in other ways. This dilemma is a pervasive feature of multilevel systems, but key features of Canadian federalism – including weak institutions of collective action and powerful regional and provincial identities – make it particularly challenging to address.

This chapter advances a potential, if partial, solution: an independent council responsible for assessing the performance of Canada's fiscal federal arrangements and advising the federal government on their reform. This proposal does not provide an immediate solution to the provincial debt dilemma, but a well-designed council might provide a partial remedy by enhancing the federation's problem-solving capacity, hardening provincial budget constraints, constraining the federal spending power, and facilitating collective action. But it could also face considerable political resistance, and there is no guarantee it would work. The design and roll out will be key.

Section two discusses the depth of the provinces' fiscal challenges and makes the case for gradual adjustment. Section three links the adjustment challenge to Canada's fiscal federal framework. Section four describes the provincial debt dilemma. Section five describes the deeper governance challenge. Section six advances a partial solution. Section seven summarizes the discussion.

2. The Case for Gradual Fiscal Adjustment

Provincial debts are widely considered unsustainable (Tombe 2020; MacPhee et al. 2022). How bad is the situation? What does it imply for the ideal pace of fiscal consolidation?

Cross-nationally, gross provincial debt to gross domestic product (GDP) is the highest of any subnational sector in the Organisation for Economic Cooperation and Development (OECD; de Mello and Ter-Minassian 2022). Historically, net provincial debts have never been higher. They rose substantially after the 2008 global financial crisis and have collectively hovered between 30 and 31 per cent of GDP since 2017. And the situation is expected to get worse. Debt sustainability analyses from the Parliamentary Budget Office (PBO) and others consistently conclude that the debts of most provinces, and the sector as a whole, are unsustainable, meaning most provinces will have to cut spending, raise taxes, or both in order to prevent their debt ratios from rising. It is little wonder some are calling for aggressive consolidation.

But we need to put provincial debt in context. Take, for starters, the cross-national comparison. It is true – provinces are far more indebted than their peers. But they never would have amassed the debt if domestic and international investors were not confident they would be repaid. Granted, investors' confidence stems, in part, from the implicit bailout guarantee (generally not a good reason to borrow). But it also reflects the provinces' sovereign-like capacities to adjust revenues and expenditures, along with a host of other stand-alone features that provincial credit rating reports regularly mention (Moody's 2010). Fitch Ratings (2021) categorizes the provinces as "type A" subnational borrowers: ones with "sovereign-like" capacity to run structural deficits.

Now consider the intertemporal comparison. Net provincial debts are slightly higher than they were in the 1990s, a period in which credit ratings were plummeting and provinces were forced to adopt radical austerity measures. But interest rates are also considerably lower today – so much so that provincial interest payments to revenues have been more or less flat since 2008, despite a substantial increase in provincial debt (see Figure 9.1).

Finally, the pandemic, as Trevor Tombe's chapter 4 in this volume shows, has not made the provinces' long-run financial situation significantly worse. The provinces have run substantial deficits during the pandemic, but they have not borrowed nearly as much as the federal government. Ottawa has also provided

Figure 9.1. Net Provincial Debt to GDP and Interest Payments to Revenues

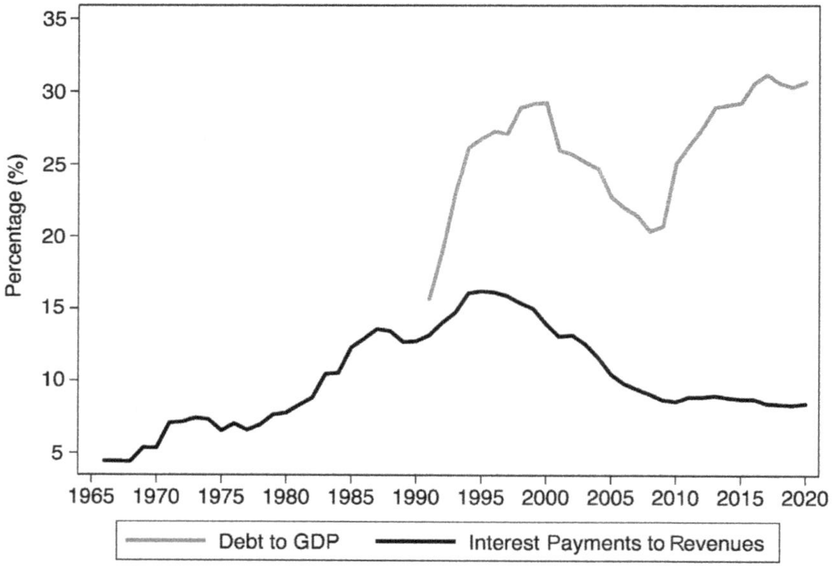

Sources: Fiscal Reference Tables, Department of Finance, Government of Canada; author's calculations.
Note: Net debt figures refer to fiscal year ending 31 March; interest payment figures refer to calendar year ending 31 December.

the provinces with a substantial infusion of one-time transfers and supported their economies and budgets indirectly with unprecedented income supports for businesses and households. Provincial budgets have also benefited from the recent surge in inflation, which, for all its other faults, has increased nominal revenues and GDP substantially.[1] It would appear, for all these reasons, that the provinces can afford to adjust slowly, at least for the time being.

But should they? This is a harder question. There is widespread agreement that governments can and should run bigger and longer deficits than they have in the past, and not just because they are in the midst of a pandemic. Blanchard, Felman, and Subramanian (2021) boil the new thinking down to three propositions. The first is that aggregate demand in the advanced economies is fragile. Desired global savings consistently exceed desired levels of global investment, leading to a low-growth, low-inflation trap in which demand is consistently at risk of falling below supply. This condition, widely known as secular stagnation (Summers 2014; Hansen 1939), appears to be at stark odds with the current environment in which inflation is elevated and demand is clearly outstripping supply. But a number of leading economists (Blanchard 2023; Summers 2022) believe secular stagnation remains the most likely long-run equilibrium. The assumption is that many of the current sources of inflation will eventually dissipate,[2] while the long-term sources of sluggish demand – including aging populations, income inequality, and the global savings glut – will likely persist.

The second proposition is that, with interest rates at or near the zero lower bound, fiscal policy has become the principal tool for supporting demand. Central banks cannot sustain or resuscitate demand because their principal means of doing so – cutting interest rates – has been largely exhausted (even the recent and rapid hikes of central bank policy rates leave central banks with little scope for cuts). Thus, central governments will need to run bigger and longer deficits than they have in the past.

The third proposition is that the deficits are affordable. While government debts are high, long-term economic growth rates in the advanced economies have reliably exceeded interest rates on long-term government bonds for some time. If this trend continues, as theories of secular stagnation suggest they will, governments can run modest primary deficits indefinitely without necessarily seeing their debt-to-GDP ratios rise (Blanchard 2023).

The argument, to be clear, is not that debt has become riskless. Far from it. Rather, it is that the balance of risks has shifted, and the risks of borrowing too little often exceed the risks of borrowing too much (Gopinath 2020). Proponents of the new consensus also believe that, if current macroeconomic conditions do shift – and the inequality between growth and interest rates flips – advanced economies have the capacity to make the necessary fiscal adjustments (Blanchard 2023; Delong 2016).

But the new thinking was developed with central governments in mind. What does it imply for the provinces? Like the federal government, the provinces are responsible for significant shares of government spending and revenue generation. Their borrowing has profound implications, therefore, for aggregate demand. They also borrow on very favourable terms, with interest rates near or below long-term growth rates in several provinces in recent years (Hanniman and Tombe 2020).

But there are strong efficiency arguments for centralizing fiscal stabilization (Oates 2005), even if full centralization is not always practical (Rodden and Wibbels 2010). What is more, the provinces are not central government borrowers. Their bonds are less creditworthy than federal debt, even if the federal government is unlikely to let them default (more on this point below). They are also less liquid or easy to trade on secondary markets. Several implications follow (Hanniman 2020b).

First, over the short term, the provinces are more vulnerable to liquidity shocks. They pay a higher interest rate than the federal government, and that spread increases with volatility in global financial markets as investors seek safety and liquidity in federal bonds. If the volatility is severe enough, provinces may struggle to borrow, which they briefly did during the global financial crisis of 2008, the commodity bust of 2015–16, the stock market meltdown of late 2018, and the financial crisis of early 2020 (Hanniman 2018, 2020a).

Second, over the long run, Ottawa is in a better position to stabilize its debt. In a recent analysis, Hanniman and Tombe (2020) show that the long-run growth rate was greater than the long-run interest rate in several provinces from 2006 to 2018. But they also find that growth was less than the interest rates in New Brunswick and Nova Scotia, and roughly equal to the interest rates in Ontario and Quebec. Provincial differentials were also more volatile, on average, than the federal differential, especially in the resource-based provinces of Alberta, Newfoundland and Labrador, and Saskatchewan. According to our projections, this volatility implied a more than 50 per cent chance of provincial debt rising above current levels, even if the provinces take measures to fully fund their program expenditures without borrowing.

Third, the provinces are more vulnerable to structural changes in macroeconomic conditions. There is no guarantee growth will continue to exceed interest rates for many borrowers. If the inequality does flip, it is the provinces, rather than the federal government, that will suffer most, partly because provinces are likely to face more punishing growth-interest rate differentials. But it is also because they have less capacity to raise revenues and cut expenditures, given their narrow tax bases and growing health-care responsibilities.

But the risks are not limited to provinces. Comparative and case study literatures link subnational debt to a variety of macroeconomic ills, including inflation (Rodden and Wibbels 2002), macroeconomic instability (Wibbels 2005), higher debts nationally (Samuels 2003), and higher borrowing costs for other governments (Jenkner and Zhongjin 2014).

In short, provinces can and probably should borrow more than they did in the 1990s. They should also adopt a slower path to fiscal consolidation. But their debts are uncomfortably high, given the sector's vulnerabilities and the macroeconomic risks. What brought the provinces to this state?

3. The Problem with Fiscal Federalism

The answer lies, in large part, in the fiscal federal framework. At some risk of simplification, it can support the provinces' fiscal sustainability in two ways: supplying fiscal capacity and discipline. Currently, it does not supply enough of either.

The capacity deficit is due, in large part, to the vertical fiscal imbalance. The provinces are on the hook for the country's rising health-care costs, while the federal government occupies a disproportionate share of the country's revenue-raising capacity and space. Federal transfers address the imbalance to some degree, but not nearly enough. The imbalance is expected to grow in coming years as population aging causes provincial health-care costs to rise. The provinces can raise taxes and will have to, but the tax base is finite and shared, and Ottawa enjoys first-mover advantage over rates (Boadway 2004). Ottawa can also unilaterally cut transfers, and while it is generally reluctant to do so, the threat always exists, particularly if its own finances come under strain, as they did in the 1990s.

The discipline deficit stems, in large part, from investors' bailout beliefs. A provincial default would have potentially devastating consequences for Canada's economy, given the provinces' significant presence in domestic and international capital markets. It would also undermine Ottawa's capacity to realize its social welfare commitments, given the importance of provincial solvency for the quality of social provision (Hanniman 2018). Most bondholders, therefore, are betting that Ottawa is unlikely to let a province default, making it easier for provinces to borrow more than they otherwise could.

Bailout expectations do not insulate the provinces from market discipline entirely, as students of provincial finances well know. There is always some possibility, however slight, that Ottawa would fail to pull a teetering province from the brink, which is why provincial credit conditions always depend on provinces' stand-alone creditworthiness to some degree. Provincial bonds are also less liquid than federal debt, and investors pay a premium for that liquidity, particularly when global financial conditions deteriorate. As I note above, this situation can make it difficult, at times, for provinces to borrow, even if their credit ratings are high.[3] But the disruptions are generally short lived; blips, you might say, in an otherwise cheap and stable credit market that the implicit bailout guarantee helps create.

Of course, provinces need not wait for bond markets to induce adjustments. Recent Quebec governments have taken measures to stabilize provincial debt, for example, even going so far as to establish a debt retirement fund. And several advanced economies prematurely withdrew stimulus after the global financial crisis – often under little or no pressure from bond markets (Romer and Romer 2019). But if the implicit guarantee is not a sufficient condition for accumulating large debts, it is likely a necessary one. Any fair reading of the provinces' fiscal history suggests they have all taken advantage of it at one point or another.

4. The Provincial Debt Dilemma

Many believe the simplest solution to provinces' fiscal ills is to increase federal transfers. On the structural side are calls for a larger and needs-based Canadian Health Transfer (CHT), particularly for provinces with rapidly aging populations (Béland et al. 2020). On the cyclical side are calls for an enhanced

Fiscal Stabilization Program to help offset provincial revenue shocks. There is no doubt these measures would boost provincial fiscal capacity. But are they affordable? Will the federal government deliver them? Would they work?

Additional transfers are clearly affordable. The latest PBO projections suggest the federal government can stabilize its debt to GDP and substantially increase provincial support without raising taxes or cutting spending (MacPhee et al. 2022). As with all exercises of this nature, there is no guarantee the underlying assumptions about interest rates and other economic and fiscal variables will pan out. Nor do the projections account for the possibility of future recessions. This uncertainty is why some would like to see active measures to reduce the debt ratio, while others would like to see it fall naturally (without raising taxes or cutting spending) without any net new spending outside of a recession. That would require additional transfers to come from higher taxes but would not necessarily make additional transfers unaffordable. Even a modest federal tax increase could go a long way towards closing the vertical fiscal imbalance.

Will the federal government increase transfers? To some extent, it already has. Direct federal transfers to provinces increased by roughly $23 billion in 2020–1, primarily through the $19 billion Safe Restart Agreement funds. Although the support was temporary, it provided provinces with substantial relief. Ottawa has also enriched the Fiscal Stabilization Program, provided significant transfers for childcare, and increased health-care funds. Yet, relative to provincial needs, *permanent* increases have been fairly modest. And they may continue to be if provinces continue to refuse federal health-care conditions.

But suppose the transfers do come. Would they work? The question is rarely asked, and yet a substantial cross-national literature suggests increasing transfers generally results in higher, rather than lower, deficits at the subnational level (Rodden 2006). Why? The most common explanation revolves around the notion of a soft budget constraint (Rodden, Eskeland, and Litvack 2003): a situation in which units borrow recklessly because they assume that, if anything goes wrong, the central government will bail them out. This outcome is only plausible, of course, if recipients interpret transfer increases as open-ended commitments. The provinces' pandemic-related transfers were temporary and unlikely, therefore, to have this effect. Ottawa can mitigate bailout expectations associated with permanent increases by allocating them according to clear and fixed criteria that provinces cannot easily game. But the pressure for ad hoc measures is strong, as recent bailouts of Newfoundland and Labrador's Muskrat Falls project attest. And no amount of fiscal engineering will substantially lower investors' bailout expectations or eliminate moral hazard entirely, since virtually any reliable transfer shields recipients from irresponsible choices to some extent. Additional transfers may increase the capacity to balance provincial budgets. Incentives are another matter.

5. The Deeper Problem: Governance

The discipline-capacity dilemma is not unique to Canada, but at least two features of Canadian federalism make it particularly sharp. The first is sociological. Canada is a deeply federal and multinational society with powerful provincial and regional identities. These characteristics put brute force solutions to provincial debt, including combining a significant increase in transfers with constraints on provincial borrowing autonomy, out of reach.

The second is institutional. Provincial debt is a classic collective action problem. Containing it would yield substantial collective benefits (including a reduction of macroeconomic risk), but it would also impose material and political costs on provinces. Certain institutions – including a vertically integrated national party system – can help resolve or attenuate these distributional conflicts (Rodden 2006), but in Canada, this institutional machinery is notoriously absent.[4]

The problems with Canada's fiscal federal governance do not end here. Canada's weak system of shared rule gives the federal government almost exclusive authority over most aspects of the transfer system, even if it feels compelled, for the sake of national unity and re-election, to take provincial views into account. The upshot is a tense mix of federal unilateralism and highly informal and self-interested intergovernmental bargaining, replete with ad hoc bailouts, intergovernmental blame shifting, and a striking lack of policy initiative. Debates over the transfer system have become so politicized in recent years that even some of the most obvious and pressing problems have become too sensitive to address (see Tombe's discussion of the federal Equalization Program in chapter 4 of this volume to appreciate the depth and consequences of this neglect). Any solution to the provincial debt dilemma needs to address this governance challenge.

6. A Potential, If Partial, Remedy

This section suggests a potential, albeit partial, solution: the establishment of an independent council responsible for assessing the performance of Canada's federal transfer system and advising the federal government on its reform. A body along these lines could address the provincial debt dilemma in four ways: strengthening the federation's problem-solving capacity, hardening provincial budget constraints, limiting unilateral federal transfer cuts, and facilitating collective action. This section discusses these potential benefits, as well as potential concerns about the body's political feasibility, effectiveness, and legitimacy.

Strengthening the federation's problem-solving capacity: Governance of Canada's federal-provincial transfer system is highly politicized (Béland and Lecours

2013). Strikingly absent is any semblance of what Fritz Scharpf (1988) calls a problem-solving approach: a style of bargaining in which actors retain but temper their self-interest with an orientation towards common values, norms, and interests. The modest hope is that an independent council might tilt a highly politicized debate in a more deliberative and cooperative direction, making it easier to reconcile fiscal capacity and discipline, and a variety of other challenges as well.

The council could evaluate the transfer system (as well as proposals to improve it) along several dimensions (Hanniman 2015). Does the system adequately measure and equalize provincial fiscal capacity? Does it promote fiscal discipline and effort? Does it provide provinces with adequate insurance against negative revenue shocks? Does it adequately address the vertical fiscal imbalance? Does it conform to national standards of equity, efficiency, and fairness?

Analysis along these lines could enhance the federation's problem-solving capacity in several ways. It could improve the technical quality of policy and policy debates; identify neglected issues; increase trust in the policy process, particularly among the transfer system's critics; generate political cover or consensus to pursue controversial reforms; and provide a neutral and broadly national perspective – one that appeals to national values, identities, and interests – on a highly provincialized debate.

Hardening provincial budget constraints: As I note above, substantially increasing transfers might increase provincial capacity to stabilize debts, but it might soften provincial budget constraints as well. The centre can mitigate this risk by allocating transfers according to fixed criteria, but no system of fiscal federal contracts can avoid renegotiation forever, and defective or outmoded systems require reform. Any solution to the soft budget constraint needs, therefore, to manage expectations around this contracting process. An independent council can help in three ways: (1) increase the odds of principled expansions of fiscal envelopes, such as ones that address unexpected or evolving challenges; (2) decrease the odds of problematic or ad hoc expansions, such as ones that insure or compensate provinces against bad fiscal decisions; and (3) disincentivize intergovernmental blame shifting, which distracts provinces and their publics from identifying solutions.

What we are describing, in essence, is a solution to the classic tension between discretion and rules (Kydland and Prescott 1977). Discretion allows policy makers to adapt policies to changing conditions but also drives a wedge between the desire to commit now and the temptation to renege later. Credible rules remove this wedge but also make it harder to correct for policy errors and adapt to new conditions. An independent council can potentially resolve this tension by coordinating expectations around a process (one that increases the odds of certain reforms and decreases the odds of others) rather than a fixed set of rules.

It might help to make the idea more concrete. Suppose a province with above-average fiscal capacity demands equalization payments on the grounds of a high budget deficit. The federal government could request the opinion of the council, which might conclude that neither the deficit nor its causes are grounds for a transfer increase. If provincial voters or journalists find the council persuasive, then the province would be wise to reduce the deficit rather than trying to shift the blame. The council would remain open to the possibility of increasing transfers, of course, but only if the reasons were sound.

Limiting unilateral federal transfer cuts: One reason Ottawa has yet to substantially increase transfers is provinces' resistance to conditions. In some cases, particularly Quebec, this reluctance reflects a deep-seated commitment to provincial autonomy (see Alain Noël's chapter 19 in this volume). In others, it partly reflects the risk of transfer cuts. Although transfers have become substantially more reliable, smaller, and arbitrary, changes still occur (see Tracy Snoddon's chapter 20 in this volume), and the drastic cuts of 1995 still loom large (see Alan Fenna's chapter 22 in this volume). Why should provinces commit to federal priorities if they cannot rely on federal support?

Facilitating collective action: An independent council could increase the credibility of federal commitments. In addition to evaluating the quality of existing transfer arrangements, it can also name and shame harmful and unjustified cuts. This surveillance would not give provinces formal influence over the federal spending power. But it could provide some additional predictability – potentially easing opposition to conditions and paving the way for higher transfer increases.

More generally, the council may be able to supply the federation – and its weak institutions of collective action – with a much-needed commitment device. It could credibly commit the federal government to supporting fiscal capacity and the provinces to fiscal discipline – addressing both aspects of the capacity-discipline dilemma and increasing the odds of agreements on transfer increases. (Ottawa is more likely to increase transfers if provinces agree to conditions, but it will also be more amenable if provinces reliably balance their budgets.)

Political feasibility, effectiveness, and legitimacy: How likely is the federal government to establish such a body? The council could provide a number of federal benefits, including cover for controversial reforms, and be a helpful interlocutor in negotiations with provinces. But it might also limit federal discretion over the transfer system and provoke opposition from provinces, which might worry about their loss of influence.[5]

The body's design – including its regional composition and appointment procedures – will be key to gaining provinces' trust. So will its remit. Ottawa could limit the body's mandate to disseminating information on the transfer system and its effects (Mendelsohn 2012). It could also have it provide advice on meeting program objectives – or even designing or redesigning specific transfers – or on the system as a whole. This holistic approach would have a number of technical and strategic advantages (Feehan 2020), but it might also prove more controversial with provinces.

What about effectiveness and legitimacy? For a number of observers, notably Béland and Lecours (2012), the Australian Commonwealth Grants Commission (CGC) is cause for hope. The Commonwealth generally accepts the CGC's arm's-length advice on distributing the pool of goods and services tax (GST) revenues, and it rarely gets any pushback from states. On its face, this model looks like a good solution for Canada. The territorial solidarity appears to be present (strong majorities in each province consistently support the Equalization Program). But many do not trust the federal government to redistribute the resources fairly. Accepting the advice of a disinterested council might, therefore, provide a significant source of depoliticization and trust.

The Canada-Australia comparison, however, is anything but a textbook case in most-similar research design. The CGC might be partially responsible for Australia's harmonious intergovernmental relations, but it might also play second fiddle to deeper cultural and institutional variables, including a relatively homogenous federal culture and a vertically integrated party system.

The council would also arrive at a difficult time for experts. While growing disillusionment with partisan politics has clearly increased demand for technocratic governance in some quarters (Bertsou and Caramani 2020), the recent upsurge in right-wing populism in many countries has clearly weakened it in others. It is not inconceivable that a populist premier would challenge an independent body's views – not unlike Saskatchewan Premier Scott Moe did, for example, when the PBO concluded that the federal carbon tax would cause most residents to come out ahead. Some premiers might go even further and question the body's political independence, as prominent members of the federal Conservatives have done, for example, with the country's independent central bank.

The risk of a populist backlash might be grounds to limit the body's advisory scope. More than anything, however, it might be grounds to keep our expectations in check. The council is unlikely to fundamentally depoliticize Canada's fiscal federal system. But it might be able to push it in a slightly more deliberative and cooperative direction.

7. Conclusion

Canada's provincial debts are unsustainable. Ideally, provinces will stabilize them gradually. But even a gradual approach requires substantial levels of fiscal capacity and discipline. Currently, Canada's fiscal federal framework does not supply enough of either, and the best way to bolster provincial fiscal capacity – increasing transfers – will not improve fiscal discipline and may even make it worse. This dilemma exists in all federations, but the governance of Canada's fiscal federal system – and the deeper sociological and institutional factors underpinning it – make it particularly difficult to address. An independent council responsible for monitoring and advising the federal government on the transfer system might provide a partial remedy by enhancing the federation's problem-solving capacity, hardening provincial budget constraints, constraining the federal spending power, and facilitating collective action. The body will face considerable political obstacles, however, and there is no guarantee it will work. The design and roll out will be key.

Regardless of the solution, the stakes are high. Low interest rates provide provinces with an opportunity for gradual fiscal adjustment, but they also weaken incentives for federal and provincial action. Debts and other fiscal vulnerabilities may continue to mount, increasing the risk of a more abrupt and painful solution, especially if the inequality between growth and interest rates flips. Simple and forceful ways of getting ahead of the problem, including the imposition of national fiscal rules, will continue to elude us. Subtle and partial solutions – including ones that tackle the problem at a governance level – will have to do the work.

NOTES

1 It has done so, at least to date, without triggering a corresponding increase in the inflation premium on government debt. This outcome is evident in the narrow spread between the interest rate on the federal government's inflation-protected and non-inflation–protected bonds. It appears markets expect inflation to return to target over the medium to long term, though it is always possible their expectations will shift.
2 These sources of inflation might include supply bottlenecks, excess stimulus, and higher energy costs.
3 The demand for liquidity was so overwhelming in early 2020 that a standard "flight to liquidity" quickly morphed into a "dash for cash," causing even sovereign bond markets in advanced economies to crash. This affair is one reason why I disagree with Tombe's suggestion (chapter 4 in this volume) that an enriched Fiscal Stabilization Program (FSP) might have helped stabilize provincial bond markets – potentially providing an alternative to central bank interventions. An enhanced FSP would have bolstered provincial creditworthiness, but fire sales of virtually riskless US and Government of Canada debt suggest that liquidity, rather than default risk, was investors' primary concern in early 2020. For a general account of the dash for cash, see the Financial Stability Board (2021). For an account of the dynamics in Canadian capital markets, see Macklem et al. (2021).

4 Several studies have found subnational governments run smaller deficits when they share the central government's party label (Rodden and Wibbels 2002), but it is unlikely this relationship, which does not hold in all countries, has much effect in Canada. Not only is the incidence of same-party rule low, but many of the devices used to discipline provincial co-partisans – including national control over provincial nominations, appointments, and other career levers – are absent (Bakvis 1994; Chandler 1987; Thorlakson 2009).

5 The Expert Panel on Equalization and Territorial Formula Financing (2006), also known as the O'Brien Commission, which dealt with the reform of the federal equalization system, decided not to recommend the establishment of an independent council precisely because of this provincial concern.

REFERENCES

Bakvis, Herman. 1994. "Political Parties, Party Government, and Intrastate Federalism in Canada." In *Parties and Federalism in Australia and Canada*, edited by Campbell Sharman, 1–22. Canberra: Federalism Research Centre, Australian National University.

Béland, Daniel, and André Lecours. 2012. *Equalization at Arm's Length*. Fiscal Transfers Series. Mowat Publication No. 48. Toronto: Mowat Centre, University of Toronto.

– 2013. "The Institutional Politics of Territorial Redistribution: Federalism and Equalization Policy in Australia and Canada." *Canadian Journal of Political Science* 46, no. 1: 93–113. https://doi.org/10.1017/S000842391300019X.

Béland, Daniel, André Lecours, Mireille Paquet, and Trevor Tombe. 2021. "A Critical Juncture in Fiscal Federalism? Canada's Response to COVID-19." *Canadian Journal of Political Science* 53, no. 2: 239–43. https://doi.org/10.1017/S0008423920000323.

Bertsou, Eri, and Daniele Caramani. 2020. "People Haven't Had Enough of Experts: Technocratic Attitudes among Citizens in Nine European Countries." *American Journal of Political Science* 66, no. 1: 5–23. https://doi.org/10.1111/ajps.12554.

Blanchard, Olivier. 2023. *Fiscal Policy under Low Interest Rates*. Cambridge, MA: MIT Press.

Blanchard, Olivier, Josh Felman, and Arvind Subramanian. 2021. "Does the New Fiscal Consensus in Advanced Economies Travel to Emerging Markets?" *Peterson Institute for International Economics Policy Brief* 21, no. 7. https://www.piie.com/sites/default/files/documents/pb21-7.pdf.

Boadway, Robin. 2004. "Should the Canadian Federation be Rebalanced?" Working Paper 2004(1). Institute of Intergovernmental Relations, Queen's University. https://www.queensu.ca/iigr/sites/iirwww/files/uploaded_files/2004-1Robinboadway.pdf.

Chandler, William. 1987. "Federalism and Political Parties." In *Federalism and the Role of the State*," edited by Herman Bakvis and William Chandler, 149–70. Toronto: University of Toronto Press.

Delong, Bradford J. 2016. "On the Proper Size of the Public Sector and the Level of Public Debt in the Twenty-First Century." In *Progress and Confusion: The State of Macroeconomic Policy*, edited by Olivier Blanchard, Raghuram Rajan, Kenneth Rogoff, and Lawrence H. Summers, 197–209. Cambridge, MA: MIT Press.

de Mello, Luiz, and Teresa Ter-Minassian. 2022. *Improving Subnational Governments' Resilience in the Wake of the COVID-19 Pandemic*. Organisation for Economic Co-operation and Development (OECD) Working Papers on Fiscal Federalism, No. 37. Paris: OECD Publishing. https://www.oecd.org/tax/improving-subnational-governments-resilience-in-the-wake-of-the-covid-19-pandemic-6b1304c8-en.htm.

Expert Panel on Equalization and Territorial Formula Financing. 2006. *Achieving a National Purpose: Putting Equalization Back on Track*. Ottawa: Department of Finance. https://publications.gc.ca/collections/Collection/F2-176-2006E.pdf.

Feehan, James P. 2020. "Canada's Equalization Program: Political Debates, and Opportunities for Reform." *IRPP Insight* 30, 28 January 2020. Montreal: Institute for Research on Public Policy. https://doi.org/10.26070/zp9t-zt92.

Financial Stability Board. 2021. "Holistic Review of the March Market Turmoil." Financial Stability Board, 17 November 2020. https://www.fsb.org/wp-content/uploads/P171120-2.pdf.

Fitch Ratings. 2021. "Fitch Affirms Province of Saskatchewan, Canada's IDRs at 'AA'; Outlook Stable." *FitchRatings*, 10 February 2021. https://www.fitchratings.com/research/international-public-finance/fitch-affirms-province-of-saskatchewan-canada-idrs-at-aa-outlook-stable-10-02-2021.

Gopinath, Gita. 2020. "Global Liquidity Trap Requires a Big Fiscal Response." *Financial Times*, 2 November 2020. https://www.ft.com/content/2e1c0555-d65b-48d1-9af3-825d187eec58.

Hanniman, Kyle. 2015. *Calm Counsel: Fiscal Federalism, and Provincial Credit Risk*. Mowat Research No. 104. Toronto: Mowat Centre, School of Public Policy and Governance, University of Toronto. https://hdl.handle.net/1807/99325.

– 2018. "Is Canadian Federalism Market-Preserving? The View from Bond Markets." In *Federalism and the Welfare State in a Multicultural World*, edited by Elizabeth Goodyear-Grant, Richard Johnston, Will Kymlicka, and John Myles, 49–72. Montreal and Kingston: McGill-Queen's University Press.

– 2020a. "COVID-19, Fiscal Federalism and Provincial Debt: Have We Reached a Critical Juncture?" *Canadian Journal of Political Science* 53, no. 2: 279–85. https://doi.org/10.1017/S0008423920000621.

– 2020b. *Strengthening Canada's Fiscal Resilience*. Essay no. 4, Inaugural Essay Series. Montreal: Institute for Research on Public Policy. https://centre.irpp.org/research-studies/strengthening-canadas-fiscal-resilience/.

Hanniman, Kyle, and Trevor Tombe. 2020. Fiscal Risks and Government Debt in Canada: The Implications of Interest Rate and Growth Volatility." *Finances of the Nation*, 10 December 2020. https://financesofthenation.ca/2020/12/10/fiscal-risks-and-government-debt-in-canada-the-implications-of-interest-rate-and-growth-rate-volatility/.

Hansen, Alvin. 1939. "Economic Progress and Declining Population Growth." *American Economic Review* 29, no. 1: 1–15. https://www.jstor.org/stable/1806983.

Jenkner, Eva, and Lu Zhongjin. 2014. "Subnational Credit Risk and Sovereign Bailouts – Who Pays the Premium?" International Monetary Fund Working Paper No. 2014/020. https://www.imf.org/en/Publications/WP/Issues/2016/12/31/Sub-National-Credit-Risk-and-Sovereign-Bailouts-Who-Pays-the-Premium-41294.

Kydland, Finn E., and Edward C. Prescott. 1977. "Rules Rather than Discretion: The Inconsistency of Optimal Plans." *Journal of Political Economy* 85, no. 3: 473–91. https://doi.org/10.1086/260580.

Macklem, Tiff, Timothy Lane, Lawrence Schembri, Paul Beaudry, and Toni Gravelle. 2021. *Financial System Review – 2021*. Bank of Canada, 20 May 2021. https://www.bankofcanada.ca/2021/05/financial-system-review-2021/.

MacPhee, Sarah, Régine Cléophat, Albert Kho, and Caroline Nicol. 2022. *Fiscal Sustainability Report 2022*. Ottawa: Office of the Parliamentary Budget Officer. https://www.pbo-dpb.ca/en/publications/RP-2223-012-S–fiscal-sustainability-report-2022–rapport-viabilite-financiere-2022.

Mendelsohn, Matthew. 2012. *Back to Basics: The Future of Fiscal Arrangements*. Mowat Publication No. 58. Toronto: Mowat Centre, School of Public Policy and Governance, University of Toronto. https://tspace.library.utoronto.ca/bitstream/1807/99235/1/Mendelsohn_2012_Back_to_Basics.pdf.

Moody's Investors Service. 2010. "Canadian Provinces: Conditions Remain Challenging." Announcement, 16 February 2010. https://www.moodys.com/.

Oates, Wallace. 2005. "Toward a Second-Generation Theory of Fiscal Federalism." *International Tax and Public Finance* 12: 349–73. https://doi.org/10.1007/s10797-005-1619-9.

Rodden, Jonathan. 2006. *Hamilton's Paradox: The Promise and Peril of Fiscal Federalism*. New York: Cambridge University Press.

Rodden, Jonathan A., Gunnar S. Eskeland, and Jennie Litvack (eds.). 2003. *Fiscal Decentralization and the Challenge of Hard Budget Constraints*. Cambridge, MA: MIT Press.

Rodden, Jonathan, and Erik Wibbels. 2002. "Beyond the Fiction of Federalism: Macroeconomic Management in Multitiered Systems." *World Politics* 54, no. 4: 494–531. https://doi.org/10.1353/wp.2002.0016.

– 2010. "Fiscal Decentralization and the Business Cycle: An Empirical Analysis of Seven Federations." *Economics and Politics* 22, no. 1: 37–67. https://doi.org/10.1111/j.1468-0343.2009.00350.x.

Romer, Christina D., and David H. Romer. 2019. "Fiscal Space and the Aftermath of Financial Crises: How it Matters and Why." Working Paper 25768. National Bureau of Economic Research (NBER) Working Paper Series. https://www.nber.org/papers/w25768.

Samuels, David. 2003. *Ambition, Federalism, and Legislative Politics in Brazil*. Cambridge: Cambridge University Press.

Scharpf, Fritz. 1988. "The Joint-Decision Making Trap: Lessons from German Federalism, and European Integration." *Public Administration* 66, no. 3: 239–78. https://doi.org/10.1111/j.1467-9299.1988.tb00694.x.

Summers, Lawrence. 2014. "Reflections on the 'New Secular Stagnation Hypothesis.'" In *Secular Stagnation: Fact, Causes, and Cures*, edited by Coen Teulings and Richard Baldwin, 27–38. London: CEPR Press.

– 2022. "Secular Stagnation after COVID-19." Stamp Memorial Lecture. London School of Economics (LSE) Online Event, 12 November 2022. https://www.youtube.com/watch?v=yQMSlLTsaHI.

Thorlakson, Lori. 2009. "Patterns of Party Integration, Influence, and Autonomy in Seven Federations." *Party Politics* 15, no. 2: 157–77. https://doi.org/10.1177/1354068808099979.

Tombe, Trevor. 2020. "Finances of the Nation: Provincial Debt Sustainability in Canada: Demographics, Federal Transfers, and COVID-19." *Canadian Tax Journal* 68, no. 4: 1083–1122. https://doi.org/10.32721/ctj.2020.68.4.fon.

Wibbels, Erik. 2005. *Federalism and the Market: Intergovernmental Conflict and Economic Reform in the Developing World*. Cambridge: Cambridge University Press.

10 Fiscal Federalism in Canada's North: Understanding Territorial Formula Financing

CHRISTOPHER YURRIS, DANIEL BÉLAND, AND TREVOR TOMBE

Introduction

Fiscal federalism, especially equalization, has long been a widespread source of contention and debate in Canadian politics (Béland et al. 2017; chapter 2 by Mary Janigan in this volume). In 2021, in the context of province-wide municipal elections, Alberta even organized a referendum on whether the principle of equalization should be removed from the constitution (Bellefontaine 2021). According to then premier Jason Kenney, the objective of this referendum was to use equalization as an issue to gain additional political leverage for Alberta in intergovernmental relations, especially in debates over oil and pipeline policies (Bennett 2021). This remark points to the fact that many controversies over equalization in Canada involve natural resources, especially non-renewable ones. Much of this rhetoric can be attributed to the symbolic importance of natural resources in Canada, especially in Alberta, as they are considered, oil in particular, a marker of provincial autonomy and prosperity (Béland et al. 2017, 42).

Yet, many of the debates on fiscal federalism have been centred on the ten provinces; the three Northern territories – Yukon, Northwest Territories (NWT), and Nunavut – have been largely ignored in public debates (and the academic literature) on fiscal federalism. The lack of discussion on the territories in debates surrounding fiscal federalism exists despite the rich natural resource potential of the region, which is home to various mineral deposits "including diamonds, gold, base metals and silver, tungsten, uranium, rare earth elements, iron ore, zinc, and copper" (CanNor 2021). For instance, according to Natural Resources Canada, in 2019 the value of natural resources production in the North was projected to exceed $3 billion, including over $1.8 billion in the NWT, $1.3 billion in Nunavut, and $169 million in the Yukon (CanNor 2021). Moreover, the energy sector is a significant contributor to the Northern Canadian economy, with the potential for major growth: "Northern Canada is estimated to contain one third of Canada's remaining potential for conventional oil and natural gas," primarily in the NWT and Nunavut (CIRNAC 2020; CER 2022). Yet, this lack of focus on the territories is not that puzzling, considering the difficulty associated with developing resources in the territories, including high start-up costs (Henderson and White 2015, 339).

Overlooking the territories in the study of fiscal federalism is a great disservice, as the three territories represent an interesting case study of fiscal federalism on two accounts. First, studying the territories' distinctive constitutional status, with their lack of constitutional control over natural resources, could improve our broader understanding of fiscal federalism in Canada. Second, with many Indigenous peoples in the territories, fiscal federalism and the related issue of natural resource devolution in the territories are intimately linked with both reconciliation and multilevel governance; in fact, the Northwest Territories Devolution Agreement was signed between the federal government, the government of the Northwest Territories (GNWT), and several signatory Aboriginal groups.[1] This agreement is also relevant for Territorial Formula Financing (TFF) design and implementation, as there could be future self-government agreements with Indigenous peoples that may lead to federal adjustments to the formula, which might lower funding levels to the GNWT. These issues may also matter for Nunavut, as that territory is a product of the 1993 Nunavut Land Claims Agreement (NLCA); Article 4 of the NLCA, "Nunavut Political Development," calls for the government of Canada to

> recommend to Parliament, as a government measure, legislation to establish, within a defined time period, a new Nunavut Territory, with its own Legislative Assembly and public government, separate from the Government of the remainder of the Northwest Territories.[2]

Likewise, the Nunavut devolution negotiations have involved the Nunavut Tunngavik Incorporated (NTI), representing the Inuit of Nunavut, which is listed as a party to the Nunavut devolution process (CIRNAC 2019).

Overall, Territorial Formula Financing is much less openly contentious than equalization. As argued in this chapter, this situation is related to the fact that TFF is not a zero-sum game, since all three territories receive money on a constant basis. This consistency is a strong contrast to equalization, a program that only transfers money to provinces with a fiscal capacity that falls under a national average (Béland et al. 2017).[3] However, that does not mean the formula cannot be improved. We will argue in this chapter that future challenges, primarily related to population aging and health-care expenditures, are potentially not well reflected in the current formula. Political conflict over this funding arrangement may increase, especially if future self-government agreements lead to lower funding to territorial governments – as previously noted. Simultaneously, as we also argue, there is political conflict over fiscal federalism in the territories, centred primarily on the devolution process as it relates to natural resources. Devolution is a contentious issue in the North as much as in the provinces but in a different way due to the constitutional framework and the politics of reconciliation, although more so in Nunavut than in the two other territories. The emphasis on devolution in the debates around fiscal federalism in the North aligns with the provinces' experience, where natural resources are a key point of contention when debating fiscal federalism, especially equalization (Béland et al. 2017, 42).[4]

The first section of this chapter will provide a literature review on the territories. The second section will introduce the territories as a case study on fiscal federalism in Canada, including an overview of the territories' differing economies, demographics, and politics. The third section will discuss fiscal federalism in the territories, focusing on TFF and natural resource devolution. The main conclusion is that, while the dynamics of fiscal federalism in the territories are distinctly different from the dynamics in the provinces due to the territories' unique historical and institutional legacies, the experience of fiscal federalism in the territories is still very much natural resource centric, as evidenced by the devolution process. This emphasis on natural resources aligns with the provincial experience, albeit manifesting itself in different ways due to distinct institutional legacies such as the lack of zero-sum logic associated with federal equalization payments to the provinces.

Lay of the Land and Framework

Valuable political science work has been done on devolution in the territories, but this scholarship is not centred on fiscal federalism. For example, Alcantara, Cameron, and Kennedy (2012) explore the devolution negotiations between the Yukon and the federal government. They provide a thorough historical background of Yukon devolution. Moreover, Alcantara (2013) provides an overview of devolution in the three territories. Alcantara's article does not really touch on fiscal federalism; however, it provides a valuable historical account of devolution in the territories, explaining why devolution occurred differently in the three territories, as well as an assessment of the current state of devolution.

To summarize this work, the Yukon's ability to negotiate devolution agreements sooner than Nunavut and the NWT can be attributed to various factors. First, the Yukon Umbrella Agreement, which was signed in 1993, made it easier to gain what was considered acceptable Indigenous consent in the Yukon compared to the NWT. Second, there are differing views on the maturity of the Yukon versus the NWT government, with the prevailing view being that the Yukon was more politically mature and ready to inherit additional powers (Alcantara 2013). Yet, importantly for the present chapter, these articles do not put a major emphasis on fiscal federalism.

Cameron and Campbell (2009) focus on Nunavut devolution, including transfers of administrative responsibilities from the federal to territorial governments and the constitutional status of Nunavut. The authors argue for the importance of renewed efforts to devolve land and resource administration and control to the government of Nunavut. From a fiscal federalism perspective, their article is relevant in its examination of how the devolution of lands and natural resources to the territories can result in Nunavut's decrease in federal dependency in the long term (205-7).

Considering that relatively little has been written about the politics of fiscal federalism in the territories, this chapter turns to the growing political science literature on fiscal federalism as it deals with the provinces. Particularly interesting here is the work on equalization policy, as it is an explicitly redistributive program that has generated much intergovernmental conflict between Ottawa and the provinces, and among the provinces (Béland et al. 2017).

While the provinces and the territories all receive federal money under the Canada Health Transfer (CHT) and the Canada Social Transfer (CST), the Equalization Program only applies to the provinces. Territorial Formula Financing (TFF) is the territorial equivalent of equalization because, like equalization and unlike both the CHT and the CST, TFF offers *unconditional* payments to the territories to help them provide public services to their residents.

A comparison between how the Constitution Act, 1982 defines the principle of equalization and how the federal government explains the nature of TFF stresses the strong parallels between the two federal programs. First, in subsection 36(2) of the Constitution Act, 1982, the principle of equalization is justified regarding the provinces in this way: "Parliament and the government of Canada are committed to the principle of making equalization payments to ensure that provincial governments have sufficient revenues to provide reasonably comparable levels of public services at reasonably comparable levels of taxation" (Department of Finance Canada 2011a).

By contrast, the federal government defines TFF as an "annual unconditional transfer from the Government of Canada to the three territorial governments to enable them to provide their residents a range of public services comparable to those offered by provincial governments, at comparable levels of taxation" (Government of Canada, 2011). Yet, while equalization payments reduce fiscal inequalities among provinces by providing payments only to provinces located below a national fiscal capacity average (Béland et al. 2017), TFF is legitimized in the above quote through a direct comparison between the provinces and the territories.

The implicit point here is that, taken as a whole, territories have a much lower fiscal capacity than the provinces in general, and simultaneously, they must pay much more on average to provide the same basic public services due to well-known factors such as geographical remoteness. In this context, while only some provinces receive equalization payments to improve their relative position vis-à-vis wealthier provinces with a greater fiscal capacity, which helps them finance public services to their residents, all three territories qualify for TFF payments, which are much larger than the average equalization payment to the receiving provinces on a per capita basis. Overall, the territories depend much more on federal transfers than the provinces. Yet, in general, fiscal federalism seems to be less contentious in the territories than in the provinces, which is particularly striking when we compare equalization to its territorial equivalent, TFF.

Drawing on insight from the institutionalist political science literature on how policies shape politics over time (Béland, Campbell, and Weaver 2022; Pierson 1993), it is possible to argue that differences in policy design between equalization and TFF account at least in part for the lower level of territorial conflict over the latter program. In other words, since all the territories receive substantial TFF payments every year, potential tensions among these units and between them and the federal government are reduced. While provinces that do not receive or lose access to equalization payments can criticize the federal equalization formula or even turn against receiving provinces (Béland et al. 2017), territories all rely massively on TFF each year. This uniformity also makes TFF more stable and predictable over time, a situation that is likely to reduce political tensions over these transfers.

Yet, beyond these powerful institutional and temporal effects, there is evidence from the existing literature on fiscal federalism in Canada that other factors do affect the intergovernmental politics of federal transfers to subnational units. For example, in their *Publius* article on the politics of equalization policy in Canada, André Lecours and Daniel Béland claim that, beyond institutional factors such as executive discretion, which is directly related to policy design, factors like the territorial distribution of natural resources can affect intergovernmental relations. This dispute arises because economic and fiscal inequalities stemming from the uneven distribution of natural resources among the provinces shape political conflict over equalization in strong ways. The recurring criticisms of equalization in Alberta, a province that has not received equalization payments since the early 1960s due largely to its oil wealth, illustrate this claim (Lecours and Béland 2010).

Simultaneously, the work of Lecours and Béland (2010) on equalization suggests that, beyond policy design and the distribution of natural resources, broad ideological and political factors can impact the politics of fiscal federalism in Canada. For example, subnational political actors such as parties and their ideological and electoral agendas can affect mobilization over transfer payments in the three territories. Therefore, when turning to the politics of fiscal federalism in the territories, we must pay close attention to how electoral political mobilization is organized. Of particular interest is the non-partisan adaptation of Westminster parliamentary democracy, known as "consensus government," which exists in the NWT and Nunavut, but not in the provinces or even in the Yukon, which has its own party system.

Finally, from a demographic standpoint, overall the territories are different from the provinces due to their higher proportion of Indigenous peoples, a situation that makes reconciliation an even more central political issue than in the provinces. Therefore, in addition to policy design, natural resources, and electoral politics, our analysis of the politics of TFF does take Indigenous politics into consideration, especially in the context of the devolution debate in the territories, which brings both reconciliation and the exploitation of natural resources to the fore.

The Territories

As the above remarks about natural resources and electoral systems suggest, the three territories must not be treated as a monolith. They each have distinctive demographics, economies, political development, and political institutions. This section will outline the policy design of fiscal federalism in the territories, along with the territories' differing economies, political cultures, and demographics. These characteristics are important to understanding the varying political and institutional factors involved in the politics of fiscal federalism and natural resource devolution.

Fiscal Challenges

The territories have several key institutional differences compared to provincial governments. Unlike the provinces, which have their jurisdictions outlined in section 91 of the Constitution Act, 1982, the three territories are creatures of the federal government, with powers devolved through acts of Parliament. They also face unique and fundamental geographic and economic challenges. We highlight three factors that are particularly relevant when considering fiscal arrangements and transfer design with respect to the territories: limited revenue-generating capacity, unique infrastructure needs, and demographics.

The territories' revenue-generating powers are limited for several reasons. First, and most important historically – though still quite relevant today – control over Crown lands in the territories, unlike in the provinces, is constitutionally within the federal government's jurisdiction, which limits the scope for natural resource revenues for territorial governments. While recent devolution agreements have eased this fiscal constraint somewhat, they have not eliminated it. The Northwest Territories Lands and Resources Devolution Agreement between the Northwest Territories, the federal government, and six signatory Aboriginal groups in 2013, for example, allows the territorial government to keep half of resource revenues up to a fixed share of their budget needs (Government of Canada and GNWT 2013; GNWT n.d.). The rest flows to the federal government. In addition, territorial economies have relatively limited private sector employment compared to the provinces, with the public sector being the predominant source of high-paying white-collar employment. This employment pattern may affect the relative size of important tax bases – such as personal and corporate income taxes – that are a key source of revenues for provincial governments, especially when compared to the uniquely high fiscal needs of territorial governments.

Second, the remote nature of the territories means that the cost of providing services to the territories is much higher than in southern Canada. The high cost of living and provision of services is perhaps best encapsulated by Nunavut. Nunavut's isolated nature presents a plethora of challenges that are not experienced in southern Canada. Sprawling geographically, Nunavut covers over 2 million kilometres in area, roughly the size of Western Europe (White 2006). Limited transportation infrastructure inhibits economic development, contributing to the high cost of living and provision of government services in the territory (Henderson and White 2015). There are no roads connecting Nunavut's twenty-five communities together or to the rest of Canada. For example, in 2017–18, Nunavut spent $60 million on medical travel (Frizzell 2019).[5]

Third, the high cost of providing social services is amplified by the social indicators in the region. The dispersed and rapidly growing population poses a challenge, requiring considerable spending on infrastructure and services. In addition, there has been a high birth rate in the territories, resulting in additional budgetary concerns, especially for the provision of health and social services. Both the NWT and Nunavut have total fertility rates per capita higher than the national average per capita (with the Yukon just below the national average).

The unique challenges in the territories were recognized by both the Expert Panel on Equalization and Territorial Formula Financing (EPETFF 2006) and the *Mayer Report on Nunavut Devolution* (Mayer 2007), which explored the prospects of natural resource devolution in Nunavut. They also have long motivated a unique, and often ad hoc, approach to territorial financing in Canada and originally were accounted for in the federal government's own public accounts. Today, the TFF program provides the bulk of support.

Policy Design – Territorial Formula Financing

These unique circumstances require a unique fiscal arrangement. Therefore, unlike the provinces, the territories are not a part of the equalization formula.

Instead, they receive Territorial Formula Financing transfers, which have been in place since 1985–6. Fiscal federalism in the North subsequently received little attention from policy makers. However, in 2006, the Expert Panel on Equalization and Territorial Formula Financing published a report on improving TFF (EPETFF 2006). The expert panel report provided one of the most comprehensive overviews of TFF up to that point. It outlined the unique challenges in the territories, including population growth that outpaces the rest of Canada, the geographically dispersed population, health-care challenges (high costs and poor outcomes), challenging social indicators, and infrastructure limitations. Moreover, it recognized the potential for developing the territories' rich natural resources, along with devolution. It also made specific recommendations regarding transfer design, which were implemented in 2007–8 and most recently renewed in 2014.

Before exploring the details of this specific transfer arrangement, some high-level points must be made. First, there are important similarities between TFF and equalization. They are both unconditional transfers from the federal government (Department of Finance Canada 2011b), and, like equalization, eligible revenues of TFF are based on a measure of fiscal capacity, which is a measure of how much ease territorial government could raise at national average tax rates (Department of Finance Canada 2011b). However, unlike equalization – which is received by some provinces and not by others – TFF is not a zero-sum game. Every territory receives funding, albeit in differing amounts, and increases to one do not mechanically imply decreases to the others. Another difference concerns natural resource revenues, which, in contrast to what happens with equalization, are negotiated separately by each territory as part of broader federal-territorial devolution negotiations. Finally, a measure of expenditure need is incorporated into the TFF formula to help ensure territorial governments can deliver comparable levels of public services to their residents.

Detailed exploration of the recent fiscal data and the TFF formula may shed important light on its functioning. In Table 10.1 we report the several categories featured within, and steps taken to arrive at, each territory's TFF grant entitlement for the 2022–3 fiscal year. First, a measure of expenditure need is set through the gross expenditure base (GEB). The GEB is not a detailed accounting of actual expenditures by each territorial government. Rather, it is a proxy for expenditure needs that was set in legislation, effective in April 2015 and subsequently adjusted annually to reflect population growth and an average of national provincial-local government expenditures. For example, in 2022–3, payments reflect a simple average annual growth of aggregate provincial-local expenditures between 2018–19 and 2020–1 of 4.2 per cent. This amount is then adjusted up or down depending on whether a territory's population grew faster or slower than the national population growth rate. The resulting values are displayed in the first row of Table 10.1, which range from just over $1.4 billion

Table 10.1. Summary of TFF Grant Calculation for 2022–3

	Millions of Dollars			
TFF Components	Yukon	NWT	Nunavut	Total
Gross Expenditure Base	1,431.7	1,886.5	2,068.6	5,386.9
Fiscal Capacity				
Personal Income Taxes	116.9	155.6	88.5	361.0
Business Income Taxes	24.6	16.7	21.2	62.5
Consumption Taxes	149.7	168.6	111.0	429.3
Payroll Taxes	12.7	23.4	20.5	56.6
Property Taxes and Misc.	66.3	115.8	57.9	240.0
Total Fiscal Capacity	370.1	480.2	299.1	1,149.4
Economic Development Incentive	111.0	144.1	89.7	344.8
Resource Revenue Offset	0.0	33.2	0.0	33.2
Other Adjustments	1.3	1.7	0.0	3.0
Final TFF Grant Entitlement	1,174.1	1,519.2	1,859.4	4,552.8

Source: Authors' calculations using formula financing grants summary data provided by Finance Canada.
Note: Numbers may not add up due to rounding.

for the Yukon to nearly $2.1 billion for Nunavut. The future evolution of the expenditure base may represent an important challenge to federal-territorial fiscal arrangements if territorial fiscal needs grow more rapidly than the rest of the country, a real possibility that we will discuss in a later section.

On the revenue side, territorial fiscal capacity is calculated to reflect the underlying ability to raise revenue, rather than the actual revenues they choose to raise. This method of calculation balances a desire to maintain territorial autonomy, just as equalization attempts to do for provincial governments, with an equally important desire to support regions in need. Various tax categories are included, such as personal and corporate income taxes, consumption taxes (which here also include tobacco taxes, gasoline taxes, diesel fuel taxes, and revenues from the sale of alcoholic beverages), payroll taxes, property taxes, and some miscellaneous items. As for equalization, the size of each territory's tax base is measured, and an estimate of revenues that could be raised if national average tax rates were applied to those bases is calculated. These are reported in the second to seventh rows of Table 10.1. In total, at national average tax rates, Nunavut is estimated to be able to raise nearly $300 million, while the Yukon and the NWT are estimated to be able to raise $370 million and $480 million, respectively.

Some additional final adjustments are made before the TFF grant entitlements are established. First, and most importantly, is an economic development incentive. This adjustment reflects an understanding that national average tax rates may be inappropriate to apply in the territories, given the challenging circumstances that private businesses and individuals face there. This incentive is equal to 30 per cent of the territories fiscal capacity and is added to the grant calculation. Effectively, territorial fiscal capacity is thus evaluated at 70 per cent of the national average tax rates. Other adjustments include an offset for resource revenues – relevant only for the NWT – and some other minor adjustments. In total, the Yukon receives the smallest TFF grant at $1.174 billion, the NWT receives the second largest at $1.519 billion, and Nunavut receives the largest at $1.859 billion.

On a per capita basis, there are important differences between the territories in the size of the TFF grant to which they are entitled. These range from just under $27,000 per capita for the Yukon to nearly $47,000 for Nunavut. In addition, and as discussed, territorial governments also receive CHTs and CSTs, as do provincial governments. Overall, each territory receives significantly more than provincial governments do on a per capita basis. In 2022–3, the Yukon received $28,497 per capita in major transfers from the federal government, while the NWT received $34,716 and Nunavut received $48,353. The bulk of the transfers to the territorial governments, to be clear, comes through TFF, with significantly smaller amounts coming from the CHT and the CST (Hicks 2018, 355). For example, in 2022–3, the territories together received $152 million in CHT payments and $54 million in CST payments. By contrast, the provinces that receive the most federal transfers per capita are the three Maritime provinces, which received between $4,096 and $4,607 per capita from the federal government in 2022–3. In fact, the three territories all receive more total transfers than Prince Edward Island, despite PEI's population being larger than the three territories combined.[6]

Though the territories receive large sums of federal transfers on a per capita basis, these transfers aim to mitigate potentially significant economic and fiscal challenges the territories uniquely face. We attribute the territories' transfer dependency to three main factors, which we describe below.

Economy and Natural Resources

The three territories have a differing reliance on natural resources, although they are all more heavily resource-based than most provinces. Nunavut's economy is balanced between being service-based (51.6 per cent of the gross domestic product [GDP]) and goods-based (48.4 per cent of the GDP in 2020). Non-renewable resource extraction dominates Nunavut's private sector, with mining, quarrying, and oil and gas extraction contributing 36.7 per cent of the total GDP in 2020 (Richards 2021d). Despite the discovery of substantial oil and gas deposits in the Arctic Islands, logistical and financial barriers have stymied development (Henderson and White 2015).

Mining is a particularly promising industry, with deposits of coal, diamonds, iron ore, silver, uranium, and other valuable minerals. One challenge with resource extraction is ensuring that Nunavummiut derive benefit from these developments and maintain regulatory control. Both the government of Nunavut and the NTI have favoured increasing mining activity in the territory, with the NTI reversing its opposition to uranium mining in 2007 (Henderson and White 2015).

By contrast, the NWT and the Yukon have more service-based economies, with services accounting for 73.9 per cent of total GDP in both territories. The NWT and the Yukon economies are less dependent on natural resources than Nunavut, with mining, quarrying, and oil and gas extraction contributing less than 15 per cent of total GDP in 2020 in both territories (Richards 2021c, 2021e).[7]

The significance of natural resources in the territories, along with the potential for future resource extraction projects, raises the question of whether fiscal federalism and devolution in northern Canada align with the provincial experience of intergovernmental political quarrels being centred on natural resource revenues.

Demographics

The territories have varying levels of urbanization and Indigenous populations. On one end, the Yukon has the most urbanized and non-Indigenous population of the three territories; approximately 70 per cent of the Yukon's population resides in Whitehorse, with 23 per cent of Yukon residents identifying as Indigenous (Yukon, Northwest Territories, and Nunavut 2019; Indigenous Services Canada 2020). By comparison, about 22 per cent of Nunavut's population resides in Iqaluit, and 50 per cent of the NWT's population is in Yellowknife (Yukon, Northwest Territories, and Nunavut 2019). Likewise, according to the 2016 census, 51 per cent of NWT residents identify as Indigenous, whereas 86 per cent of Nunavut residents identify as Indigenous (Indigenous Services Canada 2020).

The composition of Indigenous peoples varies significantly; in Nunavut, most of the Indigenous population identifies as Inuit (30,140 of 30,550 Indigenous residents identify as Inuit according to the 2016 census). The NWT's population is 30.3 per cent First Nations, 8.1 per cent Métis, and 9.9 per cent Inuit (Inuvialuit). Indigenous peoples in the Yukon are primarily First Nations (Statistics Canada 2016). The relatively large Indigenous population in the territories means that Indigenous-settler relations and reconciliation are especially pertinent when examining fiscal federalism and natural resource devolution in northern Canada.

Another important aspect of demographics in the territories concerns the age distribution of their populations and the fiscal pressure from future population

Figure 10.1. Per Capita Government Health Expenditures, 2019

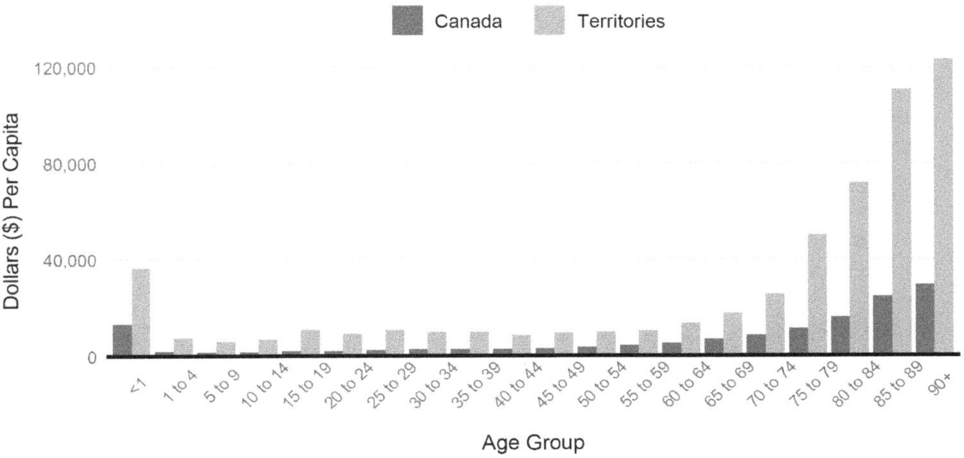

[Chart: Bar chart comparing Canada and Territories per capita government health expenditures by age group, from <1 to 90+. Y-axis: Dollars ($) Per Capita, ranging 0 to 120,000.]

Source: Own calculations from CIHI (2021).

aging. While the three territories have a smaller share of their respective populations over the age of sixty-five, they are projected to experience a roughly similar pace of aging as the rest of Canada. In 2021, for example, approximately 9 per cent of their population was aged sixty-five and over compared to 18.5 per cent of the national population. But by the early 2040s, Statistics Canada projects that roughly 15 per cent of the territorial population will be aged sixty-five and over (Statistics Canada 2019). This increase of six percentage points is slightly higher than the five percentage point increase in the national share. While not a particularly large difference in terms of the potential effect of aging on economic growth rates, there will be large effects on health-care expenditure pressures in the three territories over the next two decades.

Aging populations may increase health expenditures in all jurisdictions, but the territories may see particularly large increases. In Figure 10.1, we display information from the Canadian Institute for Health Information on government health expenditures across the age distribution (CIHI 2021). While spending is higher in the territories than the Canadian average, it is particularly elevated among higher age cohorts. Nationally, an average of approximately $12,000 per year is spent for individuals over the age of sixty-five, which rises to an average of $21,500 per year for individuals over the age of eighty. The territories, however, spend an average of over $35,000 annually for individuals over age sixty-five, and this amount rises to over $90,000 per year for individuals over age eighty. And, relative to expenditures on prime-age individuals, the territories see a sharper increase. Population aging will therefore increase the expenditure needs of territorial governments more than provincial governments. This increased expenditure need concerns fiscal arrangements specifically because, as discussed previously, the TFF grant grows each territory's expenditure base along with the national average for provincial and local governments. It may mean that the expenditure base within TFF becomes increasingly misaligned with territorial expenditure needs. Indeed, using the projected age distribution of the territories combined with the latest age-specific expenditure data displayed in Figure 10.1, we find real per capita health expenditures in the territories may increase by over $3,700 by 2043, relative to 2020 expenditures – more than double the $1,400 real per capita increase projected for the ten provinces.

Political Institutions

The three territories also have differing histories of the development of political institutions. Settler politics in the Yukon and the NWT have developed at different rates, which is relevant to studying fiscal federalism and devolution. The Yukon Gold Rush led to massive mobilization in the territory (Dickerson 1992, 15; Coates and Morrison 2005, 100). As noted by Jerald Sabin (2016, 48), in 1901 the first Canadian census taken in the territory documented the population at 27,200, 88 per cent of whom were non-Indigenous; these settlers aimed to establish a territorial government to displace federal control over the region (Alcantara 2013, 169; Sabin 2016, 48).

The Northwest Territories' path towards responsible government was much more arduous than the Yukon's (Coates and Powell 1989, 69). The Yukon's territorial government maintained a wholly elected territorial council beginning in 1908, over half a century before the NWT did in 1975 (Alcantara, Cameron, and Kennedy 2012, 330). In 1979, the Yukon received responsible government, and the NWT followed in 1986 (Cameron and White 1995, 47; Alcantara, Cameron, and Kennedy 2012, 330; Alcantara 2013, 168).

Nunavut developed differently from the other two territories as a by-product of the NLCA, a comprehensive land claim signed between the Canadian government and the NTI, representing the Inuit of Nunavut. The NLCA is protected under section 35 of the Constitution Act, 1982 (Hicks and White 2015, 42). Article 4 of the NLCA mandated the establishment of the new territory through an act of Parliament (Henderson and White 2015, 318). The NLCA opted for a public government model (where all Nunavummiut, regardless of whether they are NLCA beneficiaries or not, can vote and run for office).

Due to Nunavut's demographic composition, the government of Nunavut is ostensibly an Inuit-controlled government within Canada's federal structure (Henderson 2005, 2007; Wilson 2008). The government of Nunavut is not protected under section 35 of the Constitution Act, 1987. Nunavut was established through the 1993 Nunavut Act, with the first elections held on 15 February 1999; it officially separated from the NWT on 1 April 1999.

These differing histories of political development, as well as the demographic compositions of the territories, have resulted in differing political institutions. Since the 1978 territorial election, the Yukon Legislative Assembly has operated with political parties. The main three political parties in the Yukon are the Liberal Party, the New Democratic Party (NDP), and the Yukon Party. The Yukon Party, currently led by Currie Dixon, is the centre-right party, with fiscal conservatism as one of its core values (Windeyer 2020). The main centre-left party is the Yukon Liberal Party, led by Sandy Silver, who has been the premier since 2016. Following the 2021 territorial election, the Yukon Liberals have a minority government, with eight of the nineteen seats in the assembly; in April 2021, it was announced that the Liberals entered into a confidence and supply agreement with the three-seat NDP (CBC News 2021). The Yukon Party is currently the main opposition party with eight seats.

Meanwhile, the NWT and Nunavut operate using a non-partisan adaptation of Westminster parliamentary democracy known as "consensus government." One of the key components of consensus government is that it does not feature the same concentration of power in the executive as in Parliament and other provincial legislatures. Unlike in the traditional Westminster system, the premier does not select the cabinet; ministers are both selected and removed by members of the Legislative Assembly (MLAs). However, the premier does have the power to assign ministerial portfolios, which can be used as a reward or as punitive action (Dickerson 1992, 122; White 2000, 19). The less than dominant position of the premier (and the Premier's Office) more closely resembles the Westminster ideal of the first minister being a "first among equals" (White 2000; Kulchyski 2005, 104).

The non-partisan nature of the legislature features some differences in terms of cabinet selection. Specifically, it ensures that competent people are not excluded from cabinet based on partisan considerations (Dacks 1986, 352).[8] The less overtly partisan nature of cabinet in consensus government is relevant to intergovernmental relations and fiscal federalism because it lends itself to fewer hyper-partisan and ideological debates compared to the provinces, which then spill into relations with the federal government (the relationship between the Trudeau Liberal government and Conservative premiers in Western Canada and Ontario is a prime example of such contentious relations).

Analysis

Political Debates

The territorial premiers have tended to present a coherent, united stand towards the federal government regarding TFF, with limited conflict between the territories. They provided the Expert Panel on Equalization and Territorial Financing Formula with a joint submission, for example. However, approaches have differed across the territories. For example, a reduction in 2015 of TFF, which would have resulted in a major budget shortfall for the three territories, was met with a swift response by the territorial premiers (CBC News 2016). All three premiers came out in opposition to the reduction, although the responses differed in their content.

On one hand, Bob McLeod, then NWT premier, responded with a conciliatory statement, refusing to blame the federal finance minister Bill Morneau for the reduction, instead focusing on the "methodological changes" to Statistics Canada's preparation of expenditure data, "permanently lowering each territory's Gross Expenditure Base over two percent from what was previously expected" (GNWT 2015). It is also worth noting that, in McLeod's statement, the federal finance minister was only mentioned in a relatively positive light:

> In meetings this week, Minister Morneau committed to addressing territorial concerns prior to March 15, 2016. I thank Minister Morneau for his attention to this matter and his government's commitment to working directly with the territories on issues of concern to us. Together we can ensure Canada's northern citizens continue to share in the benefits of living in a united and prosperous country. (GNWT 2015)

By contrast, the statement from then Yukon premier Darrell Pasloski (who belongs to the centre-right Yukon Party) was less amicable in its tone, asserting that "reducing the transfer by millions of dollars without any notice is unacceptable" and arguing that the reduction in transfers violates the key principles of the territorial financing arrangement of "stability and predictability" (Government of Yukon 2015). Notwithstanding the political posturing, the reduction of TFF was quickly addressed, with the federal government restoring the $67 million that was cut from the transfers for the 2016–17 fiscal year (CBC News 2016).

A Research Agenda

This chapter introduces Canada's three Northern territories to the study of fiscal federalism. However, there are several research areas that have yet to be explored to their full potential, mainly surrounding natural resource devolution in the territories. A key issue of fiscal federalism in the territories is the devolution of lands and natural resources.

The three territories are currently at differing stages of natural resource devolution. The Northwest Territories and the Yukon have both completed devolution and resource-sharing agreements. The Yukon was the first territory to reach a lands and resources devolution agreement, coming into effect on 1 April 2003 (CBC News 2003). According to Alcantara (2013), the Yukon's ability to reach an agreement first can be attributed to the territorial and federal governments' perceived ability to acquire sufficient Aboriginal consent, which was noted as the main obstacle to the reaching of devolution agreements; this consent was facilitated by the Yukon Umbrella Final Agreement (UFA) signed in 1993 (Alcantara, Cameron, and Kennedy 2012, 329). The signing of the UFA was followed by additional treaties, "which were seen by federal and territorial officials as clear indicators that aboriginal consent had been achieved" (Alcantara 2013, 175).

Devolution in the NWT took a similarly arduous path; the 1960s and 1970s saw several strides towards devolution. In 1967 the seat of government was moved to Yellowknife from Ottawa, and in 1975 the NWT Council (renamed the Legislative Assembly in 1979) became fully elected. Further programs and responsibilities were devolved to the NWT in the late 1980s, including health care (CIRNAC 2014). However, it was not until 1988 that negotiations on natural resource devolution picked up, with the signing of the Northern Accord between the federal government and the Yukon and NWT governments "regarding oil and gas devolution and shared management offshore" (Cameron and Campbell 2009, 201). In the Yukon, the Northern Accord was followed by the 1993 Canada-Yukon Oil and Gas Accord and passage of the 1998 Canada-Yukon Oil and Gas Accord Implementation Act (201). In the NWT, negotiations were not as successful, with the negotiations breaking down in 1993–4, partially over the issue of net fiscal benefit (215).

Negotiations in Nunavut are less advanced than in the Yukon and the Northwest Territories. These negotiations between the federal government and Nunavut are ongoing; Nunavut is currently in the third phase of devolution negotiations – the final agreement. Negotiation protocols for devolution were signed in 2008 between Canada, the government of Nunavut, and NTI.[9] The Nunavut Agreement-in-Principle (AIP) was signed in 2019 (CIRNAC 2019). The varied paces of the negotiations align with the historical development of the three Northern territories.

Devolution is an important issue for the territories as it pertains to fiscal federalism because it is a step towards reducing transfer dependency. As argued by Cameron and Campbell (2009, 207–8), reducing dependency is a matter of political autonomy, because reducing reliance on the federal government reduces vulnerability. For example, previously, the territories have been impacted by the federal government's austerity, with unilateral cutbacks to territorial transfers in the 1990s (Hicks and White 2015; Hicks 2018).

Devolution is also seen by some as a step towards further political autonomy for Indigenous peoples in the region. According to the *Mayer Report on Nunavut Devolution* (Mayer 2007, 18), the government of Nunavut sees devolution as a step towards the Inuit's desire to gain control over land and natural resources. This desire for devolution was demonstrated through political discourse, including in a 2007 address to the Legislative Assembly by Nunavut's Commissioner (the equivalent to the Lieutenant Governor; Mayer 2007, 18).

Devolution raises two key questions regarding fiscal federalism in the territories. First, a potentially interesting research area going forward is the value of the territories' situation in fiscal federalism as it pertains to Indigenous-settler relations, reconciliation, and multilevel governance. Devolution negotiations in the territories are a pertinent example of multilevel governance in fiscal federalism in Canada. Devolution negotiations are not merely a bilateral exercise between the federal and territorial governments; all three territories have had Indigenous governments and organizations involved in the devolution process in official capacities

In the NWT and the Yukon, Indigenous organizations in the territory were involved in the devolution negotiations and were included as signatories to the final agreements. Moreover, the agreements have resulted in the formation of formal mechanisms for Indigenous and public governments to interact on issues regarding natural resource devolution. For example, the Northwest Territories Devolution Agreement established an intergovernmental council to allow for cooperation and collaboration between public and Aboriginal governments on issues regarding land and resource management. The NWT Intergovernmental Council demonstrates the potential natural resource devolution in the territories has towards fostering Indigenous reconciliation, and presents an interesting case study of multilevel governance.[10]

Second, fruitful discussions surrounding the fiscal impacts of natural resource devolution could be explored in greater detail, namely the net fiscal benefits of devolution. An important aspect of natural resource devolution as it pertains to fiscal federalism is the net fiscal benefits (NFBs) of devolution, which is "the extent to which territorial natural resource revenues resulting from devolution are offset by reductions in the TFF grant from the federal government" (Feehan 2009).

In addition to devolution, another increasingly important issue for fiscal federalism in Canada will be reforms to fiscal arrangements in general and TFF in particular. As discussed in this chapter, aging populations will strain many governments' health-care systems, and they will be especially costly for territorial governments. The material higher level of health expenditures among older individuals in the territories means aging may substantially increase overall spending at a pace that exceeds what is observed in provinces. Adjusting TFF grants to reflect differential health expenditure needs in the North may soon become a pressing issue. Examining potential options and weighing their trade-offs will be an important research agenda for researchers, policy analysts, and practitioners of fiscal federalism in Canada.

While not an exhaustive exploration of fiscal federalism and Canada's Northern territories, this chapter argues that natural resource development and demographics are central issues. More research is warranted, not only to better understand the historical experiences of each territory but also to inform future policy reforms. The unique historical and institutional legacies of the three territories also mean an improved understanding of the political dynamics and policy development in these regions will improve our understanding of fiscal federalism in general.

Acknowledgments

The authors thank Margaret Melhorn for her detailed comments and suggestions.

NOTES

1 For the text of the Northwest Territories Land and Resources Devolution Agreement, see Government of Canada and GNWT (2013).
2 The text of the Nunavut Agreement is available online at https://nlca.tunngavik.com/.
3 As the territories are included in the Canada Health Transfer and the Canada Social Transfer but not in equalization, which is only for the provinces, and TFF is an explicitly redistributive mechanism, it makes sense to compare it with equalization.
4 Another interesting issue surrounding devolution is the financing of Indigenous self-government. For a further discussion of First Nations and fiscal federalism, see chapter 11 by Donn. L. Feir and David Scoones in this volume.
5 As mentioned by Fellows and Tombe (2018, 28), "the season for ice roads, currently used in much of the North to transport goods to and from remotely located industrial/mining production and communities, has become shorter and less predictable, implying greater reliance on air transport with a higher associated per tonne-km cost compared to trucking."
6 All transfer totals are provided by the government of Canada: "Major Federal Transfers," https://www.canada.ca/en/department-finance/programs/federal-transfers/major-federal-transfers.html.

7 For context, the province with the largest percentage of GDP from natural resources in 2020 was Newfoundland and Labrador, with 24.3 per cent of GDP from mining, quarrying, and oil and gas extraction (Richards 2021b). Alberta is the second most resource-heavy provincial economy by percentage of GDP, with mining, quarrying, and oil and gas extraction making up 14.4 per cent of total GDP in 2020 (Richards 2021a).
8 Yet, the NWT has a convention to ensure regional representation in the cabinet, with two members of cabinet from the southern region and two from Yellowknife, which may result in the most qualified MLAs being in cabinet.
9 The text of the agreement, Lands and Resources Devolution Negotiation Protocol, between the government of Canada, the government of Nunavut, and Nunavut Tunngavik Incorporated, is available online at https://www.gov.nu.ca/sites/default/files/files/Devolution%20Protocol_eng.pdf.
10 For more on the Intergovernmental Council, see "Strengthening Relations with Indigenous Governments: Intergovernmental Council" on the government of the Northwest Territories website, https://www.eia.gov.nt.ca/en/priorities/strengthening-relations-indigenous-governments/intergovernmental-council.

REFERENCES

Alcantara, Christopher. 2013. "Preferences, Perceptions, and Veto Players: Explaining Devolution Negotiation Outcomes in the Canadian Territorial North." *Polar Record* 49, no. 2: 167–79. https://doi.org/10.1017/S0032247412000125.

Alcantara, Christopher, Kirk Cameron, and Steven Kennedy. 2012. "Assessing Devolution in the Canadian North: A Case Study of the Yukon Territory." *Arctic* 65, no. 3: 328–38. https://www.jstor.org/stable/41758939.

Béland, Daniel, Andrea Louise Campbell, and R. Kent Weaver. 2022. *Policy Feedback: How Policies Shape Politics*. Cambridge. Cambridge University Press.

Béland, Daniel, André Lecours, Gregory P. Marchildon, Haizhen Mou, and Rose Olfert. 2017. *Fiscal Federalism and Equalization Policy in Canada: Political and Economic Dimensions*. Toronto: University of Toronto Press.

Bellefontaine, Michelle. 2021. "Albertans Support Bid to Change Equalization, Narrowly Turn Down Year-Round Daylight Time." *CBC News*, 26 October 2021. https://www.cbc.ca/news/canada/edmonton/referendum-alberta-equalization-daylight-time-senate-1.6225309.

Bennett, Dean. 2021. "Alberta's Vote on Whether to Reject Equalization Is About Leverage, Premier Says." *CBC News*, 17 October 2021.https://www.cbc.ca/news/canada/edmonton/alberta-equalization-referendum-1.6214401.

Cameron, Kirk, and Alastair Campbell. 2009. "The Devolution of Natural Resources and Nunavut's Constitutional Status." *Journal of Canadian Studies* 43, no. 2: 198–219. https://doi.org/10.3138/jcs.43.2.198.

Cameron, Kirk, and Graham White. 1995. *Northern Governments in Transition: Political and Constitutional Development in the Yukon, Nunavut and the Western Northwest Territories*. Montreal: The Institute for Research on Public Policy.
CanNor (Canadian Northern Development Agency). 2021. "Resource Development: Fostering Resource Development in the Territories." Ottawa: CanNor. https://www.cannor.gc.ca/eng/1368816364402/1368816377148.
CBC News. 2003. "It's Official: Yukon Devolution in Effect." *CBC News*, 1 April 2003. https://www.cbc.ca/news/canada/north/it-s-official-yukon-devolution-in-effect-1.361649.
– 2016. "Federal Gov't to Restore $67M in Territorial Formula Funding." *CBC News*, 16 February 2016. https://www.cbc.ca/news/canada/north/federal-goverment-restores-territorial-formula-funding-1.3450621.
– 2021. "Yukon Liberals, Reduced to Minority, Embrace the NDP." *CBC News*, 28 April 2021. https://www.cbc.ca/news/canada/north/yukon-liberal-ndp-announcement-government-1.6006387.
CER (Canada Energy Regulator). 2022. *Provincial and Territorial Energy Profiles – Nunavut*. Ottawa: CER. Accessed 13 July 2022. https://www.cer-rec.gc.ca/en/data-analysis/energy-markets/provincial-territorial-energy-profiles/provincial-territorial-energy-profiles-nunavut.html.
CIHI (Canadian Institute for Health Information). 2021. "National Health Expenditure Trends." Open Data on Health Spending, Table O.2, Provincial/Territorial Government Health Expenditures by Age and Sex and Use of Funds, by Province/Territory and Canada. Ottawa: CIHI. https://www.cihi.ca/en/national-health-expenditure-trends.
CIRNAC (Crown-Indigenous Relations and Northern Affairs Canada). 2014. "Short History of Northwest Territories Devolution." Ottawa: CIRNAC. https://www.rcaanc-cirnac.gc.ca/eng/1395946093734/1539627184054.
– 2019. "Nunavut Devolution." Ottawa: CIRNAC. https://www.rcaanc-cirnac.gc.ca/eng/1352471770723/1537900871295.
– 2020. "Oil and Gas in Canada's North – Active Exploration and New Development." Ottawa: CIRNAC. https://www.rcaanc-cirnac.gc.ca/eng/1100100037301/1583413745571.
Coates, Ken, and William R. Morrison. 2005. *Land of the Midnight Sun: A History of the Yukon*. Montreal and Kingston: McGill-Queen's University Press.
Coates, Ken, and Judith Powell. 1989. *The Modern North: People, Politics and the Rejection of Colonialism*. Toronto: James Lorimer.
Dacks, Gurston. 1986. "Politics on the Last Frontier: Consociationalism in the Northwest Territories." *Canadian Journal of Political Science* 19, no. 2: 345–61 https://doi.org/10.1017/S0008423900054068.
Department of Finance Canada. 2011a. "Equalization Program." Ottawa: Department of Finance. https://www.canada.ca/en/department-finance/programs/federal-transfers/equalization.html.

- 2011b. "Territorial Formula Financing." Ottawa: Department of Finance. https://www.canada.ca/en/department-finance/programs/federal-transfers/territorial-formula-financing.html.
Dickerson, Mark. 1992. *Whose North? Political Change, Political Development, and Self-Government in the Northwest Territories*. Vancouver: UBC Press.
EPETFF (Expert Panel on Equalization and Territorial Formula Financing). 2006. *Achieving a Natural Purpose: Putting Equalization Back on Track*. Ottawa: Department of Finance. https://publications.gc.ca/collections/Collection/F2-176-2006E.pdf.
Feehan, James. 2009. "Natural Resource Devolution in the Territories: Current Status and Unresolved Issues." In *Northern Exposure: Peoples, Powers and Prospects in Canada's North*, edited by Frances Abele, Thomas J. Courchene, F. Leslie Seidle, and France St-Hilaire, 345–472. Montreal: Institute for Research on Public Policy.
Fellows, G. Kent, and Trevor Tombe. 2018. "Opening Canada's North: A Study of Trade Costs in the Territories." *SPP Research Paper* No. 11/17. School of Public Policy, University of Calgary. https://doi.org/10.2139/ssrn.3217725.
Frizzell, Sara. 2019. "Nunavut Government Hopes for New Bidders to Drum Up Competition in Airline Market." *CBC News*, 16 January 2019. https://www.cbc.ca/news/canada/north/airline-competition-nunavut-medical-duty-travel-1.4979563.
Government of Canada. 2011. "Territorial Formula Financing." Ottawa: Government of Canada. https://www.canada.ca/en/department-finance/programs/federal-transfers/territorial-formula-financing.html.
Government of Canada and GNWT (Government of Northwest Territories). 2013. "Northwest Territories Land and Resources Devolution Agreement." Agreement 25 June 2013. https://www.eia.gov.nt.ca/sites/eia/files/final-devolution-agreement.pdf.
Government of Yukon. 2015. "Premier Calls on Federal Government to Restore Yukon's Funding." News Release, 22 December 2015. https://open.yukon.ca/sites/default/files/20151222PremierCallsOnCanGovToRestoreYTFunding.pdf.
GNWT (Government of Northwest Territories). n.d. "Implementing the Devolution Agreement." Accessed 26 April 2023. https://www.eia.gov.nt.ca/en/priorities/implementing-devolution-agreement/resource-revenue-sharing-after-devolution.
- 2015. "Statement from Premier Bob McLeod on Federal Transfer Payments." News Release, 22 December 2015. https://www.gov.nt.ca/en/newsroom/news/statement-premier-bob-mcleod-federal-transfer-payments.
Henderson, Ailsa. 2005. "Support for (Quasi) Self-Government: Assessments of Northern Political Life Ten Years after the Nunavut Land Claim Agreement." Paper presented at the Canadian Political Science Association Annual Meeting, London, Ontario, 2–4 June 2005. https://assembly.nu.ca/library/Edocs/2005/001486-e.pdf.
- 2007. *Nunavut: Rethinking Political Culture*. Vancouver: UBC Press.
Henderson, Ailsa, and Graham White. 2015. "Managing the Moraine: Political Economy and Political Culture Approaches to Assessing the Success of Nunavut." In *Transforming Provincial Politics: The Political Economy of Canada's Provinces and*

Territories in the Neoliberal Era, edited by Bryan M. Evans and Charles W. Smith, 315–46. Toronto: University of Toronto Press.

Hicks, Jack. 2018. "Nunavut: Conceived in Austerity." In *The Public Sector in an Age of Austerity Perspectives from Canada's Provinces and Territories,* edited by Bryan M. Evans and Carlo Fanelli, 315–49. Montreal-Kingston: McGill-Queen's University Press.

Hicks, Jack, and Graham White. 2015. *Made in Nunavut: An Experiment in Decentralized Government.* Vancouver: UBC Press.

Indigenous Services Canada. 2020. *Annual Report to Parliament.* Ottawa: Indigenous Services Canada. https://www.sac-isc.gc.ca/eng/1602010609492/1602010631711.

Kulchyski, Peter. 2005. *Like the Sound of a Drum: Aboriginal Cultural Politics in Denendeh and Nunavut.* Winnipeg: University of Manitoba Press.

Lecours, André, and Daniel Béland. 2010. "Federalism and Fiscal Policy: The Politics of Equalization in Canada." *Publius: The Journal of Federalism* 40, no. 4: 569–96. https://doi.org/10.1093/publius/pjp030.

Mayer, Paul. 2007. *Mayer Report on Nunavut Devolution.* https://www.rcaanc-cirnac.gc.ca/eng/1357676177444/1537901029178.

Pierson, Paul. 1993. "When Effect Becomes Cause: Policy Feedback and Political Change." *World Politics* 45, no. 4: 595–628. https://doi.org/10.2307/2950710.

Richards, Simon. 2021a. *Trade and Investment: Alberta.* 2020 Data Series. Publication 2021-501-E. Ottawa: Library of Parliament. https://publications.gc.ca/collections/collection_2021/bdp-lop/ti/YM32-7-2021-501-eng.pdf.

– 2021b. *Trade and Investment: Newfoundland and Labrador.* 2020 Data Series. Publication 2021-509-E. Ottawa: Library of Parliament. https://publications.gc.ca/collections/collection_2021/bdp-lop/ti/YM32-7-2021-509-eng.pdf.

– 2021c. *Trade and Investment: Northwest Territories.* 2020 Data Series. Publication 2021-512-E. Ottawa: Library of Parliament. https://lop.parl.ca/sites/PublicWebsite/default/en_CA/ResearchPublications/TradeAndInvestment/2021512E.

– 2021d. *Trade and Investment: Nunavut.* 2020 Data Series. Publication 2021-511-E. Ottawa: Library of Parliament. https://lop.parl.ca/sites/PublicWebsite/default/en_CA/ResearchPublications/TradeAndInvestment/2021511E.

– 2021e. *Trade and Investment: Yukon.* 2020 Data Series. Publication 2021-510-E. Ottawa: Library of Parliament. https://lop.parl.ca/sites/PublicWebsite/default/en_CA/ResearchPublications/TradeAndInvestment/2021510E.

Sabin, Jerald. 2016. "Contested Colonialism: The Rise of Settler Politics in Yukon and the Northwest Territories." PhD diss., Department of Political Science, University of Toronto.

Statistics Canada. 2016. "Focus on Geography Series, 2016 Census." Ottawa: Statistics Canada. https://www12.statcan.gc.ca/census-recensement/2016/as-sa/fogs-spg/Index-eng.cfm.

– 2019. "Table 17-10-0057-01: Projected Population, by Projection Scenario, Age and Sex, as of July 1 (x 1,000)." https://doi.org/10.25318/1710005701-eng.

White, Graham. 2000. "And Now For Something Completely Northern: Institutions of Governance in the Territorial North." *Journal of Canadian Studies* 35, no. 4: 80–99. https://doi.org/10.3138/jcs.35.4.80.

– 2006. "Traditional Aboriginal Values in a Westminster Parliament: The Legislative Assembly of Nunavut." *Journal of Legislative Studies* 12, no. 1: 8–31. https://doi.org/10.1080/13572330500483930a.

Wilson, Gary N. 2008. "Nested Federalism in Arctic Quebec: A Comparative Perspective." *Canadian Journal of Political Science* 41, no. 1: 71–92. https://doi.org/10.1017/S0008423908080116.

Windeyer, Chris. 2020. "Currie Dixon Wins Yukon Party Leadership Race." *CBC News*, 23 May 2020. https://www.cbc.ca/news/canada/north/currie-dixon-wins-yukon-party-leadership-1.5582357.

Yukon, Northwest Territories, and Nunavut. 2019. *Arctic and Northern Policy Framework: Pan-Territorial Chapter – Yukon, Northwest Territories, Nunavut.* https://www.eia.gov.nt.ca/sites/eia/files/2019-06-10_anpf_-_pan-territorial_chapter_-_en_-_final.pdf.

11 Leading the Way: First Nations in Canadian Fiscal Federalism

DONN. L. FEIR AND DAVID SCOONES

Introduction

The legal jurisdiction and capacity for Indigenous governments in Canada to generate own-source revenues has been limited historically. The Constitution Act, 1867, section 91(24) assigns matters of "Indians, and Lands reserved for Indians" to the exclusive legislative authority of the Parliament of Canada. Among other things, this section means that the federal government has jurisdiction over many matters for Indigenous peoples that, for other Canadians, are the responsibility of other levels of government. Given the limited scope of government activity in 1867, it would have been hard to imagine the resulting complex patchwork of programs and arrangements that have emerged over the years since. However, the past fifty years, particularly the last fifteen, have seen substantial changes in the fiscal powers of Indigenous nations.

In this chapter, we briefly describe the history of First Nations fiscal powers since contact and discuss how these powers have evolved in the context of the colonial Canadian enterprise. We focus on the last thirty years and First Nations–led legislative alternatives to the Indian Act, self-governance agreements, and the creation of independent First Nations institutions. We briefly discuss the small but growing literature by economists examining the impact of these alternatives and add to it by offering suggestive evidence that fiscal powers may increase First Nations ability to respond to local crises by associating COVID-19 pandemic response laws with the uptake of taxation powers. We conclude by discussing the fiscal relationship that exists between Canada and First Nations outside of these Indian Act alternatives and offer some thoughts on important policy and research questions moving forward.

There is much this short chapter does not cover. First, we focus on First Nations specifically and do not discuss the fiscal relationship with Métis or Inuit nations. Second, given that First Nations finances are not included in government finance statistics, we have limited ability to discuss them in the context of other government actors in Canada. Third, we focus on taxation powers and not on revenues generated from other sources, such as First Nations enterprises or private revenue-sharing agreements, or on the federal government's policy in relation to First Nations own-source revenue streams. Finally, and most importantly, we do not discuss or quantify the transfers from First Nations to the Canadian state: when we discuss grants and contribution agreements, we caution the reader against thinking these "transfers" have been one sided. While significant numbers of Canadians continue to view government spending on First Nations as "handouts" (Neuman 2016, 11, 13), a substantial portion of Canadian government revenues arguably have been generated from the seizure, sale, and subsequent development of First Nations land and associated resources (Yellowhead 2021). In addition, many of these obligations directly stem from the treaty-making process, which is a key legal foundation for the Canadian state. We aim to offer the unfamiliar reader an introduction to the institutions and fiscal mechanisms available to First Nations, describe how these relate to the position of First Nations in Canada's system of fiscal federalism, and offer some simple evidence on the importance of recent changes in these relationships.

A Broad Institutional and Historical Overview

Indigenous peoples have rights protected, if not clearly defined, in the Canadian Constitution that extend beyond those of other citizens. This recognition builds upon the historical facts of how governments came to exercise their sovereignty over the territory that is now Canada. In addition, the statutory actions of past governments have created a fiduciary duty on governments beyond that duty in its civil dealings with other citizens, opening the door to a range of legal remedies for First Nations not available to other subnational governments (Hurley 2000). Furthermore, Indigenous peoples worldwide have successfully asserted rights through the United Nations, which, when ratified by governments, brings international law to bear on the negotiation and clarification of Indigenous rights and government powers. These facts complicate any simple analogies between First Nations governments and other Canadian orders of government. We begin with a brief overview of this history.

Treaties

When Europeans first arrived, Indigenous nations existed in an extensive network of treaty relationships, among which European powers were offered a place. These first treaties focused on "peace and friendship" and the sharing of resources that allowed colonists to survive. Among First Nations, a wide variety of systems of governance had evolved to balance the demands of individual autonomy, family and clan structures, and the broader need for coordination (Borrows 2005). The functionality of these structures was not entirely lost on the more perceptive of the newcomers. The Haudenosaunee Confederacy served as a direct inspiration for the United States Constitution and therefore indirectly influenced the design of federations throughout the world.[1] Indigenous democratic practices more broadly have been shown to be associated with the existence of contemporary representative democracy globally (Bentzen, Hariri, and Robinson 2019).

The British Royal Proclamation of 1763 formalized the British Crown's treaty process with Indigenous nations. It acknowledged the land west of the Appalachian Mountains outside of other colonial and Hudson Bay "control" as "reserved" for Indigenous peoples and specified that only the Crown, not private parties or lower orders of government, could negotiate with Indigenous nations regarding the use of their lands. This proclamation altered the process of land acquisition from one in which individuals would purchase land as private property from First Nations to one where these lands could only be transferred between sovereigns, because these transfers had implications for sovereign jurisdiction (Carlos, Feir, and Redish 2022).

While the Royal Proclamation of 1763 was a unilateral announcement from the British Crown, it was quickly followed by an agreement among sovereigns in the 1764 Treaty of Niagara, signed by 2,000 chiefs from twenty-four nations in eastern North America (Slattery 2014; Tidridge 2015). By clearly recognizing Indigenous nations' rights to land and mandating a formal nation-to-nation land surrender process, the Royal Proclamation of 1763 and the Treaty of Niagara did more than require a particular negotiated method of moving lands into the jurisdiction of the Crown and outline its obligations to Indigenous nations. They also recognized the autonomy of Indigenous nations as self-governing actors within the British imperial system in North America (Redish 2019; Borrows 1997).

Even though the territory included in the 1763 Royal Proclamation and the Treaty of Niagara represented only a small component of what would become Canada, when Parliament asked the British Crown to admit Rupert's Land and the North-Western Territory to the Dominion of Canada, they committed to the principles in the Royal Proclamation across Canada (Redish 2019).

Treaty-making with Indigenous nations proceeded for over one hundred years, with the last historic treaty signed in 1923.[2] While these treaties varied in their terms, they often retained Indigenous rights to hunt and fish, and generated an ongoing obligation on the part of the Canadian state to deliver education or other public goods in exchange for access and use of Indigenous lands. Indigenous nations retained reserves of land to be used for their benefit. The content and interpretation of these historic treaties is still a point of contention between First Nations and the Crown, and continues to evolve through court cases and the specific claims process.[3]

Statutes

Under Canadian law, Indigenous peoples have never been mere "collections of private individuals like other Crown subjects; they were distinct peoples – political units within the larger political unit that was eventually to become Canada" (Royal Commission on Aboriginal Peoples 1996, 1:240). However, there is a tension between Canadian law and fiscal policies and the principles of Indigenous self-government. The Constitution Act, 1867, section 91 states: "It is hereby declared that (notwithstanding anything in this Act) the exclusive Legislative Authority of the Parliament of Canada extends to all Matters coming within the Classes of Subjects next hereinafter enumerated; that is to say ... (24) Indians, and Lands reserved for the Indians." This section delegated responsibility for all Canadian law and policy to that of the federal government and left First Nations no articulated fiscal powers in Canada's Constitution other than those "devolved" by Parliament.

The inherent sovereignty of Indigenous nations and their rights to govern themselves on their traditional lands was further eroded by an 1887 Supreme Court decision in which First Nations were not directly involved. The decision addressed which level of government in Canada could regulate "Indian lands." The court ruled that the Indigenous possession of their land was at the discretion of the Crown in right of Canada and, despite the Royal Proclamation, endorsed the Doctrine of Discovery espoused by the United States Marshall decisions.[4]

In 1876, Canada passed the Indian Act, amalgamating all existing Canadian law regarding Indigenous peoples and nations.[5] Until recently, the Indian Act, 1876 has governed all matters pertaining to Indigenous citizenship in their own nations, defined who "counts" as "Indians" in Canadian law, and determined the legal and fiscal infrastructure of First Nations "bands" – the sole "governments" created and recognized by the Indian Act. For most of its existence, the Indian Act left First Nations with no fiscal instruments at their disposal. Their land, assets, and monies were all held in trust by the federal government for their "beneficial use," and band councils had limited authority to allocate federal monies transferred to them. In later years, the court found this trust structure to create a fiduciary duty of the federal government to First Nations, which is not present in its relationship with other Canadians (Hurley 2000; *R. v. Guerin* [1984][6]). Indigenous nations were also actively prevented from administering tax systems to raise their own revenue (Tulo 2014, 154–5). Indigenous nations have felt the consequences of these restrictions, and leaders have fought for their rights in the courts for self-government – their rights to govern themselves and the territories they viewed as theirs. Because of the existing tensions in Canadian law, Indigenous nations launched early legal battles over land and self-governance. However, in 1927, under the guise of concern for "Indians" being swindled by white lawyers, the Indian Act was amended to restrict nations from raising funds to hire lawyers to pursue these legal challenges.[7]

The Indian Act has never been static and has been used as a tool of oppression. For example, it was amended in 1884, 1895, 1914, and 1933 to prohibit traditional dances and customs (Bartlett 1978) and in 1920 to mandate the removal of children from their communities to residential schools.[8] Many have called for the Indian Act's abolition, arguing that this piece of Canadian law runs counter to the ideal of a nation-to-nation relationship and is discordant with the principles of self-determination. Abolition, though, has been strongly resisted by Indigenous groups, in part because the act facilitates the current functioning of many local First Nations governments and the flow of federal funds.[9]

The first broad step towards providing political and fiscal space for First Nations self-governance came with the 1951 significant amendments to the Indian Act, which resulted from the 1946–8 Joint Committee of the Senate and House of Commons review of Indian Affairs (Bartlett 1978). While still tightly controlling who had citizenship in any First Nation and introducing new and non-trivial jurisdictional issues with some extension of provincial law to "Indians in the province" (Wilkins 2000), the 1951 amendment to the Indian Act allowed band councils to have powers like those of municipalities – and importantly, the power to tax. Specifically, section 82(1)[10] states: "Where the Governor in Council declares that a band has reached an advanced stage of development, the council of the band may, subject to the approval of the Minister, make by-laws for ... (a) the raising of money by (i) the assessment and taxation of interests in land in the reserve of persons lawfully in possession thereof, and (ii) the licensing of businesses, callings, trades and occupations."[11] In addition, the amendment removed the restrictions on raising funds to hire lawyers for land claims.

The Modern Landscape

When the restrictions on hiring lawyers was removed from the Indian Act in 1951, Indigenous nations once again began pursuing their claims under Canadian law, both in areas covered by historic treaties and those that were not. These cases have led to a sea change in Indigenous rights and title in Canada.

The decision in *R v. Calder* [1973][12] was the first time the courts acknowledged that "Aboriginal title" to land was inherent, overturning previous Supreme Court rulings, and suggested that Indigenous nations that had never surrendered land by treaty or were never conquered still had lawful jurisdiction over their lands – although the court was evenly split on whether title continued to exist in the specific case considered (Milne 2017). This case paved the way for addressing Aboriginal title in Canada through the courts and, in the shadow of this law, through renewed negotiation. Shortly after, the federal government developed the Comprehensive Land Claims Policy, and the first modern treaty, the James Bay and Northern Quebec Agreement, was signed in 1975 (Government of Canada 2016; CIRNAC 2023). In 1982, a Special Committee of the House of Commons on Indian Self-Government was appointed. The committee ultimately recommended that First Nations should be recognized as a distinct order of government within the Canadian federation (CIRNAC 2016). Indigenous rights in Canada were affirmed in the Constitution Act, 1982, section 35(1): "The existing aboriginal and treaty rights of the aboriginal peoples of Canada are hereby recognized and affirmed." The courts have subsequently defined "Aboriginal title" as the inherent Indigenous right to land or a territory. "Aboriginal rights" are collective rights that flow from continued use and occupation of certain areas. They are inherent rights that were practised before European contact (such as self-government). The explicit inclusion of self-government as an "Aboriginal right" was acknowledged explicitly in federal government policy in the 1990s (Wherrett 1999). Aboriginal rights are inherently tied to the land.

Subsequent court decisions filled in the details of the content of Indigenous rights and title during the 1990s including, importantly, *Delgamuukw v. British Columbia* (1997),[13] which expressed the duty to consult when Aboriginal rights may be adversely impacted. *Haida Nation v. British Columbia*[14] in 2004 established that the Crown has a duty to consult Indigenous peoples when it intends to act in a manner that may affect established or *potential* Aboriginal rights (Brideau 2019). The duty to consult Indigenous nations is grounded in the legal foundation of the Honour of the Crown: "It recognizes that the tension between the Crown's assertion of sovereignty and the pre-existing sovereignty, rights and occupation of Aboriginal peoples creates a special relationship that requires that the Crown act honourably in its dealings with Aboriginal peoples."[15] In 2014, the Supreme Court recognized and affirmed Aboriginal title for the first time in *Tsilhqot'in Nation v. British Columbia*.[16] It also determined that Aboriginal title conveyed all the rights of fee simple ownership of the relevant territory and erases the Crown's assumed beneficial interest in the land (Borrows 2015).[17] In 2016, the government of Canada endorsed the United Nations *Declaration on the Rights of Indigenous Peoples* (UNDRIP) without qualification and committed to its full and effective implementation, which includes the right of self-determination. All these court and political decisions increased the potential economic power of Indigenous nations and their abilities to potentially generate own-source revenues. However, the strategies to generate economic power may differ between nations that have historic treaties and those that do not. In areas not covered by treaty, many nations have chosen to pursue comprehensive land claims along with self-government agreements.[18]

As of January 2022, twenty-six comprehensive land claim agreements have been signed. Of the twenty-six signed agreements, eighteen included provisions related to self-government. Four separate self-government agreements have also been signed (CIRNAC 2015).[19] First Nations with a self-governance agreement obtain a broad range of decision-making and fiscal powers in their jurisdiction. Their nations are no longer governed by the Indian Act and acquire powers such as taxation powers, including personal income and property tax, setting of their own election structures, land codes, education, health care, and other public services. Currently, fifteen of these nations have personal income tax, money that formerly would have accrued to the province or territory that contains their nation (Department of Finance 2008). Individuals within their jurisdiction, regardless of membership in the First Nation, pay these taxes. While some of these income tax arrangements have the tax go completely to the First Nation, others involve revenue-sharing agreements with the provinces. It has been argued that these self-government agreements effectively create a constitutionally recognized third order of government in Canadian federalism (Graben 2007). The negotiation of a comprehensive land claim not only comes with increased local fiscal powers but also with or without a self-government agreement, and it clarifies jurisdiction over formerly unsurrendered land.

Aragón (2015, 50) provides high-quality evidence on the effect of settling comprehensive land claims. He finds that a "conservative estimate suggests that treaty implementation increases real income by around 13%" and as much as 25 per cent. While Aragón argues that these real income gains are in part a consequence of reduced transaction costs for firms, it is possible that changes in local jurisdiction, taxation powers, and provision of public goods may also drive increases in growth.

While the modern treaty process seems like a clear way for First Nations to have a constitutionally protected and recognized nation-to-nation relationship with the federal government and substantially increased fiscal powers relative to being under the Indian Act, the modern treaty and comprehensive land claims process is extremely lengthy and costly. For example, negotiations of the Yukon Umbrella Final Agreement started in 1973; the agreement was not signed until 1993, and the implementation of the last subagreement took place in 2006 (Slowey 2021). The Nisga'a Final Agreement has roots in the fight of the Nisga'a since colonialization and started the Comprehensive Land Claims Policy in 1976, with a final agreement only being reached in 1998 (Hurley 1999). While we do not believe the total cost to each First Nation of negotiating these agreements is publicly known (or necessarily even fully calculated), as part of the Nisga'a Final Agreement, the federal government transferred $30 million 1998 dollars to help pay Nisga'a legal costs for the negotiations – which only covered fees for the last two decades of negotiations (Tekawennake News 1998).[20]

The frustration with the fiscal, political, and economic position of First Nations in Canada post-colonization has also manifested outside of the modern treaty process. For example, at the Seventh General Assembly of the Union of

BC Indian Chiefs (UBCIC) in 1975, the assembly passed the resolution to reject all external federal government funds. This refusal signified a rejection of federal control over Indigenous government (UBCIC n.d.). This dramatic stand also emphasized to many nations the fiscal dependence that had developed due to the political organization of Canada (Tulo 2014, 8). This resolution was the foundation that led to legislative changes, alongside the treaty process, to increase First Nations fiscal autonomy from the federal government.

In 1988, an Indigenous-led amendment to the Indian Act to implement greater property taxation powers on reserve under section 83 of the Indian Act, known as the Kamloops amendment, was passed. Before this amendment, First Nations governments could not levy taxes or fees on reserve land leased to non-members – this amendment changed that.[21] But the amendment did not allow First Nations to use the resulting stream of revenue to secure debt like other governments. Over time, this same political leadership led to the implementation of the First Nations Fiscal Management Act (FMA) in 2005, an opt-in piece of legislation that allows First Nations to remove themselves from several provisions of the Indian Act, and to the creation of three independent First Nations–led institutions to support financial governance. Adding one's nation to the FMA schedule enables that nation to implement all the taxation powers available under the Indian Act but also to pledge these revenue streams to borrow for infrastructure and economic development projects. The evidence presented by Enid Slack (chapter 13 of this volume) suggests that these municipal-like fiscal powers alone will not be a panacea, even for the challenges of local government facing many First Nations, but they are a clear move in the direction of self-determination.

The FMA also created the First Nations Tax Commission, the First Nations Financial Management Board, and the First Nations Finance Authority. The First Nations Tax Commission (n.d.) supports nations in the development of their tax codes and regulates their implementation either under the Indian Act, section 83 or the FMA.[22] It addresses the difficulties faced by small communities lacking the resources to act individually and also seeks to protect the overall financial reputation of First Nations (Jules 2000).[23] The First Nations Financial Management Board (n.d.-a) supports First Nations in conducting transparent and high-quality financial administration capacity in order for them to be eligible to borrow through the First Nations Finance Authority. The Finance Authority's purpose is to provide First Nations governments investment options, capital planning advice, and, perhaps most importantly, capital markets to give their members access to low-rate interim loans below bank prime and long-term fixed-rate loans with repayment terms up to thirty years. These rates and terms parallel those available to provincial and local governments; this function is effectively tax-exempt bond financing (First Nations Financial Authority n.d.). One of the key advantages of the FMA and related institutions is that they

Leading the Way: First Nations in Canadian Fiscal Federalism 223

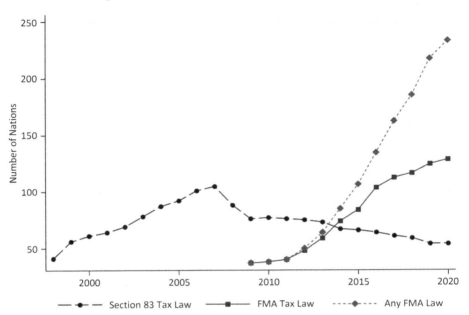

Figure 11.1. Increases in Fiscal Capacity – The Cumulative Number of First Nations Passing a Tax Law

Source: Calculations by authors.

lower transaction costs associated with developing a tax code and borrowing (Le Dressay 2021), which is arguably critical, given the relatively small population sizes of currently politically autonomous First Nations.

As of 2021, 309 First Nations have opted in to the FMA, representing nearly half of all 634 First Nations across Canada (First Nations Tax Commission 2021, 14). However, implementation takes time. Figure 11.1 shows the number of First Nations who have passed a tax law either under the FMA or under section 83 of the Indian Act and published it in the *First Nations Gazette*.[24] We can see that, as of 2019, well over 100 nations have established a tax law under the FMA, with more nations moving away from tax laws under section 83 of the Indian Act. The number of nations with any law (a tax law or a financial administration law) under the FMA has reached almost 250 nations. This figure does not account for the 38 nations who are currently implementing goods and services tax (GST) on reserve lands under the First Nations Goods and Services Tax Act (FNGST) of 2003 (status First Nations people are exempt from federal and provincial GST/HST collected on reserve; Government of Canada 2023). As of 2021, the First

Nations Finance Authority had 121 members, with 74 having outstanding loans, and had lent roughly $1.3 billion for economic development, infrastructure, and other First Nations projects (First Nations Finance Authority 2021, 6).

Before the FMA and the FNGST, First Nations also fought for legislative change to gain greater jurisdiction over their lands and worked to pass the 1999 First Nations Land Management Act (LMA), another important piece of opt-in legislation. In addition to the inherent value of self-government, the LMA also sought to enable First Nations to have greater control of their lands and how they are managed. Before the passage of the LMA, in the absence of a self-government agreement, First Nations lands were subject to the Indian Act and generally lacked regulatory frameworks present in municipalities for land management; any development required a lengthy federal approval process. Richard, Calla, and Le Dressay (2008) conducted three illustrative case studies of First Nations that wanted to start a business on their lands. The First Nations included as case studies had favourably located reserves, a history of active management of their land and resources, and additional capacity in administrating business deals from prior experience. The results from this research suggested that it takes four times as long to get a business up and running on reserve than off, even under favourable conditions. A significant amount of the time spent to complete the projects studied was found to be due to regulatory gaps, lengthy delays in land designation and leasing approvals required by Indigenous Services Canada, and the inadequacy of the current land registry system. The LMA was meant to address these regulatory gaps and federal delays in land designation and leasing approvals, while recognizing individual First Nations' right to design land laws in alignment with their own customs, values, and surrounding economic environments.

When First Nations choose to add themselves to the schedule of the LMA, they can development their own land codes and acquire many powers similar to those of municipalities. The First Nations Land Management Board, an independent First Nations–led institution established by the LMA, supports First Nations through the process. When a First Nation enacts a land code, about one-third of the Indian Act ceases to apply. Roughly ninety-four nations have implemented land codes under the LMA as of 2021. A 2014 study by KPMG on the impact of the LMA suggests that nations that implemented their land code completed land management activities significantly faster than under the Indian Act: "Processes previously reported to take months or years are now taking days" (KPMG 2014, 9). Somewhat curiously, as of 2020, roughly only 25 per cent of those with a tax law had an operational land code under the LMA, despite the evidence suggesting that participation in both the LMA and FMA can have economic returns. Pendakur and Pendakur demonstrate that implementing both in conjunction is correlated with increases in incomes (2018) and decreases in income inequality (2021). While the returns are not as large as having a self-government agreement with a comprehensive land claim, the time window in this study to evaluate the use of these opt-in arrangements has been relatively brief, and more gains may be seen over time.

Capacity for Governance

The development of tax codes (or land codes) may have returns not quantifiable in income returns. Arguably, the main advantages of the recently developed opt-in legislation and creation of First Nations institutions is their ability to reduce the transactions costs to First Nations governments of taking up greater self-governance. Using a sample of First Nations that had both property taxation and a custom election code, Hickey (2021) demonstrates that, on average, the property tax law preceded the election code. Hickey suggests that building governance capacity through taxation can support better self-governance that is more closely aligned with First Nations values.

Increasing the fiscal capacity of First Nations may have other, potentially unexpected, benefits beyond leading to improved economic conditions and electoral reform. Increased own-source revenue and the associated capacity building for self-government may allow First Nations to be more responsive to local conditions and changes (Graham and Bruhn 2010). We offer some suggestive empirical evidence that this benefit may be the case: we assess whether nations that have implemented taxation powers under either the FMA or the Indian Act were more likely to pass a COVID-19 response law in 2020-1. We make this assessment by linking data collected from the *First Nations Gazette* on all taxation laws since 1998 and COVID-19 by-laws to data from Indigenous Services Canada (ISC)'s 2011 Community Well-Being Index (CWB) dataset, which contains data on population, income, education, and housing conditions. Data were linked using the band census-subdivision (CSD) linkage file from ISC and manually matching the names of the First Nations passing laws to the First Nations names in the band linkage file.[25] We also added data on which bands have operationalized land codes under the First Nations Land Management Act. Finally, we computed the distance of the centroid from each of the census subdivisions to the nearest census metropolitan area (CMA). We estimated the association between passing a COVID-19 response law and whether the nation had ever exercised its taxation authority by passing a tax law. The results, a set of ordinary least squares regressions with heteroskedasticity robust standard errors, are presented in Figure 11.2.[26] The vertical axis depicts the percentage point change in the likelihood of passing a COVID-19 response law in 2020-1 with implementing a tax code in years prior. Each point on the horizontal axis depicts a separate estimated coefficient on an indicator variable of whether the nation has a taxation law (under the Indian Act or under the FMA). The first square point is the unconditional point estimate and its 95 per cent confidence interval. The second is the point estimate conditional on 2011

Figure 11.2. Estimated Percentage Point Change in the Likelihood of Passing a COVID-19 Response Law in 2020–1

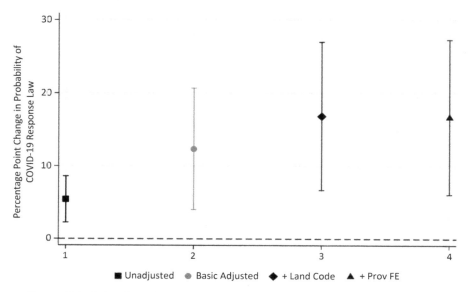

Source: Calculations by authors.

reserve population size, average income, CWB educational index, housing index, labour force participation index, and distance to the closest CMA. The third diamond point also controls for whether the nation has an operational land code; and the final triangle point conditions on a set of province indicators.[27] In all cases, the association between passing a tax law and a COVID-19 emergency response law is statistically significant and positive – the probability of passing a COVID-19 response law is 5.4 to 16.7 percentage points more likely if the First Nation has also exercised tax jurisdiction in the past. This probability is conditional on the local economic conditions facing the First Nation and the province in which it is located. While these findings are merely associative and preliminary, they are in alignment with increased local fiscal power resulting in greater responsiveness to community needs.[28]

The "New Fiscal Relationship"

The Royal Commission on Aboriginal Peoples called the relationship of the Crown to Indigenous nations paradoxical (1996, 1:241–2) and stated that "this original paradox raises the dilemma of the Crown and Indian nations simultaneously having sovereign rights to the same land. Through sharing the land, they shared sovereignty in a way that was unique to the situation in North America." However, as later recognized by the commission, Canadian and American models of federalism are exactly governments "sharing the same territory but with different or shared powers in relation to that territory" (1:241-2).

Resolving this paradox means clarifying powers and responsibilities. As pointed out by the Office of the Auditor General (OAG 2011), criticizing the state of service delivery on reserve, "many of the problems facing First Nations go deeper than the existing programs' lack of efficiency and effectiveness. We believe that structural impediments severely limit the delivery of public services to First Nations communities and hinder improvements in living conditions on reserves. We have identified four such impediments: lack of clarity about service levels, lack of a legislative base, lack of an appropriate funding mechanism, and lack of organizations to support local service delivery" (2). As discussed above, the federal government provides services on reserves that are typically delivered by provinces or municipal governments in other contexts. However, as pointed out by the OAG, it is not always clear what services the federal government is committed to providing on reserve, the extent to which these services are comparable to those delivered by provinces and local governments, and who is accountable if they are not delivered. The federal government has historically funded services such as education, health, and drinking water quality through contribution agreements or grants where the First Nation receives a certain amount of funding to deliver these services. However, these agreements often need to be renewed yearly, and OAG audits found the funds were not available until several months into the funding period because of the need for the federal government to review the First Nation's use of the monies from the previous year (2–3). These funding arrangements are problematic due to the additional administrative burdens they put on First Nations – many of whom have less than 500 members (4–5). Finally, it is not always clear to First Nations members who to hold accountable when they do not receive the services they require – their band council or Indigenous Services Canada (4).

The legislative changes discussed above, the corresponding First Nations institutions, and self-government agreements and comprehensive land claim settlements have increased the fiscal and governance capacity of many First Nations and may have helped to resolve some of this lack of clarity on the ability to provide services. In addition, in July 2016, the national chief of the Assembly of First Nations and the minister of then Aboriginal and Northern Affairs Canada signed a memorandum of understanding (MOU) concerning the development of a "new fiscal relationship" to enhance the predictability and quality of funding for First Nations communities (AFN and ISC 2017). One of the most obvious outcomes of this process was the creation of ten-year grants rather than the previous short-term grants to reduce the administrative burden on communities and enhance their ability to make forward-looking decisions. However, to access these ten-year grants, First Nations still need to go through an eligibility process. The First Nations Financial Management Board supports First Nations through this process and determines whether a nation is eligible. However, the final decision on whether a ten-year grant is offered is still with Indigenous Services Canada (First Nations Financial Management Board n.d.-b). This requirement implies that not all First Nations will be able to have access to the opportunities these grants may offer.

Predictable access to long-term funding is critical for government operations, and government-to-government transfers remain an important source of revenues for First Nations. While First Nations have increased fiscal powers through taxation and other forms of own-source revenue, grants and contribution agreements through Indigenous Services Canada are extremely important: property taxation and related payments raised approximately $96 *million* in 2018–19, but budgeted grants and contributions through Indigenous Services Canada in 2021–2 totalled $15.28 *billion* (Woolley et al. 2021). In addition, nearly half of the $96 million in tax revenue was raised by only ten nations. The median revenue for a nation through property tax was $130,000 (Woolley et al. 2021), implying that, at the moment, grants and contributions remain a necessary funding source.

In December 2020, the government of Canada introduced legislation to implement the UNDRIP. Budget 2021 proposed to provide $31.5 million over two years, starting in 2021–2, to support the co-development of an action plan to implement this legislation and to achieve UNDRIP objectives. While no dollar value was attached, the government announced its intention to work on a framework for negotiating agreements to implement fuel, alcohol, tobacco, and cannabis sales taxes on reserve or settlement lands. However, otherwise, the budget had little funding dedicated to building First Nations fiscal and governance capacity: of the planned spending in 2021–2, approximately 2 per cent goes directly to building Indigenous self-governance capacity and approximately 0.36 per cent to building the Indigenous land base.[29]

Research and Policy Questions Moving Forward

The changes described earlier have been contemporaneous with the broader trend towards decentralization among federal states in recent decades (Madariaga 2021). The motives behind these changes were also, for some people at least, consistent with motives in other areas: for example, the desire to foster greater accountability to taxpayers among "subnational" governments and to reduce bureaucratic overlap and inefficiencies. However, many Indigenous peoples resist this narrow interpretation of changes and prefer to focus on Indigenous rights, treaty obligations, and the fiduciary duty of governments.

Rather than seeing the changes described above as a starting point towards control and self-government, some Indigenous leaders see the focus on reserves, government-legislated commissions, federal institutions, and taxation as a further concession to colonial assimilation (Jobin and Riddle 2019).

Thus, there remain many unresolved big questions for First Nations and others in Canada concerning the best path forward in the context of Canadian fiscal federalism. What does true Indigenous self-determination look like in the context of the Canadian state? How can or should First Nations fit into Canada's constitutional structure? Will the opt-out agreements, which have come with First Nations institution-building, create the foundation for a recognized Federation of First Nations within Canada's political structure? Could this First Nations Federation, if it were to evolve, form the foundation of a "First Nations Province" (Courchene and Powell 1992), and should it? If it does, how would infrastructure funding (as discussed by Eric Champagne and Aracelly Denise Granja for municipalities in chapter 15) and equalization payments (whose national history is discussed by Mary Janigan in chapter 2) work for them? How does the creation of urban reservations, such as the eight created in Saskatchewan as of 2021, complicate or simplify any of these challenges? All these big questions are important in order to answer the pressing questions facing First Nations peoples every day about clean and reliable water supply, accessible health care, education, and overall community well-being systemically.

Answering some smaller questions is critical as a first step towards answering these bigger questions. For example, has the creation of the Tax Commission, the Finance Authority, the Financial Management Board, the Land Management Board, and fiscal powers under modern treaties increased First Nations access to quality public infrastructure, housing, and economic outcomes in the near term, and will they overall? Do the advantages of increasing local flexibility of First Nations governments outweigh the general economic concerns about competition across jurisdictions? Are there complementarities between the Indian Act fiscal opt-out arrangements such as the 2014 First Nations Election Act and others?[30] Are the land provisions in the Indian Act or the flexibility under the LMA sufficient to generate tax revenue to meet community needs? What are the practical alternatives? How can additions to reserves and the creation of urban reserves support fiscal capacity?[31] While there is some evidence as to the answers to each of these questions, they are currently largely unresolved.

For those simply interested in understanding models of fiscal federalism and institutional design, the First Nations context in Canada offers an opportunity for building knowledge and applications and, when explored in partnership with First Nations themselves, the opportunity for real change.

We hope this brief discussion will support First Nations and their allies in working towards gaining their rightful fiscal place with greater autonomy, clarity, and equity.

NOTES

1 This legacy was acknowledged in 1988 with a resolution passed by the US Senate: H.Con.Res.331 – A concurrent resolution to acknowledge the contribution of the Iroquois Confederacy of Nations to the development of the United States Constitution and to reaffirm the continuing government-to-government relationship between Indian tribes and the United States established in the Constitution. 100th Congress (1987–1988), https://www.congress.gov/bill/100th-congress/house-concurrent-resolution/331/.
2 This treaty was the Williams Treaty, which was arguably not a negotiated treaty. The end of historical treaty-making is often identified as 1921, with the last "numbered treaty."
3 The specific claims process allows First Nations to seek compensation through negotiation for the failures of the government of Canada to provide promised reserve land, responsibly manage First Nations assets, or deliver on treaty obligations if the claim is less than a specific dollar value. As of 2018, 460 of these claims have reached a settlement, but hundreds remain outstanding. See Crown-Indigenous Relations and Northern Affairs Canada, "Specific Claims," https://www.rcaanc-cirnac.gc.ca/eng/1100100030291/1539617582343.
4 Supreme Court of Canada, *St. Catharine's Milling and Lumber Co. v. R*, (1887) 13 S.C.R. 577.
5 Specifically, the Indian Act consolidated the Gradual Civilization Act of 1857 and the Gradual Enfranchisement Act of 1869.
6 Guerin v. The Queen, 1984 CanLII 25 (SCC), [1984] 2 SCR 335, https://canlii.ca/t/1lpfn.
7 "But from one end of Canada to the other it is becoming a common practice to represent to the Indians that they have certain rights, and those making the representations usually manage to get the Indians to enter into a contract providing substantial remuneration for their advisers. We think it is to the advantage of the Indians that these contracts should be scrutinized by the department in order to protect them from exploitation." Charles Stewart, MP, Superintendent-General of Indian Affairs. *Debates, House of Commons, First Session–Sixteenth Parliament, Volume 1, 1926–27*, 15 February 1927, 325 (Ottawa: F.A. Acland, 1927). https://parl.canadiana.ca/view/oop.debates_HOC1601_01/327.
8 Indian Act, 1920, section A10(1).
9 For example, the 1969 white paper, *Statement of the Government of Canada on Indian Policy, 1969* (Ottawa: Queen's Printer, 1969), advocated for the dismantling of the Indian Act, which was strongly resisted by Indigenous groups. For the text of the white paper, see https://oneca.com/1969_White_Paper.pdf.
10 An Act Respecting Indians, 21st Parliament, 4th session, 1951.
11 Section 82, originally section 97 of Bill 267, 21st Parliament, 2nd session, 1950. See *House of Commons Debates* (7 June 1950) at 3334. Bill 267 was the bill under consideration to revise the Indian Act in 1951.

12 R. v. Calder, 1996 CanLII 232 (SCC), [1996] 1 SCR 660, https://canlii.ca/t/1frbf.
13 Delgamuukw v. British Columbia, 1997 CanLII 302 (SCC), [1997] 3 SCR 1010, https://canlii.ca/t/1fqz8.
14 Haida Nation v. British Columbia (Minister of Forests), 2004 SCC 73 (CanLII), [2004] 3 SCR 511, https://canlii.ca/t/1j4tq.
15 See *Mikisew Cree First Nation v. Canada* (Governor General in Council), 2018 SCC 40 (CanLII), [2018] 2 SCR 765 at 21.
16 Tsilhqot'in Nation v. British Columbia, 2014 SCC 44 (CanLII), [2014] 2 SCR 257, https://canlii.ca/t/g7mt9.
17 See [2014] S.C.J. No. 44, [2014] 2 S.C.R. 257 (S.C.C.). It is important to note that Aboriginal title did not apply to privately owned or underwater lands (Borrows 2015).
18 In areas covered by historical treaties, nations can claim their rights under treaty that were never delivered upon or unjustly violated through the specific claims process and/or through treaty land entitlement agreements. Using these processes, nations can re-acquire land through the additions to reserve process, which has led to large numbers of settlements and the creation of 120 new urban reserves (see Government of Canada, "Urban Reserves," https://www.sac-isc.gc.ca/eng/110010 0016331/1611939200241). The additions to reserve process was created in 1972, since it was not possible to add land to reserves under the Indian Act (see Government of Canada, "Additions to Reserve," https://www.sac-isc.gc.ca/eng/1332267668 918/1611930372477).
19 "The current Government of Canada policy for the settlement of Aboriginal land claims had its genesis in the 1973 *Statement on Claims of Indian and Inuit People*. The policy divides claims into two broad categories: specific and comprehensive. *Specific* claims, made by First Nations against Canada, relate to the administration of land and other assets, or to the non-fulfilment of historic treaties. *Comprehensive* land claims are based on the assertion of continuing Aboriginal rights and/or title to lands and natural resources. The Comprehensive Land Claims Policy stipulates that land claims may be negotiated with Aboriginal groups in areas where claims to Aboriginal title have not been addressed by treaty or through other legal means." Government of Canada, "General Briefing Note on Canada's Self-Government and Comprehensive Land Claims Policies and the Status of Negotiations," https://www.rcaanc-cirnac.gc.ca/eng/1373385502190/1542727338550.
20 The real cost of the Nisga'a Final Agreement to the federal and provincial governments is estimated to be $500 million in 1998 dollars when direct and indirect costs are accounted for. However, some have put the cost at $1 billion in 1998 dollars (Hurley 1999). We are not aware of any public estimates of the cost to the Nisga'a.
21 Tk'emlúps te Secwépemc, *Tax*, 2021, https://tkemlups.ca/departments/lands-leasing-tax/tax/. See also First Nations Tax Commission, "30th Anniversary of Bill C-115," 20 July 2018, https://fntc.ca/30th-anniversary-of-bill-c-115/.
22 The First Nations Tax Commission also facilitates service and infrastructure agreements between First Nations local governments (Tulo 2014, 203).

232   Donn. L. Feir and David Scoones

23 First Nations governments are routinely represented in the media as inefficient, corrupt, or nepotistic. Some academic research has furthered these impressions. See, for example, Flanagan (2017), who conceded that comparative data on corruption for similarly situated non-Indigenous governments is lacking. Even less is known about corruption and nepotism in non-Indigenous businesses, which often have the incentive to cover up embezzlement to maintain reputation. The oversight provided by the First Nations Tax Commission can help limit the consequences of public beliefs regarding one First Nation impacting the ability of all to borrow.
24 Authors' calculations.
25 CSDs are the equivalent of political units such as reserves or municipalities.
26 The results are quantitatively similar to using probit or logit models.
27 The sample size of the first estimate is 1,134. The sample size of the remaining estimates is 384. The reason for the difference is that the CWB data on economic conditions is restricted to only CSDs above 250 people. Restricting the sample to be the same in the first unconditional estimate increases it from 5.4 percentage points (t-statistic 3.32) to 7.1 percentage points (t-statistic 2.19).
28 Perhaps the most significant threat to interpreting this association causally is whether nations that are used to publishing tax laws through the *First Nations Gazette* are also more likely to publish all their laws there than nations without a tax law.
29 The 2021 budget allotted $104.8 million over two years, starting in 2021–2, to support the administrative capacity of First Nations governments and other organizations that deliver critical programs and services. Budget 2021 also proposed to invest $151.4 million over five years, starting in 2021–2, to provide wrap-around supports for First Nations with the greatest community development needs; $33.4 million in 2021–2 to support the First Nations Finance Authority's pooled borrowing regime; and $73.5 million over three years, starting in 2021–2, to continue work towards the development and implementation of a First Nations Data Governance Strategy.
30 The First Nations Election Act, passed in 2014, allows First Nations additional freedom to opt-out of the Indian Act election codes by reducing the costs associated through providing alternative template election codes. See First Nations Elections Act (S.C. 2014, c. 5), https://laws.justice.gc.ca/eng/acts/F-11.65/.
31 For a description and more information about urban reserves, see City of Saskatoon, "Urban Reserves in Saskatoon: Frequently Asked Questions," August 2022, https://www.saskatoon.ca/sites/default/files/documents/community-services/planning-development/future-growth/urban-reserves-treaty-land-entitlement/urban_reserve_faq.pdf.

REFERENCES

AFN (Assembly of First Nations) and ISC (Indigenous Services Canada). 2017. *A New Approach: Co-Development of a New Fiscal Relationship between Canada and First*

Nations. Gatineau, PQ: AFN and ISC. https://publications.gc.ca/collections/collection_2017/aanc-inac/R5-601-2017-eng.pdf.

Aragón, Fernando M. 2015. "Do Better Property Rights Improve Local Income? Evidence from First Nations' Treaties." *Journal of Development Economics* 116: 43–56. https://doi.org/10.1016/j.jdeveco.2015.03.004.

Bartlett, Richard H. 1978. "The Indian Act of Canada." *Buffalo Law Review* 27, no. 4: 581–615. https://digitalcommons.law.buffalo.edu/buffalolawreview/vol27/iss4/3/.

Bentzen, Jeanet Sinding, Jacob Gerner Hariri, and James A. Robinson. 2019. "Power and Persistence: The Indigenous Roots of Representative Democracy." *The Economic Journal* 129, no. 618: 678–714. https://doi.org/10.1111/ecoj.12568.

Borrows, John. 1997. "Wampum at Niagara: The Royal Proclamation, Canadian Legal History, and Self-Government." In *Aboriginal and Treaty Rights in Canada: Essays on Law, Equality and Respect for Difference*, edited by Michael Asch, 155–72. Vancouver: UBC Press.

– 2005. "Indigenous Legal Traditions in Canada." *Washington University Journal of Law and Policy* 19, no. 1: 167–223. https://openscholarship.wustl.edu/law_journal_law_policy/vol19/iss1/13.

– 2015. "Aboriginal Title and Private Property." *Supreme Court Law Review: Osgoode's Annual Constitutional Cases Conference* 71, no. 1: 91–134. http://digitalcommons.osgoode.yorku.ca/sclr/vol71/iss1/5.

Brideau, Isabelle. 2019. *The Duty to Consult Indigenous Peoples*. Background Paper, Library of Parliament. Publication No. 2019-17-E. https://lop.parl.ca/sites/PublicWebsite/default/en_CA/ResearchPublications/201917E.

Carlos, Ann M., Donna L. Feir, and Angela Redish. 2022. "Indigenous Nations and the Development of the US Economy: Land, Resources, and Dispossession." *Journal of Economic History* 82, no. 2: 516–55. https://doi.org/10.1017/S0022050722000080.

CIRNAC (Crown-Indigenous Relations and Northern Affairs Canada). 2015. "Comprehensive Claims." Government of Canada. https://www.rcaanc-cirnac.gc.ca/eng/1100100030577/1551196153650.

– 2016. "General Briefing Note on Canada's Self-Government and Comprehensive Land Claims Policies and the Status of Negotiations." Government of Canada. https://www.rcaanc-cirnac.gc.ca/eng/1373385502190/1542727338550.

– 2023. "Treaties and Agreements." Government of Canada. https://www.rcaanc-cirnac.gc.ca/eng/1100100028574/1529354437231.

Courchene, Thomas J., and Lisa M. Powell. 1992. "A First Nations Province." Political Economy Research Group. Papers in Political Economy, No. 26. London, ON: Department of Economics, University of Western Ontario. https://ir.lib.uwo.ca/economicsperg_ppe/20/.

Department of Finance. 2008. "First Nations Personal Income Tax Administration Agreements." Government of Canada. https://www.canada.ca/en/department-finance/programs/tax-policy/aboriginal/tax-administration-agreements/first-nations-personal-income-tax.html.

First Nations Finance Authority. n.d. "About the FNFA." FNFA. Accessed 1 August 2022. https://www.fnfa.ca/en/about/.
– 2021. *Stronger Together: 2020/21 Annual Report*. FNFA. https://www.fnfa.ca/wp-content/uploads/2021/07/FNFA-Annual-report-2020-21-English-Web.pdf.
First Nations Financial Management Board. n.d.-a. "About FMB." FMB. Accessed 1 August 2022. https://fnfmb.com/en/about-fmb.
– n.d.-b "Ten-Year Grant." FMB. Accessed 1 August 2022. https://fnfmb.com/en/services/10-year-grant.
First Nations Tax Commission. n.d. "First Nations Tax Commission: Overview." FNTC. Accessed 1 August 2022. https://fntc.ca/functions-services/.
– 2021. *Building a New Path: 2020/2021 Annual Report*. FNTC. https://fntc.ca/wp-content/uploads/ARs/FNTC_ANNUAL_REPORT_20-21_EN_WEB_july23.pdf.
Flanagan, Tom. 2017. "Corruption and First Nations in Canada." *Canadian Foreign Policy Journal* 23, no. 1: 15–31. https://doi.org/10.1080/11926422.2016.1229685.
Government of Canada. 2016. "James Bay and Northern Quebec Agreement." Ottawa: Government of Canada. https://www.canada.ca/en/impact-assessment-agency/corporate/james-bay-northern-quebec-agreement.html.
– 2023. "First Nations Goods and Services Tax." Government of Canada. https://www.canada.ca/en/revenue-agency/services/tax/businesses/topics/gst-hst-businesses/charge-collect-indigenous-peoples/first-nations-goods-services-tax.html.
Graben, Sari. 2007. "The Nisga'a Final Agreement: Negotiating Federalism." *Indigenous Law Journal* 6, no. 2: 63–94. https://jps.library.utoronto.ca/index.php/ilj/article/download/27672/20403/62700.
Graham, John, and Jodi Bruhn. 2010. "In Praise of Taxes: The Link between Taxation and Good Governance in a First Nations Context." In *Aboriginal Policy Research*. Vol. X, *Voting, Governance, and Research Methodology*, edited by Jerry P. White, Julie Peters, Dan Beavon, and Peter Dinsdale, 45–86. Toronto: Thompson Educational Publishing. http://thompsonbooks.com/wp-content/uploads/2020/02/APR_Vol_10Ch3.pdf.
Hickey, Ross. 2021. "Policy Forum: First Nation Property Taxation and Governance in British Columbia." *Canadian Tax Journal* 69, no. 3: 873–87. https://doi.org/10.32721/ctj.2021.69.3.pf.hickey.
Hurley, Mary C. 1999. *The Nisga'a Final Agreement*. Parliamentary Research Branch, PRB 99–2E. Ottawa: Library of Parliament. https://publications.gc.ca/collections/Collection-R/LoPBdP/PRB-e/PRB992-e.pdf.
– 2000. *The Crown's Fiduciary Relationship with Aboriginal Peoples*. Parliamentary Research Branch, PRB 00–09E. Ottawa: Library of Parliament. https://publications.gc.ca/collections/Collection-R/LoPBdP/PRB-e/PRB0009-e.pdf.
Jobin, Shalene, and Emily Riddle. 2019. *The Rise of the First Nations Land Management Regime in Canada: A Critical Analysis*. Toronto: Yellowhead Institute.
Jules, Clarence T. 2000. "Responding to Challenges: The Future of the Indian Taxation Advisory Board." *Canadian Tax Journal* 48, no. 5: 1470–95.

KPMG. 2014. *Framework Agreement on First Nation Land Management: Update Assessment of Socio/Economic Development Benefits (Final Report)*. Ottawa: KPMG. https://labrc.com/wp-content/uploads/2014/03/FNLM-Benefits-Review-Final-Report_Feb-27-2014.pdf.

Le Dressay, André. 2021. "Policy Forum: In Defence of the First Nations Fiscal Management Act." *Canadian Tax Journal* 69, no. 3: 829–33. https://doi.org/10.32721/ctj.2021.69.3.pf.ledressay.

Madariaga, Amuitz Garmendia. 2021. "Fiscal Decentralization." In *Handbook on the Politics of Taxation*, edited by Lukas Hakelberg, 146–64. Cheltenham, UK: Edward Elgar Publishing.

Milne, Thomas. 2017 "Case Brief: Calder et al. v. Attorney-General of British Columbia, [1973] SCR 313." CanLII 4 (SCC), [1973] SCR 313. *CanLII Connects*, 15 May 2017. https://canliiconnects.org/en/summaries/45549.

Neuman, Keith. 2016. *Canadian Public Opinion on Aboriginal Peoples (Final Report)*. Toronto: Environics Institute for Survey Research. https://www.environicsinstitute.org/docs/default-source/project-documents/public-opinion-about-aboriginal-issues-in-canada-2016/final-report.pdf.

OAG (Office of the Auditor General of Canada). 2011. "Programs for First Nations on Reserves." In *Status Report of the Auditor General of Canada to the House of Commons*, chap. 4. Ottawa: OAG. https://publications.gc.ca/collections/collection_2011/bvg-oag/FA1-10-2011-4-eng.pdf.

Pendakur, Krishna, and Ravi Pendakur. 2018 "The Effects of Modern Treaties and Opt-In Legislation on Household Incomes in Aboriginal Communities." *Social Indicators Research* 137, no. 1: 139–65. https://doi.org/10.1007/s11205-017-1593-5.

– 2021. "The Impact of Self-Government, Comprehensive Land Claims, and Opt-In Arrangements on Income Inequality in Indigenous Communities in Canada." *Canadian Public Policy* 47, no. 2: 180–201. https://doi.org/10.3138/cpp.2020-004.

Redish, Angela. 2019. "Treaty of Paris vs. Treaty of Niagara: Rethinking Canadian Economic History in the 21st Century." *Canadian Journal of Economics* 52, no. 4: 1325–48. https://doi.org/10.1111/caje.12405.

Richard, Greg, Jason Calla, and André Le Dressay. 2008. "The High Costs of Doing Business on First Nation Lands in Canada." Publications and Reports, Fiscal Realities Economists. https://www.fiscalrealities.com/_files/ugd/1611b1_75070e7b498c4ea981b1cb2d49e12933.pdf.

Royal Commission on Aboriginal Peoples. 1996. *Looking Forward, Looking Back*. Vol. 1 of *Report of the Royal Commission on Aboriginal Peoples*. Ottawa: Canadian Communication Group Publishing. https://publications.gc.ca/collections/collection_2016/bcp-pco/Z1-1991-1-1-eng.pdf.

Slattery, Brian. 2014. "The Aboriginal Constitution." *Supreme Court Law Review: Osgoode's Annual Constitutional Cases Conference* 67, no. 9: 319–36. https://digitalcommons.osgoode.yorku.ca/sclr/vol67/iss1/9/.

Slowey, Gabrielle A. 2021. "Indigenous Self-Government in Yukon: Looking for Ways to Pass the Torch." *IRPP Insights* 37: 1–20. Montreal: Institute for Research on Public Policy. https://doi.org/10.26070/xzhy-p935.

Tekawennake News. 1998 "Nisga'a Treaty to Cost $311 M: Negotiator." *Tekawennake News*, 29 July 1998. https://vitacollections.ca/sixnationsarchive/3236735/data?n=23.

Tidridge, Nathan. 2015. *The Queen at the Council Fire: The Treaty of Niagara, Reconciliation, and the Dignified Crown in Canada*. Toronto: Dundurn Press.

Tulo Centre of Indigenous Economics. 2014. *Building a Competitive First Nations Investment Climate*. www.tulo.ca/textbook.

UBCIC (Union of BC Indian Chiefs). n.d. "UBIC 7th Annual General Assembly, April 21–25, 1975, Chilliwack, BC." Union of BC Indian Chiefs. https://www.ubcic.bc.ca/ubcic_7th_annual_general_assembly.

Wherrett, Jill. 1999. *Aboriginal Self-Government*. Government of Canada Publication 96-2E. https://publications.gc.ca/collections/Collection-R/LoPBdP/CIR/962-e.htm.

Wilkins, Kerry. 2000. "'Still Crazy After All These Years': Section 88 of the Indian Act at Fifty." *Alberta Law Revenue* 38, no. 2: 458–503. https://doi.org/10.29173/alr1442.

Woolley, Frances, River Doxtator, Alan McNaughton, and Daniel Sandler. 2021. "Policy Forum: Editor's Introduction – First Nation Property Taxation." *Canadian Tax Journal* 69, no. 3: 791–7. https://doi.org/10.32721/ctj.2021.69.3.pf.editors.

Yellowhead Institute. 2021. *Cash Back: A Yellowhead Institute Red Paper*. Yellowhead Institute. https://cashback.yellowheadinstitute.org/wp-content/uploads/2021/05/Cash-Back-A-Yellowhead-Institute-Red-Paper.pdf.

12 Long-Term Care Reform in Canada in the Wake of COVID-19: The Poverty of the National Standards Solution

ANTHONY BRETON AND PATRIK MARIER

Introduction

The COVID-19 pandemic has had a devastating impact on seniors, most notably on those living in residential long-term care (LTC) facilities in Canada and other countries around the world. As of 15 January 2022, 61 per cent of all Canadian COVID-related deaths occurred among those aged eighty and above. The proportion increases to 92.7 per cent if one refers simply to individuals aged sixty and above (PHAC 2021). LTC residents have been particularly impacted. In Quebec, they represented 44 per cent of all known COVID-19 deaths (INSPQ 2022). This aspect of the crisis gathered substantial attention, especially with the exceptional mobilization of the Armed Forces in long-term care. The role of private for-profit LTC facilities has also been intensively scrutinized with evidence showing higher rates of resident deaths (Stall et al. 2020). While the weakness of LTC policies had been the subject of multiple inquiries and reports across Canadian provinces in the past, the COVID-19 pandemic played the role of a "focusing event" for LTC reform on the political agenda of governments (Béland and Marier 2020).

Amidst this renewed attention to LTC, the COVID-19 pandemic has shown the difficulty of tackling this policy issue within the Canadian federal structure, with Ottawa aiming to take a leadership role in a policy area it has ignored for decades. This chapter analyses the possibilities to improve LTC quality within a context of federal collaboration. All federal parties have engaged in this debate and made various promises during the 2021 election campaign, such as deprivatizing the entire sector (New Democratic Party, NDP), instituting national standards (Liberal), or simply increasing the size of health-care transfers while preserving provincial autonomy (Conservative), which have been analysed elsewhere (Marier 2021b).

This chapter complements Marier's (2021b) previous study by focusing on the envisaged introduction of federally sponsored minimum national standards

238 Anthony Breton and Patrik Marier

for residential LTC, as featured in the most recent mandate letter of the federal health minister (Prime Minister's Office 2021). In March 2021, the Standards Council of Canada, the Health Standards Organization, and the Canadian Standards Association – three groups that set health industry standards used to accredit residential LTC homes – formed a partnership to update their LTC standards (Health Standards Organization 2021). The federal government has pledged $3 billion over five years to support the implementation of these standards (Cousins 2021).[1] This chapter seeks to assess and compare the envisaged federal standards with the residential LTC standards in place in four provinces (British Columbia, New Brunswick, Ontario, and Quebec). It also seeks to analyse the major hurdles in the creation of pan-Canadian standards.

The chapter includes five sections. The first section presents a succinct overview of LTC policies in Canada. The second features a review of quality of care standards. The third analyses and compares the standards for residential LTC facilities in four provinces (British Columbia, New Brunswick, Ontario, and Quebec). It demonstrates that, while these provinces have enacted standards to regulate quality of care in residential LTC homes, wide discrepancies in the number and scope of standards exist between and within them. The fourth section presents the standards envisaged to be nationalized while projecting their impact onto provincial frameworks. The conclusion summarizes the findings and outlines political obstacles to, and considerations for, the implementation of those standards.

Canadian Federalism and Long-Term Care

Canadian provinces employ different terms to describe the same type of establishment. For the purposes of this chapter, residential LTC facilities refer to organizations that provide accommodation, high levels of care, 24-hour nursing care, meals, and housekeeping, along with social and recreational activities for their residents (Health Standards Organization 2023). Such facilities ought to be distinguished from retirement homes, private seniors' residences, assisted living residences, and other types of nursing homes that offer less care and fewer services than residential facilities.

There are many distinctive features when it comes to residential LTC in Canada. First, LTC is considered an "extended service" in the Canada Health Act (CHA), meaning that provinces are not subjected to federal standards or obligations. Consequently, provinces have constructed their own LTC policies and infrastructure over past decades, resulting in a policy landscape much more fragmented than the thirteen health systems that operate under the CHA. One of the most notable differences across Canada arising from this decentralized system is the diversity of ownership of LTC facilities. The private for-profit sector represents the most common form of ownership in British Columbia (37 per cent), Prince Edward Island (47 per cent), and Ontario (57 per cent); the presence of the public sector is overwhelming in Quebec (88 per cent) and Newfoundland and Labrador (98 per cent); and the not-for-profit sector dominates in New Brunswick (86 per cent) (CIHI 2021).

There are also some commonalities. The primary responsibility for LTC is, with the noticeable exception of New Brunswick, typically embedded within provincial health-care systems, meaning that regional health authorities frequently oversee them. New Brunswick is an exception, with LTC integrated within a social department (Marier 2021a). This nearly homogenous treatment of LTC is quite surprising since, for instance, some provinces could have opted to delegate this responsibility at the local level, which is the norm in many European countries. In addition, all provinces spend the bulk of their LTC budget – over 80 per cent – in residential facilities rather than home care services, something that has not really changed since the 1970s, and total LTC expenditure occupies a marginal portion of health expenditure (13 per cent; Grignon and Spencer 2018). As a result of chronic underfunding and the marginalization of this policy area, there have been multiple reports from various public inquiries in all provinces to enact reforms well before the pandemic (Estabrooks et al. 2020).

This chapter explores the extent to which the creation of federal standards would represent a realignment and improvement of standards currently in place. As such, it presents an overview of provincial standards in four jurisdictions: British Columbia (BC), New Brunswick (NB), Ontario, and Quebec. The four provinces have different regulatory schemes. Ontario and NB have enacted legislation specifically focused on residential LTC homes, which applies to all types of homes regardless of their ownership status (FLTCA, s. 2[1] "long-term care home"; NHA, s. 1 "nursing home"). BC has enacted general legislation that applies to many facilities, including but not limited to residential LTC homes (CCALA). However, privately owned homes are treated differently and subject to fewer standards. Finally, Quebec has enacted general legislation that mandates residential LTC homes be accredited (ARHSSS, s. 107.1).

Quality of Care Standards

This section reviews the construction and measurement of quality of care standards. The dominant approach is Donabedian's structure-process-outcome (SPO) approach (Donabedian 1966, 1988; Castle and Ferguson 2010; Unruh and Wan 2004; Kane 1998). Donabedian posits that good health outcomes are caused by good, adequate treatments (process), which are in turn made possible by a good care setting (structure). Specifically, structure refers to the environment in which care is given, including an organization's material resources (dimension of rooms, available equipment, budget), human resources (quantity, skills, and education of personnel), and its organizational structure (division of labour, methods of reimbursements). Process, on the other hand, refers to care delivery and includes the actual treatment given to the patient as well as interactions among staff to prepare treatment. Process-related activities range from providing information to diagnosis and care giving. In contrast to structure and process, outcomes are patient-oriented (Donabedian 1988). Suggested categories of outcomes include physiological (for example, blood pressure, blood sugar, skin condition), functional (for example, activities of daily living [ADLs], instrumental activities of daily living [IADLs]), pain and discomfort, cognition, affect, social activities, social relationships, and satisfaction (Kane 1998, 235).

SPO Approach to Long-Term Care

Donabedian's SPO approach is not without critiques (Castle and Ferguson 2010). Donabedian's (1988) SPO approach was developed to measure quality of care within the health-care system with acute care in mind. Unruh and Wan (2004) build on scholarly efforts to assess quality of care in a LTC context and elaborate an expanded SPO framework for nursing home quality. They ground their theory in a broader definition of quality of care. Care involves "not only clinical care (medical and nursing care), but also social and environmental support to the residents" (198). Further, quality of care outcomes comprise elements beyond health to include "a good quality of life, which includes social and emotional health" (198)

The expanded framework refines Donabedian's theory by offering adapted examples of elements falling within the structure, process, and outcome categories. Structure, for example, is composed of organizational factors/facility characteristics (such as ownership, chain affiliation, size of beds, certification status) and nurse staffing, education, and proficiency (for example, resident-nurse ratio). Process is composed of adequate assessment of resident status (comprehensive resident assessment), adequate care planning (comprehensive care plan development), and nursing care adequacy (sufficient and appropriate nursing care). Outcomes are composed of a multitude of subcategories ranging from quality of life, freedom from abuse, and proper nutrition and hydration, to cognitive, emotional, and behavioural health (Unruh and Wan 2004).

Applying the SPO Approach to Provinces' Quality of Care Standards

To date, little research has compared the quality of care standards applicable to residential LTC homes in Canadian provinces. Gallant et al. (2020) examined the legislation of provinces and the academic literature to identify the legislative and regulatory standards related to assessing and managing pain among residents living in Canadian residential LTC facilities. They found that Ontario, NB, and Newfoundland and Labrador are the only provinces to specifically refer to pain management and assessment in their legislation, regulation, or policies. To our knowledge, no other study compares the legislation of provinces with respect to any other aspect of quality of care.

Quality of Care Standards in British Columbia, New Brunswick, Ontario, and Quebec

Canadian provinces regulate quality of care by setting standards through statutes, regulations, policies, mandatory accreditation, and/or case law. All provinces regulate and closely monitor residential LTC homes (Morris, Clarke, and Marrison 2021, 24; Library of Parliament 2020). This section compares the scope and depth of the quality of care standards set by British Columbia, New Brunswick, Ontario, and Quebec. Table 12.1 lists the sources consulted for each province. The appendix explains the methodology used to identify the relevant legal sources and the sections examined during the analysis.

Ontario and NB have enacted legislation specifically focused on residential LTC homes that – together with regulations and policies – applies to all types of homes, regardless of their ownership status. BC has enacted general legislation that applies to many facilities, including residential LTC homes. However, privately owned homes are subject to fewer standards, hence they were treated separately. Finally, Quebec has enacted general legislation that mandates homes to get accredited by either the Conseil Québécois d'agrément (CQA) or Accreditation Canada (AC). As a result, the standards set by both accreditation bodies were analysed separately.

Limitations of the Scope of the Analysis

Some sources were excluded from the analysis, such as LTC facility design and building code standards specific to residential LTC homes, since they are often non-binding, technical, and voluminous. Some sections found in the legislations were also excluded from the analysis, explaining why, for example, the number of sections selected for analysis within a statute is lower than the total number of sections it contains. Two main exclusions are worth noting. First, to ensure the reliability of the comparison, sections regulating other types of residential LTC homes were excluded from the analysis. They include Ontario's municipal and First Nations LTC homes as well as senior housing with some support, such as assisted living residences in BC and private seniors' residences in Ontario and Quebec.

Table 12.1. Characteristics of the Provincial Quality of Care Standards Analysed (as of 6 July 2022)

Characteristic	Ontario	NB	BC (public)	BC (private)	Quebec	Conseil Québécois d'agrément (CQA)	Accreditation Canada (AC)
Legislation	Fixing Long-Term Care Act, 2021, S.O. 2021, c. 39, Sched. 1 (FLTCA)	Nursing Homes Act, R.S.N.B. 2014, c. 125 (NHA)	Community Care and Assisted Living Act, S.B.C. 2002, c. 75 (CCALA)	(i) Hospital Act, R.S.B.C. 1996, c. 200 (HA); (ii) CCALA (to the extent provided by HA, s. 4[3][a])	Act Respecting Health Services and Social Services, RLRQ, c. S-4.2 (ARHSSS)	n/a	n/a
Regulation	O. Reg. 246/22: General	(i) N.B. Reg. 85-187; (ii) N.B. Reg. 2001-59	B.C. Reg. 96/2009	B.C. Reg. 96/2009 (to the extent provided by B.C. Reg. 37/2010, s. 2[2])	No	n/a	n/a
Policy	No	Standards Manual: Nursing Home Services	No	No	(i) Cadre de référence et normes relatives à l'hébergement dans les établissements de soins de longue durée (Quebec 2018);	Rapport d'agrément CHSLD Villa Val des Arbres (13 juin 2017) (CQA 2017)	HSO 21001:2020(e) Long-Term Care Services standard (HSO 2020)

Accreditation	Optional	Optional	Optional	Optional	(ii) May 8th, 2014 Notice (Quebec 2018, annex) Mandatory: Conseil Québécois d'Agrément or Accreditation Canada	
Type of home excluded from study	(i) Municipal Homes; (ii) First Nations Homes; (iii) Private Seniors' Residences	n/a	Assisted Living Residences	Assisted Living Residences	Private Seniors' Residences	n/a
No. sections analysed (excluding rights) (n =)	258	131	84	11	31	35
					24	
No. rights analysed (n =)	29	0	19	19	15	n/a

Second, provincial statutes, regulations, and policies regulating residential LTC homes contain a broad variety of sections that, for the most part, can arguably be interpreted as standards even though they differ from Unruh and Wan's (2004) conception of structure, process, and outcome. For instance, compliance and enforcement mechanisms such as inspections are found in all four provincial statutes (FLTCA, ss. 144–53; CCALA, s. 9; NHA, s. 25; ARHSSS, s. 413.2) and easily fit into the definition of structure standards. However, their purpose is to induce compliance with other quality standards. Hence, their relative importance to other structure standards (such as staffing) is lower, and they were accordingly excluded from this study. Also excluded from the scope of the analysis were sections regulating nursing home licensing, funding, and eligibility/admission/discharge of residents.

Coding

Once the relevant statutes, regulations, policies, and accreditation instruments were identified for each province, an exhaustive review and classification of their content was performed according to Donabedian's (1988) SPO approach as adapted by Unruh and Wan (2004). Each section/article/clause was read, analysed, and then classified into (i) structure, (ii) process, or (iii) outcome. Residents' rights were assimilated to outcome quality standards. Within structure-process-outcome categories, subclassification of standards around common themes was done according to the scope and breadth of the standards identified. Unruh and Wan's (2004) and Castle and Ferguson's (2010) classifications were used as guidance while coding.

Categorized quality standards were extracted from sections/articles/clauses and labelled accordingly. One section may entail more than one standard. For example, section 6 of Ontario's FLTCA arguably contains more than ten distinguishable standards. When this situation occurred, as many standards as necessary were created to reflect the different regulatory nuances. Conversely, sometimes many sections could be aggregated to form one standard. For example, sections 119 and 120 of O. Reg. 246/22 were merged to form one standard related to limiting the use of restraint. When sections referred to policies, the provisions of that policy were not analysed. Instead, the standard was classified as mandating its establishment.

Findings

Table 12.2 describes the distribution of standards identified in each province. All four provinces and both accreditation bodies have enacted structure-, process-, and outcome-related standards. Moreover, structure-related standards are twice as numerous as process-related or outcome-related standards in the legislation and policies of all four provinces as well as in the standards set by

Long-Term Care Reform in Canada in the Wake of COVID-19   245

Table 12.2. Summary of Standards Identified in the Four Provinces

	Ontario	NB	BC (public)	BC (private)	Quebec	CQA	AC
Number of sections analysed	258	131	84	11	31	24	35
Number of residents' rights analysed	29	0	19	19	15	n/a	n/a
Number of standards identified	253	130	124	33	51	27	48
Structure	137	80	68	6	31	20	15
%	54.15	61.54	54.84	18.18	60.78	74.07	31.25
Process	65	34	23	6	10	4	18
%	25.69	26.15	18.55	18.18	19.61	14.81	37.50
Outcome	51	16	33	21	10	3	15
%	20.16	12.31	26.61	63.64	19.61	11.11	31.25

the CQA. Only AC and private homes in BC have a different distribution of standards. It should be noted, however, that the unusual distribution of standards for private homes in BC is explained by the fact that approximately 63.64 per cent (21/33) of the analysed sections are residents' rights (categorized as outcomes).

As was expected from the vastly different number of sections found in the four provinces, the number of standards identified in each province varies significantly. In Ontario's statute and regulation, 253 standards were identified, compared to 130 standards in NB, 124 standards applicable to public homes in BC, and 51 standards in Quebec. Accreditation bodies have established a low number of standards (27 standards by the CQA and 48 standards by AC). Private homes in BC are regulated by the lowest number of standards (33 standards), the vast majority of which are found in the outcome category (21 standards, or 63.64 per cent).

Structure-Related Standards

Five categories compose structure-related standards: organizational structure, material resources, human resources, mandatory policies, and miscellaneous. Most categories were inspired by Donabedian's (1988) discussion regarding the components of structure and include Unruh and Wan's (2004) classification. Mandatory polices and miscellaneous were created during coding to adapt the theory to what was found in the legislation (see Table 12.3).

Table 12.3. Structure-Related Standards Categories

	Total Number of Distinguishable Standards Identified (%)	Description
Organizational structure	71 (35.86)	Standards of an administrative nature unrelated to human resources and organizational policies. Includes mission statement/organizational strategy; governance, leadership, and accountability; organizing the provision of care; managing complaints; managing resident and family councils; quality improvement; and records management.
Material resources	43 (21.72)	Standards related to the residential LTC facility, including its accessibility, safety and emergency preparedness, comfort, regulation of areas (work areas, bedrooms, bathrooms, dining areas, outside activity areas), as well as regulation of storage and stocking of supplies, and utilities. Restrictions of activities within the facility (e.g., smoking) are included.
Human resources	38 (19.19)	Standards related to human resources sufficiency (staffing), qualifications, training and orientation, supervision, continuity, communication, and management (in general).
Mandatory policies*	42 (21.21)	Standards related to policies, procedures, or plans that every home must adopt. They include policies that are care related (e.g., zero tolerance on abuse and neglect, minimum use of restraint, falls prevention and management, skin and wound care, continence care and bowel management, pain management, care transitions, suicide prevention, and care provision guidance for staff), as well as drug-related policies, risk management–related policies, and other miscellaneous policies.
Miscellaneous	4 (2.02)	Residual category of standards. The four residual standards include building external partnerships, pursuing innovative practices, public relations management, and maximum number of residents.
Total	198 (100)	

* When policies mandated by law were significantly related to another category (that is, a mandatory policy on staff training: see, for example, B.C. Reg. 96/2009, s. 85[2][c]), then they were categorized in this other category.

Ontario regulates structure extensively, with 137 standards covering each of the first four categories of standards (organizational structure, material resources, human resources, and mandatory policies) with at least 20 different standards. Its biggest emphasis is on organizational structure. The Ontarian legislation establishes approximately 25 standards mandating the organization of a wide array of residents' services. It goes as far as mandating housekeeping services seven days a week, identifying what must be cleaned, what must be disinfected, and regulating the stocking of cleaning equipment (O. Reg. 246/22, s. 93). Ontario even regulates laundry service (O. Reg. 246/22, s. 95). No other province or accreditation body regulates the provision of housekeeping services.

Even though Ontario enacted the most standards, the scope of NB's and BC (public)'s structure-related standards are roughly as broad as Ontario's. In fact, NB and BC have established at least 14 and 8 standards in the first four categories, respectively. NB has enacted a similar number of standards as Ontario with respect to material resources (19 vs. 22) and – to a lesser extent – mandatory policies (21 vs. 30). Moreover, NB extensively regulates the organization of residents' services like Ontario, having enacted approximately 17 standards in this category, representing 21.25 per cent of its structure-related standards. The categories in which NB significantly falls short when compared to Ontario are governance, leadership, and accountability (organizational structure) and staff qualification (human resources). This shortfall stems from the fact that NB does not mandate the nomination of accountable heads for the different organized services or mandate minimum qualifications for every type of staff in the LTC home like Ontario does. Interestingly, NB is the only province capping the number of residents – to 150 residents per facility (NHA, s. 11).

Although BC (public) has enacted a smaller number of structure-related standards than Ontario and NB, it frequently went beyond both provinces' standards, especially with respect to material resources. For example, both Ontario and BC (public) regulate minimum bedroom furnishings (O. Reg. 246/22, ss. 15[2], 16; B.C. Reg. 96/2009, s. 29). BC (public), NB, and Ontario mandate the existence of an operational communication and response system in every room (O. Reg. 246/22, s. 20; B.C. Reg. 96/2009, s. 19[2]; N.B. Reg. 85-187, s. 32). However, only BC (public) establishes that each resident has a separate bedroom, sets a minimum bedroom size, mandates bedroom accessibility, and regulates the bedroom lock and the bedroom window (B.C. Reg. 96/2009, ss. 25[1], 26[1], 27, 26[2], 26[3], 28, respectively).

Material resources standards are absent from Quebec's legislation and policies as well as from the standards set by both the CQA and AC. In fact, a substantial proportion of Quebec's and the CQA's standards are found in the human resources category: 12 out of 31 structure-related standards (38.71 per cent) identified in Quebec's legislation and policies regulate human resources. The proportion is even bigger in CQA's standards (11 out of 20 structure-related standards regulate human resources, or 55 per cent). This is a significant difference from Ontario, NB, and BC (public), which have allocated no more than 20 per cent of their structure-related standards to human resources (respectively, 25 out of 137 standards, or 18.25 per cent; 14 out of 80 standards, or 17.50 per cent; 12 out of 68 standards, or 17.65 per cent). Further, while Ontario and BC (public) heavily regulate staff qualification (60.00 per cent and 41.67 per cent of human resources standards, respectively), Quebec has enacted only one standard (8.33 per cent) in this category, and the CQA has not enacted a single one.

With respect to human resources staffing, all four provinces have established mandatory 24/7 nursing care availability (FLTCA, s. 11[3] and O. Reg. 246/22, s. 49; B.C. Reg. 96/2009, ss. 42[3], 43; N.B. Reg. 85-187, s. 18[b] and NB 2020: Standards Manual, # B-I-1; Quebec 2018, annex [Notice of 2014-05-08]). No province or any accreditation body regulate the minimum nurse/resident ratio, but most have set a minimum number of daily direct care hours for residents. Ontario and NB, for example, have enacted into law a minimum of 4.00 hours (FLTCA, s. 8[2]) and 2.89 hours (NB 2020: Standards Manual, #B-I-1[3]) of daily direct care hours for residents. British Columbia has set a soft target of a minimum of 3.36 hours of direct daily care per resident (British Columbia Ministry of Health 2017). Lastly, private homes in BC are subject to only 6 structure-related standards, of which 5 (83.33 per cent) are focused on organizational structure. The sixth standard establishes minimum furnishings of bedrooms (B.C. Reg. 96/2009, s. 29; B.C. Reg. 37/2010, s. 2[2]). Everything else (notably human resources and mandatory policies) is left unregulated.

Process-Related Standards

Process-related standards were divided into four categories, three of which are based on Unruh and Wan's (2004) adapted SPO approach: adequate assessment of residents (10 standards, or 13.70 per cent), adequate care planning (27 standards, or 36.99 per cent), and nursing care adequacy (28 standards, or 38.36 per cent). Only information and referral assistance (8 standards, or 10.96 per cent) is a new category (see Table 12.4).

Ontario's second biggest standard category is process-related, with 65 standards representing 25.69 per cent of its quality of care standards. Again, Ontario has by far the largest number of process-related standards, enacting a minimum of 8 standards in each process-related grouping, up to 25 standards. However, Ontario's biggest process-related standards group – adequate care planning (38.46 per cent) – is hardly significant because 18 of 25 adequate care planning standards are duplicates of the same 9 standards identically regulating the temporary plans of care developed upon admission and the permanent plans of care developed afterward (for example, compare FLTCA, s. 6 to O. Reg.

Table 12.4. Process-Related Standards Categories

	Total Number of Distinguishable Standards Identified (%)	Description
Adequate assessment	10 (*13.70*)	Frequency of resident assessments and their scope (for example, health, emotional wellness, and so forth).
Adequate care planning	27 (*36.99*)	Development of a temporary care plan upon admission, followed by an initial plan of care to be regularly reassessed. This category also includes the planning of other types of care, such as care transitions.
Nursing care adequacy	28 (*38.36*)	Minimum amount of care residents are entitled to receive, including assistance with performance of activities of daily living, hygiene of personal items and rooms, safety, restorative care, nutrition and hydration, use of restraint, administration of medication, and palliative and end-of-life care.
Information and referral assistance	8 (*10.96*)	Information that the home and the staff must provide to residents as well as the mandatory notification of certain incidents to residents, families, representatives, the licensor, and other organizations.
Total	73 (*100*)	

246/22, s. 27). On the other hand, Ontario's 24 nursing care adequacy standards, representing 38.36 per cent of its process-related standards, testifies to its regulatory strength. The following nursing care adequacy standards are left unregulated everywhere except in Ontario's legislation: each resident is entitled to two weekly baths (O. Reg. 246/22, s. 37); preventive and basic foot care (O. Reg. 246/22, s. 39); assistance to insert dentures (O. Reg. 246/22, s. 38[2]), to use personal aids (O. Reg. 246/22, s. 41[2]), and for dressing (O. Reg. 246/22, s. 44); have their linens changed at least once a week (O. Reg. 246/22, s. 95[1][a][i]); and more.

Even though NB and BC (public) have enacted fewer process-related standards, their scope is roughly as broad as Ontario's. NB has established a minimum of 5 standards in every category, up to 13; and BC (public) has enacted a minimum of 3 standards in every category, up to 10. AC has also established standards along a similar distribution (minimum 3, up to 8). However, NB, BC (public), and AC weakly regulate nursing care adequacy. BC (public)'s applicable standards provide for a general obligation to "assist persons in care in maintaining health and hygiene" (B.C. Reg. 96/2009, s. 54[1]). They also regulate dining services and mandate oral care (B.C. Reg. 96/2009, s. 54[3][b][i]), assistance for eating (B.C. Reg. 96/2009, s. 67), minimal use of restraint (B.C. Reg. 96/2009, ss. 73–5), and safe administration of medication (B.C. Reg. 96/2009, s. 70). The rest is left unregulated. NB does not go much further than BC (public), and it does not even regulate mouth care. NB (2020) does, however, provide for the respect of residents' meal routines (Standards Manual, #B-X-3), the safe manipulation of equipment (Standards Manual, #D-I-4, #D-I-6[3]), and the offering of restorative care (N.B. Reg. 85-187, ss. 15, 16). AC's standards do not go beyond respecting residents' routines (HSO 2020, #2.6.1), regulating dining services (HSO 2020, #2.6.4), and mandating minimal use of restraint (HSO 2020, #2.4.1).

Once again, Quebec's legislation and policies have a limited focus, similarly to the CQA's. Having enacted 10 and 4 standards, respectively, Quebec and the CQA avoid regulating residents' assessments, and the CQA also avoids regulating information and referral services. Moreover, the extent to which they regulate nursing care adequacy is very vague. Quebec mandates that every institution shall ensure "that the required services are offered within its facilities" (ARHSSS, s. 83[2]), while the CQA, under the rubric "*la qualité dans la prestation de services*," establishes that staff must "*accueillir la clientèle et traiter les demandes de services*" (CQA 2017, Norm 9, Process 21). CQA's only other nursing care adequacy standard mandates the safe provision of services in general terms (CQA 2017, Norm 10, Process 26).

BC's private homes are subject to 6 process-related standards, all of which are exclusively aimed at care planning and overlap with those of other provinces and accreditation bodies. Adequate assessment, information and referral services, and nursing care adequacy are left unregulated.

Outcome-Related Standards

We found 18 categories of outcome-related standards. Most were taken from Unruh and Wan's (2004) adapted SPO approach, but many were added to adapt to the standards identified. The category "quality of life" was changed to "pain management." Outcome-related standards identified in provincial legislation and accreditation instruments are either rights-based or documentation-based. The latter originate from the obligation of licensees to monitor, document, or keep record of health outcomes. Even though such information is usually considered to be part of a resident's health record and thus confidential (see, for example, B.C. Reg. 96/2009, s. 93), the fact that the information must be recorded was considered sufficient for coding the section/article/clause as an outcome-related standard. Table 12.5 outlines the 18 categories and provides an example for each.

Table 12.5. Outcome-Related Standards Categories

Outcome-Related Standards Categories	Total Number of Distinguishable Standards Identified	Examples
Adequate care	4	Right to be cared for (e.g., FLTCA, s. 3[1][16])
Pain management	2	Duty to monitor pain (e.g., HSO 2020, #2.3.3 – guidelines)
Human dignity and self-determination	7	Right to participate in the development of one's own intervention plan (e.g., ARHSSS, s. 10)
Privacy	5	Right to have personal privacy respected (e.g., Schedule of CCALA, s. 2[d])
Freedom from abuse and negligence	2	Duty not to subject resident to abuse or neglect (e.g., B.C. Reg. 96/2009, s. 52[1])
Safety/prevention of injury	2	Duty to record minor accidents, illnesses, and medication errors (e.g., B.C. Reg. 96/2009, s. 88)
Safe and clean environment	4	Duty to maintain room and equipment hygiene (e.g., CQA 2017, Norm 6, Process 13)
Individualized care	5	Right to have lifestyle and choices respected (e.g., FLTCA, s. 3[1][2])
Proper nutrition and hydration	3	Duty to monitor hydration of residents (e.g., HSO 2020, #2.3.3 – guidelines)
Appropriate medication use	2	Duty to record all medication incidents (e.g., O. Reg. 246/22, s. 147[2])
Freedom from restraint	4	Duty to document use of restraint, its type, and the duration (e.g., B.C. Reg. 96/2009, s. 73[2])
Satisfaction	2	Duty to conduct survey of resident satisfaction (e.g., CQA 2017)
Skin status	1	Duty to monitor skin infections (e.g., O. Reg. 246/22, s. 55[1][2])
Responsive behaviours	1	Duty to monitor responsive behaviours of residents (e.g., O. Reg. 246/22, s. 58[1][3])
Infection control	1	Duty to monitor and record infections (e.g., O. Reg. 246/22, s. 102[9])
Information	7	Duty to provide specific information (e.g., HSO 2020, #2.2.7)
Heath-related illnesses	1	Duty to monitor heat-related illness symptoms (e.g., O. Reg. 246/22, s. 23[2][b])
Miscellaneous rights	9	Right to keep and display personal possessions, pictures, and furnishings in resident's bedroom (e.g., Schedule CCALA, s. 2[f])
Total	62	

With 51 outcome-related standards, representing 20.16 per cent of its total number of standards, Ontario has established standards in all but one category of outcome-related standards – safety/prevention of injury – leaving only 5.56 per cent of categories unregulated. Moreover, the only standards enacted by other provinces or accreditation bodies that have been omitted by the Ontarian legislation are pain monitoring (pain management), fall and reportable incident monitoring (safety/prevention of injury), height monitoring (proper nutrition and hydration), the right to have a personalized plan of care and to receive care in one's official language (individualized care), and the right to be informed of what care is available in one's community (information). Otherwise, Ontario has enacted outcome-related standards that minimally match and frequently go beyond those of other provinces.

Outcome-related standards are second to structure-related standards in BC (public)'s legislation with 33 standards (26.61 per cent of total) and first in BC (private)'s legislation with 21 standards (63.64 per cent of total). Nevertheless, BC's public homes remain more regulated than its private ones, with only 5 categories out of 18 (27.78 per cent) unregulated compared to 11 categories (61.11 per cent) unregulated, respectively.

NB's legislation and policies regulate outcome-related standards the least, with 16 standards representing 12.31 per cent of NB's total number of standards. Of the 18 categories, 7 (38.89 per cent) are left unregulated. This proportion is identical to AC's, although its 15 standards occupy different fields than those of NB. Quebec's 10 outcome-related standards leave 12 out of 18 categories (56.67 per cent) unregulated, while the CQA's 3 outcome-related standards leave 16 (88.89 per cent) unregulated. This time, the categories regulated by Quebec's legislation and policies do not overlap with CQA's.

National Standards amidst Pre-existing Provincial Standards: A New Minimum?

In January 2023, the *CAN/HSO 21001:2023 Long-Term Care Services* standards were published, replacing AC's HSO 2020 standards for future accreditations (HSO 2023). Significantly more far-reaching, the updated standards contain 117 clauses divided into six parts: (1) governing LTC homes' strategies, activities, and outcomes (15 clauses); (2) upholding resident-centred care (25 clauses); (3) enabling a meaningful quality of life for residents (11 clauses); (4) ensuring high-quality and safe care (42 clauses); (5) enabling a healthy and competent workforce (19 clauses); and (6) promoting quality improvement (5 clauses). In total, 192 different standards were extracted from the updated standards, most of which regulate structure (112 standards, or 58.33 per cent), followed by process (44 standards, or 22.92 per cent) and outcome (36 standards, or 18.75 per cent).

Among the 112 updated standards regulating structure, almost half (51 standards, or 45.54 per cent) mandate the establishment of a policy, procedure, or plan, making this the major focus of this type of standards. Moreover, an important number of them (approximately 27) have no equivalent in the four provinces. They mandate the establishment of policies that regulate care giving and human resources in general and include, for example, mandating the adoption of a procedure to determine residents' capacity to make their own care decisions (HSO 2023, #2.1.5) and mandating the establishment a comprehensive human resources plan (#1.1.5).

The second focus of the structure-related updated standards is the organizational structure of LTC homes, with 38 applicable standards (or 33.93 per cent of its total number of structure-related standards). Again, many of them have no equivalent in the four provinces under study. They focus on leadership commitments (for example, to advancing environmental stewardship [HSO 2023, #1.1.15]; to equity, diversity, and inclusion [#2.2.2]; to cultural safety and humility [#2.2.3]; and to implementing a trauma-informed approach to care [#1.1.8]) as well as on quality of care measuring and monitoring (see, for example, #1.1.9, #6.1.2, #6.1.3).

The updated standards' second biggest category is process-related, with 44 standards representing 22.92 per cent of its quality of care standards. Those standards are well dispersed throughout each process-related category, providing a minimum of 5 standards in each of them, up to 16 standards. Process-related standards that have no equivalent in all four provinces coalesce around two themes: ensuring the resident is assessed for specific purposes (for example, the residents' ability to meet their basic needs [HSO 2023, #4.1.3]; past experiences of trauma [#2.2.4]; and sensory abilities [#4.1.5]) and mandating the assistance of residents for specific actions (for example, to access transportation services [#3.1.10] and to use new technologies [#3.1.9, #4.3.4]).

With 36 outcome-related standards, representing 18.75 per cent of its total number of standards, HSO's updated standards regulate all but two categories of outcome-related standards – safety/prevention of injury and temperature – leaving only 11.11 per cent of categories unregulated. As such, they stand second to Ontario with respect to the extent to which they regulate outcomes.

The Impact of Introducing New National Standards in the Provinces

The impact of introducing new minimum national standards varies according to the regulatory regime in place in each province. With over 200 standards distributed broadly across the SPO spectrum, Ontario has the most extensive regulatory regime. Moreover, its standards apply equally to public and private homes. NB is in a similar position since its 130 standards are applicable to both public and private (for- or not-for-profit) homes. In these cases, the added value of new minimum national standards will be small. Although

HSO's updated standards do contain several new structure- and process-related standards, their importance is often peripheral.

Conversely, the introduction of new minimum national standards would have a greater impact in provinces with either few standards like Quebec or with a dual legislative regime based on the public/private status of ownership like BC. Mandating Quebec's LTC homes to be accredited by HSO's updated standards instead of AC's or CQA's would greatly increase the number of standards they would have to comply with. Moreover, the number of standards applicable to BC's private homes would be multiplied manifold if the updated standards apply to both public and private homes, assuming that the federal government mandates the accreditation of both public and private facilities.

Still, the added value of HSO's updated standards remains limited because their wording is open-textured and vague compared to Ontario's, NB's, and BC's legislation. HSO's 2023 standards (as well as AC's and CQA's standards) are almost always composed of clauses spanning one sentence. For example, they regulate dining-related care by establishing that "the LTC home leaders enable meaningful mealtime experiences that meet residents' needs and preferences" (HSO 2023, #3.1.4). By contrast, Ontario's legislation lists 11 elements that must minimally be respected at any meal, from assisting residents while eating to the minimum furnishings in the dining room to serving food at a temperature that is "both safe and palatable to the residents" (O. Reg. 246/22, s. 79; see also B.C. Reg. 96/2009, s. 63). In short, even when they regulate quality, the updated standards usually employ vague language that may loosen accountability, which is precisely what they are designed to tighten.

One limitation of this study concerns the absence of inter-coder reliability checks. Only one author proceeded to the coding of the statutes, regulations, policies, and accreditation instruments, with the consequence that no independent reliability check could be performed on the results. Given the interpretative nature of the process of extracting standards from sections/articles/clauses, errors and biases may have impacted the results. Readers should keep this in mind when interpreting the exact number of standards found in each province and in each SPO category.

A second limitation of this study concerns the effectiveness of enacting SPO standards on LTC quality. Assessing the impact of SPO standards on quality would require extending our focus beyond micro standards – standards that regulate day-to-day caregiving through structure, process, and outcome – to include Unruh and Wan's (2004, 202) "contextual components," defined as the social, legal, and political context in which residential LTC homes operate. These macro parameters, like home ownership type, arguably have a much more important influence on care quality than micro standards. In fact, Banerjee and Armstrong (2015, 7) argue that Ontario's dense regulations impede care and that insufficient attention is granted to the "structural aspects of care that set the conditions for care – funding, ownership, and staffing levels." In other words, it is important to distinguish between regulatory improvements and quality of care improvements in long-term care. While imposing HSO's 2023 standards across Canada can increase the number of standards applicable to residential LTC homes in some provinces, it will not change the structural weaknesses of residential facilities documented abundantly by scholars and practitioners (see, for example, Estabrooks et al. 2020; Marrocco, Coke, and Kitts 2021) and may sometimes even decrease care quality by adding another layer of regulatory burden. Hence, the poverty of the national standards solution.

Conclusion

This chapter illustrates the wide diversity of quality of care standards applicable to LTC homes in four provinces (BC, NB, Ontario, and Quebec). In doing so, it highlights the multiple obstacles faced by the federal government to create national standards and improve LTC across the country. Ontario and NB have enacted broad and strong quality of care standards. Ontario has the most standards as well as the broadest scope of regulated fields. While NB's number of outcome-related standards is low, the scope and strength of the province's structure- and process-related standards is similar to Ontario's. Both provinces' standards apply equally to public and private homes. For this reason, federally sponsored minimum standards would likely have a small impact in these provinces.

While BC's legislation applicable to public homes establishes significantly fewer structure-, process-, and outcome-related standards than Ontario's, it nevertheless has enacted a significant (and sometimes very detailed) number of standards in a wide variety of fields. By contrast, Quebec has legislated a limited number of structure-, process-, and outcome-related standards. Moreover, Quebec's small number of structure- and process-related standards is skewed towards certain themes to the exclusion of others. Its mandatory accreditation policy does not remedy this lacuna. CQA's structure- and process-related standards were found to be similarly limited in number and scope, resulting in overlaps. AC's HSO 2020 standards are more numerous and balanced throughout the SPO spectrum. This finding raises the concern that residential long-term care homes in Quebec can choose between two highly unequal options of quality of care standards. Surprisingly, private homes in BC are the least regulated. This situation stands in stark contrast to BC's public homes, which must comply with a very large number and broad scope of standards. While all the rights outlined in CCALA's schedule are applicable to BC's private homes, the fact remains that BC's private homes face a disproportionately low number of structure-related standards and a limited variety of process-related standards when compared to Quebec and the CQA. In this context, federal minimum national standards could greatly enhance the regulatory landscape of BC's private LTC homes and Quebec's homes.

As a policy instrument, standards come with noticeable constraints to achieve objectives such as improving LTC policies. Federal and provincial policy makers should keep in mind the vagueness of HSO standards. Moreover, improving quality of care standards is likely insufficient to sustainably improve the quality of care in LTC homes. The structural aspects of care that set the conditions for care – funding, ownership, and staffing levels – should be considered at least as important as the standards themselves (Banerjee and Armstrong 2015).

Standards aside, a consensus exists among provinces and the federal government regarding the need for a significantly greater fiscal involvement of the latter in long-term care (Marier 2021b), not least given the long-term fiscal unsustainability of provinces caused in great part by population aging and rising health costs (Parliamentary Budget Officer 2020). The main issue revolves around the appropriate level of provincial accountability in improving LTC quality using federal funds. If the fiscal tools available to the federal government to channel more funds to provinces are thought along an accountability spectrum, conditioning federal LTC funding upon the respect of HSO's 2023 standards would undoubtedly be located in the upper, more accountable end of the spectrum. At least two political obstacles stand in the way of the federal government if it seeks to attach this level of provincial accountability to its LTC funding.

First, contrary to health care, the LTC policy area has been ignored by the federal government for decades, meaning that each province's residential LTC sector has developed organically with its own characteristics (for example, ownership of LTC facilities) and needs. As a result, the legacy of each individual province looms large in any discussion of minimum LTC national standards, expressed clearly by NB's Premier Higgs, who mentioned that he "didn't want to be restrained by standards based on the reality in other provinces" (CBC News 2020). Seeking national standards results in different costs and benefits for each province. Students of federalism in the European Union are familiar with the long-standing issues surrounding attempts to create harmonized standards across member states. Even with mechanisms such as the open method of coordination with incentives to sustain benchmarks, it is difficult to escape fears of a race to the bottom with the lowest common denominators in the field of social policy.

Second, and in line with the previous point, the federal government could mitigate some of these concerns by introducing a new federal transfer with specific LTC conditions akin to the Canada Health Transfer. However, federal leadership in health care has been tarnished by the gradual and substantial cut in health transfers, with the federal portion only accounting for less than 25 per cent instead of the 50/50 cost-share agreement when it was launched in the late 1960s (see Boadway, chapter 5 of this volume). Moreover, negotiations over LTC occur in the context of growing political polarization among political parties at both provincial and federal levels, making it challenging to secure a pan-Canadian agreement between the provinces and the federal government.

In closing, establishing new minimum federal standards in the residential LTC policy area may have the unintended consequence of strengthening the lobbying power of large corporate LTC corporations. As revealed in a comparative study of Canada and the United States, lobbyists in federal systems concentrate their activities at the governmental level that holds most legislative responsibilities (Constantelos 2010). While the COVID-19 pandemic accentuated criticism on the role and importance of the private sector in LTC, a transfer of key responsibilities in Ottawa may paradoxically enhance the lobbying power of large private LTC corporations. Such corporations possess higher incentives and resources to secure federal standardizations than not-for-profit organizations, for instance, which operate at the local level.

Appendix: Provincial Quality of Care Standards Analysed in BC, NB, Ontario, and Quebec (as of 6 July 2022)

British Columbia

British Columbia's standards are found in the Community Care and Assisted Living Act, S.B.C. 2002, c. 75 (CCALA) and its regulation B.C. Reg. 96/2009.[3] Any facility providing care to "vulnerable adults dependent on caregivers for continuing assistance or direction" must be licensed and is therefore subject to both instruments (CCALA, ss. 1 "community care facility," "care," 5, 13[1][a]; Office of the Ombudsperson [BC] 2009). Privately owned residential long-term care homes are considered "private hospitals" governed by the Hospital Act, R.S.B.C. 1996, c. 200 (HA) (CCALA, s. 2[d]; HA, ss. 5 "private hospital"; Office of the Ombudsperson [BC] 2009). Private homes must nevertheless obtain a licence (HA, s. 6[1]; BC 2021) and are subject to (i) the schedule of the CCALA, which consists of a bill of rights for residents; and (ii) 11 sections of B.C. Reg. 96/2009 (HA, s. 4[3][a]; B.C. Reg 37/2010, s. 2[2]). Whether publicly or privately owned, accreditation is not mandatory. In total, 84 sections for publicly owned homes and 11 for privately owned homes were analysed, based on the roughly 180 sections of the CCALA and its regulation.

New Brunswick

The operation of residential long-term care homes in New Brunswick is regulated by the Nursing Homes Act, R.S.N.B. 2014, c. 125 (NHA) and its relevant regulations (Reg. 85-187; Reg. 2001-59) through the licensing mechanism (NHA, s. 3[2]). The standards established by the NHA and its regulations are complemented by the *Standards Manual: Nursing Home Services* ("Standards Manual" [NB 2020]) established by the Department of Social Development in 2019. Accreditation is not mandatory. All standards set by the act, its regulations, and the Standards Manual apply to for- and not-for-profit homes (NHA,

s. 1 "nursing home"). In total, 91 sections were identified and analysed from the 131 sections contained in the NHA, its 2 regulations, and the Standards Manual. There is no resident's bill of rights in NB.

Ontario

Ontario's standards are found in the Fixing Long-Term Care Act, 2021, S.O. 2021, c. 39, Sched. 1 (FLTCA) and its regulation O. Reg. 246/22. Both apply to all types of long-term care homes, whether publicly or privately owned. Under Ontario's law, all homes providing twenty-four-hour nursing care must be licensed and are therefore subject to both instruments (FLTCA, ss. 2[1] "long-term care home," 11[3], 98[1]; O. Reg. 246/22, s. 172[1][c]). Accreditation is not mandatory. In total, around 258 sections were analysed from the over 400 sections of both instruments. Section 3 of the FLTCA, which establishes a resident's bill of rights, was also analysed.

Quebec

Whether publicly or privately owned, under or without agreement, Quebec's Act Respecting Health Services and Social Services, RLRQ, c. S-4.2 (ARHSSS) mandates the licensing of residential long-term care homes, or *Centres d'hébergement et de soins de longue durée* – CHSLD. The act does not establish many standards specific to residential long-term care homes (see, for example, ARHSSS, ss. 83, 437) but outlines several user rights (s. 3 et ss.). Moreover, the government refrained from enacting quality of care standards through regulation despite having the power to do so (ss. 446[4], 505). Rather, standards applicable to Quebec's homes are scattered throughout different sources. Quebec has outlined some guiding principles for care in its policy framework, *Un milieu de vie de qualité pour les personnes hébergées en CHSLD: Orientations ministérielles* (Quebec 2003). The province also enacted some sections/articles/clauses in its policy titled *Cadre de référence et normes relatives à l'hébergement dans les établissements de soins de longue durée* (Quebec 2018), as well as through notices (Quebec 2018, Annex I). Further, the ARHSSS mandates the accreditation of homes (ARHSSS, s. 107.1) and recognizes both the Conseil Québécois d'agrément (CQA) and Accreditation Canada (AC) for accreditation purposes (Quebec 2006).

In total, 41 sections/articles/clauses were identified and analysed in the act, the policies, and the notice.[4] All standards apply equally to public as well as private (with and without agreement) residential long-term care homes (Quebec 2016; Library of Parliament 2020). A report authored by the CQA (2017) identifies 24 sections used for accreditation purposes. AC used the Health Standards Organization's *HSO 21001:2020(e) Long-Term Care Services* standards (HSO 2020) – which are composed of 35 clauses – to certify Quebec's homes (Standards Council of Canada 2021). In January 2023, the standards were replaced by the Health

Standards Organization's new *CAN/HSO 21001:2023 Long-Term Care Services* standards which are composed of 117 clauses (HSO 2023). Given that the replacement is recent, this paper considers HSO's 2020 standards to be reflective of the standards in force for LTC homes accredited by AC at the time of publication.

NOTES

1 For a discussion of COVID-19-related federal fiscal commitments and expenditures, see Tombe, chapter 4 of this volume.
2 To be reached no later than 31 March 2025: FLTCA, s. 8(3).
3 Chapter 6 of the BC Ministry of Health's *Home and Community Care Policy Manual* (British Columbia Ministry of Health 2019) defines the role and responsibilities of health authorities with respect to the application of the CCALA and its regulation. For this reason, it was excluded from the scope of this study.
4 There are well over 600 sections in the ARHSSS. Of the act, approximately 350 sections apply to "institutions" running residential long-term care homes (ARHSSS, ss. 79–338). The vast majority have no incidence on Quebec's residential long-term care homes because they impose obligations on public integrated centres. For example, sections 119 to 182 of the act regulate the board of directors of the integrated health and social services centres. These sections were considered insufficiently linked to long-term care quality. Those that directly impact public and private long-term care quality were identified through Quebec's licence application guide for private homes (Quebec 2016). Excluding rights, roughly 18 sections from the ARHSSS were identified as relevant and analysed.

REFERENCES

Banerjee, Albert, and Pat Armstrong. 2015. "Centring Care: Explaining Regulatory Tensions in Residential Care for Older Persons." *Studies in Political Economy* 95, no. 1: 7–28. https://doi.org/10.1080/19187033.2015.11674944.

Béland, Daniel, and Patrik Marier. 2020. "COVID-19 and Long-Term Care Policy for Older People in Canada." *Journal of Aging & Social Policy* 32, no. 4/5: 358–64. https://doi.org/10.1080/08959420.2020.1764319.

British Columbia. 2021. "Residential Care Facilities – Legislation and Standards of Practice." Province of British Columbia. https://www2.gov.bc.ca/gov/content/health/accessing-health-care/finding-assisted-living-or-residential-care/residential-care-facilities.

British Columbia Ministry of Health. 2017. *Residential Care Staffing Review*. Victoria, BC: BC Ministry of Health. https://www.health.gov.bc.ca/library/publications/year/2017/residential-care-staffing-review.pdf.

– 2019. "Chapter 6: Long-Term Care Services." In *Home and Community Care Policy Manual*. Victoria, BC: BC Ministry of Health. https://www2.gov.bc.ca/gov

/content/health/accessing-health-care/home-community-care/accountability/policy-and-standards/home-and-community-care-policy-manual.
Castle, Nicholas G., and Jamie C. Ferguson. 2010. "What Is Nursing Home Quality and How Is It Measured?" *The Gerontologist* 50, no. 4: 426–42. https://doi.org/10.1093/geront/gnq052.
CBC News. 2020. "Labour Group Calls for N.B. Cooperation on National Care Home Standards." *CBC News*, 6 November 2020. https://www.cbc.ca/news/canada/new-brunswick/labour-group-care-home-1.5792581.
CIHI (Canadian Institute for Health Information). 2021. "Long-Term Care Homes in Canada: How Many and Who Owns Them?" CIHI. https://www.cihi.ca/en/long-term-care-homes-in-canada-how-many-and-who-owns-them.
Constantelos, John. 2010. "Playing the Field: Federalism and the Politics of Venue Shopping in the United States and Canada." *Publius: The Journal of Federalism* 40, no. 3: 460–83. https://doi.org/10.1093/publius/pjq010.
Cousins, Ben. 2021. "Here's What Trudeau's Liberals Have Promised for Their Third Term." *CTV News*, 20 September 2021. https://www.ctvnews.ca/politics/federal-election-2021/here-s-what-trudeau-s-liberals-have-promised-for-their-third-term-1.5593437.
CQA (Conseil québécois d'agrément). 2017. *Rapport d'agrément: CHSLD Villa Val Des Arbres*. Quebec: CQA. http://vvda.ca/wp-content/uploads/2018/08/rapportdagrement-juin2017.pdf.
Donabedian, Avedis. 1966. "Evaluating the Quality of Medical Care." *The Milbank Memorial Fund Quarterly* 44, no. 3: 166–206. https://doi.org/10.2307/3348969.
– 1988. "The Quality of Care: How Can It Be Assessed?" *JAMA* 260, no. 12: 1743–8. https://doi.org/10.1001/jama.260.12.1743.
Estabrooks, Carole A., Sharon Straus, Colleen Flood, Janice Keefe, Pat Armstrong, Gail Donner, Véronique Boscart, Francine Ducharme, James Silvius, and Michael Wolfson. 2020. *Restoring Trust: COVID-19 and the Future of Long-Term Care*. Ottawa: Royal Society of Canada.
Gallant, Natasha L., Allie Peckham, Gregory Marchildon, Thomas Hadjistavropoulos, Blair Roblin, and Rhonda J.N. Stopyn. 2020. "Provincial Legislative and Regulatory Standards for Pain Assessment and Management in Long-Term Care Homes: A Scoping Review and in-Depth Case Analysis." *BMC Geriatrics* 20, no. 1: 458. https://doi.org/10.1186/s12877-020-01758-7.
Grignon, Michel, and Byron G. Spencer. 2018. "The Funding of Long-Term Care in Canada: What Do We Know, What Should We Know?" *Canadian Journal on Aging / La Revue canadienne du vieillissement* 37, no. 2: 110–20. https://doi.org/10.1017/S0714980818000028.
HSO (Health Standards Organization). 2020. *HSO 21001:2020 Long-Term Care Services Standard*. Ottawa: HSO.
– 2021. "National Long-Term Care Services Standard." News Release. HSO Health Standards Organization, 31 March 2021. https://healthstandards.org/uncategorized/national-long-term-care-services-standard/.

- 2023. *CAN/HSO 21001:2023 (E) Long-Term Care Services Standard.* Ottawa: HSO. https://healthstandards.org/standard/long-term-care-services-can-hso21001-2023-e/.
INSPQ (Institut national de santé publique). 2022. "Données COVID-19 au Québec (mise à jour du 21 janvier 2022)." Quebec: INSPQ. Accessed on 24 January 2022. https://www.inspq.qc.ca/covid-19/donnees.
Kane, Robert L. 1998. "Assuring Quality in Nursing Home Care." *Journal of the American Geriatrics Society* 46, no. 2: 232–37. https://doi.org/10.1111/j.1532-5415.1998.tb02545.x.
Library of Parliament. 2020. "Long-Term Care Homes in Canada – How Are They Funded and Regulated?" *HillNotes*, 22 October 2020. https://hillnotes.ca/2020/10/22/long-term-care-homes-in-canada-how-are-they-funded-and-regulated/.
Marier, Patrik. 2021a. *The Four Lenses of Population Aging: Planning for the Future in Canada's Provinces.* Toronto: University of Toronto Press.
- 2021b. "How Will COVID-19 Alter the Politics of Long-Term Care? A Comparative Policy Analysis of Popular Reform Options." *Canadian Journal on Aging / La Revue canadienne du vieillissement* 40, no. 4: 651–60. https://doi.org/10.1017/S0714980821000489.
Marrocco, Frank N., Angela Coke, and Jack Kitts. 2021. *Ontario's Long-Term Care COVID-19 Commission: Final Report.* Toronto: Long-Term Care COVID-19 Commission. https://files.ontario.ca/mltc-ltcc-final-report-en-2021-04-30.pdf.
Morris, John J., Cynthia Clarke, and Anna L. Marrison. 2021. *Law for Canadian Health Care Administrators.* 3rd ed. Markham, ON: LexisNexis Canada.
New Brunswick. 2021. *Standards Manual: Nursing Home Services.* Fredericton, NB: Department of Social Development. Accessed 6 July 2022. https://www2.gnb.ca/content/dam/gnb/Departments/sd-ds/pdf/Standards/NursingHomesStandardsManual.pdf.
Office of the Ombudsperson (British Columbia). 2009. *The Best of Care: Getting It Right for Seniors in British Columbia (Part 1).* Public Report No. 46 to the Legislative Assembly of British Columbia. Victoria, BC: Office of the Ombudsperson. https://bcombudsperson.ca/assets/media/Public-Report-No-46-The-Best-of-Care-Getting-it-Right-for-Seniors-in-B.C.pdf.
Parliamentary Budget Officer. 2020. *Fiscal Sustainability Report 2020: Update.* Ottawa: Office of the Parliamentary Budget Officer. https://www.pbo-dpb.ca/en/publications/RP-2021-033-S--fiscal-sustainability-report-2020-update--rapport-viabilite-financiere-2020-mise-jour.
PHAC (Public Health Agency of Canada). 2021. *Weekly Epidemiology Update (14 to 20 February 2021).* Ottawa: Public Health Agency of Canada. https://www.publichealthontario.ca/-/media/Documents/nCoV/epi/2021/02/covid-19-weekly-epi-summary-report-feb-20.pdf.
Prime Minister's Office. 2021. "Minister of Health Supplementary Mandate Letter." Prime Minister of Canada, 13 January 2021. https://pm.gc.ca/en/mandate-letters/2021/01/15/archived-minister-health-supplementary-mandate-letter.
Quebec. 2003. *Un milieu de vie de qualité pour les personnes hébergées en CHSLD: Orientations ministérielles.* Québec: Ministère de la Santé et des Services sociaux. https://publications.msss.gouv.qc.ca/msss/document-000808/.

- 2006. *Lignes directrices sur l'agrément des services offerts par les établissements de santé et de services sociaux*. Québec: Ministère de la Santé et des Services sociaux. https://eweb.uqac.ca/bibliotheque/archives/24856223.pdf.
- 2016. *Demande de permis pour l'exploitation d'un centre d'hébergement et de soins de longue durée privé: guide d'information*. Québec: Ministère de la Santé et des Services sociaux. https://numerique.banq.qc.ca/patrimoine/details/52327/2699230.
- 2018. *Cadre de référence et normes relatives à l'hébergement dans les établissements de soins de longue durée*. Québec: Ministère de la Santé et des Services sociaux. https://publications.msss.gouv.qc.ca/msss/document-002029/.

Stall, Nathan M., Aaron Jones, Kevin A. Brown, Paula A. Rochon, and Andrew P. Costa. 2020. "For-Profit Long-Term Care Homes and the Risk of COVID-19 Outbreaks and Resident Deaths." *CMAJ* 192, no. 33: E946–55. https://www.cmaj.ca/content/192/33/E946.

Standards Council of Canada. 2021. "Long-Term Care Services." Standards Council of Canada – Conseil Canadien Des Normes, 12 March 2021. https://www.scc.ca/en/standards/notices-of-intent/hso/long-term-care-services.

Unruh, Lynn, and Thomas T.H. Wan. 2004. "A Systems Framework for Evaluating Nursing Care Quality in Nursing Homes." *Journal of Medical Systems* 28, no. 2: 197–214. https://doi.org/10.1023/B:JOMS.0000023302.80118.74.

Legal References

BRITISH COLUMBIA
Community Care and Assisted Living Act, S.B.C. 2002 c. 75 (CCALA).
Hospital Act, R.S.B.C. 1996, c. 200 (HA).
Patients' Bill of Rights Regulation, B.C. Reg 37/2010.
Residential Care Regulation, B.C. Reg. 96/2009.

NEW BRUNSWICK
General Regulation, Reg. 85-187.
Nursing Homes Act, R.S.N.B. 2014, c. 125 (NHA).
Services and care to be provided to residents of Nursing Homes, Reg. 2001-59.

ONTARIO
Fixing Long-Term Care Act, 2021, S.O. 2021, c. 39, Sched. 1 (FLTCA).
O. Reg. 246/22.

QUEBEC
Act Respecting Health Services and Social Services, RLRQ, c. S-4.2 (ARHSSS).

13 Cities in Canadian Fiscal Federalism: The Forgotten Partner

ENID SLACK

Introduction

COVID-19 has shown how much cities are on the front line when it comes to delivering essential services. They have been most visible in delivering public health and social services, but they are also responsible for public transit, waste collection and disposal, police and fire protection, and much more. And cities are expected to be significant players in the economic recovery, in part by investing in municipal infrastructure. Yet, they are responding to the crisis with limited sources of revenue – largely property taxes, user fees, and transfers from the federal and provincial governments. Higher expenditures and lower revenues, what UCLG, LSE, and Metropolis (2021) refer to as the scissor effect, have meant that municipalities, particularly the larger ones, faced significant, unanticipated operating deficits for 2020. Given its greater fiscal capacity, the federal government transferred funding to municipalities and transit authorities to meet their operating deficits for 2020. Is the current fiscal model sustainable for cities?

Notwithstanding the important role that cities play in the federation, local governments do not have any fundamental role or voice in Canada's federal structure – they are generally not included in federal-provincial fiscal discussions or negotiations. Yet, as the External Advisory Committee on Cities and Communities (2006, 22) noted, "devolution stopping at the provincial and territorial level misses the point" because municipalities are central to service delivery and taxation in this country.[1] They are the governments that are closest to the people; the services they deliver have an immediate and clear impact on the economic and social well-being of Canadians; and the opportunities for engagement at the local level are more immediate. Are cities the forgotten partner?

This chapter sets out the emerging fiscal issues facing Canadian cities and suggests ways to address them in the context of Canadian federalism. It begins in the first section with a review of the division of powers and resources among the federal, provincial/territorial, and local governments in Canada, followed by a more detailed description of what services municipalities make expenditures on and what revenues they use to pay for them in the second section. The third section considers vertical fiscal imbalance in Canada as it affects municipalities and suggests what the imbalance means for their fiscal health. The fourth section looks at which taxes are appropriate for local governments. Is the property tax enough, or do cities need access to other taxes? The fifth section makes the case for setting up a collaborative process to clarify the roles and responsibilities of each order of government and the revenues to pay for them so that cities have the means to deliver services and invest in infrastructure. The sixth section provides a brief conclusion.

1. Division of Powers

The Constitution Act sets out the division of powers between the federal and provincial governments. The federal government makes laws with respect to unemployment insurance, trade and commerce, national defence, Indigenous affairs, and criminal law. Provincial governments control regional and local affairs including education, health, social services, property rights, administration of justice, local public works, and municipal institutions. Some responsibilities are shared between the federal and provincial governments such as immigration, agriculture, and pensions. Local institutions do not have independent status in the Constitution. Rather, provincial governments have the exclusive authority to make laws in relation to municipal institutions (Slack et al. 2019).[2]

In terms of revenues, the Constitution gave the federal government comprehensive powers to raise money "by any mode or system of taxation," whereas the provinces were given authority to levy "direct taxation within the province" (for example, income, sales, property, and commodity taxes) for provincial purposes. Municipalities are limited to the taxing authority that is delegated to them by the provincial government, and this authority can vary by province. In practice, the result has been that municipalities are largely restricted to levying property taxes and user fees, and they receive transfers from the provincial and federal governments. Some cities have broader taxing powers, such as the City of Toronto, which can levy a land transfer tax, vehicle fees, a billboard tax, and taxes on alcohol, tobacco, and amusements.[3]

According to the Constitution, the federal government has no role to play in cities. It can, however, spend money wherever it likes, and over the years, some federal governments have chosen to do so. For example, the federal government came to the rescue of municipalities facing significant operating deficits in 2020 in the face of COVID-19, even though funding municipal operating expenditures has not been a traditional role for the federal government. Rather, it has been involved in recent years in supporting infrastructure funding mainly for transportation, transit, and housing but also for economic development, immigrant settlement, Indigenous communities, and ecological resilience.[4] The Canada Community-Building Fund (formerly known as the Gas Tax Fund), as an example, provides funds for local transportation infrastructure investments, allocated on a per capita basis to designated signatories – provinces, territories, municipal associations, and the City of Toronto – twice a year. In 2008, the fund was made permanent, and in 2013, it was indexed to grow at 2 per cent per year.[5]

The federal government has also engaged with cities and provinces through tri-level agreements dating back to the 1980s. Bradford (2020) describes three types of agreements. The first are site-specific agreements (urban development agreements) that target specific neighbourhoods and have been used in Vancouver, Edmonton, and Winnipeg. The second are sector-oriented agreements that implement national programs in homelessness and immigration settlement policy through localized governance entities in a few large and medium-sized cities. The third, a hybrid of the first two, are national programs available to all municipalities but require local governance collaboration. This hybrid includes the Canada Community-Building Fund mentioned above. These tri-level agreements have been praised for "bringing a place-based dimension to the theory and practice of Canadian federalism" (35) and aligning federal and provincial government policies, programs, and investments with municipal priorities. From a fiscal perspective, however, with the exception of the Canada Community-Building Fund, there are not a lot of federal resources attached to these agreements.

Provincial governments play a much more significant role than the federal government in the affairs of municipal governments in Canada.[6] Provincial governments may create, dissolve, amalgamate, or alter the boundaries of local governments in other ways without consulting local residents (Taylor and Bradford 2020).[7] In terms of municipal finance, provincial governments assign responsibilities to local governments and determine which revenues they can raise. Municipalities are not permitted to budget for an operating deficit, and, if over the course of the year they do run a deficit, they are required to cover it immediately in the next fiscal year. Provincial governments also restrict the amount that municipalities can borrow to meet capital expenditures. For example, in Ontario (with the exception of Toronto), the rule is that debt charges cannot exceed 25 per cent of own-source revenues.[8] Compared to the federal and provincial governments, municipal governments have much less power to borrow and less capacity to pay back the funds.

Lastly, provincial governments provide transfers to municipalities, many of which have conditions attached to them. The problem for local governments with conditional transfers is that the province can dictate how the funds are to be spent, thus distorting local decision-making. Furthermore, the accountability is unclear. When the transit service in Toronto, Montreal, or Vancouver stops, whom do you call to complain – the federal, provincial, or municipal government? When it comes to funding, construction, or planning, accountability is even more blurred.

All provinces provide at least some unconditional funding to municipalities. Six provinces, in particular, provide equalization grants to municipalities, generally based on a formula. In most of the provinces that provide municipal equalization grants, the formula is based on municipal fiscal capacity. In two provinces – New Brunswick and Nova Scotia – a measure of fiscal need is also included in the equalization formula.[9] These grants are unconditional – no strings are attached to how the money can be spent – but they, like conditional grants, are not always predictable.

The high degree of provincial control over local governments in Canada means that there cannot be any visible fiscal crisis at the local level (Slack and Bird 2007–8). Municipal governments are strictly held to balanced budgets for operating purposes, and their borrowing for capital expenditures is restricted by provincial regulations. The other side of the coin, however, is that municipal governments in Canada are constrained from solving any real fiscal problems they may have. Local governments are autonomous in the sense that they are responsible to local citizens both for how they spend and how they raise revenues. The reason is that the bulk of their revenues come from own sources – property taxation and user fees – rather than intergovernmental transfers. However, they are constrained in terms of fiscal flexibility because they rely largely on only those two sources of revenue.[10]

Taylor and Bradford (2020) argue that, through the 2000s, provinces have increasingly recognized municipalities as democratic and accountable orders of government, empowered them through legislative change, and expanded their fiscal resources. As shown below, however, it is not clear that the expansion of fiscal resources has been sufficient to meet their increasing expenditure needs.

2. What Do Municipalities Do, and How Do They Pay for It?

There are over 3,700 municipal governments in Canada, with considerable variation in terms of their size (Taylor and Bradford 2020).[11] Although there is some variation across provinces, local governments are generally responsible for a wide range of functions that include water, sewers, and waste management; roads and transit; fire and police protection; recreation and culture; and planning and development (see Table 13.1). The largest municipal expenditure is for transport (roads and transit), followed by general public services (that is, general administration) and policing.

Table 13.1. Distribution of Municipal Expenditures, Canada, 2020

Municipal Expenditure	% of Total Municipal Expenditures
General Public Services	16.9
Public Order and Safety	18.7
Police services	11.1
Fire protection services	5.8
Other	1.8
Economic Affairs	19.0
Transport	17.6
Other	1.4
Environmental Protection	9.2
Waste management	4.1
Wastewater management	4.1
Other	1.0
Housing and Community Services	9.0
Housing and community development	3.2
Water supply	4.9
Street lighting	0.7
Other	0.2
Health	2.9
Outpatient services	1.6
Public health	1.1
Other	0.2
Recreation and Culture	11.3
Social Protection	12.8
Old age	1.9
Family and children	2.5
Housing	3.4
Social exclusion	4.5
Other	0.5
Total Municipal Expenditures	100.0

Source: Statistics Canada, Table 10-10-0024-01.
Note: Totals may not add due to rounding.

There are differences across provinces in the distribution of municipal expenditures.[12] In Ontario, for example, municipalities spend almost one-quarter of their budget on social services, whereas municipalities in most other provinces spend little or nothing on social services. In these other provinces, the provincial government takes on that responsibility. Municipalities in Quebec spend 24 per cent of their total expenditures on transportation, which is considerably more than the average of 18 per cent for the country. Municipalities in British Columbia, Alberta, and Saskatchewan spend more on recreation and culture than municipalities in other provinces. Municipalities in Ontario, Quebec, and Alberta make expenditures on housing, whereas municipalities in most other provinces do not.

Figure 13.1. Distribution of Municipal Revenues, Canada, 2009–20

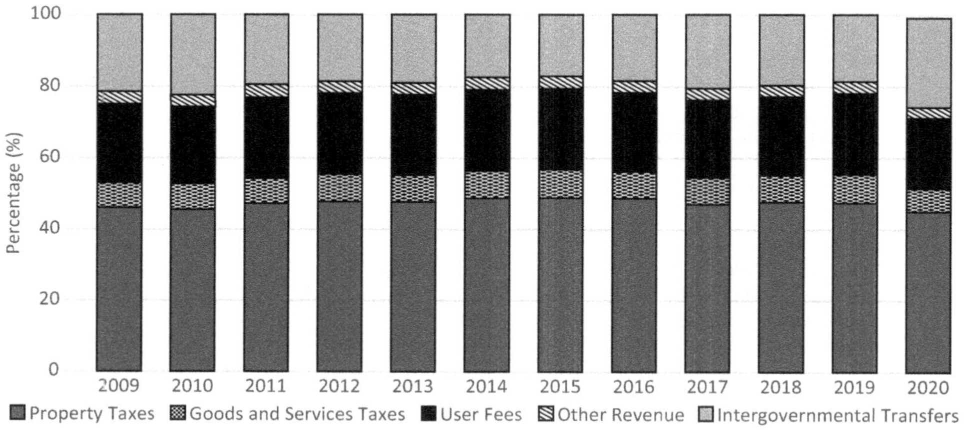

■ Property Taxes ▨ Goods and Services Taxes ■ User Fees ▨ Other Revenue ▨ Intergovernmental Transfers

Source: Statistics Canada, Table 10-10-0020-01.

Figure 13.1 shows the main sources of revenue for municipalities in Canada from 2009 to 2020. Revenues include property and property-related taxes (almost 46 per cent of revenues, on average, across the country in 2020), followed by provincial and federal transfers (25 per cent). Transfers have generally accounted for less than 20 per cent of total municipal revenues, except for 2020 when they rose to 25 per cent in response to the pandemic. User fees were 20 per cent of municipal revenues in 2020.

As with municipal expenditures, there is a wide variation in sources of revenue across Canadian municipalities (Meloche and Vaillancourt 2021). User fees represent a somewhat smaller percentage of municipal revenues in Quebec, where property taxes are largely used to pay for water. Provincial and federal transfers range from a low of 12 per cent of revenues in BC municipalities to a high of over 50 per cent in Prince Edward Island. Transfers account for 30 per cent of total municipal revenues in Ontario, where social services are cost-shared with the provincial government. Lot levies (also known as development charges) are used to pay for growth-related capital costs associated with new development. They are significant in Ontario, Saskatchewan, Alberta, and British Columbia. Lastly, land transfer taxes (included in property taxes) are levied by municipalities in Quebec and Nova Scotia, and by the City of Toronto.

In provinces that permit additional revenue-raising powers, some local governments levy other taxes, as shown in Table 13.2. With the exception of the land transfer tax, however, these additional taxes bring in very little revenue

Table 13.2. Selected Additional Municipal Revenues by Province

Tax	Manitoba	Ontario	Quebec	Nova Scotia	Prince Edward Island	Newfoundland and Labrador
Accommodation Tax	X	X	–	Halifax only	X	St. John's only
Land Transfer Tax	X	Toronto only	X	X	–	–
Vehicle Registration Tax	–	Toronto only (discontinued)	–	–	–	–
Billboard Tax	Winnipeg only	Toronto only	–	–	–	–
Electricity and Natural Gas Consumption Tax	Winnipeg only	–	–	–	–	–
Poll Tax	–	–	–	–	–	X

Source: Based on Taylor and Dobson (2020).

to those municipalities that are permitted to raise them (Meloche and Vaillancourt 2021).[13] At the end of the day, the main revenue sources for Canadian municipalities remain property taxes, user fees, and intergovernmental transfers.

3. Vertical Fiscal Imbalance and Municipal Fiscal Health

Canada has been referred to as a "radical fiscal federation" because it is one of the most decentralized countries in the world (Milligan 2019). The federal government accounts for only 29 per cent of expenditures, with provinces and municipalities combined accounting for 71 per cent (Hachard 2020). It is not possible with existing data to estimate the distribution of expenditures between provincial and local governments.[14] We do know, however, that local governments in Canada own more than 60 per cent of public infrastructure (see chapter 15 of this volume). With respect to taxation, municipal governments accounted for only 10 per cent of all taxes collected in 2020; the federal government accounted for 45 per cent and provincial governments for 45 per cent.[15] These numbers point to a vertical fiscal imbalance, but better data are needed to confirm it.

The question of how well Canadian municipalities are faring is also tricky to answer because of a lack of data. Issues around how to measure fiscal health and where to find comparable data for Canadian cities make it difficult to undertake the required analysis. Nevertheless, some efforts to date suggest that, on average, Canadian municipalities are doing well (Bird and Slack 2015). An analysis of the fiscal health of the City of Toronto before the pandemic, for example, suggested that it was sound by most measures: expenditures per capita adjusted for inflation have not increased very much over the last decade; property taxes per capita adjusted for inflation have been declining; and debt is manageable for a city of its size (Slack and Côté 2014; IMFG 2018). Similar findings can be found for other cities in Ontario as well as for cities in other provinces (Bird and Slack 2015).

Even for cities that appear to be doing well, however, the story may not be so rosy. Their apparent fiscal health may have been achieved at the expense of their overall health, which has less to do with whether they balance their budget (which they must do by law) than with the quantity and quality of the services they provide and the state of their infrastructure. A city that balances its budget, has modest tax increases from year to year, and has little or no debt may seem fiscally healthy, but its infrastructure may be crumbling. The need for infrastructure investment, both to maintain a state of good repair and to invest in new, presents a huge financial challenge to municipalities in Canada.[16]

Others have argued that municipal governments in Canada are in excellent fiscal shape, better than most provinces. For example, Robson and Wu (2021) estimate that thirty-one of the largest municipalities in Canada ran an aggregate budget surplus (a measure of net worth) of almost $11 billion in 2019.[17] The concept of municipal net worth is somewhat misleading, however, because it is largely made up of physical assets and committed funds. In Ontario, for example, the Municipal Finance Officers' Association of Ontario (MFOA 2021) has estimated that 93 per cent of municipal net worth comprises equity in tangible capital assets. As noted above, municipalities in Canada own the vast majority of public infrastructure and must maintain and operate these assets (for example, transit infrastructure, libraries, recreational facilities) to deliver services. Nevertheless, the financial margin remains limited since the only way to realize the value of the assets would be to sell them.

With respect to committed funds, reserves and reserve funds are mostly set aside for specific purposes and cannot be used for other purposes. An estimate for municipalities in Ontario shows that 95 per cent of reserves and reserve funds are earmarked for specific purposes and only 5 per cent are available for budget stabilization (FAO 2020). So, although it appears that municipalities are in better shape than their provincial counterparts, their surpluses cannot be used to plug operating deficits.[18]

At the end of the day, cities need to have revenue-raising tools that match their expenditure responsibilities, and they need to have the autonomy to make decisions that will make them prosperous.

4. Which Taxes for Local Government?

How local governments pay for services depends, at least in part, on what services they are providing. The European Charter of Local Self-Government (article 9, paragraph 2) states that "local authorities' financial resources shall be commensurate with the responsibilities provided for by the constitution and the law." In other words, finance should follow function (Bahl and Bird 2018).

Theory and experience point to a funding model that links expenditure and revenue decisions. For the public sector to operate efficiently, it is important to establish a clear link between expenditure and revenue decisions – to strengthen what Breton (1996) called the Wicksellian connection.[19] The "benefit principle" requires a link between taxation and spending to achieve the goals of fiscal decentralization, charging for public services, and earmarking revenues to specific services, all of which are central to a sound local finance system (Bird and Slack 2014). In short, expenditure responsibilities must be matched with revenue resources.

The expenditure and tax assignment literature goes back to Musgrave (1983), whose expenditure framework assigned distribution and stabilization functions to the central government and some responsibility for allocation to subnational governments. In terms of taxation, progressive taxes that redistribute income and taxes with automatic stabilizers (income and sales taxes) were considered to be best levied by the national government; local government taxes were seen as charges for the use of services that should be financed by taxes on immobile tax bases, such as the property tax.[20]

Clearly, rapid urbanization and globalization have meant that local governments are now doing more than simply delivering services, and thus a broader assessment of tax assignment than the conventional model may be necessary (Bahl and Bird 2018). The conventional wisdom used to be that, if local governments taxed mobile factors (that is, with income or consumption taxes), they might drive away jobs and capital but, on the other hand, they might have an incentive to lower tax rates if they feared losing their tax base. Oates (1996) suggested that local governments should tax non-resident beneficiaries, based on the benefits received from local services. Subsequently, the "second generation" approach to fiscal federalism suggested that self-interested politicians would prefer to shift the tax burden on to non-residents, perhaps a reason to put some constraints on their ability to do so.[21] Finally, mobility may be less of a constraint where the taxing region is larger, such as is the case when a metropolitan or regional government levies the tax.

The remainder of this section evaluates the property tax, the tax most commonly levied by local governments, based on the following characteristics of a good local tax:

- fairness in terms of the benefits received by beneficiaries of local public services;
- immobile tax base so that the tax will be borne by local residents and not passed on to people living in other jurisdictions (except where they are beneficiaries of services provided by the taxing jurisdiction);
- no harmful competition among local governments or between local governments and other orders of government;[22]
- sufficient, stable, and predictable revenues;
- visible, transparent, and accountable so taxpayers can hold governments accountable; and
- ease of administration at the local level.

This evaluation is followed by a discussion of why a mix of taxes, including income and sales taxes, for example, might also be appropriate for Canadian municipalities.[23]

Property Taxes

The property tax satisfies many of the characteristics of a fiscally sound local tax, as defined above. Its base is largely immobile – the residential portion cannot be exported to taxpayers in other jurisdictions – and, therefore, relatively efficient because distortions in economic behaviour are minimal.[24] It is at least partly effective in funding services for which the collective benefits accrue to the local community; hence, it satisfies the fairness criterion based on benefits received. Revenues are relatively stable and predictable. It is highly visible, so it makes local governments accountable for the tax levied.

Although the need for local governments to get citizen support for highly visible tax increases certainly makes them more accountable than federal or provincial/territorial governments, it also makes it more difficult for them to increase the tax to cope with rising expenditures. Another potential downside of a local property tax is that it may be more expensive to administer than other local taxes (income, sales, fuel, for example), which can be piggybacked onto existing provincial taxes.

There is some evidence that the property tax may be able to provide sufficient revenues to fund municipal services in Canada. For example, a study of Alberta municipalities concluded that the property tax is the only tax that municipalities need (Dahlby and McMillan, 2019). Furthermore, if the provincial education portion of the property tax in Alberta were eliminated, cities would have more than enough tax room to finance their services now and in the future. A study of the City of Toronto's finances noted that property tax revenues have grown more slowly than inflation since 2000 and that the tax burden per household has fallen over this time (Slack and Côté 2014). A study of the Greater Toronto Area concluded that there is room to increase residential property taxes in most municipalities in the region, though not the property tax on businesses (Tassonyi, Bird, and Slack 2015). The real question, however, is not whether the property tax is *adequate*, but whether it is the *best* tax for funding all city services.

A Mix of Taxes

Some authors have called for a mix of taxes at the local level that might, for example, include income or sales taxes (Kitchen and Slack 2016). A tax mix would give cities more flexibility to respond to local conditions such as changes in the economy, evolving demographics and expenditure needs, changes in the political climate, and other factors.[25] For example, local politicians might choose to levy sales taxes for local services that are enjoyed by commuters or a hotel tax to pay for services used by visitors.[26] An employee-based personal income tax (often referred to as a payroll tax) would tax commuters who work in the city and use services there but live outside. From an equity perspective, an income tax is likely to be more progressive than a property tax. A mix of taxes would allow cities to increase or stabilize revenue, on the one hand, while maintaining equity, on the other (Bahl 2010; Kitchen 2016; Slack 2011).

Relying on a number of different revenue sources means that a city can set lower tax rates for any single tax to levy a given amount of revenue, thereby reducing the burden of that tax. Moreover, with a range of tax sources, distortions in one tax may be counteracted by distortions in other taxes. For example, the property tax may discourage investment in housing, whereas an income tax may encourage investment in owner-occupied housing because the imputed income of owner-occupied housing is not taxed in Canada.

There are two ways that cities might levy income or sales taxes. They could set up and administer their own tax systems or piggyback onto the existing provincial system.[27] It would be much easier and cheaper to piggyback on to the provincial system. In terms of a local income tax, the External Advisory Committee on Cities and Communities (2006) proposed that the tax be piggybacked onto the provincial income tax. It recommended that the federal government reduce its personal income tax to make the change revenue neutral. Under current fiscal arrangements, if it did so, municipalities could not raise an income tax without provincial permission. The report thus recommended a process of "double devolution," whereby the federal government would provide tax room to provinces, which, in turn, would provide tax room to local governments, who would piggyback onto the provincial personal income tax system. Clearly, this mechanism would require a lot of intergovernmental cooperation. It is an open question if that would work in the Canadian context.

In terms of sales taxes,[28] it would be costly for municipalities to introduce their own tax. There may also be problems with cities piggybacking in Canadian provinces that have the harmonized sales tax (HST) or the goods and services tax (GST) because of the way in which these taxes are administered in Canada.[29] Municipalities are often more interested in taking a share of provincial (or federal) government sales tax revenues than levying their own tax rates. Tax sharing is not the same as local taxation, however, because the local government has no control over the tax base or tax rates. It simply receives a portion of provincial taxes and, for this reason, is pretty much the same as a transfer.

As noted earlier, income and sales taxes would be best levied at a regional scale to avoid cross-border shopping in response to a local sales tax or movement across municipal boundaries in response to a local income tax. Regional governments in some provinces could take on the taxing responsibility, but in others, there would need to be cooperation among municipalities in the region.

Finally, some municipalities, such as small, rural, and remote communities, will not be able to collect much revenue from income or sales taxes. It may thus be necessary to allow only larger municipalities to levy these taxes and provide provincial and/or federal transfers to smaller municipalities. New or enhanced provincial-municipal equalization transfers may also be required when new taxes are levied at the local level to ensure that all municipalities can provide a standard level of local public services at a standard tax rate.[30]

5. A Process for Clarifying Federal-Provincial-Municipal Roles and Responsibilities

The starting point for new tax sources for Canadian municipalities, as noted earlier, is the assignment of expenditure responsibilities among the orders of government. The discussion of new sources of revenue for local governments needs to start with what they are actually paying for. How do we go about clarifying federal-provincial-municipal roles and responsibilities?

Municipalities deliver a wide range of services, but provinces are involved in every aspect through cost-sharing, policy setting, regulation, or other forms of entanglement. In Ontario alone, no fewer than 280 provincial statutes and countless provincial regulations, policy frameworks, and service standards affect how municipalities in that province deliver services (Wilson 2019). Indeed, the current cost-sharing arrangements between the Province of Ontario and municipalities have been described as a "tangled web" of overlapping obligations (Fenn and Côté 2014). When federal government funding is added to the mix, the web is even more entangled. In some cases, it may be beneficial to disentangle provincial and municipal involvement by assigning responsibility to one government or the other. Some services, though, may benefit from greater coordination and cooperation among orders of government.[31]

A recent paper on clarifying provincial-municipal responsibilities in one province (Ontario) recommends a principles-based approach to sorting out who does what – what cities do best, what the province does best, where they can work together, and what resources cities need to fulfil their responsibilities (Eidelman, Hachard, and Slack 2020). One of the key principles is to follow the pay-for-say principle and avoid unfunded mandates. A government's input into how a service functions should be matched with a corresponding responsibility to pay for that service. Unfunded mandates, whereby provincial regulations require local government to perform certain actions or meet technical standards without providing money to meet those requirements, should be avoided. Another principle is to consider local revenue capacity – any proposal to increase municipal service responsibilities should consider whether local governments have the necessary and appropriate resources to meet those responsibilities. A third is to take account of differences across regions, because the cost of delivering services differs in different places. In other words, asymmetrical arrangements may be required.

COVID-19 has highlighted how the division of powers among the federal, provincial, and local governments plays out in the face of a public health crisis. In particular, the federal government used its spending powers in 2020–1 to assist provinces and municipalities, which faced considerable fiscal pressure to address critical responsibilities but without the necessary revenue sources to meet them. As noted in the introduction to this volume, this misalignment of revenues and expenditures is particularly acute for municipalities that rely mainly on property taxes and user fees. It is time to revisit the role of all orders of government, and to this end, an independent, non-governmental commission was proposed to rethink the architecture of Canadian fiscal federalism (Béland, Dahlby, and Orsini 2020).

Recalibrating our federal fiscal structure will hopefully put municipalities and provinces on better footing, but there will still be areas where coordination between orders of government will be required. Such coordination needs to be trilateral, rather than bilateral (Slack and Hachard 2020). In the aftermath of COVID-19, the Organisation for Economic Co-operation and Development (OECD) is urging national governments to "introduce, activate or reorient existing multi-level coordination bodies that bring together national and subnational government representatives, in order to minimize the risk of a fragmented crisis response" (OECD 2020, 2).

Canada has a history of establishing trilateral agreements in areas such as homelessness and urban development, but these agreements are the exception rather than the rule (Bradford 2020). Decisions taken on immigration, infrastructure, and public health, to name a few examples, have significant effects on municipalities. In cases where there is insufficient funding for programs, municipalities often bear the cost of filling gaps in services. Municipalities, and particularly large cities, should not need to wait to see what arrangements the provinces and Ottawa agree to in areas such as infrastructure, public health, and immigration. Municipalities need to be part of intergovernmental discussions on these issues. As Eidelman (2020) notes, we need a new intergovernmental infrastructure that enables policy makers at all levels to understand cities' needs and respond. In short, municipalities need a seat at the intergovernmental table (Hachard 2022).[32]

6. Conclusion

Municipalities in Canada are responsible for an ever-increasing number of services and for maintaining and adding to municipal infrastructure. Yet, their sources of revenue have remained largely untouched for decades. They are limited to property taxes, user fees, and intergovernmental transfers. COVID-19 has highlighted the vital role that local governments play in the federation, but it has also shone a light on the cracks in the outdated federal fiscal structure. Municipalities have turned to the federal government to help them cover their operating deficits, but funding cities in this way may not be sustainable.

It is time to revisit local governments' roles, responsibilities, and revenues, especially in the large cities and city-regions. Although the federal government has recently shown interest in cities, and it can transfer money to cities, it can change neither their expenditure responsibilities nor their revenue-raising powers. Any real reform of municipal finance in this country will essentially depend on provincial involvement and agreement to make changes in what municipalities do and how they pay for it. All three orders of government thus need to be involved in clarifying responsibilities and revenues.

NOTES

1 The External Advisory Committee on Cities and Communities was established by the Honourable Paul Martin in 2004 and reported in 2006. The committee, chaired by Michael Harcourt, focused on creating a long-term vision for cities and communities in Canada. Many of its recommendations are still relevant today.
2 A number of authors have suggested that the Canadian Constitution be amended to give original powers to municipalities. For a review of some of these proposals

and the debate around giving municipalities recognition in the Constitution, see IMFG (2020).
3 For a description of other taxes in selected cities across Canada, see Meloche and Vaillancourt (2021).
4 For information about other federal transfers generally, see Taylor and Bradford (2020). See chapter 14 in this volume for a history of federal funding for housing.
5 The Gas Tax Fund was incorrectly named because it is not based on gas tax revenues but rather started out as $2 billion per year, now indexed for inflation. For more information and an analysis of the Gas Tax Fund, see chapter 15 in this volume and Bradford (2020). As noted, in March 2021, it was renamed the Canada Community-Building Fund.
6 In addition to the provincial legislation that applies to all municipalities in a province, some municipalities in some provinces have specific legislation in a freestanding specific law: Vancouver, Calgary, Edmonton, Toronto, Winnipeg, and Montreal (Taylor and Dobson 2020). Special legislation does not seem to have increased the revenue-raising powers of the affected cities in a significant way, however (Taylor and Dobson 2020; Kitchen 2016).
7 Perhaps the best known example of this phenomenon was the amalgamation of Metro Toronto and the six constituent municipalities in 1998, against the wishes of the municipalities and residents. For more on the impact of the amalgamation on municipal finances, see Slack and Bird (2013).
8 For more details on provincial constraints on municipal borrowing across Canada, see Slack and Tassonyi (2017).
9 For more information on provincial-municipal transfers in Canada, see Bird and Slack (2021).
10 A comparison of Toronto and seven other international cities shows that, with the exception of London, UK, the major cities have more tax options than Toronto (Slack 2017).
11 This number is based on information from provincial websites. For a breakdown of the number of local governments, by province, see Taylor and Bradford (2020).
12 The source of information in this paragraph is Statistics Canada, Table 10-10-0024-01.
13 The land transfer tax has been criticized largely because it provides a disincentive for people to move, thereby resulting in potential inflexibilities in the labour market and encouraging people to stay in properties of a size and location that they might not have otherwise chosen. For other criticisms of the land transfer tax, see Kitchen and Slack (2016); Haider, Anwar, and Holmes (2016); and Dachis (2012).
14 Statistics Canada provides consolidated provincial-local expenditure and revenue data but does not separate provincial governments from local governments. Moreover, there is no source for comparable municipal finance data for cities in Canada.
15 The source for these numbers is Statistics Canada, Table 10-10-0015-01.

16 There is much discussion about the poor state of municipal infrastructure in Canada – roads are congested, transit systems call for major investments, several bridges are crumbling, many water treatment plants still need to be replaced, and more. See FAO (2021) for estimates of the current replacement value (CRV) and current condition of infrastructure assets in Ontario, as well as an estimate of the costs of bringing them into a state of good repair.
17 This amount reflects financial and non-financial assets minus liabilities.
18 There is an ongoing debate about how to measure municipal surpluses based on cash versus accrual accounting. For a discussion of the merits of accrual accounting at the local level, see Dachis (2018).
19 For more on the Wicksellian connection in financing local public services, see Bird and Slack (2014); and Slack and Bird (2018).
20 User fees are appropriate where beneficiaries can be identified, and those who do not pay can be excluded. For more on user fees, see Tassonyi and Kitchen (2021).
21 As Bahl and Bird (2018) note, the desires of the median voter of the first-generation approach and the self-interested politician in the second-generation approach may not be all that different: both prefer to export the tax burden to non-residents. They may both also prefer to shift the cost to future generations through borrowing or development charges that likely impact future voters rather than present ones.
22 Of course, competition is to some extent beneficial in terms of accountability.
23 Municipalities in Canada levied an income tax prior to the Second World War. In the 1930s, the provincial government in Ontario took over the income tax from municipalities because it needed the revenue. In Quebec, Montreal and Quebec City had also levied municipal income taxes, but these taxes were repealed under the Wartime Tax Agreements during the Second World War and have not been reintroduced since that time (Perry 1990). Municipal income taxes are currently levied in many Nordic countries, but these are mainly unitary countries.
24 The same is not true of the non-residential property tax, however, which can be exported to other jurisdictions. See Smart (2012); and Dahlby, Ferede, and Khanal (2021).
25 New taxes at the local level in Canada would require provincial approval and possibly new legislation.
26 US evidence suggests that the cost of inner-city services used by people who live in the suburbs and commute to work exceeds, sometimes substantially, what they pay for inner-city services. Local income and consumption-based taxes could be used to alleviate this disparity. See Chernick and Tkacheva (2002).
27 Piggybacking onto the provincial tax can still mean that cities levy their own tax rates.
28 An alternative to the sales tax is a business value tax (BVT). The base can be calculated as sales minus the purchase of inputs from other businesses (including capital inputs less a depreciation allowance). Although the base is similar to the GST/HST, it is a tax on income (not consumption) because it taxes profits as well as wages. For more on the BVT, see Bird (2014).

29 GST and HST revenues collected in each province are not tracked by the federal government and remitted to that province. Rather, all GST/HST revenues are collected annually by the federal government, and the entitlement for each province is calculated by a formula that estimates the consumption expenditure base in that province and then applies the tax rate for that province to its calculated share of the base. Revenues allocated to each HST/GST province are thus driven by the estimated taxable consumption base in that province. In short, how the revenue is allocated is completely unrelated to how the HST actually works (Bird 2012). If a city were to "piggyback" a municipal sales tax onto the HST, estimates of the taxable consumption base would be required for that city.

30 For more on provincial-municipal equalization transfers in Canada, see Bird and Slack (2021). Of course, it is not possible to provide a comparable level of services to all small, rural, and remote communities, even with intergovernmental transfers.

31 Multilevel governance carries significant possible benefits, including the ability to profit from pooled resources while still creating opportunity for local input. However, risks of sacrificing accountability and wasting resources also exist (see Horak 2012).

32 Hachard (2022) explores how to reform Canada's intergovernmental infrastructure to include municipalities, based on lessons learned from other countries.

REFERENCES

Bahl, Roy. 2010. "Financing Metropolitan Areas." In *Local Government Finance: The Challenges of the 21st Century. Second Global Report on Decentralization and Local Democracy* (*Global Observatory of Local Finance [GOLD] II*), 285–307. United Cities and Local Governments (UCLG). Cheltenham, UK: Edward Elgar Publishing.

Bahl, Roy, and Richard M. Bird. 2018. *Fiscal Decentralization and Local Finance in Developing Countries*. Cheltenham, UK: Edward Elgar Publishing.

Béland, Daniel, Bev Dahlby, and Steve Orsini. 2020. "COVID-19 Will Force a Change to Canada's Fiscal Arrangements." *Policy Options*, 7 May 2020. https://policyoptions.irpp.org/magazines/may-2020/covid-19-will-force-a-change-to-canadas-fiscal-arrangements/.

Bird, Richard M. 2012. "The GST/HST: Creating an Integrated Sales Tax in a Federal Country." *SSP Research Papers* 5, no. 12. Calgary: School of Public Policy, University of Calgary. https://www.policyschool.ca/wp-content/uploads/2016/03/bird-gst-hst.pdf.

– 2014. "A Better Local Business Tax: The BVT." *IMFG Papers on Municipal Finance and Governance*, No. 18. Toronto: Institute on Municipal Finance and Governance, University of Toronto. https://hdl.handle.net/1807/81249.

Bird, Richard M., and Enid Slack. 2014. "Local Taxes and Local Expenditures in Developing Countries: Strengthening the Wicksellian Connection." *Public Administration and Development* 34, no. 4: 359–69. https://doi.org/10.1002/pad.1695.

- eds. 2015. *Is Your City Healthy? Measuring Urban Fiscal Health*. Toronto: Institute on Municipal Finance and Governance, and Institute of Public Administration of Canada.
- 2021. "Provincial-Local Transfers in Canada: Time for a Change?" *IMFG Papers on Municipal Finance and Governance*, No. 57. Toronto: Institute on Municipal Finance and Governance, University of Toronto. https://hdl.handle.net/1807/108373.

Bradford, Neil. 2020. "Policy in Place: Revisiting Canada's Tri-Level Agreements." *IMFG Papers on Municipal Finance and Governance*, No. 50. Toronto: Institute on Municipal Finance and Governance, University of Toronto. https://hdl.handle.net/1807/102474.

Breton, Albert. 1996. *Competitive Governments*. Cambridge: Cambridge University Press.

Chernick, Howard, and Olesya Tkacheva. 2002. "The Commuter Tax and the Fiscal Cost of Commuters in New York City." *State Tax Notes* 25, no. 6: 451–6. https://ssrn.com/abstract=321081.

Dachis, Benjamin. 2012. *Stuck in Place: The Effect of Land Transfer Taxes on Housing Transactions*. Commentary, No. 364. Toronto: C.D. Howe Institute. https://www.cdhowe.org/sites/default/files/attachments/research_papers/mixed/Commentary_364_0.pdf.

- 2018. *A Roadmap to Municipal Reform: Improving Life in Canadian Cities*. Policy Study 46. Toronto: C.D. Howe Institute. https://www.cdhowe.org/public-policy-research/roadmap-municipal-reform-improving-life-canadian-cities.

Dahlby, Bev, Ergete Ferede, and Mukesh Khanal. 2021. "The Impact of Property Taxation on Business Investment in Alberta." *SPP Research Paper* 14, no. 8. Calgary: School of Public Policy, University of Calgary. https://doi.org/10.11575/sppp.v14i.69686.

Dahlby, Bev, and Melville McMillan. 2019. "What Is the Role of Property and Property-Related Taxes? An Assessment of Municipal Property Taxes, Land Transfer Taxes, and Tax Increment Financing." In *Funding the Canadian City*, edited by Enid Slack, Lisa Philipps, Lindsay M. Tedds, and Heather L. Evans, 45–73. Toronto: Canadian Tax Foundation.

Eidelman, Gabriel. 2020. *Reimagining the Canadian Federation through an Urban Lens*. Montreal: Institute for Research on Public Policy, Centre of Excellence on the Canadian Federation. https://centre.irpp.org/research-studies/reimagining-the-canadian-federation-through-an-urban-lens/.

Eidelman, Gabriel, Tomas Hachard, and Enid Slack. 2020. *In It Together: Clarifying Provincial Municipal Responsibilities*. Toronto: Ontario 360, Institute on Municipal Finance and Governance, and Urban Policy Lab. https://imfg.munkschool.utoronto.ca/research/doc/?doc_id=525.

External Advisory Committee on Cities and Communities. 2006. *From Restless Communities to Resilient Places: Building a Stronger Future for All Canadians*. Final Report. Ottawa: Infrastructure Canada.

FAO (Financial Accountability Office of Ontario). 2020. *Ontario Municipal Finances: An Overview of Municipal Budgets and an Estimate of the Financial Impact of the COVID-19 Pandemic*. Toronto: Financial Accountability Office of Ontario. https://www.fao-on.org/en/Blog/Publications/municipal-finances-2020.
- 2021. *Municipal Infrastructure: A Review of Ontario's Municipal Infrastructure and an Assessment of the State of Repair*. Toronto: Financial Accountability Office of Ontario. https://www.fao-on.org/web/default/files/publications/EC2103%20Municipal%20Infrastructure/Municipal%20Infrastructure%20Review-EN.pdf.
Fenn, Michael, and André Côté. 2014. "Provincial-Municipal Relations in Ontario: Approaching an Inflection Point." *IMFG Papers on Municipal Finance and Governance*, No. 17. Toronto: Institute on Municipal Finance and Governance, University of Toronto. https://imfg.munkschool.utoronto.ca/research/doc/?doc_id=275.
Hachard, Tomas. 2020. "It Takes Three: Making Space for Cities in Canadian Federalism." *IMFG Perspectives*, No. 31. Toronto: Institute on Municipal Finance and Governance, University of Toronto. https://hdl.handle.net/1807/103012.
- 2022. "A Seat at the Table: Municipalities and Intergovernmental Relations in Canada." *IMFG Papers on Municipal Finance and Governance*, No. 69. Toronto: Institute on Municipal Finance and Governance, University of Toronto. https://imfg.munkschool.utoronto.ca/research/doc/?doc_id=591.
Haider, Murtaza, Amar Anwar, and Cynthia Holmes. 2016. "Did the Land Transfer Tax Reduce Housing Sales in Toronto?" *IMFG Papers on Municipal Finance and Governance*, No. 28. Toronto: Institute on Municipal Finance and Governance, University of Toronto. https://hdl.handle.net/1807/81207.
Horak, Martin. 2012. "Conclusion: Understanding Multilevel Governance in Canada's Cities." In *Sites of Governance: Multilevel Governance and Policy Making in Canada's Big Cities*, edited by Robert Young and Martin Horak, 349–70. Montreal and Kingston: McGill-Queen's University Press.
IMFG (Institute on Municipal Finance and Governance). 2018. "A Check-Up on Toronto's Fiscal Health, 2018." Institute on Municipal Finance and Governance. https://imfg.munkschool.utoronto.ca/imfg/research/a-check-up-on-torontos-fiscal-health-2018/.
- 2020. "Charting a New Path: Does Toronto Need More Autonomy?" *IMFG Forum Paper*, No. 10. Toronto: Institute on Municipal Finance and Governance, University of Toronto. https://imfg.munkschool.utoronto.ca/research/doc/?doc_id=529.
Kitchen, Harry. 2016. "Is 'Charter-City Status' a Solution for Financing City Services in Canada – Or is that a Myth?" *SPP Research Paper* 9, no. 2. Calgary: School of Public Policy, University of Calgary. https://doi.org/10.11575/sppp.v9i0.42566.
Kitchen, Harry, and Enid Slack. 2016. "More Tax Sources for Canada's Largest Cities: Why, What, and How?" *IMFG Papers on Municipal Finance and Governance*, No. 27. Toronto: Institute on Municipal Finance and Governance, University of Toronto. https://hdl.handle.net/1807/81209.
Meloche, Jean-Philippe, and François Vaillancourt. 2021. "Municipal Financing Opportunities in Canada: How Do Cities Use Their Fiscal Space?" *IMFG Papers on*

Municipal Finance and Governance, No. 52. Toronto: Institute on Municipal Finance and Governance, University of Toronto. https://hdl.handle.net/1807/105277.

MFOA (Municipal Finance Officers' Association). 2021. "Fixated on a Tree, Missing the Forest: A Response to C.D. Howe Institute's Rating of Municipal Budgets and Financial Statements." Toronto: Municipal Finance Officers Association and Ontario Regional and Single Tier Treasurers. https://www.mfoa.on.ca/mfoa/MAIN/MFOA_Policy_Projects/MFOA_Responds_CD_Howes_2020_Municipal_Scorecard.

Milligan, Kevin. 2019. "Canada's Radical Fiscal Federation: The Next Fifty Years." In *Policy Transformation in Canada: Is the Past Prologue?*, edited by Carolyn Hughes Tuohy, Sophie Borwein, Peter John Loewen, and Andrew Potter, 87–96. Toronto: University of Toronto Press.

Musgrave, Richard A. 1983. "Who Should Tax, Where and What?" In *Tax Assignment in Federal Countries*, edited by Charles McClure, 2–19. Canberra: Centre for Research on Federal Financial Relations, Australian National University.

Oates, Wallace. 1996. "Taxation in a Federal System: The Tax-Assignment Problem." *Public Economics Review* 1: 35–60.

OECD (Organisation for Economic Co-operation and Development). 2020. *The Territorial Impact of COVID-19: Managing the Crisis across Levels of Government*. Paris: OECD. https://www.oecd-ilibrary.org/deliver/d3e314e1-en.pdf.

Perry, J. Harvey. 1990. *Taxation in Canada*. 5th ed. Canadian Tax Papers, No. 89. Toronto: Canadian Tax Foundation.

Robson, William B.P., and Miles Wu. 2021. *Puzzling Plans and Surprise Surpluses: Canada's Cities Need More Transparent Budgets*. Commentary, No. 592. Toronto: C.D. Howe Institute. https://www.cdhowe.org/sites/default/files/attachments/research_papers/mixed/Commentary_592_0.pdf.

Slack, Enid. 2011. "Financing Large Cities and Metropolitan Areas." *IMFG Papers on Municipal Finance and Governance*, No. 3. Toronto: Institute on Municipal Finance and Governance, University of Toronto. https://hdl.handle.net/1807/81275.

– "How Much Local Fiscal Autonomy Do Cities Have? A Comparison of Eight Cities around the World." *IMFP Perspectives*, No. 18. Toronto: Institute on Municipal Finance and Governance, University of Toronto. https://tspace.library.utoronto.ca/bitstream/1807/82864/1/imfg_perspectives_no19_localfiscalautonomy_slack_2017.pdf.

Slack, Enid, and Richard M. Bird. 2007–8. "Cities in Canadian Federalism." *Policy Options*, 29, no. 1. https://policyoptions.irpp.org/magazines/the-mood-of-canada/.

– 2013. "Merging Municipalities: Is Bigger Better?" *IMFG Papers on Municipal Finance and Governance*, No. 14. Toronto: Institute on Municipal Finance and Governance, University of Toronto. https://hdl.handle.net/1807/81253.

– 2018. "Financing Regional Public Transit in Ontario: The Case for Strengthening the Wicksellian Connection." In *Canada: The State of the Federation 2015: Canadian Federalism and Infrastructure*, edited by John R. Allen, David L.A. Gordon, Kyle Hanniman, André Juneau, and Robert A. Young, 45–74. Montreal and Kingston: McGill-Queen's University Press.

Slack, Enid, and André Côté. 2014. "Is Toronto Fiscally Healthy? A Check-Up on the City's Finances." *IMFG Perspectives*, No. 7. Toronto: Institute on Municipal Finance and Governance, University of Toronto. https://hdl.handle.net/1807/82786.

Slack, Enid, and Tomas Hachard. 2020. "Now, with a Deal Made to Help Cities, the Work Begins." *Policy Options*, 17 August 2020. https://policyoptions.irpp.org/magazines/august-2020/now-with-a-deal-made-to-help-cities-the-work-begins/.

Slack, Enid, Lisa Philipps, Lindsay M. Tedds, and Heather L. Evans. 2019. "Introduction." In *Funding the Canadian City*, edited by Enid Slack, Lisa Philipps, Lindsay M. Tedds, and Heather L. Evans, 1–20. Toronto: Canadian Tax Foundation.

Slack, Enid, and Almos T. Tassonyi. 2017. "Financing Urban Infrastructure in Canada: Overview, Trends, and Issues." In *Financing Infrastructure: Who Should Pay?*, edited by Richard M. Bird and Enid Slack, 21–53. Montreal and Kingston: McGill-Queen's University Press.

Smart, Michael. 2012. "The Reform of the Business Property Tax in Ontario: An Evaluation." *IMFG Papers on Municipal Finance and Governance*, No. 10. Toronto: Institute on Municipal Finance and Governance, University of Toronto. https://imfg.munkschool.utoronto.ca/research/doc/?doc_id=202.

Tassonyi, Almos, Richard M. Bird, and Enid Slack. 2015. "Can GTA Municipalities Raise Property Taxes? An Analysis of Tax Competition and Revenue Hills." *IMFG Papers on Municipal Finance and Governance*, No. 20. Toronto: Institute on Municipal Finance and Governance, University of Toronto. https://imfg.munkschool.utoronto.ca/research/doc/?doc_id=319.

Tassonyi, Almos, and Harry Kitchen. 2021. "Addressing the Fairness of Municipal User Fee Policy." *IMFG Papers on Municipal Finance and Governance*, No. 54. Toronto: Institute on Municipal Finance and Governance, University of Toronto. https://imfg.munkschool.utoronto.ca/research/doc/?doc_id=561.

Taylor, Zack, and Neil Bradford. 2020. "Governing Canadian Cities." In *Canadian Cities in Transition: Understanding Contemporary Urbanism*, edited by Markus Moos, Tara Vinodrai, and Ryan Walker, 33–50. Don Mills, ON: Oxford University Press.

Taylor, Zack, and Alec Dobson. 2020. "Power and Purpose: Canadian Municipal Law in Transition." *IMFG Papers on Municipal Finance and Governance*, No. 47. Toronto: Institute on Municipal Finance and Governance, University of Toronto. https://imfg.munkschool.utoronto.ca/research/doc/?doc_id=526.

UCLG (United Cities and Local Government), LSE (London School of Economics), and Metropolis. 2021. "The Impact of the COVID-19 Pandemic on Subnational Finances: Emergency Governance for Cities and Regions." *Analytics Note*, No. 3. https://www.lse.ac.uk/Cities/publications/Policy-Briefs-and-Analytics-Notes/Analytics-Note-03-The-Impact-of-the-Covid-19-pandemic-on-Subnational-Finances.

Wilson, Matthew. 2019. "Municipal Money Matters: Our Fiscal Future." Presentation at the Association of Municipalities of Ontario (AMO) Annual Conference, 19 August 2019, Ottawa.

14 Coming Full Circle: Federalism and Responsibility for Housing

STEVE POMEROY

Introduction

A critically important aspect of Canada's housing system is that it exists within a federal system of government. Within the Canadian Constitution, the allocation of responsibility for both social welfare generally and housing more particularly is not explicit. Housing is a multidimensional, complex topic. While the term "housing" is not present in the constitutional division of powers (British North America [BNA] Act, sections 91–2), activities related to housing permeate constitutional responsibility.

Notable for the federal role, responsibility includes taxation, which underpins the so-called spending powers; census and statistics (housing need); banking and interest (mortgage finance); and Indians and lands reserved (Aboriginal and Indigenous housing). Meanwhile, provinces have exclusive jurisdiction over municipal institutions (local planning and development); local works and undertakings (infrastructure); property rights and civil rights; and generally all matters of a merely local or private nature in the province (see Slack, chapter 13, this volume). Provinces also have exclusive jurisdiction over provincial taxation (own revenues and cost-sharing capacity).

The lack of explicit jurisdiction is not surprising given the prevailing conditions of the latter nineteenth century when the BNA Act was drafted. Social welfare issues were largely a private matter, with the public sphere confined to rudimentary relief at the municipal level (Banting 1990). Responsibility has consequently evolved, influenced by circumstances and the larger federal revenue collecting and thus *spending powers*, which emerged as a key element in the Canadian version of the welfare state. This development enabled the emergence of a dominant federal role in housing in the immediate post-war period.

As noted by Banting (1990), the federal spending powers are central to the way responsibilities evolved (see also Oliver, chapter 3, this volume). The spending powers allow the federal government to make payments to individuals, institutions, and other levels of government for purposes that the federal Parliament does not necessarily have the power to regulate.[1]

Having capacity to spend, and to attach conditions to that spending, significantly expanded the reach of scope of the federal government across a number of decades. Again, this expanded scope is seen in the housing sphere in the more recent National Housing Strategy, as well as in *Budget 2022*, a budget labelled by some as a "housing budget" (Hogue 2022). In the National Housing Strategy, unilateral federal programs again dominate – despite the lack of a formal constitutional responsibility for housing.

This chapter uses a historical lens to describe the evolving nature of federalism in the housing area. It first highlights the activist federal role in the context of post-war reconstruction and the gradual shift towards a competitive unilateralism with parallel policy and programming efforts concurrent at the federal and provincial level. This path continued through a period of cooperative federalism in which provincial and territorial governments were coerced into more expansive roles, prior to wholesale withdrawal of the federal government in 1993. Finally, the chapter describes how, despite thirty years of withdrawal and devolution, the federal government under Justin Trudeau's administration has re-engaged and has reasserted a leadership role in housing policy, programming, and funding.

The chapter seeks to make the case that this federal re-engagement is not good policy, and the efforts to return to direct, unilateral federal program delivery have exposed the erosion of capacity and competencies within the federal housing agency, the Canadian Mortgage and Housing Corporation (CMHC). Rather than pursue a return to unilateralism, a more collaborative form of federalism is required, treating provincial and territories as strong partners and maximizing on their accumulated expertise. Such an approach would be more consistent with the concept of a truly national rather than assertive federal housing strategy.

Post-War Reconstruction

The current context roles and relationships that characterize Canada's housing system, especially its intergovernmental roles, have their roots in the immediate post–Second World War period. It was at this time that much of the institutional infrastructure that we now take for granted was created. This infrastructure includes creating a federal housing agency in 1946 (Central Mortgage and Housing, renamed from Central to Canada in 1979), provincial housing corporations and subsequently ministries and the formative role of public policy in nurturing a housing industry, and a housing finance system that has enabled a strong market system to be in place. There are also important legacy effects, both in terms of institutional structures and relationships and the shifting roles and competencies (Miron 1993; CMHC 1986).

The immediate post-war period was dominated by the federal government, which focused on transition to a peacetime economy and the need to create housing for returning veterans following almost a decade with minimal home construction (Rose 1980). During the war, federal authorities had proved themselves effective in the housing sector, with a federal Crown corporation, Wartime Housing Ltd., producing over 19,000 temporary dwellings between 1941 and 1945 to house wartime manufacturing workers.[2]

CMHC was created in 1946 to help in this process, aided by new federal legislation, the 1945 National Housing Act (NHA). At that time, there was very limited provincial capacity or expertise – it began to emerge only in the 1960s. CMHC over time created a large network of local offices (at their peak in 1984, there were ninety-five branch offices across the country), staffed with multidisciplinary expertise, which established a presence that reinforced a strong federal role, especially in the 1970s under a more centralist federal administration.

During this period, these powers enabled CMHC to establish mortgage loan programs to assist individual household home purchase. It also created financing to fund necessary municipal infrastructure to support development and, with a staff of architects and engineers, developed model home plans and assisted builders to construct housing to meet pent-up demand – in effect, helping to establish the private home construction system.

While both the Curtis and Marsh reports[3] on post-war reconstruction identified the need to create public housing, there was ambivalence and some reluctance, especially from federal finance officials, fearing the associated expenditure impact (Rose 1980; Banting 1990). This reluctance is reflected in the early elements of the NHA that enabled CMHC to create direct lending and some cost-shared subsidy programs *provided that* the lead in undertaking public housing came from the provinces or municipalities. Indeed, Canada's earliest and ultimately largest public housing development, Regent Park near downtown Toronto, was initiated in 1949 in a partnership between CMHC and the City of Toronto (not the province). Overall, however, this separation of responsibilities was ineffectual, and little low-rent public housing was created before the 1964 amendments to the NHA that revised the financing and subsidy conditions (Rose 1980; Banting 1990).

Increasingly capable and proactive provincial bureaucracies emerged in the 1960s, initially in Ontario and Quebec. Resulting federal-provincial tensions led to efforts to curtail the federal use of the spending powers as a way to work directly with municipalities. Ontario and Quebec established public housing corporations to lead public housing development, a practice subsequently following in other provinces.

This practice resulted in shifting responsibility, with the larger provinces developing and managing public housing, removing CMHC from project-level decision-making. Public housing ultimately created some 206,000 public housing units, most between 1964 and 1974 and disproportionately in Ontario. Provinces also became more assertive and took on more active policy roles, establishing provincial ministries and ministers in the early 1970s.

The support for assisted "public housing," however, was a small part of CMHC's role, which remained focused on enabling and expanding homeownership. This focus was substantially abetted in 1954 with the introduction of public mortgage insurance, effectively a risk guarantee to protect private mortgage lenders, which encouraged private lending (and reduced pressures on direct federal lending and associated capital requirements) to support the continued expansion of home purchase and the growth of homeownership in parallel with a process of urbanization.

Again, seeking to minimize federal subsidies for social (public) housing activities, CMHC extended credit to private investor-builders and non-profit borrowers to build moderate-rent rental housing. This credit provided no direct subsidy but did provide forgiveness of 10 per cent of the loan principal if the return on equity was maintained below 5 per cent per annum. This limited dividend (and parallel non-profit) loan program played an important role in helping to expand rental supply, especially as the baby boom generation began forming new households and created urban rental demand in the mid-1960s. This rental activity was also assisted by favourable federal tax treatment of rental investment (accelerated depreciation, soft cost deductibility, no tax on capital gain, and so on).

1970s Shift to Competitive Unilateralism

The concept of *competitive unilateralism* (coined by Banting 1990) saw the cessation of joint programming in public housing, which was replaced by distinctly separate programming at the provincial versus the federal level. This shift was also influenced by a 1969 federal task force on housing and urban development, the Hellyer Task Force, prompted by concerns about the stigmatization and concentration of poverty in large-scale provincially developed public housing. The federal government was also concerned about uneven provincial capacity, which had seen Ontario and Quebec absorb a disproportionate share of public housing loans and subsidies.

The federal response to the concerns about provincially delivered larger scale public development and concentrated poverty and stigmatization was to seek partnerships with the community-based non-profit and cooperative sector as proponents of smaller scale mixed-income community-based affordable housing. Again, this response was paralleled by new federal initiatives to enable lower income households to access ownership (Assisted Home Ownership Program [AHOP] in 1975) and new incentives for private rental development (Assisted Rental Program [ARP] in 1975–8; and the Multiple Unit Residential Building [MURB] tax incentives in 1974–81).

Meanwhile, the provinces identified their priorities and accordingly designed their own unilateral initiatives, albeit with smaller and uneven outputs across jurisdictions compared to the more richly funded federal programs (again reflecting spending power). According to one count, by 1976, there were fifty-three housing programs administered by the provinces independently of the National Housing Act, including direct construction and rental subsidies, housing rehabilitation, capital financing, and rental controls (CMHC 1984; Banting 1990).

The late 1970s through the mid-1980s were the peak years of growth for "social housing," distinguished from "public housing" by their non-governmental organization (NGO) community-based ownership (although there was also a role for public municipal corporations to utilize these new federal programs, so a quasi-public continuation – but at a smaller scale and with mixed income). The non-profit and co-op programs covered 100 per cent of the capital cost via private lender CMHC-insured loans, and received ongoing subsidies to ensure rents could be affordable to a minimum of 25 per cent of tenants at only 25 per cent of gross income.

While pursuing unilateral initiatives, the federal government gave tacit acknowledgement to provinces' interests and desires, inviting provinces to participate in the 1978 reframing of social housing programs. They were invited to match federal subsidies and take on responsibility to deliver some programming. In an effort to sustain their public housing activities, provinces took on the municipal non-profit program except in Prince Edward Island, Nova Scotia, Newfoundland and Labrador, and Manitoba. Quebec and Saskatchewan delivered the private non-profit program, and in British Columbia, the delivery of the private non-profit program was split, with CMHC delivering it to families while the province delivered seniors projects. This arrangement set a precedent for the subsequent cooperative federalism in the mid-1980s.

1980s Engagement of Provinces and Territories through Cooperative Federalism

By early 1980, housing policy had come to be produced by eleven governments (plus two territories, albeit at a smaller scale) acting in varying degrees of unilateralism with ongoing tensions and intergovernmental conflict.

As federal unilateral programs expanded with layering of long-term (thirty-five-year) subsidy commitments, on top of earlier fifty-year public housing subsidies, there was an exponential growth in the amount of federal expenditure on housing, rising from only $150 million annually in 1971, to over $1.4 billion annually by 1984, and to over $2 billion by 1990 (Carter 1997). This increase was primarily driven by subsidies to the expanding non-profit and cooperative housing organizations that were building and operating social housing. These were financed with loans covering 100 per cent of cost, at a time of high and rising mortgage rates (exceeding 20 per cent by 1980), such that the subsidies required to carry this debt were substantial (Pomeroy 1995; Wolfe 1998). This financing was occurring at a time when the federal deficit was also rising, prompting concern and efforts to rein in spending (Carter 1997; Suttor 2016) – a process subsequently initiated with the election of the Conservative Mulroney government in 1983.

The new Mulroney administration in 1985 initiated a comprehensive program review, the Nielsen Task Force, including a review of all federal housing programs. Notably, with a title *Housing Programs in Search of a Balance* (Government of Canada, 1985), the housing review went beyond just social programs to also encompass the function of the mortgage market, ways that government can use housing as an economic lever, and energy conservation in homes. It sought to find balance between social and market objectives; between new construction versus housing assistance and renewal of the existing stock; and, notable to the current theme, between the respective roles of the federal versus provincial/territorial jurisdictions.

This review culminated in a reframing of the approach in the 1985 policy document *A National Direction for Housing Solutions* (CMHC 1986). It is notable that, in framing and presenting these new directions, the minister responsible for CMHC, William McKnight, stated: "The principle upon which federal housing policy is founded is that Canadians in all parts of the country be able to have decent and adequate shelter at a level of payment that is affordable within their means" (2). While implicit, highlighting the aspiration to provide all with decent and adequate shelter, there was no explicit reference to housing as a basic need, nor as a fundamental right. A rights-based approach was not part of the policy discourse at that time.

The *National Direction* included policies related to the housing market, including continued commitment to strengthen access to financing through a new mortgage securitization initiative that would improve access to capital for private lenders. Notably, in the area of market stimulus and incentives, and in response to briefs from industry, the government agreed to minimize market disruptions (that is, short-term stimulus incentives) seen to be damaging to the long-term health of the housing industry (CMHC 1986). As a consequence, the *National Direction* emphasized interventions to address need and social challenges (much like the more recent *National Housing Strategy* [CMHC 2017]).

Intent on reining in expenditure growth, the review also highlighted the mixed-income feature of the 1979–84 programs and reversed that policy, determining that limited resources should be directed to the most needy. The 1985 changes also took advantage of the demands from some (the larger) provinces for a more active role in program design and delivery, relegating the federal role more to one of funder (albeit on a cost-shared basis).

This change in the federal role created a new intergovernmental framework, with global and operating agreements executed in all provinces and territories (PTs). These agreements yielded considerably more direct and active roles to the PTs in exchange for cost-sharing at a minimum of 25 per cent of each program that the PT elected to deliver (Pomeroy 1989). CMHC remained responsible for residual programs (including federal cooperatives, the Urban Native Housing Program in many jurisdictions, and rehabilitation in some jurisdictions). As a result, many CMHC staff transferred into provincial ministries and agencies, and CMHC began a process of downsizing and substantially reduced its network of field offices.

1980s Spending Constraint and Constitutional Challenges

Over the following eight years, the Department of Finance sought to stall the growth in federal spending on social housing subsidies. Through a series of eight spending cuts from 1985 through 1992, there were a series of reductions in federal funding commitments. In aggregate, these reductions immediately cut federal spending by $560 million annually and, projecting the reductions forward, were estimated to lower planned federal spending between 1992 and 1998 by a further $1.265 billion (Carter 1997).

Together, these cuts reduced the trajectory of federal spending and made gradual reductions in annual outputs of new social housing (Carter 1997). Driven by concerns in the Department of Finance about the continued growth of federal housing expenditures (which reached $2 billion annually in 1993), these pressures to contain spending culminated in the 1993 federal budget. This budget terminated all new federal funding for social housing construction, except for on-reserve programs.[4]

While deficit concern and spending constraint were key factors, officials in the Department of Finance were aided and abetted by parallel constitutional negotiations. Housing was one of the "six-sisters," areas of exclusive jurisdiction claimed by the provinces (most emphatically by Quebec) in the Charlottetown Accord. While the accord was defeated in the Canadian and Quebec referenda, it nonetheless placed housing in the target for negotiated withdrawal.

Mid-1990s Devolution and a Declining Federal Role

Because most social housing programs were cost-shared and delivered by the PTs, the termination of federal funding in 1993 was followed by parallel reduction or termination of PT spending. Only British Columbia and Quebec (and Ontario until a 1995 change in government) continued to deliver unilaterally, but with a much-reduced budget and output.

While the federal spending power in combination with cost-sharing arrangements initially levered PT investment, when federal spending terminated, it had the opposite effect, relieving PTs of spending obligations and reinforcing cuts at the federal level.

With the PTs having taken on more active delivery of programs and responsible for ongoing oversight for subsidy and portfolio administration since 1986 (and in some cases since 1978), there was inevitable administrative overlap with similar CMHC functions related to the pre-1985 federal unilateral portfolios. For example, many housing providers had a number of federal funding agreements and subsequently agreements with their province, creating two parallel streams of compliance reporting. In order to pursue administrative simplification, the federal government directed CMHC to transfer this administrative responsibility to the PTs, as well as freezing the ongoing federal subsidies associated with historic commitments.

As noted, most programs had originally been funded with long-term (thirty-five and fifty years) operating agreements, which committed the federal government to ongoing subsidy payments (as these pre-existed at the time of termination for new project funding). The PTs were leery of potential risks and subsidy liabilities in taking on the federal administrative role and absorbing all future inflationary increases in subsidy cost. CMHC's negotiating strategy was that interest rates were falling, and upon mortgage renewals (most on five-year renewing terms), there would be substantial savings to offset any other operating cost increases. This strategy required a new set of bilateral agreements to define roles, liabilities, and obligations. Despite cabinet direction to implement these arrangements in 1996, for the aforementioned reasons, negotiations of the transfer bilateral social housing agreements (SHAs) were protracted, extending from 1997 beyond 2000. British Columbia did not execute an SHA until 2006, and Alberta eventually signed only in 2016. Quebec has persisted in refusing to execute a transfer agreement, as has Prince Edward Island.

The overall effect of first the 1986 global agreements, then the 1993 termination, and subsequently the post-1997 SHAs was an increasingly substantial reduction in the federal role and expertise in social and affordable housing and direct program delivery – a context that is important in the current onerous and slow implementation of the renewed federal role under the more recent National Housing Strategy (NHS), discussed below.

Modest Federal Re-engagement 1999–2001

By the latter 1990s, the Chrétien government had successfully tackled the deficit and, aided by a strong economic cycle, found itself in a new fiscal environment of budgetary surplus. This situation enabled the governing Liberals to revert to more centralist policy making, exploring ways to invest the fiscal dividend and repay voters for the suffering imposed by earlier program cuts – much of which impacted social spending (Suttor 2016; see also Prince's chapter 6 in this volume). Cognizant of lingering constitutional dynamics in the aftermath of the Meech Lake and Charlottetown Accords, the revitalization of federal social spending was framed in the 1998 Social Union Framework Agreement (SUFA). It required that any new social programming be developed in close negotiation with the PTs and yielded control over design and delivery to them (chapter 6, this volume).

Critics and observers of the 1993 termination of federal social housing funds associated the subsequent rise in visible homelessness to the cuts to social housing, and a variety of activist organizations (for example, the Toronto Disaster Relief Fund) as well as mainstream organizations like the Federation of Canadian Municipalities (at that time Jack Layton was president) mounted extensive campaigns to reinstate federal funding for social housing.

Following extensive analysis and recommendations from the Toronto Mayor's Homelessness Action Task Force in 1998, and stimulated by public outrage over deaths of homeless persons on the steps of Queens Park, the federal government in 1999 made a tentative re-entry, announcing a new National Homeless Initiative (NHI). Located in then Human Resources and Skills Development Canada (HRSDC; now Employment and Social Development Canada [ESDC]), rather than in CMHC, the initiative focused more on supporting the expansion of emergency and transitional shelters, with a deliberate attempt to manage and avoid the spending that would result from funding the construction of housing.

Then, in 2001, a new federal-provincial-territorial (FPT) Affordable Housing Framework Agreement set the stage to negotiate bilateral agreements with the PTs for the creation and delivery of a new Affordable Housing Initiative (AHI). At the insistence of the PTs, the framework agreement clearly identified the primary jurisdiction of the PTs in a set of principles that included the following:

- Provinces and territories have the primary responsibility for the design and delivery of housing programs within their jurisdiction.
- Provinces and territories require flexible programs to address their affordable housing needs and priorities.
- Nothing in this document shall be construed to derogate from the respective governments' jurisdictional responsibilities. (Affordable Housing Framework Agreement 2001)

In an effort to avoid exponential expenditure growth, the agreement avoided long-term ongoing subsidy (which can become non-discretionary) in favour of upfront capital funding (where the funding taps can be quickly shut off). The housing lexicon eschewed the term "social housing" in favour of "affordable housing." As explained by a CMHC vice president at the time, they associated the term "social housing" with ongoing subsidy; affordable housing had no such commitment.

PTs were required to match the federal capital on a 50/50 basis (unlike in 1986, when only a minimum 25 per cent commitment was required), and the initiative was delivered entirely via PT housing ministries and agencies.

Again, this arrangement provided opportunity for PTs to be active and to rebuild their expertise and competencies in program design and delivery (certain provinces, notably British Columbia and Quebec, were still active, but most had eroded capacity through the 1994–2001 period, other than managing ongoing operating subsidies and portfolio oversight).

Meanwhile, the CMHC role was mainly one of providing funding and oversight for the series of bilateral agreements that facilitated these arrangements, although, notwithstanding the above-noted principles, CMHC also sought to retain some control through prescriptive conditions over program design in the bilateral agreements.

A broad concern from sector stakeholders as well as from the PTs, which was emphasized in the later NHS consultations, was that these funding arrangements were time limited, initially for five years (2001–5) with subsequent extensions varying from one to three years. This uncertainty and unpredictability made it difficult to plan and create a pipeline of new affordable development.

Also, while the initial affordable housing bilateral agreements were quite prescriptive, through subsequent extensions the PTs gradually negotiated increased flexibilities, and funding could be used for a broader set of initiatives based on provincial needs and priorities – including rehabilitation, rental allowances, and assisted homeownership, in addition to new affordable rental development.

The funding quantum overall was quite modest (generally around $120 to $130 million annually) and at the project level up to $75,000 per unit, plus PT match, such that the resulting "affordable" rent levels were typically in the 80 to 100 per cent of the average market rent (AMR), which is substantially higher than the more deeply targeted rent-geared-to-income (RGI) levels in pre-1994 social housing.

The reporting on outcomes was weak, and there is a lack of detail on how many units were constructed or households assisted under different program options (Leone and Carroll 2010; Suttor 2016). CMHC published only a running total of households assisted, with no details. It is estimated that this agreement generated on average 7,500 units per year nationally (Suttor 2016) – far lower than the 25,000 to 30,000 under pre-1994 social housing and insignificant compared to the over one million renter households defined to be in need in 2011 under the CMHC core housing need measure.

During the Paul Martin–led minority Liberal government in 2004–5, the activist and centralist tendencies of the Liberals were further provoked by pressures from the New Democratic Party (NDP), by then led by Jack Layton, which held the balance of power. This conflict culminated in a budget agreement between Layton and Martin in 2005 to substantially increase funding for affordable housing in a one-off arrangement that created a series of three affordable housing trusts, totalling $1.4 billion to be invested over two years in the territories ($300 million); Indigenous off-reserve ($300 million); and $800 million to PTs on a per capita basis. Unlike the AHI funding, there was no cost-sharing obligation; these funds were simply conditional block transfers to the provinces, territories, and Indigenous organizations.

Although the Martin government fell in the fall of 2005, this budgetary commitment was honoured by the new Harper minority presaging the new government's policy stance on housing – one of expediency and pragmatism characterized by a "let sleeping dogs lie" approach. The federal spending on housing, while high due to the trusts, remained less than 1 per cent of federal program spending. It made no sense to expend political capital to terminate or reduce such a small budget (Pomeroy and Falvo 2013). And by funding these trusts as a block transfer to PT treasuries, rather than through formal agreements, any potential expansion of the federal (CMHC) role was minimized.

This period was followed by the global financial crisis and the need for economic stimulus, in which the Harper government saw social housing as a convenient tap to quickly open. With the FPT delivery framework already in place, it was easy to bolster the budget allocations under the AHI.

The Canada Economic Action Plan (CEAP) included $1 billion to help retrofit an aging social housing stock (most of which was owned or overseen by PT housing agencies) and a further $1.1 billion to support targeted affordable construction for seniors, First Nations, persons with disabilities, and the North. The primary motivation was employment generation; there was no policy commitment to address unmet housing needs, but again, as a case of political pragmatism, this government was able to take credit for both.

Following the maturing of the CEAP boost and the maturing of the AHI bilateral agreements, a new set of bilateral agreements were negotiated in 2011 to extend this initiative, but reverted it to the lower 2001–5 levels of funding. In a somewhat Machiavellian twist, a notable change in the 2011 bilateral agreements was the folding in of the renovation funding envelope into the bilateral arena. Prior to 2011, there was a parallel Residential Rehabilitation Assistance Program (RRAP) budget of an almost equal size ($128 million annually) that remained delivered and unilaterally funded mainly by CMHC. By moving this amount inside the bilateral agreements, it triggered a PT cost-sharing that effectively levered a further $125 million annually from PT budgets.

In a surprising but politically astute announcement in the 2013 budget, the Harper government announced, one year in advance, a five-year extension of the bilateral agreements: for the period 2014–19, Investments in Affordable Housing (IAH) would be allotted a total budget of $1.9 billion (essentially the same annual level of funding as the prior 2011–14 agreement framework when combining IAH and RRAP). This announcement occurred just as advocates were designing advocacy around renewing and strengthening the IAH agreements, which were scheduled to expire in March 2014, and accordingly pre-empted any advocacy.

Towards a National (Federal?) Housing Strategy 2017

Following the 2015 election, the Trudeau Liberals inherited these agreements. They immediately doubled the annual funding level in the 2016 budget alongside a commitment towards a national strategy outlined in the ministerial mandate letter to Jean-Yves Duclos, minister of Families, Children and Social Development. The letter tasked the minister "to develop a strategy to re-establish the federal government's role in supporting affordable housing ... [followed by an extensive list that included] finding ways to support the municipal construction of new housing units and refurbishment of existing ones; providing support to municipalities to maintain rent-geared-to-income subsidies in co-ops; providing communities the money they need for Housing First initiatives that help homeless Canadians find stable housing" (Office of the Prime Minister 2015). To paraphrase the prime minister's pronouncements to the international community, "we're back," this new mandate signalled a significant re-engagement of the federal government in the housing arena, with language that again captured the provisions of the old spending powers to leapfrog the PTs and work directly with municipalities and community organizations.

To pursue this mandate, Duclos, the minister responsible for CMHC, instructed CMHC officials, in collaboration with the ESDC Homeless Secretariat, to embark on an extensive consultation on how this renewed federal role should be shaped. It included working with an FPT Strategic Working Group to review and assess ideas submitted in the consultation.

While a CMHC (2016) report, *What We Heard*, suggested active collaboration and participation of the PTs, it seems these discussions were not necessarily harmonious. As described below, last-minute changes to the funding and allocations to the PTs caused consternation (removing $2 billion from the rebranded IAH and shifting these funds into a newly announced Canada Housing Benefit, but without PT concurrence).

Despite assertions that CMHC had worked in close partnership with the PTs, it took an additional five months until April 2018 to come to agreement on the

NHS Framework Agreement and over a year to execute some of the bilateral agreements needed to implement the cost-shared parts of the NHS. As it had in prior FPT communiques, Quebec explicitly announced it would not sign onto the proposed NHS Framework "unless the strategy fully respects Quebec's programs and jurisdiction in the matter" (CMHC 2018a).

Quebec's aspirations (and possibly those of other provinces) conflicted with many long-term stakeholders and advocates, who harkened back to the "good old days" when CMHC was delivering social housing, with peak outputs in the 1980s exceeding 25,000 social housing units per year, and advocated for a return of federal leadership. Cognizant of PT tensions, the *What We Heard* report (released in November 2016) downplayed this aspect but did include a short chapter, "The Role of Government," in which it stated: "Canadians told us that roles and responsibilities for housing should be clarified and collaboration strengthened. In general, respondents favor an expanded role for CMHC in support of a federal leadership role in housing" (CMHC 2016, 40).

While the NHS was not released until November 2017, it was presaged by the 2017 federal budget in March, which identified planned spending to support the strategy. In a speech to the Canadian Club on 1 June 2017, CMHC CEO Evan Siddall (2006) proudly promoted the forthcoming NHS, stating: "All in all, combining Budget 2016 and 2017, the government has committed over $30 billion to housing in Canada from 2016–17 until 2027–2028, on top of the $18 billion previously committed. *We can confidently call that a renewed federal leadership role in housing*" (emphasis added).

In sum, at the political level, there were federal aspirations for a more engaged and activist federal role, and these were largely encouraged by many stakeholders, especially outside of Quebec. Concurrently, CMHC officials were excited by the prospect of getting back into direct delivery – despite having lost much of the expertise and field infrastructure to support such a role.

But the extent of CMHC attempts to control the design of the NHS and to deliver much of the new spending begs the question as to whether this program is a national or a federal strategy.

The 2017 Announcement of the National Housing Strategy

In November 2017, following almost two years of consultations, the federal government unveiled a new National Housing Strategy. It was announced as the first-ever national strategy and largest-ever federal funding commitment to housing in Canada. Both assertions have been contested as hyperbole (Pomeroy 2017; Young 2019; PBO 2019).

The NHS is more narrowly an affordable housing strategy, rather than a fully comprehensive housing strategy (Hulchanski 2017), with a specific focus on vulnerable households, and it contains only token discussion of the housing market and issues related to rental supply and access to ownership (under the rubric of "balanced markets").

It sets two overarching goals to accomplish:

1. reduce the severity of housing need for 530,000 renter households (this number was 50 per cent of the 2011 estimate of renter need, the most recent data available at that time); and
2. reduce chronic homelessness by 50 per cent (subsequently revised to 100 per cent reduction in the 2020 Fall Economic Statement).

To achieve these goals, it outlined a range of programs directed to

- preserve and improve the legacy stock of public and social community housing created mainly between the early 1960s and 1994;
- address persisting unmet housing needs through a combination of programming to support new construction of affordable housing and a new demand-side approach of housing allowances, branded as the Canada Housing Benefit;
- strengthen the federal response to homelessness via enhancements to the federal homeless partnering strategy (subsequently rebranded as "Reaching Home"); and
- undertake a number of ancillary initiatives, including expanding funding to access surplus federal lands, improving housing market data, and strengthening the university-based research capacity (which is almost non-existent in the housing area since the late 1980s).

It also introduced the concept of the gender-based analysis (GBA+) lens, committed to evidence-based research and data reporting, and announced future legislation to embed a commitment to the progressive realization of the right to housing.

The NHS, framed as a national rather than a federal strategy, sought to present a united front with PTs through joint programming; it also reversed the long trend of federal devolution and disentanglement with significant re-engagement of CMHC in the design and delivery of unilateral federal initiatives. This change can be seen in the structure of initiatives in the NHS, overviewed below.

It is also important to note that the NHS, while seeking a significant announcement as "the largest ever level of funding and so on," achieves that claim through creative accounting. First, it uses a ten-year budget window, compared to the more standard five years. It also adds in PT expenditures linked via cost-shared programs, counts pre-existing ongoing legacy funding commitments from the earlier thirty-five- to fifty-year subsidy agreements, and conflates budgetary (grants and contributions) and non-budgetary expenditures (low-rate loans that take advantage of the federal governments' credit rating and financing facility – $11.2 billion of initial $40 billion was in the form of loans – now $34.4 billion in an increased total of $70 billion).

NHS Dual Funding Streams, with Diminished PT Transfers

The NHS embraces two primary funding streams:

- programs delivered under bilateral agreements with provinces and territories that require cost-matching funding from PTs; and
- unilateral federal funding.

The intent and objective of each program/initiative are detailed in the bilateral agreements, which also dictate that all PTs prepare an action plan detailing how the fund will be allocated between eligible purposes, with specific annual targets intended to contribute to the overall goals of the NHS.

The bilateral initiatives include funding for a rebranded Affordable Housing Initiative, funding to preserve legacy social housing where long-term subsidies are expiring, and a new Canada Housing Benefit (CHB). Together, these streams are budgeted to receive $7.4 billion in federal funding, cost-matched by PTs to total $14.8 billion.

The unilateral federal programs include a new unilateral National Housing Co-Investment Fund (NHCF), intended to support expansion of affordable housing development ($13.2 billion);[5] an incentive program to stimulate private rental construction;[6] Reaching Home – the rebranded Homeless Partnering Strategy – through which unilateral federal homeless funding is delivered; and a number of smaller ancillary initiatives.

The elements of the NHS were implemented gradually, commencing in April 2018 with the federal unilateral NHCF and the smaller ancillary initiatives, while the federal lands program was implemented in June 2018.

The initiatives under the bilateral agreements commenced April 2019, except the CHB, which was scheduled to be implemented in April 2020. This initiative is now being implemented, with all PTs having signed amendments to the NHS bilateral agreements to encompass this activity.

While it is still early in the implementation phase, there is already some experience and insight into the various components of the NHS and some useful lessons. These suggest a number of potential refinements to strengthen and enhance the NHS and improve the trajectory of outcomes towards realizing the goals of the NHS – reducing housing need and chronic homelessness, each by at least 50 per cent. Notably, while reducing chronic homelessness (by 50 per cent) is one of the two main objectives of the NHS, Reaching Home received only $2.2 billion of the initial $40 billion announced funding.

Under subsequent budgets since 2017 through 2022, the NHS funding has been expanded to just over $72 billion. Most of this increase is via increased ($23.75 billion) loan authority for the unilateral federal Rental Construction Financing Initiative (RCFI) and capital contribution to cover 100 per cent of the cost to build permanent supportive housing for those exiting homelessness under the Rapid Housing Initiative (total $4 billion in three budgets 2020, 2021, 2022). Smaller temporary funding was also announced for the federal homeless initiative Reaching Home to address costs associated with COVID-19 measures in emergency shelters. *Budget 2022* also presented a series of additional initiatives, mostly outside of the NHS, including a $4 billion fund intended to address lack of new housing supply (claimed to be the cause of excessive home price increases) and initiatives to stall speculative investment (Department of Finance 2022).

Discussion

Lack of Federal Delivery Capacity

Through the period of devolution commencing in 1986 and extending after 1994, CMHC lost much of its capacity to deliver programs. This loss included the closure of a vast network of over ninety field offices, most staffed with expertise in underwriting, project management, appraisal, market analysis, and program administration and all with strong local knowledge and relationships. In addition, under the 1986 devolution, many experienced staff transferred to work in provincial/territorial/municipal housing ministries/agencies, and many have since retired.

As a result, CMHC has very limited experience and has faced a considerable learning curve in returning to direct delivery. There have been extensive delays, weak project management, and extensive frustration among community-based providers and private rental developers seeking to access these new programs (PBO 2019, 2021).

There are also distributional concerns. Unlike other funding programs, the budget for the federal initiatives that account for 85 per cent of the now $72 billion NHS is not geographically allocated across the PTs; rather, it is a first-come-first-served model and caters only to regions/communities that are able to contribute significant funds as "co-investment," notably Ontario, where municipalities have a larger statutory role and involvement. In addition, in jurisdictions that have been very proactive and have extensive expertise and working relationships, as well as unilateral programs outside of the NHS (especially British Columbia and Quebec), potential partners – community-based non-profit and co-op groups – seem to prefer to pursue options via the province, eschewing the federal programs, their cumbersome application processes, and minimal grant assistance.

At the same time, because they have been delivering programs since 2001, the PT organizations have built expertise and competencies in program delivery (processing time under PT-delivered IAH [now the Provincial-Territorial Priorities Fund (PTPF)] is substantially shorter than the CMHC-delivered NHCF) and have extensive local relationships. Rather than build on this capacity, the NHS belittled it.

Initially, a modest expansion on funding under the IAH cost-shared program was signalled in the 2017 federal budget. This expansion would have raised annual funding from $253 million per year to $310 million and thereby levered PT cost-sharing while taking advantage of the existing delivery expertise.

But in an eleventh-hour decision to add the Canada Housing Benefit (CHB) into the suite of new initiatives, CMHC unilaterally withdrew its $2 billion from the cost-shared IAH pot in order to fund the CHB. This decision meant that the quantum of funding in IAH (rebranded as PTPF) was reduced below the average levels of the pre-2016 era.

Meanwhile, two CMHC unilateral programs, the National Housing Co-Investment Fund (NHCF) and the Rental Construction Financing Initiative (RCFI) have emerged as the flagships of renewed federal engagement.

The RCFI was only tangentially mentioned in the NHS document and was initially subsumed within the NHCF envelope, even though it is not targeted to meet low-income need. It is a market supply initiative, with a very modest affordability component. This program has been strongly criticized for pretending to address affordability when the design completely misses the mark on any reasonable definition of affordability (PBO 2019; Pomeroy 2021). As of late 2020, the RCFI has become the single largest element in the NHS with a budget of $27.75 billion, over one-third of NHS funding (which now exceeds $72 billion), albeit exclusively in the form of low-rate loans.

Meanwhile, the NHCF is also primarily a loan fund with minimal grant (structured as a forgivable loan). As such, the subsidy level is insufficient to penetrate to low-income affordable need without considerable complementary contributions from other parties – including non-profits with land that can be intensified; some capital reserves; faith-based organizations with land; municipal contributions, again including land as well as waiving development fees and charges; and notably, substantial PT contributions.

The latter is ironic and an affront to the PT expertise. Having diminished the funding for the PPF delivery, the NHCF subsequently relies on PT contributions to the unilateral federal flagship program.

The evidence to date reveals that, in order to achieve viable projects with some modicum of affordability, it is often necessary to rely on PT contributions. Indeed, all but two of the final approved projects to March 2019 include PT contributions, and often significant ones. For example, one NHCF project in British Columbia involved a $3.9 million NHCF contribution (primarily in the form of a loan), while the province is contributing $8.7 million in grants, along with a small in-kind contribution (fee waiver) from the City of Kelowna.

Lack of Transparency and Objective Reporting

One of the key commitments in the NHS was towards collecting sound data and using objective data to support empirically based policy development or refinement. Despite this goal, reporting to date has been minimal and heavily politicized.

Progress reports have been released by the minister's office, and reporting aligned with the term of the Trudeau government (which presents spending since fourth quarter 2015; see, for example, CMHC 2018b). There is no publicly available data set that objectively reports on units created/retrofit, households assisted by jurisdiction or by year, or the nature of assistance, whether rents are affordable, and to what income level. The "progress to date" page of the CMHC-NHS website simply lists the total budget for each initiative and the aggregate of funding announced and units associated as of the current quarter and removes data from prior quarters, so monitoring of incremental or annual progress is impossible (Government of Canada n.d.).

With the NHS being quite recent, minimal progress has been made to date, so reporting is mainly in the form of announced funding commitments rather than units built or households subsidized.

Other than the aforementioned web page progress summary, two progress reports have been issued to date. The first was released on the one-year anniversary in November 2018 (prior to commencement of the bilateral initiatives) and the second in June 2019, immediately prior to the federal election. Both included exaggerated claims, counting all units delivered prior to 1994, simply because new NHS funds can now be used to retrofit some of these units. The progress reports also included pre-NHS commitments under IAH. This practice, for example, enabled the headline in the 2018 anniversary report to read "Government of Canada Provides Housing Support for Almost 1 Million Canadian Families."

Summary and Conclusions

This chapter has traced the evolving roles of the federal and provincial-territorial governments in the area of housing policy and programming, most particularly in the area of assisted housing. It highlights the early domination of the federal government, drawing on the federal spending powers to carve its role, and the subsequent ascendance of the provinces, through periods of competitive unilateralism, cooperative federalism, and subsequently devolution to the provinces and territories.

Contrary to the view of Leone and Carroll (2010) that, once a policy area is devolved, the likelihood that it becomes recentralized is remote, we have witnessed a substantial re-engagement of the federal government, increasingly stepping on the toes of the provinces and territories, and sweeping aside PT consternation with a single-minded goal of reasserting a substantial federal role. Perhaps a centralist tendency is in the DNA of the Trudeau bloodline.

The National Housing Strategy is the primary evidence in this federal aspiration and begs the question: While paying homage to the need to work collaboratively and to have strong partnerships, is it really a national strategy or a federal one?

The reduction of the established cost-shared funding model – Investments in Affordable Housing (IAH) – has diminished the PT role as well as the level of PT investment in some jurisdictions. In others, the traditional powerhouses in social housing, British Columbia and Quebec, are essentially ignoring the NHS unilateral initiatives and continue to hoe their own roads and build and subsidize their own houses.

As the unilateral federal part of the NHS, the co-investment fund should not be seeking to impose additional financial contributions from the PTs beyond those in the bilateral arrangement (unless enhancing the federal contribution to these PT-delivered initiatives).

Rather than the federal funds helping to rebalance investment and capacity, we see the emergence of a very uneven set of playing fields, especially in the absence of a fair share or needs-based allocation formula in the use of federal funds. Because the design of the flagship National Housing Co-Investment Fund relies on co-investment, it is inevitably skewed in favour of those jurisdictions that are better resourced co-funding partners – to the detriment of other jurisdictions.

Arguably, in the early phase of the NHS, we have returned to an era of unilateral federalism. The attempt for federal domination overrides federal leadership, which might more effectively help to address need more evenly across the country and enable and encourage rather than dissuade PT involvement.

While the implementation of the NHS is still in its early days, and objective reporting on progress to date remains lacking, there is hope that this situation will improve. CMHC officials repeatedly speak of "taking stock" to assess the implementation and, hopefully, to refine and adjust.

One area they should carefully examine is the role and established capacity of the PTs in program delivery in juxtaposition to their own delivery struggles. This examination should be accompanied by realignment in funding to provide increased quantum of funds to the bilateral programs and reduction in the federal unilateral pot, which would both lever additional PT resources as well as better utilize established PT capacity and, as an aside, respect the Constitution.

NOTES

1 This federal view was rejected by Quebec as unconstitutional and was central to the tensions between Canada and Quebec that have persisted; it was one of five main concerns in the constitutional debates that commenced in the mid-1980s (Banting, 1990).
2 The fact that these dwellings were temporary and usually located in proximity to wartime factories created subsequent pressures and opportunities for urban renewal and redevelopment of these well-located areas.
3 The Advisory Committee on Reconstruction included subcommittee reports on Social Security for Canada, named after Leonard Marsh as the "Marsh Report" (1943), and on Housing and Planning, named the "Curtis Report" (1944) after its chair.
4 With some delay in completing funded projects, the portfolio of public and social housing peaked in 1995 at 6.4 per cent of all housing in Canada. Since then, due to construction of market housing, the relative scale of the social housing sector has declined (now under 5 per cent of all housing).
5 NHCF was initially announced as a $15.7 billion initiative, but this amount included the previously (2016) announced $2.5 billion Rental Construction Finance Initiative (RCFI), which was subsequently separated out and expanded. It also included $200 million for the Federal Lands Initiative. Adjusting for these initiatives reduces NHCF to $13.2 billion, of which $8.1 million is in loans.
6 Initially announced in 2016 at $2.5 billion, the Rental Construction Finance Initiative (RCFI) was enhanced first with an addition of $1.25 billion in the 2018 budget and, subsequently, with a further $10 billion in the 2019 budget and $12 billion in the 2019 Fall Economic Statement (FES) over nine years to 2028.

REFERENCES

Affordable Housing Framework Agreement. 2001. "A Framework to Guide Housing Initiatives in Canada by the Provincial and Territorial (P/T) Ministers Responsible for Housing." https://scics.ca/en/product-produit/a-framework-to-guide-housing-initiatives-in-canada-by-the-provincial-and-territorial-pt-ministers-responsible-for-housing/.
Banting, Keith. 1990. "Social Housing in a Divided State." In *Housing the Homeless Poor: New Partnerships among the Private, Public, and Third Sectors*, edited by Alex L. Murray and George Fallis, 115–63. Toronto: University of Toronto Press.
Carter, Tom. 1997. "Current Practices for Procuring Affordable Housing: The Canadian Context." *Housing Policy Debate* 8, no. 3: 593–631. https://doi.org/10.1080/10511482.1997.9521268.
CMHC (Canada Mortgage and Housing Corporation). 1984. *Social Housing Review: Background Document for Federal Consultations on Housing*. Ottawa: CMHC.
– 1986. *A National Direction for Housing Solutions*. Ottawa: CMHC.

- 2016. *What We Heard: Shaping Canada's National Housing Strategy*. Ottawa: CMHC.
- 2017. *National Housing Strategy*. Ottawa: CMHC.
- 2018a. "Federal, Provincial and Territorial Ministers Endorse New Housing Partnership Framework." News Release, 9 April 2018. https://scics.ca/en/product-produit/news-release-federal-provincial-and-territorial-ministers-endorse-new-housing-partnership-framework/.
- 2018b. *Getting Housing Right: A Progress Report on Federal Housing Investments*. Ottawa: CMHC.

Department of Finance Canada. 2022. *Budget 2022: A Plan to Grow Our Economy and Make Life More Affordable*. Ottawa: Queens Printer. https://www.budget.canada.ca/2022/home-accueil-en.html.

Government of Canada. n.d. "Progress on the National Housing Strategy." https://www.placetocallhome.ca/progress-on-the-national-housing-strategy.

- 1985. *Housing Programs: In Search of Balance: A Study Team Report to the Task Force on Program Review*. Task Force on Program Review, Erik Nielsen, chair. Ottawa: Task Force on Program Review.

Hogue, Robert. 2022. "Budget 2022 Is Big on Housing But Won't Immediately Relieve Affordability Crisis." Special Housing Reports, Royal Bank of Canada, 8 April 2022. https://thoughtleadership.rbc.com/budget-2022-is-big-on-housing-but-wont-immediately-relieve-affordability-crisis/.

Hulchanski, J. David. 2017. "No, Ottawa Has Not Put Forth a National Housing Strategy." *Globe and Mail*, 4 December 2017. https://www.theglobeandmail.com/opinion/no-ottawa-has-not-put-forth-a-national-housing-strategy/article37173057/.

Leone, Roberto, and Barbara Carroll. 2010. "Decentralizing and Devolution in Canadian Social Housing Policy." *Environment and Planning C: Government and Policy* 28, no. 3: 389–404. https://doi.org/10.1068/c09153.

Miron, John. 1993. *House, Home, and Community: Progress in Housing Canadians*. Montreal and Kingston: McGill-Queen's University Press.

Office of the Prime Minister. 2015. "Minister of Families, Children, and Social Development Mandate Letter." 12 November 2015. Ottawa: PMO. https://pm.gc.ca/en/mandate-letters/2015/11/12/archived-minister-families-children-and-social-development-mandate.

PBO (Parliamentary Budget Officer). 2019. *Federal Program Spending on Housing Affordability*. Ottawa: Office of the Parliamentary Budget Officer. https://www.pbo-dpb.gc.ca/web/default/files/Documents/Reports/2019/Housing_Affordability/Federal%20Spending%20on%20Housing%20Affordability%20EN.pdf.

- 2021. *Federal Program Spending on Housing Affordability in 2021*. Ottawa: Office of the Parliamentary Budget Officer. https://distribution-a617274656661637473.pbo-dpb.ca/c14c97d8ca19d3036782918415de2bd3c976a66ed53e0030daf83b206c8d36e1.

Pomeroy, Steve. 1989. "The Recent Evolution of Social Housing in Canada." *Canadian Housing* 6, no. 1: 6–13.

- 1995. "Influences on Housing Policy through the Year 2000: A Canadian Perspective on Housing Policy." *Housing Policy Debate* 6, no. 3: 619–53. https://doi.org/10.1080/10511482.1995.9521198.
- 2017. "Making Sense of the Funding Allocations in the National Housing Strategy." *CURE Brief*, no. 9. Ottawa: Centre for Urban Research and Education (CURE), University of Carleton. https://carleton.ca/cure/wp-content/uploads/CURE-Brief-9-Assessing-the-Funding-in-the-National-Housing-Strategy.pdf.
- 2021. "Toward Evidence Based Policy: Assessing the CMHC Rental Housing Finance Initiative." *CURE Brief*, no. 12. Ottawa: Centre for Urban Research and Education (CURE), University of Carleton. https://carleton.ca/cure/wp-content/uploads/CURE-Brief-12-RCFI-1.pdf.

Pomeroy, Steve, and Nick Falvo. 2013. "Pragmatism and Political Expediency: Housing Policy under the Harper Regime." In *How Ottawa Spends, 2013–2014: The Harper Government: Mid-Term Blues and Long-Term Plans*, edited by Christopher Stoney and G. Bruce Doern, 184–95. Montreal and Kingston: McGill-Queen's University Press.

Rose, Albert. 1980. *Canadian Housing Policies (1935–1980)*. Toronto: Butterworth.

Siddall, Evan. 2006. "No Solitudes: A Canadian National Housing Strategy." Speech to the Canadian Club, 1 June 2006. https://www.cmhc-schl.gc.ca/en/corp/nero/sp/2017/2017-06-01-1245.cfm.

Suttor, Greg. 2016. *Still Renovating: A History of Canadian Social Housing Policy*. Montreal and Kingston: McGill-Queen's University Press.

Wolfe, Jeanne M. 1998. "Canadian Housing Policy in the Nineties." *Housing Studies* 13, no. 1: 131–4. https://doi.org/10.1080/02673039883524.

Young, Margot. 2019. "Policy Brief: The National Housing Strategy." Broadbent Institute, 6 September 2019. https://www.broadbentinstitute.ca/margotyoung/policy_brief_national_housing_strategy.

15 Public Infrastructure Financing and Multilevel Governance in Canada

ERIC CHAMPAGNE AND ARACELLY DENISE GRANJA

Introduction

Financing infrastructure has increasingly become a vital recourse employed by both central and local governments as a means of injecting the necessary financial assets to maintain and/or fortify a state's economy (Lee 2019). Governments are elected to finance public infrastructure, facilitate infrastructural growth, safeguard their national interests, and ensure their ability to provide their citizenry with essential goods and services. Public infrastructure is essentially a set of goods and services that the private sector (on its own) would be unable to adequately supply. In addition, public infrastructure also encompasses key welfare benefits (Lee 2019). It has been demonstrated historically that, in Canada, the financing of public infrastructure is heavily reliant on collaboration between the different levels of government (Doern, Stoney, and Hilton 2021). The degree of governmental cohesion normally dictates whether the outcome of the investment will be negative or positive. Therefore, for an exercise of financing to be effective, all three levels of government must work together. Historically, the importance of multilevel governance has proven to be particularly vital in public infrastructure funding (Champagne 2013).

This chapter seeks to address three questions. First, what are the existing federal, provincial, and municipal public policies in terms of financing public infrastructure? Second, what are the institutional arrangements, intergovernmental pacts, and policy instruments in place that allow the federal government to intervene in municipal affairs? And third, how do federal investments influence municipal infrastructure planning and management? In order to respond to these questions, this chapter concentrates its examination on the Canadian context. Canada has a federal political system in which the responsibilities are divided between the federal, provincial/territorial, and municipal governments. Consequently, it is a prime example of multilevel governance at work. In addressing these questions, this chapter intends to highlight the role of local governments, which are too often overshadowed by their federal and provincial counterparts. The study of investments in basic infrastructure allows for the integration of municipalities into research on fiscal federalism (multilevel governance) that goes beyond constitutional issues. The need for municipal-level integration is because, even though municipalities can be dubbed the "creatures" of the provinces as they remain under provincial jurisdiction, through their continual development they have gained greater recognition as a governmental power. The municipal level of government has taken on great importance, particularly if one examines Canada's larger cities, which are often bigger in population size than some provinces. However, while our analysis emphasizes the growing role of municipalities, we also acknowledge that, structurally, municipalities continue to be devalued and have considerable limits in authority along with limited fiscal revenue sources and spending. As Enid Slack describes in chapter 13, "Cities in Canadian Fiscal Federalism," local governments remain confined by old funding models, are heavily dependent on conditional transfers, and have a limited role in policy discussions. In the housing sector, Steve Pomeroy's chapter 14 does a good job of describing the challenges of policy development and the funding of social housing and homelessness policies by addressing accountability issues between levels of government. In a recent book, Alison Smith (2022) clearly describes the "barriers" to homelessness policies that are greatly explained by the issues associated with multilevel governance in Canada. Based on previous works (Champagne 2012, 2013, 2014; Champagne and Choinière 2016), we describe in this chapter how municipal infrastructure financing requires collaboration between the three levels of government in the policy and spending process and discuss the challenges of multilevel governance in this policy sector.

This chapter is divided into three sections. The first section provides a brief literature review in which the key concept of multilevel governance is discussed. This section also outlines the roles of political actors at the federal, provincial/territorial, and municipal levels. Additionally, it stresses the importance of policy coherence in public infrastructure policies and management. The second section explores the investment shares in public infrastructure spending by the order of government. Finally, the third section provides an overview of federal policies and funding instruments. The chapter concludes by discussing the possible infrastructural responses in the face of new challenges.

Multilevel Governance: The Three Levels of Government

To begin our analysis of financing infrastructure, it is important that we clearly outline our conceptualization of multilevel governance. This section serves to examine the roles and responsibilities of each level of government. This discussion is essential to illustrate the need for policy coherence as a way of financing public infrastructure in Canada.

Multilevel Governance

The term multilevel governance (MLG) was first employed in the early 1990s. It was coined by political scientist Gary Marks in the making of the European Union: "The concept aimed in particular to capture and understand political processes related to the emergence of supranational institutions such as the European Union and to facilitate analysis of decentralized decision-making processes, in which sub-national level governments and civil society have come to have increasing influence" (Saito-Jensen 2015, 2).

Explicitly, "the concept of MLG comprises numerous State and non-state actors located at different levels, such as the local (sub-national), the national and the global (supranational)" (Saito-Jensen 2015, 2). This chapter focuses on the interactions that take place at the subnational and national levels.

Within the literature, there are two prominent approaches that constitute multilevel governance theory. First, scholars like Hooghe and Marks (2003) focus their analysis on the origins and structures of MLG, mainly as it applies to the Westphalian order. These authors focus on the role of political mobilizations and lobbying (Hooghe 1995), as well as on the importance of creating political coalitions between the different levels of government within the state (Christiansen 1997). This group of academics contends that the structural implications of multilevel governance are the result of globally historic circumstances, which can be used to formulate a theory of state transformation (Tortola 2017). Although the procedural and transformative nature of multilevel governance is important, this chapter bases its examination on the second theory in the literature, which looks at multilevel governance as a means of explaining the implementation of public policy.

MLG as it relates to the elaboration of public policy focuses on how ideas, advocacy coalitions, policy networks, and the stages of the policy cycle are all responsive to how the different levels of government interact and work together (Tortola 2017). This line of reasoning investigates how policy is created, how it is placed on the government agenda, and how it is implemented in response to state institutions, processes, and structures. In other words, MLG implements a specific federally constituted political system. Specifically, it discusses how different political and economic actors, both from the public and private sectors, develop and advocate for a proposed policy solution. It considers how the interactions between these agents are influenced by the level of government to which they belong, their partisan political interests, and the outcome they wish to achieve. Overall, with reference to public policy, MLG is impacted by the roles, responsibilities, and interactions between key political actors at the local, regional, and national levels.

In Canada, a new way of studying intergovernmental relations, inspired by the notion of MLG, emerged in the early 2000s. Under the leadership of Robert

Young (Horak, Sancton, and Bramwell 2021), several Canadian researchers have devoted part of their research to MLG in many public policy areas such as urban issues, infrastructure, immigration, emergency management, social housing, immigration, and Aboriginal issues, to name a few (Tolley and Young 2011; Harvey and Young 2012; Horak and Young 2012; Peters 2012; Henstra 2013; Ircha and Young 2013; Andrew and Graham 2014). Our research perspective borrows from and is part of this research tradition.

As mentioned above, Canada's political system is divided into three levels of government: federal, provincial/territorial, and municipal. Subsequently, this section identifies the key players at each level and examines their mandated roles and responsibilities as it relates to infrastructure.

Federal Level of Government

From an MLG perspective, the federal government is the highest level of political authority in Canada. One of the federal government's main roles is to ensure the national citizenry's well-being through the use of social programs. This function is fulfilled with the provinces/territories, which is why the government spends approximately 20 per cent of its federal funding on transfers to the other levels of government to fund health care and other social programs (Azzi 2006). Over the past few decades, a proportion of federal transfers have been employed to finance infrastructure development in the provinces/territories and their respective municipalities. The allocation of federal funding for infrastructure is primarily carried out by Infrastructure Canada, the national ministry of infrastructure.

Infrastructure Canada provides federal funding to the provinces/territories for projects "across a variety of sectors such as transportation, water, energy, and social infrastructure" (Siemiatycki 2021). However, despite the central government's financial support, it has minimal jurisdiction over basic infrastructure decisions. The federal government's role in relation to basic public infrastructure is limited to the funding programs it develops and implements.

In other words, through the implementation of federal programs like the Investing in Canada Plan, Infrastructure Canada can exert some influence over the provinces by establishing bilateral agreements that dictate how federal funds will be allocated across the country's provinces and subsequently to their municipal affiliates. The central government's superior financing capabilities allow it to engage more closely with both provincial and municipal development. Therefore, even though the federal government's infrastructural ownership is scarce, its funding power allows it to exercise a certain degree of influence over provincial and municipal policy issues. Yet, the extent of this influence consistently remains an issue of contention with the provincial/territorial governments.

Provincial/Territorial Level of Government

The provincial/territorial level of government is second only in power to the federal government. In the context of this chapter, we will focus more on provincial jurisdictions rather than on territorial governments as both have different administrative and power arrangements with the federal government. Among the three levels of government, the provincial and federal levels of government overlap the most, a fact that continues to cause political tension and disputes. As is best illustrated by Alain Noël's chapter 19 and Ken Boessenkool's chapter 21 in this volume, since Confederation, the provinces (most consistently Quebec and Alberta) have sought to gain greater equality of power in comparison to the central government. They have maintained that the federal government should not intervene in provincial matters as these areas are not in its constitutional purview or jurisdiction. The question of whether or not the federal government is legally able under the Constitution to interfere in provincial matters has been an issue of much debate, especially when it comes to the division of resources and the allocation of public funds.

The request for greater federal funding in basic infrastructure stems mainly from the fact that the provinces must ensure that their populations have equitable access to social programs and that the federal financing they receive is adequately distributed among their municipalities. Hence, even though the provinces remain firm on wanting to limit federal interference in regional affairs, they opportunely recognize their need for federal support and dub it the central government's responsibility to provide provincial funding. Consequently, through federal shared-cost programs and transfer payments, provincial investments in infrastructure have been stimulated by the central government since the mid-1990s. The provinces/territories rely on federal support to supplement their regional income, which derives mainly from direct taxation and regional fiscal programs. It is through multilevel governance and economic cost-sharing that the provincial governments have been able to partly fund the massive infrastructural needs of both their region and municipal subsidiaries (Champagne 2013, 2014).

Municipal Level of Government

As is well described by Enid Slack's chapter 13 in this volume, the municipal level of government is the most subordinate and dependent of the three levels of government. Constitutionally, municipal government power is reliant on the jurisdiction of the provinces. But over time, provinces have transferred many responsibilities of local nature to the municipalities. Today, Canadian municipalities are commonly responsible for overseeing the parks, parking, libraries, roadways, public transportation, community waterways, sewers, garbage collection, local land use, and police and fire services (Government of Canada 2017). The municipal governments are led by mayors who are elected in local elections. Other administrative bodies such as school boards, municipal councils, and police commissions are also often elected at the local level (Magnusson 2006). All of these electoral processes contribute to the continual fortification of Canadian democracy and have given municipal governments greater political legitimacy, especially since local governments are held more accountable to their communities as they are perceived to be members of the same social groups. Overall, municipal governments embody the most visible representation of local initiatives, political involvement, and citizen participation.

In relation to their sources of revenue, municipalities have limited power regarding taxation and borrowing when compared to the more senior levels of government. As such, they are highly dependent on federal and provincial transfers (Slack 2017). These transfers are conditional in connection with the specific programs from which they emanate. Furthermore, federal transfers are normally wired to the provinces/territories, which then distribute the money to their municipalities in relation to population size and financial need. In relation to municipal infrastructure, the federal government's support is normally directed towards the maintenance and renovation of old and run-down structures, for instance in the transportation, sewage, and building sectors. Without federal and provincial assistance, cities across the country would be unable to sustain, let alone encourage, municipal development. Yet, despite their reliance on federal and provincial support, municipalities are able to generate some income independently. Though limited, municipalities can proceed with some income through the imposition of property taxes and service pricing (Horak and Young 2012).

Collectively, all three levels of government must contribute to the maintenance of a stable economic system and the promotion of infrastructural development. In order to fulfil this role, however, cohesion among the three levels of government is needed so as to efficiently invest public funds and ensure that the continued production of goods and services remains relatively unscathed.

Public Infrastructure Financing in Canada

The literature on the financing of public infrastructure as well as multilevel governance is quite extensive. Here is how Jones and Llewellyn (2019, R61–2) have recently defined the term "infrastructure": "Infrastructure encompasses both tangible and non-tangible assets. It amounts to the structures that enable people, capital, commodities, manufactures, water, energy, information and more to move efficiently both within, and into and out of, a country. It therefore includes the assets that underpin the networks for transportation; power generation, distribution and storage; communications; waste management; and water distribution and treatment."

Governments at all levels work (at least partially) to ensure the healthy development of infrastructure as it contributes to the overall preservation of a strong economy. In Canada, multilevel cooperation to finance infrastructure, particularly at the local level, was not always prevalent. In the 1970s, the federal government neglected the importance of cities (Andrew, Graham, and Phillips 2002). During this time, the central and provincial governments did not prioritize municipal infrastructural projects; on the contrary, they actually reduced their overall investment in public infrastructure (Champagne 2014). Subsequently, multilevel governance remained for a long time in a state of infancy (Horak and Young 2012). Throughout Brian Mulroney's Conservative government (1984–93), the federal government remained unwilling to intervene in provincial-municipal affairs and did not provide municipalities with funding for infrastructure (Bojorquez, Champagne, and Vaillancourt 2009). This situation has since changed, as Canadian cities have seen major growth in population and have developed into cultural and economic metropolitan hubs: "Economically, their weight in the national totals of employment and production steadily increases. They continue to be the centres of cultural life. In most provinces, laws that stipulate the range of their functions have been amended to provide more scope for autonomous political action" (Horak and Young 2012, 3).

Consequently, collective infrastructural investment between the federal and municipal governments has developed significantly since the mid-1990s. Champagne (2013) discusses this development through a historical analysis of the country's infrastructure programs, claiming that the Canada Infrastructure Works Program, created in 1994 by Jean Chrétien's Liberal government, represents an example of multilevel governance in Canada. The program was initiated in order to solidify a partnership between the federal and local governments in which the former committed "significant federal public expenditure of several billion dollars" (Champagne, 2014, 164). The objective of the program was "assisting in the maintenance and development of infrastructure in local communities and the creation of employment" (Bojorquez, Champagne, and Vaillancourt 2009, 440). In addition, the Infrastructure Canada program was created in 2002, an initiative in which a federal department was put in charge of managing the infrastructure transfer programs for municipalities (Stoney and Graham 2009).

The federal government cited four reasons for committing funds to the development of local infrastructure: (1) investing in infrastructure can serve to stimulate the economy and provide employment opportunities in the interim within the construction sector; (2) the development of infrastructure can also increase productivity rates and facilitate labour conditions through improved transportation and communications; (3) better quality and more modern infrastructure is needed in local communities; and (4) the costs associated with infrastructural development are too large for any one level of government to take on alone. Thus, the cohesion of efforts was considered essential and beneficial to increase the level of investments in basic infrastructure in Canada.

The program was structured as a cost-share initiative and originally began with a budget of $2 billion dollars (Champagne 2014). Many predicted that the program would eventually lose support, particularly when a change of administration would occur. However, when the Liberal governments of Prime Ministers Chrétien and Martin ended and Stephen Harper came to power in 2006, Harper's Conservative government pledged to continue to supply public expenditures to the cause of infrastructural growth: "The new regime not only maintained most federal grants to municipalities, along with the Gas Tax Fund programs to the municipalities, but prolonged or enhanced these programs. The Conservative government replaced some of the federal grant programs to municipalities with other similar programs but did not cut the level of funding. Quite the contrary, infrastructure investments became a political priority of the Conservative government to stimulate the Canadian economy" (Bojorquez, Champagne, and Vaillancourt 2009, 442).

The interest by the Liberal and (surprisingly) Conservative political parties for municipal affairs demonstrates the strong link between financing infrastructure and maintaining/stimulating the economy. It is a relationship that has not only led to the expansion of the 1994 Infrastructure Works Program over time but has also made political actors at all three levels of government overtly aware that public expenditures can serve as a political tool to win elections as much as a policy instrument to ensure economic and financial stability.

By analysing Canada's public infrastructure policies and instruments, this chapter intends to show how multilevel governance is used as a mechanism that has provided the federal government with greater avenues for fiscal and policy intervention at the local level. To illustrate this mechanism, the following section examines the investment shares in public infrastructure spending by each order of government.

Investment Shares in Public Infrastructure Spending

There are several different types of infrastructure that overlap with major public sectors such as education, health, state-owned businesses, and defence. However, for the purposes of this chapter, these major sectors will not be our focal point. Instead, we have opted to concentrate on what is dubbed by Statistics Canada as "basic infrastructure." Basic infrastructure focuses on the provision of roads, bridges, tunnels, cultural centres, sports and recreation facilities, drinking water, storm-water, wastewater, solid waste, public transportation, and social/affordable housing (Statistics Canada 2018). All of these public services come at a relatively high cost through capital expenditures. Consequently, in order for municipalities in Canada to be able to provide the public with these

Figure 15.1. Basic Infrastructure Investments, 2009–20

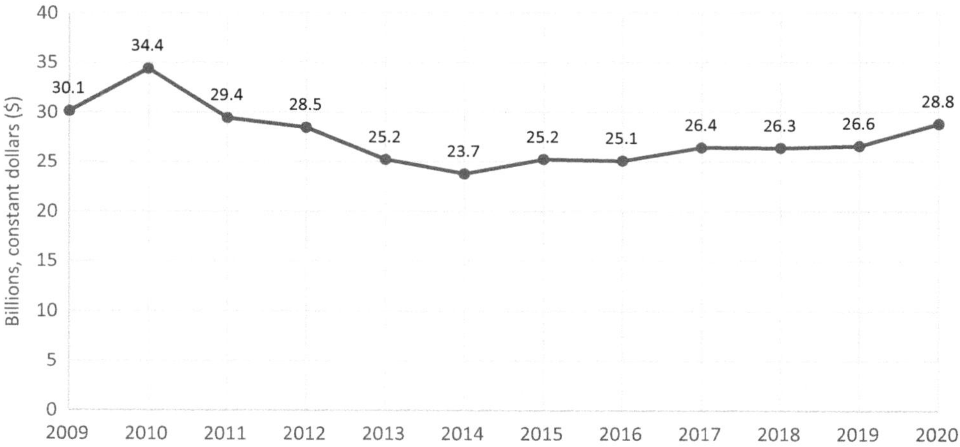

Year	Billions, constant dollars ($)
2009	30.1
2010	34.4
2011	29.4
2012	28.5
2013	25.2
2014	23.7
2015	25.2
2016	25.1
2017	26.4
2018	26.3
2019	26.6
2020	28.8

Source: Statistics Canada (2023).

essential amenities, a coordinated financial effort from all three levels of government is required.

As a result, annually in Canada, the nation spends approximately $30 billion on financing basic infrastructure (Figure 15.1). Obviously, each level of government contributes differently in proportion to the political and especially economic power they represent. Additionally, as can be seen in Figure 15.1, public investment in basic infrastructure varies from year to year. It is not always constant, as factors such as economic recessions, health crises, or changes in administration and political priorities can have an impact.

Figure 15.2 illustrates a comparison between government investments in basic infrastructure and the above-mentioned major sectors (health, defence, education, privately owned and publicly owned enterprises). This comparison illustrates that the highest levels of public investments in the country are directed towards basic infrastructure. Although spending in the private sector is comparable, spending in basic infrastructure is still more dominant, principally during the years in which the nation has faced economic turmoil, such as during the 2008–12 financial crisis. This trend can be attributed to the fact that investing in infrastructure acts as a financial stimulus that not only maintains but impulses economic development.

Once basic infrastructure projects are funded, the question of who owns them comes to the forefront. In Canada, the answer is that basic infrastructure is predominantly owned by the three levels of government. However, as Figure

Figure 15.2. Infrastructure Investments, Comparison between Major Sectors, 2009–20

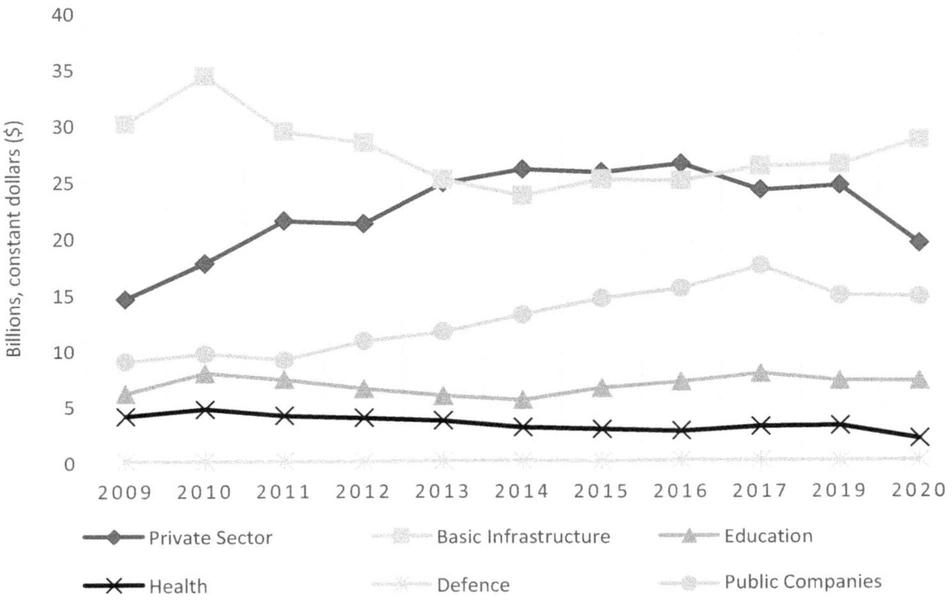

Source: Statistics Canada (2023).
Note: Percentages do not add up exactly to 100 due to rounding.

15.3 illustrates, infrastructural ownership is not equitable nor is it reflective of the amount of money invested by each level of government. As we can see, even though the municipal level of government is the most financially dependent, it has the largest share of infrastructural stock at a rounded 62 per cent. Although this amount is the result of all the subsidies and infrastructural investments made by the federal, provincial, municipal, and Indigenous governments, the fact remains that a rounded 62 per cent of basic infrastructure in Canada is municipal property, while only approximately 31 per cent is provincial, 5 per cent federal, and 3 per cent Indigenous. These figures demonstrate why municipalities are becoming more financially significant, especially for the operating, maintenance, and repair of these assets, as the weight of their infrastructural stocks continue to accumulate over time.

Although there are various benefits to financing basic infrastructure, there are also some issues. The most noticeable problem is related to the growing cost of maintaining and renewing aging infrastructure. For the last decade, Canada

Figure 15.3. Net Stock of Basic Infrastructure by Level of Government, 2020

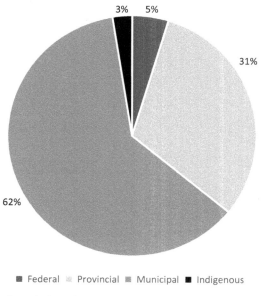

Source: Statistics Canada (2023).
Note: Percentages do not add up exactly to 100 due to rounding.

has been on a trajectory of renewal, attempting to replace and/or repair older infrastructure facilities constructed between the 1950s and the1980s: "Canada invests billions of dollars a year to repair, upgrade and expand its public infrastructure. Whether it involves paving roads, renovating bridges or upgrading sewer and water systems, all levels of governments and the private sector work together to ensure that Canada's public infrastructure is safe and meets the needs of a growing population and economy" (Statistics Canada 2008).

As a result, the lifespan of a large proportion of infrastructure stock in Canada is exhausted, and the majority of public expenditures designated towards financing basic infrastructure are used for upkeep, mainly within major cities where the need for basic infrastructure is massive and the assets are generally old. Municipal infrastructure management is central to the nation's operational functions as it deals with issues of public health, quality of life, economic growth, productivity, and international competitiveness. Therefore, municipal infrastructure is not only a local issue since it affects the vitality, well-being, and competitiveness of the country as a whole. Its importance puts additional pressure on political leaders, who must balance the costs of urban planning, infrastructural development, and contributing to overall community well-being (Andrew, Graham, and Phillips 2002). It is difficult for decision-makers to adhere to public expectations for new infrastructural developments such as the construction of a new sports arena or community centre when most of their funds must go towards the maintenance of aging infrastructure.

To respond to the issue mentioned above, new investments are necessary; continual flow of funds is required not only to cover the costs of maintaining/renewing infrastructure but also to meet the financial costs that arise from an aging population, increased mobility, adaptation to the consequences of climate change, and going green (to name a few). Therefore, the federal government has implemented several policies and funding instruments to outline the procedures related to transferring funds.

Federal Policies and Funding Instruments

This section provides an overview of the federal policies and funding instruments that have been used to promote infrastructure in Canada. The focus is on the federal spending programs/instruments that are used to invest in the public infrastructure of Canadian municipalities. As outlined in Table 15.1, this section will examine three such instruments: fiscal transfer (formally known as tax sharing), shared tripartite funding, and public-private partnerships.

Fiscal Transfer: The Canada Community-Building Fund

The Canada Community-Building Fund (formerly known as the Gas Tax Fund) is a permanent source of indexed federal funding that aims to lessen the financial burden placed on Canadian municipalities. The fund was made permanent in 2011. It provides over $2 billion annually for local priorities to approximately 3,600 communities (Government of Canada 2022). It is typically allocated twice a year on a per capita basis to the provinces and territories, which then distribute the funds to their cities, towns, and boroughs in proportion to their respective populations. This form of public spending is meant to support local infrastructure initiatives, primarily in eighteen different project categories (Government of Canada 2022). In 2014–15, it was indexed at 2 per cent per year, with increases to be applied in $100 million increments from 2014–15 to 2023–4. Over time, the fund has so far represented $21.8 billion in flexible, long-term funding for municipal infrastructure (Government of Canada 2021a).

Furthermore, the fund is now accepted as a federal-provincial-municipal fiscal transfer. The program is structured to minimize the possibility for the funds to be redirected by provincial governments. At times, it can be used as

Table 15.1. Types of Policy Instruments for Federal Investment in Municipal Infrastructure

Types of Instruments	Federal Funding Programs	Description
Fiscal transfer	Canada Community-Building Fund (formerly the Gas Tax Fund)	The federal transfer is provided in the form of a basic grant to municipalities. This fund aims to be a stable, predictable, and long-term support program to help municipalities build and repair public infrastructure. The Canada Community-Building Fund is distributed to all Canadian municipalities nationwide with a permanent, stable, and indexed source of infrastructure funding. It is divided between them in proportion to the population and is indexed annually. The fund was made permanent in 2011 at $2 billion per year. In 2014–15, it was indexed at 2 per cent per year, with increases to be applied in $100 million increments from 2014–15 to 2023–4. This transfer represents $21.8 billion in flexible, long-term funding for municipal infrastructure.
Shared tripartite funding	Investing in Canada Plan (formerly Canada Community-Building Fund)	This fund was created in 2014 under the name Canada Community-Building Fund, which in 2016 was renamed the Investing in Canada Plan. The fund is allocated on a project-by-project basis. It relies on the principle of shared funding. The basic structure of the program is tripartite, that is to say, a project submitted by a municipality and accepted by the other levels of government will be funded up to one-third by the federal, one-third by the province, and the other third by the municipality. More recently, some federal funding has accounted for as much as 50 per cent of financing.
Public-Private Partnerships	Canada Infrastructure Bank (CIB) (formerly PPP Canada)	This plan focuses on accelerating Canada's transition to a low-carbon economy. Its funding targets public transportation, clean power, green infrastructure, expanding broadband connections, and improving the conditions for trade and transportation. The CIB's growth plan is worth $10 billion (for three years), $1 billion of which is allocated towards the Indigenous Community Infrastructure Initiative (ICII). The CIB partners with the provinces/territories, municipalities, Indigenous communities, and private sector in order to work towards a *greener* and financially stable future.

loan collateral, borrowing against future stipends. Municipalities can invest the funds in the infrastructure projects of their choosing within a broad range of criteria; yet in some cases, such as in Quebec, provincial governments have stipulated in which sectors their municipalities should invest (Government of Canada 2022). However, despite these occasional restrictions, most municipalities enjoy substantial flexibility with regards to their investments.

The Canada Community-Building Fund has proven to be a vital source of revenue for municipalities. It has had significant structural success by illustrating the efficiency of multilevel governance. As a result, within the 2019 budget, the fund was expanded, given the public health context. The federal government opted to include a one-time doubling of the Canada Community-Building Fund, allocating an additional $2.2 billion to local communities. In 2020, due to the devastating financial repercussions of the COVID-19 global pandemic, the government announced that it would be accelerating the distribution of the money. Instead of providing its usual two payments, the central government would be providing the municipalities with a single payment in an effort to minimize the financial strain (Government of Canada 2022). The overall effectiveness of this financial mechanism has called for its further expansion by municipal governments as an alternative to the other two instruments.

Shared Funding: Investing in Canada Plan

The Investing in Canada Plan (formerly Canada Community-Building Fund) is a fund integrated under the confines of the Building Canada Plan, which is a broader federal financial development program. The fund was first established in 2007 to fund projects for the duration of seven years, from 2007–14. The fund was originally allocated $8.8 billion to address national, regional, and local infrastructure projects in three specific areas: (1) developing a stronger economy; (2) building a cleaner environment; and (3) reinforcing the creation of strong and affluent communities (Government of Canada 2011). The money in the fund is allocated to public infrastructure projects mandated by the provinces, territories, and municipalities.

The fund seeks to provide resources for research, knowledge, planning, and infrastructure delivery through the implementation of two central components; the Major Infrastructure Component (MIC) and the Communities Component. The MIC is the dominant component of the Building Canada Fund. This component focuses on providing funding to infrastructural programs that are of major significance to Canadians' everyday lives. For example, it provides funding for projects related to drinking water, wastewater, public transportation, the National Highway System, and green energy (Government of Canada 2011).

In 2014, after the initial seven-year period of the program ended, the fund was renewed. The 2014 New Building Canada Fund pledged $14 billion to the continuation of infrastructural development at all three levels of government. Under the new fund, two new components were created: the National Infrastructure Component (NIC), worth $4 billion, and the Provincial-Territorial Infrastructure Component (PTIC), worth $10 billion. The NIC concentrates on investing in projects of national importance that will have overarching public benefits and contribute to long-term economic growth. The PTIC is divided into two areas of interest: national and regional projects, worth $9 billion, and small local projects, worth $1 billion (Government of Canada 2020).

The latest iteration of the Investing in Canada Plan was launched in 2016, soon after the election of Liberal Party of Canada, with a goal to invest over $180 billion in infrastructure over twelve years. The strategy aims to fulfil three goals: creating long-term economic growth, supporting resilience and a clean growth economy, and building social inclusion and socio-economic outcomes. The investment is delivered through five investment streams: public transit, green, social, trade and transportation, and rural and northern communities. The plan also aims to create 100,000 jobs each year (Government of Canada 2023).

As a funding instrument, the Investing in Canada Plan, and those that preceded it, is a tripartite cost-sharing tool in which the federal government shoulders a percentage of the costs of regionally and locally owned infrastructure projects (Government of Canada 2020). The fund is allocated on a project-by-project basis. It relies on the principle of shared tripartite funding. The basic structure of the program is tripartite, that is to say, a project submitted by a local or regional government and accepted by the other levels of government will be funded up to one-third by the federal, one-third by the province, and the other third by the local or regional government. More recently, some federal funding has accounted for as much as 50 per cent of financing. The fund also invests in privately owned (not-for-profit) infrastructure projects, covering up to 25 per cent of the costs. Overall, this program is a prime example of multilevel governance and of how all three levels of government need to collaborate to ensure long-term investments in basic infrastructure.

Public-Private Partnerships (PPP) – Canada Infrastructure Bank (CIB)

The last multilevel transfer program we examine in this section is the Canada Infrastructure Bank (CIB; formerly Public-Private Partnerships Canada). The CIB is an example of public-private partnerships (PPPs) in Canada. Before instituting the CIB, the federal government created a public enterprise called PPP Canada and the Public-Private Partnership Fund in 2007, a program meant to manage public funds and invest them in private infrastructure projects (Champagne 2013). The idea behind the creation of this fund was that, by integrating both private and public investments, the financial risk would, in principle, decrease while the prospect of economic growth would increase.

The CIB was created in 2017. Similar to its predecessor (PPP Canada), this program demonstrates how the public and private sectors can come together in order to promote the expansion of infrastructure in Canada. The CIB puts the onus of investment transfers on both private corporations and the government. It seeks to attract considerable private and institutional investment in infrastructural development, advising public actors on infrastructural needs and incrementing the pool of research and knowledge (CIB 2021).

Of the previously discussed programs, the CIB is arguably the most expansive and well-rounded with regards to its five main target sectors: public transit, clean power, green infrastructure, broadband, and trade and transportation (CIB 2021). In order to invest in these sectors, the CIB has allocated $10 billion over the next three years and an additional $1 billion towards the Indigenous Community Infrastructure Initiative (ICII; CIB 2021).

The principal target of this instrument is to fortify a partnership between the public and private sectors so as to promote mutual investment in infrastructure projects that will contribute to national economic growth and facilitate Canada's transition towards a low-carbon economy. Finding the optimal conditions to develop marketable/commercial projects is not always easy for the CIB. Therefore, one of the primary objectives of the fund is to motivate the different levels of government and corporations to make an ecological change in the infrastructural projects they invest in. It is the hope of the CIB that, by supporting green infrastructure, the ecological transformation of Canada's economy will be accelerated. With this goal in mind, the CIB has pledged to invest an initial $35 billion in infrastructure programs over the next years.

As has been demonstrated through the examination of these three infrastructural policy instruments, multilevel governance is essential to the public policy process in Canada. Yet, this new generation of infrastructure programs has been paved on the back of stringent pacts and negotiations. In order to come to these infrastructural bi/multilateral agreements, the federal government (under the confines of Infrastructure Canada) has had to enter into long-term arrangements that clearly stipulate a respectful jurisdictional divide between the central government and the provinces/territories. Unfortunately for the municipalities, during these negotiations, they have been given little control/influence (with the exception of the Association of Municipalities of Ontario [AMO] and the Union of British Colombia Municipalities [UBCM]). In sum, the federal transfer programs have created a ripple effect on the provincial and municipal governments whereby the public financing of basic infrastructure in Canada continues to increase.

Conclusion

In conclusion, this chapter has sought to address the challenges of financing basic public infrastructure in Canada, an obligation that, through multilevel governance, is shared among the three levels of government in the country. Through a brief examination of multilevel governance as a theory, our chapter illustrates that, for public infrastructure in Canada to continue to effectively develop, intergovernmental cooperation is vital. This point was further demonstrated through our overview of the economic interdependencies that the federal, provincial/territorial, and municipal governments share – a fact that we emphasized through our discussion of three major federal policy and funding instruments: (1) fiscal transfer, (2) shared tripartite funding, and (3) public-private partnerships.

Our chapter illuminates the strong connection that exists between financing basic infrastructure and conserving a strong economy. Therefore, since the mid-1990s, all three levels of government have opted to continue (and increase) investments in public infrastructure. More recently, infrastructure policy responses to combat issues related to climate change have increasingly been a priority of Canada's three levels of government. A green initiative has been increasingly incorporated into all infrastructure funding programs. Attempting to lower its carbon footprint and meet the objectives set forth in the 2015 Paris Climate Agreement, Canada has been working towards going green with mixed results – meaning the federal government has been allocating more funding to the province/territories and municipalities with the specific purpose of encouraging green infrastructural development.

A recent example of the federal government's efforts to accomplish this goal has been the creation of the Green and Inclusive Community Buildings Program (GICB). The GICB was established in 2021 and is currently in the process of being implemented. It is (provisionally) a five-year program intended to assist in the construction of more community buildings and the restoration of existing ones (Government of Canada 2021b). The construction of these buildings is meant to be "more energy efficient, lower carbon, more resilient, and higher performing. This program will support green and accessible retrofits, repairs or upgrades of existing public community buildings and the construction of new publicly-accessible community buildings that serve high-needs, underserved communities across Canada" (Government of Canada 2021b).

The GICB, like the majority of Canada's green development programs, is under the purview of Infrastructure Canada, to which the federal government has allocated $1.5 billion. With approximately $100,000 to $3 million available per project, the federal government is encouraging both provinces and municipalities with retrofit community projects to apply for funding. In addition, as the

GICB was designed to support the first pillar of the Strengthened Climate Plan, an initiative meant to support green jobs and make it more accessible for Canadians to make green renovations on their homes, the commitment the federal government is making towards helping provincial and municipal governments invest in green projects is evident.

Looking towards the future, it is a safe projection to say that growing amounts of federal, provincial, and municipal funding will have to be designated towards the fight against climate change. This focus will mean increasing funds especially targeted towards the development and implementation of green technologies, promoting the green job market, building low-carbon properties, and converting old structures to be more environmentally friendly.

Overall, the three levels of government in Canada will need to increase cooperative measures to meet these issues head-on. What is overtly obvious is that, for these challenges to be addressed effectively, the federal, provincial, and territorial governments will have to increasingly assist and support municipalities to make this shift. It is important to emphasize that any political and economic strategy will require (at least partially) a multilevel infrastructural policy response.

REFERENCES

Andrew, Caroline, and Katherine A. Graham. 2014. *Canada in Cities: The Politics and Policy of Federal-Local Governance*. Montreal and Kingston: McGill-Queen's University Press.
Andrew, Caroline, Katherine A. Graham, and Susan D. Phillips. 2002. *Urban Affairs Back on the Policy Agenda*. Montreal and Kingston: McGill-Queen's University Press.
Azzi, Stephen. 2006. "Federal Government." *The Canadian Encyclopedia*. https://www.thecanadianencyclopedia.ca/en/article/federal-government.
Bojorquez, Fabio, Eric Champagne, and François Vaillancourt. 2009. "Federal Grants to Municipalities in Canada: Nature, Importance and Impact on Municipal Investments, from 1990 to 2005." *Canadian Public Administration* 52, no. 3: 439–55. https://doi.org/10.1111/j.1754-7121.2009.00091.x.
Champagne, Eric. 2012. "L'organisation et les structures gouvernementales dans le contexte canadien: Fédéralisme, centralisation et décentralisation." In *L'administration contemporaine de l'État: Une perspective canadienne et québécoise*, edited by Pierre P. Tremblay, 17–39. Quebec: Presses de l'université du Québec.
– 2013. "Les programmes d'infrastructures municipales du gouvernement fédéral: Une analyse de la gouvernance multiniveau au Canada." *Télescope* 19, no. 1: 43–61. https://doi.org/10.7202/1017151ar.
– 2014. "Tracking the Growth of the Federal Municipal Infrastructure Program under Different Political Regimes." In *Canada in Cities: The Politics and Policy of*

Federal-Local Governance, edited by Katherine A.H. Graham and Caroline Andrew, 164–92. Montreal and Kingston: McGill-Queen's University Press.

Champagne, Eric, and Olivier Choinière. 2016. "Le financement des infrastructures municipales et les défis du fédéralisme fiscal canadien." *Revue Gestion et Management Public* 4, no. 3: 25–36. https://doi.org/10.3917/gmp.043.0025.

Christiansen, Thomas. 1997. *Reflective Approaches to European Governance*, edited by Knud Erik Jørgensen, 1–22. Basingstoke, UK: Palgrave Macmillan.

CIB (Canada Infrastructure Bank). 2021. "Priority Sectors." Canada Infrastructure Bank. https://cib-bic.ca/en/sectors/priority-sectors/.

Doern, Bruce G., Christopher Stoney, and Robert Hilton. 2021. *Keeping Canada Running: Infrastructure and the Future of Governance in a Pandemic World*. Montreal and Kingston: McGill-Queen's University Press.

Government of Canada. 2011. "Building Canada Fund." Infrastructure Canada. https://www.infrastructure.gc.ca/prog/bcf-fcc-eng.html.

– 2017. "Government." Immigration and Citizenship Canada. https://www.canada.ca/en/immigration-refugees-citizenship/services/new-immigrants/learn-about-canada/gcvernement.html.

– 2020. "The 2014 New Building Canada Fund: Focusing on Economic Growth, Job Creation and Productivity." Infrastructure Canada. https://www.infrastructure.gc.ca/plan/nbcf-nfcc-eng.html.

– 2021a. "Canada Community-Building Fund Allocation Table." Infrastructure Canada. https://www.infrastructure.gc.ca/prog/gtf-fte-tab-eng.html.

– 2021b. "Green and Inclusive Community Buildings." Infrastructure Canada. https://www.infrastructure.gc.ca/gicb-bcvi/index-eng.html.

– 2022. "The Canada Community-Building Fund." Infrastructure Canada. https://www.infrastructure.gc.ca/plan/gtf-fte-eng.html.

– 2023. "Investing in Canada Plan – Building a Better Canada." Infrastructure Canada. https://www.infrastructure.gc.ca/plan/about-invest-apropos-eng.html.

Harvey, Jean, and Robert Young. 2012. *Image-Building in Canadian Municipalities*. Montreal and Kingston: McGill-Queen's University Press.

Henstra, Daniel. 2013. *Multilevel Governance and Emergency Management in Canadian Municipalities*. Montreal and Kingston: McGill-Queen's University Press.

Hooghe, Liesbet. 1995. "Subnational Mobilisation in the European Union." *West European Politics* 18, no. 3: 175–98. https://doi.org/10.1080/01402389508425097.

Hooghe, Liesbet, and Gary Marks. 2003. "Unraveling the Central State, But How? Types of Multi-Level Governance." *The American Political Science Review* 97, no. 2: 233–43. https://doi.org/10.1017/S0003055403000649.

Horak, Martin, Andrew Sancton, and Allison Bramwell. 2021. "Bob Young, Big Projects and the Study of Local and Urban Politics in Canada." In *Across Boundaries: Essays in Honour of Robert A. Young*, edited by André Blais, Cristine de Clercy, Anna Lennox Esselment, and Ronald Wintrobe, 15–32. Montreal and Kingston: McGill-Queen's University Press.

Horak, Martin, and Robert Young. 2012. *Sites of Governance: Multilevel Governance and Policy-Making in Canada's Big Cities*. Montreal and Kingston: McGill-Queen's University Press.

Ircha, Michael C., and Robert Young. 2013. *Federal Property Policy in Canadian Municipalities*. Montreal and Kingston: McGill-Queen's University Press.

Jones, Russell, and John Llewellyn. 2019. "Improving Infrastructure." *National Institute Economic Review* 250, no. 1: R61–8. https://doi.org/10.1177/002795011925000119.

Lee, Simon. 2019. "Public Investment Government Policy." *Encyclopedia Britannica*. https://www.britannica.com/topic/public-investment.

Magnusson, Warren. 2006. "Local Government." *The Canadian Encyclopedia*. https://www.thecanadianencyclopedia.ca/en/article/local-government.

Peters, Evelyn J. 2012. *Urban Aboriginal Policy Making in Canadian Municipalities*. Montreal and Kingston: McGill-Queen's University Press.

Saito-Jensen, Moeko. 2015. *Theories and Methods for the Study of Multilevel Environmental Governance*. Center for International Forestry Research (CIFOR). https://www.cifor.org/publications/pdf_files/Books/BCIFOR1502.pdf.

Siemiatycki, Matti. 2021. *Canada: The Role of the Federal Government in Infrastructure Planning*. Milan: Italian Institute for International Studies. https://www.ispionline.it/en/pubblicazione/canada-role-federal-government-infrastructure-planning-24441.

Slack, Enid. 2017. *How Much Local Fiscal Autonomy Do Cities Have? A Comparison of Eight Cities around the World*. Toronto: Institute on Municipal Finance and Governance, Munk School of Global Affairs.

Smith, Alison. 2022. *Multiple Barriers: The Multilevel Governance of Homelessness in Canada*. Toronto: University of Toronto Press.

Statistics Canada. 2008. "Age of Public Infrastructure: A Provincial Perspective." Statistics Canada. https://www150.statcan.gc.ca/n1/pub/11-621-m/11-621-m2008067-eng.htm.

– 2018. "Concepts, Definitions and Classifications." Statistics Canada. https://www150.statcan.gc.ca/n1/pub/13-607-x/2016001/1364-eng.htm.

– 2023. "Table 36-10-0608-01 Economic Infrastructure Accounts, Investment and Net Stock by Asset, Industry and Asset Function." Statistics Canada. https://www150.statcan.gc.ca/t1/tbl1/en/tv.action?pid=3610060801.

Stoney, Christopher, and Katherine A.H. Graham. 2009. "Federal-Municipal Relations in Canada: The Changing Organizational Landscape." *Canadian Public Administration* 52, no. 3: 371–94. https://doi.org/10.1111/j.1754-7121.2009.00088.x.

Tolley, Erin, and Robert Young. 2011. *Immigrant Settlement Policy in Canadian Municipalities*. Montreal and Kingston: McGill-Queen's University Press.

Tortola, Pier D. 2017. "Clarifying Multilevel Governance." *European Journal of Political Research* 56, no. 2: 234–50. https://doi.org/10.1111/1475-6765.12180.

16 Financing Education in Canada

JENNIFER WALLNER

Introduction

"Education," understood as the formally provided programs that enable and assist an individual to develop the skills, competencies, knowledge, and aptitudes deemed necessary for life, is traditionally broken down into three main stages: (1) early childhood education and care (ECEC) for children between the approximate ages of one to five; (2) mandatory schooling, also known as elementary and secondary education, which takes place between the ages of six and seventeen; and (3) advanced education, or post-secondary education (PSE), offered through vocational training programs, colleges, and universities. In most countries, the education arena constitutes one of the largest areas of state-led activity, and Canada is no exception. According to data from the World Bank (2022), Canada in 2020 spent 5.2 per cent on education as a percentage of its gross domestic product (GDP) and was thus aligned with other countries such as the United Kingdom, Finland, France, the Netherlands, Switzerland, and Austria. Canada also has some of the most impressive participation rates, particularly in the second and third stages of education. For example, at 59.96 per cent in 2020, Canada records the highest proportion of tertiary education graduates among Organisation for Economic Co-operation and Development (OECD) countries (Statista Research Department 2022).

Like most federations, in Canada the responsibility for the education sector was constitutionally allocated to the provinces and has been devolved in more recent years to the territories. Unlike most federations, however, Canada's federal government does not maintain a dedicated department for the education sector to help coordinate, influence, or assess in a systematic fashion the actions and activities of the provinces and territories in the arena. While many other sectors, like health care and pensions, have witnessed considerable formal or informal jurisdictional adjustments or rebalancing of roles and responsibilities between the orders of government, education is one sector where adjustments

Financing Education in Canada 327

have not occurred. To be sure, certain federal ministries are engaged in the education sector in a piecemeal fashion through targeted programs aimed at specific stages or directed towards particular segments of the population. However, due to this non-centred configuration, one of the largest areas of policy activity in Canada is broken down into more than thirty-six separate systems for ECEC, elementary and secondary education, and advanced education, operating concurrently with minimal pan-Canadian oversight across the thirteen provinces and territories.[1] To the extent that coordination occurs in the sector, it is facilitated under the auspices of the Council of Ministers of Education, Canada (CMEC), an intergovernmental body comprised of the thirteen provincial and territorial ministers of education.[2]

If we take a bird's eye view across the three main stages of education in Canada, a series of striking features becomes immediately apparent. Whereas two of the stages operate according to a market model of delivery and exhibit considerable variation across and within the jurisdictions, one stage – that of elementary and secondary education – does not. Furthermore, while the federal government's role in the education sector overall is heavily circumscribed, it nevertheless looms large for very specific populations in the Canadian body politic. Finally, in elementary and secondary education, where the provinces and territories retain almost complete control, we uncover remarkable interjurisdictional consistency to the principles of universal service delivery, reinforced by the fiscal arrangements at work supporting that stage of the sector.

This chapter advances in four parts. It opens with a brief overview of the two stages of education that operate according to market models, namely ECEC and PSE. The second section proceeds to sketch out the very specific ways in which the federal government is directly implicated in elementary and secondary schooling, with dedicated interventions in the schooling of First Nations children living on reserves and support for official minority-language education programs across the country. Section three then details the arrangements at work across the provinces and territories to support the delivery of elementary and secondary education within their respective jurisdictions. The fourth section concludes, offering some overarching observations highlighting the significance of baseline principles that influence the stability of fiscal arrangements, the importance of transcending commitments to particular models, and the value of consistent leadership to help stabilize while elevating components of the education sector.

Patchwork Practices, Uneven Arrangements: ECEC and Advanced Education in Canada

Across the overwhelming majority of the country, as intricately presented in Jennifer Robson's chapter 17 of this volume, childcare is primarily delivered by privately run operators, regulated by the province or territory within which they operate, and paid overwhelming by individual families. While in the rest of the OECD countries 85 per cent of three- to five-year-olds are enrolled in publicly financed ECEC programs, Canada lags significantly behind such an achievement (Mahon 2019, 83). Across the country as a whole, 70 per cent of childcare is delivered by not-for-profit organizations with the remaining 30 per cent supplied by commercial operators. However, as Prentice and White (2019, 63) underscore, the relative balance between operators varies enormously among the provinces and territories: "Commercial operators provide 72 per cent of all spaces in Newfoundland and Labrador but not a single space in Nunavut and the Northwest Territories." The authors add: "Despite federal and provincial investments, licensed childcare spaces are scarce in Canada ... When parents manage to secure a scarce childcare space, they are responsible for the cost (unless they qualify for a fee subsidy)" (62). Fees across the country vary dramatically, both among and within jurisdictions. In its review on fees in Canada, the Centre for Canadian Policy Alternatives reported that fees for toddlers range from a low in the Quebec cities of Gatineau, Laval, Montreal, Longueuil, and Quebec City, where families pay $179 a month, to a high in Toronto with a median monthly fee of $1,457 (Macdonald and Friendly 2019, 13). Finally, the lack of space in regulated ECEC providers means that a significant number of parents end up turning to unlicensed childcare facilities through home-based providers where there is no proactive monitoring and few, if any, regulations, often translating into lower quality services than what is offered by licensed providers.

In 1997, the province of Quebec spearheaded a new childcare regime, introducing affordable childcare through *centres de la petite enfance* or through family childcare homes at an initial cost of $5 per day for parents. It is important to note that these providers are still non-state actors who are responsible for actually delivering childcare services. While fees have increased over the past decade, the arrangements in Quebec have helped keep costs significantly lower for residents in the province. In 2019, following Quebec's lead, Prince Edward Island introduced a similarly structured set of arrangements to lower childcare costs in that province. Furthermore, after decades of signalling its intention to help address the costs and availability of childcare (see Robson, chapter 17 of this volume), the federal government in 2021 announced its formal commitment to establishing a Canada-wide Early Learning and Child Care Plan. To accomplish this goal, the federal government signed bilateral intergovernmental agreements with each of the provinces and territories to send new funding to lower costs of childcare, strengthen the provision of early learning through expanding regulated childcare spaces, and help equalize opportunities for families with young children throughout the country (Employment and Social Development Canada 2017). While this development is encouraging,

Prentice and White (2019, 61) nevertheless offer a sobering analysis: "In relying on non-state actors (primarily not-for-profit organizations) to implement public policy, governments therefore have only indirect mechanisms to encourage service expansion in underserved areas, to promote quality, or to regulate costs. For these reasons, Canada's existing childcare policy architecture is profoundly inadequate for meeting child, family, women's and social needs."

The advanced education sector across Canada exhibits many similar features, characteristics, and results as those outlined above in the ECEC sector. In this sector, governments once again rely on non-state actors to provide post-secondary programs. A dizzying panoply of private and not-for-profit institutions offer a range of certification, recertification, and accredited degree-granting programs for adults throughout the country. Many of these institutions operate according to government-mandated regulations and receive significant public funds. However, public funding from both orders of government to the advanced education sector has been steadily decreasing since 2009 (Usher 2018). For example, in its 2021 budget, Alberta cut 1.4 per cent of funding for advanced education and indicated that, in 2022, the province would cut an additional 5.4 per cent of funding, which translates into 750 full-time equivalent job losses in the sector (Herring 2021). To compensate for the loss of public funds, institutions are now increasingly relying on student tuition and, in the case of many major universities, international student fees at rates significantly higher than those applied to domestic residents. Statistics Canada (2023) reported that the average undergraduate tuition in 2022–3 for a resident of Canada was $6,834 per year, but topped over $36,000 annually for international students. What is more, according to Statistics Canada, much like the patterns observed in the ECEC sector, tuition fees for post-secondary education vary dramatically. The most affordable rates are found in Newfoundland and Labrador and Quebec at $3,400 and $3,359, respectively, while the higher ends are in Saskatchewan and Nova Scotia at $8,854 and $9,328, respectively. Finally, it is important to note that universities across the country charge significantly higher tuition rates for undergraduates in professional degree programs. Statistics Canada (2022) reports that, in 2022–3, the highest average fees were dentistry ($23,963), medicine ($15,182), veterinary medicine ($14,838), law ($13,222), pharmacy ($12,291), and optometry ($10,398).

Funds for post-secondary education (PSE) are allocated by both federal and provincial governments. The federal government earmarks funds along three avenues. First, funds are allocated to provinces through the loosely conditional Canada Social Transfer (CST), an equal per capita transfer to the provinces and territories, which then in turn use the funds to support their respective post-secondary institutions according to their own discretion. It is important to note, however, that the CST is designed to support a series of government services beyond PSE, including social assistance and social services, early childhood development, and early learning and childcare, as defined under the terms of the Federal-Provincial Fiscal Arrangements Act (FPFAA; Parliamentary Budget Officer 2020). Furthermore, similar to other conditional grants in the federation, the reporting requirements associated with the funds are weak at best, meaning that accountability for these transfers is murky and opaque. The second avenue of federal funding for PSE flows through individuals via a series of student loan programs designed to help support students from lower and middle-income families. The federal government also runs the Registered Education Savings Plan (RESP), which is a tax sheltered savings account eligible for top-ups from the federal government through the Canada Education Savings Grant (CESG). Third and finally, the federal government provides research funds through such arm's-length bodies as the Canadian Institutes of Health Research, the Natural Sciences and Engineering Research Council, and the Social Sciences and Humanities Research Council. In turn, principal investigator(s) use these funds to support laboratories and other research endeavours, supporting undergraduate and graduate student training and funding.

Provincial funding for PSE flows along two lines. First, funding goes directly to institutions that adhere to mandates and regulations set by the respective province. In Ontario, for example, provincial funding accounts for 25 per cent of total revenues for universities and colleges. According to Usher (2019), public funding is weaker in Ontario than elsewhere in Canada: only 0.92 per cent of Ontario's GDP, compared to 1.32 per cent of GDP in the rest of Canada. According to Usher's analysis, Ontario's arrangement resembles those at work in the United States, with a heavy reliance on private funds from individuals and philanthropic foundations, while the arrangements at work in the other provinces are more in line with those operating in European countries. In partnership with the federal government, provinces also offer support to individuals through a series of means-tested bursary and student loan programs to somewhat address equity concerns and ensure that advanced education is somewhat accessible for those from lower income households. Arrangements and relative generosity vary throughout the federation. For example, residents of British Columbia and Saskatchewan benefit from additional contributions made by those respective governments to the federal government's RESP program. Residents of other provinces, however, receive no such benefits.

Put together, across the ECEC and PSE sectors, we uncover marked variations; considerable differences in principles, designs, and delivery mechanisms; and significant inequalities across the country in terms of access and affordability. Considerable financial burdens are born by families and individuals attending PSE programs. Public funding, moreover, from federal-provincial-territorial governments appears somewhat inconsistent and at times even erratic, as recently exhibited in Alberta in the PSE sector.

Specific Populations, Shifting Arrangements: The Federal Role in Elementary and Secondary Education

While it is accurate to say that the federal government plays a very restrained role in the education sector, particularly in the area of elementary and secondary education, it nevertheless looms large for two groups of people in particular: First Nations children living on reserves and children registered in official minority-language education programs.

As a settler-colonial country, Canada was established through a process by which "a permanent settler society takes control of a territory previously occupied by an indigenous population and incrementally imposes its laws, governing institutions, and economic system onto the original inhabitants" (Papillon 2019, 141). Part of acquiring control included first allocating through the Constitution responsibility for "Indians and lands reserved for Indians" to the federal government, which in turn enacted the Indian Act in 1870. Here we find one of Canada's most egregious legacies, documented in the report of the Truth and Reconciliation Commission released in 2015 (TRC 2015). For more than 100 years, the government of Canada funded residential schools operated by Catholic, Anglican, Methodist, and Presbyterian churches. Indigenous children were required by federal law to attend these schools, and it is estimated that approximately 150,000 First Nations, Inuit, and Métis children were separated from their families and communities to attend such schools scattered throughout the country. In these institutions, children were "forced to abandon their language, cultural beliefs, and way of life. They were compelled to adopt the European languages of either English or French, foreign religious denominations, and new habits" (Union of Ontario Indians 2013, 5). In addition to these tactics of forced assimilation, the federal government also turned a blind eye to the unrelenting reports of abuse, starvation, and neglect endured by these children at the hands of those responsible for managing the schools over generations (Milloy 1999). The last residential school that operated under this regime, located in Saskatchewan, finally closed its doors in 1996.

In 2008, on behalf of the government of Canada, Prime Minister Stephen Harper issued an apology to Indigenous peoples, which acknowledged Canada's direct role in the residential school system (Government of Canada 2008). The social, cultural, and economic damage caused by the legacy of residential schools nevertheless persists today. Furthermore, despite maintaining the responsibility for the schooling of First Nations children living within their communities on what are referred to as "reserves," the federal government fails to fulfil its obligations. Specifically, where non-Indigenous children outside of reserve schools benefit from stable, reliable, and predictable funding arrangements (which will be detailed below), funding for schools in First Nations communities has been typically allocated through proposal-based programs, on an annual basis, without any alignment to the funding provided by provincial governments to their respective programs. This ad hoc and fluid arrangement translated into chronic underfunding of First Nations schools relative to those operating for non-Indigenous children throughout the provinces and territories (Indigenous Services Canada n.d.) – underfunding, even though the costs associated with providing quality schooling to First Nations children living within their communities is significantly higher due to smaller population size and remoteness.

In 2016, in an effort to address this persistent problem and ongoing inequality, the federal government announced an injection of $2.3 billion of new money into First Nations education over five years and started moving towards a formula-based funding model for schools in Indigenous communities, informed by provincial allocations, while endowing expanded language and cultural programming on a more consistent basis. Under the Elementary and Secondary Education Program, the government of Canada is committed to "supporting elementary and secondary education for First Nations students, schools and communities, by working in partnership with First Nations to help close the education outcome gaps between First Nations peoples and other Canadians" (Indigenous Services Canada n.d.). The implementation of this new arrangement began on 1 April 2019 under a protocol known as the Interim Funding Approach. However, as detailed by Leslee White-Eye (2019, 1), significant problems remain: "There is no funding to govern education; the resources that are there may boil down to a wage increase for some First Nations; few supports for sustainable long-term change to student outcomes; yet, full responsibility for the whole system." And, most damningly, "the glaring lack of meaningful First Nation control" (2). Put simply, despite decades of apologies and commitments from federal leaders to improve the provision of schooling for First Nations children living in Indigenous communities, considerable work still needs to be done.

The second area in elementary and secondary education where the federal government is more directly implicated is in the provision of educational programs for official minority-language communities spread across the country. Federal engagement in this area emerges from its role as the primary overseer of official languages, specifically English and French. Since 1970, the federal Department of Canadian Heritage has maintained a series of agreements with provincial governments to help offset the additional costs associated with minority-language education and second-language instruction in each of their jurisdictions. These dedicated and ongoing intergovernmental arrangements aim to ensure that English communities in Quebec and French communities outside of Quebec have the "opportunity to be educated in their own language and to experience cultural enrichment through exposure to their own culture" (Canadian Heritage 2020). Multiyear agreements accompanied by an action plan are negotiated either bilaterally with each relevant government or – when interprovincial, inter-territorial, or even pan-Canadian projects have emerged – under the auspices of the Council of Ministers of Education, Canada (CMEC).

There are two major critiques of federal arrangements in this arena: insufficient funding and a lack of meaningful central oversight. The Standing Committee on Official Languages (2016, 3) pointed out in its 2016 report: "The difficulty lies in the fact that there is no central agency responsible for official languages, and each department is responsible for managing its own official languages programs and budgets." In a brief to the Standing Committee on Official Languages, the Fédération nationale des conseils scolaires francophones (FNCSF) affirmed these critiques and called for greater accountability and transparency: "Today, 35 years after section 23 of the charter was adopted, the protocol still fails to meet the needs of communities or shed light on how federal funding is spent on French minority-language education in the country" (quoted in Standing Committee on Official Languages 2016, 5). Similar concerns were raised by other organizations, such as the Quebec English School Boards Association (QESBA), which underscored the general lack of reporting and accountability for federal funds. Consequently, there appears to be a double-edged and persistent challenge of insufficient reporting and insufficient funding in the area of minority-language education where the federal government plays a greater and more formal role.

In June 2019, Melanie Joly, minister of Tourism, Official Languages and La Francophonie, announced that $60 million over four years has been set aside to increase funding to the provinces and territories for minority-language education. These funds are projected to add to the more than $235 million in funding that was already allocated in the federal government's 2019 budget and marks the first substantial increase in this area in more than ten years (Canadian Heritage 2019). Access to these funds is contingent upon a province or territory successfully signing the Protocol for Agreements in Minority-Language Education and committing to a certain action plan. However, enforcement mechanisms to assure provincial-territorial compliance and ongoing reporting of achievements remain obscure. Consequently, while perhaps addressing – in the short-term – the issue of funding adequacy for minority-language education, the new protocol does little to address the supplemental issue of accountability and reporting for these funds and to strengthen the quality of minority-language schooling across the country.

Relative Consistency and Relative Equity: Elementary and Secondary Education in Canada

Of the three educational stages, it is only in elementary and secondary education that we see a strong commitment to a singular principle guiding the actions of decision-makers: that of universality (Wallner and Marchildon 2019). Across the country, the overwhelming majority of Canadians receive their elementary and secondary education in public institutes overseen by provincial and territorial decision-makers. Despite the lack of central oversight or formal coordination, in broad brush strokes the main arrangements governing elementary and secondary education in Canada are remarkably consistent across the thirteen jurisdictions (Wallner 2014). In each provincial and territorial legislature, a member of the governing party is appointed to head a ministry of education, thus assuring dedicated representation of the education sector within the political executive. As such, when provincial and territorial governments are making budgetary decisions or determining fiscal priorities, education has a guaranteed seat at the table, and the sitting government is collectively responsible for the elementary and secondary education sector of their territory. The minister of education is supported by a substantial staff of professional public servants working within the department, who are responsible for crafting the core policies that govern schools, including curriculum and assessment, teacher preparation and certification, supervision and oversight, and – most pertinent here – the financing of the system itself.

School boards, traditionally – but not exclusively – locally elected, in turn serve as an intermediary between individual schools and the central ministry of each of the thirteen systems.[3] While quite powerful in the past, today's school boards are tasked with such things as tailoring curriculum to local needs, overseeing school maintenance, hiring and managing staff and support services for the schools, and maintaining local transportation policies. While in most provinces these entities are exclusively "public" and non-denominational, in Alberta, Saskatchewan, and Ontario separate publicly funded Roman Catholic school boards operate alongside the larger public non-denominational systems. Importantly, because these bodies receive full public funds, they are required to adhere to provincial regulations, curricula, and labour market rules.

Due to section 23 of the Charter of Rights and Freedoms (Government of Canada n.d.), all provinces and territories maintain at least one French-language or English-language school board reserved for "minority-language communities." In Ontario, for example, there are twelve French-language school boards with more than 470 French-language schools. The Ontario Ministry of Education (2022) states: "In these schools the curriculum is taught exclusively in French, except for courses taught in international languages, English, Indigenous languages curricula, and Québec sign language (LSQ). French-language schools have a mandate to protect, enhance and transmit the French language and culture." Such school boards thus help assure some form of local control for minority-language communities within each province.

The critical difference separating elementary and secondary education from the other educational stages in Canada is that it rests firmly upon the principle of universal provision and access. This principle means that public authorities are fully responsible for financing the arena. Interestingly, early in Canadian history the financing of elementary and secondary education shared many similarities with the contemporary practices at work in ECEC and PSE. Costs were borne primarily by families and individuals, which translated into uneven and unequal participation and financial instability for individual schools, with conditions in rural areas being particularly grim, further exacerbating poor educational outcomes outside of urban centres (Wallner 2014, 138). Within a generation, however, this inequity would change.

Lacking any fiscal levers, governments could exert little influence to try to standardize and strengthen the quality of educational programs in their jurisdictions. As the goal of free elementary education for all gained currency in the late 1800s, provincial officials and education leaders needed to find a way to stabilize funding for schools. Debates ensued in various provincial legislatures across the country, and one idea in particular took hold. Advanced by Mahlon Burwell in the Ontario legislature (inspired by the arrangements at work in New York State), a system of local taxes was to be instituted whereby school boards would have the authority to set and collect property taxes to finance and administer the education system, which would in turn be regulated by the provincial government (Wilson 1978, 34–8). This idea to institute local property taxes set and collected by school boards quickly spread across the provinces such that, by 1930, it was fully implemented throughout the ten jurisdictions.

Stable funding helped promote the rapid expansion of elementary schooling in the opening decades of the twentieth century. By the 1920s, spending on public schooling had outstripped government allocations for all other social programs. As schools expanded, costs increased, and provinces realized that they would need to provide supplemental funds to the various school boards to assure sufficient funding. British Columbia, for example, started this practice in 1933 with the introduction of a weighted population grant, which took into account such things as the number of pupils in a school board, classrooms, and teachers, and was further adjusted according to local resources benchmarked to local property values (Wallner 2014, 140). Decision-makers from other provinces learned from BC's approach and gradually implemented comparable conditional grants to help support elementary schooling. Thanks to these decisions, school boards in various parts of the country gained considerable power and influence, particularly those with strong tax bases, like Toronto and Edmonton.

That said, it is worth underscoring that, in the early decades of the twentieth century, there were marked variations in the relative expenditures on elementary schooling made by the provinces. In 1945, Prince Edward Island spent $37.00 per student, while British Columbia invested significantly more at $107.00 per student. Furthermore, it was at this time that decision-makers within each of the provinces became attuned to the internal discrepancies among school boards and were increasingly concerned about the sustainability of existing financial arrangements. Sustainability was particularly a concern given that, throughout the 1950s and into the 1960s, governments across the country were working to expand universal education up through the secondary level. In 1955, the Canadian School Trustees' Association released a report advocating for equalization grants among boards and uniform tax rates to finance basic programs in all the provinces (LaZerte 1955). Similar recommendations were made by other stakeholder organizations throughout the various provincial systems.

In 1967, New Brunswick decided to institute a new approach to education finance in order to address many of these concerns: centralized education funding. Rather than local property taxes set and collected by the school boards, the province took on full responsibility for education finance. Admittedly critiqued as an anti-democratic move that handcuffed the autonomy of individual school boards, the change nevertheless achieved the key goals of reducing internal disparities and expanding universal secondary schooling. Within a few short years, all the eastern provinces had followed New Brunswick's lead. As stakeholder organizations in other parts of the country witnessed the transformation ushered in through full provincial funding, the other provinces gradually followed suit, such that today all provinces and territories use essentially the same arrangement to fund elementary and secondary education. Some provinces in Western Canada, such as British Columbia and Manitoba, continue to maintain a residential school tax rate whereby local taxes still constitute a significant portion of education revenues (Statistics Canada 2020b). Although on paper this arrangement technically appears as a shared-cost approach to education finance because the tax rate is set by the province and the revenues are collected by the province, in practice it essentially amounts to full provincial funding.

According to Statistics Canada (2020b), in 2017–18 Canadian public elementary and secondary schools received $45.3 billion from government sources, accounting for 93.8 per cent of their total revenue nationally. Provincial and territorial sources account for almost three-quarters of total government funding. Across the country, resources devoted to education represented 3.0 per cent of GDP, and public school expenditures as a percentage of provincial or territorial GDP ranged from 2.3 per cent in British Columbia to 4.4 per cent in the Yukon. In other words, it appears as if the relative investment burdens borne by each province and territory to invest in elementary and secondary education are somewhat aligned, despite markedly different economic capacities among the jurisdictions. It is possible that the Equalization Program, administered by the federal government since the 1950s, has indirectly helped in this regard since its stated purpose is to help align provincial capacities to provide services at reasonably similar rates of taxation (see also Mary Janigan, chapter 2 of this volume). Finally, across the provinces in 2017–18, per-student expenditures ranged from $12,109 in British Columbia to $17,161 in Saskatchewan. In the territories, where the costs of education are significantly higher due to smaller populations, remote areas, and harsher conditions, expenditures start at $20,762 in Nunavut, ranging to $30,002 in the Yukon (Statistics Canada 2020a).

Strong investments seem to have helped secure positive results in elementary and secondary education. In general, the provinces have high graduation rates and achieve strong results on major international tests, including the Program for International Student Assessment (PISA) run by the OECD, the lodestar of international assessments. Over multiple years, Canada has been signalled out, not only for its high performances throughout the provinces but also for achieving very equitable results (Schleicher 2018). According to the OECD's measures, a student's socioeconomic background matters significantly less in terms of educational achievements in Canada, relative to achievements in other countries.

Assessing the Quilt: Transcending Observations of the Financing of the Education Arena in Canada

Pulling back the lens once again to assess dynamics and trends in the financing of the three stages of education in Canada reveals an important lesson. It seems undeniable that the combination of clear executive control combined with a strong commitment across the provinces and territories to the principle of universal provision and access to elementary and secondary schooling has generated remarkable consistency and produced good results in that specific stage of education. While ECEC and PSE have been beset by underfunding, erratic or even declining investments by some federal-provincial-territorial governments over the past two decades, investments in elementary and secondary education have demonstrated remarkable stability and have generally kept pace with inflation over the same period (Hill, Li, and Emes 2020). Given that all sectors have faced comparable pressures and all governments are in relatively similar fiscal predicaments, the stability displayed for elementary and secondary education is likely attributable to the consistent leadership of ministers of education and the clear ideational consensus to public provision that serves to stabilize this stage of the arena.

ECEC and PSE, on the other hand, have neither consistent leadership within the provinces and territories nor a strong consensus on what either stage should look like in terms of delivery and access. For the most part, across the majority of jurisdictions, the financial burden for ECEC and PSE falls to families and individuals. What is more, as emphasized by Prentice and White (2019), the delivery of ECEC is largely outsourced by governments to the non-profit sector, which somewhat compromises the levers available to governments to control costs. It remains to be seen whether the new federal initiatives to enter into detailed intergovernmental agreements with all the provinces and territories to invest in ECEC will translate into long-term cost reductions and increased quality and equity in the field (see also Robson, chapter 17 of this volume). PSE, in the meantime, appears to be at a bit of a standstill in terms of government innovations and investments. To be sure, it is impossible for governments to tackle all policy problems simultaneously. However, the absence of clear intergovernmental collective and collaborative engagement, even though promoted by the CMEC, seems to be undermining the financing of the sector.

Lastly and arguably of most concern and significance, for those directly affected by the federal government, it is clear that circumstances must change. For the government of Canada to secure its goal of reconfiguring relations with Indigenous peoples in the country, it is vital that new fiscal arrangements be institutionalized to increase funding while expanding self-government for those communities. Similarly, to uphold its responsibilities to preserve and protect official language communities in the country, the federal government must reform the support it gives while strengthening accountability for government funds. All of these reforms must be undertaken with the participation and engagement of both the communities affected and the provinces and territories that are ultimately responsible for education.

NOTES

1 To date, the provision of advanced education is extremely limited in the three northern territories. The main provider is Aurora College, which is connected through transfer agreements and partners in a network of technical schools, colleges, and universities throughout Canada and the circumpolar world.
2 The territories now enjoy full membership in the CMEC and are even capable of chairing the organization on an equal footing with the provinces.
3 While school boards in fact pre-date Confederation, they are nevertheless a source of contention. Since the 1990s, various provincial governments have either consolidated boards or endeavoured to end them completely. New Brunswick, for example, attempted to close school boards permanently in the 1990s but ended up reinstating them due to public response and for pragmatic reasons. More recently, in 2020, Quebec passed Bill 40, which calls for the abolishment of school boards and replacing them with "service centres" (CBC News 2020). It remains to be seen what will come from these new arrangements in the province. Further complicating the place of school boards in Canada is the fact that provinces and territories are constitutionally bound to assure the education rights of minority-language

communities, which includes their right to control the provision of education for their populations within a province or territory. Consequently, simply terminating democratically elected school boards without establishing some form of complementary organization that secures the representation of minority-language communities would likely be subjected to a challenge in the courts.

REFERENCES

Canadian Heritage. 2019. "Government of Canada Increases Support for Quality Minority-Language Education." News Release, 25 June 2019. https://www.canada.ca/en/canadian-heritage/news/2019/06/the-government-of-canada-increases-support-for-quality-minority-language-education.html.
– 2020. "Intergovernmental Cooperation on Minority Language Education." https://www.canada.ca/en/canadian-heritage/services/funding/official-languages/intergovernmental-minority-language-education.html.
CBC News. 2020. "Quebec Passes Education Reforms Abolishing School Boards." *CBC News*, 8 February 2020. https://www.cbc.ca/news/canada/montreal/quebec-education-reform-school-boards-1.5457100.
Employment and Social Development Canada. 2017. *Multilateral Early Learning and Child Care Framework*. https://www.canada.ca/content/dam/canada/employment-social-development/programs/early-learning-child-care/reports/2017-multilateral-framework/MEL_and_CCF-EN.pdf.
Government of Canada. n.d. "Section 23 – Minority Language Educational Rights." *Canadian Charter of Rights and Freedoms*. https://www.justice.gc.ca/eng/csj-sjc/rfc-dlc/ccrf-ccdl/check/art23.html.
– 2008. "Prime Minister Harper Offers Full Apology on Behalf of Canadians for the Indian Residential Schools System." Statement of the Prime Minister of Canada, 11 June 2008. https://www.rcaanc-cirnac.gc.ca/eng/1100100015644/1571589171655.
Herring, Jason. 2021. "Budget 2021: Post-Secondary Sees Further Cuts, 750 Job Losses." *Calgary Herald*, 25 February 2021. https://calgaryherald.com/news/local-news/0226-budget-postsec.
Hill, Tegan, Nathaniel Li, and Joel Emes. 2020. *Education Spending in Public Schools in Canada, 2020 Edition*. Vancouver, BC: The Fraser Institute. https://www.fraserinstitute.org/sites/default/files/education-spending-in-public-schools-2020.pdf.
Indigenous Services Canada. n.d. "Elementary and Secondary Education Program." https://www.sac-isc.gc.ca/eng/1450708959037/1531319458607.
LaZerte, Milton Ezra. 1955. *School Finance in Canada, 1955*. Edmonton: Finance Research Committee of the Canadian School Trustees' Association.
Macdonald, David, and Martha Friendly. 2019. *Developmental Milestones: Child Care Fees in Canada's Big Cities*. Ottawa: Canadian Centre for Policy Alternatives. https://www.policyalternatives.ca/publications/reports/developmental-milestones.

Mahon, Rianne, with Michael J. Prince. 2019. "From Family Allowances to the Struggle for Universal Childcare in Canada." In *Universality and Social Policy in Canada*, edited by Daniel Béland, Gregory P. Marchildon, and Michael J. Prince, 83–102. Toronto: University of Toronto Press.

Milloy, John S. 1999. *A National Crime: The Canadian Government and the Residential School System, 1879 to 1986*. Winnipeg: University of Manitoba Press.

Ontario Ministry of Education. 2022. "French-Language Education." https://www.ontario.ca/page/french-language-education.

Papillon, Martin. 2019. "Segmented Citizenship: Indigenous Peoples and the Limits of Universality" In *Universality and Social Policy in Canada*, edited by Daniel Béland, Gregory P. Marchildon, and Michael J. Prince, 137–54. Toronto: University of Toronto Press

Parliamentary Budget Officer. 2020. *Federal Support through Major Transfers to Provincial and Territorial Governments*. Ottawa: Office of the Parliamentary Budget Officer. https://www.pbo-dpb.gc.ca/web/default/files/Documents/Reports/RP-2021-020-S/RP-2021-020-S_en.pdf.

Prentice, Susan, and Linda A. White. 2019. "Childcare Deserts and Distributional Disadvantages: The Legacies of Split Childcare Policies and Programmes in Canada." *Journal of International and Comparative Social Policy* 35, no. 1: 59–74. https://doi.org/10.1080/21699763.2018.1526700.

Schleicher, Andreas. 2018. *PISA [Programme for International Student Assessment] 2018: Insights and Interpretations*. Organisation for Economic Co-operation and Development (OECD). https://www.oecd.org/pisa/PISA%202018%20Insights%20and%20Interpretations%20FINAL%20PDF.pdf.

Standing Committee on Official Languages. 2016. *Toward a New Action Plan for Official Languages and Building New Momentum for Immigration in Francophone Minority Communities*. Report of the Standing Committee on Official Languages to the House of Commons of Canada, 42nd Parliament, 1st Session, December 2016. https://www.ourcommons.ca/DocumentViewer/en/42-1/LANG/report-3/.

Statista Research Department. 2022. "Share of People with Tertiary Education in OECD Countries 2020, by Country." Statista. https://www.statista.com/statistics/1227287/share-of-people-with-tertiary-education-in-oecd-countries-by-country/.

Statistics Canada. 2020a. *Education Indicators in Canada: An International Perspective*. Catalogue no. 81-604-X. https://www150.statcan.gc.ca/n1/en/pub/81-604-x/81-604-x2020001-eng.pdf.

– 2020b. "Public Elementary and Secondary School Board Revenues and Expenditures, 2017–2018." *The Daily*, 15 July 2020. https://www150.statcan.gc.ca/n1/daily-quotidien/200715/dq200715b-eng.htm.

– 2021. "Tuition Fees for Degree Programs, 2021–2022." *The Daily*, 8 September 2021. https://www150.statcan.gc.ca/n1/daily-quotidien/210908/dq210908a-eng.htm.

– 2022. "Tuition Fees for Degree Programs, 2022–2023." *The Daily*, 7 September 2022. https://www150.statcan.gc.ca/n1/daily-quotidien/220907/dq220907b-eng.htm.

- 2023. "Table 37-10-0045-01 Canadian and International Tuition Fees by Level of Study (Current Dollars)." https://doi.org/10.25318/3710004501-eng.
TRC (Truth and Reconciliation Commission of Canada). 2015. *Honouring the Truth, Reconciling for the Future: Summary of the Final Report of the Truth and Reconciliation Commission of Canada*. Ottawa: TRC. https://ehprnh2mwo3.exactdn.com/wp-content/uploads/2021/01/Executive_Summary_English_Web.pdf.
Union of Ontario Indians. 2013. *An Overview of the Indian Residential School System*. http://www.anishinabek.ca/wp-content/uploads/2016/07/An-Overview-of-the-IRS-System-Booklet.pdf.
Usher, Alex. 2018. "The State of Canadian Post-Secondary Education, 2018." Higher Education Strategy Associates, 28 August 2018. https://higheredstrategy.com/the-state-of-canadian-pse-2018/.
- 2019. "Canadian PSE Funding Is Weirder Than You Think." Higher Education Strategy Associates, 3 September 2019. https://higheredstrategy.com/canadian-pse-funding-is-weirder-than-you-think/.
Wallner, Jennifer. 2014. *Learning to School: Federalism and Public Schooling in Canada*. Toronto: University of Toronto Press.
Wallner, Jennifer, and Gregory P. Marchildon. 2019. "Elementary and Secondary Education: The First Universal Social Program in Canada." In *Universality and Social Policy in Canada*, edited by Daniel Béland, Gregory P. Marchildon, and Michael J. Prince, 63–82. Toronto: University of Toronto Press.
White-Eye, Leslee. 2019. "Education and Crown Paternalism: Reviewing the New On-Reserve Education Funding Model." *Policy Brief* 27, 26 April 2019. Yellowhead Institute. https://yellowheadinstitute.org/2019/04/29/education-and-crown-paternalism-reviewing-the-new-on-reserve-education-funding-model/.
Wilson, J. Donald. 1978. "The Pre-Ryerson Years." In *Egerton Ryerson and His Times*, edited by Neil McDonald and Alf Chaiton, 9–42. Toronto: Macmillan Press.
World Bank. 2022. "Government Expenditure on Education, Total (% of GDP) – Canada." https://data.worldbank.org/indicator/SE.XPD.TOTL.GD.ZS?locations=CA.

17 Childcare in a Decentralized Federation: Who Pays?

JENNIFER ROBSON

Introduction

The 2021 federal budget made a significant change to the intergovernmental fiscal arrangements related to early learning and childcare (ELCC). The federal government committed to dramatically higher and eventually permanent spending on childcare services through conditional transfers to provinces and territories. This commitment was in addition to the 2017 bilateral agreements signed with all provinces and territories that had increased federal transfers for ELCC and included goals for increasing ELCC spaces set by provinces and territories.[1] The federal government has since concluded new agreements with all provinces and territories.[2]

Much of the decades-long debate over ELCC in Canada has focused on the merits of public investment in services versus instruments that simply transfer cash to families with children under the label of "choice" or on the disputes over estimates of the costs and true returns on investment in Quebec's ELCC policy (Finley 2006; Fortin 2017). But this debate has taken place somewhat divorced from the literature on fiscal federalism and the use of the federal spending power.[3]

There is general agreement that ELCC policy, as an educational service aimed at our youngest children, is an area of provincial jurisdiction under section 93 of the Constitution Act.[4] This fact is also widely recognized among ELCC advocates and experts (Friendly et al. 2021).[5] However, the federal Parliament retains the residual power, subject to limits, to spend public funds in areas that it chooses, including with an intent to advance certain social policy objectives (Gauthier 2017). It is on the nature and extent of that spending power and, conversely, the limits on that spending power, where debate continues.

Some advocates and experts have taken a more normative view of the question of federal spending power in ELCC, calling on the federal government to exercise leadership to compensate for provincial inaction or even to reshape

Childcare in a Decentralized Federation: Who Pays?   343

provincial policy priorities. For example, Yalnizyan and McCuaig (2020, 4) called for federal funding to "buy change and build a high-quality, publicly managed system. Absence of required reporting that tracks progress towards negotiated targets will void the arrangement for future funding."[6] In late June 2021, several high-profile ELCC experts co-signed an open letter[7] calling on federal policy makers to place conditions on all federal ELCC funding to prohibit provinces from using it to support for-profit providers (Early Child Development Funders Working Group 2021).[8] The national ELCC coalition Child Care Now has stated that "substantial federal funds must be used to drive transformational change in ELCC with regard to public responsibility for funding, management and delivery" and recommended a detailed list of conditions that should be attached to combined federal and provincial funding destined for provincially licensed ELCC providers, including for-profit providers with existing licences (Child Care Now 2021). Such calls to reshape which providers receive government support as well as conditions required of funded services might be interpreted as overlapping with provincial regulatory powers over ELCC delivery. Others have warned that, while ELCC systems across Canada demand significant increases in public spending, intergovernmental arrangements on ELCC must continue to respect the constitutional division of roles and responsibilities (Boessenkool and Robson 2021). Similarly, Cameron (2009, 141) cautioned: "In advocating for standards to link together the various provincial systems, it is important not to call on the federal government to do more than it can do constitutionally or politically. Without cooperation from the provinces, the federal government has no authority to oblige them to provide child care services."

The 2021 federal budget committed to spending $27.2 billion over five years to reach new bilateral agreements with provinces and territories with certain target milestones on reducing average fees for licensed spaces and increasing their supply (Department of Finance Canada 2021a, 102). On the one hand, this statement could be read as an endorsement of the normative view that federal spending power can and should be put to use to change provincial ELCC policy and standards. On the other hand, it can be read as a statement of policy goals that leaves the methods of achieving those goals subject to negotiations with the subnational governments responsible for ELCC. Whether the budget will, in practice, set shared standards for ELCC and fundamentally transform the size and composition of ELCC services will only be determined in the coming years as the text of the new agreements is evaluated alongside measurable changes to ELCC delivery in Canadian communities. Such an analysis is beyond the scope of this chapter until new data become available. But we can observe and learn from provincial responses to bilateral agreements on ELCC and consider them in the context of fiscal federalism as it applies to ELCC. At least one previous review of the state of ELCC concluded that the 2017 federal investment and bilateral agreements with provinces had directly led to an increase in provincial spending (Akbari, McCuaig, and Foster 2021).[9] This chapter revisits the question of the impact of federal spending by presenting data on spending in the four largest provinces and constructing more detailed case studies of the two largest provinces, jurisdictions that have historically taken very different policy directions on ELCC. The chapter starts from a theoretical framework of Canadian federalism and the federal spending power. Next, using public accounts and other public data sources, it seeks to understand how ELCC policy is shaped by fiscal arrangements between orders of government and, in turn, between government and citizens.

Fiscal Federalism and Limits on the Federal Spending Power

The power of a legislature to allocate public funds in areas of policy exists for both provincial and federal orders of government but has more often, and sometimes controversially, been exercised by the federal Parliament in Canada, owing to a range of political as well as fiscal considerations.[10] The exercise of that power may take many forms, including direct transfers to individuals or organizations, transfers to other orders of government, or cost-shared programs (Hogg 2013; Oliver, chapter 3, this volume). Where the legislature allocates funding, or more precisely approves of allocations initiated by the government, it may attach conditions, sometimes enumerated in legislation to create a statutory program or transfer (such as the Canada Health Act) or by adopting (via a ways and means motion) a budget that describes conditions and later passing implementation and appropriation bills. In the context of ELCC, federal spending is exercised through the Income Tax Act, the Federal-Provincial Fiscal Arrangements Act, and more recently, in the expression of parliamentary confidence in the 2017 and 2021 budgets.

As Oliver (chapter 3, this volume) notes, there are competing arguments regarding the scope or limits on the federal spending power. Generally, in assessing the legality of federal spending in areas of provincial jurisdiction, it is important to distinguish between the effect of the spending and the intent. The courts have, as Oliver points out, recognized the existence and legitimacy of a federal spending power, including the right of Parliament to impose conditions on that spending, "provided that those conditions do not in fact amount to what is, in pith and substance, regulation or control of a matter outside federal authority." Federal conditions might encourage provincial action that is consistent with federal policy aims, but the conditions cannot dictate or direct provincial actions. This limitation has at least two important components. The first is that the conditions not be so directive as to amount to a regulatory intent. The second is that the acceptance of the funding and the attached conditions must be voluntary by the recipient.

As Gauthier (2017, 265–6) notes, "when strict and specific conditions are added to the provision of funds by the federal government to a province, an exercise of spending power could create improper constraints." Even the Canada Health Act, often cited as a model for strong federal conditions on transfers to provinces, imposes an even stronger test on federal officials before payments can be reasonably reduced or delayed to a province (see Oliver, chapter 3, this volume).[11] In pith and substance, the aims of the health transfer are to ensure the availability and affordability of minimally acceptable health services across the country, not to regulate how provincial health services go about meeting these policy outcomes.

When a province willingly adopts the same policy goals as the federal government, and the conditions attached to the federal transfer to support those shared goals are not so specific as to dictate *how* the province might meet the shared goals, there is little reason for concern about overstepping the limits to the spending power. But this arrangement implies that a recipient party must conversely be free to refuse the funding and the conditions attached to it (Anand 2005). For example, payments to individuals in the Employment Insurance system may require that they complete regular reporting of their job search efforts or their benefits will be stopped. Individuals who dislike the reporting requirements are able to choose not to accept the benefit and therefore avoid the conditions attached to it (Anand 2005; Courchene 2008).[12]

When the spending power is applied to provincial governments that have their own head of power, the question of voluntary cooperation in adopting shared goals attached to new funding is even more important. When funding and conditions are linked, but conditions cannot be directly imposed by the federal government in areas of provincial jurisdiction, the federal government can offer or withhold conditional funding. But it must ultimately rely on willing provinces to adopt compatible policy objectives of their own and to willingly provide evidence that they are meeting the conditions of the funding. The federal government can withhold funding, but it cannot compel policy action or reporting in areas of provincial jurisdiction. More recently, federal governments have recognized the right of provinces and territories to opt out of new conditional federal spending plans, even with full compensation to be spent on other policy goals, when the subnational government substantially meets the same policy objectives as those established by the federal government (First Ministers' Meeting 1999).

Applying these principles regarding limits to the spending power, Cameron (2009, 134) concludes that "while the federal government cannot force a province to accept its offer of financial support, history shows that the provinces will accept money targeted to child care services when it is offered." In short, federal spending power can indeed "buy change" in ELCC, as advocates have suggested (Yalnizyan and McCuaig 2020). It is important, however, to remember that it will be the ELCC change that provinces and territories are interested in making and not necessarily what federal policy makers might prioritize. The federal government, as a funder and not a regulator, can threaten to reduce or withhold federal transfers if it is not satisfied that provincial or territorial actions are meeting federal conditions. But this power is a blunt instrument and one best used infrequently if the federal government is sincere in wanting to meet its policy and political objectives in ELCC. In the following section, this chapter turns to the recent historical record to see how federal and provincial spending on ELCC have jointly evolved and how provinces have responded to changes in federal conditional spending.

Previous Quantitative Studies on ELCC Spending in Canada

There have been previous efforts to compile and present data on the state of ELCC in Canada. These have included broader performance evaluations that consider system performance against a series of target indicators including measures of public spending (Akbari, McCuaig, and Foster 2021), periodic surveys of providers to estimate ELCC costs facing households (Macdonald and Friendly 2020), as well as periodic descriptive reports that permit comparisons between provinces and within provinces over time, again including measures of public spending (Friendly et al. 2021).

Two reports from the Atkinson Centre provide estimates of gross spending in the same four provinces of interest included in this chapter (Akbari, McCuaig, and Foster 2021; Akbari and McCuaig 2018). The authors of those reports used government budget documents[13] and included amounts for a wider range of programs that support early child development outside of childcare services, for example kindergarten and services for children with autism. Their results suggest that spending on ELCC in 2020 was 37 per cent higher in Ontario than in Quebec.[14]

Researchers at the Childcare Resource and Research Unit have published twelve reports on childcare since 1992, including a summary of annual spending in each province and territory. In Table 27 of their 2021 report, the authors present their estimates of government budgetary allocations for regulated childcare between 1992 and 2018–19 (Friendly et al. 2021, 244). Their totals include spending on kindergarten in some but not all jurisdictions and for some but not all years, reflecting changing policy regimes across provinces. Results from Friendly et al. (2021) suggest that, in the most recent fiscal year (2018–19), spending on ELCC was 40 per cent higher in Quebec than in Ontario.[15]

In the most recent edition in a series of reports, Macdonald and Friendly (2020, 9–10) have surveyed a sample of ELCC providers across the country to estimate median monthly fees for parents. The authors present provider-reported fees for different age groups of children and show regional or community level differences. But, as the authors' note, their data do not include any individual subsidies or refundable tax credits tied to ELCC expenses. As such, their data cannot be interpreted as evidence of what families actually pay out of pocket, net of government spending.[16]

The current chapter appears to be the first to present longitudinal data on actual spending, rather than budgetary allocations, on ELCC in four provinces. This chapter also offers disaggregated analyses of federal and subnational spending, including municipal spending in Ontario. These data differ from results published in previous studies in at least a few important ways. First, this report relies primarily on public accounts and tax expenditure data to capture actual public spending at the end of the fiscal or tax year, rather than projected spending in government budgets or estimates. As described later in the results section and illustrated in the data appendix, there can be important variances between projected and actual annual expenditures. Second, this report provides detailed and interprovincially comparable data by applying the same set of parameters to all jurisdictions studied.[17] Third, past reports on ELCC spending in Canada have generally been cross-sectional – that is, reports are produced periodically but only examine data for a given year of interest. This chapter instead creates a panel dataset, with adjustments for constant dollars, to permit analysis of trends over the full study period. Finally, this chapter presents analyses of the interactions of federal, provincial, and municipal spending on ELCC over time. To understand total spending trends in the presence of intergovernmental transfers, it is important to distinguish between gross spending that includes the transfer and net spending that reflects the unique contribution of each order of government.[18]

Methods and Data Sources

I construct a longitudinal dataset of reported spending on ELCC using the public accounts for the governments of Canada (Receiver General of Canada, 2010–11 to 2019–20), Quebec (Ministère des Finances, 2010–11 to 2019–20), Ontario (Treasury Board Secretariat of Ontario, 2010–11 to 2019–20), Alberta (Alberta Children's Services, 2010–11 to 2019–20), and British Columbia (Government of British Columbia, 2010–11 to 2019–20) for fiscal years 2010–11 through 2019–20. I include direct spending on transfers to other governments and to service providers, including operating grants and fee or wage subsidies. Capital spending is included but reported without amortization for consistency, given differences in public accounting standards across jurisdictions. Any dedicated government revenues related to ELCC, such as licensing fees or restricted amounts received from another order of government, are not reported but are, where possible, netted against reported government expenditures. Fee-based revenues are not evenly reported by provinces, and differences in this regard are noted in the results section. Internal government costs, such as any salary and benefits paid to public servant employees administering ELCC programs, are excluded for consistency across jurisdictions and to focus on observable ELCC service impacts for Canadian families.

Federal spending includes transfers to provinces under bilateral agreements signed in 2017. In fiscal year 2019–20, total federal spending under these agreements was $399.7 million. In addition to these agreements, I also include a portion of the Canada Social Transfer (CST) that is notionally earmarked for ELCC.[19] In the 2007 federal budget, the CST base was increased by $250 million per year "for the creation of child care spaces," with a further commitment to apply the 3 per cent annual escalator to the new amount starting in the 2009–10 fiscal year (Department of Finance Canada 2007, 128). I also include direct transfers to ELCC providers or associations, as reported in the public accounts, through programs administered by various federal departments. This last category of spending may directly or indirectly support ELCC services and will exclude transfers to organizations that could not be clearly identified as an ELCC organization.

In my estimates of government spending, I also include longitudinal data on tax expenditures for tax measures related to ELCC from the Quebec, Ontario, and federal governments. In Quebec, eligible families can receive a refundable tax credit to cover eligible fees outside of provincially subsidized spaces (Revenu Québec n.d.). A similar, though less generous, provincial credit was also introduced in Ontario for the 2019 tax year (Government of Ontario n.d.). Data for these two credits are taken from the respective Quebec and Ontario expenditure data (Ministère des Finances 2010–11 to 2019–20; Treasury Board Secretariat of Ontario 2010–11 to 2019–20). The federal tax expenditure of interest is the childcare expenses deduction (CCED), as reported in annual federal tax expenditure reports (Department of Finance Canada 2021b).

While some have argued that the CCED should be excluded from an analysis of spending on ELCC, the deduction is not part of Canada's benchmark tax system. Cleveland (2021) argues that the deduction serves a horizontal equity objective, reducing the disincentive effect of childcare fees for mothers to join the paid workforce instead of forgoing paid employment to provide unpaid care to dependent children. In this view, the CCED might instead be treated as an expenditure supporting female labour market participation. However, as illustrated in Figure 17.1, the relationship between the value of the deduction and the labour force participation of women in childbearing years is at best unclear. Since it was created in 1972, the deduction has evolved significantly in ways that greatly reduce its relationship to workforce entry for secondary earners, presumed to be female. For example, expenses incurred to retain a childcare spot, even if the parent is on leave from work, are eligible for the deduction. Furthermore, the deduction is permitted for parents who are in education or

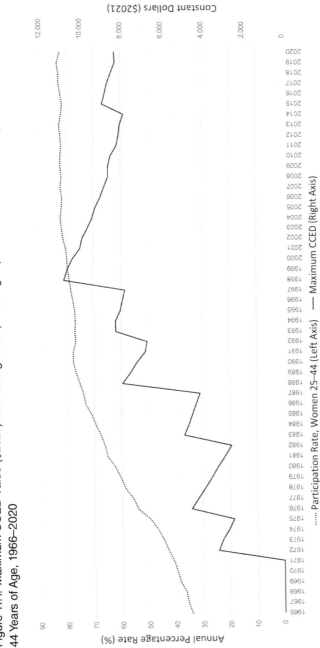

Figure 17.1. Maximum CCED Value ($2021) for a Young Child (under Age 7) and Labour Force Participation of Women 25 to 44 Years of Age, 1966–2020

Sources: Author's calculations using Statistics Canada (2022); data published for 1966 to 1974 in Denton (2018, 22); Canada Revenue Agency (1985–2021); and CCED data published in Gagné (2001).

Note: CCED = childcare expenses deduction.

research, or receiving Canada Pension Plan (CPP) disability benefits, and not necessarily earning employment income. Other rules permit primary earners in a couple to claim the deduction in some circumstances.

Take-up of the deduction is concentrated among parents with higher education, who already enjoy better wage incentives to participate in the labour market (Heidinger, Findlay, and Guèvremont 2020). Evaluations of the deduction also find significant evidence of eligible non-participation, that is parents who report use of paid childcare but who do not claim the CCED (Heidinger, Findlay, and Guèvremont 2020; Department of Finance Canada 2021b). Other tax credits and deductions now exist to recognize various and more general costs incurred to participate in the labour market, such as the Canada employment credit and the deduction for using the home as a workplace. Compared to the CCED, these are more clearly direct tax measures to offset the costs of engaging in paid work. Framing the CCED as a female labour market participation measure requires that we assume mothers have a true choice to forgo paid work. This assumption was perhaps defensible in 1972 when labour force participation of women in childbearing years was 42.8 per cent (as illustrated in Figure 17.1), but it seems an unusual assumption in the context of participation rates of over 80 per cent and when the income of secondary earners is not discretionary but rather makes up roughly 40 per cent of market income for couples with children.[20] In fact, this framing of "choice" is more typical of horizontal equity arguments against supply-side funding for ELCC in favour of direct cash supports to all families, including those with a parent outside of the labour market. Past studies of ELCC spending in Canada have also included the CCED (Friendly et al. 2021). For all of these reasons, I include the federal expenditure in my estimates. The federal share spent within a province is estimated from the proportion of total claims for the deduction arising from that province. The provincial share of forgone tax revenues is not reported because both Ontario and Quebec, the provinces of interest for the detailed results, have replacement measures in their tax and transfer system, as described earlier.

In Ontario, childcare funding and oversight is largely devolved to municipal governments. Friendly et al. (2021) report that municipal service managers are required to match allocations from the province at $0.20 per $1 received. In practice, municipalities may not be meeting that expectation. To estimate actual municipal spending on ELCC, I sampled municipal budgets for the cities of Toronto, Peel, and Ottawa during the years 2010 to 2020 for their reporting on the previous year. I find that actual amounts reported by cities range from 13 per cent to 18 per cent (with a mean of 15 per cent) of reported provincial transfer revenues. In my estimates, municipal spending is imputed at 15 per cent of provincial transfers for grants to providers (both operational and capital) and subsidies to families.

Table 17.1. Mean Variance between Provincial ELCC Spending Allocations and Actual Expenditures Reported in Public Accounts

Province	x̄ Variance
British Columbia	−0.10441
Alberta	−0.00818
Ontario	−0.02001
Quebec	−0.00317

Sources: Author's calculations using data from Ministère des Finances (2010–11 to 2019–20), Treasury Board Secretariat of Ontario (2010–11 to 2019–20), Alberta Children's Services (2010–11 to 2019–20), and Government of British Columbia (2010–11 to 2019–20).

To estimate private household spending on ELCC, I use the Canadian Income Survey, a cross-sectional annual survey conducted by Statistics Canada. Analysis was completed using the public use microdata files for the survey years 2012 through 2017 inclusive (Statistics Canada 2012–17).[21] Data on ELCC spending by the economic family is self-reported by survey respondents and refers to all out-of-pocket spending on childcare incurred in the year. Amounts per year reflect the aggregate amount reported by all households resident in the province.

All dollar amounts in a given twelve-month fiscal or tax year are attributed to the federal fiscal year running April to March to harmonize the data. All dollar amounts are adjusted to constant dollar values for 2021 using the Consumer Price Index.

As indicated earlier, and in contrast to previous reports on ELCC spending in Canada, I report on actual amounts spent rather than amounts allocated through public budgeting or estimate processes. To illustrate why this methodological choice is important, in Table 17.1 I report the mean variance between annual amounts allocated and actual amounts spent on ELCC in the four provinces of interest over the fiscal years 2014–15 through 2019–20. Mean variance is negative in all cases, indicating the actual expenditures are generally less than amounts allocated. The difference is especially important in the case of British Columbia, with over 10.4 per cent in the average difference between allocations and actual expenditures.

To understand the policy outputs achieved for the spending, I report on the number of licensed spaces in each province of interest. I also calculate the annual value of public and total spending in a province per licensed space. Provincial data on the number of licensed spaces are taken from provincial departmental reports on childcare (Ontario Ministry of Education 2020; Alberta Children's Services, 2010–11 to 2019–20; Ministère de la Famille, 2021b; Ministry of Children and Family Development, 2010–11 to 2019–20). Readers should note that these data exclude ELCC providers who are not required to obtain a licence. For example, in Ontario, a provider caring for five or fewer children (who are not the dependent children of the caregiver) must follow certain regulations to protect the welfare of the children but is not subject to licensing requirements.[22]

Results

In Table 17.2, I present total public spending, in real dollars, for the federal and four provincial governments of interest. It represents the total value of transfers to other orders of government, organizations, and individuals (in the form of subsidies), as well as tax expenditures. It excludes amounts spent on internal costs, such as government staffing and administration, and is net of any ELCC-specific revenues within the jurisdiction, such as licensing fees. Amounts net of transfers received are presented later in Tables 17.4 and 17.5.

Table 17.3 presents the data on total licensed spaces in each of the four provinces of interest. Readers should note that the BC data, as reported by the provincial government (Ministry of Children and Family Development 2010–11 to 2019–20), includes only those licensed spaces that received provincial operating funding. The data shown are as reported at December of the fiscal year. Other jurisdictions report all licensed spaces instead. In Quebec, three-quarters of all licensed spaces receive operating funding to subsidize parental fees (Ministère de la Famille 2021b).

According to Akbari, McCuaig, and Foster (2021), the 2017 bilateral agreements on ELCC resulted in significant increases to provincial spending on ELCC. I find that, in the three fiscal years following the 2017 bilateral agreements signed on ELCC, federal spending remained essentially unchanged in real terms, while it increased to varying degrees in the four provinces of interest. The largest increase was in British Columbia (122 per cent), followed by Ontario (35 per cent). The increase in British Columbia appears to be mainly due to the introduction of the province's Affordable Child Care Benefit in 2018, which replaced the previous fee subsidy system with a portable and more generous income-tested benefit for families. In Ontario, most of the spending increase, as I illustrate in detail later in this section, was attributable to the introduction of the provincial refundable tax credit.

The impact of the 2017 agreements on the volume of licensed spaces was more modest. Using the counts of spaces reported in Table 17.3, I find that spaces increased by less than 2 per cent in Quebec, by 8 per cent in both Ontario and British Columbia, and by just under 11 per cent in Alberta. This relative change in spaces is, however, significantly larger than the targets agreed to in the federal-provincial deals. The increase in licensed spaces in Alberta at 13,543 between the fiscal years 2017–18 and 2019–20 was roughly quadruple the target number (3,000) of new spaces cited in the 2017 Canada-Alberta

Table 17.2. Summary of Total Public Real Spending on ELCC, Selected Jurisdictions ($ millions; 2021 constant dollars)

	2010–11	2011–12	2012–13	2013–14	2014–15	2015–16	2016–17	2017–18	2018–19	2019–20
Federal	1,342	1,382	1,426	1,417	1,438	1,837	1,763	2,193	2,193	2,192
Ontario	1,005	1,017	1,109	1,161	1,298	1,403	1,482	1,845	2,100	2,486
Quebec	2,917	3,121	3,140	3,268	3,360	3,327	3,226	3,220	3,218	3,441
Alberta	262	282	295	298	315	319	340	405	428	422
British Columbia	n/a	n/a	277	269	267	271	274	308	496	683

Sources: Author's calculations using data from Receiver General of Canada (2010–11 to 2019–20), Ministère des Finances (2010–11 to 2019–20), Treasury Board Secretariat of Ontario (2010–11 to 2019–20), Alberta Children's Services (2010–11 to 2019–20), and Government of British Columbia (2010–11 to 2019–20).

Table 17.3. Summary of Licensed ELCC Spaces, Selected Jurisdictions

	2010–11	2011–12	2012–13	2013–14	2014–15	2015–16	2016–17	2017–18	2018–19	2019–20
Ontario	264,201	275,873	294,490	317,868	350,801	389,286	406,395	427,032	446,596	462,802
Quebec	232,628	245,107	258,366	268,624	279,310	285,315	293,434	301,174	305,083	306,152
Alberta	n/a	n/a	n/a	n/a	105,310	109,482	116,714	124,824	131,624	138,367
British Columbia	92,242	95,597	98,447	100,281	104,353	106,456	109,313	111,558	113,675	120,005

Sources: British Columbia Ministry of Children and Family Development (2010–11 to 2019–20), Quebec Ministère de la Famille (2021b), Ontario Ministry of Education (2020) and Alberta Children's' Services (2010–11 to 2019–20).

agreement (Employment and Social Development Canada 2017a).[23] Likewise, the agreement with British Columbia had promised to result in 1,960 new childcare spaces, and during the life of the agreement, the province added 8,447 spaces (Employment and Social Development Canada 2017b).[24]

In Tables 17.4, 17.5, and 17.6, I present the more detailed data on ELCC spending federally and in the two largest provinces, Ontario and Quebec. These tables offer disaggregated data and permit analysis of trends in the components of total public spending, including transfers to providers, transfers to other orders of government, and tax measures.

In Table 17.4, I present detailed data for real federal spending for fiscal years 2010–11 through 2019–20. During the period examined, the largest share of

Table 17.4. Details of Federal Real Spending on ELCC ($ millions, constant 2021 dollars)

Category of Spending	2010–11	2011–12	2012–13	2013–14	2014–15	2015–16	2016–17	2017–18	2018–19	2019–20
CCED, federal portion of forgone tax revenues	1,021	1,058	1,100	1,087	1,103	1,494	1,415	1,414	1,420	1,425
Federal direct transfers to provinces/territories for ELCC, total*	–	–	–	–	–	–	–	428	419	408
Federal direct transfers to ELCC providers/associations[†]	2	3	3	2	2	2	2	2	2	1
Federal CST portion earmarked for ELCC[‡]	319	321	322	328	334	342	346	349	352	357
Total federal spending	1,342	1,382	1,425	1,417	1,439	1,838	1,763	2,193	2,193	2,191

Sources: Author's calculations using data from Receiver General of Canada (2010–11 to 2019–20) and Department of Finance Canada (2007).

* Actuals for 2017 bilateral agreements, as reported in the Public Accounts for fiscal years 2017–18 to 2019–20.

[†] 2010–13 transfers are for Indigenous ELCC providers or associations as well as ELCC sector council; in 2012–12 some non-Indigenous providers received funding; in 2013 the ELCC human resources council funding was discontinued. Amounts exclude very small transfers via Foreign Affairs for international ELCC organizations. Organizations were identified by a text search for "child care" and "garderie," and may exclude transfers to organizations also providing care but not reflected in their name. Transfers may not be for childcare activities of recipient organizations.

[‡] Author's calculation using the formula outlined in the 2007 federal budget (Department of Finance Canada 2007).

Table 17.5. Details of Provincial Real Spending on ELCC in Quebec ($ millions, constant 2021 dollars)

Category of Spending	2010–11	2011–12	2012–13	2013–14	2014–15	2015–16	2016–17	2017–18	2018–19	2019–20
Infrastructure subsidy	29	30	31	34	36	37	39	41	42	43
Total operating grants	2,411	2,536	2,486	2,516	2,532	2,463	2,336	2,306	2,283	2,520
Benefits for workers	68	69	66	91	129	130	134	134	142	134
Refundable tax credit for childcare expenses	409	486	558	627	662	696	718	739	751	745
Total provincial spending	2,917	3,121	3,140	3,268	3,360	3,327	3,226	3,220	3,218	3,441
Federal transfers received for ELCC*	74	74	75	77	77	79	79	174	170	170
Total provincial spending net of federal transfers for ELCC	2,843	3,047	3,065	3,191	3,283	3,248	3,147	3,046	3,048	3,271

Sources: Author's calculations using data from Ministère des Finances (2010–11 to 2019–20), Receiver General of Canada (2010–11 to 2019–20) and Department of Finance Canada (2007).
* Author's calculation of provincial share of notional envelope within the Canada Social Transfer plus amounts transferred under the 2017 bilateral ELCC agreement.

Table 17.6. Details of Provincial Real Spending on ELCC in Ontario ($ millions, constant 2021 dollars)

Category of Spending	2010–11	2011–12	2012–13	2013–14	2014–15	2015–16	2016–17	2017–18	2018–19	2019–20
Transfers to providers	1,004	1,015	1,099	1,093	1,291	1,394	1,482	1,804	2,001	1,976
CARE Tax credit	–	–	–	–	–	–	–	–	–	503
Childcare capital spending (including amortization)	1	2	10	68	7	9	1	41	99	6
Total provincial spending	1,005	1,017	1,109	1,161	1,298	1,403	1,482	1,845	2,100	2,486
Federal transfers received for ELCC*	123	125	125	126	129	131	133	292	289	290
Total provincial spending net of federal transfers for ELCC	882	893	984	1,035	1,170	1,271	1,349	1,553	1,811	2,196
Municipal incremental spending on ELCC†	151	152	165	164	194	209	222	271	300	296
Total subnational net spending on ELCC	1,032	1,045	1,149	1,199	1,363	1,481	1,571	1,824	2,111	2,492

Sources: Author's calculations using data from Treasury Board Secretariat of Ontario (2010–11 to 2019–20), Receiver General of Canada (2010–11 to 2019–20) and Department of Finance Canada (2007).
* Author's calculation of provincial share of notional envelope within the Canada Social Transfer plus amounts transferred under the 2017 bilateral ELCC agreement.
† Author's estimate of municipal spending as 15 per cent of transfers received from the province.

federal spending is consistently the Child Care Expenses Deduction (CCED), a tax measure described earlier in this chapter. At roughly $1.4 billion annually in recent years, it accounts for nearly two-thirds of all federal spending on ELCC. The 2017 bilateral agreements began in the 2017–18 fiscal year and more than doubled transfers to provinces and territories for ELCC over the baseline CST portion that is earmarked for childcare. However, the agreements were for nominal amounts without an escalator clause or indexation, and so spending effectively fell by $20 million over the three-year period of the agreements. The introduction of the deals in 2017 increased total federal spending by nearly 25 per cent, relative to the 2016–17 fiscal year, but because of the decline in the real value of those transfers, total federal spending was unchanged during the period of those bilateral agreements.

In Table 17.5, I present detailed data for real provincial spending in Quebec for fiscal years 2010–11 through 2019–20; in Table 17.6, comparable data are presented for Ontario. In both tables, amounts received by the province as a transfer for ELCC are reported and then subtracted from the estimate of total net provincial spending. Spending in both provinces includes direct spending for ELCC operations as well as more modest spending to create new ELCC services. During the lifetime of the 2017 bilateral agreements with the federal government, spending on transfers to childcare providers for operations and fee subsidies in Ontario increased 10 per cent between 2017–18 and 2019–20. However, Ontario's capital spending on new spaces plummeted from a high of $99 million in 2018–19 to just $6 million in 2019–20. In Quebec, transfers to providers increased 9 per cent during the life of the bilateral agreement, but funding to create new spaces was essentially flat. Total net provincial spending is significantly larger in Quebec compared to Ontario. At $3.3 billion per year, in the most recent year, Quebec's ELCC spending is equivalent to 1 per cent of provincial gross domestic product (GDP), while it is much lower at just 0.4 per cent of provincial GDP in Ontario.

Both provinces have some important differences in the composition of their ELCC spending. Since 2003, Quebec has offered a group pension plan and a benefits plan for many ELCC workers (Ministère de la Famille 2021a). These plans cover workers in the same ELCC settings that receive provincial operating transfers – non-profit centres de la petite enfance (CPEs), subsidized for-profit centres, and subsidized self-employed home-based care providers. In total, 77 per cent of ELCC spaces in the province are subsidized, and their staff benefit from the enhanced compensation package subsidized by the province (Dubé 2021). Over the fiscal years included in this study, the cost of this compensation package has risen much faster than the amount the province allocates for the start-up costs of new CPEs in the province. But these labour force programs might indirectly contribute to increases in the volume and quality in the supply of ELCC services by reducing staff turnover in both centre and home-based settings, and providing an indirect subsidy to providers, including eligible for-profit ELCC centres.

In Ontario, it is important to note the unique feature of the role played by municipal governments. In contrast to the three other provinces considered in this chapter, Ontario has devolved much of its responsibility for administration of ELCC funding to municipal governments. Provincial transfers for capital and operating costs are allocated to municipal governments across the province, and they in turn match amounts from their own revenues. As noted in the discussion on data sources and methods, using a sample of detailed municipal budget documents, I estimate that actual municipal spending is approximately 15 per cent of provincial spending, rather than the prescribed 20 per cent in provincial directives for operating grants to providers.[25]

As of the 2019-20 fiscal year, both Ontario and Quebec also have tax expenditures for ELCC in the form of refundable credits paid to families for out-of-pocket ELCC costs. In the most recent fiscal year, refundable credits account for 23 per cent of all provincial spending (net of federal transfers) in Quebec and 20 per cent of all provincial plus municipal funding (again, net of federal transfers) in Ontario. In short, refundable credits now occupy a similar share of fiscal room in ELCC spending in both jurisdictions. Over the full decade under review for this study, Quebec's refundable tax credit experienced the fastest rate of growth (at 112 per cent) of any component of its ELCC spending. The actual costs of Ontario's refundable credit are only available for one fiscal year, but it is worth noting that the cost, at $503 million, is already substantially higher than originally projected in the 2019 provincial budget.[26] Absent this new expenditure in Ontario, real provincial spending (including shares from municipalities) on ELCC would have fallen substantially between 2018-19 and 2019-20 in the final year of the bilateral agreement with the federal government.

Finally, in Figures 17.2 and 17.3, I first integrate data on federal and provincial spending, reported above, with estimates of the annual totals of household spending on ELCC services in both Ontario and Quebec. Rather than dollar amounts reported thus far, I now consider relative shares of total spending, in order to understand how governments have been sharing the costs of these services and what portion is left to households to absorb privately. Then I present a per-space average of both total and all government spending on ELCC services. Because the data for households is drawn from the Canadian Income Survey (Statistics Canada 2012-17), these figures reflect the shorter time series over which data on household spending is available.

Figures 17.2 and 17.3 illustrate the relative shares of spending on ELCC by households and governments in both Quebec and Ontario over the six-year period from 2012-13 to 2017-18. In both provinces, household spending on ELCC simply dwarfs public spending and, in Ontario, is relatively impervious

Figure 17.2. Relative Shares of Real Total Spending on ELCC, Quebec, 2012–18

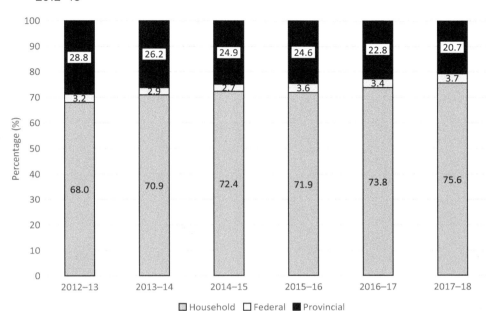

Sources: Author's calculations using data from Statistics Canada (2012–17), Receiver General of Canada (2010–11 to 2019–20), Department of Finance Canada (2007), and Ministère des Finances (2010–11 to 2019–20).
Note: ELCC = early learning and childcare.

to the real changes in public spending illustrated earlier in Table 17.6. However, there are important interprovincial differences in the relative burden borne by households for ELCC services. In Ontario, household spending hovers at roughly 90 per cent of all spending on ELCC in the province until 2016–17 before falling to just under 87 per cent in 2017–18. Readers will note that the last year for which household spending data are available is also the first year in which the federal-provincial agreement was in place. However, because the decline in the relative share of household over public spending seems to begin in 2016–17, it is difficult to attribute this shift in relative cost burdens to the bilateral agreement.

In Quebec, despite significantly higher real public spending at the provincial level, the relative share of ELCC costs borne by households in the province has increased over time from 68 per cent in 2012–13 to 76 per cent in 2017–18. The relative share of total spending from provincial coffers is roughly double

Figure 17.3. Relative Shares of Real Total Spending on ELCC, Ontario, 2012–18

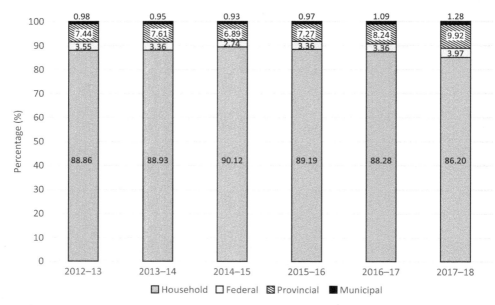

Sources: Author's calculations using data from Statistics Canada (2012–17), Treasury Board Secretariat of Ontario (2010–11 to 2019–20), Receiver General of Canada (2010–11 to 2019–20) and Department of Finance Canada (2007).
Note: ELCC = early learning and childcare.

in Quebec what it is in Ontario, even when combining provincial and the increment from municipal budgets in Ontario. But the proportion of ELCC costs absorbed by the provincial government in Quebec clearly declined over time between 2012–13 and 2017–18, from nearly 29 per cent to 21 per cent, despite the fact that, as illustrated earlier in Table 17.5, real provincial spending (net of federal transfers) was essentially unchanged.

Federal spending from 2016–17, before the bilateral agreements on ELCC, to 2017–18, the first year of the bilateral agreements, remains a sliver of total spending in both jurisdictions in this study. This result holds even though federal funding more than doubled, in real terms (as illustrated earlier in Tables 17.5 and 17.6), during this period in both Quebec and Ontario.

In Figures 17.4 and 17.5, I illustrate changes over time in the per-space average of total spending in both Quebec and Ontario. Again, these figures

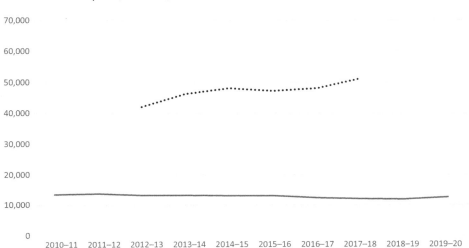

Figure 17.4. All Public Spending and Public Plus Household Spending per Licensed Space, Quebec, 2010–11 to 2019–20

Sources: Author's calculations using data from Statistics Canada (2012–17), Receiver General of Canada (2010–11 to 2019–20), Department of Finance Canada (2007), Ministère des Finances (2010–11 to 2019–20), and Ministère de la Famille (2021b).

represent the sum of household and government spending (at all orders) divided by the count of licensed spaces in the province, over time. Because households are self-reporting their ELCC spending, there may be both under- and over-counting of the net spending after credits and deductions paid directly to households for ELCC.

These figures show two very different patterns in public and total spending on ELCC in the two provinces of interest. In Quebec, there is a decline in total public spending (the sum of federal and provincial), per ELCC space, over the decade. In fiscal year 2010–11, public spending per licensed space was just over $13,500, falling to just over $12,500 by 2019–20. As illustrated earlier in Figure 17.2, the relative share of provincial spending fell during this time, while the federal share remained small and largely unchanged. Yet, as noted in Table 17.5, provincial real spending did grow by about $400 million from fiscal year 2010–11 to 2019–20. Taken together, this finding suggests that spaces in the province grew faster than public investment. As noted earlier in Table 17.3, Quebec added nearly 74,000 new licensed spaces during

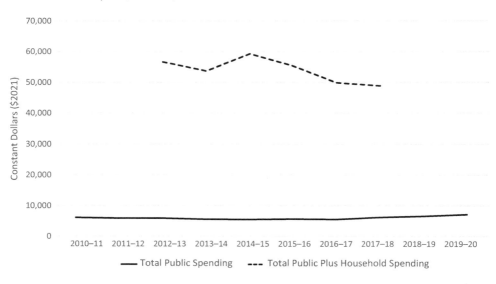

Figure 17.5. All Public Spending and Public Plus Household Spending per Licensed Space, Ontario, 2010–11 to 2019–20

Sources: Author's calculations using data from Statistics Canada (2012–17), Treasury Board Secretariat of Ontario (2010–11 to 2019–20), Ontario Ministry of Education (2020), Receiver General of Canada (2010–11 to 2019–20) and Department of Finance Canada (2007).

this decade, but it appears that it was families who absorbed the costs of this expansion.

By contrast, total spending per licensed space in Ontario declined over the same period, while public spending (including all three orders of government) increased slightly. In 2010–11, governments collectively spent just over $6,100 per licensed space in Ontario, rising to $7,200 by 2019–20. These public investment levels are, however, almost half the amounts spent per space in Quebec. Quebec spends more public dollars for the ELCC services it has, and it invests its spending in a wider range of tools, including transfers to providers, benefits for ELCC workers, and cash transfers to parents. Whether this higher per-space public spending in Quebec over Ontario is indicative of better quality services or not is beyond the scope of this study, but measures of quality and child outcomes have been examined elsewhere in the literature (Baker, Gruber, and Milligan 2008, 2019; Duval et al. 2020; Haeck, Lefebvre, and Merrigan 2015; Japel 2012; Lehrer, Lemay, and Bigras 2015; Lemay, Bigras, and Bouchard 2015;

Verreault 2019). Finally, both provinces appear to be spending less, including both public and private spending, than some estimates of the per-space cost of quality care (Cleveland 2012).[27]

Finally, there is a remarkable convergence of total spending per licensed space across the two provinces. Again, this is the sum of aggregate public and household spending divided by the number of licensed spaces in the province. In Quebec, it rose from $42,000 in 2012–13 to $51,000 in 2017–18. In Ontario, it declined from $57,000 to $49,000 over the same period. As noted earlier, given the outsized role of household spending in both provinces, some of the convergence reflects shifts in who is absorbing the costs of expansion of new licensed spaces. In Quebec, it appears that it has been primarily households.

Readers will also note that this estimate of total spending is many times higher than public spending and higher than estimates of the cost to operate a quality space. But it is important to note that many forms of childcare, such as homecare services (outside of licensed agencies) and private nannies, are not part of licensed care in any province. In other words, an important portion of total spending – particularly household spending and tax expenditures at both federal and provincial levels – is flowing to unlicensed care. If licensing of care leads to better quality and outcomes for children, then this finding suggests that Canada is not currently at an optimal allocation of total resources for ELCC. On the other hand, the results may also provide some information of the distribution of family preferences, a distribution that may (or may not) shift as governments roll out new public spending under the 2021 bilateral agreements.

Discussion and Conclusion

This study has presented detailed temporally and geographically comparable data on real ELCC spending in Canada. The data provide a baseline for monitoring financial changes to ELCC systems as a result of new federal spending starting in 2021. The federal government set some clear policy goals for ELCC in the 2021 budget and bilateral agreements on ELCC – first, to increase the quantity and quality of childcare services across the country and to redistribute the burden of paying for childcare so that families with young children bear a smaller direct share of the total costs. This latter goal proved to be an important talking point for a federal government under pressure to reduce financial pressures for Canadian households in the high inflation environment of 2022 (Freeland 2022). Looking ahead, by tracking the relative share of total ELCC spending in a province, we can gain an indication of progress on that goal, one shared by both federal policy makers and ELCC advocates alike. There will also be merit to tracking both the volume of new licensed spaces created and the trend lines in both public and total spending per licensed space. If public spending per licensed space continues to decline in some provinces, such as

364   Jennifer Robson

Quebec, it should raise concerns about where new federal money is actually being directed. Others may also see it as a proxy indicator for quality of ELCC services, but I am more cautious in making that assertion. That total spending per licensed space is so much higher than estimates of the cost to operate good quality care is an indication that an important share of household spending on ELCC is happening outside of licensed spaces. For some families, this cost will reflect preferences that will compete with policy goals to expand licensed ELCC services. But for many families, it likely reflects constrained optimization in which they are paying for the care they are able to find. If licensed spaces can expand enough, if the care is of good quality, and if licensed ELCC fees are affordable to parents, then we might see more household resources directed towards licensed versus unlicensed care.

The 2021 federal budget also set a goal of raising federal spending to eventually become an equal partner with provinces on ELCC spending. The results of this study suggest that it could be a very challenging goal to meet. The challenge is not, as some have misunderstood the federal fiscal commitment, that it requires provinces to match new federal spending at $0.50 for each dollar. Instead, the challenge is that federal spending is starting from such a modest level, even using the most generous definition that includes the CCED tax expenditure and CST. Matching the ELCC spending of the four largest provinces in 2019–20 would cost the federal purse just over $7 billion. The 2021 federal budget projected a maximum and permanent federal transfer for all provinces and territories of just $9.2 billion by 2025 (Department of Finance Canada 2021a, 102).[28] The federal funding formula for all agreements with provinces and territories is clearly stated in the text of the published agreements. Provinces and territories will all receive a baseline of $2 million plus a share of the annual allocations ($2.9 billion in 2021–2, rising to $7.7 billion in 2025), based on the local share of the Canadian population aged under one year to twelve years. While this formula may be sufficient to bring federal spending to equality with provincial spending in some smaller jurisdictions, it will not bring federal spending to par in the highest-spending province of Quebec. Still, the federal government was able to conclude an agreement with Quebec.

Even if it does not appear to match provincial spending, the Canada-Quebec agreement is consistent with the federal spending power in the context of asymmetrical federalism. When the federal government reached an agreement with the government of Quebec in August 2021, the federal press release was quick to state that the federal funding was being agreed upon while "recognizing that Quebec will maintain its role in setting priorities in early learning and child care, an area exclusive to Quebec and in which it already has a proven track record" (Office of the Prime Minister 2021). Previously, both the prime minister and Quebec's minister of finance had stated that any federal transfer for ELCC to Quebec would be unconditional, sparking anger from the government of Alberta, which demanded the same style of agreement (Canadian Press 2021; French 2021). This demand was political theatre, and it rested on a misunderstanding of subtle but important aspects of the federal spending power. Because the new federal spending in 2021 was attached to certain policy objectives that Quebec had already adopted as its own and largely met before the federal 2021 budget was even drafted, no additional conditions on the transfer to Quebec could be required or justified. Other provinces and territories that have reached agreements with the federal government have now likewise voluntarily adopted the agreed-upon ELCC policy goals laid out in the bilateral agreements. These goals are provincial policy goals, and all provinces and territories were free to refuse the federal offer of conditional money.

I began this chapter by noting that childcare advocates have hoped that new federal spending could be used to buy change in provincial ELCC policy. The bilateral agreements clearly position the new federal funding as a contribution towards costs incurred by a subnational government for the provision of ELCC. The agreements are also clearly rooted in an understanding of asymmetrical federalism, allowing different subnational governments to agree to different conditions. For example, in British Columbia, the agreement sets shared objectives for fee reductions in provincially licensed providers and spaces, which include non-profit as well as private for-profit ELCC providers in the province (Employment and Social Development Canada, 2021a). However, the deal negotiated with Nova Scotia's government instead specifies that the fee reduction objective applies to "provincially funded, regulated" spaces (Employment and Social Development Canada, 2021b).[29] Similarly, the BC agreement commits to using federal funds "exclusively to support licensed child care,"[30] while the Nova Scotia agreement commits to using federal funding "exclusively to support non-profit private and public child care providers/operations, as well as family-based child care."[31]

What remains unknown is whether the federal government will be willing to withhold a planned transfer for ELCC if ever federal officials believe that a province has broken a condition of the bilateral agreement. If the province disagrees with the claim about an area over which it has exclusive policy jurisdiction, the dispute may be a very interesting test of federal spending power. To what extent is the federal government prepared to fight for certain kinds of policy change or fight against others? Here it may be helpful to consider the recent historical example of the 2017 bilateral agreements.

One policy goal set by the federal government is growth in the number of licensed and quality ELCC spaces available. But did the 2017 agreements lead to an expansion of ELCC services? Given the nature of the largest spending increases in these provinces, and the targets set in the transfer agreements, it is difficult to attribute growth in spaces in the provinces of interest in this study to a causal effect from the 2017 bilateral agreements. Provinces increased their own spending, but often to introduce cash benefits for parents, measures with, at best, an indirect effect on the supply of spaces. Further, Alberta, the province that saw the smallest relative increase in spending during the 2017–20 period, actually saw the largest relative increase in licensed spaces in the jurisdiction (see Table 17.3, earlier in this chapter). I suggest that other and unobserved factors, such as regulations, training and compensation for ELCC workers, and even costs of real property to house ELCC services, might all influence the rate at which new licensed ELCC spaces can be created. It is provinces that directly determine regulations and can shape the training and wages of ELCC workers. Here, the federal government has no regulatory power at all. An attempt to use federal transfers to direct provincial regulations would exceed any reasonable understanding of the limits of federal spending power.

Another stated goal of the federal government is growth in the supply of quality ELCC services rather than increases in cash transfers to parents to subsidize demand. This goal is enthusiastically shared by ELCC advocates who understandably warn that demand-side measures will not create new spaces, enhance the quality of services, or improve working conditions in the sector. Advocates might hope that the spending power could be used as a bulwark against provincial instincts to use demand-side tools rather than investing in ELCC supply. However, here the lesson from recent history is very clear. In the final year of the 2017 bilateral agreement between the federal and Ontario governments, the newly elected government of Ontario slashed capital spending to build new spaces, froze operating transfers to providers, and instead directed the savings towards a new refundable tax credit. The federal transfer for ELCC was still paid as expected. The federal government could not have done otherwise without violating the limits on its spending power.

Looking ahead at potential impacts from the 2021 round of agreements, federal policy may indeed "buy change" in ELCC systems across the country, but it will be the change that has been willingly chosen by provinces and territories. In signing agreements with the federal government, provinces and territories have clearly expressed different directions and priorities for change that reflect their own assessments and preferences for the medium and longer term. Now that the ELCC transfers will be larger and eventually permanent, when provincial and territorial governments change political hands, the priorities and preferences of those governments on ELCC may change as well. The agreements appear to be written with enough flexibility to adapt. Hopefully, advocates will see this resilience as a strength of Canadian federalism rather than characterizing it as a failure of federal leadership.

NOTES

1 The full texts of all 2017 bilateral agreements and renewals were published by Employment and Social Development Canada and are available online at https://www.canada.ca/en/early-learning-child-care-agreement/agreements-provinces-territories.html.
2 Multiyear (2021 to 2025) bilateral agreements were signed beginning in July 2021 with all provinces and territories. The final 2021 agreement, signed with Ontario (until 2026), was concluded in May 2022 and retroactive to 2021. For simplicity, I will refer to this round of agreements as "2021 agreements." Copies of the full texts of all agreements were eventually made available online at https://www.canada.ca/en/early-learning-child-care-agreement/agreements-provinces-territories.html.
3 A notable exception is Cameron (2009).
4 See the Constitution Acts, 1867 to 1982, Consolidated Statutes of Canada, available online at https://laws-lois.justice.gc.ca/eng/const/index.html.
5 See pages x–xiv of the report by Friendly et al. (2020) for a discussion on the division of roles in ELCC in Canada.
6 It is important to note that Yalnizyan and McCuaig use the term "publicly managed" rather than "publicly delivered." The former denotes public planning and oversight of services, while the latter suggests direct public provision of a service.
7 The author was approached to sign this letter but respectfully declined given time constraints to consider or discuss the wording and context.
8 Provinces regulate ELCC services in their jurisdiction and have licensing requirements for the majority of service providers with more than a small number of spaces usually operated in a private home. The *Early Childhood Education Report 2020* reported that 57 per cent of regulated providers were for-profit operators, including family care providers. See Akbari, McCuaig, and Foster (2021), British Columbia profile, https://ecereport.ca/en/profiles/british-columbia/. The government of Quebec reported that 39 per cent of ELCC spaces in centres are run by for-profit providers, with an additional 30 per cent in family care settings (Dubé 2021). In Ontario, the provincial government reported that 21 per cent of spaces in centres and 20 per cent of spaces in licensed homecare agencies operate on a for-profit basis (Ontario Ministry of Education 2020).
9 The authors found that provincial spending increased by over $3 billion between 2017 and 2020, increasing faster than double the rate of federal transfers earmarked for ELCC. See Akbari, McCuaig, and Foster (2021), Overview, 8, https://ecereport.ca/media/uploads/2021-overview/overview2020_final2.pdf.
10 For a detailed discussion of federal and provincial fiscal capacity, see Trevor Tombe, chapter 4 of this volume.
11 In 2019–20, federal deductions from the Canada Health Transfer (CHT) totalled $16.8 million (or 0.0004 per cent of total CHT payments) before reimbursements and $734,000 net after reimbursements applied in that year (Health Canada 2021).

12 In the case of the Unemployment Insurance Act (since replaced by the Employment Insurance Act), a constitutional amendment was required to address limitations on federal spending power. As a system of insurance, contributions had to be made compulsory, but the insurance itself was deemed part of provincial head of power on the regulation of property and civil rights (Anand 2005; Courchene 2008).

13 It is important to note that budget documents will present planned spending rather than reporting actual expenditures. The political nature of budget documents also makes it difficult to use them to effectively track changes in spending over time as amounts can be reported in ways to dissemble new allocations from existing planned levels.

14 Author's calculation using figures reported in Akbari, McCuaig, and Foster (2021). For 2020, they report total Ontario spending of $6,268,232,949 and total Quebec spending of $4,561,738,379.

15 Author's calculation using data reported in Friendly et al. (2021, 244), Table 27. For 2018–19, they report total Ontario spending of $1,894.3 million and total Quebec spending of $2,653.8 million.

16 Readers will note, later in the methods and results section, that data used in the present study also may not adjust household spending for the value of all subsidies and tax measures tied to ELCC. Data used reflect self-reported fees paid, and different respondents may or may not be including subsidies or tax savings in their estimate.

17 The dataset created for this study is available on request and may be posted online at a future date. The dataset includes metadata on how variables were created and the analytical decisions required to harmonize spending across jurisdictions with different public accounting practices.

18 For example, Friendly et al. (2021) report Ontario's spending on childcare including federal transfers in amounts for capital and operating funding spent by the province. They report a total of $1,894,305,507 in combined federal and provincial funding, but the details of the federal and provincial shares cannot be inferred from their figures.

19 For a detailed discussion of the Canada Social Transfer, see Michael J. Prince, chapter 6 of this volume.

20 Author's calculation using the Canadian Income Survey 2017, public use microdata file, Statistics Canada, accessed through the Ontario Data Documentation, Extraction Service and Infrastructure.

21 Analysis was completed using Stata 16 with survey-adjusted weights provided by Statistics Canada.

22 See also "Types of child care," Government of Ontario, available online at https://www.ontario.ca/page/types-child-care.

23 See Employment and Social Development Canada (2017a), "Annex 2: Alberta's Action Plan," Table "Areas of Investment: Affordability, Accessibility, Quality and Improvements."

24 See Employment and Social Development Canada (2017b), Annex 2: British Columbia's Action Plan, Table Details of Expected Results: Indicators and Targets.
25 According to Friendly et al. (2021), local service managers in Ontario municipalities are expected to match provincial allocations for operating transfers to ELCC providers at $0.20 per $1. According to the City of Toronto (2020, 121) budget, as of the 2020–1 fiscal year, the province will require all ELCC funding, including funding for service expansion, to be cost-shared 80:20 with municipalities.
26 The Ontario 2019 budget projected the annual cost of the credit at $390 million per year; see Government of Ontario (2019, 338), Annex: Details of Tax Measures, Table A.4: Income Tax Deduction Before and After the Immediate Writeoff Measure.
27 Using American data, Cleveland (2012) calculates the cost of care at between $6,717 and $11,231 per year (in 1997 prices), depending on the age of the child. Adjusting for inflation, this cost would be between $10,572 and $17,677 in 2021 dollars. Quebec's total spending in the fiscal year 2019–20 is just within the lower bound of this range for children aged three to five years but well below the cost estimates for very young children.
28 See Chart 3.3.
29 See Employment and Social Development Canada (2021b), paragraph 1.2(a), page 3.
30 See Employment and Social Development Canada (2021a) paragraph 2.1.1, page 3.
31 See Employment and Social Development Canada (2017b), paragraph 2.1.1, page 3.

REFERENCES

Akbari, Emis, and Kerry McCuaig. 2018. *Early Childhood Education Report 2017*. Toronto: The Atkinson Centre for Society and Child Development. https://ecereport.ca/en/early-years-studies/ece-report-2017/.
Akbari, Emis, Kerry McCuaig, and Daniel Foster. 2021. *Early Childhood Education Report 2020*. Toronto: The Atkinson Centre for Society and Child Development. https://ecereport.ca/en/.
Alberta Children's Services. 2010–11 to 2019–20. "Ministry Annual Reports." Edmonton: Government of Alberta. https://www.alberta.ca/government-and-ministry-annual-reports.aspx.
Anand, Raj. 2005. "MISWAA – Development of New Architecture for Income Security in Canada." Toronto: WeirFoulds LLP. https://openpolicyontario.s3.amazonaws.com/uploads/2021/08/MISWAA-opinion-ltr_v1-1.pdf.
Baker, Michael, Jonathan Gruber, and Kevin Milligan. 2008. "Universal Child Care, Maternal Labor Supply, and Family Well-Being." *Journal of Political Economy* 116, no. 4: 709–45. https://doi.org/10.1086/591908.
– 2019. "The Long-Run Impacts of a Universal Child Care Program." *American Economics Journal: Economic Policy* 11, no. 3: 1–26. https://doi.org/10.1257/pol.20170603.
Boessenkool, Ken, and Jennifer Robson. 2021. *Aggressive Incrementalism: Strengthening the Foundations of Canada's Approach to Childcare*. Commentary, No. 595. Toronto:

The C.D. Howe Institute. https://www.cdhowe.org/public-policy-research /aggressive-incrementalism-strengthening-foundations-canada%E2%80%99s -approach-childcare.

Cameron, Barbara. 2009. "Political Will, Child Care, and Canadian Federalism." *Our Schools / Our Selves* 18, no. 3 (Spring): 129–44. Ottawa: Canadian Centre for Policy Alternatives. https://socialrightscura.ca/documents/publications/cameron /BC-Political-Will-Child-Care.pdf.

Canada Revenue Agency. 1985–2021. "Tax Packages for All Years." Ottawa: Government of Canada. https://www.canada.ca/en/revenue-agency/services/forms -publications/tax-packages-years.html.

Canadian Press. 2021. "Trudeau Can Spend Federal Money on Child Care without Conditions, Trudeau Says." *Montreal Gazette*, 26 April 2021. https://montrealgazette.com/news/local-news/quebec-can-spend-federal -money-on-child-care-without-conditions-trudeau-says.

Child Care Now. 2021. "Canada's Roadmap to Affordable Child Care for All." 6 July 2021. https://childcarecanada.org/documents/research-policy-practice/21/07 /canada%E2%80%99s-roadmap-affordable-child-care-all.

City of Toronto. 2020. *Budget TO: City of Toronto 2020 Budget Summary*. Toronto: City of Toronto. https://www.toronto.ca/wp-content/uploads/2020/08/8de8-2020 -city-of-toronto-budget-public-book.pdf.

Cleveland, Gordon. 2012. "The Economics of Early Childhood Education and Care in Canada." In *Perspectives on Early Childhood Education and Care in Canada*, edited by Nina Howe and Larry Prochner, 80–108. Toronto: University of Toronto Press.

– 2021. "Another Poorly Conceived Childcare Proposal from the C.D. Howe Institute." *Childcare Policy* (blog), 31 March 2021. https://childcarepolicy.net /another-poorly-conceived-child-care-proposal-from-c-d-howe/.

Courchene, Thomas. 2008. *Reflections on the Federal Spending Power: Practices, Principles, Perspectives*. IRPP Working Paper Series, No. 2008-01. Montreal: Institute for Research on Public Policy. https://irpp.org/wp-content/uploads/2014/09 /wp2008-01.pdf.

Denton, Frank T. 2018. "Table D205-222 Civilian Labour Force Participation Rates, by Age and Sex, Annual Averages, 1946 to 1975." Section D: The Labour Force, Historical Statistics of Canada, Statistics Canada. https://www150.statcan.gc.ca/n1 /pub/11-516-x/pdf/5500094-eng.pdf.

Department of Finance Canada. 2007. *Budget Plan 2007: Aspire to a Stronger, Safer, Better Canada*. Ottawa: Department of Finance Canada. https://www.budget.canada .ca/2007/pdf/bp2007e.pdf.

– 2021a. *Budget 2021: A Recovery Plan for Jobs, Growth, and Resilience*. Ottawa: Finance Canada. https://www.budget.gc.ca/2021/home-accueil-en.html.

– 2021b. "Report on Federal Tax Expenditures." Ottawa: Government of Canada. https://www.canada.ca/en/department-finance/services/publications/federal -tax-expenditures.html.

Dubé, Diane. 2021. "Les services de garde éducatifs à l'enfance." Presentation on ELCC services by the Ministère de la Famille at a roundtable hosted by the Public Policy Forum, Ottawa, 26 March 2021.

Duval, Stéphanie, Caroline Bouchard, Lise Lemay, and Gilles Cantin. 2020. "Examination of the Quality of Interactions as Observed in Childcare Centers and Reported by Early Childhood Educators." *SAGE Open* 10, no. 2. https://doi.org/10.1177/2158244020932914.

Early Child Development Funders Working Group. 2021. "Charitable, Academic, and Private Sector Leaders Urge Ottawa Limit Child Care Funds to Non-Profit/Public Providers." Press Release, 30 June 2021. https://www.newswire.ca/news-releases/charitable-academic-and-private-sector-leaders-urge-ottawa-limit-child-care-funds-to-non-profit-public-providers-843035001.html.

Employment and Social Development Canada. 2017a. "Canada-Alberta Early Learning and Child Care Agreement 2017–2020." Ottawa: Government of Canada. https://www.canada.ca/en/early-learning-child-care-agreement/agreements-provinces-territories/alberta-2017.html.

– 2017b. "Canada-British Columbia Early Learning and Child Care Agreement 2017–2020." Ottawa: Government of Canada. https://www.canada.ca/en/early-learning-child-care-agreement/agreements-provinces-territories/british-columbia-2017.html.

– 2021a. "Canada-British Columbia Canada-Wide Early Learning and Child Care Agreement – 2021 to 2026." Ottawa: Government of Canada. https://www.canada.ca/en/early-learning-child-care-agreement/agreements-provinces-territories/british-columbia-canada-wide-2021.html.

– 2021b. "Canada-Nova Scotia Canada-Wide Early Learning and Child Care Agreement – 2021 to 2026." Ottawa: Government of Canada. https://www.canada.ca/en/early-learning-child-care-agreement/agreements-provinces-territories/nova-scotia-canada-wide-2021.html.

Finley, Diane. 2006. "Choice in Child Care Plan: Notes for Remarks by The Honourable Diane Finley, Minister of Human Resources and Social Development, at a Debate on the Speech from the Throne." Press Release, 7 April 2006. Ottawa: Minister of Human Resources and Social Development. https://www.canada.ca/en/news/archive/2006/04/choice-child-care-plan.html.

First Ministers' Meeting. 1999. "Agreement: A Framework to Improve the Social Union for Canadians." Ottawa: Canadian Intergovernmental Conference Secretariat. https://scics.ca/en/product-produit/agreement-a-framework-to-improve-the-social-union-for-canadians/.

Fortin, Pierre. 2017. "What Have Been the Effects of Quebec's Universal Childcare System on Women's Economic Security?" Brief Submitted to the Standing Committee on the Status of Women of the House of Commons, Ottawa. https://www.ourcommons.ca/content/Committee/421/FEWO/Brief/BR8806290/br-external/FortinPierre-e.pdf.

Freeland, Chrystia. 2022. "Keynote Address by The Hon. Chrystia Freeland, Canada's Deputy Prime Minister and Minister of Finance." Empire Club of Canada, Toronto, 16 June 2022. https://empireclubofcanada.com/event/chrystia-freeland-2022-2/.

French, Janet. 2021. "Alberta Premier Demands Federal Child-Care Deal with No Strings Attached." *CBC News*, 6 August 2021. https://www.cbc.ca/news/canada/edmonton/alberta-kenney-federal-child-care-1.6133095.

Friendly, Martha, Laura Feltham, Sophia S. Mohamed, Ngoc Tho Nguyen, Rachel Vickerson, and Barry Forer. 2021. *Early Childhood Education and Care in Canada 2019*. Toronto: Childcare Resource and Research Unit. https://childcarecanada.org/sites/default/files/ECEC-Canada-2019-full-publication-REV-12-2-21.pdf.

Gagné, Lynda G. 2001. "Potential Income and the Equity of the Child-Care Expense Deduction." *Canadian Tax Journal* 49, no. 3: 636–73. https://www.ctf.ca/ctfweb/Documents/PDF/2001ctj/2001ctj3_gagne.pdf.

Gauthier, Éléonore. 2017. "Spending Power, Social Policy and the Principle of Subsidiarity." *Review of Constitutional Studies* 22, no. 2: 261–80. https://www.constitutionalstudies.ca/wp-content/uploads/2019/08/06_Gauthier-6.pdf.

Government of British Columbia. 2010–11 to 2019–20. "Public Accounts of British Columbia, Consolidated Revenue Fund Extracts." Victoria: Government of British Columbia. https://alpha.gov.bc.ca/gov/content/governments/finances/public-accounts/archive.

Government of Ontario. n.d. "Ontario Child Care Tax Credit." Taxes and Benefits. Toronto: Government of Ontario. https://www.ontario.ca/page/ontario-child-care-tax-credit.

– 2019. *2019 Ontario Budget: Protecting What Matters Most*. Toronto: Government of Ontario. https://budget.ontario.ca/pdf/2019/2019-ontario-budget-en.pdf

Haeck, Catherine, Pierre Lefebvre, and Philip Merrigan. 2015. "Canadian Evidence on Ten Years of Universal Preschool Policies: The Good and the Bad." *Labour Economics* 36 (October): 137–57. https://doi.org/10.1016/j.labeco.2015.05.002.

Health Canada. 2021. *Canada Health Act Annual Report 2019–20*. Ottawa: Government of Canada. https://www.canada.ca/en/health-canada/services/publications/health-system-services/canada-health-act-annual-report-2019-2020.html.

Heidinger, Loanna, Leanne C. Findlay, and Anne Guèvremont. 2020. "Uptake of the Child Care Expense Deduction: Exploring Factors Associated with the Use of the Child Care Expense Deduction among Families with a Child under 12 Years." *International Journal of Child Care and Education Policy* 14: article 12. https://doi.org/10.1186/s40723-020-00076-0.

Hogg, Peter. 2013. *Constitutional Law of Canada: 2013 Student Edition*. Toronto: Carswell.

Japel, Christa. 2012. "The Quebec Child Care System: Lessons from Research." In *Perspectives on Early Childhood Education and Care in Canada*, edited by Nina Howe and Larry Prochner, 285–307. Toronto: University of Toronto Press.

Lehrer, Joanne S., Lise Lemay, and Nathalie Bigras. 2015. "Parental Perceptions of Child Care Quality in Centre-Based and Home-Based Settings: Associations with External Quality Ratings." *International Journal of Early Childhood* 47, no. 3: 481–97. https://doi.org/10.1007/s13158-015-0147-8.

Lemay, Lise, Nathalie Bigras, and Caroline Bouchard. 2015. "Quebec's Child Care Services: What Are the Mechanisms Influencing Children's Behaviors across Quantity, Type, and Quality of Care Experienced?" *Journal of Research in Childhood Education* 29, no. 2: 147–72. https://doi.org/10.1080/02568543.2015.1009201.

Macdonald, David, and Martha Friendly 2020. *In Progress: Child Care Fees in Canada 2019*. Ottawa: Canadian Centre for Policy Alternatives. https://www.policyalternatives.ca/publications/reports/progress.

Ministère des Finances. 2010–11 to 2019–20. *Public Accounts*. Vol. 2, *Financial Information on the Consolidate Revenue Fund: General Fund and Special Funds*. Quebec City: Ministère de Finances, Government of Quebec. https://avispublication.finances.gouv.qc.ca/prwext02/f?p=119.

Ministère de la Famille. 2021a. "Avantages sociaux." Quebec: Government of Quebec. https://www.mfa.gouv.qc.ca/fr/services-de-garde/personnel/etre-educateur/avantages-sociaux/Pages/index.aspx.

– 2021b. "Développement du réseau des services de garde éducatifs à l'enfance." Quebec: Government of Quebec. hhttps://www.mfa.gouv.qc.ca/fr/services-de-garde/developpement-du-reseau/Pages/index.aspx.

Ministry of Children and Family Development. 2010–11 to 2019–20. "Child Care Operating Funding – Facilities and Spaces Over Time." Open data set, monthly data. Government of British Columbia. https://catalogue.data.gov.bc.ca/dataset/b67255a7-8040-43c0-935c-d74f168af215/resource/63d9b10c-ec0b-432c-9291-e7b3db8c7e96.

Office of the Prime Minister. 2021. "New Agreement to Strengthen the Early Learning and Child Care System in Quebec." Press Release, 5 August 2021. Ottawa: Office of the Prime Minister. https://pm.gc.ca/en/news/news-releases/2021/08/05/new-agreement-strengthen-early-learning-and-child-care-system-quebec.

Ontario Ministry of Education. 2020. *Ontario's Early Years and Child Care Annual Report 2020*. Toronto: Government of Ontario. https://www.ontario.ca/page/ontarios-early-years-and-child-care-annual-report-2020.

Receiver General of Canada. 2010–11 to 2019–20. *The Public Accounts of Canada*. Vol. 2, *Details of Expenses and Revenues*. Ottawa: Receiver General of Canada. https://www.tpsgc-pwgsc.gc.ca/recgen/cpc-pac/index-eng.html.

Revenu Québec. n.d. "Tax Credit for Childcare Expenses." Quebec: Government of Quebec. https://www.revenuquebec.ca/en/citizens/tax-credits/tax-credit-for-childcare-expenses/.

Statistics Canada. 2012–17. "Canadian Income Survey: Public Use Microdata File." Ottawa: Statistics Canada. https://doi.org/10.25318/72m0003x-eng.

- 2022. "Table 14-10-0327-01 Labour Force Characteristics by Sex and Detailed Age Group, Annual." Ottawa: Statistics Canada. https://doi.org/10.25318/1410032701-eng.
Treasury Board Secretariat of Ontario. 2010–11 to 2019–20. "The Public Accounts of Ontario: Past Editions." Toronto: Treasury Board Secretariat, Government of Ontario. https://www.ontario.ca/page/public-accounts-ontario-past-editions.
Verreault, Catherine. 2019. "Measuring the Impact of Universal Childcare Program on Mental Health and Substance Use Behaviors in Adolescents: Evidence from a Longitudinal Cohort in Quebec." MA thesis. McGill University.
Yalnizyan, Armine, and Kerry McCuaig. 2020. "A Year by Year Approach to Investing in Early Learning and Child Care." Memorandum to the Ministry of Finance, the Privy Council Office, and the Prime Minister's Office, 16 October 2020. Toronto: Atkinson Foundation. https://atkinsonfoundation.ca/atkinson-fellows/posts/a-year-by-year-approach-to-investing-in-early-learning-and-child-care/.

18 Diversity in Adversity: Fiscal Federalism, the Four Atlantic Provinces, and Canada's Great Demographic Imbalance

RICHARD SAILLANT

Introduction

Since the turn of the millennium, the discussion around fiscal federalism in Canada has mostly focused on the issue of the *vertical fiscal imbalance*, with provinces claiming that Ottawa has more resources than it needs to meet its responsibilities while they don't have enough. Although more intense in the 2000s, the debate around this issue is heating up again – witness the recent call by provinces and territories for Ottawa to immediately boost its annual payments under the Canada Health Transfer (CHT) by nearly two-thirds, from $41.9 billion in 2020–1 to $69.5 billion (Council of the Federation 2021).

While not entirely absent, the issue of the *horizontal fiscal imbalance* – differences in the ability of the provinces to carry out their responsibilities – has received much less attention recently. However, all has not necessarily been well on that front. As this chapter will make clear, for at least one part of the country, the situation has deteriorated considerably over the past decade. The culprit: population aging.

Canada's regions are aging at highly different speeds. This phenomenon, which I have called elsewhere Canada's "great demographic imbalance" (Saillant 2016), is nothing new; it has been unfolding steadily over the last half century or so. Yet, until the turn of the last decade, it did not matter much that some regions were aging faster than others since the whole country was enjoying the demographic dividend that flowed from the fact that all baby boomers were still of working age. This period was a time not only when demography was making its peak contribution to prosperity but also when the relative burden of caring for dependents was at its lowest. The situation began to change a few years ago, when the demographic tide that lifted all provincial boats started to recede. As the tide continues to ebb over the next few decades, it will affect the economies and the public purses of older, faster-aging provinces much more than younger, slower-aging ones.

This chapter examines the consequences of population aging on the public finances of Canada's four easternmost provinces, all of which find themselves at the wrong end of Canada's great demographic imbalance. The chapter is structured as follows. First, it briefly reviews population aging dynamics in the four provinces, contrasting them with the rest of the country. Second, it reviews the provinces' economic trajectories since the turn of the last decade. Third, it does the same for public finances, illustrating stark differences in how the four provincial governments have responded to the great demographic imbalance and other negative shocks. Fourth, it peers into the future by examining the ability of the four provinces to deal with the pressures of population aging. Finally, the chapter examines a range of options available to Ottawa to address the consequences of the great demographic imbalance, particularly as it relates to Canada's four easternmost provinces.

Canada's Four Atlantic Provinces in the Age of the Great Demographic Imbalance

Faster aging in the four Atlantic provinces is often attributed reflexively to the fact that they have been chronically losing people to the rest of the country. This rationale, however, tells only one part of the story: also of key importance is that these provinces generally experienced bigger baby booms. As a rule, Canada's baby boom was loudest in provinces whose populations were more rural and Catholic.

As the four Atlantic provinces came out of the baby boom younger, it took them a long time to grow older than the rest of the country. Indeed, as late as the turn of the millennium, when baby boomers were in the prime of their adult lives, the age structures of the four provinces were not meaningfully different from those elsewhere in Canada. Two decades later, however, the four Atlantic provinces are now significantly older than most other provinces, with Newfoundland and Labrador leading the way (Table 18.1). The median resident in that province was over forty-seven years old in 2020, nearly ten years above the age of the median Prairie resident.

A similar story applies to the share of seniors. In 2000, this proportion was similar across nearly all provinces. Twenty years later, deep regional differences are evident, with the four Atlantic provinces exceeding the share of the Prairies by roughly 50 per cent. Looking forward, the gap separating younger from older provinces is expected to grow for another fifteen years. According to Statistics Canada's "high growth" population scenario (which best reflects recent demographic trends), by 2030, 27.5 per cent of residents in the four Atlantic provinces will be seniors, compared to 17.6 per cent in the Prairies. Beyond 2030, the share of seniors in the latter is not projected to grow meaningfully, while in the former it is projected to continue growing until the middle of the

Table 18.1. Selected Population Age Structure Characteristics, Canada and Provinces, 1946–2040

	1946 Median Age	1946 65+ (%)	1966 Median Age	1966 65+ (%)	1980 Median Age	1980 65+ (%)	2000 Median Age	2000 65+ (%)	2020 Median Age	2020 65+ (%)	2030 (p)* 65+ (%)	2030 (p)* 75+ (%)	2040 (p)* 65+ (%)	2040 (p)* 75+ (%)
NL	n/a	n/a	19.3	5.9	24.7	7.4	37.4	11.9	47.4	22.3	29.4	14.1	32.9	19.0
PEI	26.5	9.8	24.0	10.8	28.2	11.9	37.1	13.4	42.9	20.0	24.2	11.7	24.7	14.3
NS	26.5	8.2	24.7	8.9	28.7	10.6	37.9	13.5	45.0	21.3	26.9	12.9	28.1	16.8
NB	24.4	7.2	22.2	8.2	27.5	9.8	37.6	13.1	46.1	21.9	27.8	13.6	29.2	17.4
QC	24.6	5.5	23.9	6.1	29.2	8.5	38.1	12.9	42.7	19.7	24.5	11.9	24.8	14.9
ON	30.4	8.3	27.2	8.2	30.0	9.7	36.5	12.5	40.4	17.6	21.7	10.2	22.7	13.1
MB	28.6	7.3	26.7	9.2	29.4	11.5	36.0	13.6	37.6	16.1	18.6	8.7	18.6	10.5
SK	26.4	6.5	25.6	9.3	28.3	11.7	35.9	14.7	37.8	16.2	18.0	8.3	17.6	10.1
AB	27.2	6.3	24.5	7.1	26.7	7.3	34.5	10.1	37.5	13.8	17.2	7.7	18.0	10.0
BC	31.3	8.9	28.2	9.5	30.4	10.5	37.5	13.1	42.2	19.2	23.4	11.2	24.3	14.1
Canada	27.7	7.2	25.4	7.7	29.1	9.4	36.8	12.6	40.9	18.0	22.0	10.4	22.7	13.2

Sources: Saillant (2016, 6); Statistics Canada (2022a, 2022c). Projections for 2030 and 2040 based on Statistics Canada "high growth" (HG) scenario.
Note: AB = Alberta; BC = British Columbia; MB = Manitoba; NB = New Brunswick; NL = Newfoundland and Labrador; NS = Nova Scotia; ON = Ontario; PEI = Prince Edward Island; QC = Quebec; SK = Saskatchewan
* p = projection

decade, plateauing at around 29 per cent. Nationally, the share of seniors is projected to grow from 18 per cent in 2020 to 22 per cent by 2030 and to plateau at a little below 23 per cent towards the middle of the next decade. In other words, the share of seniors in Canada as a whole is not projected to ever grow much beyond the current level in the four Atlantic provinces. In the Prairies, it is not expected to grow beyond the current national level (Statistics Canada, 2022c[1]).

Growing Apart: The Recent Economic Trajectories of the Four Atlantic Provinces

In this chapter, I refrain from referring to the four Atlantic provinces as "Atlantic Canada." Two reasons motivate this choice. The first is that, unlike the Maritimes, Atlantic Canada's existence as a region is questionable. The Maritimes emerged as a Canadian region early in the twentieth century as people living on that territory mobilized around commonly held grievances regarding their position within the Dominion (see Forbes 1979). Newfoundland, for its part, remained a British colony until 1949, turning its gaze towards the sea and the British Empire. The second reason is that, since the turn of the millennium, Newfoundland and Labrador's[2] economic geography has been thoroughly transformed by a single commodity, oil. The province's economy – and, as it turns out, its public finances – can now more or less be summed up as a highly leveraged bet on the fate of its offshore oil industry. To be sure, Newfoundland and Labrador faces a severe demographic headwind. However, the role of demographics in shaping its economic trajectory takes a back seat to its offshore oil industry.

In the Maritimes, the impact of demographics on the economy is much easier to discern. From 1981 to 2010, real gross domestic product (GDP) grew on average 2.2 per cent annually, a rate only slightly below that of Canada as a whole (see Table 18.2). On a per capita basis, the region was actually converging with the Canadian average at a robust clip. However, since the turn of the last decade, as baby boomers began to retire in droves, growth in the Maritimes fell precipitously while Canada as a whole posted a much more modest decline. Nearly all of the Maritimes' sharp slowdown was accounted for by labour force growth, which essentially stalled.

Looking forward, the ongoing exit of baby boomers from paid work should continue to severely constrain the region's growth potential for at least another decade. The actual magnitude of its slowdown, however, will depend on flows. On this count, the news is fairly encouraging, particularly so for Prince Edward Island, which stands as an eloquent case study of the power of immigration in improving demographic and economic outcomes. Since the mid-2000s, the province went from Canadian laggard to leader, its net immigration rate escalating from 0.2 per cent in 2004–5 to a country-leading 1.4 per cent right

The Four Atlantic Provinces and Canada's Great Demographic Imbalance 379

Table 18.2. Growth in Real GDP, Real GDP Per Capita, and Labour Force, 1981–2010 and 2010–19

	Real GDP (%)		Real GDP Per Capita (%)		Labour Force (%)	
	1981–2010	2010–19	1981–2010	2010–19	1981–2010	2010–19
NL	2.6	0.5	3.0	0.4	0.7	–0.1
PEI	2.5	2.3	2.0	1.1	1.3	1.2
NS	2.1	1.0	1.8	0.6	1.1	0.0
NB	2.2	0.5	2.0	0.2	1.0	0.0
Canada	*2.4*	*2.1*	*1.3*	*1.0*	*1.4*	*1.0*

Sources: Statistics Canada (2022a, 2022b, 2022d, 2023a). Author's calculations.
Note: NB = New Brunswick; NL = Newfoundland and Labrador; NS = Nova Scotia; PEI = Prince Edward Island

before the pandemic. As a result, Prince Edward Island's population has grown slightly faster than the national average, and so has its economy (Statistics Canada 2022a). Moreover, as newcomers tend to be young adults of child-rearing age, immigration has put the province on a slower-aging trajectory. Yet, fifteen years of booming immigration have not proven enough to fully erase prior decades of poor migratory outcomes. Although lower than in the other two Maritime provinces, Prince Edward Island's share of seniors remains higher than the Canadian average.

Nova Scotia and New Brunswick have also posted considerable improvements in their migration outcomes. Up until as late as the middle of the last decade, immigration to both provinces was marginal. Just prior to the pandemic, in 2019, immigration rates were close to the national average. In fact, if we consider overall migration (including net interprovincial migration and net inflows of non-permanent residents), outcomes in both provinces were actually better than the national average. So far, however, these improvements have only produced modest growth in the number of working-age residents.[3]

Both New Brunswick and Nova Scotia have expressed aspirations to emulate Prince Edward Island in driving economic and demographic growth through immigration. Whether they can effectively do so is unclear. As economist Herb Emery (2020) recently pointed out, given its small size and the concentration of its population around Charlottetown, Prince Edward Island's immigration performance should not be compared to that of its two sister Maritime provinces but rather to regions sharing similar characteristics. Comparing Prince Edward Island to southeastern New Brunswick (which is dominated by Moncton), Emery shows that both exhibited similar performances in recent years. The rub is that southeastern New Brunswick happens to be New Brunswick's economic and demographic growth leader. With the exception of the capital, Fredericton, other regions – where two-thirds of the population live – continue to record much poorer outcomes (Statistics Canada 2023b).

If the prospects of stronger immigration-led growth for Nova Scotia and New Brunswick are unclear, what does seem clear is that they cannot expect immigration to work wonders to the same extent it did for Prince Edward Island. That's because, even if they succeeded in bringing their immigration flows to the latter's levels – a big "if" – they cannot make up for the lost time. Prince Edward Island's younger and slower-aging population is a reflection of a decade and a half of booming immigration. To make up for the lost time, the two provinces would have to ramp up their immigration levels well beyond those achieved by Prince Edward Island since the mid-2000s – a very tall order.

Finally, there is Newfoundland and Labrador. As indicated earlier, the most important force shaping the province's economic performance in the years ahead is likely to remain its oil industry. Unlike in the Maritimes, the prospects for an immigration-led economic revival of sorts are bleak. The last few years illustrate this point. From a purely demographic standpoint, Newfoundland and Labrador is the province that most needs to rely on migration to maintain its labour force. Yet, with an economy in the doldrums until recently and a heavily indebted government downsizing its labour force, net migration is much weaker than in the Maritimes, and the province has lost population in the 2021 Census – the only province in the country to have done so.

Provincial Public Finances: Diversity in the Midst of Demographic Adversity

At the turn of the last decade, the aging of the baby boom generation represented roughly the same economic and fiscal headwind for all four Atlantic provinces, a headwind that was much stronger than in the rest of Canada. Yet, they have since followed sharply contrasting fiscal trajectories. To understand why, one has to recall that a province's fiscal trajectory reflects not only external shocks – negative or positive – but also how successive governments have responded to them.

Nova Scotia: From Laggard to Leader

A decade ago, Nova Scotia stood among the provinces fiscally least well-prepared to face the future. As one of Canada's oldest provinces, its economy was bound to hit a major speed bump when baby boomers would begin to retire in droves. This demographic shift, in turn, did not bode well for a province with an already high tax burden and Canada's second-highest debt-to-GDP ratio after Quebec. Yet, far from worsening, Nova Scotia's fiscal position has since improved considerably, with its debt-to-GDP ratio dropping from 37.1 per cent

Table 18.3. Net Debt in the Four Atlantic Provinces, Fiscal Years 2009–10 and 2019–20

	Total ($ millions)		Percentage of GDP (%)		Per Capita ($)	
	2009–10	2019–20	2009–10	2019–20	2009–10	2019–20
NL	8,220	14,400*	32.9	40.7*	15,907	27,508*
PEI	1,581	2,205	32.0	29.3	11,302	14,021
NS	12,992	15,242	37.1	32.7	13,848	15,718
NB	8,538	13,922	29.5	36.3	11,385	17,921

Sources: Finance Canada (2020); Statistics Canada (2022a, 2022d).
Note: NB = New Brunswick; NL = Newfoundland and Labrador; NS = Nova Scotia; PEI = Prince Edward Island
* In 2019–20, Newfoundland and Labrador booked an extra $2.5 billion in revenues from Ottawa to be received under a revised Atlantic Accord over the 2019–56 period, thus lowering its net debt (Province of Newfoundland and Labrador 1997–98 to 2019–20).

in 2009–10 to 32.7 per cent in 2019–20 (Table 18.3). This decrease was the second-best improvement after Quebec (Finance Canada 2020).

It is likely not a coincidence that Canada's two fiscal laggards of a decade ago are the ones that subsequently performed best. Having started off the decade with heavy debt loads, they could ill afford to let their fiscal positions deteriorate much further as their demographics turned from tailwind to headwind.

In 2010, Nova Scotia's first-ever New Democratic Party (NDP) government, led by Darrell Dexter, announced a two percentage point increase in its portion of the harmonized sales tax (HST). In doing so, it became the first provincial government to fully scoop up the fiscal room vacated by the federal government when it lowered the goods and services tax (GST) by one percentage point in 2006 and 2008. The fact that Nova Scotia was compelled to raise taxes early on improved its fiscal dynamics considerably. A good way to illustrate this change is by comparing its trajectory to that of its neighbour, New Brunswick, which otherwise experienced similar demographic, economic, and federal transfer trends.

New Brunswick's Lost Fiscal Decade

When the Great Recession struck in 2008, New Brunswick was in arguably the best fiscal position of all four Atlantic provinces. Since the turn of the millennium, the government had posted a surplus in all but two fiscal years. Net debt, which had doubled in the 1990s, had stopped growing. With the economy growing strong and all baby boomers still of working age, the province's debt-to-GDP ratio had been on a firm downward trajectory, dropping from 33 per cent in 2000–1 to 25 per cent six years later.

Following the Great Recession, however, New Brunswick entered what can be aptly named a "lost decade," which stretched over fiscal years 2007–8 to 2016–17. During this period, the government recorded nine consecutive deficits, nearly doubling its net debt along the way. The main reason for New Brunswick's much weaker fiscal outcomes compared to Nova Scotia is that it waited longer to raise taxes, particularly in bringing back the HST to 15 per cent, which it only did in 2016. In no small part because it increased taxes sooner, Nova Scotia ran fewer and smaller deficits. Between 2007–8 and 2016–17, Nova Scotia's accumulated deficit (sum of annual deficits and surpluses) stood at $473 million, a small amount compared to New Brunswick's $3.3 billion. In turn, Nova Scotia's smaller deficits meant less borrowing and, as interest rates went down, declining debt servicing charges (Saillant and Emery 2019, 1017–18).

Prince Edward Island: Reaping the Immigration Dividend

Thanks to its booming immigration, Prince Edward Island is the Atlantic province whose finances have been least affected by the gradual retirement of its baby boomers from paid work. Despite posting the smallest tax increases, Prince Edward Island saw the strongest growth in own-source revenues over the last decade. With strong population growth, it also saw the fastest growth in CHT and Canada Social Transfer (CST) payments (Receiver General for Canada 2011, 2020). In turn, the province's stronger revenue performance allowed it to grow its program spending faster than the national average while also lowering its debt-to-GDP ratio. Of note, as Prince Edward Island's economy was fueled more by strong population than business sector productivity growth, its equalization payments grew at roughly the same pace as its two neighbours. As a result, despite its much better economic performance, the province remains the most reliant on federal transfers in the country.

Newfoundland and Labrador: The Blessing of Oil Turns into a Fiscal Curse

As previously noted, towards the turn of the millennium, Newfoundland and Labrador's economic geography was profoundly reshaped by a single commodity, oil. Although oil first started flowing through the Hibernia platform in 1997, it is only around the mid-2000s that it really began to spill over the province's books. In four short years, royalties grew twelvefold, from $126 million in 2003–4 to $1.7 billion in 2007–8 (Province of Newfoundland and Labrador, 1997–8 to 2019–20). They reached an all-time high of $2.8 billion in 2011–12, accounting for 39 per cent of the province's own-source revenues.

This sharp escalation in royalties had two major effects, one that was welcome but transient and another much less welcome but long lasting. First, the increase in royalties brought down the province's net debt sharply, from a high of $11.9 billion in 2004–5 to $8.0 billion in 2008–9. Second, the wealth effect that came with booming revenues led to a dramatic escalation in program spending, from $4.0 billion in 2004–5 to $7.0 billion in 2011–12. By 2011–12, Newfoundland and Labrador had by far the highest per capita spending among Canadian provinces.

With such an inflated cost base, Newfoundland and Labrador was exposed to a major downturn in its oil industry. This downturn occurred after 2011–12 in two stages. The first, which lasted until late 2014, was caused by production declines amidst strong prices. By 2014–15, annual royalty revenues were down to $1.6 billion. The next stage came with the sharp decline in oil prices of late 2014. From 2015–16 to 2019–20, royalty payments averaged $0.9 billion annually.

To deal with collapsing royalties, Newfoundland and Labrador acted mostly on the revenue side of the ledger. Its biggest move on this count came in the 2016–17 budget, which raised numerous taxes and fees, and brought the HST and personal income taxes in line with the three other Atlantic provinces. On the spending side, despite constantly repeating it did not have a revenue but a spending problem, the provincial government has mostly managed through wage moderation and attrition. Yet, despite posting the lowest program spending growth among Canadian provinces, Newfoundland and Labrador remains by far the biggest spender.

Inevitably, the province's inability to bring down its cost structure amidst sharply lower revenues has led to very large annual deficits and ballooning debt. The province's debt challenge, which is exacerbated by massive taxpayer-supported cost-overruns for the Muskrat Falls project, is now such that, in the early days of the pandemic, then-premier Dwight Ball wrote to Prime Minister Trudeau to notify him that Newfoundland and Labrador was unable to secure the financing it sought from financial markets (Ball 2021). For a Canadian provincial government, that's likely as close to bankruptcy as it gets.

Looking Ahead: How Well-Equipped Are the Four Atlantic Provinces to Face the Future?

Having reviewed the demographic, economic, and fiscal trajectories of the four Atlantic provinces, what can we say about the future? Are their public finances on sustainable paths? To answer this last question, we must start by defining *fiscal sustainability*. A definition is the easy part: *a government's finances are said to be sustainable if they allow it to provide existing services indefinitely without having to increase taxes*. The much harder – some would say, the nearly impossible – part is to actually assess fiscal sustainability. That's because doing so requires peering into the future and, as Yogi Berra is said to have quipped, "it's tough to make predictions, especially about the future."

To illustrate this difficulty, just consider the case of the four Atlantic provinces at the turn of the millennium. Looking at their economic, demographic, and fiscal landscapes at the time, who could have predicted that immigration would soon explode in Prince Edward Island but not in Nova Scotia and New Brunswick? And with the price of oil trading at around $20 per barrel over much of the 1990s, who would have been bold enough to forecast that Newfoundland and Labrador would witness a decade-long royalty boom, only to leave fiscal devastation in its wake?

In assessing how well provinces are equipped to face future pressures, one must also make a clear distinction between fiscal sustainability and *fiscal position*. In a recent monograph, economist Trevor Tombe (2020) examines the fiscal sustainability of senior Canadian governments and concludes that, among all provinces, only Quebec has sustainable finances. Yet, this conclusion does not by any means imply the latter is in a better fiscal position than all of its counterparts. As Tombe notes, Quebec's distinct status is attributable to the fact that it taxes its residents much more than other provinces. With the highest tax burden and a debt burden above the average of Canadian provinces, Quebec has less room to raise its taxes further or go deeper into debt than, say, British Columbia. Its fiscal position is thus more precarious.

Despite its limitations, sustainability analysis remains an important tool to assess the fiscal trajectories of governments and, if applicable, estimate the magnitude of the changes needed to put their finances on a more solid footing. As the future is unknown, fiscal sustainability analysis relies by necessity on assumptions about a wide range of factors that affect revenue generation and spending patterns, such as productivity and labour force growth, interest rates, inflation, technological change, population age structure, collective bargaining dynamics, and so on. Needless to say, the results of any fiscal sustainability analysis depend on the various assumptions made about the evolution of these factors, thus the importance of sensitivity analysis. Typically, such assumptions are formulated based on past trends and informed guesses about their future evolution.

Tombe's recent analysis of the sustainability of Canadian senior government public finances is the most elaborate I have seen to date. Tombe (2020) computes what he calls "fiscal gaps," that is, the adjustments needed to stabilize each government's debt-to-GDP ratio, expressed in terms of immediate tax increases and/or spending cuts as a percentage of GDP. His results suggest that, despite the massive fiscal cost of the pandemic, the federal government's finances remain sustainable by a comfortable margin. Unsurprisingly, he finds that, among provincial governments, Newfoundland and Labrador has by far the highest gap, at 9.4 per cent of GDP. By comparison, fiscal gaps in the Maritimes, which range from 3.0 to 4.0 per cent of GDP, look quite small. However, it is not really the case. Revenue increases or spending cuts of that magnitude represent very large sums. For example, in the case of New Brunswick, it is the equivalent of raising own-source revenues by a bit over 20 per cent immediately. For a province with an already high tax burden, that would be no small task. Of note, Tombe finds that, unlike in Newfoundland and Labrador, fiscal gaps in the Maritimes are entirely attributable to population aging.

Interestingly, Tombe's (2020) results suggest that, among the three Maritime provinces, Prince Edward Island has the least sustainable public finances. This finding re-emphasizes the importance of distinguishing between fiscal position and fiscal sustainability. As we've already seen, with an economy expected to grow faster and a younger population expected to age slower than in its sister Maritime provinces, Prince Edward Island is in a better position to meet its future fiscal challenges. Ironically, it is likely for this very reason that the island province ranks lower on fiscal sustainability. Here, comparing the recent fiscal trajectories of Prince Edward Island with New Brunswick is highly instructive. Faced with much greater fiscal pressures, New Brunswick has had to curb spending growth to a much greater extent than its island neighbour since the Great Recession. Over the ten years from 2008 to 2018, Prince Edward Island grew its health-care spending on average by 5.1 per cent annually, twice as fast as New Brunswick at 2.5 per cent. As a result of its health-care spending moderation, New Brunswick is now considered to have more sustainable finances than Prince Edward Island. However, this disparity does not mean the former is better equipped than the latter to face the future. On the contrary, New Brunswick's recent success in slowing spending growth will likely make future success harder to achieve, since many of the low-hanging fruits in terms of efficiency savings have likely been harvested (Saillant and Emery 2019, 1021).

Except perhaps for Prince Edward Island, health-care spending is a sword of Damocles hanging over the fiscal heads of Atlantic provinces. As Figure 18.1 shows, provincial health-care spending is highly sensitive to population age structure, with expenditures growing more or less linearly after the first year of birth up to the age of sixty and then geometrically afterwards. In 2021, Canada's oldest baby boomers turned seventy-five. Over the next two decades, the population of Canadians aged seventy-five or over is projected to more than double (+126 per cent). The four Atlantic provinces are projected to witness similar growth. The difference is that, west of New Brunswick, the number of working-age people available to support these growing ranks of older seniors is projected to grow by more than one-fifth (22.3 per cent), while the number is set to decline by 5 per cent in the four Atlantic provinces.

Despite its pivotal importance, population aging is far from the only factor that will determine the sustainability of health-care spending in Atlantic Canada. Historically, provincial health-care spending has grown fast, but it did not follow a straight line: moderation in the 1990s was followed by exuberance in the 2000s and a return to moderation over the last decade. Although other

Figure 18.1. Provincial Health-Care Spending Per Capita by Age Groups, Canada, 2018

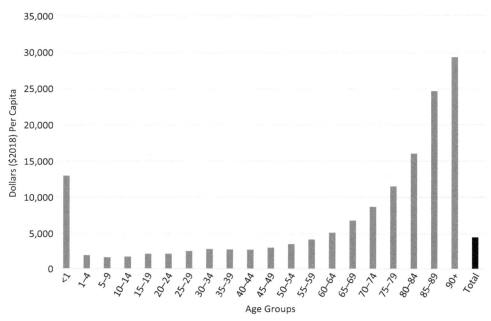

Source: CIHI (2022a).

factors were in play, the main driver of health-care spending volatility has been compensation costs. For instance, between 2002–3 and 2012–13, total clinical payments to physicians have nearly doubled, with the bulk coming from the amounts paid per service performed, a rough proxy for wage growth[4] (CIHI 2022b). Of note, all provinces took part at the time in this compensation escalation, which suggests that provincial governments compete – or at least perceive they are competing – with each other to secure health professionals (Saillant 2016, 80–3; Saillant and Emery 2019, 1022).

Looking forward, the path of non-aging provincial spending growth appears highly uncertain. On one hand, with chronic shortages in many health professions, a fast-growing population of seniors aged seventy-five and over, and the pandemic having exposed serious flaws in the country's elderly care system, competition for scarce health-care human resources is likely to heat up. On the other hand, with most provincial governments facing major fiscal challenges, their ability to escalate health spending without major tax increases or meaningfully faster-growing transfers from Ottawa remains constrained.

Although uncertain, the path of non-aging spending growth will matter a great deal to the fiscal sustainability of the four Atlantic provinces. If exuberance in health-care spending returns, the latter will not be in a position to emulate their richer, slower-aging counterparts without jeopardizing their fiscal futures.

Policy Options

Canada's great demographic imbalance exacerbates its horizontal fiscal imbalance since it disproportionately affects the revenue-raising capacities and spending needs of older, faster-aging provinces. At the same time, all of Canada is aging, which in turn alters the vertical fiscal balance between Ottawa and the provinces, since the latter are primarily responsible for health care.

The fact that population aging has both vertical and horizontal fiscal implications matters a great deal in assessing policy options for addressing the effects of the great demographic imbalance on Canada's four easternmost provinces. That's because any measure to deal with the vertical fiscal imbalance – real or perceived – is bound to affect the fiscal positions and fiscal sustainability of all provinces, often in unintended ways.

It is worth expanding on this point using two recent examples. The first relates to the evolution since the turn of the millennium of the Canada Health and Social Transfer (CHST) and, after 2004, its successors, the CHT and the CST. In the 2000s, following major cutbacks in the previous decade, the federal government dramatically ramped up the money paid to provinces under those transfers. On average, funding grew by a staggering 10.6 per cent annually from 2000–1 to 2010–11 (Finance Canada 2020). Needless to say, such explosive growth altered the fiscal balance between Ottawa and the provinces. Yet, this massive influx of federal dollars, combined with fast-growing provincial own-source revenues, also produced a sharp escalation in provincial health spending, making health-care systems harder to sustain just as baby boomers began to retire in droves.

A second example of a federal move that altered the vertical fiscal (im)balance, yet had a very different impact on provincial fiscal dynamics, is the decision by the Harper government to lower the GST by one percentage point in 2006 and 2008. Tellingly, given the uneven fiscal pressures exerted by Canada's great demographic imbalance, Harper's GST cuts divided Canada along the Ottawa River, with all provinces to its east fully scooping up the newly vacated fiscal room and none to the west of the river having to do so. Forced to ask for more money from their taxpayers themselves, richer provinces proved hesitant. As a result, they had greater incentives to lower spending growth, thus dampening health-care inflationary pressures.

With this important caveat about the importance of broader developments in fiscal federalism on provincial fiscal dynamics, we can now turn our attention to policy options for explicitly addressing Canada's growing horizontal fiscal imbalance, starting with needs-based equalization.

Needs-Based Equalization

Since 1982, Parliament and the government of Canada are constitutionally committed to the principle of ensuring that "provincial governments have sufficient revenues to provide reasonably comparable levels of public services at reasonably comparable levels of taxation" (Constitution Act, 1982, s. 36[2]). Nowhere in the Constitution is it mentioned that Ottawa is committed to ensuring provinces have reasonably comparable revenues. Yet, this idea has been the main focus of Ottawa's Equalization Program since its inception in 1957. Unlike some other federations such as Australia and, to a lesser extent, Germany, Canada's approach to equalization does not explicitly take into account the fact that constituent units require different levels of resources to provide comparable services.

Conceptually speaking, implementing an explicit needs-based approach to equalization is very appealing. After all, what could be more effective in ensuring a single Canadian social citizenship than taking into account all the factors that supposedly influence the ability of provinces to provide comparable services at comparable levels of taxation? In practice, however, it turns out that implementing such an approach could well work out against the Maritimes and provide no further assistance to Newfoundland and Labrador. At least, that is the conclusion from a seminal paper written by a former World Bank economist, Anwar Shah (1996), who developed an elaborate econometric model to estimate the impact of different needs on provincial spending requirements. At the time, Shah concluded that a needs-based approach would work to Ontario and Quebec's advantage and that, for the fiscal year 1991–2, it would have resulted in payment reductions ranging from 32 per cent to 49 per cent in the four Atlantic provinces. To be sure, Shah's model would need to be respecified and calculations updated to ensure they reflect today's conditions rather than those of thirty years ago. It is unclear, however, whether the situation has since changed to the point where the four Atlantic provinces would now benefit by amending the Equalization Program to take spending needs into account.

If we assume that Shah was right, then a logical question is, why did smaller recipient provinces such as the Maritimes and Newfoundland and Labrador "overspend" on public services if it is not because they had greater spending needs? Shah does not provide a firm answer. Rather, he limits his comments on this topic to an endnote in which he asks the following question: "Could it be that the equalization program may be encouraging the recipient provinces to provide higher public employment and wages rather than improved provision of public services?" (Shah 1996, 114).

Shah was certainly not alone in suggesting this answer. Among the others was Thomas Courchene (for example, 1984, 1998), who notably argued that governments in richer provinces may ultimately have greater spending needs than those in poorer ones since they must pay higher wages to compete with the private sector. The rub, of course, is that many public sector unions in poorer provinces (those representing well-paid professionals in particular) do not benchmark their wages against the local private sector but rather against public sector compensation trends in other provinces, including richer ones. The result is that total compensation in the public sector in the Maritimes is on average 65 per cent above the local private sector, compared to 30 per cent on average in the provinces west of New Brunswick (Statistics Canada 2023c).

Beyond the fact that explicit needs-based equalization may not turn out to favour the four Atlantic provinces, there is another reason for its lack of promise as a policy solution for addressing the consequences of the great demographic imbalance: politically, it would likely stir up a hornet's nest. A number of scholars have pointed to the central importance of the idea of provincial autonomy in Canadian politics as a likely insurmountable obstacle to implementing a needs-based approach to equalization (Leslie 1988; Béland and Lecours 2011). Furthermore, as history has reminded us on numerous occasions – including recently, with the reactions of some provincial western leaders to Quebec's resistance to the Energy East pipeline just as it was receiving an equalization payment windfall – equalization policy is an extremely polarizing topic. As such, it is likely that the future path of the Equalization Program will resemble that of the past, following the logic of "muddling through," that is, of incremental rather than radical change. This probability suggests the Equalization Program is likely to stay focused on the revenue side of the ledger.

Amending the CHT to Take Population Age Structures into Account

An alternative approach to addressing uneven aging-induced provincial spending pressures without opening up the Pandora's box of needs-based equalization would be to amend the allocation formula for the CHT to take into account the age structures of provincial populations. There are countless ways to do so. Tombe (2020, 1112–18) examines three possibilities: (1) allocating the CHT on the basis of the provincial population aged sixty-five and over; (2) indexing CHT growth to demographics; and (3) supplementing the CHT to cover extra aging-induced health-care costs. Tombe finds that the third approach would best assist older, faster-aging provinces in improving their fiscal sustainability.

Although such approaches are conceptually appealing, they too face a big political hurdle. That's because any move away from a per capita formula would mark a major departure from the recent trend in fiscal federalism of treating equality and equity as synonymous in dispensing major federal transfers to all provinces. This trend goes back to the turn of the millennium, when the federal government began to spend the "fiscal dividend" resulting from its efforts to address its structural deficits in the 1990s. Outside the CHST and its successors, the CHT and the CST, the default approach of both Chrétien and Martin for sending extra cash to provinces, from targeted initiatives in the health-care sector to the Gas Tax Fund (now the Canada Community-Building Fund) transfer, was to allocate funding on a per capita basis. Their successor, Stephen Harper, completed the "per capita revolution" by applying it to both the CHT and the CST. This revolution was politically attractive in parts of the country where most voters live, particularly in the faster-growing and slower-aging provinces west of the Ottawa River (see Saillant 2016, 132–7).

A New Atlantic Accord?

If moving away from the per capita approach to dispensing major federal transfers to all provinces is likely to be perceived in Ontario and the Prairies as robbing Peter to pay Paul, then an alternative may be to work outside the existing major federal transfer apparatus and to focus federal action for dealing with the great demographic imbalance on the "region" that is most affected, Atlantic Canada. Such an approach would also prove a relatively inexpensive way of dealing with the reality of regionally uneven aging in the country, since the four Atlantic provinces account for only 6.4 per cent of Canada's population, a proportion that is set to decline further in the years ahead.

A number of considerations would need to be taken into account in devising a formula for allocating funding under a new Atlantic Accord. First, the formula should be *principle-based* so that future governments in Ottawa would find it harder to undo the special assistance to this part of the country. Notably, assistance should be tied to the spending side of the equation, since Canada's Equalization Program already compensates poorer, faster-aging provinces for the consequences of poorer demographics on their revenue-raising capacities.

Second, assistance should provide incentives for recipient provinces to improve efficiency. For instance, the allocation formula for taking demographics into account in funding should be based on the national distribution of health-care spending by age groups rather than those of individual provinces. That way, Prince Edward Island and Newfoundland and Labrador would not be "rewarded" for having higher cost structures than New Brunswick and Nova Scotia.

Third, the assistance formula should take into account the national dynamics of provincial health spending, which suggest that Canada-wide non-aging expenditure trends (compensation in particular) have an impact on the ability of the four Atlantic provinces to control costs. Tombe (2020) calculates that health-care–specific inflation (over and above the overall inflation of about 2 per cent) grew 1.3 per cent annually since 1998. However, this rate has been highly unstable over time, with alternating bouts of exuberance and moderation (Saillant 2016, 80–3; Saillant and Emery 2019, 1022). Given their high tax burdens, the four Atlantic provinces will have very limited ability to follow suit if other provinces trigger a renewed escalation in health-care spending. A principle-based approach to special assistance to the four Atlantic provinces should recognize this reality. One way to do so would be to grant them an increase in their special assistance when health-care–specific inflation exceeds a certain threshold, such as the long-term rate of 1.3 per cent.

Conclusion

Since provinces are primarily responsible for health care, population aging poses a challenge to fiscal federalism as it alters the vertical balance between Ottawa and the provinces. As this chapter has made clear, however, Canada is aging at a regionally uneven pace, which has significant horizontal implications.

This chapter has examined the fiscal trajectories and prospects of the part of the country most affected by Canada's great demographic imbalance, the four easternmost provinces. It has also examined options for addressing its consequences on their provincial public finances. Since an effective mechanism, the Equalization Program, already exists to deal with the horizontal implications of faster population aging on revenue-generation capacity, the chapter has focused on the uneven pressures on spending across provinces.

A number of key points or findings are worth emphasizing here. First, although all four Atlantic provinces faced a similar negative shock as Canada's oldest baby boomers turned sixty-five towards the turn of the last decade, they responded very differently to this shock. In turn, their different policy responses resulted in sharply different fiscal trajectories. One province, Prince Edward Island, actually managed to considerably alter its demographic dynamics through booming immigration: although older than the Canadian average, it is no longer aging faster. Second, among the four Atlantic provinces, the two that fared worst in facing a rising demographic headwind were those that entered the decade in arguably the strongest fiscal positions: New Brunswick and Newfoundland and Labrador. Conversely, the one that fared best, Nova Scotia, was in arguably the worst fiscal position. This chapter has suggested that this situation may not be a coincidence. Third, this chapter has made an important distinction between fiscal position and fiscal sustainability: a province may fare better on fiscal sustainability calculations, yet find itself in a much weaker fiscal position.

The last part of the chapter discusses policy options for addressing the implications of Canada's great demographic imbalance, focusing on the growing horizontal fiscal imbalance resulting from regionally uneven aging-induced provincial spending pressures. Of note, these options are not likely to fully restore the fiscal sustainability of the four Atlantic provinces – they are not meant to. Other policy responses from the federal and provincial governments will likely be required to ensure the fiscal sustainability of all senior Canadian governments, including, in many instances, higher provincial taxes. As this chapter has stressed, any approach for dealing with Canada's horizontal fiscal imbalance must take into account the potential impact of measures taken to address the vertical fiscal imbalance – real or perceived.

Finally, there is Newfoundland and Labrador. Canada's easternmost province is in dire fiscal straits. Its future fiscal trajectory is inextricably tied to the fortunes of its oil industry – and Ottawa. For reasons discussed in this chapter, Newfoundland and Labrador most likely does not find itself on the wrong end of Canada's horizontal fiscal imbalance. Rather, its central problem is its inability to bring down its cost structure in line with its lower, but still above-average revenues since the mid-2010s. Looking forward, the potential for renewed strength in the province's oil industry in the near to mid-term could provide it with some breathing room to restructure its public finances. Clearly, none of the policy options presented in this chapter would by themselves come anywhere near close to restoring the province's fiscal sustainability. As indicated earlier, Newfoundland and Labrador's economy and public finances have become a highly leveraged bet on the price of a single commodity, oil. If the bet fails, only intervention from Ottawa to enable fiscal consolidation will prevent it from going over the proverbial fiscal cliff.

NOTES

1 For ease of reading and concision, the data source for each specific indicator (for example, population, real GDP, net debt) is only listed the first time reference is made to it. Unless indicated otherwise, this source is also used for subsequent references to this indicator.
2 Newfoundland was renamed Newfoundland and Labrador in 2001.
3 More recently, starting in the first quarter of 2021, the interprovincial migratory balances of the Maritimes have nearly tripled compared to the years immediately prior to the pandemic. This dramatic improvement was fueled almost entirely by a strong influx of residents from Ontario moving to the region to secure more affordable housing. It is too early at this point to determine whether and for how long such inflows can be sustained. What seems clear is that they cannot go on at this pace indefinitely. The housing market in the Maritimes is relatively small, and all indicators are pointing to the fact that supply is simply not keeping up with demand. As a result, prices are growing significantly faster than the national average. If this trend continues, the price gap between southern Ontario and the Maritimes should

eventually narrow to a point where moving from the former to the latter will lose much of its financial appeal (Saillant 2022a, 2022b).
4 I say this estimate is a rough proxy for wage growth because it does not take into account changes in the mix of medical services offered. I also refer to wage growth rather than compensation growth because, for most physicians, compensation is not only determined by the fees they receive but also by the number of services they perform.

REFERENCES

Ball, Dwight. 2021. "Letter to Prime Minister Justin Trudeau." 20 March 2020. St. John's: Office of the Premier, Government of Newfoundland and Labrador. https://www.documentcloud.org/documents/6823548-Letter-to-Prime-Minister.html.

Béland, Daniel, and André Lecours. 2011. "The Ideational Dimension of Federalism: The 'Australian Model' and the Politics of Equalisation in Canada." *Australian Journal of Political Science* 46, no. 2: 199–212. https://doi.org/10.1080/10361146.2011.567974.

CIHI (Canadian Institute for Health Information). 2022a. "National Expenditure Trends – Health Spending." https://www.cihi.ca/en/national-health-expenditure-trends.

– 2022b. "Physicians: National Physician Database – Data Tables." https://www.cihi.ca/en/physicians.

Council of the Federation. 2021. *Increasing the Canada Health Transfer Will Help Make Provinces and Territories More Financially Sustainable Over the Long Term.* Report of the Provincial and Territorial Ministers of Finance to the Council of the Federation. Ottawa: Council of the Federation. https://www.canadaspremiers.ca/increasing-the-canada-health-transfer-will-help-make-provinces-and-territories-more-financially-sustainable-over-the-long-term/.

Courchene, Thomas. 1984. *Equalization Payments: Past, Present, and Future.* Toronto: Ontario Economic Council.

– 1998. *Renegotiating Equalization: National Policy, Federal State, International Economy.* CD Howe Institute Commentary, 1 September 1998. https://www.cdhowe.org/public-policy-research/renegotiating-equalization-national-polity-federal-state-international-economy.

Emery, Herb. 2020. "Emery: P.E.I.'s Economy Holds No Lessons for New Brunswick." *Telegraph Journal*, 2 December 2020. https://tj.news/telegraph-journal/101425662.

Finance Canada. 2020. *Fiscal Reference Tables 2020.* Ottawa: Finance Canada. https://www.canada.ca/en/department-finance/services/publications/fiscal-reference-tables/2020.html.

Forbes, Ernest R. 1979. *The Maritime Rights Movement, 1919–1927: A Study in Canadian Regionalism.* Montreal and Kingston: McGill-Queen's University Press.

Leslie, Peter M. 1988. *National Citizenship and Provincial Communities: A Review of Canadian Fiscal Federalism.* Kingston, ON: Institute of Intergovernmental Relations.

Province of Newfoundland and Labrador, Office of the Comptroller General. 1997–98 to 2019–20. *Public Accounts Consolidated Financial Statements*. St. John's, NL: NL House of Assembly. https://www.gov.nl.ca/exec/tbs/working-with-us/publications/public-accounts/.

Receiver General for Canada. 2011. *Public Accounts of Canada 2011*. Vol. 1, *Summary Report and Consolidated Financial Statements*. Ottawa: Public Services and Procurement Canada. https://publications.gc.ca/collections/collection_2011/tpsgc-pwgsc/P51-1-2011-1-eng.pdf.

– 2020. *Public Accounts of Canada 2020*. Vol. 1, *Summary Report and Consolidated Financial Statements*. Ottawa: Public Services and Procurement Canada. https://epe.lac-bac.gc.ca/100/201/301/public_accounts_can/html/2020/recgen/cpc-pac/2020/index-eng.html.

Saillant, Richard. 2016. *A Tale of Two Countries: How the Great Demographic Imbalance Is Pulling Canada Apart*. Halifax: Nimbus.

– 2022a. "Saillant: House Prices May Drop – But Not in New Brunswick." *Telegraph Journal*, 22 June 2022. https://tj.news/telegraph-journal/101901871.

– 2022b. "Saillant: Province Faces Big-City Prices on Small Town Wages." *Telegraph Journal*, 6 July 2022. https://tj.news/telegraph-journal/101912216.

Saillant, Richard, and Herb Emery. 2019. "Policy Forum: Is New Brunswick Heading Over the Fiscal Cliff?" *Canadian Tax Journal* 67, no. 4: 1011–24. https://doi.org/10.32721/ctj.2019.67.4.pf.saillant.

Shah, Anwar. 1996. "A Fiscal Need Approach to Equalization." *Canadian Public Policy* 22, no. 2: 99–115. https://doi.org/10.2307/3551902.

Statistics Canada. 2022a. "Table 17-10-0005-01 Population Estimates on July 1st, by Age and Sex." Statistics Canada. https://doi.org/10.25318/1710000501-eng.

– 2022b. "Table 17-10-0008-01 Estimates of the Components of Demographic Growth, Annual." Statistics Canada. https://doi.org/10.25318/1710000801-eng.

– 2022c. "Table 17-10-0057-01 Projected Population, by Projection Scenario, Age and Sex, as of July 1 (x1.000)." Statistics Canada. https://doi.org/10.25318/1710005701-eng.

– 2022d. "Table 36-10-0222-01 Gross Domestic Product, Expenditure-Based, Provincial and Territorial, Annual (x 1.000.000)." Statistics Canada. https://doi.org/10.25318/3610022201-eng.

– 2023a. "Table 14-10-0023-01 Labour Force Characteristics by Industry, Annual (x 1.000)." Statistics Canada. https://doi.org/10.25318/1410002301-eng.

– 2023b. "Table 17-10-0135-01 Population Estimates, July 1, by Census Metropolitan Area and Census Agglomeration, 2016 Boundaries." Statistics Canada. https://doi.org/10.25318/1710013501-eng.

– 2023c. "Table 36-10-0480-01 Labour Productivity and Related Measures by Business Sector Industry and by Non-Commercial Activity Consistent with the Industry Accounts." https://doi.org/10.25318/3610048001-eng.

Tombe, Trevor. 2020. "Provincial Debt Sustainability in Canada: Demographics, Federal Transfers, and COVID-19." *Canadian Tax Journal* 68, no. 4: 1083–1122. https://doi.org/10.32721/ctj.2020.68.4.fon.

19 Quebec's Fiscal Federalism Trilemma

ALAIN NOËL

Introduction

Consistently, over the years, the Quebec government has advocated for a more balanced distribution of revenues between the federal and provincial governments, against the use of the "federal spending power" to dictate conditions to provincial governments in their areas of jurisdiction, and for a fair distribution of financial resources across the land. These three objectives belonged to a coherent vision of federalism as a political regime where sovereignty and financial resources are divided among governments that are autonomous but committed to a reasonable level of regional solidarity.

Consider, for instance, the reaction of Quebec Minister of Finance Éric Girard to the April 2021 federal budget (Ministère des Finances 2021). Girard acknowledged and endorsed the different measures announced by Ottawa to sustain the post-pandemic economic recovery, but he insisted these new initiatives should respect Quebec's autonomy in its areas of jurisdiction and take the form of "unconditional transfers." With respect to enhanced federal funding for childcare services, notably, Girard "reiterated that Quebec will take advantage of its right of withdrawal with full compensation." In health care, the minister insisted on the provision of "stable, appropriate, long-term" funding and noted that the provinces unanimously demanded improved federal transfers.

In a few words, the minister expressed the basic, enduring orientations of the Quebec government with respect to fiscal federalism: the affirmation of autonomy in provincial domains of jurisdiction; the need for an adequate sharing of financial resources, consistent with the division of powers; and collaboration and solidarity with other provincial governments. In the language of fiscal federalism, the Quebec government sought autonomy, vertical equity (between orders of government), and horizontal equity (among provinces).

Seeking to make progress on these three fronts is certainly not inconsistent. Winning on all fronts, however, is not easy. In this chapter, I argue that the Quebec government is confronted with an enduring fiscal federalism trilemma, a situation where it is difficult, and perhaps impossible, to pursue the three favoured objectives at once. A trilemma is like a dilemma, but with three rather than two conflicting ends. In a trilemma, an actor can make gains on two fronts, but these gains are usually at the expense of the third objective (Iversen and Wren 1998). A trilemma can be hard, when winning on all fronts is simply impossible, or soft, when pursuing three goals remains feasible but unlikely to succeed. Because the three objectives are valued, there can never be a decision to drop one definitively for the sake of the other two. What takes place, instead, is a sort of institutionalized hesitancy, an enduring cycle leading to shifting priorities and strategies over time. Once this trilemma is identified, the instability in strategic choices can at least be better understood. It becomes possible, as well, to characterize the trajectory of Quebec over time, as context and choices lead to different interpretations of the government's "traditional" position.

The first part of this chapter presents the structure of Quebec's fiscal federalism trilemma, which is anchored in a principled understanding of federalism, and contrasts it with the choices made by other governments in Canada that are less preoccupied by the preservation of autonomy. The second part goes back to the origins of the trilemma, with the development of the welfare state in the 1950s and 1960s. In its 1956 report on constitutional problems, the Tremblay Commission was hardly confronted with this trilemma. The federal Equalization Program did not exist yet, and the question of horizontal equity was largely overlooked, leaving only autonomy and vertical equity as core concerns. The situation changed in the following years, but the priorities of the Quebec government remained autonomy and vertical equity. The third section covers the constitutional debates of the 1980s and 1990s, which extended the reading of the situation developed in the 1960s into a period of neoliberalism and welfare retrenchment, as well as the debates on the social union in the late 1990s. The fourth section considers the 2002 report of the Séguin Commission, which, perhaps for the first time, articulated clearly the three aims of the Quebec government in fiscal federalism. The Séguin Commission expressed and formalized Quebec's fiscal federalism trilemma. This section also considers recent developments in intergovernmental relations to see more closely the trilemma at work. The conclusion wraps up and points to the inherent fragility of the Quebec government's position on fiscal federalism, a fragility that is not due to unclear objectives or to incoherence but rather to the intrinsic difficulty of achieving three objectives in tension with one another.

Principles in Tension

If the Canadian federation had not included Quebec, it would have become less contentious, more centralized, and more uniform (Courchene 2009; Rodden

2006, 264). From the very beginning, the Quebec government constituted a force of resistance to centralization in the name of a distinct nation that sought to preserve its autonomy within Canada (Silver 1997). By comparison, other provincial governments repeatedly accepted to compromise on autonomy in exchange for additional transfers. Quebec's resistance was so sustained and solid that the country became by far the most decentralized federation in the world, with both the highest share of revenues raised autonomously by subnational governments and the highest share of public spending by subnational and municipal governments (Boucher and Noël 2021, 14–16).

Intergovernmental relations constituted for the Quebec government what foreign affairs were to a country: a policy domain that was the object of debates and amendments through the years but remained anchored in a strong, lasting partisan consensus over core principles. These principles can be summarized around three notions that define federalism, understood as a regime that allows peoples to live together and separately: the principle of separation, the principle of autonomy, and the principle of participation (Croisat 1999; Noël 2009a, 275). The principle of separation implies that sovereignty is divided among different orders of government and is embodied in a constitutional division of legislative powers. The principle of autonomy expresses the understanding that there is no hierarchy among orders of government, as there would be in a merely decentralized regime; each order of government is truly sovereign over its own competences. The principle of participation entails that, however separate, the peoples of a federation do live in a common country. They should be represented adequately in shared institutions and associated in country-wide mechanisms of solidarity. Over the years, the Quebec government has jealously guarded the division of powers and Quebec's autonomy within the federation, and it has stood for a good representation in federal institutions, bilingualism, and a fair share of revenues (Secrétariat aux affaires intergouvernementales canadiennes 2001, 2016).

Fiscal federalism concerns the rules governing the distribution of revenues and expenditures within a federation. The principles of separation, autonomy, and participation also apply to these rules, but they take a specific meaning. The principle of separation gives rise to the question of vertical equity, whereby the distribution of financial resources between orders of government should correspond, in the end, to the financial responsibilities associated with the division of powers (Anderson 2010, 6). Vertical equity can be achieved through an adequate distribution of tax bases, through fiscal transfers from one order of government to another, or, theoretically, through adjustments in the division of powers. When vertical equity is not obtained, there is fiscal imbalance. The principle of autonomy concerns primarily the protection of the constitutional division of powers against the pressures and conditions that can be associated with fiscal transfers. In Canada, this principle is primarily challenged by references to the federal spending power, a "power" that is not established by the Constitution but allows Ottawa to dictate orientations in matters of provincial jurisdiction (Noël 2008). Finally, in fiscal federalism, the principle of participation raises the issue of horizontal equity, which refers to the distribution of resources among regions, especially in a country with important geographical disparities (Beramendi 2012).

These three principles of fiscal federalism are all important, but they coexist uneasily. More precisely, advances made on any two of the three objectives may well jeopardize the other one. Suppose, for instance, that the federal government abided by the Council of the Federation's recent proposal to increase the Canada Health Transfer (CHT) so as to reach 35 per cent of aggregate provincial and territorial expenditures, compared to an estimated 21.7 per cent in 2021-2 (Council of the Federation 2021). This decision, which would call for additional expenditures of $21.7 billion in 2021-2 alone, would automatically improve the fiscal balance between the two orders of government for a gain in vertical equity. Because the CHT benefits all provinces and territories equally, on a per capita basis, horizontal equity would also be well served. Provincial autonomy, however, would be put at risk since the share of own-source revenues in provincial budgets would diminish substantially. The federal government would probably not make such a hefty commitment without introducing some new conditions, which is precisely why, in its 2002 report, the Quebec Commission on Fiscal Imbalance (Séguin Commission) favoured a reallocation of tax fields over enhanced social transfers (Commission on Fiscal Imbalance 2002b). The Séguin Commission proposition constituted a way to improve vertical equity, with better safeguards to protect provincial autonomy. With unequal regional economies and provinces with significantly different tax capacities, however, leaving more financial resources for the provinces to collect undermined horizontal equity. Sales taxes, for instance, would bring more revenues in wealthier provinces. In other words, better attending to autonomy and vertical equity would put horizontal equity under pressure. Concerned by this possibility, the Séguin Commission recommended also improving the Equalization Program to protect provincial governments with lower fiscal capacities and preserve horizontal equity. In 2021, the Quebec government, along with other provinces, opted simply for more generous transfers.

Logically, attending satisfactorily to these three fiscal federalism objectives is not impossible, but it is difficult. It is possible to juggle with three balls at once, and indeed with many more balls, but the average person is likely to drop one of the three. This uneasy position explains why I call Quebec's trilemma a soft rather than a hard one. Conciliating all objectives is conceivable, but it usually fails.

Figure 19.1 summarizes this trilemma by representing the three objectives of the government as angles in a triangle. When V and H are pursued, as is the

Figure 19.1. Quebec's Fiscal Federalism Trilemma

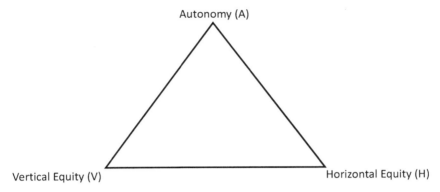

case with the Council of the Federation recent proposition, A is at risk; when A and V have priority, as with the Séguin Commission, H is under pressure.

While it is rarely acknowledged and identified, this trilemma translates into enduring policy orientations that remain coherent but prove unstable. Policies remain coherent because they hold consistently to the government's basic objectives. The Quebec government, for instance, never renounces its autonomy and always seeks a better fiscal balance. At the same time, policy orientations prove unstable because priorities change over time, the focus being on two of the three objectives at any given moment.

Fiscal Federalism before the Trilemma: The Tremblay Commission

In the 1950s, the conservative government of Maurice Duplessis vehemently contested the division of financial resources inherited from the Second World War, which left the key tax fields to the federal government. Duplessis wanted, notably, to secure a share of the new and growing personal income tax field for his government. To make his case for a better division of financial resources, Quebec's premier put together in 1953 a Royal Commission of Inquiry on Constitutional Problems, chaired by Judge Thomas Tremblay. Maurice Duplessis did not wait for the report to appear; he introduced Quebec's own income tax in 1954, a bold move that economist Thomas Courchene described as "one of the watershed moments in Canadian fiscal and political federalism." Quebec's initiative affirmed the autonomous revenue-raising capacity of the provinces and forced a reconfiguration of federal transfers (Courchene 2012, 88–9).

The Tremblay Commission report, which came almost two years after this momentous decision, was nevertheless important because it articulated better than ever a Quebec vision of federalism anchored in constitutional and fiscal autonomy. A belated response to the wartime Rowell-Sirois Commission, which emphasized national unity and efficiency, the Tremblay Commission report insisted on a classical understanding of federalism that stressed the division of powers and the autonomy of the constituents. For Quebec in particular, autonomy appeared primordial because Quebec was home to a distinct society that needed sovereign powers to protect and develop its own institutions and practices (Rocher 2009, 100). The Tremblay Commission report, noted political scientist François Rocher, devoted very few pages to what was called above the principle of participation, the idea that belonging to a federation also entailed the recognition of interdependence and of the need for effective cooperation mechanisms. The "collaboration envisioned in the Tremblay Report" aimed "only at the preservation of provincial autonomy" (Rocher 2009, 103–5).

There was, in fact, no fiscal federalism trilemma for the Tremblay Commission, because only two objectives were identified, autonomy and vertical equity. Autonomy, of course, aimed to consolidate the political and institutional capacities of the French-Canadian society anchored in Quebec, along with vertical equity because an adequate division of fiscal resources between the two orders of government was imperative to maintain provincial autonomy. The commission forcefully denounced the frequent federal reference to an alleged federal spending power that would allow Ottawa to intervene in areas of provincial jurisdiction. "In a federative state," read the report, "all the component parts should, on their own initiative and on their own responsibility, be able to procure for themselves through taxation the financial resources needed for the exercise of their respective jurisdictions. For, if that is lacking, the system loses its federative character" (Royal Commission of Inquiry on Constitutional Problems 1956, vol. 3, 2:196). Such a fiscal balance was deemed essential to maintain the constitutional division of powers and federalism itself: "What would be the good of a careful distribution of legislative powers, if one of the governments could get around it and, to some extent, annul it by its taxation methods and its fashion of spending?" (2:217).

Horizontal equity, the distribution of financial resources across provinces, was not considered. At the time, indeed, the federal Equalization Program did not exist, and there was little redistribution across provinces, except for statutory federal subsidies that had some redistributive effects (Béland et al. 2017, 16). What is more, the Tremblay Commission, headed by a judge close to Maurice Duplessis, had a strong conservative bent and did not consider the need to assure sufficient resources to develop, in each province, a modern welfare state. Quebec's autonomy within the federation was sought primarily to protect and preserve existing traditional and market-oriented institutions.

Quebec's introduction of its own personal income tax, however, challenged the existing order and forced Ottawa to adjust. First, the wartime tax rental agreements, which left income taxes to the federal government, were replaced by a new tax-sharing arrangement that allowed provinces to raise their own

Figure 19.2. Quebec Per Capita Equalization Entitlements, 1957–8 to 2021–2

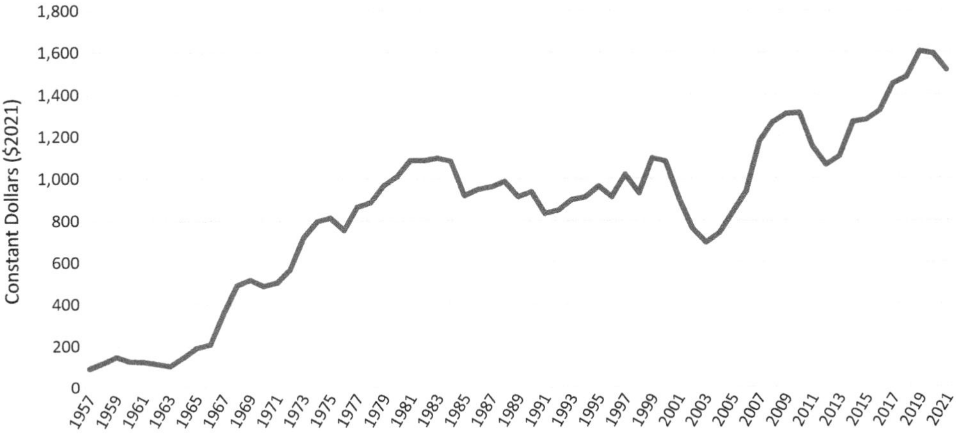

Sources: Calculated from data presented in Béland et al. 2017, 121–2 (for 1957–8 to 2015–16); data from the Department of Finance (for subsequent years), corrected for inflation with the Bank of Canada inflation calculator (using the first part of the fiscal year, that is, 1957 for 1957–8).

income taxes through the federal tax report. Unavoidably, provinces of unequal wealth obtained different revenues, which brought the federal government to introduce, in 1957, the Equalization Program (Courchene 2012, 89). According to Courchene, this enhanced provincial autonomy also encouraged the development of shared-cost programs as a way to maintain federal influence on provincial social policies (89–90).

With the rise of provincial income taxes, the introduction of equalization, and the expansion of shared-cost programs, the issue of distribution within the federation was bound to become paramount. Ironically, a process driven by the Quebec government's unaltered focus on autonomy and vertical equity brought to the forefront the third element of our triangle, the concern for horizontal equity. The creation of the Equalization Program, writes Daniel Béland and his co-authors (2017, 18), as well as the tax-sharing arrangement and the expansion of shared-cost programs, "can be understood in part as an attempt to break the recent fiscal and institutional isolation of Quebec within the Canadian federal system."

In the short term, the preoccupations of the Quebec government remained centred on autonomy and vertical equity. Even with the expansion of the welfare state in the 1960s in the wake of the Quiet Revolution, the issue of horizontal equity proved insufficiently salient to speak of a full-fledged trilemma. The evolution over time of per capita equalization entitlements, presented in Figure 19.2, helps understand this belated attention given to horizontal equity.

Prior to 1967, Quebec's per capita equalization entitlements remained below or near $200 per year (in 2021 constant dollars). The Equalization Program then was less a redistribution mechanism than a complement to top up the new tax point transfer arrangement Ottawa designed to adjust for Quebec's new personal income tax (Tombe 2018, 883). The action in those early years was centred on the expansion of shared-cost arrangements, whereby Ottawa contributed to the development of social programs in the provinces. These transfers grew rapidly, but they were not explicitly redistributive. The issue raised by shared-cost programs was not horizontal equity but autonomy, and to some extent vertical equity (Commission on Fiscal Imbalance 2002a, 38–9).

Until the mid-1960s, then, Quebec did not really face a true fiscal federalism trilemma. The government focused on two objectives, autonomy and vertical equity. It increased Quebec own-source revenues and contested federal interventions in Quebec's jurisdictions. In the following decades, these orientations would translate into epic constitutional battles.

Towards the Trilemma: The Rising Concern for Provincial Equality

In the 1960s, Quebec's Quiet Revolution raised a constitutional challenge for Canada. Bent on using the provincial state to modernize and transform social relations, Quebec governments sought to increase their powers and their financial resources in the federation. Initially, Ottawa made concessions and allowed Quebec to opt out of some shared-cost programs and, more importantly, to develop its own public pension plan. This avenue was soon closed, however, as the federal government increasingly refused to make special arrangements with Quebec. The argument for provincial equality was often raised, less by the provinces than by the federal government, as an argument against asymmetric decentralization.

Provincial autonomy was nevertheless growing. First, the tax-sharing arrangement was gradually giving more own-source revenues to the provinces. Second, the development of the welfare state, which featured important federal transfers to individuals in the 1940s and 1950s, increasingly concerned social services, health care, and education, where massive public programs were managed by the provinces. Third, the era of micromanaged cost-sharing federal programs, where Ottawa associated transfers to the provinces to detailed conditions, gradually came to an end, in part because the federal Department of Finance resented having important elements of its budget determined by provincial decisions. In 1977, shared-cost programs in health and post-secondary education were pooled into a new block grant named Established Programs Financing (EPF). EPF block funding gave provinces more autonomy, but it also disconnected federal contributions from the evolution of costs, which over time would have major consequences, in health-care financing in particular.

Block funding did not prevent federal conditions entirely. In health care, some conditions were reintroduced with the 1984 Canada Health Act.

In the 1980s and early 1990s, the constitutional question came to occupy a central place, with the adoption in 1982, against Quebec's will, of a new Constitution Act, followed by unsuccessful attempts to convince the Quebec government to sign in subsequent years. In this process, and notably during the debates over the 1987 Meech Lake Accord, the question of provincial equality took on a new meaning as a key argument against the recognition of Quebec as a distinct society. What was initially a rather implicit federal argument against asymmetry became a rallying principle for citizens and movements mobilized in favour of an undifferentiated Canada. Horizontal equity was becoming an important issue.

The 1980s and early 1990s were also marked by the rise of neoliberalism in Canada as elsewhere in the world. The welfare state was not dismantled, but its growth was contained, and the focus was increasingly on market mechanisms, fiscal deficits, and lower taxes. In 1995, the federal government presented a landmark budget that drastically reduced and restructured social transfers to the provinces. Provincial governments united and called for a new social union in which the federal government would commit to provide stable and predictable transfers to the provinces. Provincial unity did not last, however, and in 1999 the federal government convinced all provincial governments except Quebec to sign an agreement where they explicitly recognized the federal spending power in exchange for more generous transfers. Quebec remained alone to defend a demanding vision of provincial autonomy.

The growing autonomy of the provinces and two decades of constitutional and intergovernmental debates made horizontal equity a salient concern. For the Quebec government, this objective never ranked as high as the principles of autonomy and vertical equity. With the 1995 drastic cuts in federal transfers to the provinces, however, concerns with horizontal redistribution became more important. As can be seen in Figure 19.2 above, Quebec's equalization entitlements also dropped in real terms in the late 1990s and early 2000s. The stage was set for a debate centred on fiscal imbalance.

The Trilemma Identified

In the beginning of the 2000s, the constitutional debate was practically dead. All over Canada, elected officials were convinced that constitutional change was now impossible, and they concluded that, for a majority of Canadians, the status quo was perfectly acceptable. In Quebec, the narrow defeat of the 1995 referendum on sovereignty also ended an era of affirmation and demands for better terms within Canada. In public affairs, constitutional lawyers were about to give ground to economists.

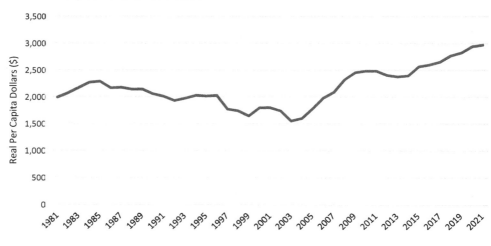

Figure 19.3. Major Social Transfers to Quebec (Cash Component) in Real Per Capita Dollars, 1981–2021

Source: Finances of the Nation (2022).

Indeed, tensions in the federation resurfaced as conflicts over the distribution and redistribution of financial resources. The trigger, as mentioned above, was the February 1995 federal budget presented by Paul Martin. This budget announced that the block grant known as Established Programs Financing (EPF) and the last remaining major shared-cost program (the Canada Assistance Plan, which funded social assistance and social services) would be merged into a new and much reduced block grant, the Canadian Health and Social Transfer (CHST). This new social transfer would be substantially lowered, dropping from $18.5 billion in 1995–6 to $12.5 billion in 1997–8. This dwindling federal commitment would be maintained for the following years, allowing the federal government to reach budgetary balance "on the back of the provinces" (Courchene, quoted in Noël 2009a, 285). As can be seen in Figure 19.2, the value of provincial entitlements in the Equalization Program also dropped as a result of bilateral side agreements and various manipulations in the formula. Overall, as Figure 19.3 indicates, federal transfers to the Quebec government dropped significantly. By 2003, they reached the lowest per capita value in the forty year period from 1981 to 2021.

Given the failure of the social union interprovincial initiative, which concluded with an accord that turned out to be insignificant (Noël 2000, 2003), the Quebec government was on its own. In May 2001, the government of Bernard

Landry created a Commission on Fiscal Imbalance, presided by former Liberal minister Yves Séguin, to analyse the situation and propose avenues for change.[1] The Séguin Commission defined fiscal balance as a situation where one order of government has enough own-source revenues given its legislative responsibilities or where transfers are sufficient to compensate this lack of financial resources, provided that these transfers do not encroach on the autonomy of each order of government (Commission on Fiscal Imbalance 2002b). When the vertical fiscal gap between orders of government is too wide, or when transfers are insufficient or conditional, there is fiscal imbalance.

The Séguin Commission observed a growing fiscal imbalance in the Canadian federation. The costs of provincial programs, in health care notably, grew faster than that of programs managed by the federal government, and own-source revenues and transfers did not correct for this gap. Without corrective measures, the federal government would realize growing budgetary surpluses over time, while the provinces would face rising deficits.

In line with its own definition of fiscal balance, the Séguin Commission's preferred solution was to reallocate tax fields to reinforce provincial financial capacity. Merely increasing social transfers, as provincial governments had proposed in August 2001, would not bring about a durable solution because it would provide no guarantee of sufficient funding for subsequent years. Transfers would remain discretionary. They would also remain conditional. With higher levels of transfers, the weight of conditionality would in fact increase. All in all, noted the commission, there would be no logic in allowing the federal government to raise revenues so that it could return the proceeds to the provinces to finance programs in their jurisdiction. The best option was to abolish the inadequate CHST and compensate the loss of this transfer by a reallocation of tax fields, which would leave more tax room to the provinces (Commission on Fiscal Imbalance 2002b).

The reallocation of sales taxes would be optimal in this respect because the entire tax field could be left to the provinces, with fewer disparities in income than if a portion of the federal income taxes was given to the provinces. The role of the Equalization Program would increase because the value of this tax field varies from one province to the other, but the effect on equalization entitlements would remain acceptable.

Compared to the Tremblay Commission report, the Séguin Commission report had to consider horizontal equity in its recommendations because, as can be seen in Figure 19.2 above, equalization entitlements had become important components of Quebec's budgets. The report estimated the effect on equalization of the reallocation of tax fields, and it also made recommendations to improve the Equalization Program. The Séguin Commission argued, in particular, for a return to a formula based not on the fiscal capacity of five "representative" provinces but on the capacity of all ten provinces.

Quebec's fiscal federalism trilemma was thus fully articulated. The three objectives of autonomy, vertical equity, and horizontal equity were considered jointly in an integrated argument that sought to advance on all three dimensions. This balance was difficult to hold because it involved a careful assessment of various federal and provincial interventions and a set of reforms that required much goodwill from the federal government. From then on, however, there was no going back to the simple two-dimensional representation put forward by the Tremblay Commission report.

In the short term, the fate of the Séguin Commission report was not favourable. Within Quebec, the conclusions were well received, and they were supported by a joint motion of all parties represented in the National Assembly. The idea of a fiscal imbalance made sense and rallied most social actors (Noël 2005). Elsewhere in Canada, the reception was less positive. Immediately, the federal government dismissed the report as "pseudo science" and as a political exercise that "almost no one has discussed" (Noël 2005). Given Ottawa's lack of interest, the discussion indeed never started outside Quebec. In the media, the report was considered to be Quebec news only.

For the first time in a long period, the Quebec government had released a document that considered Quebec's situation in a pan-Canadian, federalist perspective and offered demanding but feasible reforms to address a problem broadly recognized by provincial governments. The spirit of 1982 nevertheless prevailed, and the status quo was affirmed as the only option. Efforts were made, afterward, to enrol the other provincial governments through the Council of the Federation, but the debate never took off until the election of Stephen Harper's Conservative Party in 2006.

Cycles of Shifting Priorities

As head of a minority Liberal government, following the 2004 federal election, Paul Martin made important concessions. While he avoided talking about a fiscal imbalance, he made a commitment in 2004 to provide stable and predictable funding for health care, with a 6 per cent annual increase for the next ten years. Although this arrangement came short of what the Commission on Fiscal Imbalance had recommended, it brought a notable improvement, and it came as well with a symbolic acknowledgement of asymmetry whereby Quebec could use its own statistics to report progress. Modifications were implemented in the Equalization Program as well, but they made the program more, rather than less, arbitrary than before. Implicitly acknowledging this difficulty, Martin appointed an Expert Panel on Equalization and Territorial Formula Financing, headed by Al O'Brien, a former deputy treasurer with the government of Alberta. The report of this panel would be later received by Stephen Harper. At stake, then, were the three aims of Quebec's trilemma. In a context where the federal government had the initiative, however, vertical and horizontal equity prevailed over autonomy.

During the following election campaign, in December 2005 Stephen Harper promised to go further with "a new style of open federalism," more respectful of the division of powers and of provincial prerogatives. This new, open federalism would restore fiscal balance in the federation and curtail the use of the federal "spending power" (Noël 2006). The Harper government's first two budgets did bring improvements, but these were more in line with Paul Martin's late reforms than with a truly new form of federalism. Social transfers were improved with formulas similar to what had been done for health-care transfers, and the Equalization Program was reformed in accordance with the recommendations of Al O'Brien's panel. More generous social transfers were particularly beneficial to Alberta and Ontario because they were almost entirely distributed on a per capita basis, leaving aside the reference to needs built into the old shared-cost and block transfers. Changes to the Equalization Program, on the other hand, were a gain for Quebec, because the program was once again based on the fiscal capacity of the ten provinces and also considered half of the revenues from non-renewable resources (Noël 2009a). In the October 2007 Speech from the Throne, the Harper government reiterated as well its intention to circumscribe the federal "spending power," but it only did so with respect to new shared-cost programs in areas of exclusive provincial jurisdiction. This engagement was at best symbolic, because shared-cost programs constituted a feature of a bygone era; they had not been used in more than ten years and were very unlikely to reappear. This proposition to fix something that no longer existed evoked little interest in Quebec, and the matter was rapidly dropped (Noël 2008).

One after the other, Paul Martin and Stephen Harper improved the transfer system by making health and social transfers more legible, predictable, and stable and by tying once again equalization entitlements to a formula based on a representative provincial tax system. Overall, federal transfers increased, as can be seen in Figures 19.2 and 19.3 above. These reforms, however, did not reflect the Quebec government's preoccupation with autonomy. They were indeed driven by federal priorities, and they emphasized vertical and horizontal equity. True enough, following the 1995 referendum defeat, the Quebec government did not have much bargaining power.

The reforms also remained fragile and very much dependent on Ottawa's goodwill. In its 2009 budget, the Harper government introduced a new ceiling on equalization to limit the growth of the program to a moving average of gross domestic product (GDP) growth. This measure, which distorted the newly adopted formula, was introduced without warning or consultation with the provinces (Noël 2009b). Likewise, following the end of Paul Martin's ten-year commitment to increase health-care transfers by 6 per cent a year, on par with the actual rise of costs in the health-care system, both the Conservatives and the Liberals agreed to limit the growth of the federal contribution by linking it not to health-care costs but to economic growth. This shift was announced by the Harper government and implemented by the Trudeau government. What Ottawa gives, Ottawa can take back. The absence of consideration for autonomy in recent fiscal arrangement reforms left the provinces at the mercy of the ups and downs of federal politics.

When Jean Charest was Quebec's premier in 2007, he converted a $700 million transfer made by Ottawa to improve fiscal balance temporarily into tax cuts. Charest also hesitated before recuperating the two percentage points of the goods and services tax (GST) abandoned by the Harper government, undermining further his claims regarding fiscal imbalance (Rioux Ouimet 2014, 64–5). Gradually, the issue faded.

In June 2017, the Liberal government of Philippe Couillard outlined its own vision, with an ambitious statement on Quebec's objectives in Canadian intergovernmental relations entitled *Quebecers, Our Way of Being Canadian: A Policy for Quebec's Affirmation and for Canadian Relations* (Secrétariat aux affaires intergouvernementales canadiennes 2017). Taking stock of the academic work on federalism and diversity done by Quebec scholars in recent years, this document presented a sophisticated version of Quebec's place in the federation and called for a new conversation among Canadians. The considerations on fiscal federalism, however, remained very limited. The document deplored the fiscal imbalance between the two orders of government but did not elaborate and offered no way out. *Our Way of Being Canadian* did not, for instance, consider the solution proposed by the Séguin Commission and focused instead on improving health-care transfers. Likewise, it suggested circumscribing the federal spending power without specifying how exactly that could be done. The statement on intergovernmental relations focused on two endpoints of the fiscal federalism trilemma, autonomy and horizontal equity, leaving largely aside the question of vertical equity. Non-committal on fiscal federalism, this policy paper left the Quebec government on fragile grounds and contributed to bringing intergovernmental relations back to the main objectives of the federal government and of other provinces, vertical and horizontal equity. Autonomy remained a wish.

For all its talk about autonomy, the Legault government stands rather close to this perspective, focusing mostly on improving health transfers and equalization at the expense, precisely, of autonomy. As chair of the Council of the Federation for 2020, François Legault led the premiers to demand a major increase in Ottawa's contribution to health-care financing. In the 2021 federal election campaign, the main contenders remained short of such a contribution. The Conservative Party proposed to bring back a 6 per cent annual increase, which would still leave the provinces with unsustainable financial situations (Behro and Tombe 2021). The Liberals evoked ad hoc increases associated with a number of stringent conditions, contrary to the federal principle. Once again,

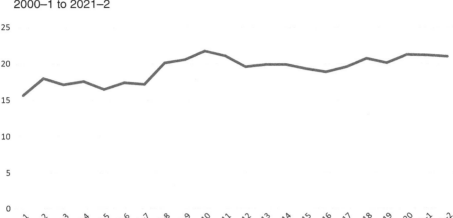

Figure 19.4. Share of Federal Transfers in Quebec's Consolidated Revenues, 2000–1 to 2021–2

Source: Ministère des Finances 2023.

the whole debate left unadressed the autonomy component of Quebec's fiscal federalism trilemma.

Conclusion

For the Quebec government, finding the right balance among contending fiscal federalism objectives is never easy. In earlier days, when the Tremblay Commission did its work, it was easier to combine autonomy and vertical equity, because horizontal equity remained largely a non-issue. As equalization entitlements per capita grew, however, the incidence of changes in redistribution within the federation could no longer be omitted.

The weight of federal transfers also grew over time. As is mentioned above, Canadian provinces are the most autonomous federal entities in the world of federations, relying strongly on own-source revenues. Federal transfers nevertheless remain important, and their presence is growing. Figure 19.4 presents the share of federal transfers in Quebec's consolidated revenues in this century.

Federal transfers now count for more than 20 per cent of Quebec's consolidated revenues. According to the Parliamentary Budget Officer, the federal and provincial governments face very different financial outlooks. Even with the shock of COVID-19 expenditures, the federal government's financial situation is sustainable in the long term, whereas that of the provinces is not (Parliamentary Budget Officer 2021). Quebec's situation, like that of Nova Scotia and Ontario, appears relatively sustainable, but like all provinces, Quebec is faced with rising health-care costs that will represent a growing constraint over time.

Like other provincial governments, the Quebec government remains dependent on the goodwill of the federal government to balance its budget in the long term. In this context, achieving the three aims of Quebec's fiscal federalism trilemma will be increasingly difficult. Of all the objectives, autonomy is the most difficult to reach and the most likely to be forgotten. With a developed welfare state, an aging population, slower growth, and a limited influence over federal finances, the Quebec government no longer faces the conditions that prevailed when the Tremblay Commission wrote its report. Quebec pursues objectives in tension with one another, and it cannot easily win on all fronts.

The federal ideal of Quebec political elites, writes François Rocher (2009, 109, 121), is not shared by their Canadian counterparts, and it may well be impossible to realize: "One has to be quite clever to discern new paths in Canadian federalism not already identified by generations of analysts." With respect to fiscal federalism, this impasse appears indeed serious.

The major contradiction in Quebec's situation, for the time being, rests in the tension between the demand for much higher health transfers and the will to protect and enhance autonomy. As the Séguin Commission identified almost twenty years ago, the logical solution to this problem would be to rely less on enhanced transfers and seek instead a new division of financial resources. Both options present difficulties because they depend on the will to compromise of the federal government. Sharply increased transfers, however, would be more likely to come with strings attached. From the standpoint of the Quebec government, a new division of tax fields thus appears more promising. After twenty years, it would be time to update the evaluation and the recommendations proposed by the Séguin Commission when it identified and tried to solve the fiscal federalism trilemma faced by the Quebec government.

NOTE

1 The author was a member of the Commission on Fiscal Imbalance.

REFERENCES

Anderson, George. 2010. *Fiscal Federalism: A Comparative Introduction*. Oxford: Oxford University Press.

Behro, Ayaka, and Trevor Tombe. 2021. "Unpacking the Conservative Party's Proposal to Boost Health Transfers to the Provinces." *Finances of the Nation*, 24 August 2021. https://financesofthenation.ca/2021/08/24/unpacking-the-conservative-partys-proposal-to-boost-health-transfers-to-the-provinces/.

Béland, Daniel, André Lecours, Gregory P. Marchildon, Haizhen Mou, and M. Rose Olfert. 2017. *Fiscal Federalism and Equalization Policy in Canada*. Toronto: University of Toronto Press.

Beramendi, Pablo. 2012. *The Political Geography of Inequality: Regions and Redistribution*. Cambridge: Cambridge University Press.

Boucher, François, and Alain Noël. 2021. "Introduction: Sub-State Nationalism and Fiscal Relations in Plurinational States." In *Fiscal Federalism in Multinational States: Autonomy, Equality, and Diversity*, edited by François Boucher and Alain Noël, 3–31. Montreal and Kingston: McGill-Queen's University Press.

Commission on Fiscal Imbalance (Séguin Commission). 2002a. *Fiscal Imbalance in Canada: Historical Background*. Quebec: Commission on Fiscal Imbalance.

– 2002b. *A New Division of Canada's Financial Resources: Report*. Quebec: Commission on Fiscal Imbalance.

Council of the Federation. 2021. *Increasing the Canada Health Transfer Will Help Make Provinces and Territories More Financially Sustainable over the Long Term: Report of the Provincial and Territorial Ministers of Finance to the Council of the Federation*. Ottawa: Council of the Federation.

Courchene, Thomas. 2009. "Where Would Canada Be without Quebec?" *Globe and Mail*, 29 September 2009. https://www.theglobeandmail.com/opinion/where-would-canada-be-without-quebec/article1202906/.

– 2012. "Reflections on the Federal Spending Power: Practices, Principles, Perspectives." In *Canada: The State of the Federation 2008: Open Federalism and the Spending Power*, edited by Thomas J. Courchene, John R. Allan, and Hoi Kong, 85–117. Montreal and Kingston: McGill-Queen's University Press.

Croisat, Maurice. 1999. *Le fédéralisme dans les démocraties contemporaines*. 3rd ed. Paris: Montchrestien.

Finances of the Nation. 2022. "Major Federal Transfers." *Finances of the Nation*. https://financesofthenation.ca/transfers/.

Iversen, Torben, and Anne Wren. 1998. "Equality, Employment, and Budgetary Restraint: The Trilemma of the Service Economy." *World Politics* 50, no. 4 (July): 507–46. https://doi.org/10.1017/S0043887100007358.

Ministère des Finances. 2021. "Minister Girard Reacts to the Federal Budget." Press Release, 20 April 2021. http://www.finances.gouv.qc.ca/documents/Communiques/en/COMEN_20210420.pdf.

– 2023. *Statistiques budgétaires du Quebec*. Québec: Government of Québec. http://www.budget.finances.gouv.qc.ca/budget-en-chiffres/fr-CA/Mars-2023/Document-t%C3%A9l%C3%A9chargeable/.

Noël, Alain. 2000. "General Study of the Framework Agreement." In *The Canadian Social Union without Quebec: Eight Critical Analyses*, edited by Alain G. Gagnon and Hugh Segal, 9–35. Montreal: Institute for Research on Public Policy.

– 2003. "Power and Purpose in Intergovernmental Relations." In *Forging a Canadian Social Union: SUFA and Beyond*, edited by Sarah Fortin, Alain Noël, and France St-Hilaire, 47–68. Montreal and Kingston, McGill-Queen's University Press.

- 2005. "'A Report That Almost No One Has Discussed:' Early Responses to Quebec's Commission on Fiscal Imbalance." In *Canadian Fiscal Arrangements: What Works, What Might Work Better*, edited by Harvey Lazar, 127–51. Montreal and Kingston: McGill-Queen's University Press.
- 2006. "Il suffisait de presque rien: Promises and Pitfalls of Open Federalism." In *Open Federalism: Interpretations, Significance*, edited by Keith G. Banting, Roger Gibbins, Peter M. Leslie, Alain Noël, Richard Simeon, and Robert Young, 25–37. Kingston, ON: Institute of Intergovernmental Relations.
- 2008. "How Do You Limit a Power That Does Not Exist?" *Queen's Law Journal* 34, no. 1 (Fall): 391–412.
- 2009a. "Balance and Imbalance in the Division of Financial Resources." In *Contemporary Canadian Federalism: Foundations, Traditions, Institutions*, edited by Alain-G. Gagnon, 273–302. Toronto: University of Toronto Press.
- 2009b. "Feu le fédéralisme d'ouverture." *Options politiques* 30, no. 3 (March): 68.

Parliamentary Budget Officer. 2021. *Fiscal Sustainability Report 2021*. Ottawa: Office of the Parliamentary Budget Officer.

Rioux Ouimet, Hubert. 2014. "Quebec and Canadian Fiscal Federalism: From Tremblay to Séguin and Beyond." *Canadian Journal of Political Science* 47, no. 1: 47–69. https://doi.org/10.1017/S0008423914000237.

Rocher, François. 2009. "The Quebec-Canada Dynamic or the Negation of the Ideal of Federalism." In *Contemporary Canadian Federalism: Foundations, Traditions, Institutions*, edited by Alain-G. Gagnon, 81–131. Toronto: University of Toronto Press.

Rodden, Jonathan. 2006. *Hamilton's Paradox: The Promise and Peril of Fiscal Federalism*. Cambridge: Cambridge University Press.

Royal Commission of Inquiry on Constitutional Problems (Tremblay Commission). 1956. *Report*. Quebec: Government of Quebec.

Secrétariat aux affaires intergouvernementales canadiennes. 2001. *Positions du Québec dans les domaines constitutionnel et intergouvernemental de 1936 à 2001*. Québec: Gouvernement du Québec.
- 2016. *Positions du Québec dans les domaines constitutionnel et intergouvernemental de 2001 à 2008*. Québec: Gouvernement du Québec.
- 2017. *Quebecers, Our Way of Being Canadian: A Policy for Quebec's Affirmation and for Canadian Relations*. Québec: Gouvernement du Québec.

Silver, Arthur I. 1997. *The French-Canadian Idea of Confederation, 1864–1900*. 2nd ed. Toronto: University of Toronto Press.

Tombe, Trevor. 2018. "'Final and Unalterable' – But Up for Negotiation: Federal-Provincial Transfers in Canada." *Canadian Tax Journal* 66, no. 4: 871–917.

20 Fiscal Fortunes: An Ontario Perspective on Federal-Provincial Transfers

TRACY SNODDON

1. Introduction

Fiscal arrangements are a critical feature of fiscal federalism in Canada. These arrangements help manage and coordinate government activities and address efficiency and equity issues that arise in the federation. Practical considerations such as affordability and accountability also play a role in their design and implementation. In the past, changes in fiscal fortunes in the country have led the federal government to make fundamental, and sometimes controversial, changes to Canada's fiscal arrangements. The recent COVID-19 pandemic, and the economic upheaval that accompanied it, may similarly spark changes in fiscal arrangements as governments at all levels try to tackle its aftermath.

The primary objective of this chapter is to provide an Ontario perspective on fiscal arrangements in Canada. Ontario, as Canada's most populous province, has a unique fiscal role in the federation, both in terms of its contribution to federal revenue and its effect on federal spending on transfers to provinces. To set the stage, the chapter begins with an overview of the evolution of major federal transfers to provinces over the past forty years. Significant program changes and the fiscal and economic pressures that contributed to them are highlighted. An Ontario perspective on fiscal federalism is formulated through an examination of provincial government budgets since 1980. Budget documents offer a historical record of the Ontario government's policy priorities and concerns, and are a useful data source for uncovering Ontario's reactions to changes in federal transfers. The analysis reveals that the province has several persistent concerns about Canada's fiscal arrangements that colour its perspective on the need for fiscal federalism reform. These concerns are critically evaluated, taking into consideration not only Ontario's perspective but also the role of fiscal arrangements in the federation as a whole. Finally, the chapter considers the implications of the changing fiscal fortunes in the post-pandemic era and what they might mean for federal-provincial transfers and Ontario moving forward.

2. Fiscal Fortunes and the Evolution of Canada's Fiscal Arrangements

This section describes the major federal transfers to provinces, identifying key changes to these transfers and important fiscal and economic influences at the federal government level and in select provinces since 1980.[1] Three types of federal transfers are examined: transfers that address fiscal imbalances, insurance-like arrangements, and infrastructure support. Canada's social transfers, the Canada Health Transfer (CHT) and the Canada Social Transfer (CST), are motivated in part by the presence of a *vertical* fiscal imbalance, a situation where provinces and territories are responsible for major expenditure programs but the federal government has comparatively greater fiscal capacity.[2] The Equalization Program is designed to address *horizontal* fiscal imbalances that arise when provinces differ in their ability to raise revenue to finance their spending responsibilities. Federal transfers in support of provincial infrastructure spending are often motivated by a vertical fiscal imbalance and benefit spillovers. Other arrangements, like the Fiscal Stabilization Program (FSP) and the Disaster Financial Assistance Arrangements (DFAA), offer insurance-like protection to provincial governments in response to different types of shocks. Recent transfers to provinces, such as the monies provided under the Safe Restart Agreements, while time-limited, also provide insurance-like protection to help cushion provinces from pandemic-related fiscal shocks.

To begin, consider some broad trends. Federal transfer programs are designed and paid for by the federal government. Ottawa's spending on these transfers, therefore, is sensitive to its fiscal circumstances. Figure 20.1 shows the federal government's net debt and major cash transfers to provinces as a percentage of the gross domestic product (GDP) since 1981–2. Cash transfers include health and social transfers, equalization, and in 2020–1, pandemic-related transfers to provinces.[3] The period from 1981–2 to 2002–3 is one of fiscal retrenchment. The ratio of federal net debt to GDP increases quite significantly, peaking in 1996, and then declines over the next several years as the federal government's actions to tackle the deficit and debt take hold. Over this same period, the ratio of cash transfers to GDP falls, slowly at first and then more dramatically. By contrast, the period from 2004 to 2020 is characterized by a relatively low and stable federal net debt to GDP ratio and increasing cash transfers to provinces as a percentage of GDP.

Some of the pandemic's fiscal impacts are evident in Figure 20.1. Federal net debt as a ratio of GDP is forecast to increase from about 33.4 per cent in 2019–20 to over 50 per cent in 2020–1, primarily due to massive increases in federal spending on COVID-19 support programs. With the infusion of $24 billion in extra cash to the provinces under the federal government's time-limited COVID-19 arrangements, the ratio of cash transfers to GDP jumps from 3.2 per cent in 2019–20 to 4.6 per cent in 2020–1. The sharp increase in federal

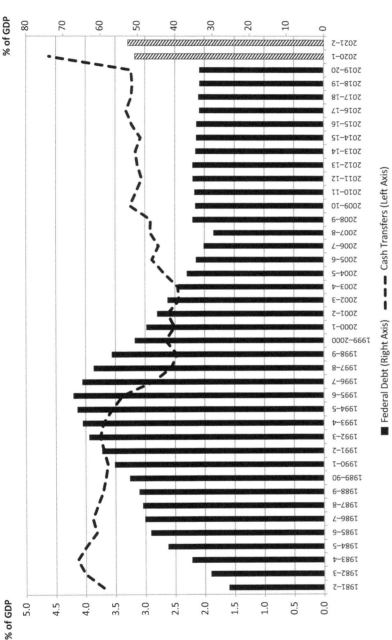

Sources: Authors' construction. Federal net debt as a percentage of GDP taken from Finance of the Nation (n.d.); cash transfers from Department of Finance Canada (2022); estimates of net debt to GDP for 2020–1 and 2021–2 from RBC (n.d.); and nominal GDP from Statistics Canada (2023a).
Notes: CAP = Canada Assistance Plan; CHST = Canada Health and Social Transfer; CHT = Canada Health Transfer; CST = Canada Social Transfer; EPF = Established Programs Financing. Major cash transfers include EPF, CAP, CHST, CHT, CST, Equalization, and associated equalization. For 2020–1, cash transfers include $24.3 billion in federal transfers to tackle the pandemic ($19 billion Safe Restart; $3.3 billion COVID Resiliency; and $2 billion Safe Return to School).

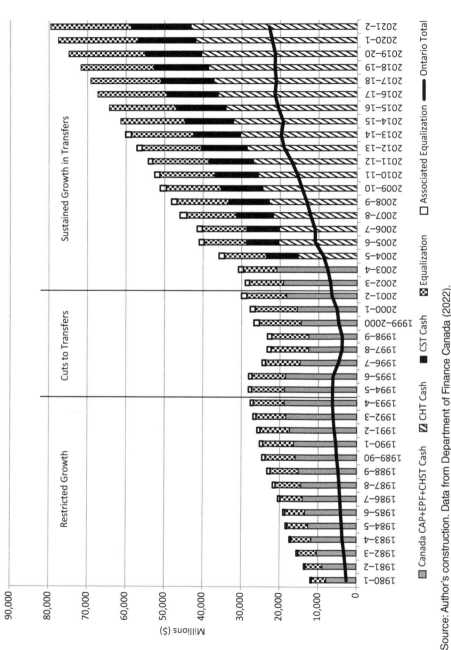

Figure 20.2. Federal Cash Transfers to Provinces and Ontario

Source: Author's construction. Data from Department of Finance Canada (2022).
Note: CAP = Canada Assistance Plan; CHST = Canada Health and Social Transfer; CHT = Canada Health Transfer; CST = Canada Social Transfer; EPF = Established Programs Financing

net debt is potentially worrisome for the provinces if the federal government decides to tackle its net debt by targeting federal spending on transfers to provinces.

Of course, fiscal pressures at the federal level are sensitive to economic circumstances in the provinces, particularly in Ontario and Alberta. Ontario's influence is due to its size. The federal government's ability to finance spending, including spending on major transfers, depends on Ontario's contributions to federal revenues. About 41 per cent of federal government tax revenue comes from Ontario, although this share has varied since 1980 from a low of about 37.5 per cent in 1981 to a high of 45 per cent in 1989.[4] With its 39 per cent population share, Ontario also has a sizeable effect on federal transfer spending since key transfers are allocated on an equal per capita basis. Alberta's influence stems primarily from its volatile oil and gas revenues and the fact that oil and gas endowments are very unevenly distributed across provinces.[5] As discussed below, the impact of Alberta's changing fiscal fortunes on the federal government's Equalization Program has been an ongoing source of controversy.

Figure 20.2 shows federal cash transfers to all provinces and to Ontario since 1980. Similar to Figure 20.1, two periods are evident. A retrenchment period between 1980 and 2003, characterized first by restrictions in the growth in transfers and then cuts to transfers, is followed by a subsequent period of sustained growth in cash transfers.

The Social Transfers

Social transfers in support of health, post-secondary education (PSE), and social assistance have existed in one form or another for decades. Although all provinces (and territories) have entitlements to these transfers, federal government changes to social transfers over time have affected the aggregate level of funding and the allocation of funds across provinces.

In 1980, the federal government supported provincial spending on health care and post-secondary education via the Established Programs Financing (EPF) arrangements, originally introduced in 1977 to replace cost-sharing grants for health and PSE. Provinces received an equal per capita entitlement, comprised of a cash transfer and a tax point transfer. The move to block funding limited the federal government's financial obligation at a time of increasing deficit and net debt to GDP ratios (Figure 20.1) and gave the provinces more flexibility. The per capita entitlement was intended to grow annually based on an escalator. During the 1980s and 1990s, however, the federal government made numerous changes to limit growth in (and eventually freeze) per capita EPF transfers.[6]

The federal government also provided matching grants under the Canada Assistance Plan (CAP) in support of provincial expenditures on social assistance.

CAP was originally introduced in 1966 and changed little during the 1980s. In 1990, however, the federal government imposed a 5 per cent ceiling on the annual growth in payments to provinces that did not qualify for equalization – Alberta, Ontario, and British Columbia. This "cap on CAP" remained until 1994–5, and in 1995–6 CAP payments to all provinces were frozen.

Social transfers continued to undergo considerable change over the next decade. CAP and EPF transfers were replaced with the Canada Health and Social Transfer (CHST) in 1996–7, resulting in a dramatic reduction in total cash support for provinces over the next few years. At the time of introduction, the CHST was allocated to provinces based on their combined shares of EPF and CAP, but by 2001–2 provinces received equal per capita CHST entitlements. Starting in 2000, the federal government made frequent changes, including the introduction of an escalator, a cash floor (subsequently revised), and cash supplements (Madore 2003).

Today's CHT and CST were created in 2004 when the CHST was split once again into two block grants. Like the CHST, these transfers initially consisted of a tax point transfer and a cash component, and total entitlements were allocated on an equal per capita basis. Various adjustments were made over the next several years. An annual escalator for the CHT of 6 per cent took effect in 2006–7. A 3 per cent annual escalator for the CST started in 2009–10. Both transfers were eventually allocated on an equal per capita cash basis, in 2009–10 for the CST and in 2014–15 for the CHT. The last major change came in 2012 when the federal government announced a reduction in the CHT escalator from 6 per cent to a three-year moving average of GDP, with a 3 per cent minimum annual rate of growth, starting in 2017–18.

A chronology of changes to social transfers since 1980 is provided in Appendix Table 20.A1.

Equalization

The Equalization Program, introduced in 1957, was under stress heading into 1980. Alberta's resource revenue explosion in the 1970s and 1980s, and again in the 2000s, evident in Figure 20.3, prompted significant changes to the program.[7] In 1980, even though Alberta's resource revenues were only partially included in the equalization formula, the tremendous growth in the province's fiscal capacity meant Ontario would qualify for equalization, and total spending on equalization would increase significantly. In response, the federal government introduced the "personal income override" in 1981 to retroactively prevent Ontario from receiving equalization payments from 1977–8 to 1981–2. And in 1982, the ten-province standard was replaced with a five-province standard, and a 100 per cent inclusion rate for resource revenues was adopted. These changes insulated the program from Alberta's growing but volatile fiscal

Figure 20.3. Alberta's Non-Renewable Resource Revenues

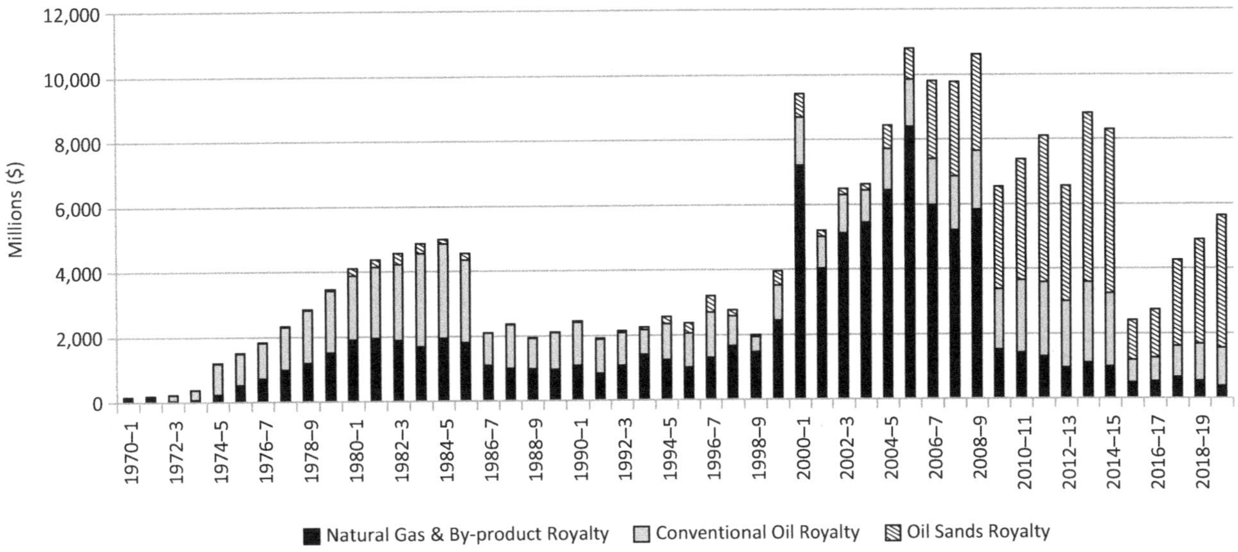

Source: Author's construction. Data from Government of Alberta (n.d.).

capacity vis-à-vis the other provinces. At the same time, a ceiling restricting the annual growth in total payments to the rate of growth in nominal GDP was introduced, as was a floor provision to protect individual provinces against significant year-over-year reductions in entitlements.[8]

The next major changes to the Equalization Program came roughly twenty years later. The ceiling on aggregate entitlements was eliminated in 2002-3. In 2004, the five-province standard was abandoned, and a new framework introduced. Total equalization was exogenously fixed for the first two years, after which it would grow at a rate of 3.5 per cent a year. Funds were allocated to provinces based on the distribution of past payments. The federal government argued that program changes were needed due to the effects of the 2002-3 slowdown in the Ontario economy on equalization payments to recipient provinces and on federal tax revenues.[9] Variability in payments was also flagged as a concern.

This new framework did not last very long. Following the recommendations of the Expert Panel on Equalization and Territorial Financing, the ten-province standard was re-adopted in 2007. Concerns about the volatility in payments were addressed by calculating fiscal capacity using a three-year weighted moving average, lagged two years. A hybrid approach was adopted with respect to the contentious issue of the resource revenue inclusion rate. Provinces would receive the higher payment from two calculations – equalization based on a 50 per cent inclusion rate and equalization based on a zero inclusion rate. A fiscal capacity cap (FCC) was also adopted to ensure that fiscal capacity based on own-source revenues and equalization for any recipient province could not exceed the fiscal capacity of the poorest non-recipient province, which at the time was Ontario.

In 2009, the year in which Ontario qualified for equalization, the federal government introduced a fixed growth rule that acts as both a ceiling and a floor on total payments. The FCC was amended to equal the fiscal capacity of the average of all recipient provinces if more than 50 per cent of the population lived in a receiving province. If the population condition does not apply, then the FCC reverts to the fiscal capacity of the poorest non-recipient province (see Nadeau 2014). As Tombe (2018) notes, the amended FCC essentially applies only when Ontario is receiving equalization.

Appendix Table 20.A2 summarizes major changes in equalization since 1980.

Insurance-Type Arrangements

The federal government provides an important insurance function through two major programs – the Fiscal Stabilization Program (FSP) and the Disaster Financial Assistance Arrangements (DFAA), introduced in 1967 and 1970, respectively. These programs differ from the more established transfer programs outlined above but nevertheless play an important role in Canada's system of fiscal arrangements.

All provinces are eligible for a fiscal stabilization payment provided they suffer a qualifying revenue shock and make a claim for payment. Since 1980, there have been three major changes to the program. In 1987, stabilization payments were capped at a maximum of $60 per person. In 1995, a 5 per cent deductible for non-resource revenues was reintroduced after having been eliminated in 1972. Today, to be eligible for a payment, a province must suffer a greater than 5 per cent decline in annual, non-resource revenue; resource revenues are included only if the decline from this source exceeds 50 per cent. The federal government recently announced that the $60 cap would increase to $169 for 2019–20 and 2020–1, and would increase in line with nominal GDP after that.[10]

In the event of a weather-related disaster, a province may request a DFAA payment to assist with disaster expenditures. Eligible disaster expenses include provincial expenditures on evacuation, emergency shelter, and repairs to public roads and bridges. The federal government's cost-share increases from 0 to 90 per cent as eligible disaster costs increase above certain thresholds. In 2015, the federal government increased the nominal thresholds (unchanged since 1970) and instituted annual inflation indexing for the thresholds moving forward.

Finally, the federal government's time-limited COVID-19 transfers helped provincial and territorial governments' cope with fiscal shocks stemming from the pandemic. Three major COVID-19–related transfers were introduced in 2020. Under the Safe Restart Agreement, the federal government provided $19 billion to provinces and territories to support spending in seven priority areas in 2020–1. Much of the funding was conditional block-type funding with provincial amounts determined on an equal per capita basis.[11] The COVID-19 Resilience Infrastructure Stream repurposed up to $3.3 billion in existing infrastructure funds to provide matching grants to provinces and territories for projects to make certain public spaces more "pandemic-resistant." And finally, under the Safe Return to Class Fund, the federal government transferred $2 billion to provinces and territories. Funds were allocated based on the number of school-aged children in the province between ages four and eighteen, with $2 million in base funding to each jurisdiction.

Appendix Table 20.A3 summarizes major changes to federal insurance-type arrangements.

Infrastructure Funding

Federal support to provinces for infrastructure has ramped up considerably over the past fifteen years and has become a more or less permanent feature in Canada's system of fiscal arrangements since 2007.[12] As shown in Figure 20.4, infrastructure funding to the provinces, territories, and municipalities accounts

Figure 20.4. Share of Federal Transfers, by Type, 2020–1

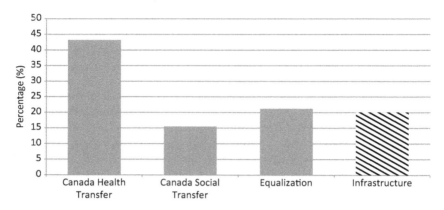

Sources: Author's tabulations. Federal infrastructure spending is based on estimates of spending under various programs including the Investing in Canada Plan, Gas Tax Fund (now Canada Community-Building Fund), and other legacy programs (see Infrastructure Canada 2018). Data for other transfers are from Department of Finance Canada (2022).

for about 20 per cent of total federal spending on social transfers, equalization, and infrastructure in 2020–1. Infrastructure funding is typically cost-shared and time-limited, with priority areas defined by the federal government of the day. Provincial allocations of available funds are determined using a number of metrics, including population, merit, and transit ridership, and depend on the specifics of the particular infrastructure program. In contrast to the more established transfers, infrastructure funding for a province is the result of bilateral agreements between the federal government and each province.

In 2007, the federal government launched its Building Canada Fund, promising $33 billion over seven years. In 2009, the federal government made available another $4 billion in infrastructure funding as part of its economic stimulus package. Provincial allocations were based on population, conditional on the project's merits and readiness. When this fund expired, a new Building Canada Fund was introduced in 2014, providing an additional $14 billion over ten years. In 2016, the federal government introduced new funding under its Investing in Canada Plan (IICP). The federal government also flows infrastructure funds through the provinces to municipalities using the Canada Community-Building Fund (previously called the Gas Tax Fund). Originally introduced in 2005, these funds are allocated to provinces on an equal per capita basis with some adjustments.

3. An Ontario Perspective

The previous section summarizes major federal transfer programs and the changes made to them since 1980. Important fiscal drivers include federal government budgetary pressures and changes in provincial economic and fiscal circumstances, particularly in Ontario and Alberta.[13] Against this backdrop, an Ontario perspective on fiscal federalism and major federal transfers to provinces is formulated by undertaking an analysis of provincial government budget documents over the past four decades. Budgets are typically released on an annual basis and provide information on government revenues, expenditures, federal transfers, deficits, and other economic data. These documents lay out the government's priorities and identify areas of concern, including those related to the federal government and fiscal arrangements. Finally, an analysis of budgets over time helps distinguish between persistent and more transitory concerns that have played a role in shaping the province's current perspective on fiscal arrangements.

The analysis reveals that Ontario has some long-standing issues with Canada's fiscal arrangements. Four key concerns are identified: an inadequate level of federal transfer support; unfair treatment of Ontario; too high net contributions to equalization and to the federation; and the need for stable, long-term, and sustainable federal support. Of course, Ontario budgets reflect Ontario's interests, but fiscal arrangements are designed to address efficiency and equity issues within the federation. Each concern is therefore critically evaluated while considering the possible tension between Ontario's interests and the broader interests of the federation.

Inadequate Level of Federal Support

Ontario budgets have delivered a consistent message over the past forty years that the level of federal support for health care, and more recently for infrastructure, is inadequate. In the 1980s, the province opposed federal cuts to EPF, arguing that transfers to provinces were not the main source of the federal government's fiscal troubles. The 1990s were a difficult period, and Ontario's budget documents reflect this. Throughout that decade Ontario argued that federal offloading, cuts to transfers, and the inadequacy of federal funding unfairly compounded the province's financial burden from the recession. Budgets over the forty-year period repeatedly call for fair and adequate health-care funding from the federal government, including most recently a demand that the federal share of health-care spending increase from 22 per cent in 2020 to 35 per cent moving forward. From the province's perspective, more federal support is preferred to less. But it is justified?

Ontario points to a persistent and growing vertical fiscal imbalance, rising health-care costs, growing provincial deficits, and the presence of an infrastructure deficit to support its claim that more funding is needed. It is challenging, however, to measure the adequacy of the overall level of federal support to provinces in general and to Ontario specifically. Federal health transfers, for example, are typically motivated by the presence of a vertical fiscal imbalance, but there is no consensus on how to measure this imbalance. The vertical fiscal imbalance can change over time, either temporarily or permanently, compounding the measurement challenge. There is also debate as to what approach is needed to close the gap. Federal transfers are one option. A transfer of tax room is another. In 1977, when matching grants for health care were replaced by a block grant, the federal government lowered its tax rate to make room for provinces to raise taxes if they wished. This tax transfer meant that provinces would be taking on a greater share of health-care funding. But Ontario has argued over the past four decades that the federal government's share is too low. In the 1980s, 24 per cent was deemed too low. In 2021, the province called for the federal government to increase its share to 35 per cent. From the province's perspective, the desired federal share is a moving target, and the level of support is always too low.

A recent study finds that rising health-care costs due to population aging are a primary factor contributing to the deterioration of provincial governments' fiscal positions (Bergeron et al. 2020). Budget deficits reflect provincial governments' spending and taxation choices but, as Dahlby (2005) and Feehan (2020) both argue, they are not evidence per se of the need for higher levels of federal transfers. Recent studies support this argument. Eisen, Lammam, and Ren (2016) find that a significant contributing factor to persistent provincial budget deficits is provincial government spending decisions, not federal transfers.

An analysis of long-term fiscal sustainability for individual provinces finds that increases in CHT funding under various scenarios, including CHT growth in line with provincial health spending and CHT allocations based on shares of population aged eighty-five years and over, will not solve the fiscal sustainability problems in most provinces (Shaw 2018). While the evidence does indicate that population aging contributes to the deterioration of provincial governments' fiscal positions, Bergeron et al. (2020) show that Ontario is one of three provinces with sustainable fiscal policy, at least prior to the pandemic. This study also finds that the aging population problem is most acute in the Atlantic provinces, not in Ontario. In chapter 18 of this volume, Richard Saillant observes that the median age and the share of seniors are both higher in the Atlantic provinces as compared to the national average. Additionally, between 2020 and 2030, the percentage of the population over sixty-five years of age is expected to grow faster in Newfoundland and Labrador, New Brunswick, and Nova Scotia as compared to the national average (and Ontario). This demographic imbalance will have serious economic and fiscal implications for provinces east of Quebec, particularly with respect to provincial government spending on health care.[14]

Federal infrastructure funding has increased quite dramatically since 2007, but there is debate in the literature about how much ongoing federal infrastructure support is needed. Infrastructure transfers are often motivated by spillover benefits and by the presence of vertical and horizontal imbalances. Spillovers can, however, be positive or negative, and there is limited empirical evidence on their size. Boadway and Kitchen (2018) argue that provinces have an incentive to overinvest in infrastructure, in which case matching grants can worsen the problem. Dahlby and Jackson (2015) argue that infrastructure grants (and differential matching rates) are justified given persistent fiscal imbalances, evident from the differences in the marginal cost of public funds (MCF) across governments at both levels, despite existing equalization and social transfers. The authors note, however, that matching infrastructure grants for smaller projects come with unduly high coordination and efficiency costs. Both studies argue, for different reasons, that there are potential benefits from bolstering established fiscal transfers and reducing the heavy reliance on matching grants for infrastructure.

Over the last fifteen to twenty years, there has been steady growth in federal funding for both health and infrastructure, especially in comparison to the previous two decades. So, one could argue that Ontario's concern has at least been partially addressed. From the perspective of the federation, however, the issue of the level of funding support is arguably more pressing for other provinces. Given persistent fiscal imbalances, it may be reasonable to argue that the level of funding for health care is inadequate or that a high level of infrastructure support is needed, but the literature suggests that more of all transfers for all provinces is not necessarily justified.

Ontario Is Treated Unfairly

There are two dimensions to Ontario's fairness concern. First, the province takes issue with changes in transfer programs that specifically target Ontario, and second, the province is concerned about its unfair share of transfers.

The budget review reveals three notable instances where the federal government made changes to transfers that unfairly targeted Ontario – the adoption of the personal income override in 1981, the imposition of the cap on CAP in 1990, and the adoption of a fixed growth rule for equalization in 2009.

Ontario accepted the personal override on condition that the federal government would reform the Equalization Program to address the impact of Alberta's oil and gas revenues on payments. The federal government was motivated to do so, especially since the increases in equalization fueled by these oil and gas revenues did not directly contribute to federal or Ontario tax revenues. Equalization was reformed in 1982, but Ontario lost out on $1.3 billion in payments that it would have otherwise received between 1977–8 and 1981–2.[15]

The province was particularly unhappy about the selective cap on the growth of its CAP grants and the ad hoc use of fiscal capacity as the criteria for restricting transfers. Carter (1994) estimates that the cap cost Ontario about $5 billion in lost transfer revenue between 1990–1 and 1993–4, roughly 83 per cent of the transfer revenue forgone by the three affected provinces combined.

The fixed growth rule was implemented largely in response to Ontario's expected entry into the Equalization Program in 2009.[16] Because the province has a large population, even a small per capita deficit in revenue-raising capacity means a large increase in equalization payments for the federal government. The fixed growth rule reduced payments to Ontario (and other recipient provinces) from what they otherwise would have been for several years.[17] One study estimates that removal of the fixed growth rule would have generated an additional $14.5 billion in total payments between 2010–11 and 2019–20; $8.1 billion of this amount would have gone to Ontario (see Busby and Behrend 2020).[18]

Questions of fairness are always difficult, but the claim that Ontario is sometimes treated unfairly merits consideration. From a Canada-wide perspective, the federal government's concerns about escalating transfer costs and affordability due to Ontario's size are reasonable. Boadway and Kitchen (2018) and Courchene (2010) have both argued that social transfers could be redesigned to be conditioned on provincial fiscal capacity to address disparities that remain after equalization. Social transfers could also be designed using fiscal capacity to restrict transfers when some ceiling on the growth in transfer spending is hit. This proposal may be an equitable approach to restricting transfers when the need arises. But implementing a restriction based on fiscal capacity in a seemingly ad hoc and punitive way to target a particular province, however, is arguably unfair. Indeed, Courchene (1994) argues that, although British Columbia and Alberta were affected, the federal government's cap on CAP was designed mainly to restrain growing CAP transfers to Ontario.

Ontario's second fairness concern relates to its share of transfers. The province has vigorously argued that federal transfers for health care, and more recently for infrastructure, should be allocated on an equal per capita cash basis.

Given the province's large population share, this approach is to its advantage. The province has also on occasion argued that factors other than population, including expenditure need in equalization and transit ridership in infrastructure funding, merit consideration.

Provinces have received equal per capita cash payments under the CHT since 2014–15. Provincial maximum allotments of federal infrastructure funding are primarily, but not exclusively, determined on an equal per person basis. Other metrics like transit ridership and project merit are sometimes used. Some infrastructure funding involves equal allocations of "base" funding to all provinces with additional funds allocated on a per capita basis. Thus, it would seem that the province's concern about the allocation of health and infrastructure transfers has been largely addressed.

From a broader Canada-wide perspective, equal per capita transfers need not be fair (or efficient). Provincial needs may differ beyond differences in population size. For instance, fairness may require that CHT transfers be allocated based on some indicator of health-care need. Robin Boadway argues in this volume's chapter 5 on the CHT that such a proposal would help to address horizontal fiscal imbalances that remain after equalization. Conditioning the CHT on a province's age structure is also discussed in Saillant's chapter 18 as an option for tackling the Atlantic region's population-induced health-care spending pressures. Dahlby and Jackson (2015) argue that the allocation of transfers may, for efficiency reasons, depend on the presence and size of spillovers and fiscal imbalances, and differences in governments' MCFs. They find that efficiency requires matching rates for infrastructure grants that differ by province and by project type. Equal per capita infrastructure grants to provinces would be a very unlikely result based on this efficiency criterion.

Ontario has a legitimate concern that federal government changes in transfer programs have sometimes unfairly targeted the province. Its quest for equal per capita allocations for health-care transfers and infrastructure support have, to a large extent, been addressed. From the perspective of the federation, however, a fair allocation of federal transfers need not align with Ontario's view of fairness. It is important to design fiscal arrangements to balance fairness concerns with the federal government's affordability considerations in such a way as to minimize the scope for ad hoc punitive adjustments.

The Need to Address Ontario's Net Contribution to the Federation (and Equalization)

Ontario budgets have become increasing focused on the issue of the province's net contributions to the federation and to equalization since 1980. The net contribution debate centres on the fact that Ontario taxpayers send more tax revenues to the federal government than they receive in federal spending on transfers to provinces. In the case of equalization, Ontario measures its net contribution as the difference between the payments it receives and the province's contribution to financing those payments, calculated as the share of federal revenue coming from Ontario multiplied by total federal spending on transfers. In its 2019 budget, Ontario estimated its net contribution to the federation at $13 billion.

The province's net contribution is heavily influenced by equalization. In the early 1980s, Ontario was particularly concerned with the effect of Alberta's oil and gas revenues on equalization, especially since the province was precluded from receiving equalization between 1977 and 1982. Following the 1982 equalization reform, the issue fell into the background for a few decades. Starting in the 2000s, Ontario's net contribution to the federation became a core issue once again, especially so between 2009–10 and 2018–19, when the province was an equalization recipient.

The Equalization Program aims to reduce disparities in provinces' revenue-raising capacities. By design, only some provinces qualify for payments, which naturally creates tension in provinces like Ontario and Alberta since the federal taxes paid by their citizens are helping to finance federal government spending on equalization payments to other provinces.[19] However, Ontario does not directly send own-source revenues to the federal government, nor does it send cheques to other provinces to pay for equalization (or any other federal program).[20] It is fair to say, though, that some Ontario residents are net contributors – in terms of what they contribute to federal taxes and the benefits they receive from federal spending.

Several analyses have been undertaken to measure fiscal balances across provinces and/or over time. The most comprehensive study to date is that of Mansell, Khanal, and Tombe (2020). Their analysis focuses on the differences in federal fiscal balances, defined as the difference between federal revenues collected and federal expenditures, including spending on transfers, across regions over the period from 1961 to 2018. Over the period from 2009 to 2018, the authors find that Ontario and Alberta were the largest net contributors. For Ontario, the federal government's personal income tax system accounted for the largest contribution to per capita fiscal balances; the second largest contribution in per capita contribution came from the Equalization and Fiscal Stabilization Programs.

There is no obvious economic rationale for adjusting federal transfers to provinces to undo the interpersonal redistribution caused by federal taxes on individuals. Nevertheless, what is a fair level of interregional redistribution within the federation is a legitimate question. Large provincial net contributions with respect to equalization may be of concern if there are design issues that hinder the program's functioning and, at the same time, unnecessarily contribute to large fiscal imbalances related to this program. For example, Ontario received less equalization payments because of the imposition of the fixed growth rule starting in 2009. In recent years, the fixed growth rule has been acting as a floor on total equalization spending, even when provincial fiscal capacities have been converging (and Ontario no longer qualifies). Removal of the fixed growth rule arguably improves the functioning of the Equalization Program and would address some of Ontario's fairness concerns. Other Equalization Program reforms have been proposed. Feehan (2014, 2020) discusses options for the treatment of hydro resources in the Equalization Program, and Gusen (2012) considers the inclusion of expenditure need. Of course, not all reforms that improve the functioning of the Equalization Program would necessarily align with Ontario's interests or lead to a reduction in Ontario's net contribution to the program. But the adoption of the fixed growth rule when Ontario was an equalization recipient and its continued use as a floor after Ontario exited the program has increased Ontario's net contribution to equalization and to the federation in an arbitrary and unfair manner.

The Need for Stable, Long-Term, and Sustainable Federal Support

Ontario budgets, highlighting the need for stable, long-term funding, have often criticized the federal government for frequent discretionary changes to transfers. Of particular concern is the federal government's history of ad hoc cuts to transfer programs when dealing with its own budgetary pressures. The restrictions to CAP grants and health-care transfers between 1980 and 2003, for instance, were frequent, sometimes replaced previously announced changes, and were generally not announced well in advance of taking effect. The cap on CAP was particularly problematic, having been introduced when Ontario was suffering from the 1990 recession. Provinces have the option of adjusting their own taxes and spending decisions in response to changes in transfer payments. However, the less discretionary nature of much of provincial government spending means that ad hoc cuts to transfers can add to provinces' fiscal pressures, at least in the short run.

Compared to the 1980s and 1990s, the past two decades represent a period of relative stability and predictability (and mostly growth) in federal transfers to provinces. Changes in the escalator for social transfers, particularly the CHT, were announced in advance. The Equalization Program has not changed in ten years' time; it might be flawed, but it has been stable. Thus, it is reasonable to argue that the province's concerns about stability and long-term funding have been addressed.

Over the past decade, Ontario has also taken issue with federal support that is "time-limited, declines over time or ends" (Government of Ontario 2012, 214). The province expressed concern over the federal government's failure to renew wait time funding when it expired in 2013–14, despite vigorous calls from the province to do so. In 2013, the federal government eliminated the total transfer payment protection in a year in which only Ontario would have qualified for it. The province also criticized the federal government's decision to raise the per capita thresholds in the DFAA program in 2015 as offloading emergency support and recovery responsibilities onto the provinces.[21] Finally, Ontario budgets regularly call for infrastructure funding to be put on a long-term funding track.

But what about the concern that federal support needs to be long term rather than time-limited? The corollary is that federal transfers should be enduring and immune to change, but this notion is unreasonable and impractical. The purpose of health-care transfers is partially to address vertical fiscal imbalances. These transfers have changed over time in response to various fiscal pressures. Perhaps the changes could have been managed better, but overall health-care funding to provinces has been enduring. Specific purpose, time-limited funding also clearly has a role. Wait times reduction funding was intended to last ten years. Provinces knew this timeline in advance, and a ten-year time frame is perhaps long enough to encourage changes in the health-care system to address the problem. The federal government's COVID-19 supports to provinces are also time-limited; the extraordinary provincial expenditures, needed to tackle pandemic-related issues, are presumably time-limited and so too should be the federal government's special-purposed supports to the provinces.

4. Ontario's Perspective: The COVID-19 Pandemic and Beyond

The budget review suggests that Ontario has some long-standing issues with Canada's fiscal arrangements. Over the past four decades, the province has become increasingly concerned about the adequacy of federal transfers, the unfair treatment of Ontario, and the province's net contribution to the federation, particularly with respect to equalization. Stable, long-term, and sustainable federal support is also an ongoing concern. These persistent concerns have played an important role in shaping the province's current views on fiscal arrangements. The 2019 Ontario budget summarizes Canada's federal transfer system as "broken."

The pandemic has added new pressures to an already stressed system of fiscal arrangements. Now is the time for provinces and the federal government to engage in a productive discussion on how to tackle their dual problems of changing fiscal fortunes and fiscal arrangements reform. Fiscal adjustments at all levels will eventually be necessary. Changes to federal transfers are likely, and intergovernmental tensions will intensify, as is often the case in times of fiscal stress.

Ontario's experience with fiscal arrangements over the past forty years provides some valuable insights. In the past, the federal government targeted transfers to provinces as part of an overall effort to tackle its deficit and debt. This approach added to provincial governments' revenue instability and increased provinces' fiscal burdens at a time when they faced considerable fiscal pressure. For these reasons, the upward spikes in cash transfers to provinces and federal net debt in 2020–1 seen in Figure 20.1 are worrisome, particularly from an Ontario perspective. The federal government's past approach to tackling its deficit and debt problems should be avoided if possible moving forward. The federal government should also avoid unfairly targeting certain provinces, as it has done in the past.

The budget analysis shows that practical considerations to transfer design, such as affordability, predictability, and sustainability, matter. Where possible, these considerations should be explicitly addressed in any discussions of possible reforms. For instance, transfer systems can be redesigned, if desired, using fiscal capacity as a metric for limiting transfers under certain conditions (such as when an affordability indicator is triggered). Changes should be announced well in advance and phased in. The transparency of such an approach is fair to all provinces, including Ontario, especially when compared to ex post, arbitrary changes.

Intergovernmental tensions will likely intensify on both vertical and horizontal dimensions. On the vertical dimension, the federal government's pandemic fiscal supports to provinces were time-limited deals. Provinces can be expected to exert pressure on the federal government to extend or make permanent some variants of these transfers or to request that some of this funding be rolled into existing supports. However, there is no evidence to support making permanent some or all of the $24 billion in federal COVID-19 supports to provinces.

Finally, where the pandemic experience has revealed chronic weaknesses in current fiscal arrangements, reforms should be considered. For instance, the pandemic has highlighted the importance of a federal government role in helping to address public health and related spillovers and as provider of regional insurance and national equity, particularly in times of crisis. The COVID-19 crisis has also made it clear that unconditional health-care funding in no way guarantees minimum standards in, for example, long-term care or pandemic preparedness and that the consideration of need in health-care funding and/or equalization merits attention. These lessons should help inform discussions of fiscal arrangements reform moving forward.

Appendix

Table 20.A1. Changes to Federal Transfers: Health, Post-Secondary Education, and Welfare, 1980 to Present

Year	Description of Changes
1983	Growth in PSE component of EPF limited – 6 per cent in 1983–4 and 5 per cent in 1984–5.
1986	EPF escalator reduced from GNP to (GNP –2 per cent).
1990	EPF escalator reduced to GNP – 3 per cent announced in 1989 superseded by freeze in per capita entitlements for 1990–1 and 1991–2. Annual growth in CAP payments to non-equalization recipient provinces limited to 5 per cent for 1990–1 and 1991–2.
1991	Freeze in per capita EPF entitlements and cap on CAP to selected provinces extended to 1994–5.
1995	CHST replaces EPF and CAP transfers starting in 1996–7. Total CHST distributed across provinces based on shares of EPF and CAP (in 1995–6 and 1994–5).
1996	CHST entitlements fixed for next two years. For 2000–1 to 2002–3, total CHST growth based on GDP escalator (with a downward adjustment). Provincial allocation formula adjusted to move closer to equal per capita entitlements. $11 billion floor set for total CHST cash.
1998	Increase in CHST cash floor to $12.5 billion, starting in 1997–8.
1999	An additional CHST cash infusion over next five years of $11.5 billion. Cash floor and CHST total entitlement escalator eliminated (as cash amounts set directly). Adjustments to provincial allocation formula to speed up move to equal per capita entitlements.
2000	Additional CHST cash, allocated on an equal per capita basis (twice).
2003	Federal government announces CHT and CST to replace CHST. Total entitlements allocated on an equal per capita basis. Cash amounts set for 2004–5 and 2005–6.
2005	CHT cash to grow at annual rate of 6 per cent starting in 2006–7.
2007	CST cash to grow at an annual rate of 3 per cent starting in 2009–10. Move to equal per capita cash, starting in 2009–10 for CST and 2014–15 for CHT.
2012	Federal government announces CHT escalator will move to a three-year moving average of GDP (with a 3 per cent minimum) in 2017–18.

Source: Various federal budgets; Carter (1994); and Madore (2003).

Table 20.A2. Changes to Federal Transfers: Equalization, 1980 to Present

Year	Description of Changes
1981	Federal government's Bill C-24 imposes a personal income override on equalization, retroactively to cover entitlements from 1977–8 to 1981–2. Any province with above average per capita income not eligible for equalization.
1982	Equalization formula changes to include all revenues but only five provinces (Alberta, NF, NS, NB, PEI excluded); ceiling on rate of growth in aggregate entitlements; floor provision to protect individual provinces against significant year-over-year reductions in entitlements.
2003	2002–3 Equalization Program ceiling eliminated.
2004	Five-province standard abandoned; aggregate entitlements exogenously determined (fixed pool approach); allocation across provinces determined separately based on distribution of past payments. A funding floor equal to $10 billion for 2004–5; guaranteed growth in total entitlements of 3.5 per cent per year from $10.9 billion base in 2005–6 for a ten-year period.
2007	Formula-based approach reintroduced. Ten-province standard, best of 50 per cent or 0 per cent inclusion rate for resource revenues, fiscal capacity cap, three-year weighted moving average, lagged two years to calculate fiscal capacity.
2009	Fixed growth rule – total entitlements to grow in line with three-year moving average of nominal GDP (acts as both a ceiling and a floor). Change to fiscal capacity cap.

Source: Expert Panel on Equalization and Territorial Formula Financing (2006); Tombe (2018); Courchene (1983); Nadeau (2014); and various federal budgets.

Table 20.A3. Changes to Federal Transfers: FSP, DFAA, and Temporary COVID-19 Measures, 1980 to Present

Year	Description of Changes
1987	FSP: A $60 per capita cap on fiscal stabilization payments to qualifying provinces.
1995	FSP: A 5 per cent deductible for non-resource revenues, reinstated after it was eliminated in 1972; 50 per cent deductible for natural resource revenues continues to be in effect (since 1977).
2015	DFAA: Annual inflation indexing of thresholds for federal cost share.
2020	COVID-19: Temporary, time-limited federal transfers to provinces to help address extraordinary expenditures and revenue losses related to the pandemic.
2020	FSP: Indexing of the $60 per capita cap set in 1987; current level $169.82 per capita for 2019–20 and 2020–1. Cap to grow in line with nominal GDP starting in 2021–2.

Source: Author's construction and Tombe (2018).
Note: DFAA = Disaster Financial Assistance Arrangements; FSP = Financial Stabilization Program

NOTES

1 A historical overview of the evolution of fiscal federalism and the role of interregional equity from Confederation to the early 1960s is provided by Mary Janigan in chapter 2 of this volume.
2 See Robin Boadway's chapter 5 in this volume for a detailed discussion of the CHT and options for reform to better address fiscal imbalances across provinces and between federal and provincial governments.
3 Cash transfers do not include fiscal stabilization, DFAA, or infrastructure grants. A consistent series of infrastructure grants to provinces since 1980 has proven elusive. Several studies note a decline in government infrastructure investment as a percentage of GDP after 1960 and the subsequent resurgence starting in the mid-2000s. See Bazel and Mintz (2015); Dahlby and Jackson (2015); Lammam and MacIntyre (2017).
4 Based on data taken from Statistics Canada (2023b) and Hartmann (2017).
5 James Feehan's chapter 8 in this volume provides a more detailed discussion of the implications of uneven and volatile natural resource revenues for fiscal federalism. Economic circumstances in other provinces also play an important role. For example, Quebec's unique role, discussed in Alain Noel's chapter 19 of this volume, stems from its distinct language and culture, size, and lower-than-average fiscal capacity. The influence of the Atlantic provinces stems from their comparatively heavy reliance on federal transfers as a revenue source and, as Saillant notes in chapter 18 of this volume, from the region's aging population.
6 See Carter (1994) for an excellent description of EPF and the changes to it during this period.
7 Several changes were made between 1957 and 1974. In 1967, a ten-province standard was adopted, and 100 per cent of all revenues were equalized. In the 1970s, in an attempt to deal with growing equalization payments stemming from resource revenues, the inclusion rate for these revenues was reduced.
8 See Courchene (1983) for a discussion of the 1982 Equalization Program.
9 See the Department of Finance Canada (2004). At this time, Ontario's fiscal capacity, according to the budget, accounted for 50 per cent of the standard fiscal capacity under the five-province standard.
10 See the federal government's Fall Economic Statement 2020, released 30 November 2020, https://www.budget.canada.ca/fes-eea/2020/report-rapport/FES-EEA-eng.pdf.
11 Federal support for childcare for returning workers included $2 million in base funding for each jurisdiction with the remaining support allocated on an equal per capita basis. Maximum funding allocations for municipalities were equal per capita and 50 per cent cost-shared with provinces and territories.
12 Dahlby and Jackson (2015) provide an analysis of federal infrastructure funding since 2002.
13 Political considerations also play a role but are not the focus of this chapter.

14 See chapter 18 by Richard Saillant in this volume.
15 See *Ontario Budget 1981*, available online at http://www.archives.gov.on.ca/en
    /historical_documents_project/77-81/ONTARIO_1981_BUDGET.pdf.
16 There was also a ceiling (and a floor) on the growth in equalization payments
    from 1982 to 2002. According to Carter (1994), the ceiling was binding in 1988–9,
    1989–90, 1990–1, and 1993–4. The floor protection was graduated, based on the
    degree to which a recipient province's fiscal capacity was below the standard.
17 Since the fixed growth rule can also serve as a floor, Ontario received a payment in
    2018–19 when it would not have otherwise qualified (see Tombe 2018).
18 Note that Ontario did not, however, oppose the imposition of the ceiling on equalization payments when it was introduced in 1982, at a time when it was not going
    to qualify for payments under the reformed program.
19 Alberta's take on equalization and the province's net contribution to the federation
    is discussed by Ken Boessenkool in chapter 21 of this volume.
20 The federation could move to a net equalization scheme where above-average fiscal
    capacity provinces make transfers directly to below-average fiscal capacity provinces. This change would at least remove the financing of equalization from the set
    of federal government activities paid for by federal taxes, but most commentators
    think this idea is a non-starter.
21 The DFAA had received no attention in Ontario budgets up to this point. The
    province, however, was likely sensitive to changes in the program following the
    large scale and very costly winter ice storm it suffered in 2013. The federal government's $98 million DFAA payment to the province related to this event was not
    finalized until 2018.

REFERENCES

Bazel, Philip, and Jack M. Mintz. 2015. "Optimal Public Infrastructure: Some Guideposts to Ensure We Don't Overspend." *SPP Research Papers* 8, no. 37. School of Public Policy, University of Calgary. https://doi.org/10.11575/sppp.v8i0.42546.

Bergeron, Étienne, Sarah MacPhee, Carleigh Busby, Caroline Nicol, Tim Scholz, and Diarra Sourang. 2020. *Fiscal Sustainability Report 2020: Update*. Ottawa: Office of the Parliamentary Budget Officer. https://www.pbo-dpb.ca/en/publications/RP-2021-033-S--fiscal-sustainability-report-2020-update--rapport-viabilite-financiere-2020-mise-jour.

Boadway, Robin, and Harry Kitchen. 2018. "A Fiscal Federalism Framework for Financing Infrastructure." In *Canadian Federalism and Infrastructure*, edited by John R. Allan, David L.A. Gordon, Kyle Hanniman, Andre Juneau, and Robert A. Young, 75–114. Montreal and Kingston: McGill-Queen's University Press.

Busby, Carleigh, and Robert Behrend. 2020. *Federal Support through Major Transfers to Provincial and Territorial Governments*. Ottawa: Office of the Parliamentary Budget Officer. https://www.pbo-dpb.ca/en/publications/RP

-2021-020-S--federal-support-through-major-transfers-to-provincial-territorial-governments--soutien-federal-principaux-transferts-aux-gouvernements-provinciaux-territoriaux.

Carter, George E. 1994. "Federal Restraints on the Growth of Transfer Payments to the Provinces since 1986–87: An Assessment." *Canadian Tax Journal* 42, no. 6: 1504–32. https://www.ctf.ca/ctfweb/EN/Publications/CTJ_Contents/1994ctj6.aspx.

Courchene, Thomas J. 1983. "Canada's New Equalization Program: Description and Evaluation." *Canadian Public Policy* 9, no. 4: 458–75. https://doi.org/10.2307/3551131.

– 1994. "Canada's Social Policy Deficit: Implications for Fiscal Federalism." In *The Future of Fiscal Federalism*, edited by Keith G. Banting, Douglas M. Brown, and Thomas J. Courchene, 83–122. Montreal and Kingston: McGill-Queen's University Press.

– 2010. "Intergovernmental Transfers and Canadian Values: Retrospect and Prospect." *Policy Options* 31, no. 5 (May): 32–40. Montreal: Institute for Research on Public Policy. https://policyoptions.irpp.org/magazines/the-fault-lines-of-federalism/intergovernmental-transfers-and-canadian-values-retrospect-and-prospect/.

Dahlby, Bev. 2005. *Dealing with the Fiscal Imbalances: Vertical, Horizontal and Structural*. Toronto: CD Howe Institute. https://www.cdhowe.org/sites/default/files/attachments/research_papers/mixed//workingpaper_3.pdf.

Dahlby, Bev, and Emily Jackson. 2015. *Striking the Right Balance: Federal Infrastructure Transfer Programs, 2002–2015*. SPP Research Papers 8, no. 36. School of Public Policy, University of Calgary. https://doi.org/10.11575/sppp.v8i0.42547.

Department of Finance Canada. n.d. "Historical Transfer Tables: 1980 to Present." Ottawa: Department of Finance Canada. https://open.canada.ca/data/en/dataset/4eee1558-45b7-4484-9336-e692897d393f.

– 2004. *The Budget Plan 2004*. Ottawa: Department of Finance Canada. https://www.budget.canada.ca/pdfarch/budget04/pdf/bp2004e.pdf.

Eisen, Ben, Charles Lammam, and Feixue Ren. 2016. "Are the Provinces Really Shortchanged by Federal Transfers?" Fraser Institute, 12 January 2016. https://www.fraserinstitute.org/studies/are-the-provinces-really-shortchanged-by-federal-transfers.

Expert Panel on Equalization and Territorial Formula Financing. 2006. *Achieving a National Purpose: Putting Equalization Back on Track*. Ottawa: Expert Panel on Equalization and Territorial Formula Financing.

Feehan, James. 2014. *Canada's Equalization Formula: Peering Inside the Black Box … and Beyond*. SPP Research Papers 7, no. 24. School of Public Policy, University of Calgary. https://www.policyschool.ca/wp-content/uploads/2016/03/feehan-equalization.pdf.

– 2020. "Canada's Equalization Program: Political Debates and Opportunities for Reform." *IRPP Insight* 30. Montreal: Institute for Research on Public Policy. https://doi.org/10.26070/zp9t-zt92.

Finance of the Nation. n.d. "Finances of the Nation Data Sets." https://financesofthenation.ca/data/.

Government of Alberta. n.d. "Historical Royalty Revenue." https://open.alberta.ca/opendata/historical-royalty-revenue.

Government of Ontario. 2012. *Ontario Budget 2012: Strong Action for Ontario.* Toronto: Queen's Printer. https://collections.ola.org/mon/26003/316311.pdf.

Gusen, Peter. 2012. *Expenditure Need: Equalization's Other Half.* Mowat Publication No. 46. Toronto: Mowat Centre for Policy Innovation. https://hdl.handle.net/1807/99138.

Hartmann, Erich. 2017. *Ontario, Oil & Unreliable Data: The Complex Problems Confronting Equalization and Simple Solutions to Address Them.* Mowat Publication No. 149. Toronto: Mowat Centre for Policy Innovation. https://hdl.handle.net/1807/99367.

Infrastructure Canada. 2018. *Investing in Canada: Canada's Long-Term Infrastructure Plan.* Ottawa: Infrastructure Canada. https://www.infrastructure.gc.ca/plan/icp-publication-pic-eng.html#C.

Lammam, Charles, and Hugh MacIntyre. 2017. *Myths of Infrastructure Spending in Canada.* Vancouver, BC: Fraser Institute. https://www.fraserinstitute.org/sites/default/files/myths-of-infrastructure-spending-in-canada.pdf.

Madore, Odette. 2003. *The Canada Health and Social Transfer: Operation and Possible Repercussions on the Health Care Sector.* Ottawa: Library of Parliament. https://publications.gc.ca/collections/Collection-R/LoPBdP/CIR-e/952-e.pdf.

Mansell, Robert, Mukesh Khanal, and Trevor Tombe. 2020. *The Regional Distribution of Federal Fiscal Balance: Who Pays, Who Gets and Why It Matters.* SPP Research Paper 13, no. 14. School of Public Policy, University of Calgary. https://doi.org/10.11575/sppp.v13i0.69872.

Nadeau, Jean-François. 2014. *2014–15 Federal Transfers to Provinces and Territories.* Ottawa: Office of the Parliamentary Budget Officer. https://publications.gc.ca/collections/collection_2014/dpb-pbo/YN5-66-2014-eng.pdf.

RBC (Royal Bank of Canada). n.d. "Provincial Outlook and Fiscal Analysis." Accessed April 2021. http://www.rbc.com/economics/economic-reports/canadian-fiscal-reports.html.

Shaw, Trevor. 2018. *Federal Financial Support to the Provinces and Territories: A Long-Term Scenario Analysis.* Ottawa: Office of the Parliamentary Budget Officer. https://www.pbo-dpb.ca/en/publications/RP-1718-367--federal-financial-support-to-provinces-and--le-soutien-financier-du-gouvernement-federal.

Statistics Canada. 2023a. "Table 36-10-0103-01 Gross Domestic Product, Income-Based, Quarterly (x 1,000,000)." https://doi.org/10.25318/3610010301-eng.

– 2023b. Table 36-10-0450-01 Revenue, Expenditure and Budgetary Balance – General Governments, Provincial and Territorial Economic Accounts (x 1,000,000)." https://doi.org/10.25318/3610045001-eng.

Tombe, Trevor. 2018. "'Final and Unalterable' – But Up for Negotiation: Federal-Provincial Transfers in Canada." *Canadian Tax Journal* 66, no. 4: 871–917. https://www.ctf.ca/ctfweb/EN/Publications/CTJ_Contents/2018CTJ4.aspx.

21 Canadian Fiscal Federalism and Alberta's Latest Attempt to Get a Fair(er) Deal

KEN BOESSENKOOL

Introduction

Attempts by Alberta to get a fairer fiscal, economic, and constitutional deal within Canada are as old as the sentiment that Alberta was hard done by in Confederation – that is, perpetual and eternal (Janigan 2012; see also Janigan's chapter 2 in this volume).

There are numerous reasons for this outcome, and they are deeply rooted in the regional nature of Canadian politics and in several real and imagined slights many Albertans feel as part of a smaller, richer province in a large federation. Some of these slights are real – historically, more money has left the province of Alberta for the rest of the country than has come back – but even this fact has an explanation: a large part of those net transfers out of Alberta is simply because the province is richer than the rest of the country.

Alberta is undoubtedly in a stronger place today than it has been in the past. To go right to the beginning, a national railway ensured that the province's wheat could get to market. In more recent times, the 1982 patriation of the Constitution confirmed that provinces – at the insistence of Alberta and other resource-rich provinces – have ownership and control over natural resources. And the government of Stephen Harper made federal cash transfers for health and other social programs equal per capita, eliminating a "super equalization" component for poorer provinces.

Alberta's real and imagined beefs with the rest of the country also have political and partisan roots. The beefs are political in that Alberta politicians (like those anywhere else) always find it easier to blame someone else for their woes rather than take responsibility themselves (on blame avoidance, see Weaver 1986) – and the federal government is a useful target of angst. Here is where partisanship fits in. Alberta has for decades voted solidly Conservative at the federal level. The federal government has been typically Liberal. Albertans, as a result, quite often do not see themselves reflected in the federal government, which makes a "them" versus "us" narrative a bit more natural.

Then there are a myriad of cultural and symbolic elements. The leaf on our national flag is from a tree that is not native to Alberta. The maverick and/or rural and/or outdoor culture of Alberta (waning as these traits are) sets up a ready conflict with "Laurentian elites" from the Montreal-Toronto-Ottawa triangle, who seem to control our most important institutions. The "big shift" has not yet happened (Bricker and Ibbitson 2013).

And there are real slights. Aggressive pursuit of emissions reductions to meet the challenge of climate change clashes with Alberta's resource intensity and wealth. Alberta does send billions more to the rest of the country than it gets back. Quebec, both for electoral and national unity reasons, seems to get what it wants (including the lion's share of those dollars leaving Alberta) much more quickly than Alberta does. Ottawa seems all too eager to take over policy levers, or refuse to hand over policy levers, for things Albertans just want to do themselves.

Alberta has never really had a separatist movement making any real electoral threat – unlike Quebec. But its sense of alienation from the rest of the country is real (Gibbins and Berdhal 2003).

In his premiership, Jason Kenney put forward a series of proposals in the latest attempt to get a "fair deal" for Alberta within Canada. The remainder of this chapter will lay out the roots of these proposals and then evaluate their contents grouped under "destructive" and "constructive" for Alberta and its place in Canada.

The chapter will proceed by first detailing the backdrop into which these proposals fall. It will lay out the mood of the province at the time and then reach back to the origin of some of Kenney's key proposals – namely the 2001 Alberta Agenda (more commonly known as the Firewall Letter) from a group of Alberta conservatives (the author included) to then premier Ralph Klein. The chapter will then turn to an analysis of key individual items within Kenney's "fair deal" package according to whether they are destructive or constructive in relation to the avowed goal of strengthening Canada's place in Confederation.[1]

The Backdrop

The Viewpoint Alberta survey captures Alberta's alienation well (Béland et al. 2020). In short, Alberta is angry. According to that survey, conducted immediately following the 2019 federal election, just over half of those surveyed about which emotion captured their attitude about Alberta's position in Canada replied "angry." In addition, the survey showed that

- 76 per cent of Albertans felt their province received less than its fair share of federal programs and transfers;

- 75 per cent felt that Alberta was not treated with the respect it deserved in Canada;
- 70 per cent felt that the federal government treated Alberta worse than other provinces; and
- 29 per cent of Albertans agreed that Alberta should "separate from Canada and form an independent country." (Béland et al. 2020)

Anger always runs the risk of impotency; but frustration and rage are dead ends. Talk of Alberta separation is a manifestation of rage, and while it serves as an articulation of anger, it is not a constructive or useful way to address Alberta's challenges.

In this atmosphere, in mid-2020, Alberta's government-appointed Fair Deal Panel released its report, the key components of which are rooted in a similar set of proposals from the early 2000s (Fair Deal Panel 2020).

Alberta Gets "Tough Love"

In late 1998, global oil prices hit a historic low of $10.82 per barrel. Natural gas hit a low of $1.05. While both commodities slowly recovered over the next two years, these low prices sent a shockwave of angst through Alberta and formed an important backdrop to the 2000 federal election.

During the 2000 campaign, then prime minister Jean Chrétien made fun of his Alberta-based opponents. "I like to do politics with people from the East," Chrétien said. By contrast, his Albertan opponents were "a different type." After claiming he was joking, Chrétien delivered a second punchline saying, "I'm serious" (quoted in Boessenkool 2019).

Rather than find it funny, Albertans found it familiar – the bad joke echoed in TV ads that Liberals were running against Alberta's health-care system, as well as Chrétien's later comment that what the West needed was some "tough love."

In the 2000 election, Albertans expressed themselves by giving all but two seats to conservative parties (Canadian Alliance and Progressive Conservative). Mere months later, separatist sentiment was on the rise, and an enterprising Alberta separatist party known as the Alberta First Party nominated sixteen candidates for the following March 2001 provincial election. Then, as now, an apparent contempt for Alberta's concerns sparked demands for political change.

The Firewall Letter

In January 2001, six politicians, political scientists, and others of like mind (including the author of this chapter) penned a letter to Alberta premier Ralph

Klein, setting out an "Alberta Agenda." It would broadly become known as the Firewall Letter, as it called for Alberta to erect a "firewall" against unwelcome intrusions from Ottawa (Boessenkool et al. 2001).

The firewall was an Alberta project whose authors believed would tap into, as well as diffuse, the angst felt in Alberta towards the rest of the country. The intention was to turn a negative into a positive and ultimately avoid the crazy cul-de-sac of separatism.

One of the most important insights behind the Firewall Letter is that its proposals had to be doable unilaterally – they contained primarily policies or approaches that Alberta could adopt without the consent, approval, or actions of another government. The policies had to be serious ideas that could be realized reasonably quickly at a reasonable (ideally lower!) cost and with a reasonable chance of success.

The Alberta Agenda proposed that the province should withdraw from the Canada Pension Plan and create its own Alberta Pension Plan; consider setting up its own tax collection agency; withdraw from the national Royal Canadian Mounted Police (RCMP) and set up a provincial police force; instigate legal challenges to insure it retained control over health-care policy; and do more to push Senate reform onto the national agenda.

The Firewall Letter ultimately got overtaken by events. Within a year or two, energy prices soared to breathless heights, and Alberta was booming as never before – awash in government revenues and prosperity. A couple of years after that, Canada installed an Alberta firewall in 24 Sussex Drive. In short, Stephen Harper was prime minister, Alberta was booming, and the demands for structural changes diminished.

For the next fifteen years, the Alberta political consensus increasingly broke down. Progressive Conservatives who had ruled the province since the halcyon days of Peter Lougheed in the early 1970s began to splinter and bicker internally. Following Ralph Klein, they continued to win elections but cycled through new leaders in each election. A new party on the populist right – the Wildrose Party – presented a real threat, though not without its own leadership challenges. The firewall ideas played a minor role in these machinations, largely finding a home within the new Wildrose Party.

Leading up to the election of 2015, these events culminated in a series of botched attempts to bring the two parties of the right together under yet another new leader – this time from the federal Conservative bullpen. Those botched attempts plus a very poorly received budget and an unnecessary election call brought a shock to the Alberta body politic; the first non-conservative government was elected in over forty years in the form of the left-leaning New Democrats and its impressive leader Rachel Notley.

It is an understatement to say that this new left-leaning and largely competent provincial government was a shock to what many considered the conservative consensus in Alberta. And indeed, the government was formed with 41 per cent of the vote, with the Progressive Conservatives capturing 28 per cent and the Wildrose Party 24 per cent. Many more Albertans had voted conservative, but the NDP got a clear majority of fifty-four seats to the Progressive Conservative's nine and the Wildrose's twenty-one.

Following the watershed 2015 election, a federal Conservative stepped forward – Jason Kenney. Probably the most impressive Conservative political organizer in Canada and a prominent cabinet minister in the national Harper government, Kenney ran for the leadership of the Progressive Conservative Party while making it clear that this move was the first step in returning conservatives to power in Alberta. The second step would be a merger with the Wildrose Party, thereby creating a single party on the right to challenge the Notley NDP. The third step was defeating the NDP.

Kenney not only won the leadership of the Progressive Conservatives, but he skilfully engineered a merger into a single new political party – the United Conservative Party – to challenge the Notley NDP. Jason Kenney then obtained a massive electoral mandate for his new party in 2019.

Old Ideas Are New Again

By the time Jason Kenney surprised nobody by ascending to the Alberta premier's chair, the late 1990s seemed to be repeating themselves. For a number of geopolitical, social, and technological reasons, oil prices were not at the same low points globally as in 1998, but the value Alberta received for its oil was heavily discounted, and natural gas prices were near their historic lows.

As well, Alberta's largest customer became its largest competitor, with the United States shifting from a massive global importer to a net global exporter of both commodities. Both Alberta and Canada were slow to respond to this global trend. In particular, replacing American sales with global sales required something that seemed frustratingly out of reach – a pipeline to tidewater.

Hard times returned, anger was rising, and the sentiment grew that Ottawa was to blame. Pipeline projects seemed impossible to move forward. The hostility to pipelines seemed to extend to the industry itself. New regulatory requirements, bans on coastal tankers, and an aggressive climate agenda all felt like proof points for the prime minister's past musings about "phasing out" the oil sands.

Kenney's response to all this was setting up the Fair Deal Panel, whose report largely supported a basket of proposals that Kenney asked it to evaluate – from referendums on equalization to retreading several firewall proposals like an Alberta Pension Plan and an Alberta Police Force.

Alberta's fair deal proposals contained both destructive and constructive ideas to reform the federation and assert Alberta's long-standing desire for more autonomy within a united country.

On the destructive side were a series of referendums – a strange signal of timidity from a government with a stronger mandate than Ralph Klein had in all but one of his elections – that did little other than sow division and distrust within Alberta. Most blatantly silly was the referendum on the Equalization Program. It sought to exploit a broad misunderstanding between Alberta's net contribution to Canada (what I call "small-e equalization") and the Equalization Program itself ("big-E Equalization"). Worse, although the referendum yielded a majority in favour of eliminating Equalization from Canada's Constitution, it has produced no change in either equalization or Equalization.

On the constructive side were a series of policies designed to take advantage of Alberta's long-standing demographic and economic advantages by doing what is extremely normal in Canada's two largest provinces: for example creating an Alberta Pension Plan and an Alberta Police Force, gaining more control over immigration, and perhaps even collecting the province's own income tax. These are things that either should be done on their own merits or because a more autonomous Alberta is the best way to squelch a budding separatist movement.

Destructive Proposals

At the core of the destructive portions of the fair deal proposals was Kenney ignoring the central insights behind the Firewall Letter – namely that policies should be things that Alberta can do on its own and do reasonably quickly to make Albertans better off.

Referendums

Jason Kenney won a raw majority – 54 per cent – of votes in the 2019 election. He got more votes than Ralph Klein got in all but one of his elections (62 per cent in 2001). Kenney did not quite reach a Peter Lougheed–style victory (who twice got just shy of two-thirds of the popular vote), but it was right in line with Ernest Manning's seven victories at just over 50 per cent. There is a word for electoral victories that conclusive – a mandate, a strong mandate even.

Leaders with strong electoral mandates should not need to seek an additional mandate via a referendum. Leaders with strong electoral mandates do the things they ran on. And on the big things they ran on, it can safely be assumed that they have a broad base of support.

To put it another way, does anyone really doubt that Jason Kenney had a broad base of support to talk to Ottawa about the fairness of federal transfers? He had Ernest Manning and Ralph Klein type of broad-based support. He was not too far shy of Peter Lougheed's broad-based support. Proposing a referendum on an issue on which you have a clear mandate demonstrated a lack of confidence. To put it harshly, it made Kenney look like the democratic reform loser he is not. It did not add to his mandate to deal with Ottawa; in fact, it subtracted from it. The first referendum Kenney proposed was on removing the principle of equalization from the Constitution. Of all the federal programs in Alberta, Equalization is probably the most misunderstood. One of the key reasons for this problem is that Alberta politicians have conflated the actual Equalization Program with the broader structure of fiscal federalism in Canada.

As noted, the broader structure of fiscal federalism in Canada sees many more billions of dollars leave Alberta than ever come back – what might be called "small-e equalization." This is both structural and intentional. Then, there is the "Big-E Equalization," which is the Equalization Program itself. This program is paid out of federal revenues collected from all Canadians and distributed to provinces with relatively less capacity to raise revenues than other provinces. The principle behind Big-E Equalization is well summarized in section 36(2) of the Canadian Constitution: "Parliament and the government of Canada are committed to the principle of making equalization payments to ensure that provincial governments have sufficient revenues to provide reasonably comparable levels of public services at reasonably comparable levels of taxation."

The confusion between Big-E and small-e equalization is widespread and well-sown in Alberta. As a result of this confusion, it is perhaps not surprising that Big-E Equalization is not the problem most Albertans think it is. University of Calgary economist Trevor Tombe has done an enormous service by calculating the sources of redistribution in and out of various provinces.[2] Between 2007 and 2016, Alberta sent $2,168 per person more personal income tax revenue to Ottawa than the average province, $1,148 more corporate income tax, and $405 more consumption or product taxes. It happened for an obvious reason – Alberta is richer than other provinces. And it still is, despite the energy shock recently experienced. Alberta also received $45 less per person for Employment Insurance and $328 less per person in Old Age Benefits. Why? Alberta's younger population is better off, as is its older population. Ottawa also spends $90 less per person on defence in Alberta than on average elsewhere.

To eliminate all this net redistribution from Alberta would involve either making Alberta comparatively poorer or other provinces comparatively richer. Making Alberta older and making employment insurance and defence procurement fairer would help, but only at the margins. Or maybe Alberta should just be thankful that it is so much better off. Maybe Alberta should face the fact it would be better off to run more of its own programs, like an Alberta Pension Plan and an Alberta Police Force.

But Equalization? Over that period, Alberta received $450 less per person than the average in Canada (the same as British Columbia, incidentally). That is 10 per cent of the net outflow of dollars out of Alberta. It is not nothing. But

I would argue that proponents of dismantling Equalization (the ones that do it honestly, that is) are missing something very important.

Some have argued that Equalization is the glue that holds Canada together. My perspective is that Equalization is the bribe that prevents Canada from breaking up. Without Equalization, several of our provinces could not provide basic health or education services to their populations. Manitoba and the Atlantic provinces' residents received between $1,000 and $2,000 more in equalization transfers relative to the average from 2007–16. And Quebec received $600 more than the average. Without these cash infusions, these provinces would be clamouring for Ottawa to take over their health and education systems, which would produce pressure for the federal government, not the provinces, to manage more programs. This outcome would be bad, and not just for Alberta. Ten per cent of Alberta's net advantage over the rest of the country is a small bribe to make sure that Alberta gets to manage its own health and education systems without half of Canada's provinces wanting to transfer that responsibility to the federal government.

An equalization referendum is wrong analytically because it cannot address the net transfer to the rest of the country from Alberta that its proponents (Morton 2021) are calling on it to solve – eliminating the Equalization Program would only reduce Alberta's net contribution by about 10 per cent. And, of course, the proponents of the referendum formally wanted to eliminate a reference to equalization in the Constitution, for all that would do. Any non-constitutional changes would require federal consent. This proposal is the very opposite of something Alberta can accomplish on its own.

An equalization referendum was wrong tactically because Jason Kenney had all the authority he needed to implement his fair deal ideas for Alberta. Ralph Klein did not hold a referendum to cut spending to eliminate the deficit or to introduce a single rate tax. Peter Lougheed did not hold a referendum to get Ottawa to solidify provincial control over natural resources. They campaigned on these issues and then they addressed them.

For these reasons, the equalization referendum likely weakened Alberta. Among other things, the impossibility of converting strong support in the referendum into policy success for Albertans may just strengthen the hand of separatists.

Opting Out of Cost-Share Programs and Seeking Tax Points

Let us lump two fair deal ideas together and talk about health care. Health care and pharmacare is where the rubber threatened to hit the road.

Kenney proposed that Alberta opt out of shared-cost programs (programs funded by both the federal and provincial governments) with full compensation for Alberta to run its own programs. He also proposed that, instead of

Ottawa collecting taxes and then sending cheques to the provinces, the federal government should let provinces collect this revenue themselves (that is, transferring tax points to the provinces) for programs they run. And having Alberta collect federal income taxes (which Quebec is also demanding and is part of the fair deal package) is a non-starter.

I have for years called on the federal government to eliminate some or all cash transfers to provinces by giving the provinces full access to GST/HST revenues (Boessenkool 2010). Let us do a deeper dive on these ideas by focusing on health care.

Canadian health care is administered by the provinces but partially funded by the federal government. In addition, the federal government holds what some believe is the hammer – withholding cash transfers if provinces do not abide by the principles of the Canada Health Act.

It is a basic principle of accountability that the level of government running a program should be the level of government that funds that program. Canadians are understandably confused about this connection when it comes to health care.

On the one hand, they have a provincial health-care card, but constantly hear their provincial governments complain that Ottawa should pay more for health care. This jurisdictional blame game gives the provinces an out when it comes to improving health care.

On the other hand, Canadians are used to high-minded soliloquies from Ottawa about how amazing our health-care system is. They hear prime ministers wax eloquently about the "biggest investment in health care in history," but they see no connection between paying taxes to Ottawa and the stitches their kids just got at the doctor's office.

Opting out and transferring tax points were two items in Kenney's fair deal package that represented ways to solve this problem – to get the federal government out of the health-care game and make provinces more responsible for funding the programs they deliver. And the pharmacare would be a great opportunity to press this cause.

But there is a catch: Alberta cannot do either of these things on its own – only Ottawa can – so even though these are great ideas, they will not happen so long as Liberals are in control in Ottawa. In fact, they may not even happen if there was a Conservative government in Ottawa that included Jason Kenney.

Constructive Proposals

Let us now turn to some constructive ideas in the fair deal plans. These ideas mostly had to do with Alberta running programs that are currently administered federally – programs that not only contain provincial opt-out clauses but programs that other provinces – primarily Ontario and Quebec – already administer themselves.

The immediate reaction from most is that there is no way Alberta could deliver programs cheaper or more efficiently than the federal government. They argue that Alberta would lose so-called economies of scale. My perspective is that there are few things Ottawa does that Alberta could not do better. In addition, when it comes to government, bigger is not better. There is also a substantive economic case. Policies delivered by closer or smaller levels of government can be more attentive to the needs of a population than policies delivered by governments that are further away and overweening.

Matters ought to be handled by the smallest, lowest, or more proximate competent authority, since the jurisdiction closest to the people is best able to meet local preferences most efficiently. This is the lens we should use to assess the viability of various aspects of fair deal proposals.

Collecting Its Own Income Tax

For Alberta, collecting its own income taxes is an expensive idea that may make a lot of sense. Establishing a provincial revenue agency can be done unilaterally by pulling out of tax collection agreements. Of course, it will cost about $500 million or more for Alberta to set up its own tax collection agency for personal income taxes.

The question is whether the additional flexibility would outweigh these costs. Current tax collection agreements allow Alberta to set its own rates and tinker with some tax credits, but not define taxable income. Things like income splitting or making the family the basis of taxation are things Alberta could do with its own tax system that it cannot do today.

It is an expensive idea for the Alberta government, but it could create opportunities to improve economic and social benefits that are simply not available today. Alberta collects its own corporate income tax for similar reasons – it allows Alberta to tailor its corporate tax regime to the very different industrial structure of the province.

Creating an Alberta Pension Plan

When the Canada Pension Plan (CPP) was established, the province of Quebec opted out and created its own provincial pension plan. At the time, its demographics – younger than the national average – meant that Quebec could deliver pension benefits with lower premiums than the rest of the country. It also gave it the flexibility to tailor the program to its own priorities. To give other provinces the same opportunity down the road, the CPP legislation contains a three-year withdrawal provision allowing any other province to do likewise.

Today, all the arguments that held initially in Quebec hold in Alberta. Not only would it be a net gain for Alberta, but it is the best tool the Alberta government has to demonstrate the inherent unfairness of many federal policies for Alberta.

Alberta has both a younger and wealthier population than other provinces, and as a result, Albertans subsidize CPP contributors in other provinces (though not in Quebec, of course, as the province operates its own Quebec Pension Plan). An Alberta Pension Plan, according to reporting Alberta Investment Management Corporation (AIMCo) analysis, could deliver the same benefits for a much smaller premium – to be precise, a premium over 25 per cent less (7.21 instead of 9.90 per cent of payroll; Varcoe 2019).

Over a quarter of the premiums collected in Alberta pays for pensions of residents in other provinces. It works out to $2.0 billion (or $450 per Alberta resident per year) in premiums that Albertans are overpaying by not having their own identical pension plan. This is $2 billion Alberta could stop sending annually to the rest of the country – a real "small-e equalization" transfer that is equal to over four years of the average "Big-E Equalization" amount sent to the rest of the country.

CPP legislation allows a province to pull out with three years notice if it sets up a "comprehensive" and "comparable" plan. This is precisely what Alberta should do, at least in the short to medium term. But what about people who move in and out of Alberta? Would they lose their benefits? Not at all. People move between Quebec and Canada all the time without issues, and people move between private pension plans easily too.

But what about administering an Alberta Pension Plan? The operating costs of the Canada Pension Plan are 3.5 per cent of premiums raised. Costs would only be higher in Alberta if the economies of scale were lower for running a 4.3 million people pension plan versus a 29.1 million people pension plan. That seems unlikely.

That said, even if it costs Alberta twice as much to run its own Alberta Pension Plan (which is inconceivable), that is only a small fraction of the savings Alberta would see from its younger and wealthier population. Albertans would still be better off by roughly $430 per resident per year – well worth it.

Jason Kenney had said that pulling out of the CPP would also mean that Alberta would get $40 billion in investment funds from the CPP Investment Board (CPPIB) moved to AIMCo. Alberta recently proposed moving the administration of a number of public service pension plan funds into AIMCo. This massive increase in the size of AIMCo would create a financial services powerhouse in its own right – a decent diversification strategy. Having said that, removing CPP assets is not contemplated in the CPP legislation, and it will likely take some creativity and perhaps some time, even if there are private sector examples to go by.

In light of this, one option to explore could be to contract out the investment management portion of the Alberta Pension Plan to the CPPIB. In other words, one option is to just leave the money where it is and pay Alberta's share of the costs based on historic contribution shares. Contracting to CPPIB would reduce one other risk – namely that some future government would be tempted to dip into the fund for political purposes.

If Alberta pulls out of the CPP, Canadians outside Quebec and Alberta would have to raise premiums to maintain current CPP benefits – up to 10.6 per cent from 9.9 according to AIMCO. This increase would be a helpful and concrete demonstration of the size of the subsidy Alberta has been paying to the rest of the country under the existing Canada Pension Plan – a $2 billion dollar annual subsidy from CPP alone. Creating an Alberta Pension Plan is probably the single best thing Alberta could do to make itself more autonomous, while also demonstrating – and reducing – the net transfers of cash from Alberta to the rest of the country.

A Provincial Police Force

Since Ontario and Quebec already have their own police forces, the RCMP only delivers provincial and municipal policing outside the two largest provinces. This means Alberta covers 30 per cent of the RCMP contract.

The RCMP does some municipal policing, some provincial policing, and some national policing. Alberta would take over the two former functions, allowing the RCMP in Alberta to just do national policing.

Letting the RCMP contract expire and creating its own provincial force would allow Alberta-wide policing to be better integrated with, for example, municipal police forces in Calgary and Edmonton, and that function would be more efficiently done from within Alberta than from Ottawa.

There would be some initial costs to make the switch and perhaps some ongoing administrative costs – though Alberta is the second-largest jurisdiction in the current contract, so it is hard to imagine why costs would be higher.

Conclusion

Jason Kenney's fair deal proposals were partially rooted in the past and partly new. Some of those proposals only served to weaken Alberta and strengthen the hands of the separatists – in particular the referendum on equalization. Other proposals – most notably pulling out of the Canada Pension Plan and creating a provincial version – would strengthen Alberta's hand and reduce net transfers out of Alberta.

NOTES

1 This analysis is heavily influenced by my own experiences and history. For full disclosure, I worked for Preston Manning in the early 1990s and for Ralph Klein in the late 1990s. I was a co-author of the original Firewall Letter. And I was deeply involved in the creation of the federal Conservative Party of Canada in 2003 and the election of its first leader – Stephen Harper – as Canada's prime minister.
2 See Tombe (2018), Table 5 in particular.

REFERENCES

Béland, Daniel, Loleen Berdahl, Jared Wesley, and Amy Vachon-Chabot. 2020. "Alberta and the Rest of Canada." *Viewpoint Alberta*, 15 June 2020. https://www.commongroundpolitics.ca/alberta-can.

Boessenkool, Ken. 2010. "Fixing the Fiscal Imbalance: Turning GST Revenues over to the Provinces in Exchange for Lower Transfers." *SPP Research Papers* 3, no. 10. School of Public Policy, University of Calgary. https://doi.org/10.2139/ssrn.1923347.

– 2019. "How Alberta's Proposed 'Fair Deal' Could Cut Separatism Off at the Knees." *CBC News*, 11 December 2019. https://www.cbc.ca/news/canada/calgary/fair-deal-panel-firewall-letter-ken-boessenkool-1.5363753.

Boessenkool, Ken, Andrew Crooks, Stephen Harper, Rainer Knopff, and Ted Morton. 2001. "An Open Letter to Ralph Klein." *The National Post*, 24 January 2001. https://albertapolitics.ca/wp-content/uploads/firewall.pdf.

Bricker, Darrell J., and John Ibbitson. 2013. *The Big Shift: The Seismic Shift in Canadian Politics, Business, and Culture and What It Means for Our Future*. Toronto: HarperCollins.

Fair Deal Panel. 2020. *Report to Government*. Edmonton: Fair Deal Panel. https://www.alberta.ca/fair-deal-panel.aspx.

Gibbins, Roger, and Loleen Berdhal. 2003. *Western Visions, Western Futures: Perspectives on the West in Canada*. Toronto: Toronto University Press.

Janigan, Mary. 2012. *Let the Eastern Bastards Freeze in the Dark: The West versus the Rest since Confederation*. Toronto: Knopf Canada.

Morton, Ted. 2021. "Alberta's Equalization Referendum Will Start Dialogue on Canada's Future." *Calgary Herald*, 27 February 2021. https://calgaryherald.com/opinion/columnists/morton-albertas-equalization-referendum-will-start-dialogue-on-canadas-future.

Tombe, Trevor. 2018. "Final and Unalterable – But Up for Negotiation: Federal-Provincial Transfers in Canada." *Canadian Tax Journal* 66, no. 4: 871–917. https://financesofthenation.ca/wp-content/uploads/2020/06/871_18CTJ4_FON.pdf.

Varcoe, Chris. 2019. "Provincial Pension Plan Holds 'Substantial Benefit' for Albertans, Internal AIMCo Report Shows." *Calgary Herald*, 15 November 2019. https://calgaryherald.com/opinion/columnists/varcoe-provincial-pension-plan-could-offer-substantial-benefit-for-albertans-report-shows.

Weaver, R. Kent. 1986. "The Politics of Blame Avoidance." *Journal of Public Policy* 6, no. 4: 371–98. https://doi.org/10.1017/S0143814X00004219.

22 Canadian Fiscal Federalism in Comparative Perspective

ALAN FENNA

Introduction

Fiscal relations are as integral to the operation of a federal system as the division of powers – and fundamental to the way that division works in practice. How are the respective governments resourced, and how does that affect their policy capacity and autonomy as well as the overall functioning of the system? This broad question has both vertical and horizontal dimensions: between the two orders of government and among the constituent units. The issue in respect to the first dimension is vertical fiscal imbalance (VFI) and the potential for central governments to encroach upon constituent unit jurisdiction using the "spending power." The issue in respect to the second dimension is the extent, mode, and contentiousness of horizontal fiscal equalization (HFE), whereby revenue is redistributed from jurisdictions with higher fiscal capacity to those with lower. Considerable variance exists across federations in both these regards.

Just as no federal system is without its flaws and points of chronic contention, so no set of fiscal arrangements is without its issues. That said, Robin Boadway (2007, 99) has described Canada as having "the textbook best-practice system of fiscal federalism" – a bold claim indeed. This chapter takes that proposition as its point of departure and asks three questions: Is that so? If so, what explains it? And again, if so, why is there continuing instability and conflict? Paradoxically, Canada seems to experience a relatively high degree of conflict over its fiscal arrangements, notwithstanding how exemplary they might be. In addressing these questions, this chapter considers the arrangements, practices, and politics of Canadian fiscal federalism by comparison with the main other established federations: Australia, Germany, Switzerland, and the United States.

On Being Best Practice

Boadway's (2007, 99) assertion that Canada's arrangements represent best practice was based on the following propositions:

1 provinces "share with the federal government unrestricted access to all the major tax sources and are responsible for raising a high proportion of their own revenues";
2 "federal transfers are only as intrusive as is necessary to achieve national objectives";
3 there are "enviable forms of income tax and sales tax harmonization";
4 there is "an efficient internal economic union"; and
5 there is "a fair and equitable social union."

Presumably this assertion is not to be read as suggesting that Canada's arrangements are a Panglossian best of all possible worlds but merely that they are about as good as it gets in the real world. The features Boadway highlights reflect some of the main desiderata of fiscal federalism, not all of which are entirely compatible. Three of these features will be explored here: fiscal self-reliance, minimally intrusive transfers, and "a fair and equitable social union." The first two are integral to the "self-rule" aspect of federalism, while the third speaks more to the "shared rule" and shared existence aspect. None, though, is an objective criterion.

Assessing where Canada stands is made difficult by the challenges of comparative federalism, in which the diversity and paucity of even the most similar cases impose a severe limitation (Fenna 2019b). The five federations compared here are the closest to most similar cases; however, the dissimilarities are substantial. In constitutional–institutional terms, Germany is the outlier, given its administrative division of powers and system of integrated federalism (Hueglin and Fenna 2015, 61–3; Fenna 2020; Mueller and Fenna 2022). Switzerland is also distinctive for the pivotal role played by its practice of direct democracy (Linder and Mueller 2021). The United States, meanwhile, is distinct in its presidential separation-of-powers form of government, which has a considerable impact on the way its federal system functions. In societal terms, meanwhile, Canada stands out for its bi-communalism or bi-nationalism – a reality that has underpinned an enduring schism in the way Canadians view federalism (Rocher 2009). Although Switzerland is multilingual, it is not a multination federation and does not exhibit such schismatic qualities (Dardanelli and Mueller 2019). As a consequence of its bi-communal nature, Canada is, in turn, highly distinctive for the degree to which it has resisted the steady centralization experienced by the established federations more generally over the last century or more (Brady 1959; Dardanelli et al. 2019; Lecours 2019).

In political economy terms, Australia is the closest comparator to Canada, and the two countries are regularly compared on that basis (see, for example, Eccleston and Woolley 2015; Gordon 2015; Turgeon and Simeon 2015; Turgeon and Wallner 2013). Like Canada, Australia has a pair of demographically and hence electorally dominant "metropolitan" jurisdictions where manufacturing is centred; some resource-based jurisdictions; and some jurisdictions less happily off in either respect. Onshore natural resources in both countries are constitutionally the property of the constituent unit in which they are located. These are rough similarities, and as we shall see below, there are some political economy differences between the two countries that have a major impact on the politics of fiscal federalism.

Finally, it must be noted that, in addition to the question of whether comparison is really *possible*, there is the question of whether it is really *necessary*. Alain Noël (2014) has eloquently argued that Canadian scholars need not apologize for cultivating their own garden. Here the utility of comparison is seen as being twofold. First, it puts the Canadian case in a broader perspective that helps us see what is distinctive, what the range of possibilities might be, and what benchmarks we might apply (Watts 2000, 372). Second, it potentially provides some explanatory insights via application of the comparative method.

Raising Revenue

It is an axiom of fiscal federalism that "finance should follow function" (Shah 2007a, 9), and there is some empirical evidence that financial self-reliance produces better outcomes (for example, Biela, Hennl, and Kaiser 2012). Making finance follow function is not so easy, though, given the reduced applicability, efficacy, or efficiency of many forms of taxation at the constituent unit level – notably redistributive taxation of mobile sources – together with the overwhelmingly "local" logic of service delivery. The consequence is a reliance on central government transfers. These may well serve important purposes (Olson 1969; Oates 1999; Boadway, chapter 5, this volume), but they also invite opportunistic, coercive, or capricious exercise of the power of the purse.[1]

Of Gaps and Imbalances

Traditionally, this revenue/expenditure misalignment has been known as *vertical fiscal imbalance*, or VFI. However, a number of scholars have argued for a more nuanced approach that distinguishes between two closely related but ostensibly distinct concepts: vertical fiscal *gap* and vertical fiscal *imbalance*. The former is used to describe the simple monetary difference between own-source revenues and the expenditure responsibilities of the respective orders of government, while the latter refers to a gap that has somehow become "problematic" (see, for example, Noël 2005, 129). In some versions of this distinction, an imbalance is said to exist to the extent that the gap is insufficiently bridged (see, for example, Shah 2007b, 17). In others, there is much more to it than that; for a "gap" not to become an "imbalance" three criteria must be met:

> The vertical fiscal gap ... should never be so wide as to make the autonomy of one order of government illusory. When they complement own-source revenues, transfers should also be adequate, and allow governments to cover the expenditures associated with their powers. Finally, transfers should be unconditional, unless there is a valid agreement to that effect between the governments. (Noël 2005, 129)

As defined by Shah (2007b, 17), the distinction seems contrived and lacking any particular utility. Noël's conceptualization is more ambitious but, as a consequence, becomes an exercise in contorted logic. Why and at what point, if a larger gap is generously bridged by transfers and those are entirely unconditional, does that "gap" become an "imbalance"? And what sense is there in referring to the imposition of conditions as constituting "imbalance" rather than an exploitation of the power that an imbalance provides?

It is not evident, then, that the distinction is coherent, necessary, or workable. Proponents acknowledge that it is difficult to "operationalize" (see, for example, Noël 2005, 129), but they are slow to accept the necessary implications of that.[2] For these reasons, the concept of VFI will be used here in its more straightforward sense, meaning simply: the degree to which central governments have own-source revenues in excess of their budgetary needs and, vice versa, for the constituent units to have spending responsibilities in excess of their own-source revenues.[3]

Revenue Modes

As is often noted, the different orders of government can be assigned *different tax bases* to farm; they can *share access* to some of the same tax bases; and/or they can *share the revenue* from a given tax base. In Australia the first applies (although it didn't originally); in Canada and the United States the second applies quite broadly, and in Switzerland somewhat less so; and in Germany the third applies. The first mode requires suitably remunerative tax bases for each order of government. Originally, with the priority being on creating a common market, the dual federations transferred exclusive rights to the then most remunerative tax base – custom duties – to the central government. As a consequence, these federations were born with vertical fiscal imbalance (Hueglin 2020, 129; Saunders 1986). The second mode, shared access to tax bases, is likely to operate invidiously, with one order of government a second-class partner.

The third mode presents one clear solution to the constituent unit tax poverty problem: a system of joint taxation, as is the case in Germany (Spahn 2020). Governments do not have to rely on having the right tax bases, and they don't have to compete in harvesting from any given tax base. However, this mode is more in line with Germany's very different approach to the division of powers – its "administrative federalism" – whereby the *Länder* implement and administer policies made at the national level[4] and its uniquely federal second chamber, the *Bundesrat*, which gives the *Länder* co-determination rights over federal legislation affecting them (Fenna 2020).

Revenue Shares

The claim that Canada enjoys best-practice fiscal federalism is based first on the extent to which the provinces are financially self-sufficient. And, indeed, to an unusually high degree, they are. The *initial* measure of such self-sufficiency is share of total tax revenue raised by constituent units and their local governments. According to figures from the Organisation for Economic Co-operation and Development (OECD 2021, 289–326), Canada tops the charts in this regard at 54 per cent in 2019; Switzerland comes a very close second at 53 per cent; while the United States follows not too far behind at 48 per cent. Coming a distant last, at 19 per cent, is Australia.[5]

Those federations where tax revenue is split reasonably evenly are ones where the constituent units retain access to major revenue streams.[6] Australia is the outlier here, with the states having been excluded from all the major tax bases – personal income tax, corporate income tax, and sales tax – by a combination of Commonwealth unilateralism and judicial interpretation (Fenna 2008, 2017). At the other extreme lies Switzerland, where the cantons play the primary role in personal and corporate income taxation, making it the most fiscally "federal" or non-centralized of all the federations considered here. The Swiss Constitution stipulates the maximum level at which the Confederation may impose a direct tax; it stipulates that "the Confederation, in fixing the taxation rates, shall take account of the burden of direct taxation imposed by the Cantons and communes"; and, finally, it requires that these taxes be "assessed and collected by the Cantons" (article 128). As might be expected, this stipulation does lead to potentially problematic tax competition between the cantons; however, that competition is moderated to some extent by Switzerland's high level of horizontal intergovernmental coordination (Gilardi and Wasserfallen 2016).

Vertical Fiscal Imbalance

Having a good share of revenue is one thing; having a share of revenue commensurate with one's share of responsibilities is another. Despite raising such a healthy share of total tax revenue, the Canadian provinces still rely on transfers for 20 per cent of their expenditure needs (Joanis and Vaillancourt 2020, 115). This percentage is lower, though, than in the United States, where the states rely on transfers for around one-third of their resourcing (Chernick 2020, 100); and it is much lower than Australia, where the states are dependent on transfers for 45 per cent of their needs (Treasury 2022). The only federation in which constituent units have greater fiscal independence than Canada is Switzerland, where the cantons rely on federal grants for only 13 per cent of their revenue (Dafflon 2020, 136).

While comparatively low, 20 per cent is still a substantial amount and thus represents a degree of dependence that threatens two types of potential debilities for the Canadian provinces. The first is fiscal vulnerability: those funds are not guaranteed. This weakness was made starkly evident when the federal government slashed transfers in 1996 to repair its budgetary situation – as highlighted, *inter alios*, by Quebec's Commission sur le déséquilibre fiscal, the Séguin Commission (CDF 2002b, 46–55). From that perspective, an arrangement such as exists in Australia where the entire net proceeds of one main Commonwealth government tax (the goods and services tax, GST) are hypothecated by intergovernmental agreement and an Act of Parliament to the states might be considered federal best practice since it insulates constituent units from central government budgetary whims.[7] For these reasons, this practice was one of the main recommendations of the Séguin Commission (CDF 2002c, xii), which was deliberating just as the GST arrangements were being introduced in Australia.

The other main risk of vertical fiscal imbalance is the use of specific purpose or conditional grants to extend central government policy making into areas of constituent unit jurisdiction, to which we now turn.

The "Spending Power"

Fiscal federalism doctrine accords a justifiable and indeed potentially important role for central government grants in ensuring the adequate provision of public goods. Even in the Canadian case, though, the federal government is equipped with surplus revenue beyond what is necessary for such purposes, as Robson and Laurin (2018, 36) argued. There is, then, considerable potential for the spending power to be a vehicle for "coercive" and/or "opportunistic" federalism by the central government. Central governments can easily exceed their constitutional allocation of authority, either by providing conditional grants that are too costly for constituent units to refuse or by making direct "payments to people or institutions" in areas where they do not "have the power to legislate" (Trudeau 1969). And there is a perennial twofold temptation to take advantage of the spending power. First, governing parties always have an ideological mission in pursuit of which they are typically happy to exploit whatever policy levers are available. Second, there is always the electoral anxiety that, while wearing the odium for collecting taxes, the central government is not getting due credit for the services that those revenues fund.

Here, Canada is seen as best practice because conditionality is reasonably low. The majority of specific purpose funds are in the form of the Canada Health Transfer (CHT) block grants. This transfer funded around 30 per cent of "targeted" provincial health spending over the past decade, according to federal government calculations (PBO 2020). The CHT contribution to overall health spending is distinctly less by provincial government calculations, though (PTMF 2021), and of course health makes up a very large component of provincial expenditure (see Boadway, chapter 5, this volume). The Canada Social Transfer (CST), something of "a poor cousin," funds four broad programs (Prince, chapter 6, this volume; PBO 2020).[8] Canada, Australia, and the United States are fundamentally alike here. In all three federations, the largest transfer is to impose a system of public health insurance across the country along centrally determined lines. Canada requires adherence to the principles laid down in the 1984 Canada Health Act (CHA); Australia has Medicare, its public health insurance system; and the United States has its Medicare and Medicaid systems.

How intrusive is the CHT? Not particularly so, for several reasons, suggests Boadway (chapter 5, this volume). None of these, however, is particularly compelling. First, "the provinces, after all, can refuse to take the funds." Given the enormous sums involved, this notion is fanciful. Second, the requirement that CHT funds be spent on health is entirely "notional." However, the provinces have no choice but to spend that amount and more on health care. Third, the conditions laid down by the CHA "consist mainly of broad principles whose meaning is open to interpretation." They may be broad principles, but they are quite strong ones. Medicare established a pan-Canadian centrally defined system of universal health care that represents as important an exercise of the spending power as one finds in Australia or the United States. Finally, Boadway argues, the leverage the CHT provides in enforcing the terms of the Canada Health Act "wanes as the share of federal financing of provincial health spending falls." However, is that really the case? It is a basic axiom of economics that costs or spending at the margin are what count. The CHT would have to fall to very low levels before it lost its intergovernmental efficacy. Finally, it is important to note that the CHT is also exploited by the federal government to launch new initiatives of its own in this area of provincial jurisdiction – the 2022 announcement of funding for dental care being one example (see Finance Canada 2022, ch. 6).

Intrusiveness is nonetheless of a greater magnitude in Australia and the United States, where the spending power has been, and continues to be, used extensively. In Australia, energetic use of the spending power was pioneered by the Labor Party in a deliberate and determined effort to obviate the constitutional division of powers, which was seen as an illegitimate obstacle to Labor's social reform ambitions (see, for example, Whitlam 1977). Conditional, or "tied," grants soon became an entrenched part of Australian federalism. Recent Commonwealth government budget papers unabashedly note:

> The Commonwealth provides payments to the States for specific purposes in policy areas for which the States have primary responsibility. *These payments cover most areas of State and local government activity*, including health, education, skills and workforce development, community services, housing, Indigenous affairs, infrastructure and the environment. (Treasury 2018; emphasis added)

The Séguin Commission exaggerated when it declared that centralization in Australia had reached "the point of reducing it to a unitary state" (CDF 2002a, 25). Climate change politics and the COVID-19 pandemic have made clear that is not the case (Fenna 2021, 2023). However, there is no doubt that this use of the spending power goes well beyond anything conceivable in Canada and is integral to the degree to which Australian federalism has become centralized (Fenna 2019a). Similarly, "categorical" grants – those with conditions attached, often for very specific purposes – have long been an important feature of the US transfer system. Furthermore, in neither Australia nor the United States is the choice of "opting out" with financial compensation available, and thus, although grants are technically optional, in practice they are an offer that is, if not impossible, certainly very difficult, to refuse.

Best Practice?

Canada's higher level of constituent unit financial autonomy certainly makes it somewhat better practice in revenue raising than the United States and decidedly better than Australia. It might be considered better practice than Switzerland too, depending on one's views about tax competition. There is nonetheless a substantial degree of VFI, and best practice is measured, as well, by how that issue is addressed. Canada has no guaranteed set of transfers along the lines of Australia's GST arrangements. Scope for unilateralism certainly exists, and the severe transfer reductions of the mid-1990s would seem a far cry from best practice. Likewise, scope for what, following the Tremblay report (Kwavnick 1973, 165), we could refer to as "imperialism" also exists, and any assessment of Canada as best practice unavoidably depends on how legitimate or how intrusive one considers the use of the spending power. Boadway assessed Canada's arrangements as best practice in no small part because "transfers are only as intrusive as is necessary to achieve national objectives" (2007, 99). However, that statement is both tendentious and circular: what constitutes legitimate "national objectives" is an open question, particularly in a bi-communal federation. The Quebec view on that question, and hence on the intrusiveness of the federal spending power, is quite different from the view prevailing in the "rest of Canada" (Telford, Graefe, and Banting 2008). From Quebec's perspective, it is quite reasonable to ask, as the province's *premier ministre* recently did *à propos* of the CHT: "*Comment se fait-il qu'il y ait un ministre de la Santé fédéral alors que c'est un champ de compétence des provinces et des territoires?*" (Saba 2022).[9] As a general rule, the trade-off between fiscal gain and autonomy loss characteristic of conditional grants is greater for the more "distinctive" constituent units in a federal system (Schnabel and Dardanelli 2022).

Sharing the Wealth

Ensuring that jurisdictions are sufficiently resourced to provide comparable levels of key public services seems, from one perspective, an essential element of any federal system – contributing to the sense that everyone is living in the same country. It also has long been seen as helping to maintain the federal quality of the union by reducing pressures for central government provision and hence centralization (Buchanan 1950). At the same time, redistribution is an all-too-transparent zero-sum game, and the other side of federalism is that the claim of jurisdictional autonomy is usually taken as implying an onus of jurisdictional responsibility. Even simple per capita grants – such as Canada's CHT and CST – are a form of equalization, since they are funded by federal government taxes that draw proportionally more from richer jurisdictions. In the following discussion, however, the focus is on explicit rather than implicit modes of equalization – or, to use Boessenkool's (chapter 21, this volume) terms, "Big-E" rather than "small-e" equalization.

How Much Equalization?

A formal system of horizontal fiscal equalization has been operating in Canada since 1957 following a rather protracted set of debates and negotiations dating back to the Great Depression (Janigan 2020; Béland et al. 2017). The requirement was enshrined in the Constitution Act, 1982, and thus we can say that together these two realities make equalization a core element of fiscal federalism in Canada. At the same time, however, equalization is implemented far less thoroughly in Canada than it has been in Australia, where there is no constitutional requirement whatsoever.[10]

Robin Boadway (2015, 432) has described equalization as the "life-blood of federations" – but evidently some federations are more sanguinary than others, for degrees of equalization vary substantially. On the bloodless end of the scale is the United States, which for reasons to do with peculiarities of its history, society, and political system has no equalization system at all (Béland and Lecours 2014b). On the other end of the scale are Australia and Germany, with thorough-going equalization systems that seek to ensure close-to-equal fiscal capacity across the federation. The Australian system has been focused not just on bringing disadvantaged jurisdictions up to an average but on ensuring a complete levelling. It also factors in the expense needs as well as the revenue capacity of each jurisdiction.[11] In addition, a statutory federal government agency, the Commonwealth Grants Commission, does the necessary sums and recommends to the Treasury how much each state and territory should receive from the common pool (CGC 1995, 2008, 2017). The Grants Commission was established in 1933, immediately after voters in the then-disadvantaged State of Western Australia voted 66 per cent in favour of secession (for discussion, see Lecours and Béland 2019).

Canada sits somewhere between the equalizing extremes. According to OECD analyses, in 2012 the ratio of highest-to-lowest fiscal capacity in Canada was 2.4 before equalization and 1.8 afterwards (Blöchliger 2013, 105). By contrast, Germany's was 1.7 before equalization and 1.1 afterwards, while Australia's was 7.5 and 1.[12] Canada is more in line with Switzerland (4.3 to 2.6) as countries that, while practising equalization, do so only in moderation. In particular, by only lifting and not levelling, Canada allows the province of Alberta to keep its windfall petroleum royalties in a way that Western Australia, with equivalent windfall rents that are equalized away, could (until very recently, at least) only fantasize about.

And How Is It Done?

It is customary to distinguish between two modes of equalization: one occurring by more or less *direct* transfer from the wealthy to the poorer jurisdictions; the other effected *indirectly* by central government grants.[13] It is not always easy to characterize regimes in these terms. The Australian system, for example, can be seen as an instance of neither or both. It is often seen as *indirect* in nature, since equalization is executed through general revenue grants from the Commonwealth to the states. However, those grants come from a pool of funds (the total net GST revenues) pre-assigned by legislation to the states and thus constitute for all intents and purposes a *direct* transfer from richer states and territories to poorer ones. That pool provides the states with approximately one-fifth of all their revenue, and since it is much larger than is required for equalization, there is effectively no limit on how much it can equalize without incurring any extra cost for the Commonwealth government.

Similarly, while the German system was recently changed from a very explicitly direct arrangement to one that is less so (Renzsch 2019), it nonetheless has at its core a formula for assigning shares of a common funding pool and thus retains its original quality. There is also an indirect component, with the federal government providing a top-up for those jurisdictions still below the standard (Spahn 2020, 66). The Swiss Constitution, meanwhile, not only requires a combination of the two methods but also stipulates in what ratio.[14] Canada is the outlier here, relying entirely on the indirect method, with the federal government funding equalization payments entirely out of its own budget.

We might surmise that the two approaches have their respective implications. First, full equalization is substantially more feasible using direct transfers, since that brings the top down at the same time as it lifts the bottom up and does not impose a burden on the central government. Unsurprisingly, it is the mechanism relied on by the two comprehensive equalizers, Australia and Germany. Second, we might think that an unambiguously indirect system is less likely to provoke conflict than an invidiously direct one, since Peter is not being explicitly robbed to pay Paul. On that basis, we would expect Canada, *ceteris paribus*, to have less conflict over equalization than federations practising direct transfer – and even more so since the system does not equalize down. However, the veil of fiscal ignorance is easily lifted, and the richer jurisdictions in an indirect system are quick to protest that the money is nonetheless coming out of their pockets, given the proportionally greater contribution their taxpayers make to federal revenues (see, for example, Hartmann, Thirgood, and Thies 2018; Tombe 2018).

Best Practice?

How to assess Canada's equalization arrangements? Certainly, there are ways in which they look suboptimal. First, we might note that there is no independent expert body managing the system as the OECD recommends and as we find in Australia (Dougherty and Forman 2021, 7). But even that does not come close to the Swiss practice, where both chambers of the federal Parliament were involved in designing the current system. The Conference of Cantonal Governments was instrumental in negotiating between contributors and recipients; the resulting compromise was ratified by 65 per cent of voters in the required referendum and written into the Constitution, and Parliament continues to exercise a monitoring function (Schnabel and Mueller 2017, 556). Furthermore, in Canada the formula is altered in ad hoc ways to cope with changing fiscal pressures – an almost inevitable consequence of reliance on federal budget funding in a fluctuating environment; and the system does not equalize. On the other hand, perhaps full equalization is too much of a good thing, and the Canadian approach hits the compromise sweet spot. Perhaps, too, it represents the optimal degree under Canada's specific circumstances. As Benz (2021, 121) has said, "there is no single norm that applies for fiscal equalization … This follows from the conflict between autonomy and solidarity in federations."

462   Alan Fenna

Conflict Nonetheless

Notwithstanding what might be seen as best practice, fiscal federalism has been, suggest Béland and Lecours (2018, 298ff), a "burning political issue" in Canada in ways we don't see in other federations. Is this a reflection of the underlying political economy; of societal characteristics; of contingent factors; of institutional differences; or of something else?

VFI and the Spending Power

A low level of conditionality has not prevented Canada's intergovernmental grants from being contentious – as evidenced not least by the extent to which they are the subject of debate. Petter (1989, 468) inveighed against the spending power as a constitutional travesty, asserting that it had substituted administrative for coordinate federalism and given Canadians the "worst of all possible worlds [sic]. It imposes upon citizens the costs and inconvenience of supporting two orders of government while denying them the benefits of local control."[15] Telford (2003) was similarly critical of the spending power as offensive to Quebec and inimical to the principles of federalism more generally. Lajoie (2006) gamely asserted that the spending power has been one of the tools with which Canada has played the centralization "game" like a "pro." Adam (2007) insisted that federal government claims to a plenary spending power are without constitutional foundation. Courchene (2008) argued that the very language of a right to "opt out" places a reverse onus since it implicitly grants primacy to the application of the spending power rather than to the provincial jurisdiction concerned. Meanwhile, at least one spirited defence of the spending power has been mounted (Kent 2008). The prominence of the issue is also clear from the fact that it was a component of constitutional and sub-constitutional reform proposals going back to 1969, including the 1987 Meech Lake and 1992 Charlottetown Agreements (see Dunn 2018, 71).

The spending power debate has no counterpart in either Australia or the United States. In part, this absence reflects the degree to which it is constitutionally a settled issue in those two federations. Australia is the extreme case in that regard, with the Commonwealth Constitution giving the spending power explicit licence: section 96 states in unequivocal terms that "the Parliament may grant financial assistance to any State on such terms and conditions as the Parliament thinks fit." And, lest there was any doubt, the High Court very early on gave an equally – indeed brutally – unequivocal endorsement.[16] However, even without such explicit licence, it is difficult to see a domestic court instructing the national government on how, or how not, to spend its own money, and the Supreme Court of Canada has been broadly supportive (see Oliver, chapter 3, this volume). In the United States, where no constitutional provision for the spending power exists, the Supreme Court nonetheless deferred to Congress, effectively giving Washington something close to carte blanche.[17]

Béland and Lecours (2018) are surely correct to highlight the centrifugal impact of Quebec on Canadian federalism in this regard. To this must be added that Australia is a generally more homogeneous federation. That said, the crucial point is that the chief moment of conflict the authors identify in Canada was the conflict surrounding the federal government's effort at deficit reduction in the mid-1990s via, in large part, cuts in transfers to the provinces. The Australian government had never dug itself into the same fiscal hole and thus did not need to impose the same savage cuts. While in Australia the Commonwealth had brought its budget back into surplus by 1988, in Canada the federal government's deficit had reached a quite extraordinary 8 per cent of gross domestic product (GDP) in 1984 and was still at a quite substantial 5 per cent of GDP later in the decade. By the mid-1990s, net federal government debt was over 70 per cent of GDP in Canada. In response, own spending was cut by slightly under 10 per cent and transfers to the provinces by over 20 per cent. In other words, there is a very straightforward explanation for greater conflict over intergovernmental grants in Canada.

Why So Much Conflict Over Equalization?

In 2021, the Alberta government put the following question to its citizens in a plebiscite: "Should Section 36(2) of the Constitution Act, 1982 – Parliament and the Government of Canada's commitment to the principle of making equalization payments – be removed from the Constitution?" Voter turnout was only 40 per cent, but of those, 62 per cent said yes. Although equalization is not the consequence of the constitutional requirement in Canada – if anything, the other way round – this result provides a good indication of its unsettled nature.[18]

Why, with a compromise system of equalization that does not equalize or take directly from one province to give to another, has there been greater conflict in Canada than in other federations? Béland and Lecours (2018, 302) adduce a host of reasons, including various institutional and political ones. "The first, and most important, is the governance structure." In their view, "the 'Australian model' of governance for equalization, characterized by the existence since 1933 of an arm's-length federal commission that makes recommendations on 'relativities'" is one where political conflict is neutralized. Canada, they argue, pays the price for having no equivalent mechanism. Benz (2021, 136) makes the same argument.

Yes, Australia has long had the Grants Commission calculating what share of the pool each jurisdiction should receive. And, yes, the system provoked little conflict for much of its time. However, we must not overlook a key underlying difference between the political economy of equalization in Australia and Canada: *for almost the entire history of the Australian system, the two demographically and economically dominant jurisdictions have been the funders.* New South Wales (NSW) and Victoria have long received slightly less than their per capita share of the grant pool so that more can go to the smaller and less affluent jurisdictions.[19] Ontario and Quebec are the Canadian counterparts to NSW and Victoria; there, the situation has been radically different, with Quebec having been the *largest recipient* rather than a contributor for the entire sixty-four years the equalization system has so far been in operation. The difference is stark.

Having one of the populous jurisdictions as a recipient means that even a minor per capita differential can amount to a substantial total. In 1957–8, when the Canadian system was inaugurated, Quebec received fully one-third of the entire pool, and Ontario was the net contributor (Janigan 2020, 285). Since then, the imbalance has become more pronounced, with Quebec typically receiving almost half of all equalization funds and, recently, receiving more than all other jurisdictions combined. This allotment naturally raises the question of whether a major purpose of equalization in Canada is to mollify Quebec (as suggested by Béland and Lecours 2014a). For purposes here, its significance lies in the much greater burden placed on the equalization system.

By the 1970s, the petroleum transformation of Alberta's fiscal fortunes meant that it became very distinctly a "have" province.[20] A situation that makes one of the two large jurisdictions a perpetual recipient creates substantially greater pressures, which then become magnified when one of the small population jurisdictions becomes a net contributor. Exacerbating the difficulties thereby created was the way Alberta's economic interests have been diametrically opposed to much of the rest of Canada's: first, other parts of the country consume Alberta's resource exports; and second, resource production is the largest source of greenhouse gas emissions in the country. Again, here is a source of conflict that has no equivalent in Australia. And, as if all that wasn't enough, in 2008–9 the other large jurisdiction, Ontario, also became an equalization beneficiary. While in Germany the most populous jurisdiction, Nordrhein-Westfalen, is a recipient, it absorbs less than 10 per cent of the total equalization transfers, and the second and third most populous *Länder* are the main funders (BMF 2019, 24).[21]

A within-case longitudinal comparison reinforces the importance of these considerations. Things have not always been amicable in the Australian equalization system. Conflict rather than consensus prevailed for the decade to 2018. Indeed, conflict has occurred to such extent that, in their comparative analysis, Eccleston and Woolley (2015) depict the Australia–Canada comparison in terms *exactly the reverse* of those on which Béland and Lecours's analysis is predicated. For Eccleston and Woolley, what needs explaining is "the relatively successful management of regional tensions in the Canadian context" (231). Their explanation for what they see as the *less* conflictual politics of equalization in Canada is the compromise nature of the Canadian system and, in particular, the way it allows Alberta to keep its windfall resource earnings.

The reason these two analyses can come up with diametrically opposed readings of the degree of conflict in the two cases lies in the period on which each chooses to focus; both are cherry-picking their data point. Neither argument stands up in the face of more representative sampling. Australia's equalization system worked in the way Lecours and Béland describe it for a considerable period during which the two big jurisdictions were the funders and carried a small per capita cost. During a period in the early 1980s, however, tensions were high as a consequence of new resource wealth – a harbinger of things to come (Head 1983, 77). Generally, though, there was only intermittent grumbling.[22] This situation changed in the early 2000s, corresponding more to Eccleston and Woolley's characterization. When the iron ore boom transformed Western Australia (WA) into an Alberta-equivalent fifteen years ago, and its share of the funding pool declined, then plunged, the system become unstable and then untenable. In the space of a decade, WA went from earning $300 million per annum in iron ore royalties to earning almost $6 billion. As a consequence, it went from receiving more than 100 per cent of its equal per capita share of the GST revenues to being due a mere 30 per cent (CGC 2021). Rather than philosophical acceptance that this decrease was precisely how the system was designed to work, outrage at the loss of GST share become the order of the day (see, for example, Porter 2011). Contrary to Béland and Lecours's postulation, the fact that the Grants Commission made the punitive calculations did nothing to reduce the sense of grievance. Indeed, in some ways, it may have had the opposite effect because of the perceived complexity and opacity of the commission's calculations and processes (PC 2018, 89; Shah 2017, 3; Porter 2011).

The Commonwealth government washed its hands of the issue for as long as possible on the grounds that it was up to the states to resolve disagreement about their respective shares. Persistent pressure and two inquiries later, though, the Commonwealth eventually conceded – introducing changes to privilege Western Australia (PC 2018; GSTDR 2012; PM and Treasurer 2018).[23] An arbitrary floor on state relativities of 70 per cent per capita share was introduced; the benchmark was changed from the fiscally strongest jurisdiction to the fiscally strongest of NSW and Victoria; and the Commonwealth introduced an element of indirect transfer, contributing money from its own budget.[24] The incentives were very different from those that apply in Canada, where equalization is funded entirely out of the federal government's own budget. Here, the federal government responded to similar stresses by capping payments in 2009 – saving itself $16 billion over the next few years (PBO 2020, 11).

Conclusion

The most obvious comparators for an assessment of Canadian fiscal federalism are Australia and the United States; together, the three countries constitute the main examples of systems based on dualist or coordinate design. However, Switzerland and Germany also provide some useful contrasts and comparisons. It is not much to go on, but it is something. For what it's worth, Canada does set the benchmark in the group of three, although not in all regards. Canada's constituent units enjoy the highest level of fiscal autonomy and are the least subject to the spending power. At the same time, all is not perfect. In particular, as the offloading by the federal government of its fiscal problems onto the provinces in the mid-1990s shows, even a relatively modest VFI can expose constituent units to significant risk if, as is the case here, control over the transfer quantum is unilateral and at executive discretion. In addition, almost any exercise of the spending power is potentially an affront to a minority nation jurisdiction.

The explanation for the degree to which Canadian fiscal federalism represents best practice is Quebec. As Alexander Brady put it long ago:

> Quebec's devotion to the federal idea has served a national purpose; it has helped to lessen the danger of excessive centralization in Ottawa and the equal danger of a rigid framework advantageous to Ottawa. Rigid arrangements acceptable today may be intolerable tomorrow. Flexibility is a prime condition for a healthy federalism, and paradoxically Quebec by its unbending position has been its guarantor. (1959, 270)

Having ensured that Canada would be truly federal from the outset (Silver 1997), Quebec's intransigence has been fundamental to protecting provincial tax bases and keeping the spending power in check. Other factors have certainly contributed. Canada is more regionalized than Australia, particularly where distribution of natural resources is concerned. However, even there, it would seem, Quebec has played a crucial role. According to Gibbins (1992, 72), Alberta's assertiveness bore fruit at key moments because the provincial government "surfed adroitly on the constitutional waves generated by the nationalist movement in Quebec" – even if that metaphor does seem a little maladroit given the province's landlocked nature.

Equalization is a different matter. What constitutes best practice in that contentious domain is impossible to say. Each federation tends to get the system that corresponds to its structure and character, particularly in respect to how regionally egalitarian it seeks to be. There is no reason to think that Canada's compromise arrangements represent best practice; rather, they merely represent what is politically feasible within the Canadian context. Nor is there any reason to think that the unilateral and ad hoc way in which the system is managed represents best practice.

To the extent that Canada nonetheless has it generally so good, there remains the question, why is it so miserable? As Béland and Lecours note, Canada seems to have more conflict in fiscal regards with the least reason for it. The answer, in part, is the same as the reasons advanced above: the tensions that have given Canada something resembling best practice fiscal federalism are the same as the ones that make it conflictual. The paradox is easily resolved. In addition, equalization is also a much more challenging proposition in Canada than it is in the United States, where it is not regarded as part of the federal contract at all, or in Australia and Germany, where the distribution of wealth has generally been more conducive. One would like to think that a solution lies in the institutional reform suggested by Béland and Lecours, a statutory equalization agency (see also Feehan 2020, 19). Introducing something along Grants Commission lines would certainly do no harm and quite possibly some good, and could be recommended on that basis. Unfortunately, though, it is excessively optimistic to think that institutional tinkering of such a nature would somehow do away with the main underlying conflicts. Such a notion is not supported by the comparative experience.

NOTES

1 By "capricious," I mean the potential for central governments to launch programs unilaterally, perhaps in response to some current issue, only to neglect or abandon them later on, leaving the constituent units with the problem.
2 The awkwardness of the distinction is evident in the way it leads to conceptually self-contradictory statements like "the federal government uses the superior financial resources it has by virtue of the fiscal imbalance to introduce conditions and norms in fields that are not within its jurisdictions [sic]," where the "imbalance" is seen as allowing abuses that we were told earlier are what constitute an imbalance (Noël 2005, 139).
3 Technically, of course, it could be vice versa, but in that case the implications are very different.
4 *Vollzugsföderalismus* – "implementational federalism" or "executionary federalism" – as it is known in German. For elaboration and discussion, see Mueller and Fenna (2022).
5 We must be mindful that, as Richard Bird (1986) pointed out, the basic data used in these comparisons are to some extent going to be stylized, indicative, or approximate, and true comparability is difficult.
6 A peculiarity of Canada is that the British North America Act, 1867 accorded the provinces "exclusive" power to levy "direct taxation." Not only was this not an "exclusive" power, since the federal government was assigned a plenary taxation power, but it ended up being so curiously interpreted by the courts as to permit the

provinces a much broader range of taxes than the wording would normally suggest, including those that are clearly indirect.
7 The Intergovernmental Agreement on the Reform of Commonwealth–State Financial Relations, 1999 and A New Tax System (Commonwealth–State Financial Arrangements) Act 1999. Australia's strong bicameralism means that enactment is a more effective device that it would be in Canada. It does nothing, though, to insulate the conditional transfers from Commonwealth budgetary whims.
8 "Programs in respect of post-secondary education; social assistance and social services; early childhood development; and early learning and child care services" – contributing between 13 and 14 per cent of provincial spending in these areas, according to federal government calculations (PBO 2020, 10, 19).
9 "How is that there is a federal health minister at all, given that health is a power and responsibility of the provinces?"
10 Commonwealth legislation stipulates that "the respective payments to which the States are entitled ... should enable each State to provide, without imposing taxes and charges at levels appreciably different from the levels of the taxes and charges imposed by other States, government services at standards not appreciably different from the standards of government services provided by the other States;
  (ii) taking account of:
  - differences in the capacities of States to raise revenues; and
  - differences in the amounts required to be expended by the States in providing comparable government services." (States [Personal Income Tax Sharing] Act 1976, section 13[3])
11 A more dispersed population or a larger Indigenous population will, for instance, increase the jurisdiction's expenditure needs, and the Grants Commission will take such factors that are beyond the jurisdiction's control into account.
12 The very high "before" ratio in Australia reflects the impact of the resources boom on Western Australia's revenues at this time, discussed below.
13 The Germans refer to the direct transfer between constituent units as "fraternal" equalisation, which presumably makes the top-down or indirect mode "paternal" or, more appropriately perhaps, "maternal."
14 "The payments made by those Cantons with higher level of resources shall amount to a minimum of two thirds and a maximum of 80 per cent of the payments made by the Confederation" (article 125).
15 He surely meant worst of *both* worlds, not worst of *all possible* worlds.
16 The "Roads Case," *The State of Victoria and Others v. The Commonwealth* [1926] 38 CLR 39.
17 On the surely rather specious grounds that states are free to decline the offer of a conditional grant, going back to *Steward Machine Co. v. Davis*, 301 [1937] U.S. 548.
18 It's worth noting here that, while Germany's high level of equalization is underpinned by a constitutional requirement for "equivalent living conditions" across the country (originally "uniform living conditions"), Australia's exists without any constitutional requirement at all.

19 Their per capita share of the pool has generally been in the 83 to 97 per cent range over the period (CGC 2016, 3).
20 Alberta ceased receiving equalization grants in 1965, but it was not until the dramatic rise in prices after 1973 that petroleum became such a source of wealth for the province.
21 Bayern and Baden-Württemberg, respectively.
22 Expressed, as it so often is, as the economists' proposition that equalization somehow discourages good policy in both contributor and recipient jurisdictions (see, for example, Garnaut and FitzGerald 2002).
23 Treasury Laws Amendment (Making Sure Every State and Territory Gets Their Fair Share of GST) Act, 2018. The first enquiry made a status quo recommendation. The second, however, was conducted by the Productivity Commission, the Commonwealth's main economic advice agency, which was persuaded by arguments about perverse incentives lurking in such systems of wealth sharing and recommended a watering down. "The objective of the HFE system should be refocused to provide the States with the fiscal capacity to provide services and associated infrastructure of a reasonable (rather than the same) standard" (PC 2018, 39).
24 That the Commonwealth acted rather precipitously became evident in September 2021 when the Western Australian government recorded the biggest budget surplus in the state's history (and the second biggest in the country's history). Victoria and New South Wales, meanwhile, were wrestling not just with COVID-19 (which had been kept out of WA) but with the dire economic and fiscal effects of their pandemic control measures.

REFERENCES

Adam, Marc-Antoine. 2007. "Federalism and the Spending Power: Section 94 to the Rescue." *Policy Options* 28, no. 3: 30–4. http://irpp.org/wp-content/uploads/assets/po/equalization-and-the-federal-spending-power/adam.pdf.
Béland, Daniel, and André Lecours. 2014a. "Accommodation and the Politics of Fiscal Equalization in Multinational States: The Case of Canada." *Nations and Nationalism* 20, no. 2: 337–54. https://doi.org/10.1111/nana.12049.
– 2014b. "Fiscal Federalism and American Exceptionalism: Why Is There No Federal Equalization Program in the United States?" *Journal of Public Policy* 34, no. 2: 303–29. https://doi.org/10.1017/S0143814X14000038.
– 2018. "Comparative Perspectives on the Territorial Politics of Fiscal Federalism: Canada, Australia, and the United States." In *Handbook of Territorial Politics*, edited by Klaus Detterbeck and Eve Hepburn, 293–305. Cheltenham, UK: Edward Elgar.
Béland, Daniel, André Lecours, Gregory P. Marchildon, Haizhen Mou, and M. Rose Olfert. 2017. *Fiscal Federalism and Equalization Policy in Canada: Political and Economic Dimensions*. Toronto: University of Toronto Press.
Benz, Arthur. 2021. *Policy Change and Innovation in Multilevel Governance*. Cheltenham, UK: Edward Elgar.

Biela, Jan, Annika Hennl, and André Kaiser. 2012. *Policy Making in Multilevel Systems: Federalism, Decentralisation, and Performance in the OECD Countries*. Colchester, UK: ECPR Press.

Bird, Richard. 1986. "On Measuring Fiscal Centralization and Fiscal Balance in Federal States." *Environment and Planning C: Government and Policy* 4, no. 4: 389–404. https://doi.org/10.1068/c040389.

Blöchliger, Hansjörg, ed. 2013. *Fiscal Federalism 2014: Making Decentralisation Work*. Paris: Organisation for Economic Co-operation and Development.

BMF (Bundesministerium für Finanzen). 2019. *Ergebnisse des Länderfinanzausgleichs 2018*. Berlin: Bundesrepublik Deutschland. https://www.bundesfinanzministerium.de/Monatsberichte/2019/03/Inhalte/Kapitel-3-Analysen/3-3-ergebnisse-laenderfinanzausgleich_pdf.pdf.

Boadway, Robin. 2007. "Canada." In *The Practice of Fiscal Federalism: Comparative Perspectives*, edited by Anwar Shah, 99–124. Global Dialogue on Federalism Series. Montreal and Kingston: McGill-Queen's University Press.

– 2015. "Intergovernmental Transfers: Rationale and Policy." In *Handbook of Multilevel Finance*, edited by Ehtisham Ahmad and Giorgio Brosio, 410–36. Cheltenham, UK: Edward Elgar.

Brady, Alexander. 1959. "Quebec and Canadian Federalism." *Canadian Journal of Economics and Political Science* 25, no. 3: 259–70. https://doi.org/10.2307/138902.

Buchanan, James M. 1950. "Federalism and Fiscal Equity." *American Economic Review* 40, no. 4: 583–99. https://www.jstor.org/stable/1808426.

CDF (Commission sur le déséquilibre fiscal). 2002a. *The "Federal Spending Power."* Quebec: Gouvernement du Québec.

– 2002b. *Fiscal Imbalance in Canada: Historical Context*. Quebec: Gouvernement du Québec.

– 2002c. *A New Division of Canada's Financial Resources*. Quebec: Gouvernement du Québec.

CGC (Commonwealth Grants Commission). 1995. *Equality in Diversity: A History of the Commonwealth Grants Commission*. 2nd ed. Canberra: Commonwealth of Australia.

– 2008. *The Commonwealth Grants Commission: The Last 25 Years*. Braddon ACT: Commonwealth of Australia.

– 2016. *Trends in Horizontal Fiscal Equalisation*. Canberra: Commonwealth of Australia.

– 2017. *The Principle of HFE and Its Implementation*. Canberra: Commonwealth of Australia.

– 2021. *Mining Revenue and GST Distribution*. Canberra: Commonwealth of Australia.

Chernick, Howard A. 2020. "The United States Grant System." In *Intergovernmental Transfers in Federations*, edited by Serdar Yilmaz and Farah Zahir, 86–108. Cheltenham, UK: Edward Elgar.

Courchene, Thomas. 2008. *Reflections on the Federal Spending Power: Practices, Principles, Perspectives*. IRPP Working Paper Series, No. 2008-01. Montreal: Institute for Research on Public Policy. https://irpp.org/research-studies/reflections-on-the-federal-spending-power/.

Dafflon, Bernard. 2020. "Revenue and Expenditure Needs Equalization: The Swiss Answer." In *Intergovernmental Transfers in Federations*, edited by Serdar Yilmaz and Farah Zahir, 134–62. Cheltenham, UK: Edward Elgar.

Dardanelli, Paolo, John Kincaid, Alan Fenna, André Kaiser, André Lecours, Ajay Kumar Singh, Sean Mueller, and Stephan Vogel. 2019. "Dynamic De/Centralization in Federations: Comparative Conclusions." *Publius: The Journal of Federalism* 49, no. 1: 194–219. https://doi.org/10.1093/publius/pjy037.

Dardanelli, Paolo, and Sean Mueller. 2019. "Dynamic De/Centralization in Switzerland, 1848–2010." *Publius: The Journal of Federalism* 49, no. 1: 138–65. https://doi.org/10.1093/publius/pjx056.

Dougherty, Sean, and Kass Forman. 2021. *Evaluating Fiscal Equalisation: Finding the Right Balance*. Paris: Organisation for Economic Co-operation and Development.

Dunn, Christopher. 2018. "The Federal Spending Power." In *The Handbook of Canadian Public Administration*. 3rd ed., edited by Christopher Dunn, 52–74. Don Mills ON: Oxford University Press.

Eccleston, Richard, and Timothy Woolley. 2015. "From Calgary to Canberra: Resource Taxation and Fiscal Federalism in Canada and Australia." *Publius: The Journal of Federalism* 45, no. 2: 216–43. https://doi.org/10.1093/publius/pju039.

Feehan, James P. 2020. "Canada's Equalization Program: Political Debates and Opportunities for Reform." *IRPP Insight* 30. Montreal: Institute for Research on Public Policy. https://irpp.org/research-studies/canadas-equalization-program-political-debates-and-opportunities-for-reform/.

Fenna, Alan. 2008. "Commonwealth Fiscal Power and Australian Federalism." *University of New South Wales Law Journal* 31, no. 2: 509–29. https://www.unswlawjournal.unsw.edu.au/article/commonwealth-fiscal-power-and-australian-federalism.

– 2017. "The Fiscal Predicament of Australian Federalism." In *A People's Federation*, edited by Mark Bruerton, Tracey Arklay, Robyn Hollander, and Ron Levy, 134–46. Leichhardt, NSW: Federation Press.

– 2019a. "The Centralization of Australian Federalism 1901–2010: Measurement and Interpretation." *Publius: The Journal of Federalism* 49, no. 1: 30–56. https://doi.org/10.1093/publius/pjy042.

– 2019b. "What Hope for Comparative Federalism?" In *A Research Agenda for Federalism Studies*, edited by John Kincaid, 76–92. Cheltenham, UK: Edward Elgar.

– 2020. "*Modell Deutschland?* Comparative Reflections on the German Federal System." In *Reformbaustelle Bundesstaat*, edited by Felix Knüpling, Mario Kölling, Sabine Kropp, and Henrik Scheller, 209–28. Wiesbaden: Springer.

- 2021. "Australian Federalism and the COVID-19 Crisis." In *Federalism and the Response to COVID-19: A Comparative Analysis*, edited by Rupak Chattopadhyay, Felix Knüpling, Diana Chebanova, Liam Whittington, and Phillip Gonzalez, 17–29. Abingdon, UK: Routledge.
- 2023. "Climate Governance and Federalism in Australia." In *Climate Governance and Federalism: A Forum of Federations Comparative Policy Analysis*, edited by Alan Fenna, Sébastien Jodoin, and Joana Setzer, 14–40. Cambridge: Cambridge University Press.

Finance Canada, Department of. 2022. *Budget 2022*. Ottawa: Government of Canada.

Garnaut, Ross, and Vince FitzGerald. 2002. *Review of Commonwealth–State Funding: Final Report*. Melbourne: Committee for the Review of Commonwealth–State Funding.

Gibbins, Roger. 1992. "Alberta and the National Community." In *Government and Politics in Alberta*, edited by Allan Tupper and Roger Gibbins, 67–84. Edmonton: University of Alberta Press.

Gilardi, Fabrizio, and Fabio Wasserfallen. 2016. "How Socialisation Attenuates Tax Competition." *British Journal of Political Science* 46, no. 1: 45–65. https://doi.org/10.1017/S0007123414000246.

Gordon, David J. 2015. "An Uneasy Equilibrium: The Coordination of Climate Governance in Federated Systems." *Global Environmental Politics* 15, no. 2: 121–41. https://doi.org/10.1162/GLEP_a_00301.

GSTDR (GST Distribution Review). 2012. *Final Report*. Canberra: Department of the Treasury.

Hartmann, Erich, Jordann Thirgood, and Andrew Thies. 2018. *A Fair Fiscal Deal: Towards a More Principled Allocation of Federal Transfers*. Toronto: Mowat Centre.

Head, Brian. 1983. "The Political Crisis of Australian Federalism." In *Australian Federalism: Future Tense*, edited by Allan Patience and Jeffrey Scott, 75–93. Melbourne: Oxford University Press.

Hueglin, Thomas O. 2020. *Federalism in Canada: Contested Concepts and Uneasy Balances*. Toronto: University of Toronto Press.

Hueglin, Thomas O., and Alan Fenna. 2015. *Comparative Federalism: A Systematic Inquiry*. 2nd ed. Toronto: University of Toronto Press.

Janigan, Mary. 2020. *Art of Sharing: The Richer versus the Poorer Provinces since Confederation*. Montreal and Kingston: McGill-Queen's University Press.

Joanis, Marcelin, and François Vaillancourt. 2020. "Federal Finance Arrangements in Canada: The Challenges of Fiscal Imbalance and Natural Resource Rents." In *Intergovernmental Transfers in Federations*, edited by Serdar Yilmaz and Farah Zahir, 109–33. Cheltenham, UK: Edward Elgar.

Kent, Tom. 2008. "The Federal Spending Power Is Now Chiefly for People, Not Provinces." *Queen's Law Journal* 34, no. 1: 413–25.

Kwavnick, David, ed. 1973. *The Tremblay Report: Report of the Royal Commission of Inquiry on Constitutional Problems*. Toronto: McClelland and Stewart.

Lajoie, Andrée. 2006. "The Federal Spending Power and Fiscal Imbalance in Canada." In *Dilemmas of Solidarity: Rethinking Distribution in the Canadian Federation*, edited by Sujit Choudhry, Jean-François Gaudreault-Desbiens, and Lorne Sossin, 145–66. Toronto: University of Toronto Press.

Lecours, André. 2019. "Dynamic De/Centralization in Canada, 1867–2010." *Publius: The Journal of Federalism* 49, no. 1: 57–83. https://doi.org/10.1093/publius/pjx046.

Lecours, André, and Daniel Béland. 2019. "From Secessionism to Regionalism: The Changing Nature of Territorial Politics in Western Australia." *Regional & Federal Studies* 29, no. 1: 25–44. https://doi.org/10.1080/13597566.2018.1443918.

Linder, Wolf, and Sean Mueller. 2021. *Swiss Democracy: Possible Solutions to Conflict in Multicultural Societies*. 4th ed. Cham, CH: Palgrave Macmillan.

Mueller, Sean, and Alan Fenna. 2022. "Dual versus Administrative Federalism: Origins and Evolution of Two Models." *Publius: The Journal of Federalism* 52, no. 4: 525–52. https://doi.org/10.1093/publius/pjac008.

Noël, Alain. 2005. "'A Report That Almost No One Has Discussed': Early Responses to Quebec's Commission on Fiscal Balance." In *Canadian Fiscal Arrangements: What Works, What Might Work Better*, edited by Harvey Lazar, 127–52. Montreal and Kingston: McGill-Queen's University Press.

– 2014. "Studying Your Own Country: Social Scientific Knowledge for Our Times and Places." *Canadian Journal of Political Science* 47, no. 4: 647–66. https://doi.org/10.1017/S0008423914001085.

Oates, Wallace E. 1999. "An Essay on Fiscal Federalism." *Journal of Economic Literature* 37, no. 3: 1120–49. https://doi.org/10.1257/jel.37.3.1120.

OECD (Organisation for Economic Co-operation and Development). 2021. *Revenue Statistics 2021*. Paris: OECD.

Olson, Mancur. 1969. "The Principle of 'Fiscal Equivalence': The Division of Responsibilities among Different Levels of Government." *American Economic Review* 59, no. 2: 479–87. https://www.jstor.org/stable/1823700.

PBO (Parliamentary Budget Office). 2020. *Federal Support through Major Transfers to Provincial and Territorial Governments*. Ottawa: Parliament of Canada. https://www.pbo-dpb.ca/en/publications/RP-2021-020-S--federal-support-through-major-transfers-to-provincial-territorial-governments--soutien-federal-principaux-transferts-aux-gouvernements-provinciaux-territoriaux.

PC (Productivity Commission). 2018. *Horizontal Fiscal Equalisation: Inquiry Report*. Melbourne: Productivity Commission.

Petter, Andrew. 1989. "Federalism and the Myth of the Federal Spending Power." *Canadian Bar Review* 68, no. 3: 448–79. https://cbr.cba.org/index.php/cbr/article/view/3450.

PM (Prime Minister) and Treasurer. 2018. "Legislating a Fairer Way to Distribute the GST." Media Release, 1 October 2018. https://ministers.treasury.gov.au/ministers/josh-frydenberg-2018/media-releases/legislating-fairer-way-distribute-gst.

Porter, Christian. 2011. "The Grants Commission and the Future of the Federation." *Public Policy* 6, nos. 1/2: 45–70.
PTMF (Provincial and Territorial Ministers of Finance). 2021. *Increasing the Canada Health Transfer Will Help Make Provinces and Territories More Financially Sustainable over the Long Term*. Ottawa: Council of the Federation.
Renzsch, Wolfgang. 2019. *Bending the Constitution: The New Regulation of Intergovernmental Fiscal Relations in Germany*. Ottawa: Forum of Federations.
Robson, William B.P., and Alexandre Laurin. 2018. "Adaptability, Accountability, and Sustainability: Intergovernmental Fiscal Arrangements in Canada." In *The Handbook of Canadian Public Administration*, edited by Christopher Dunn, 35–51. Don Mills ON: Oxford University Press.
Rocher, François. 2009. "The Quebec–Canada Dynamic or the Negation of Federalism." In *Contemporary Canadian Federalism: Foundations, Traditions, Institutions*, edited by Alain-G Gagnon, 81–131. Toronto: University of Toronto Press.
Saba, Michel. 2022. "Le comportement de Trudeau est 'insultant,' dit Legault." *La Presse*, 12 July 2022. https://www.lapresse.ca/actualites/sante/2022-07-12/restauration-du-systeme-de-sante/le-comportement-de-trudeau-est-insultant-dit-legault.php.
Saunders, Cheryl. 1986. "The Hardest Nut to Crack: The Financial Settlement in the Commonwealth Constitution." In *The Convention Debates 1891–1898: Commentaries, Indices and Guide*, edited by Gregory Craven, 149–72. Sydney, AU: Legal Books.
Schnabel, Johanna, and Paolo Dardanelli. 2022. "Helping Hand or Centralizing Tool? The Politics of Conditional Grants in Australia, Canada, and the United States." *Governance*, 1–21. https://doi.org/10.1111/gove.12708.
Schnabel, Johanna, and Sean Mueller. 2017. "Vertical Influence or Horizontal Coordination? The Purpose of Intergovernmental Councils in Switzerland." *Regional & Federal Studies* 27, no. 5: 549–72. https://doi.org/10.1080/13597566.2017.1368017.
Shah, Anwar. 2007a. "Introduction: Principles of Fiscal Federalism." In *The Practice of Fiscal Federalism: Comparative Perspectives*, edited by Anwar Shah, 3–42. Montreal and Kingston: McGill-Queen's University Press.
– 2007b. "A Practitioner's Guide to Intergovernmental Fiscal Transfers." In *Intergovernmental Fiscal Transfers: Principles and Practice*, edited by Robin Boadway and Anwar Shah, 1–53. Washington, DC: World Bank.
– 2017. *Horizontal Fiscal Equalization in Australia: Peering Inside the Black Box*. Sydney, AU: NSW Government. https://www.pc.gov.au/__data/assets/pdf_file/0007/223495/subdr103-horizontal-fiscal-equalisation.pdf.
Silver, A.I. 1997. *The French-Canadian Idea of Confederation, 1864–1900*. Toronto: University of Toronto Press.

Spahn, Paul Bernd. 2020. "The German Model of Addressing Vertical and Horizontal Fiscal Imbalances." In *Intergovernmental Transfers in Federations*, edited by Serdar Yilmaz and Farah Zahir, 64–85. Cheltenham, UK: Edward Elgar.

Telford, Hamish. 2003. "The Federal Spending Power in Canada: Nation-Building or Nation-Destroying?" *Publius: The Journal of Federalism* 33, no. 1: 23–44. https://doi.org/10.1093/oxfordjournals.pubjof.a004976.

Telford, Hamish, Peter Graefe, and Keith Banting, eds. 2008. *Defining the Federal Government's Role in Social Policy: The Spending Power and Other Instruments*. Montreal: Institute for Research on Public Policy.

Tombe, Trevor. 2018. "'Final and Unalterable' – But Up For Negotiation: Federal–Provincial Transfers in Canada." *Canadian Tax Journal* 66, no. 4: 871–917. https://financesofthenation.ca/2018/03/01/final-and-unalterable-up-for-negotiation-federal-provincial-transfers-in-canada/.

Treasury, Department of the. 2018. *Budget Paper No. 3: Federal Financial Relations*. Canberra: Commonwealth of Australia.

– 2022. *Budget Paper No. 3: Federal Financial Relations*. Canberra: Commonwealth of Australia.

Trudeau, Pierre Elliott. 1969. *Federal–Provincial Grants and the Spending Power of Parliament*. Ottawa: Government of Canada.

Turgeon, Luc, and Richard Simeon. 2015. "Ideology, Political Economy and Federalism: The Welfare State and the Evolution of the Australian and Canadian Federations." In *Understanding Federalism and Federation*, edited by Alain-G. Gagnon, Soeren Keil, and Sean Mueller, 125–42. Abingdon, UK: Ashgate.

Turgeon, Luc, and Jennifer Wallner. 2013. "Adaptability and Change in Federations: Centralization, Political Parties, and Taxation Authority in Australia and Canada." In *The Global Promise of Federalism*, edited by Grace Skogstad, David Cameron, Martin Papillon, and Keith Banting, 188–213. Toronto: University of Toronto Press.

Watts, Ronald L. 2000. "Federal Financial Relations: A Comparative Perspective." In *Canada: The State of the Federation 1999–2000 – Towards a New Mission Statement for Canadian Fiscal Federalism*, edited by Harvey Lazar, 371–88. Montreal and Kingston: McGill-Queen's University Press.

Whitlam, E.G. 1977. "Socialism within the Australian Constitution." In *On Australia's Constitution*, edited by E.G. Whitlam, 47–71. Camberwell, AU: Widescope.

23 Pressures, Challenges, and Policy Recommendations: Improving Fiscal Federalism in Canada

ANDRÉ LECOURS, DANIEL BÉLAND, TREVOR TOMBE, AND ERIC CHAMPAGNE

Canada is one of the most decentralized federal systems in world, and fiscal federalism is a crucial aspect of public policy across the country, especially because other levels of government rely on federal transfers to provide benefits and services to their population. This situation is partly why fiscal federalism is central to so many key policy areas in Canada. To a certain extent, fiscal federalism lies at the foundation of such policy areas. Yet, citizens do not necessarily understand the fiscal mechanisms at hand, as fiscal federalism in a multinational and territorially diverse country like Canada is necessarily complex. Not only does it raise questions of efficiency and performance, but it also involves issues of legitimacy, equity, solidarity, recognition, and even, in the context of the financing of First Nations and the territories, decolonization. In that sense, the study of Canadian fiscal federalism is subject to the same types of big questions permeating the literature on Canadian federalism more broadly (Gagnon 2006; Bakvis and Skogstad 2020). For this reason, we brought together a diverse group of authors hailing from all regions of the country and various academic disciplines to analyse, evaluate, and, when appropriate, make some recommendations about fiscal federalism in Canada. In this short conclusion, we sum up the volume's contributions, discuss coming pressures upon and challenges for fiscal arrangements in Canada, and put forth some recommendations for potential reforms.

Contributions

Across its twenty-three chapters, this volume encompasses insight from some of the best specialists of fiscal federalism in the country from several different fields of knowledge: economics, political science, history, law, and public administration. It collectively unpacks numerous complexities of fiscal federalism in Canada and – never fully displayed until now –features key regional and provincial perspectives while taking into consideration Indigenous realities and municipal affairs. It offers both depth and scope, digging deep into the workings of fiscal federalism but at the same time going beyond the major transfers to examine the financing of education, cities, infrastructure, housing, and more. Together, this volume makes several original contributions to the study of fiscal federalism in Canada.

First, the volume shows that fiscal federalism is much more than simply an aggregate of individual programs and transfers. Not only are the major transfers interconnected in the context of a larger system (Béland et al. 2017), which also includes funding for more targeted policy areas, but also all this activity occurs in the context of a bigger picture featuring a diversity of actors and regional political perspectives. A multidisciplinary approach reveals these rich interdependencies throughout the volume. Health transfers, for example, are examined in detail through a fiscal lens in one chapter and through a regional equity lens in another. The broad approach of this volume also sheds new light on the wide-ranging implications of the COVID-19 pandemic in the Canadian federation.

A second contribution of the volume is to highlight the role of actors other than the federal and provincial governments in fiscal federalism. Indigenous and municipal governments are critical participants in Canada's federal system and are increasingly central to policy making. These "other" actors are an integral part of the full picture of fiscal federalism in the country. Several chapters detail fiscal relations involving municipal governments and present new data and fresh perspectives on the challenges they face. Moreover, an analysis of the ongoing renewal of fiscal arrangements between First Nations and the federal and provincial governments is a particularly original and important part of this volume.

A third contribution is to recall the importance of territoriality. Canada has always been a diverse federation, which is a central challenge when designing fiscal arrangements and managing intergovernmental relations. The views on fiscal federalism in Western Canada, Ontario, Quebec, and Atlantic Canada are quite different, as are the ways they are influenced by the broader politics and history of Canadian federalism. This diversity goes beyond differences in perception. As argued below, the future challenges faced by different regions will be markedly different. Energy transitions may disproportionately affect oil-producing provinces while aging populations disproportionately affect Atlantic provinces. The various regional perspectives on Canadian fiscal federalism are reminders that, while it has important economic, legal, and governance components (all of which are explored in this volume), it is also inseparable from politics.

Attention paid in this volume to the political dimension of fiscal federalism represents a fourth contribution. As suggested above, fiscal federalism is at the heart of the functioning of the Canadian federation in terms of funding programs through transfers, but it also indirectly provides status, or standing, and therefore has significant symbolic value (like all parts of the multinational state; Basta 2021). Hence, this volume contributes to the so-called second-generation fiscal federalism literature, even pushing its boundaries by fully incorporating its sociological and political basis into the analysis.

We hope these contributions help shape the way academics and practitioners think about Canadian fiscal federalism. Multidisciplinary thinking about fiscal federalism in Canada is particularly crucial, as mounting pressures will require thoughtful reform to current arrangements in a new social, political, and economic context of the post-pandemic. We now turn to a brief discussion of critical challenges to fiscal federalism in Canada before presenting some potential recommendations for policy reform going forward.

Pressures and Challenges

Ensuring that Canada's fiscal federalism responds well to ever-evolving economic, social, political, and fiscal pressures has always been a central challenge for policy makers. As circumstances change, so too must Canada's institutional environmental and intergovernmental relations. This process is often slow and difficult, but necessary reforms have historically led to the resilient policies in place today. Yet, several new sources of pressure – each of which may gradually grow in scale over the coming years and decades – demand a renewed effort towards examining potential reforms. A rapidly aging population, climate change, energy transitions, labour market disruptions, reconciliation with Indigenous peoples, the growing importance of municipalities (especially large cities), as well as rising regional political animosities, all challenge current fiscal federalism arrangements. Understanding these pressures, and how they interact with each other and with current policies, is necessary for implementing beneficial reforms in the years to come.

Many of these pressures are fiscal and economic in nature. As more individuals reach retirement age, for example, economic growth rates may slow while public expenditures on health care rise. Both effects are potentially large. Based on recent projections from Statistics Canada, these demographic pressures may subtract 0.3 percentage points off economic growth as a larger fraction of the population withdraws from the labour market. Accelerated population aging may also accelerate government expenditure growth in health care by approximately 1 per cent per year (Tombe 2020). Sustained over decades, these pressures represent a larger fiscal and economic shock than what resulted from the COVID-19 pandemic. Its slow-moving nature, however, makes this issue far less salient to most individuals and, therefore, creates an incentive for governments to delay action. However, action, at some point, may be unavoidable. Several chapters in this volume explore these issues and propose potential reforms, including changes that range from adjusting fiscal transfer programs to altering the distribution of expenditure responsibilities across orders of government. The importance of this analysis, and additional work that builds upon it, will only increase in the coming years.

Adding to these gradual but mounting pressures will be challenges that result from climate change, emissions reduction policies, and the coming energy transitions. Action on climate in Canada and around the world will alter the nature of economic activity in several sectors and regions. Oil- and gas-producing parts of the country are potentially the most visibly exposed, but changes throughout the economy may be inevitable. Technological developments in the manufacture of electric vehicle production, for example, are already a priority for several provincial governments. In addition, beyond economic adjustments, many regions will be directly exposed to adverse environmental damages and costs that result from climate change, as recent fires and flooding in British Columbia demonstrate.

Canada has committed, under successive governments, to help lower global emissions. Nevertheless, policies to achieve this goal in Canada are subject to a uniquely complex intergovernmental coordination problem. Multiple levels of government play a role, and the wide regional differences in emissions profiles and energy systems add to the complexity. Adjustments for several sectors will be difficult, and ensuring workers are not left behind is a key policy challenge. This issue touches upon several aspects of fiscal federalism discussed in this volume, including fiscal transfers, infrastructure programs, and the financing of education.

There are also challenges to fiscal federalism in Canada that go beyond fiscal and economic issues but directly affect intergovernmental political dynamics. A particularly deep-rooted source of pressure on Canadian fiscal federalism is the contemporary feeling of Western alienation. Centred in Alberta and, to a slightly lesser degree, Saskatchewan, this feeling is anchored in the belief that "the West" is marginalized within the federation. The contemporary politics of Western alienation have been such that equalization has become a vehicle for the Alberta and Saskatchewan governments to express frustration for what they see as the unwillingness of the federal government and of some provincial governments, like British Columbia and Quebec, to support the development of oil pipelines. The 2021 Alberta referendum on equalization reflected this frustration. It does not appear that the referendum will have significant direct consequences on Canadian fiscal federalism, despite 61.7 per cent of Alberta voters saying "yes" to a question asking if the federal government's commitment to making equalization payments should be removed from the Constitution. Regardless, what exact changes the Alberta government wished would be made to equalization was always unclear. In fact, Premier Jason Kenney had explicitly said he was not looking (despite the referendum question) to have the equalization principle taken out of the Constitution. For his United Conservative Party, equalization was instead a symbol of the perceived unfairness of Canadian federalism. Broader reforms to Canadian federalism (for example, to the Senate) are more likely to address these feelings than any adjustment to the equalization formula.

We hope that this volume will not only help increase awareness of these pressures but will also offer potentially productive ways forward. For instance, several contributors propose similar potential reforms, despite addressing different challenges. We now turn to those.

Recommendations

One idea for reform to the governance of fiscal federalism in Canada that comes up in more than one chapter is the creation of an arm's-length fiscal federal commission. This idea has been considered (and rejected) by policy makers in the past, and it has resurfaced over the last decade or so (Béland and Lecours 2012). The general idea behind arm's-length governance on equalization, which is inspired by Australia's Commonwealth Grants Commission, is that it could serve to partly depoliticize, or at least reduce the *perceptions* of politicization of, decision-making on the program (Béland and Lecours 2011). Of course, such perceptions have been particularly acute in the context of contemporary criticism of equalization from the Alberta and Saskatchewan governments.

In addition to making recommendations on equalization payments, such a commission could also be leveraged to make recommendations on other dimensions of fiscal federalism in Canada, including CHT and CST transfers as well as issues of deficit and debt. Yet, convincing the federal government to introduce a new actor into policy making on fiscal arrangements and issues remains a challenge because, in the context of a decentralized federal system, the tools available to this government for regulating the affairs of the federation are relatively few (and equalization is certainly one such tool). Moreover, although provincial approval is not constitutionally necessary to make a change to the governance of equalization, or of fiscal federalism more broadly, implementing this type of major reform to the administration of crucial elements of Canadian fiscal federalism against the wishes of most provinces would represent a significant political challenge for the federal government. In addition, provincial governments have historically preferred to have the federal government rather than an arm's-length commission oversee equalization, as they felt they could better exercise political leverage with elected federal politicians than with technocrats operating at arm's length (Béland and Lecours, 2012).

Several chapters in this volume also highlight the potential value in thinking more about measures of expenditure need in the design of future fiscal arrangements. To be sure, this idea is not a new concept in Canadian fiscal federalism, and it comes with many unique challenges. From its earlier days of cost-sharing arrangements, Canada has gradually moved away from conditionality in its transfers, leaving provincial governments with much autonomy. In addition, except for equalization, transfers are now more structurally equal across provinces on a per capita basis than at any point in Canada's recent history. There are strong merits to this state of affairs, but recognizing and more fully addressing the sometimes-large horizontal imbalances among provinces may become increasingly important in the coming years. Population demographics, including the potentially large differences across provinces in average age, will be a particularly significant challenge to overcome, as a few chapters specifically note. The issue of expenditure needs goes beyond health expenditures. Recent childcare agreements, for example, are allocated based on a particular measure of need. Needs also seem relevant when it comes to public infrastructures and social housing.

Another issue that stands out in this book is the role of municipalities and large cities in the Canadian intergovernmental fiscal dynamics. Although the role of municipalities has never been very well defined in the constitutional framework, their responsibilities have increased considerably. In addition to their traditional responsibilities (parks, parking, libraries, roadways, public transportation, community waterways, sewers, garbage collection, local land use, and police and fire services), municipalities have seen a multitude of new socioeconomic issues fall into their laps (for example, poverty, homelessness, housing, and climate change). For this reason, many authors suggest that municipalities should be part of the fiscal imbalance debate in the future.

Canada will face important economic, environmental, and political pressures that will significantly affect fiscal federalism in the years and decades ahead. Whatever specific reforms are ultimately considered to address these pressures, changes will be – as they have always been as circumstances evolve – necessary. The present volume should facilitate thinking about Canadian fiscal federalism in innovative ways, and hopefully it serves as a useful reference for scholars, policy makers, elected representatives, and many other actors interested in the future of fiscal federalism in Canada.

REFERENCES

Bakvis, Herman, and Grace Skogstad, eds. 2020. *Canadian Federalism: Performance, Effectiveness, and Legitimacy.* Toronto: University of Toronto Press.

Basta, Karlo. 2021. *The Symbolic State: Minority Recognition, Majority Backlash, and Secession in Multinational Countries.* Montreal and Kingston: McGill-Queen's University Press.

Béland, Daniel, and André Lecours. 2011. "The Ideational Dimension of Federalism: The 'Australian Model' and the Politics of Equalization in Canada." *Australian Journal of Political Science* 46, no. 2: 199–212. https://doi.org/10.1080/10361146.2011.567974.

– 2012. "Equalizing at Arm's-Length." Mowat Publication 48. Toronto: Mowat Centre. https://hdl.handle.net/1807/99225.

Béland, Daniel, André Lecours, Gregory Marchildon, Haizhen Mou, and M. Rose Olfert. 2017. *Fiscal Federalism and Equalization Policy in Canada: Political and Economic Dimensions*. Toronto: University of Toronto Press.

Gagnon, Alain-G., ed. 2006. *Le fédéralisme canadien contemporain*. Montreal: Presses de l'Université de Montréal.

Tombe, Trevor. 2020. "Provincial Debt Sustainability in Canada: Demographics, Federal Transfers, and COVID-19." *Canadian Tax Journal* 68, no. 4: 1083–122. https://doi.org/10.32721/ctj.2020.68.4.fon.

Contributors

Daniel Béland is the director of the McGill Institute for the Study of Canada and James McGill Professor in the Department of Political Science at McGill University. A student of fiscal federalism and comparative social policy, he has published more than 20 scholarly books and 175 articles in peer-reviewed journals.

Robin Boadway is an emeritus professor of economics at Queen's University. He is an Officer of the Order of Canada, Fellow of the Royal Society of Canada, Fellow of the Canadian Economics Association, and Distinguished CES Fellow at the University of Munich. He is past-president of the Canadian Economics Association and of the International Institute of Public Finance, and former editor of the *Canadian Journal of Economics* and the *Journal of Public Economics*.

Ken Boessenkool is one of Canada's leading policy strategists. He was J. W. McConnell Professor of Practice at the Max Bell School of Public Policy at McGill University and is Research Fellow at the C.D. Howe Institute. Ken Boessenkool has been front and centre in Canadian politics for almost three decades. He has worked for and founded a variety of public affairs firms, played senior roles in provincial governments, and was the architect of political campaigns nationally and in British Columbia, Alberta, and Ontario.

Anthony Breton holds a bachelor of law from the Faculty of Law of the Université de Montréal (2019) and a master's degree in public policy and public administration from Concordia University (2022). He is a member of the Quebec Bar (2023). In 2023–4, Anthony Breton will join the chamber of the Honourable Justice O'Bonsawin at the Supreme Court of Canada.

Eric Champagne is an associate professor in public administration at the School of Political Studies and director of the Centre on Governance at the

University of Ottawa. His research focuses on multilevel governance, particularly the role of municipalities and large cities in the financing and implementation of transportation, infrastructure, and public health policies, and on the digital transformation of the public sector. In 2020, he won the Pierre De Celles Award for Excellence in Teaching Public Administration presented jointly by the Institute of Public Administration of Canada (IPAC) and the Canadian Association of Programs in Public Administration (CAPPA).

James (Jim) Feehan is an honorary research professor at Memorial University of Newfoundland, having been a faculty member there for thirty-five years. He has been a visiting professor at the University of Western Ontario, Carleton University's School of International Affairs, and the National University-Mohyla Academy (now the Kyiv School of Economics). James Feehan served in various capacities on the boards of the *Canadian Journal of Economics*, Canada's National Statistics Council, and the Canadian Economics Association. His main areas of research and publication include Canadian fiscal federalism, taxation policy, public investment, and electricity economics.

Donn. L. Feir is an associate professor in the Department of Economics at the University of Victoria. An economist and economic historian who has published on reconciliation, modern Indigenous labour market experiences, health, and the impact of historical policies on Indigenous economies and people, Donn. Feir is also a research fellow at the IZA Institute of Labor Economics and has worked as a research economist for the Center for Indian Country Development at the Federal Reserve Bank of Minneapolis. Donn. Feir received their PhD from the Vancouver School of Economics at the University of British Columbia.

Alan Fenna is a professor of politics at The John Curtin Institute of Public Policy, Curtin University, Western Australia, and writes on Australian public policy, federalism, and constitutionalism, as well as on comparative federalism. He is the co-author or co-editor of *The Constitution of Western Australia: An Exploration* (Springer, 2023); *Climate Governance and Federalism: A Forum of Federations Comparative Policy Analysis* (Cambridge University Press, 2023); *Australian Government and Politics* (Pearson, 2021); *Interrogating Public Policy Theory: A Political Values Perspective* (Elgar, 2019); and *Comparative Federalism: A Systematic Inquiry* (University of Toronto Press, 2015). He served as president of the Australian Political Studies Association 2009–10.

Aracelly Denise Granja is a doctoral researcher at the University of Ottawa. Her research focuses on the criminalization of human rights defenders and civil society in Honduras and Nicaragua. Her research work at the Centre on

Governance focuses on investments in public infrastructure in Canada as well as on the impact of the COVID-19 pandemic on university governance and public policy transformations. She completed her undergraduate work at York University, Glendon Campus, where she obtained a trilingual international bachelor of arts degree in political science. She completed her master's degree in public and international affairs at the University of Ottawa.

Kyle Hanniman is an assistant professor of political studies at Queen's University as well as a fellow and the former associate director of the Institute of Intergovernmental Relations. He studies fiscal federalism and political economy, with a focus on government bond markets, subnational finance, inter-regional risk sharing and redistribution, and the politics of central banking. His work has appeared in the *Canadian Journal of Political Science*, the *British Journal of Political Science*, as well as in edited volumes and popular outlets, including the *Financial Post* and the *Globe and Mail*. His current book project is entitled *Booms, Busts and Bailouts: Fiscal Federalism and the Limits of Market Discipline*.

Mary Janigan is a former journalist who is now a historian. Her first book, *Let the Eastern Bastards Freeze in the Dark: The West versus the Rest since Confederation*, won the J.W. Dafoe Book prize in 2013 and was a finalist for the Donner Book Prize. Her most recent book, *The Art of Sharing: The Richer versus the Poorer Provinces since Confederation* is a history of equalization.

Marcelin Joanis is a full professor of economics at Polytechnique Montréal. He is also the principal researcher in public finance at the Center for Interuniversity Research and Analysis on Organizations (CIRANO) and an honorary professor at the Université de Lille, France. His research focuses on the political economy of public finance and fiscal federalism. He regularly acts as an external expert to the World Bank and Quebec's Auditor General, and he was previously an economist with Finance Canada and with Quebec's Commission on Fiscal Imbalance (2001–2). He has published in such scholarly outlets as the *Journal of Development Economics, Fiscal Studies, Public Choice, Economics of Governance, Public Finance Review, Economics and Politics, Applied Economics*, and *Energy Policy*.

André Lecours is a professor in the School of Political Studies at the University of Ottawa, past-president of the Canadian Political Science Association, and fellow of the Royal Society of Canada. His main research interests are nationalism and federalism. He is the co-author (with Daniel Béland) of *Nationalism and Social Policy. The Politics of Territorial Solidarity* (Oxford University Press, 2008); the co-author (with Daniel Béland, Gregory Marchildon,

Haizhen Mou, and Rose Olfert) of *Fiscal Federalism and Equalization Policy in Canada: Political and Economic Dimensions* (University of Toronto Press, 2017); and the author of *Nationalism, Secessionism, and Autonomy* (Oxford University Press, 2021).

Patrik Marier is a professor of political science at Concordia University and the scientific director of the Centre for Research and Expertise in Social Gerontology (CREGÉS) of the Centre intégré universitaire de santé et de services sociaux du Centre-Ouest-de-l'Île-de-Montréal. His research focuses on the impact of aging populations on a number of public policy fields including pensions, labour, and social services and programs across comparative cases. He has published in leading international journals such as the *American Journal of Political Science, Governance, Policy Sciences,* and the *Journal of European Public Policy*. His recent book, *The Four Lenses of Population Aging: Planning for the Future in Canada's Provinces* (University of Toronto Press), explores the multiple challenges of planning for an aging population.

Alain Noël is a professor of political science at the Université de Montréal. He works on social policy in a comparative perspective, as well as on federalism and on Quebec and Canadian politics. His latest book is entitled *Utopies provisoires: Essais de politique sociale* (Québec Amérique, 2019). He is also the author, with Jean-Philippe Thérien, of *Left and Right in Global Politics* (Cambridge University Press, 2008). In 2001–2, he was a member of Quebec's Commission on Fiscal Imbalance.

Peter C. Oliver is a member of the Centre de droit public uOttawa Public Law Centre and a full professor in the civil law section, Faculty of Law, University of Ottawa. He is the author of *The Constitution of Independence: The Development of Constitutional Theory in Australia, Canada and New Zealand* (Oxford University Press, 2005) and editor (with Patrick Macklem and Nathalie Des Rosiers) of *The Oxford Handbook of the Canadian Constitution* (Oxford University Press, 2017).

Steve Pomeroy is an Ottawa-based housing research consultant and part-time lecturer at Carleton and McMaster. Widely recognized as one of the leading housing policy experts and thought leaders in Canada, Steve Pomeroy has almost forty years of experience in the housing sector, working at the municipal and federal governments, in non-profit development, and since 1994, as a consultant and part-time academic. Since 1994, he has authored over 230 research reports and papers.

Michael J. Prince is Lansdowne Professor of Social Policy in the Faculty of Human and Social Development at the University of Victoria. He is also an adjunct faculty member in the Department of Political Science in the Faculty of Social Sciences. He has been an advisor to various federal, provincial, territorial, and municipal government agencies; four royal commissions; and parliamentary committees both federally and provincially. In studying intergovernmental relations, Michael Prince has theorized notions of actuarial federalism, deliberative federalism, provincial spending power, and sociopolitical province-building, and, for Indigenous peoples and their political organizations, the hide-and-seek politics of federalism.

Jennifer Robson is an associate professor and program director of the Graduate Program in Political Management at Carleton University. She has previously published policy-relevant research and analysis on parental leave, early learning and childcare, income assistance, tax policy and administration, household finances, and public budgeting. She has worked in government and in the voluntary sector before joining Carleton University. She is a fellow of the Public Policy Forum, a research advisor to the Institute for Research on Public Policy, and a member of the Royal Society of Canada's Task Force on COVID-19.

Richard Saillant is a Moncton-based public policy consultant, university lecturer, and newspaper columnist. He has spent two decades in government and academic circles, notably as vice-president at l'Université de Moncton and director of the Donald J. Savoie Institute. He has written or edited four books, including *A Tale of Two Countries: How the Great Demographic Imbalance Is Pulling Canada Apart* (Nimbus, 2016). Richard holds a BA in economics and political science from l'Université de Moncton, a masters' degree in economics from l'Université de Montréal, an MBA from McGill University, and has pursued doctoral studies in political science at Dalhousie University.

David Scoones is an associate professor of economics at the University of Victoria. He has published research in labour economics, public finance, and political economy. His work has appeared in the *Journal of Public Economics*, the *Journal of Public Economic Theory*, *Social Choice and Welfare*, *Public Choice*, and the *American Economic Review*.

Enid Slack is the director of the Institute on Municipal Finance and Governance (IMFG) at the School of Cities at the University of Toronto. Enid Slack has written several books and articles on property taxes, intergovernmental transfers, municipal restructuring, and municipal infrastructure finance. Recent co-edited books include *Funding the Canadian City, Financing Infrastructure:*

Who Should Pay? and *Is Your City Healthy? Measuring Urban Fiscal Health*. In 2012, Enid Slack was awarded the Queen's Diamond Jubilee Medal for her work on cities.

Tracy Snoddon is an associate professor of economics at Wilfrid Laurier University who specializes in public policy issues in federal settings. Her recent research focuses on fiscal federalism challenges relating to carbon pricing and equalization, and has been published in various outlets including *Canadian Tax Journal*, *Canadian Public Policy*, the C.D. Howe Institute, and *Policy Options*. She, along with co-author Trevor Tombe, was awarded the Vanderkamp Prize for the best article in *Canadian Public Policy* in 2019. In 2023, Tracy Snoddon was the recipient of the Donald F. Morgenson Faculty Award for Sustained Teaching Excellence at Laurier.

Trevor Tombe is a professor of economics at the University of Calgary and a research fellow at the School of Public Policy. He received his PhD in economics from the University of Toronto in 2011, and his research focuses on international and internal trade, public finances, and fiscal federalism. He has published in top economics journals, such as the *American Economic Review*, *Journal of Monetary Economics*, and the *Canadian Journal of Economics*, and he is the co-author of the forthcoming textbook *Public Finance in Canada*. He is also co-director of *Finances of the Nation*. He has served on several editorial boards, and he advises various governments on issues related to internal trade, public finance, carbon pricing, and more.

Jennifer Wallner is an associate professor with the School of Political Studies at the University of Ottawa and holder of the Jean-Luc Pepin Research Chair in Canadian Politics. Author of *Learning to School: Federalism and Public Schooling in Canada* (University of Toronto Press, 2014), she works on a range of policy issues within the context of federal states, including education policy, fiscal federalism, and intergovernmental relations.

Christopher Yurris graduated from St. Francis Xavier University in 2021 with a degree in political science. He is a political science masters' student at McGill University, focusing on Northern Canadian politics. Christopher was born and raised in Yellowknife, Northwest Territories. He has previous experience on Northern issues working for the government of the Northwest Territories and for the federal government.

Index

Page numbers with *t* indicate tables; page numbers with *f* indicate figures.

Aboriginal and Northern Affairs Canada, 227–8
Accreditation Canada (AC), 241, 242–3*t*, 245*t*, 249–50, 252, 254, 258–9
Adam, Marc-Antoine, 462
Advisory Committee on Reconstruction, 303n3
Affordable Child Care Benefit, 352
affordable housing. *See* housing
Akbari, Emis, 352
Alberta, 438–50; aging population compared to median, 377*t*; Alberta Agenda, 440–1, 446; Alberta First Party, 440; Alberta Investment Management Corporation (AIMCo), 448; Alberta Pension Plan, 441–4, 447–9; Alberta Police Force, 442–4, 449; Calgary, 277n6, 449; and CAP, 119, 418; and CERB, 124; Confederation, 33; default on bonds, 39; Edmonton, 265, 277n6, 335; and education, 329, 330, 334; and ELCC, 347, 351*t*, 352, 353*t*, 366; and equalization, 169, 192, 196, 417–18, 426–8, 444–5, 469n20, 479; Fair Deal Panel, 440, 442, 443–9; Firewall Letter, 440–2; fiscal stabilization payments, 168–9; Heritage Savings Trust Fund, 172n1; and housing funding, 291; lot levies/development charges, 268; natural resources, 156–7, 210n7, 419*f*; oil and gas industry, 161, 210n7, 417, 419*f*, 440, 464; opting out of shared-cost programs, 445–6; political history of, 438–42; referendums, 30, 45n2, 192, 443–5, 479; residential electricity rates, 166*t*; stabilization payments, 86–7; and taxes, 273, 443–4, 446, 447; Viewpoint Alberta, 439–40; Western alienation, 439, 479
Alcantara, Christopher, 194, 207
Aragón, Fernando, 221
Armstrong, Pat, 254
Assembly of First Nations, 227–8
Atkin, Lord, 62
Atkinson Centre (OISE), Toronto, ON, 346
Atlantic provinces, 375–94; aging population/great demographic imbalance, 376–8, 391, 424; Atlantic Accord, 172n3, 390–1; equalization payments, 445; fiscal sustainability, 380–3; future of, 383–7; and GDP, 379*t*, 381*t*; policy options, 387–91; population percentage in Canada, 390. *See also* Maritime provinces; Newfoundland and Labrador

490   Index

Aurora College, NWT, 338n1
Australia: about, 4, 453; Australian Loan Council, 38; *Chaplains* case in High Court, 56; Commonwealth Grants Commission, 43, 107, 171, 186, 460, 463, 465, 480; and COVID-19, 469n24; and deficit reduction, 463; and equalization, 388, 460–1, 464–5, 468n18; federal transfers, 456; GST (goods and services tax) in, 186, 456; and income taxes, 455; medicare and public health insurance system, 457; revenue modes and sharing, 454–5; and spending power, 457–8, 462

Bahl, Roy, 278n21
Ball, Dwight, 383
band census-subdivision (CSD), 225, 232n25, 232n27
Banerjee, Albert, 254
Bank of Canada, 84, 87–8
Banting, Keith, 284
Bégin, Monique, 67, 69
Béland, Daniel: chapter by, 3–28, 192–214; cited, 90, 171, 186, 196, 401, 462–5, 467
Bennett, R.B., 36, 37
Benz, Arthur, 461, 463
Bergeron, Étienne, 424
bilateral agreements: about, 99, 172n9; and ELCC, 342–4, 348, 352, 354t, 357–60, 363–6, 367n2; and housing, 291–6, 298; and infrastructure, 309, 442
Bird, Richard M., 278n21, 467n5
Blake, Edward, 53
Blanchard, Olivier, 178
blind persons, 116, 117
block funding, 108, 114, 120–1, 125–7, 402–3, 417. *See also* Canada Health and Social Transfer (CHST); Canada Social Transfer (CST); Established Programs Financing (EPF)

Boadway, Robin: chapter by, 93–111; cited, 121, 135, 158, 169–70, 425–7, 451–2, 457–9
Boessenkool, Ken: about, 449n1; chapter by, 438–50; cited, 310
Boychuk, Gerard W., 9
Boyer, Marcel, 168
Bradford, Neil, 265, 266
Brady, Alexander, 466
Breton, Anthony: chapter by, 237–62; cited, 271
Britain. *See* United Kingdom
British Columbia: Affordable Child Care Benefit, 352; aging population, 377t; and CAP, 119, 418; and CERB, 124; Confederation, 33; *Delgamuukw v. British Columbia*, 220; and education, 330, 335, 336, 337; and ELCC, 257, 347, 351t, 352–3, 353t, 365; *Haida Nation v. British Columbia*, 220; and housing, 288, 290, 291, 302; and long-term care, 238–9, 241, 242–3t, 245, 245t, 247–9, 257; lot levies/development charges, 268; and municipalities, 268; and natural resources, 156; NHCF project, 300–1; residential electricity rates, 166t; Seventh General Assembly of the Union of BC Indian Chiefs, 221–2; stabilization payments, 86–7; *Tsilhqot'in Nation v. British Columbia*, 220; Vancouver, 265, 277n6
British North America Act, 155, 467n6
Budget 2022, 78, 87, 285, 299
Building Canada Plan/Building Canada Fund, 319–20, 422
Burns, R.M., 40, 43
Burwell, Mahlon, 335

Cairns, Robert D., 172n5
Calgary, AB, 277n6, 449
Cameron, Kirk, 194, 195, 343
Campbell, Alastair, 195, 207–8

Index 491

Canada Assistance Plan (CAP): about/history, 30, 94, 114, 117–20, 417–18; cap on, 425–6; federal share of costs and Supreme Court, 65; as part of federal transfers, 416*f*; and Winterhaven Stables, 62
Canada Caregiver Credit, 123
Canada Child Benefit (CCB), 123, 128
Canada Community-Building Fund (CCBF, was Gas Tax Fund, now IICP): about, 317–20; as equal per capita transfer, 96, 98; fiscal transfer to municipalities, 318*t*; Gas Tax Fund, 109n7, 277n5, 313, 390, 422*f*; and infrastructure, 96, 101, 172n9, 265, 313, 317–19, 318*t*, 422; Investing in Canada Plan (IICP), 309, 318*t*, 319–20, 422, 422*f*; as model, 107–8; and vertical balance, 100
Canada Economic Action Plan (CEAP), 294
Canada Education Savings Grant (CESG), 330
Canada Emergency Response Benefit (CERB), 123–4
Canada Free Trade Agreement, 99
Canada Health Act (CHA): about, 12, 44, 66–9, 94–5, 403, 457; and Alberta Agenda, 446; constitutionality of, 65; and long-term care, 238; as model for federal transfers, 345; and Winterhaven Stables, 62
Canada Health and Social Transfer (CHST): about, 114, 120–2, 125, 415*f*, 416*f*, 418, 432; beginnings of, 94, 120, 404–5, 432; Prince Edward Island finance minister on, 137. *See also* Canada Health Transfer (CHT); Canada Social Transfer (CST)
Canada Health Transfer (CHT), 93–111; about, 5, 12, 66–7, 93–7, 122, 387; allocation formula, 389–90; as block grant, 5, 107–8, 418, 457; compared to other transfers, 79, 96, 159, 160*t*, 422*f*, 427; Council of the Federation on, 97, 104, 398–9; and debt, 415*t*; deductions from, 367n11; and federal-provincial fiscal relations, 97–9; and GDP, 89; and growth, 416*f*; to Prince Edward Island, 382; provincial requests for increase, 4, 181, 375, 398; reform options, 103–8; roles of, 99–103; to territories, 209n3; and vertical fiscal imbalance (VFI), 100, 103, 104–5, 414
Canada Housing Benefit (CHB), 298, 300
Canada Infrastructure Bank (CIB, was Public-Private Partnerships [PPP] Canada), 318*t*, 320–1
Canada Infrastructure Works Program, 312–13
Canada-Ontario Memorandum of Agreement Respecting Welfare Programs for Indians (1965), 116
Canada Pension Plan (CPP), 113, 350, 441, 447–9
Canada Recovery Benefits, 124
Canada Revenue Agency (CRA), 99
Canada Social Transfer (CST), 112–31; about, 94–6, 114, 122–4, 159–60, 418, 457; compared to other transfers, 98, 422*f*; conditions for, 108; and ELCC, 348, 357, 364; policy issues, 124–6; policy recommendations, 127–8; and post-secondary education funding, 329–30; to Prince Edward Island, 382; and vertical fiscal imbalance (VFI), 414. *See also* social assistance
Canada Workers Benefit (CWB), 122–3
Canada-Yukon Oil and Gas Accord Implementation Act, 207
Canadian Income Survey (Statistics Canada), 351
Canadian Institute for Health Information (CIHI), 90, 203

Canadian Institutes of Health Research (CIHR), 330
Canadian Mortgage and Housing Corporation (CMHC), 285, 286, 289–90, 291, 295–6, 299, 302
Canadian School Trustees' Association, 336
Canadian Standards Association, 238
Canadian Tax Journal, 140
CAP. *See* Canada Assistance Plan (CAP)
Carroll, Barbara, 302
Carter, George, 426, 435n16
CCBF. *See* Canada Community-Building Fund (CCBF)
C.D. Howe Institute, 134
census, 90n1, 204, 225–6
Centre for Canadian Policy Alternatives, 328
centres de la petite enfance (CPEs), 357
CERB. *See* Canada Emergency Response Benefit (CERB)
Champagne, Eric: chapter by, 3–28, 306–25; cited, 312
Charest, Jean, 408
Charlottetown Accord, 290, 292, 462
Charter of Rights and Freedoms, 334
Chevrette, François, 55
child care: Affordable Child Care Benefit, 352; Canada Child Benefit (CCB), 123, 128; centres de la petite enfance (CPEs), 357; childcare expenses deduction (CCED), 348, 349*f*, 350, 357, 364; Child Care Now, 343; Childcare Resource and Research Unit, Child Care Canada, 346; National Child Benefit, 123. *See also* early learning and childcare (ELCC)
Chrétien government, 291, 312–13, 390, 440
CHT. *See* Canada Health Transfer (CHT)
cities/municipalities, 263–83; about, 5, 109n1, 307; contributions to federalism, 476; division of powers, 264–6; and ELCC, 350, 358, 369n25; expenditures, 267, 267*t*; Federation of Canadian Municipalities, 292; functions and revenues, 266–9, 268*t*; Municipal Finance Officers' Association of Ontario, 270; responsibilities, 310–11, 481; revenues *versus* services, 271–4; Safe Restart Agreement, 80*t*; and taxation, 268*f*, 272–4, 278n23, 311; trilateral/tri-level agreements, 265, 269, 274–6, 320; vertical fiscal imbalance, 269–71. *See also* individual cities
Cleveland, Gordon, 348
climate change, 6, 322, 439, 479
CMHC. *See* Canadian Mortgage and Housing Corporation (CMHC)
Collier, Robert, 53
Colonial Office, 53
commodity price index, 84
common law powers, 55–6
Commonwealth Grants Commission, Australia, 43, 107, 171, 186, 460, 463, 465, 480
Community Well-Being Index (CWB), 225–6, 232n27
Comprehensive Land Claims Policy, 220, 231n19
Confederation, 30–4
Confédération des syndicats nationaux v. Canada (Procureur général) (2006), 64–5, 67–8
Conseil Québécois d'agrément (CQA), 241, 242–3*t*, 245*t*, 247–50, 252, 254, 258–9
constitution: Constitution Act (1867), 51–4, 57–8, 70, 155–6, 215; Constitution Act (1907), 34, 53; Constitution Act (1982), 195, 264–5, 403, 438, 459; Constitution Act, section 35 (1982), 204–5, 220;

Constitution Act, section 36 (1982), 50, 53, 62–3, 65, 69, 101, 105, 161, 388, 463; Constitution Act, section 91 (1982), 197; Constitution Act, section 92 (1982), 158; Constitution Act, section 93 (1982), 342; and equalization, 50, 53, 105; and federal spending power, 52–4; suggested amendments, 276n2
Consumer Price Index, 351
Corning, H.W., 35
Couillard, Philippe, 408
Council of Ministers of Education, Canada (CMEC), 327, 333, 338, 338n2
Council of the Federation: on CHT, 97, 104, 398–9; on equalization payments, 136; on Fiscal Stabilization Program (FSP), 170; and the provinces, 99, 408; on the Séguin Commission report, 406
Courchene, Thomas, 40, 106, 161, 389, 399, 401, 426, 462
Couture, Jérôme, 134
COVID-19, 77–92; in Australia, 469n24; Canada Recovery Benefits, 124; and CERB, 123–4; changes to federal transfers, 433*t*; and debt, 88–90, 177; and federal spending/transfers, 104, 114, 264–5, 421; fiscal capacity, 81–5; fiscal stabilization, 77, 85–8; fiscal supports, 78–81, 79*t*; and GDP, 414–15; and income taxes, 79; and long-term care facilities, 237; and Ontario, 430–3; Resilience Infrastructure Stream, 421; response law, 226*t*; and spending power, 275
CST. See Canada Social Transfer (CST)
Cumulative Best-of Guarantee (CBOG) payments, 144
Curtis report, 286, 303n3

Dahlby, Bev, 169, 424, 425, 427
decentralization, 4, 7–8, 100, 132, 269

Delgamuukw v. British Columbia, 220
demographic imbalance, great. *See* great demographic imbalance
dental care, 95, 104, 107, 457
Depression, the. *See* Great Depression
Deutsch, John James, 29, 45, 45n1, 46n12
Dexter, Darrell, 381
disabilities, 116, 117, 350
Disaster Financial Assistance Arrangements (DFAA), 414, 420–1, 433*t*, 434n3, 435n21
Dixon, Currie, 205
Doctrine of Discovery, 218
Dominion-Provincial Conferences, 34, 36, 37, 39, 41
Donabedian, Avedis, 239–40, 244, 245
Driedger, Elmer, 62
Duclos, Jean-Yves, 295
Duncan, Andrew/Duncan report, 35–6, 41
Dunning, Charles, 39
Duplessis, Maurice, 42–3, 46n9, 399

early childhood education and care (ECEC), 326, 327–9. *See also* early learning and childcare (ELCC)
Early Childhood Education Report 2020, 367n8
early learning and childcare (ELCC), 342–74; and Alberta, 347, 351*t*, 352, 353*t*, 366; benefits for workers, 357; and bilateral agreements, 342–4, 348, 352, 354*t*, 357–60, 363–6, 367n2; and British Columbia, 347, 351*t*, 352–3, 353*t*; Child Care Now, 343; and cities/municipalities, 350, 358, 369n25; and CST, 348, 357, 364; early childhood education and care (ECEC), 326, 327–9; federal funding of, 120, 122, 353*t*, 354*t*; and Indigenous peoples, 123, 354*t*; and Ontario, 346–8, 351*t*, 353*t*, 356*t*, 357–60, 360*t*, 362*t*, 367n8,

early learning and childcare (*cont.*) 368n18; previous funding studies, 346–7; and Quebec, 342, 346–8, 352, 357–60, 362–3, 367n8; and refundable tax credits, 358; and spending, 342–3, 344–6, 347–8, 351*t*, 353*t*, 364–5; study methods, 347–52; study results, 352–63; and taxation issues, 348. *See also* child care; licensed ELCC spaces
Eccleston, Richard, 464–5
Economic and Fiscal Update 2021, 78
Edmonton, AB, 265, 277n6, 335
education, 326–41; elementary and secondary education, 332–7; and equalization, 336; federal funding of, 94–5, 108, 109n2, 121, 122; and First Nations, 331–2, 338; and GDP, 326, 336; and minority-language communities, 332–4, 338n3; as percentage of GNP, 326; percentage of graduates, 326; per student expenditures, 337; post-secondary education, 42, 44, 46n9, 329–30, 337–8; school boards, 311, 333–6, 338n3; university fees, 329; and Winterhaven Stables, 62. *See also* early learning and childcare (ELCC)
education, associations and programs: Canada Education Savings Grant (CESG), 330; Canadian Institutes of Health Research (CIHR), 330; Canadian School Trustees' Association, 336; Council of Ministers of Education, Canada (CMEC), 327, 333, 338, 338n2; Fédération nationale des conseils scolaires francophones (FNCSF), 333; Natural Sciences and Engineering Research Council (NSERC), 330; Program for International Student Assessment (PISA), 337; Protocol for Agreements in Minority-Language Education, 333; Quebec English School Boards Association (QESBA), 333; Registered Education Savings Plan (RESP), 330; Social Sciences and Humanities Research Council (SSHRC), 330; Standing Committee on Official Languages, 333
Eidelman, Gabriel, 276
Eisen, Ben, 424
ELCC. *See* early learning and childcare (ELCC)
electricity rates across provinces, 166*t*, 167–8
Emery, Herb, 379
Employment and Social Development Canada (ESDC, was Human Resources and Skills Development Canada, HRSDC), 292
Employment Insurance, 345
Energy East pipeline, 389
equalization, 132–54; about, 5, 10, 132–4, 159, 418–20, 445, 459; and Alberta, 169, 192, 196, 417–18, 426–8, 444–5, 469n20, 479; analysis of, 134–6; annual variations and the budget cycle, 140–4; assessment of, 461; and Atlantic provinces, 445; and Australia, 388, 460–1, 464–5, 468n18; beginning of, 29–30, 36, 43–4, 401; ceiling on, 137, 140–1, 407, 433*t*, 435n16; changes to, 433*t*; compared to other federations, 463–5; compared to other transfers, 79, 96–8, 103, 160*t*, 422*f*; in the constitution, 50, 53, 105; Council of the Federation on, 136; and education, 336; Expert Panel on Equalization and Territorial Formula Financing (O'Brien report), 133, 135, 141, 145, 162–4, 188n5, 198, 206, 406–7, 420; and fiscal stabilization, 102; five-province *versus* ten-province standard, 132–3, 162, 407, 418, 420,

433, 434n7, 434n9; fixed growth rule, 420, 425–6, 429, 433*t*, 435n17; formulas for calculating, 82–4, 161–4, 172n11, 173nn13–15; and GDP, 164, 407; and horizontal fiscal imbalances, 414; and income taxes, 172; issues with, 105; and Manitoba, 134, 141, 142*t*, 143*t*, 445; and Maritime provinces, 134; medium-run fiscal plans, 144–8; and natural resources, 132, 134, 161–8; needs-based approach, 388–9; and New Brunswick, 141, 142*t*, 143*t*; and Newfoundland, 165*t*; and Nova Scotia, 141, 142*t*, 143*t*, 144–5; and Ontario, 141, 149n4, 423, 426, 428; as part of federal transfers, 416*f*; as per capita transfer, 96, 105; and Prince Edward Island, 136–41, 142*t*, 143*t*, 382; from provinces to municipalities, 266; and Quebec (tables and figures), 142*t*, 143*t*, 401*f*, 404*f*; and Quebec (text), 134–6, 141, 144, 398, 402–3, 445, 464; reforms to, 84–5; and Saskatchewan, 165*t*, 169, 479; and Séguin Commission report, 398, 405–6; and vertical fiscal imbalance, 100; and water power rentals, 167*t*, 173n17. *See also* Expert Panel on Equalization and Territorial Formula Financing (O'Brien report); fiscal capacity; Territorial Formula Financing (TFF)

ESDC. *See* Employment and Social Development Canada (ESDC)

ESDC Homeless Secretariat, 295

Established Programs (Interim Arrangements) Act, 44, 116–17

Established Programs Financing (EPF), 94, 120, 402, 404, 416*f*, 417

European Charter of Local Self-Government, 271

European Union, 308

Expert Panel on Equalization and Territorial Formula Financing (O'Brien report), 133, 135, 141, 145, 162–4, 188n5, 198, 206, 406–7, 420

External Advisory Committee on Cities and Communities, 263, 273, 276n1

Fair Deal Panel, 440, 442, 443–9

family allowances, 41

Federal Lands Initiative, 303n5

Federal-Provincial Fiscal Arrangements Act (FPFAA), 159, 330, 344

federal-provincial fiscal relations, 97–9

federal-provincial-municipal fiscal relations, 265, 269, 274–6, 320

federal spending power, 50–71; about, 284–5, 456–8; and Canadian federalism, 59–61; and the courts in the future, 65–9; and the courts in the past, 61–5; definition of, 51–2; and ELCC, 342–3, 344–6, 364–5; Harper on, 407; legal and constitutional basis, 52–9; and the principle of separation, 397–8; and vertical fiscal imbalance (VFI), 462–3

Fédération nationale des conseils scolaires francophones (FNCSF), 333

Federation of Canadian Municipalities, 292

Feehan, James: chapter by, 155–75; cited, 171–2, 424, 429

Feir, Donn. L.: chapter by, 215–36; cited, 113

Fellows, G. Kent, 209n5

Felman, Josh, 178

Fenna, Alan: chapter by, 451–75; cited, 171

Ferguson, Barry, 46n8

Finances of the Nation (Canadian Tax Foundation), 140

financial crisis (2008), 177, 314, 381

Finlay v. Canada (Minister of Finance) (1993), 63–4, 67, 68, 69

Firewall Letter, 440–2
First Nations, 215–36; band census-subdivision (CSD), 225, 232n25, 232n27; current issues, 219–26; and education, 331–2, 338; and federal funding arrangements, 226–8; and fiscal capacity, 223*t*; and GST, 223; Haudenosaunee Confederacy, 217; and infrastructure, 222, 224, 229, 231n22, 315, 321; and long-term care homes, 243; and opting out, 222, 224–5, 229, 232n30; self-governance, 225; and social assistance, 113; and social services, 123; statutes, 218–19; term usage, 17n2; treaties, 216–17, 230nn2–3; and the Yukon, 202. *See also* Indigenous peoples; Indigenous Services Canada; settlers/settler colonialism
First Nations, acts and official bodies: Assembly of First Nations, 227–8; Community Well-Being Index (CWB), 225–6; First Nations Elections Act, 232n30; First Nations Finance Authority, 222, 229, 232n29; First Nations Financial Management Board, 222, 228–9; First Nations Fiscal Management Act (FMA), 222–3; *First Nations Gazette*, 225, 232n28; First Nations Land Management Act (LMA), 224, 225, 229; First Nations Land Management Board, 224, 229; First Nations Tax Commission, 222–3, 229, 231n22, 232, 232n23; Seventh General Assembly of the Union of BC Indian Chiefs, 221–2
Fiscal Arrangements Act, 172n9
fiscal capacity: about, 161; and CAP, 118; and COVID-19, 81–5; and First Nations, 223*t*; fiscal capacity cap (FCC), 163–6, 420; fiscal capacity gap (FCG), 162; and natural resource revenues, 132; and other countries, 460; and the territories, 200–1, 200*t*; used to determine social transfers, 426; and vertical fiscal imbalance (VFI), 176, 180
fiscal efficiency/equity, 105
fiscal federalism, 476–82; about, 7–11, 159–60, 476–8; Canada as best example of, 451–3, 458–9; challenges, 478–80; equality and equity, 390–1; and provincial debt, 180–1, 183; recommendations, 480–1. *See also* Canada Community-Building Fund (CCBF); Canada Health and Social Transfer (CHST); Canada Health Transfer (CHT); Canada Social Transfer (CST); COVID-19; education; equalization; federal spending power; fiscal federalism, history of; fiscal federalism in comparative perspective; Indigenous peoples; infrastructure; social assistance
fiscal federalism, history of, 29–46; Confederation, 30–2; The Depression, 36–9, 115, 459; Maritime provinces, 35–6; into the mid-1920s, 32–4; Rowell-Sirois Commission (on Dominion-Provincial Relations), 39–41, 43, 400; tax-rental deals, 41–4
fiscal federalism in comparative perspective, 451–75; conflict nonetheless, 462–5; equalization, 463–5; raising revenue, 453–9; sharing the wealth, 459–61; vertical fiscal imbalance (VFI) and federal spending power, 462–3
Fiscal Stabilization Program (FSP): about, 98, 159, 182, 187n3, 414, 420–1, 434n3; changes to, 433*t*; and COVID-19, 77, 85–8; and equalization, 102; and natural

Index   497

resource revenues, 168–71; reform of, 105
fiscal sustainability, 383
Fitch Ratings, 177
Fitzgerald, E.A., 172n3
five-province standard, 133, 162, 418, 420, 433, 434n9
Flanagan, Tom, 232n23
Foster, Daniel, 352
FPT (Federal-Provincial-Territorial) Strategic Working Group, 295
Friendly, Martha, 346, 350, 368n15, 368n18, 369n25

Gallant, Natasha L., 240–1
Gas Tax Fund, 109n7, 277n5, 313, 390, 422f. *See also* Canada Community-Building Fund (CCBF)
Gauthier, Éléonore, 345
GDP. *See* gross domestic product (GDP)
gender-based analysis (GBA+) lens, 297
Germany, 388, 452, 454–5, 460–1, 464, 468n18
Gibbins, Roger, 466
Girard, Éric, 395
GNP. *See* gross national product (GNP)
gold rush, 204
goods and services tax. *See* GST (goods and services tax)
Granja, Aracelly Denise: chapter by, 306–25
great demographic imbalance, 376–8, 387, 424
Great Depression, 36–9, 115, 459
Green and Inclusive Community Buildings Program (GICB), 322–3
gross domestic product (GDP): in Atlantic provinces, 379t, 381t; and CHT, 89; and COVID-19, 414–15; and education, 326, 336; and equalization, 164, 407; and federal debt, 96, 414; federal transfers as percentage of, 80, 81f; and Financial Stabilization Program (FSP), 170; and infrastructure, 434n3; in Maritime provinces, 378, 384–5; and Prince Edward Island, 381t, 382; and provincial debt, 177, 178t
gross expenditure base (GEB), 199, 206
gross national product (GNP), 119, 432
GST (goods and services tax): about, 279n29; in Australia, 186, 456; decline from COVID-19, 79; and federal government, 387; and First Nations, 223; and municipalities, 268f, 274; and Nova Scotia, 381; and Quebec, 408
Gusen, Peter, 429

Hachard, Tomas, 279n32
Haida Nation v. British Columbia, 220
Hanniman, Kyle: chapter by, 176–91; cited, 105, 180
harmonized sales tax (HST), 98–9, 274, 279n28, 279n29, 318
Harper, Stephen/Harper government: about, 406–7; and cash transfers, 390, 438; and equalization for Prince Edward Island, 139; and GST, 387; and housing, 294–5; and Indigenous peoples, 331; and infrastructure, 313
Haudenosaunee Confederacy, 217
Hayashi, Masayoshi, 135
health care: and aging populations, 88, 181, 203–4, 385; in Australia, 457; Canadian Institute for Health Information (CIHI), 90, 203; Canadian Institutes of Health Research (CIHR), 330; changes to federal transfers, 432t; coverage by province, 107; dental care, 95, 104, 107, 457; Health Standards Organization, 238; mental health services, 118; per capita funding in the territories, 203–4, 203t; per

health care (*cont.*)
capita provincial spending, 386t; pharmacare/pharmaceuticals, 95, 104, 107–9, 445–6; and Quebec, 459. *See also* Canada Health Act (CHA); Canada Health and Social Transfer (CHST); Canada Social Transfer (CST); long-term care sector
Hellyer Task Force, 287
Hibernia, 159
Hickey, Ross, 225
Hobson, Paul A.R., 122, 125
Hogg, Peter, 55
home care, 80t, 94, 104, 107, 239
Homelessness Action Task Force (Toronto Mayor), 292
Hooghe, Liesbet, 308
horizontal equity, 16, 126, 148, 350, 395–6, 398–403, 405–9
horizontal fiscal equalization (HFE), 451
horizontal fiscal imbalance, 105–7, 161, 375, 387, 414, 425
Hospital Insurance and Diagnostic Services Act, 44, 93
housing, 284–305; affordable housing, 287–8, 291–8, 303n4, 313, 392; and bilateral agreements, 291–6, 298; competitive unilateralism, 287–8; current issues, 298–302; federal funding initiatives (1999–2001), 291–5; federal-provincial framework, 288–90; federal role, 290–1, 295–6; and Indigenous peoples, 294; jurisdiction for, 284; and Maritime provinces, 392n3; post-war reconstruction, 286–7; provincial funding, 287–8; public housing, 286–7; spending cuts (1980s), 290, 299
housing programs, funds, and reports: Affordable Housing Initiative (AHI), 292, 294, 298; Canada Economic Action Plan (CEAP), 294; Canada Housing Benefit (CHB), 298, 300; Canadian Mortgage and Housing Corporation (CMHC), 285, 286, 289–90, 291, 295–6, 299, 302; ESDC Homeless Secretariat, 295; Green and Inclusive Community Buildings Program (GICB), 322–3; Homelessness Action Task Force (Toronto Mayor), 292; *Housing Programs in Search of a Balance* (Nielsen Task Force), 289; Investments in Affordable Housing (IAH), 295, 302; *A National Direction for Housing Solutions* (CMHC), 289; National Homeless Initiative (NHI), 292; National Housing Act (NHA), 286, 288; National Housing Co-Investment Fund (NHCF), 298, 300–2, 303n5; National Housing Strategy (NHS), 285, 296–9; New Building Canada Fund, 320; Rapid Housing Initiative, 299; Reaching Home, 298–9; Rental Construction Financing Initiative (RCFI), 299, 300, 303n5, 303n6; Residential Rehabilitation Assistance Program (RRAP), 294; Social Union Framework Agreement (SUFA), 292; Wartime Housing Ltd., 286, 303n2; *What We Heard* (CMHC), 295–6
Howe, Joseph, 30–1, 32
Human Resources and Skills Development Canada (HRSDC, now Employment and Social Development Canada, ESDC), 292

IICP. *See* Investing in Canada Plan (IICP)
Ilsley, James, 39
Imbeau, Louis M., 134
income taxes: and Alberta, 443–4, 446, 447; and Australia, 455; and COVID-19, 79; and equalization, 172; and Established Programs Financing

(EPF), 116, 126; First Nations, 221; Income Tax Act, 344; and municipalities, 273–4, 278n23; and National Energy Policy (NEP), 157; and Newfoundland, 383; and Ontario, 428; and Quebec, 42–3, 399–402, 405; Rowell-Sirois Commission, 39; and tax harmonization, 99; territories, 200*t*; Working Income Tax Benefit, 122

Indian Act, 218–19, 221–2, 230n5, 331

Indigenous peoples: COVID-19 response law, 226*t*; *Delgamuukw v. British Columbia*, 220; and devolution, 193, 208; and education, 332, 334; and ELCC, 123, 354*t*; forced assimilation of, 331; *Haida Nation v. British Columbia*, 220; and housing, 294; Indigenous Community Infrastructure Initiative (ICII), 321; Indigenous/Aboriginal title, 219–20, 231n17, 231n19; Inuit, 17, 119, 123, 193, 202–5, 208, 331; James Bay and Northern Quebec Agreement, 220; land claims, 193, 204, 207, 219–21, 227, 231nn18–19; nation-to-nation relationship, 221; and reconciliation, 208; residential schools, 219, 331; rights, 217; *R v. Calder*, 219; self-government, 127, 193, 208, 209n4, 218–20, 222, 228–9, 338; and social assistance, 116, 119, 127–8; and taxation issues, 218–19, 221–5, 223*t*, 228, 232n28; term usage, 17n2; in the territories, 194, 197, 202; treaties, 216–17, 220, 221, 230n2, 231n18, 231n20; *Tsilhqot'in Nation v. British Columbia*, 220; Williams Treaty, 217, 230n2. *See also* First Nations; settlers/settler colonialism

Indigenous Services Canada, 224–5, 227, 228

infrastructure, 306–25; and Bennett government, 36; and bilateral agreements, 309, 442; described, 313; and First Nations, 222, 224, 229, 231n22, 315; funding of, 98, 312, 317–21, 318*t*, 421–2; and GDP, 434n3; investments in, 314*f*, 315*f*; maintenance *versus* new projects, 316–17; multilevel governance, 307–12; ownership, 269, 313–17, 316*f*; public financing, 312–13; Resilience Infrastructure Stream, 421; state of, 270, 278n16; in the territories, 198–9; and vertical fiscal imbalance (VFI), 425

infrastructure, federal programs: Building Canada Plan, 319; Canada Infrastructure Bank (CIB), 318*t*, 320–1; Canada Infrastructure Works Program, 312–13; and CCBF, 96, 101, 172n9, 265, 313, 317–19, 318*t*, 422; Green and Inclusive Community Buildings Program (GICB), 322–3; Indigenous Community Infrastructure Initiative (ICII), 321; Infrastructure Canada, 309, 312, 322–3; Investing in Canada Plan, 309, 318*t*, 319–20; Major Infrastructure Component (MIC), 319; National Infrastructure Component (NIC), 320; New Building Canada Fund, 320; Provincial-Territorial Infrastructure Component (PTIC), 320; Resilience Infrastructure Stream, 421; Strengthened Climate Plan, 323

International Monetary Fund (IMF), 145

Inuit, 17, 119, 123, 193, 202–5, 208, 331. *See also* Indigenous peoples

Investing in Canada Plan (IICP, was CCBF), 309, 318*t*, 319–20, 422, 422*f*

Investments in Affordable Housing (IAH), 295, 302

Jackson, Emily, 425, 427
James Bay and Northern Quebec Agreement, 220
Janigan, Mary: chapter by, 29–49; cited, 3
Joanis, Marcelin: chapter by, 132–54; cited, 148
Joly, Melanie, 333
Jones, John Harry, 37–8
Jones, Russell, 311
Judicial Committee of the Privy Council (JCPC), 53, 62

Kennedy, Steven, 194
Kenney, Jason, 192, 439, 442, 443–4, 479–80
Kent, Tom, 44
Khanal, Mukesh, 428
King, William Lyon Mackenzie, 35–6, 38, 39
Kitchen, Harry, 425, 426
Klein, Ralph, 440–1, 445

Lajoie, Andrée, 462
Lammam, Charles, 424
land claims. See under Indigenous peoples
Landry, Bernard, 404–5
land transfer taxes, 268–9, 277n13
language issues for minority-language communities, 332–4, 338n3
Laurier, Wilfrid, 33, 53
Laurin, Alexandre, 456
Layton, Jack, 292, 294
Lecours, André: chapter by, 3–28, 476–82; cited, 90, 186, 196, 462–5, 467
Le Dressay, André, 224
Legault, François, 408
Leone, Roberto, 302
licensed ELCC spaces: in Alberta, 352, 353t; in British Columbia, 257, 353t, 365; fees for, 343, 364–5; in Nova Scotia, 365; numbers of, 351, 352, 361, 362, 363, 365–6; in Ontario, 258, 353t, 362t, 363, 367n8; in Quebec, 352, 353t, 361t, 363; scarcity of, 328; spending per space, 363–4
Llewellyn, John, 311
long-term care sector, 237–78; about, 237–9; construction of quality of care standards, 239–41; definitions, 239–40; national standards (2023), 252–5; national *versus* provincial standards, 255–6; outcome-related standards, 250–2, 251t; private for-profit sector, 238–9; process-related standards, 248–50, 249t; residential facilities *versus* home care, 239; SPO (structure-process-outcome) approach, 240–1, 244; standards in BC, NB, ON, and QC, 241–52, 257–9; standards of care compared, 242–3t; structure-related standards, 245–8, 246t
lot levies/development charges, 268
Lougheed, Peter, 441, 445

Macdonald, Angus, 37–8
Macdonald, David, 346
Macdonald, John A., 33, 53
Mackenzie King, William Lyon. *See* King, William Lyon Mackenzie
Major Infrastructure Component (MIC), 319
Manitoba: aging population, 377t; bond default, 39; and CERB, 124; and Confederation, 32–3; and education, 336; and equalization, 134, 141, 142t, 143t, 445; and long-term care, 241; municipal revenues, 269t; natural resource revenues, 156; residential electricity rates, 166t; and social housing programs, 288; Winnipeg, 265, 277n6
Mansell, Robert, 428

marginal cost of public funds (MCF), 425, 427
Marier, Patrik: chapter by, 237–62; cited, 237
Maritime provinces: about, 30, 35–6, 378; and equalization payments, 134; and GDP, 378, 384–5; and housing, 392n3; Royal Commission on Dominion-Provincial Relations, 37–8; Royal Commission on Maritime Claims, 35–6. *See also* New Brunswick; Nova Scotia; Prince Edward Island
Market Basket Measure (MBM), 127
Marks, Gary, 308
Marsh report, 286, 303n3
Martin, Paul/Martin government, 294, 313, 390, 404, 406, 407
Mayer Report on Nunavut Devolution, 198, 208
McBride, Richard, 34
McCuaig, Kerry, 342, 352, 367n6
McIntosh, Tom, 4
McKnight, William, 289
McLelan, Archibald W., 32
McLeod, Bob, 206
Medical Care Act, 44, 93
Meech Lake Accord, 62–3, 292, 403, 462
Mella, Patricia J., 136–7
mental health services, 118
Mercier, Honoré, 33
Métis, 17n2, 202, 215, 331
Metropolis, 263
Moe, Scott, 186
Moncton-based Intercolonial Railway, 35
Montreal, QC, 277n6, 278n23, 328
Moore, Christopher, 31
Morneau, Bill, 206
mothers' allowance, 115, 117–18
Mulroney government, 289, 312
multilevel governance (MLG), 306–12

Municipal Finance Officers' Association of Ontario, 270
municipalities. *See* cities/municipalities
Murphy, Mitch, 137–9
Musgrave, Richard A., 271
Muskrat Falls project, NL, 383

National Adjustment Grants (NAGs), 30, 39, 41, 43
National Child Benefit, 123
National Direction for Housing Solutions, A (CMHC), 289
National Energy Policy (NEP), 157–8
National Homeless Initiative (NHI), 292
National Housing Act (NHA), 286, 288
National Housing Co-Investment Fund (NHCF), 298, 300–2, 303n5
National Housing Strategy (NHS), 285, 296–9, 302
National Infrastructure Component (NIC), 320
National Welfare Council, 124
nation-to-nation relationship, 221
natural resources, 155–75; about, 155–9, 172n4, 210n7; in Alberta, 156–7, 210n7, 419f; and equalization, 132, 134, 161–8; and fiscal stabilization payments, 168–71; in initial constitution, 156; in Newfoundland and Labrador, 156–9, 172n4, 210n7; ownership of, 438; in the territories, 192–3. *See also* oil and gas industry
Natural Sciences and Engineering Research Council (NSERC), 330
needs-based equalization, 388–9
neoliberalism, 403
New Brunswick, 385; aging population, 377t, 424–5; budgets, 148; and CERB, 124; and debt, 381–2, 381t, 384; and education, 336; and equalization, 141, 142t, 143t; and fiscal sustainability, 385; further subsidies (1935), 38; and

New Brunswick (*cont.*)
immigration, 379–80; interest rates and growth rates, 180; and long-term care, 239, 241, 242–3*t*, 245, 245*t*, 247–50, 252–3, 257–8; Moncton-based Intercolonial Railway, 35; and municipalities, 266; natural resource revenues, 156; residential electricity rates, 166*t*; school boards, 338n3; share of Canada Child Benefit (CCB), 123; special grants, 31–2, 52. *See also* Atlantic provinces; Maritime provinces

New Building Canada Fund, 320

New Democratic Party (NDP), 294, 381, 441

Newfoundland and Labrador: aging population, 89, 376, 377*t*, 424–5; and CERB, 124; credit market conditions, 88; and debt, 381*t*, 382–3, 384; and equalization, 165*t*; fiscal capacity, 84, 164–5, 165*t*; and immigration, 380; and income taxes, 383; long-term care facilities, 239; municipal revenues, 269*t*; Muskrat Falls project, 182, 383; naming of, 392n2; and natural resources, 156–9, 172n4, 210n7; and oil industry, 210n7, 378, 380, 382–3, 392; population shrinkage, 89; residential electricity rates, 166*t*; and social housing programs, 288; stabilization payments, 86–7; university fees, 329. *See also* Atlantic provinces

NHCF. *See* National Housing Co-Investment Fund (NHCF)

Nielsen Task Force, 289

Nisga'a Final Agreement, 221, 231n20

Noël, Alain: chapter by, 395–412; cited, 310, 453–4

Northern Accord, 207

Northwest Territories: Aurora College, 338n1; birth rate, 198; and CERB, 124; consensus government, 197; and devolution, 193, 198, 207, 208; economy, 202; natural resources, 192; political institutions, 204–5, 210n8; Territorial Formula Financing (TFF) grant calculations, 200–1, 200*t*

Notley, Rachel, 441

Nova Scotia: aging population, 377*t*, 424–5; budgets, 147–8; and CERB, 124; Cumulative Best-of-Guarantee (CBOG) payments, 144; and debt, 380–1, 381*t*; and ELCC, 365; and equalization, 141, 142*t*, 143*t*, 144–5; and GST, 381; and immigration, 379–80; interest rates and growth rates, 180; land transfer taxes, 268; and municipalities, 266, 269*t*; and natural resources, 156–8, 172n4; residential electricity rates, 166*t*; share of Canada Child Benefit (CCB), 123; and social housing programs, 288; special grants and subsidies, 31–2, 38; and sustainable finances, 409–10; university fees, 329. *See also* Atlantic provinces; Maritime provinces

Nunavut: birth rate, 198; and CERB, 124; consensus government, 197; and devolution, 195, 207–8; economy, 201–2; natural resources, 192–3; Nunavut Agreement-in-Principle, 207; Nunavut Land Claims Agreement, 193, 204; Nunavut Tunngavik Incorporated (NTI), 193, 202, 204, 207; per student expenditures, 337; political institutions, 204–5; Territorial Formula Financing (TFF) grant calculations, 200–1, 200*t*

Oates, Wallace, 271

O'Brien, Al/O'Brien report, 133, 135, 141, 145, 162–4, 188n5, 198, 206, 406

Offshore Accord, 144
oil and gas industry: Alberta, 161, 210n7, 417, 419f, 440, 464; and climate change, 479; during COVID-19, 83; Energy East pipeline, 389; National Energy Policy (NEP), 157–8; Newfoundland, 210n7, 378, 380, 382–3, 392; and Russia's invasion of Ukraine, 84; in the territories, 201–2, 207
old age programs, 35, 113, 115–16, 117, 350, 441, 447–9
Oliver, Peter C.: chapter by, 50–76; cited, 344
Omran, Farah, 134
Ontario, 413–37; aging population, 377t; Canada-Ontario Memorandum of Agreement Respecting Welfare Programs for Indians (1965), 116; and CAP, 119, 418; and CERB, 124; contributions to federal revenues, 417; and COVID-19, 430–3; and education, 330, 334; and ELCC, 346–8, 351t, 353t, 356t, 357–60, 360t, 362t, 367n8, 368n18; and equalization, 141, 149n4, 423, 426, 428; fair treatment of, 425–7; and federal support, 423–5; federal transfers to, 416f; fiscal capacity, 83–4; fiscal stabilization payments, 168; and income taxes, 428; interest rates and growth rates, 180; licensed ELCC spaces, 258, 352, 353t, 362–3, 362t, 363, 367n8; and long-term care, 239, 241, 242–3t, 245, 245t, 247–9, 252–4, 258; lot levies/development charges, 268; Municipal Finance Officers' Association of Ontario, 270; and municipalities, 268, 269t, 274–5; and natural resources, 156; net contribution, 427–9; personal income override, 85, 418, 425–6, 433t; residential electricity rates, 166t; and school boards, 334; stabilization payments, 87; and sustainable finances, 410, 424. *See also* Toronto, ON
opting out: about, 462; and Alberta, 445–6; and conditional federal spending plans, 345, 446; and Established Programs Financing (EPF), 44, 116; and First Nations, 222, 224–5, 229, 232n30; in other countries, 458; and Quebec, 116–17, 402, 447
Organisation for Economic Co-operation and Development (OECD), 145, 177, 275, 455
Organization of Petroleum Exporting Countries (OPEC), 157

Paris Climate Agreement, 322
Pasloski, Darrell, 206
Pendakur, Krishna, 224
Pendakur, Ravi, 224
pensions. *See* old age programs
Petit, Gillian, 123–4
Petro-Canada, 157
Petter, Andrew, 462
pharmacare/pharmaceuticals, 95, 104, 107–9, 445–6
Pickersgill, J.W., 30, 46n10, 46n12
Pomeroy, Steve: chapter by, 284–305; cited, 307
population, aging, 375–94; across provinces, 377t; in Atlantic provinces, 376–8, 391, 424–5; as challenge to federalism, 478; great demographic imbalance, 376–8, 424; and health care, 88, 181, 203–4, 385; in Newfoundland, 89, 376, 377t, 424–5; and provincial budgets, 424; and the territories, 203–4. *See also* long-term care sector
post-secondary education, 42, 44, 46n9, 329–30, 337–8

PPP (Public-Private Partnerships) Canada (now Canada Infrastructure Bank), 318*t*, 320–1
Prentice, Susan, 328–9, 337–8
Prince, Michael J.: chapter by, 112–31
Prince Edward Island: aging population, 377*t*; budgets, 148; and Canada Health and Social Transfer (CHST), 137; and CERB, 124; and debt, 381*t*, 382; early childhood education and care (ECEC) fees, 328; and education, 335; and equalization, 136–40, 141, 142*t*, 143*t*, 382; and federal transfer payments (CHT and CST), 382; fiscal sustainability, 385; and GDP, 381*t*, 382; and housing, 291; and immigration, 378–9, 382; and long-term care, 239; and municipalities, 268, 269*t*; and natural resources, 156; residential electricity rates, 166*t*; and social housing programs, 288; special grants and subsidies, 33, 38. *See also* Atlantic provinces; Maritime provinces
Program for International Student Assessment (PISA), 337
Progressive Conservatives, 441
Protocol for Agreements in Minority-Language Education, 333
provinces: Dominion-Provincial Conferences, 34, 36, 37, 39, 41; economic convergence, 82*f*; economic decline from COVID-19, 85; electricity rates, 166*t*; Provincial Bond Purchase Program, 87–8; provincial-municipal funding, 264–6; Provincial-Territorial Infrastructure Component (PTIC), 320; Royal Commission on Dominion-Provincial Relations (Rowell-Sirois Commission), 39–41, 43, 400; self-sufficiency of, 455, 458; trilateral/tri-level agreements, 265, 269, 274–6, 320. *See also* bilateral agreements; opting out; individual provinces
provincial debt, 176–91; and fiscal federalism, 180–1, 183; gradual fiscal adjustment, 177–80; possible solutions to, 183–6

Quebec, 395–412; Accreditation Canada (AC), 241, 242–3*t*, 245*t*, 249–50, 252, 254, 258–9; aging population, 377*t*; budgets, 145, 146*t*; and CERB, 124; *Confédération des syndicats nationaux v. Canada (Procureur général)* (2006), 64–5, 67–8; Conseil Québécois d'agrément (CQA), 241, 242–3*t*, 245*t*, 247–50, 252, 254, 258–9; and COVID-19, 237; and debt, 181; early childhood education and care (ECEC) fees, 328; and early learning and childcare (ELCC), 342, 346–8, 352, 357–60, 362–3, 367n8; and ELCC (tables), 351*t*, 353*t*, 355*t*, 359*t*, 361*t*; and equalization, 134–6, 141, 144, 398, 402–3, 445, 464; and equalization (tables and figures), 142*t*, 143*t*, 401*f*, 404*f*; Fédération nationale des conseils scolaires francophones (FNCSF), 333; fiscal capacity, 84; and health care, 459; horizontal equity, 16, 126, 148, 350, 395–6, 398–403, 405–9; and housing, 288, 290, 291, 296, 302; interest rates and growth rates, 180; and long-term care, 237–41, 242–3*t*, 245, 245*t*, 247–8, 254, 258, 259n4; Montreal, 277n6, 278n23, 328; and municipalities, 269*t*, 319; and natural resources, 156; and opting out, 116–17, 402, 447; residential electricity rates, 166*t*; school boards, 338n3; Séguin Commission (Royal Commission on Fiscal Imbalance),

10, 135–6, 398–9, 405, 410, 456, 458; share of Canada Child Benefit (CCB), 123; share of federal transfers, 409*f*; social transfers per capita, 404*t*; stabilization payments, 87; and sustainable finances, 384, 409; and taxes, 29–30, 42–3, 268, 399–402, 405, 408; Total Transfer Protection (TTP), 144; Tremblay Commission (Royal Commission of Inquiry on Constitutional Problems), 42, 399–402, 458; trilemma, 396–9, 399*f*, 403–6; university fees, 329; vertical equity, 16, 395–403, 406, 408, 409
Quebec English School Boards Association (QESBA), 333
Quebecers, Our Way of Being Canadian: A Policy for Quebec's Affirmation and for Canadian Relations, 408
Quebec sign language (LSQ), 334
Quiet Revolution (Quebec), 402

railways, 35, 438
Rapid Housing Initiative, 299
RCMP. *See* Royal Canadian Mounted Police
Reaching Home, 298–9
Reference re Assisted Human Reproduction Act (2010), 66
Regent Park, Toronto, ON, 286
Registered Disability Savings Plan, 123
Registered Education Savings Plan (RESP), 330
Ren, Feixue, 424
Rental Construction Financing Initiative (RCFI), 299, 300, 303n5, 303n6
representative tax system (RTS), 103, 132–3
residential long-term care. *See* long-term care sector
Residential Rehabilitation Assistance Program (RRAP), 294
residential schools, 219, 331
Resilience Infrastructure Stream, 421
Richard, Greg, 224
Robson, Jennifer: chapter by, 342–74; cited, 126, 327–8
Robson, William B.P., 134, 270, 456
Rocher, François, 400, 410
Roman Catholic school boards, 334
Rose, John, 32
Rowell-Sirois Commission (Royal Commission on Dominion-Provincial Relations), 39–41, 43, 400
Royal Canadian Mounted Police (RCMP), 441, 449
Royal Commissions: on Aboriginal Peoples, 226–7; on Dominion-Provincial Relations (Rowell-Sirois Commission), 39–41, 43, 400; on Fiscal Imbalance (Séguin Commission), 10, 135–6, 398–9, 405, 410, 456, 458; of Inquiry on Constitutional Problems (Tremblay Commission), 42, 399–402, 458; on Maritime Claims, 35–6; on National Development in the Arts, Letters and Sciences, 42
Rupert's Land, 156, 217
Russia, 84
R v. Calder, 219

Sabin, Jerald, 204
Safe Restart Agreement, 79–80, 80*t*, 182, 414, 421
Safe Return to Class Fund, 421
Saillant, Richard: chapter by, 375–94; cited, 424, 427
Saskatchewan: aging population, 377*t*; bond default, 39; Confederation, 33; and education, 330, 337; and equalization, 165*t*, 169, 479; fiscal capacity, 84, 164–5, 165*t*; fiscal stabilization payments, 168–9; lot

Saskatchewan (*cont.*)
  levies/development charges, 268;
  and natural resources, 156–7, 159;
  residential electricity rates, 166*t*; Roman
  Catholic school boards, 334; and social
  housing programs, 288; stabilization
  payments, 87; university fees, 329
Scharpf, Fritz, 184
school boards, 311, 333–6, 338n3
Schutz Index, 81–3
Scoones, David: chapter by, 215–36
Scott, Frank (F.R.), 55
Secession Reference (1998), 69
secular stagnation, 178–9
Séguin, Yves/Séguin Commission, 10, 135–6, 398–9, 405–6, 410, 456, 458
settlers/settler colonialism: Aboriginal and Northern Affairs Canada, 227–8; about, 331; Canada-Ontario Memorandum of Agreement Respecting Welfare Programs for Indians (1965), 116; Doctrine of Discovery, 218; Indian Act, 218–19, 221–2, 230n5, 331; Indigenous Services Canada, 224–5, 227, 228; nation-to-nation relationship, 221; and reconciliation, 208; residential schools, 219, 331; Royal Commission on Aboriginal Peoples, 226–7; treaties, 216–17, 220, 221, 230n2, 231n18, 231n20. *See also* Indigenous peoples
Seventh General Assembly of the Union of BC Indian Chiefs, 221–2
Shah, Anwar, 388, 454
Sheridan, Wesley J., 139–40, 148
Siddall, Evan, 296
Silver, Sandy, 205
Simeon, Richard, 172n2
Slack, Enid: chapter by, 263–83; cited, 222, 307, 310
Smith, Alison, 307
Snoddon, Tracy: chapter by, 413–37

social assistance, 112–31; about, 112–14, 417–18; and COVID-19, 123–4; federal spending on, 468n8; history of, 115–17; history of CAP (1966–96), 117–20; history of Canada Health and Social Transfer (CHST; 1996–2020s), 120–2; history of spending on, 432*t*; outside the CST, 122–4; policy recommendations, 127–8. *See also* Canada Social Transfer (CST)
Social Sciences and Humanities Research Council (SSHRC), 330
Social Union Framework Agreement (SUFA), 65, 292
spending power. *See* federal spending power
SPO (structure-process-outcome) approach to long-term care, 239–40, 244, 250, 254
Standards Council of Canada, 238
Standing Committee on Official Languages, 333
Statement on Claims of Indian and Inuit People, 231n19
St-Hilaire, France, 122, 125
St-Laurent, Louis, 30, 41–4, 45
Strengthened Climate Plan, 323
Subramanian, Arvind, 178
Supreme Court of Canada, 58, 60, 61–5, 69, 119, 218
Switzerland, 100, 452, 454–5, 456, 458, 460–1

taxation issues: and Alberta, 273, 443–4, 446, 447; asymmetric tax competition, 158–9; and cities/municipalities, 268*f*, 272–4, 278n23, 311; and ELCC, 348; Federal-Provincial Fiscal Arrangements Act, 344; First Nations Tax Commission, 222–3, 229, 232; harmonized sales tax (HST), 98–9, 274, 279n29, 318; Income Tax Act,

344; and Indigenous peoples, 218–19, 221–5, 223*t*, 228, 232n28; land transfer taxes, 268–9; local taxes, 272; in Nova Scotia, 380–1; property taxes, 268, 335; provincial income tax, 401; provincial-municipal areas, 264; and Quebec, 29–30, 42–3, 268, 399–402, 405, 408; refundable tax credits, 358; and rental investment, 287; representative tax system (RTS), 103, 132–3; revenue modes and sharing, 454–5; revenues *versus* services, 271–4; Séguin Commission, 10, 135, 398–9, 405, 410, 456, 458; tax collection agreements (TCAs), 98–9; tax-rental deals, 29–30, 36, 40–5, 80; and vertical fiscal imbalance (VFI), 182; wartime programs, 30, 36, 40–1, 80, 278n23; Working Income Tax Benefit, 122. *See also* GST (goods and services tax); income taxes

Taylor, Zack, 266
Tedds, Lindsay, 123–4
Telford, Hamish, 462
ten-province standard, 132, 162, 418, 420, 433, 434n7
Territorial Formula Financing (TFF), 192–214; about, 198–201; compared to equalization payments, 193–6, 209n3; grant calculations, 200*t*; specific grants, 172n10
territories: and CHT, 209n3; fiscal capacity, 200–1, 200*t*; income taxes, 200*t*; infrastructure, 198–9; oil and gas industry, 201–2. *See also* Territorial Formula Financing (TFF); individual territories
Tilley, Leonard, 31
Tombe, Trevor: chapter by, 3–28, 77–92, 192–214; cited, 114, 168, 169, 171, 180, 187n3, 209n5, 384–5, 389–91, 428, 444

Toronto, ON: and amalgamation, 277n7; early learning, 328, 350; and education, 335; fiscal health, 270; Regent Park, 286; and specific legislation, 277n6; and taxes, 264, 268, 273
Total Transfer Protection (TTP) payments, 144
treaties, 216–17, 220, 221, 230n2, 231n18, 231n20
Tremblay, Thomas/Tremblay Commission, 42, 399–402, 458
trilateral/tri-level agreements, 265, 269, 274–6, 320
Trudeau (Justin) government, 295, 301, 408
Truth and Reconciliation Commission, 331
Tsilhqot'in Nation v. British Columbia, 220
Tupper, Charles, 31

Ukraine, 84
unemployment insurance, 41, 44, 61, 68, 116, 117, 368n12
United Cities and Local Government (UCLG), 263
United Conservative Party, 442, 480
United Kingdom, 31, 70, 217
United Nations Declaration on the Rights of Indigenous Peoples (UNDRIP), 216, 220, 228
United States, 5, 217, 230n1, 452, 454–8, 460, 462–3
Unruh, Lynn, 240
Usher, Alex, 330

Vancouver, BC, 265, 277n6
vertical equity, 16, 395–403, 406, 408, 409
vertical fiscal gap, 5, 8, 10, 100, 103, 160, 180, 453–4

vertical fiscal imbalance (VFI): about, 375, 424, 451, 453–4, 455–6; and CHT, 100, 103, 104–5, 414; and cities/municipalities, 269–71; and CST, 414; and equalization, 100; and federal spending power, 462–3; and fiscal capacity, 176, 180; and GST, 387; and infrastructure, 425; Séguin, Yves/Séguin Commission, 10, 135, 398–9, 405, 410, 456, 458; and taxation, 182
Viewpoint Alberta, 439–40

Wallner, Jennifer: chapter by, 326–41; cited, 9
Wan, Thomas T.H., 240, 244, 245, 248, 250, 254
Wardhaugh, Robert, 46n8
wartime programs: tax agreements, 30, 36, 40–1, 80, 278n23; War Measures Act, 39; Wartime Housing Ltd., 286, 303n2; war veteran's allowance, 115
Westphalian order, 308
What We Heard (CMHC), 295–6
White, Linda A., 328–9, 337–8
White, Thomas/White report, 37–8, 41

White-Eye, Leslee, 332
Whitney, James, 33
Wicksellian connection, 271, 278n18
Wildrose Party, 441, 442
Williams Treaty, 217, 230n2
Winnipeg, MB, 277n6
Winterhaven Stables v. A.G. Canada (1989), 62
Woolley, Timothy, 464–5
Working Income Tax Benefit, 122
World Bank, 326
Wu, Miles, 270

Yalnizyan, Armine, 342, 367n6
Young, Robert, 308–9
Yukon: about, 202, 204–5; Canada-Yukon Oil and Gas Accord Implementation Act, 207; and CERB, 124; and devolution, 207; per student expenditures, 337; Territorial Formula Financing (TFF) grant calculations, 200–1, 200t; Yukon Umbrella Agreement, 194, 207, 221
Yurris, Christopher: chapter by, 192–214

Milton Keynes UK
Ingram Content Group UK Ltd.
UKHW022214040324
438897UK00023B/215